P9-CRS-428

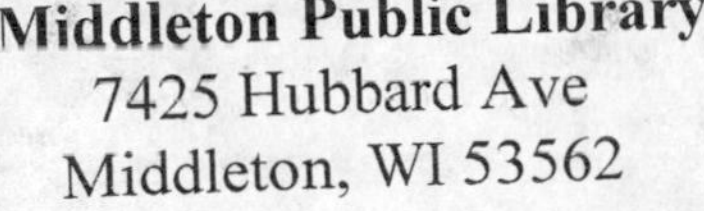
Middleton Public Library
7425 Hubbard Ave
Middleton, WI 53562

LOCAS

THE MAGGIE AND HOPEY STORIES

A LOVE AND ROCKETS BOOK

Jaime Hernandez

APE
SEX

LOCAS

Edited by Gary Groth
Design by Unflown
Promotion by Eric Reynolds
Published by Gary Groth
and Kim Thompson

FANTAGRAPHICS BOOKS

 For a free full-color catalogue of comics and cartooning, call 1-800-657-1100. Our books may be viewed — and purchased — on our web site at: www.fantagraphics.com.

First Fantagraphics Books edition: September, 2004

ISBN 1-56097-611-X

Printed in Korea

7563 Lake City Way NE • Seattle, WA 98115 USA

TABLE OF

Contents

MECHANICS

DEAR HOPEY,

SURPRISE! IT'S ME! I'M STILL ALIVE. I'LL BET YOU THOUGHT I WAS DEAD OR KIDNAPPED OR SOMETHING. WELL, I'M NEITHER. I'M WRITING FROM AN OLD, DECREPIT HOTEL CLEAR ACROSS THE GLOBE IN ZIMBODIA!! IT WAS REALLY WEIRD, LAST FRIDAY WHEN YOU AND IZZY WENT TO MAD-DOG'S WITHOUT ME, I WAS SITTING THERE ALL SENTIDA WATCHING TV WHEN THE PHONE RANG. IT WAS RAND RACE. HE SAID WE HAD A BIG, BIG JOB SOMEWHERE OUTSIDE OF THE COUNTRY AND THAT I HAD TO BE AT THE AIRPORT IN FIFTEEN MINUTES. SORRY I DIDN'T LEAVE A NOTE, BUT I BARELY HAD TIME TO EVEN PACK (I DIDN'T HAVE ENOUGH CLEAN UNDERWEAR, SO I BORROWED SOME OF YOUR OLD ONES, OK?). I'LL BET YOU THOUGHT I GOT SO SENTIDA THAT NIGHT THAT I WENT OUT AND KILLED MYSELF, HUH?

I'M SO EXCITED, BECAUSE WE'RE JUST STOPPED HERE FOR A NIGHT. WE REALLY HAVE TO GET TO, GET THIS... ZHATO!! AND I DON'T MEAN THE FUN, POPULATED, CITY ZHATO, I MEAN THE JUNGLE, WILD ANIMALS, CANNIBALS ZHATO. IT'S SOME BIG GOVERNMENT JOB WE'RE ON. I'M NOT EVEN SURE IF I'M ALLOWED TO TELL YOU ABOUT IT. ESPECIALLY SINCE YOU'RE THE MOST ANTI-GOVERNMENT PERSON I KNOW. YOU'RE EVEN ANTI-ANTI (HA HA).

I'LL ONLY BE GONE FOR ABOUT A WEEK, SO IF YOU COULD PLEASE FEED TIC TAC AND WASH THE DISHES THIS WEEK AND I'LL DO THEM NEXT WEEK.

OH YEAH, AND PLEEEEEZZZ...

(OVER)

TAKE OUT THE TRASH, OK? THANKS A LOT. SEE YOU IN ABOUT A WEEK.

LOVE YOU,
MAGGIE

P.S. I'VE FINALLY SEEN A REAL LIVE ZIMBODIAN. THEY REALLY DO HAVE SKIN LIKE OLIVES. THEY ALSO HAVE THE BIGGEST FEET IN THE WORLD. ≡ WHEW ≡

P.S.S. SAY HI TO IZZY AND PENNY FOR ME AND I'LL BRING YOU ALL SOUVENIERS FROM ZHATO REAL SOON.

DEAR HOPEY,

TODAY WE ARRIVED AT THE BUBÉ (PRONOUNCED BOO-BEH) AIRPORT JUST OUTSIDE ZHATO. WE'LL BE SPENDING THE NIGHT IN THE JUAN PANADERO HOTEL (UGH, WHAT A DUMP) BEFORE WE TAKE A CHOPPER INTO THE JUNGLE WHERE WE'LL BE WORKING. THERE WE MET THIS FUNNY GUY WHO WAS SUPPOSED TO FILL US IN ON WHERE WE WERE STAYING AND STUFF LIKE THAT, BUT HE DIDN'T KNOW HIS ASS FROM HIS SHIT. WE WAITED AROUND FOUR HOURS BEFORE WE GOT ANY INSTRUCTIONS. IT WASN'T SO BAD WAITING BECAUSE THEY HAD THIS LITTLE JUKE BOX IN THE AIRPORT CAFÉ AND ON IT WAS THE THEME SONG TO THAT HILLBILLY PROGRAM YOU LIKE. I PLAYED IT EIGHT TIMES. OH YEAH, I SAW A PICTURE OF THE DAMAGES ON THE ROCKET SHIP WE WILL BE FIXING, AND I HAVE A SLIGHT FEELING WE'LL BE MORE THAN A WEEK (WHAT A MESS). I'LL WRITE YOU IN A COUPLE OF DAYS. TAKE CARE, HAH?

LOVE YOU,
MAGGIE

P.S. THIS IS THE BUBENESE GREETING: "BUBÉ, BUBÉBE BU." THAT MEANS, "DON'T COUNT YOUR CHICKENS BEFORE YOUR BRITCHES IS HATCHED." HA HA.

P.S.S. IN CASE YOU HAVEN'T NOTICED, OUR JOB IS TO FIX A ROCKET THAT CRASHLANDED IN THE JUNGLE YEARS AGO.

DAY 1

WELL, HERE WE ARE. SORRY I'VE TAKEN SO LONG TO WRITE, BUT WE HAVE TO GO ABOUT NINETY MILES INTO ZHATO TO MAIL A LETTER AND THE EXPRESS HERE IS SO SLOW. BUT ANYWAY, REMEMBER WHEN I TOLD YOU WE WERE WORKING IN THE DEEP JUNGLE? WELL, EVEN I DIDN'T KNOW IT WOULD BE THE DEEP, DEEP, DEEP, JUNGLE WHERE THE LOCAL NATIVE LANGUAGE IS SO COMPLEX THAT EVEN THE CLOSEST TRIBES WHICH ARE SEVERAL MILES AWAY CAN'T MAKE IT OUT.

I MEAN, THIS JUNGLE IS SO DEEP, THAT IF THE ROCKET WE HAVE TO FIX DIDN'T OPEN SOME SPACE WHEN IT CRASHLANDED, WE'D ALL BE LIVING IN THE TREES.

OUR HUTS ARE VERY NICE. THEY'RE JUST LIKE THE ONES IN THE MOVIES, ONLY THEY SMELL JUST LIKE KA KA. I GUESS I'LL JUST HAVE TO GET USED TO THE STENCH HERE IN LOWER PELLUCIDAR. I MEAN, THIS JUNGLE IS SOOOOOO DEEP THAT NEXT TO THIS BIG, BIG, BIG ROCKET SHIP WE HAVE TO FIX THAT IS STUCK IN THE SLIMEY MUCK, IS A BIG, BIG, BIG, OLD, FAT, SMELLY, FAT, OLD, BLACK DINOSAUR!

NO KIDDING. IT KIND OF LOOKS LIKE A BRONTOSAURUS REX EXCEPT IT'S GOT A BUMP ON IT'S HEAD. THEY SAY IT'S BEEN SITTING THERE SINCE THE BIG, BIG BIRD OUT OF THE SKY (THE ROCKET SHIP) CRASHED INTO IT MANY YEARS AGO. AND THEY BOTH HAVE BEEN SITTING THERE SINCE. IT SEEMS THE BIG TWISTED ROOTS UNDERWATER GREW AROUND AND TANGLED IT UP, SO IT'S THERE FOR GOOD. ANYWAY, WE TALKED WITH A MR. ESCARENO, AND HE FILLED US IN ON THE SITUATION. HE SAID IT'S ONLY THE ENGINE. HE'S CRAZIER THAN THE LAST GUY.

SO, BEFORE WE STARTED WORK THE NEXT MORNING, WE HAD THE REST OF THE DAY TO LOOK AROUND AND GET A FEEL OF THE PLACE. WELL, THE MEN DID. THEY WENT TO CHECK OUT THE DINOSAUR. ME, I GOT STARTED ON MY TAN. HUH, SOME TAN.

DAY 2-11

IT'S HOT!! LEMME OUTA HERE!! I HATE THIS PLACE ALREADY. WE HAVE TO DRINK BEER CONSTANTLY OR WE'LL DRY UP. THE CLIMATE IS SO STRANGE HERE, AND THE SMELL, IT'S DONE SOME WEIRD THINGS TO MY STOMACH. THE LIZARD, I THINK IS CALLED A BRACKINOSAURUS, OR SOMETHING LIKE THAT. IT'S ALREADY GETTING ON MY NERVES. BAD. THE NATIVES, THOUGH, USE IT AS A TEMPLE FOR PRAYING. AND DO THEY HAVE GREAT PARTIES AFTER MASS! I JUST LOVE THEIR MUSIC. IT'S A CROSS BETWEEN MARIACHI AND CORRACOBAÑ MUSIC. HARD TO BELIEVE, HAH? BUT, NOW IF IT SOUNDS LIKE I'M HAVING A BALL, I'M NOT. ALL WE DO ALL DAY LONG IS WORK, PLAN, GET INSTRUCTIONS, AND WORK. I HATE IT.

I FINALLY FOUND OUT WHY THIS JOB IS SO HUSH-HUSH. THIS SHIP WE'RE WORKING ON IS THE LEGENDARY SATURN STILLETTO. MANY YEARS AGO, DURING THE ZYMBODIAN REVOLUTION, IT WAS HIRED TO TRANSPORT THE BIGGEST LOAD OF PITO IN THE WORLD OUT OF ZHATO, BUT CAUGHT ITSELF IN A BATTLE AND WAS BLASTED. IT WAS LICKED...

BUT IT HAD ENOUGH SPARK LEFT TO FLY SO FAR INTO THE JUNGLE WHERE NO ONE WOULD EVER FIND IT. THE SHIP AND CREW WERE NEVER HEARD FROM AGAIN. MANY EXPEDITIONS WERE FORMED TO FIND IT BUT ALWAYS VANISHED IN THE JUNGLE. DUE TO WAR, THEY COULD NEVER SEARCH BY AIR. WHAT IT BOILS DOWN TO IS, WE'RE HIRED TO FIX THE SHIP, SO THEY CAN FLY IT OUT AND RETRIEVE THE PITO. I THINK IT'S STUPID. BY PULLING OUT THE STILLETTO, IT COULD KILL THE LOCAL'S ONLY CONTACT TO THEIR MESSIAH. BUT I GUESS A LARGE, DEAD HUNK OF JUNK IS FAR MORE IMPORTANT THAN A LIVING THING. DAMN, THE STUPID THING WILL NEVER FLY AGAIN. WE'RE WASTING OUR TIME. BUT, WHAT THE HELL, WE'RE GETTING PAID FOR IT. THE LOCALS CALL IT THE MOUTH OF HELL, BECAUSE THEY SAY MANY HAVE VENTURED INSIDE BUT NEVER RETURNED. KINDA SPOOKY.

I'LL BET YOU'RE WONDERING HOW I KNOW SO MUCH ABOUT THE NATIVES AND I DON'T EVEN UNDERSTAND THE LINGO. WELL, WE HAVE OUR VERY OWN GUIDE FROM ZHATO, A YOUNG GIRL CALLED TSE TSE. SHE'S ONE OF THE ONLY PEOPLE IN THE WORLD WHO SPEAKS BOTH OURS AND THESE PEOPLE'S LANGUAGES.

AFTER DAYS OF JUST WORKING, WE FINALLY GOT A DAY OFF AND WENT INTO ZHATO. I LOVE THIS TOWN. BUT, WE ALL GOT SO DRUNK, THE LAST I REMEMBER, I WAS DANCING AND THESE GEEKS KEPT PINCHING MY BUTT. THEN THEY WANTED ME TO GO WITH 'EM, BUT RACE BEAT THEM UP. SO I JUMPED OFF A TABLE INTO RACE'S ARMS AND ALMOST SWALLOWED HIS FACE BY KISSING HIM. THEN I THINK I PASSED OUT. GOD, I WAS PENNY CENTURY FOR A NIGHT. BUT, THE NEXT MORNING MY POOR HEAD FELT LIKE WORLD WAR THREE, AND I WAS SO EMBARRASSED ABOUT THE NIGHT BEFORE THAT I HID MY FACE FROM RACE THE WHOLE DAY.

DAY 12-15

IT RAINED LIKE CRAZY THE PAST FEW DAYS SO WE'VE HARDLY WORKED AT ALL. I BORE MYSELF WHILE THE MEN TALK JOB.

TODAY THEY SENT OVER A HORNY DOCTOR WHO GAVE US SHOTS SO WE WOULDN'T CATCH ANY OF THE JUNGLE DISEASES. OF COURSE HE GAVE THEM TO THE MEN ON THEIR ARMS, BUT TOLD ME IT'S BETTER FOR FEMALES TO GET IT YOU-KNOW-WHERE. AND LIKE A STUPID SHIT I FELL FOR IT, TILL HE STARTED DROOLING ALL OVER MY BUTT. THE BOYS THOUGHT IT WAS KIND OF CUTE. I HATE MEN. ANYWAY, THE RAIN STOPPED AND IT WAS BACK TO WORK. EVEN IF EVERYTHING IS NOW SOGGY, THE RAIN DID CLEAR UP A LOT OF THINGS. THE DINOSAUR HAS A RICH TAN AND THE SHIP IS A PRETTY PURPLE. IF YOU CAN'T SEE THESE COLORS, I SUGGEST YOU ADJUST YOUR TV SET. AND AS FAR AS THE WEATHER IS CONCERNED, IT'S HOTTER THAN EVER NOW. SO THE FASHION OVER HERE IS NOW LITTLE AS POSSIBLE.

BUT SERIOUSLY, FOLKS, I'LL NEVER FORGET THIS DAY AS LONG AS I LIVE. DUKE, YAX AND TSE TSE WENT INTO ZHATO FOR SUPPLIES. RACE AND I WERE ALONE (HO'D IT, MAGGIE)...

I FOUND THAT THIS MUD IS GREAT FOR MY SKIN. I'M GOING TO TRY TO BRING SOME WITH ME WHEN I FINALLY COME HOME. ANYWAY...

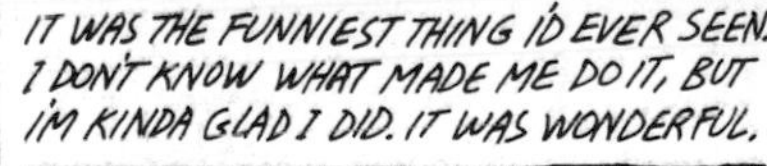

RACE WAS FINE, ONLY TOO WEAK TO GET UP. I SAT THERE AN HOUR HOLDING ON TO HIM. I DIDN'T WANT TO LET GO, BECAUSE I DIDN'T THINK I'D HAVE ANOTHER CHANCE. I MEAN, WAS HE MAKING A PASS EARLIER OR NOT? IT ALL WENT SO FAST. I GUESS I'LL NEVER KNOW, WILL I? STUPID SNAKE.

END OF PART I

DAY 16 DAMN IT! THINGS ARE GETTING WORSE HERE! IT'S GETTING HOTTER, WE HAVEN'T HAD A DAY OFF IN DAYS UPON DAYS, AND JUST BECAUSE WE'VE HAD A FEW CHANGES IN OUR JOB, AND RACE IS LAID UP FOR A COUPLE OF DAYS, DUKE MORALES HAS BEEN ON YAX'S AND MY ASS MORE THAN EVER NOW. SHIT! THAT'S ALL I NEED. WELL, ONE GOOD THING HAS COME OUT OF ALL THIS. I'VE ACTUALLY LOST, THAT'S RIGHT, LOST THREE WHOLE POUNDS!! I THOUGHT FOR SURE WITH ALL THAT BEER, I'D BE A BALLOON RIGHT NOW.

MECHANICS PART 2 MECHANICS PART 2 JAIME 82 7

DAY 17

TODAY WAS FULL OF SURPRISES. FIRST, RACE RECOVERED COMPLETELY FROM THAT MUD WRESTLING MATCH. SECOND, TODAY WAS ANOTHER DAY OFF. THAT'S RIGHT, "WAS." BY SOME FREAK ACCIDENT OF NATURE, SOMETHING JUST HAD TO SCREW UP MY PLAN. OH, YES, MEN ARE THE ABSOLUTE WORST THINGS EVER PUT ON THIS PLANET.

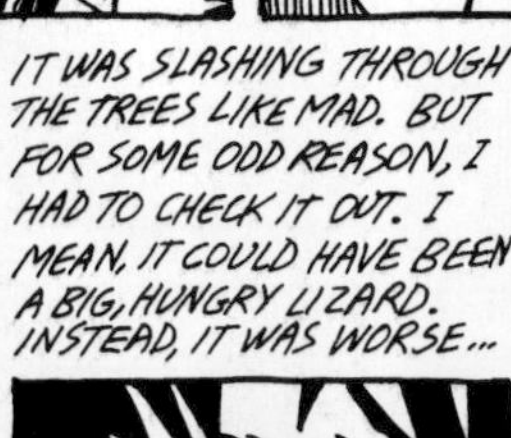

OOPS! I'M SORRY! I... OH, HI, MAGGIE! WHAT ARE YOU DOING HERE?
PENNY CENTURY!
ZOWIE! EUREKA! I FOUND IT! AND I DIDN'T EVEN USE A COMPASS!
PENNY! WHO...? HOW DID YOU...? PENNY?!
SO THAT'S IT, EH? THEY WERE RIGHT! BUT THAT'S NO MONSTER! THAT'S JUST A BRACHIOSAURUS! THIS IS WILD! I'LL GO DOWN IN HISTORY! BUT, WHAT DO I DO NOW?
PENNY! SPUT... SPUT... SPUTTER...
OH, HI, MAGGIE! WHAT ARE YOU DOING HERE?
DUH...
PENNY?
RACE! YOU'LL NEVER BELIEVE IT, BUT THIS IS MY FRIEND FROM...
HELLO, PENNY!
RAND RACE?
Y-YOU'RE LOOKING REAL GOOD! UM... HOW'VE YOU...
JUST FINE, THANK YOU!
C'MON, MAGGOT! THERE'S A BEACH NOT TOO FAR FROM HERE! LET'S GO FOR A SWIM! I'LL TELL YOU ALL ABOUT MY ADVENTURE!
HEY, RACE! WHAT'S UP? DON'T WE HAVE A BALL GAME TO PLAY?
NOT ANYMORE, BOSS! I THINK THE DINOSAUR ATE THE BALL!
ZOWIE!
PENNY! YOU STILL HAVEN'T TOLD ME WHAT YOU'RE DOING HERE! I MEAN YOU CAN'T JUST... CAN YOU?
HERE'S HOW IT WENT...
"IT STARTED IN FRITO'S CAFE, WHERE I WAS DINING WITH A FRIEND, AND I COULDN'T HELP OVERHEARING SOME ZHATOANS WHISPERING ABOUT THE LARGEST LOAD OF PITO IN THE WORLD LOST IN THE DEEP ZHATO JUNGLE.
"NATURALLY, I WAS INTRIGUED. SO I PERSUADED MY FRIEND TO HIRE ME A BOAT AND CREW, AND I WAS SET.
"THEY SAID IT WAS INSIDE A GIANT DEAD BIRD NEXT TO THE GIANT MONSTER! FEH! MONSTER OR NOT, I WAS DETERMINED TO FIND IT, AND NOTHING WAS TO STAND IN MY WAY! WELL, ALMOST NOTHING.
9

"WE WERE ALMOST TO THE END OF THE RIVER, WHEN MY CREW TURNED AGAINST ME! THEY WOULDN'T GO ANY FURTHER BECAUSE IT WAS TABOO (CHICKENS). SO WHEN I DEMANDED THAT THEY GO ON AHEAD, THEY WERE GONNA MAKE ME WALK THE PLANK! BUT THAT WAS POSTPONED...

"I THINK THE CREW WERE BEING EATEN WHILE I MADE IT TO DRY LAND, BUT I DIDN'T CARE TO LOOK BACK! I JUST KEPT RUNNING. I ATE AND SLEPT IN THE TREES WITH THE MONKEYS AT NIGHT, AND RAN ALL DAY. I RAN TILL SOON THERE WAS NO MORE DAYLIGHT!

"AND FINALLY WHEN I COULD RUN NO MORE, I CAME ACROSS A CLEARING, AND THERE LAY SOME OLD MAN BONES WITH A MAP TO THE TREASURE AND A MACHETE! TALK ABOUT PERFECT! SO, NOW IT WAS THOSE JUNGLE BEASTIES WHO HAD TO RUN FOR THE HILLS! THEN I CHOPPED MY WAY TO WHERE I AM NOW."

AND NOW I FIND YOU HERE ON SOME KIND OF JOB AND EVERYTHING! IT'S WONDERFUL!
HMM... I GUESS I SHOULDN'T BE TOO SURPRISED TO SEE YOU! YOU'VE ALWAYS HAD A KNACK FOR GETTING AROUND!

SO, TELL ME, WHAT ARE THE LOCALS LIKE HERE?
WILD! THESE PEOPLE ARE NUTS! THEY'RE ALWAYS HAVING PARTIES, DANCES, AND STUFF LIKE THAT! AND THEY'RE ALSO HEAVY INTO MAGIC! THEY'RE ALWAYS CONJURING UP LIGHT SHOWS AND STUFF! WILD, HUH?

MAGIC, HUH? YOU MEAN LIKE, THE KIND THAT CAN GIVE SOMEONE SUPER POWERS ???
HERE COMES ME, ROCKET'S GIRL!
UM, GEE... I DUNNO! I NEVER THOUGHT OF THAT! HEY, PENNY...?

WHAT DO YOU THINK OF THE BIG MONSTER THAT GUARDS THE FORBIDDEN TREASURE NOW?

HAH! HE'S NOT SO TOUGH! WE'LL SHOW 'IM WHO'S TOUGH!

THINGS ARE GONNA GET FUN AROUND HERE, NOW THAT PENNY'S ARRIVED. NO MORE BORING WORK DAYS, JUST FUN, FUN, FUN! AND THE BEST PART OF ALL IS, SHE CAN'T STAND THE SIGHT OF RACE. ANYWAY, I WISH YOU WERE HERE. IT SURE IS A BREAK FROM CIVILIAN LIFE. NOT A PROBLEM IN THE WORLD.
EAST SIDE BAD GIRLS

DAILY JUEVIN
IT'S WAR

DAY18-19→

THIS IS A PICTURE OF THE FINALISTS OF THE MISS BIG BRA CONTEST. GUESS WHO WON? PENNY AND I WERE THE FINALISTS BECAUSE WE WERE THE ONLY CONTESTANTS. NONE OF THE LOCAL WOMEN WANTED TO ENTER BECAUSE THEY WERE SCARED. I JUST THINK THEY WERE AFRAID OF BEATING US (HA HA). FOR DAYS, WORK HAS BEEN REALLY SLOW SO I'VE BEEN DRUNK OFF MY ASS THE WHOLE TIME, SCREWING AROUND WITH PENNY AND THE LOCALS, TRYING TO GET SOMETHING GOOD OUT OF THIS TRIP. RACE HAS BEEN REALLY QUIET LATELY. PENNY BROKE THE POOR BOY'S HEART AWHILE BACK. HM, SERVES HIM RIGHT. BY THE WAY, THE MAN HOLDING US UP IS NOT A ROBBER, BUT BEN RUBEN, THE VILLAGE WRESTLER.

AND SPEAKING OF WRESTLING, IN A COUPLE OF DAYS WE'RE EXPECTING A COUPLE OF PEOPLE TO JOIN US FOR AWHILE, AND GUESS WHO ONE OF THEM IS? NONE OTHER THAN QUEEN RENA TITAÑON! YOU KNOW, THE WORLD PRO WRESTLING CHAMPION, FROM WHOM MY AUNT VICKI STOLE THE TITLE. RENA WOULD STILL BE CHAMP IF MY TIA WOULD HAVE WRESTLED SCIENTIFICALLY (SHE USED THE ROPES). SMALL WORLD, HAH? AND DID YOU KNOW THAT WHEN SHE WASN'T IN THE RING SHE WAS TROTTING THE GLOBE FIGHTING MONSTERS AND CROOKS, STARTING REVOLUTIONS AND ALL OTHER TYPES OF HEROICS? AND TO THINK SHE PICKED THIS HOLE FOR HER NEXT SHINDIG. THIS WOMAN I'VE GOT TO MEET.

RENA'S HERE TO FIND OUT HOW DINOSAURS HAVE KEPT ALIVE HERE FOR SO MANY YEARS, AND WHY ONES FROM DIFFERENT TIME PERIODS COEXIST. I SAY IT'S BECAUSE THEY WERE WRONG ALL ALONG AND THAT DINOSAURS NEVER BECAME EXTINCT. THEY JUST GOT TIRED OF WORKING EIGHT HOUR SHIFTS AND MOVED TO THE WILD TO LIVE OFF THE LAND LIKE FLEABAG HIPPIES.

WELL, HOPITA, IT LOOKS LIKE IT'S GONNA BE A LONG TIME BEFORE I'LL BE SEEING GOOD OL' HOPPERS THIRTEEN AGAIN. OUR EMPLOYER IS NUTS!! HE MUST TRULY BE THE MONSTER FROM THE PADDED CELL. HE'S GOT US NOW TAKING THE WHOLE DAMN SHIP APART. THIS JOB JUST MIGHT FINISH US BEFORE WE FINISH IT. THERE'S SOMETHING FISHY GOING ON.

11

DAY 20

TODAY I WOKE UP WITH THE FEELING OF IMPENDING DOOM. I CAN ALWAYS TELL WHEN SOMETHING'S GOING TO GO WRONG, BECAUSE I WAKE UP WITH ALL MY COVERS ON THE FLOOR. SO, FOR THE WHOLE DAY I WAS EXTRA CAUTIOUS, AND IT GOT SO BAD THAT I SOON BECAME AFRAID OF MY OWN SHADOW.

END OF PART II

MECHANICS

JAIME 82

DAY 21

TODAY PENNY'S PET WAS DISCOVERED AND CAPTURED BY THE LOCALS. I DON'T DARE TELL PENNY HE'S BEING SAVED FOR THANKSGIVING, IT WOULD BREAK HER HEART. ANYWAY, OUR NEW VISITORS HAVE FINALLY SETTLED DOWN. FIRST, THERE'S PEDERO RODRIGUEZ SAN JO. HE'S THE SON OF OUR EMPLOYER. WHICH MEANS WE'RE WORKING FOR NONE OTHER THAN SANCHO CONRADO SAN JO! THE MAN WHO IS SO RICH, THE WHOLE ZYMBODIAN GOVERNMENT IS UNDER HIS FOOT. THE MAN WHO HAS PUT ZHATO, ZYMBODIA THROUGH SO MANY REVOLUTIONS, ASSASSINATIONS, ETC... THESE PAST FORTY YEARS, ALL BECAUSE HE THINKS ZHATO IS THE FUNNEST CITY IN ALL ZYMBODIA. HIS SON IS HERE JUST TO CHECK OUT DADDY'S PROGRESS. AND TALK ABOUT HORNY GOONS... YEESH...

THE FIRST DAY HE GOT HERE, HE CORNERED ME WHILE I WAS WASHING CLOTHES AND STARTED FEEDING ME THE OLD "WOULDN'T-YOU-RATHER-BE-WITH-ME-AT-A-DISCO" LINES. THEN HE STARTED GETTING DIRTY, SO I THREW SOAP IN HIS FACE (I KNOW, ♫ CHIVA RIVA RI, A PUN PUN PUN ♫). I'M PRETTY SURE HE GOT THE MESSAGE, BECAUSE NOW HE ONLY MAKES GOO GOO EYES AT ME. AND FINALLY, THERE'S BIG OL' RENA TITAÑON. ALL THE MEN GO GA GA OVER HER. WELL, SHE IS ATTRACTIVE, I GUESS, FOR AN ELDERLY WOMAN, THAT IS. ALTHOUGH, THERE'S ONE THING I'LL SAY FOR HER, SHE OUTDOES EVEN PENNY IN THE THINGS SHE'S DONE, THE PEOPLE SHE'S MET, AND THE PLACES SHE'S BEEN. BUT THE REAL TOPPING OFF THE CAKE IS THAT RENA WAS ONCE A SUPER HERO. AND AS YOU'VE PROBABLY ALREADY FIGURED OUT, PENNY CAN'T STAND THE SIGHT OF HER.

WHEN WE SHOWED OUR VISITORS THE SATURN STILETTO, IT LOOKED AS IF RENA TITAÑON HAD SEEN A GHOST. WELL, SHE MAY AS WELL HAVE BECAUSE WOULDN'T YOU KNOW IT, IN THE OLD DAYS SHE USED TO TRAVEL IN IT DURING THE WESTSIDE WARS. IT SEEMS SHE HAD A LOVE AFFAIR WITH THE CAPTAIN OF THE SHIP. THEY PLANNED TO WED, BUT THAT WAS DAYS BEFORE THE SHIP WAS THOUGHT LOST. AND NOW EVERYBODY HERE IS DISCUSSING VENTURING DOWN INTO THE SHIP TO SEE IF THE CREW DIED WITH IT. WELL, I HOPE THEY CAN COUNT ME OUT, BECAUSE WHEN I WAS LITTLE, WE WERE PLAYING HIDE AND SEEK, AND THERE WAS THIS OLD REFRIGERATOR, AND WELL...

LATER TODAY SANCHO SAN JO SENT MS. TITAÑON SOME FLOWERS ON HER ARRIVAL. (THE MAN IS MAD ABOUT HER). IF HE'S ANYTHING LIKE HIS SON, THOSE ORCHIDS WERE BOOBY TRAPPED. I ASKED PEDERO WHY HE DOESN'T GO AFTER PENNY, AND HE SAID MY SHAPE WAS MORE HIS IDEA OF A WOMAN. I SHOULD BE FLATTERED, BUT I'M NOT. WAIT! I'LL HAVE TO WRITE YOU ABOUT IT LATER. RIGHT NOW, THE GHOUL HIMSELF IS PEEKING IN MY WINDOW. I WONDER IF THERE'S MORE AT HOME.

DAY 22

TODAY IT WAS MINE AND RACE'S TURN TO GET SUPPLIES IN TOWN. RENA TITAÑON HAD TO COME ALONG TO TRANSLATE FOR US. Y'KNOW, I DIDN'T THINK TOO MUCH OF HER WHEN SHE FIRST ARRIVED, BUT NOW SHE'S MY HERO. MY GOD, SHE'S FANTABULOUS. I THINK I WAS JUST A BIT JEALOUS BECAUSE OF THE WAY EVERYBODY LOOKS UP TO HER. NOW I'M KINDA ASHAMED OF MYSELF. ANYWAY... WE WALKED INTO AN OLD AIRPLANE HANGER, AND THERE WAS AN OLD MAN SITTING BEHIND AN OLD DESK. AND WHEN HE SAW US COMING, HE STARTED TO BACK AWAY.

THIS GUY WAS HYSTERICAL! NEITHER RACE OR I COULD UNDERSTAND HIS LANGUAGE TOO WELL, BUT THE NAME "SAN JO" WAS PRETTY CLEAR...

NO!! GO AWAY!! I KNOW YOU'RE WORKING FOR SAN JO! WHY DON'T YOU PEOPLE LEAVE ME ALONE? BECAUSE OF YOU, MY WIFE HAS GONE CRAZY! AND MY KIDS...
CALM DOWN, OLD TIMER! WE HAVE ONLY COME FOR SUPPLIES!
NO!
I KNOW WHAT YOU WANT! BUT YOU'RE NOT GOING TO GET IT!
HO'D IT, RUBEN!

THE SCUFFLE WAS OVER QUICKLY, AND WE GOT OUR SUPPLIES. AND AS WE WERE LEAVING, I COULD HEAR THE OLD MAN MUMBLING SOMETHING ABOUT NOT GETTING "IT". I WONDER IF HE WAS TALKING ABOUT THE PITO. THIS WHOLE SITUATION'S BECOME PRETTY SPOOKY.

ON THE WAY BACK RENA EXPLAINED TO US THAT THE LAND BELOW USED TO BE A VILLAGE THAT GREW COFFEE BEANS BEFORE IT WAS WIPED OUT BY MORTARS. SAN JO THOUGHT THEY WERE TOO MUCH COMPETITION FOR HIS PAN PIXLEY PEANUT COFFEE INVESTMENT.

AND A FEW MILES AWAY IN THE TOWN OF WINZENA, SAN JO CLOSED DOWN THE LARGEST FACTORY FOR MILES AROUND LEAVING THOUSANDS OF EMPLOYEES OUT OF WORK AND ALL NEWLYWEDS HOMELESS, ALL BECAUSE HIS NEW BROTHER-IN-LAW WHO WORKED IN THE FACTORY OWED HIM FIFTY DOLLARS. OH YES, HIS SISTER WAS STERILIZED (HIS ORDERS).

AND NOW WE'RE WORKING FOR THIS GHOUL. I DON'T MIND TELLING YOU, I'M ABSOLUTELY SCARED SHITLESS. SO WHEN WE WERE GETTING SUPPLIES, I STOLE A TV SET TO TAKE MY MIND OFF THIS JERK. BUT, WOULDN'T YOU KNOW IT, SAN JO OWNS ALL THE LOCAL NETWORKS, SO HE'S A HERO ON ALL CHANNELS.

THIS GUY CRACKS ME UP!
15

DAY 23-24

THIS CHICK'S BLOWING IT. I'VE BEEN DRINKING MYSELF SILLY THESE PAST COUPLE OF DAYS, AND I'VE BEEN FUCKING UP AT MY JOB. DUKE HAS ALMOST DECKED ME PLENTY OF TIMES, BUT I DON'T CARE. THIS IS SO RIDICULOUS!! EVERYBODY'S GOING AROUND AS IF NOTHING'S WRONG. THEY'RE ALL PRETENDING THEY DON'T KNOW ANY DAY NOW SAN JO WILL DROP AN H-BOMB ON US AND THEN HAVE HIS LUNCH. HIS SON EVEN KNOWS HE'S OFF HIS FLAMING ROCKER.

HA! DAD WOULD NEVER DO ANYTHING TO HURT ME! THE ONLY REASON YOU'RE ALL ALIVE RIGHT NOW IS BECAUSE I'M HERE! BUT THE DAY I LEAVE, KABLOOIE!

YOU'RE LYING...

HIS LAUGHTER WAS JUST AS SICKENING AS HIS OLD MAN IS. I HAD TO GET AWAY FROM THERE FAST, OR I'D THROW UP. THIS IS GETTING OUT OF HAND.

THE NEXT MORNING I WOKE UP WITH A BIG, BIG, BIG HANGOVER WONDERING IF PEDERO WAS BULLSHITTING ME. DUKE WAS ON MY BACK AGAIN, YELLING MY HEAD OFF AS I PRAYED TO THE PORCELAIN GOD. POOR ME.

I COULDN'T TAKE ANY MORE. I NEEDED STRENGTH. SO THAT NIGHT I LOOKED FOR PENNY. SHE'S ONE PERSON I COULD USUALLY TURN TO FOR ASSURANCE. BUT WHEN I FOUND HER, IT WASN'T THE SAME. THE NATIVES HAD HER PET FOR TONIGHT'S SUPPER. UGH.

PENNY'S OUT OF IT AND EVERYBODY ELSE IS TOO BUSY TO KNOW WHAT THE HELL IS REALLY GOING ON. SO, IT'S UP TO ME TO GET US OUT OF THIS. NOW, INSTEAD OF BEING SCARED, I'M GONNA GET MAD! I'M GONNA GET THINGS DONE! THIS GHOUL IS NOT GONNA GET AWAY WITH MURDER! I'M GONNA... I'M GONNA GET ANOTHER BEER AND SLEEP IT OFF AND GO TO WORK IN THE MORNING...

DAY 25

TODAY IS THE DAY I TAKE SHIT FROM NO ONE. NOT FROM SAN JO, HIS SON, DUKE MORALES, OR EVEN THAT DAMN DINOSAUR THAT KEEPS ME UP ALL NIGHT HUMMING AT THE MOON. EVEN RACE, WHO, EVER SINCE PENNY AND RENA SHOWED UP, WON'T GIVE ME A SECOND GLANCE. JUST LET THEM TRY TO GET IN MY WAY. I'LL SHOW 'EM. YAX IS OK, BUT HE DOESN'T SAY MUCH. AND TSE TSE SPENDS MOST OF HER TIME COOKING AND WASHING CLOTHES. NOW THAT ONLY LEAVES PENNY, WHO JUST TODAY DECIDED TO SPLIT THIS JIVE-ASS SCENE.

I'VE FINALLY BECOME GOOD FRIENDS WITH RENA TITAÑON. SHE HELPED ME WASH OUT HER BLOUSE AFTER I THREW UP ALL OVER IT. I WAS PRETTY DRUNK, I GUESS. WELL, AT LEAST DUKE GOT THE MESSAGE.

17

WAIT A MINUTE! THIS ONE IS DAY TWELVE TO FIFTEEN! I DON'T WANT TO READ "MUD WRESTLING LOVE" AGAIN!
I'M HUNGRY! TAKE ME TO OKI-NUTS!
SHADDAP, WILL YA? I'M TRYING TO READ!
HOPEY? WHERE IS THAT DAMN TURN OFF? HOPEY! WILL YOU PLEASE TELL ME WHERE... HOPEY?
GIMME A BEER!
IS THAT A COP? I THINK WE SHOULD STASH THE BEERS! WAIT! IS THAT A COP?
HEY, HOPEY! PASS ME DAY EIGHTEEN TO NINETEEN! I WANNA READ ABOUT THE CONTEST PENNY WON! AND PASS ME A BEER, TOO!
I WANT TO READ WHAT THAT CRAZY GUY IS DOING TO THEM NOW! OUCH! FUCKIN' HOPEY! WHY WON'T YOU LET ONE OF US SIT UP FRONT WITH YOU?
JUST BE GLAD YOU HAVE A RIDE HOME! HEY, IZZY! SINCE WHEN HAS YOUR PEESASHIT CAR LIGHTER WORKED?
LET'S GO GET SOMETHING TO EAT! REWIND THE TAPE! IZZY, REWIND THE...
ARE THOSE COP HEADLIGHTS BEHIND US? THEY LOOK SQUARE!
OH, MAN... GOING OUT OF MY MIND... GOTTA CALM DOWN... RELAX... OK... TALK ABOUT... MAGGIE'S JOB... OK... WHERE THE HELL IS THAT TURN OFF... CAN'T SEE... OK... WAIT... GOTTA PEE NOW... GREAT...
DON'T THINK I SHOULD HAVE TAKEN THAT ACID AT HUERO'S, HOPITA!
I DON'T THINK YOU SHOULDA DOWNED THAT WHOLE SIXER OF VATO'S GOLD! THAT BEER'LL KILL YOU, Y'KNOW?
HEY! LISTEN TO THIS... MAGGIE GOT DRUNK AND TOLD THAT OLD...
YEOW! WATCH IT!!
WELL, MOVE YOUR... OUCH!!
IT'S A HIGHWAY PATROLMAN! LOOK!
THAT DID IT! IF YOU GUYS DON'T ST... OH, SHIT... IT IS A COP!!
DAY 26
TODAY I MADE A HAT. WOW.
DON'T PULL OVER! JACK OUT AND LOSE HIM!
OHH... SHIT, IZZY! I'M A MINOR! IS HE GONNA BUST US??
I TOLD YOU! I TOLD YOU!
MY DAD'S GONNA KILL ME!
W-WHAT'LL I DO... I CAN'T... I-I CAN'T TAKE IT ANY LONGER... I JUST GOTTA SCREEEEEEE
RELAX! JUST HIDE THE BEER!
18
END OF PART III

LATELY I'VE BEEN HAVING THESE AWFUL DREAMS ABOUT THE STILLETTO. THEY STARTED WHEN WE GOT ORDERS TO VENTURE INSIDE TO THE BACK OF THE SHIP.

LAST NIGHT OUTSIDE MY HUT I HEARD DUKE AND RENA, TALKING ABOUT THE STILLETTO WHEN IT FLEW, AND ABOUT ITS PILOT, HER ONCE SOON TO BE HUSBAND, BERNIE CARBO.

SOON THE THREE OF THEM BECAME KIND OF A TEAM, BUT DUKE SOON DROPPED OUT BECAUSE HE FIGURED THREE WAS A CROWD. POOR DUKE, I THINK HE LOVED HER, TOO. ANYWAY, BEING DRUNK AND REMEMBERING OLD TIMES GOT DUKE ALL CHOKED UP, SO HE EVEN APOLOGIZED TO ME FOR ALWAYS GIVING ME A HARD TIME. THAT WAS NICE, BUT I'M STILL BUGGED ABOUT THAT SHIP. I DON'T THINK SAN JO IS MY ONLY WORRY ANY MORE. MAYBE I'M PSYCHIC.

FOR INSTANCE, IT SAYS THAT RECENTLY ALL THE PEOPLE IN THE TOWN OF JINTÍN GAVE SAN JO A VERY WARM RECEPTION WHEN HE STAYED AT THE MAYOR'S HOUSE. BUT THEN SAN JO OWNS ALL THE NEWSPAPERS IN THE COUNTRY. I WONDER WHAT REALLY HAPPENED. I WONDER WHAT THE PEOPLE OF ZYMBODIA REALLY THINK OF SANCHO CONRADO SAN JO.

MANY YEARS AGO CARBO NEEDED MECHANICAL HELP FOR HIS NEW ROCKET SHIP AND DUKE GOT THE JOB. THEY BECAME GOOD FRIENDS FOR THE YEARS TO FOLLOW. THEN ONE DAY, DUKE INTRODUCED CARBO TO A FRIEND OF HIS NAMED RENA. IT WAS LOVE AT FIRST SIGHT.

THE NEXT DAY TSE TSE CAME RUNNING WITH SOMETHING IN HER HAND. IT WAS THE LATEST COPY OF THE DAILY PANADERON, A ZHATO NEWSPAPER. AT LAST I'D FIND OUT WHAT THE OUTSIDE WORLD WAS UP TO. IT WAS FULL OF FUN AND FASCINATING FACTS.

WHAT DOES S-A-N-J-O SPELL?

DID THEY GET HIM?
NO! HE HAD A TRAP DOOR!
19

DAY 30

SOMETHING FISHY IS GOING ON AGAIN. RENA TITAÑON HAS BEEN HERE TEN DAYS AND SHE HASN'T HAD ANYTHING TO DO WITH LIZARDS. AND MOST OF THE TIME SHE'S OFF IN ZHATO DOING WHO KNOW'S WHAT. ANYWAY, TODAY EVERYBODY WENT INTO TOWN BUT ME, RACE AND OL' HORNDOG. Y'SEE, I'VE BEEN LETTING PEDERO GET AWAY WITH A LOT. LIKE, NOT RATTING ON HIM WHEN I SHOULD, JUST SO HE WON'T GET DADDY ON US. WELL, TODAY WAS THEEEE STRAW THAT BROKE THE DINOSAUR'S BACK.

OK, BIG MAN! YOU'RE GONNA SEE WHAT HAPPENS WHEN YOU FUCK WITH A SAN JO!
NO FAIR!

NO FAIR! DON'T...
GET OFF, BITCH!

KRUNCH!

RACE! WAIT! I THINK HE'S HAD ENO... RACE!
AKK!

RACE! OOF! NEVER MIND!

WANT SOME MORE, HAH? OK! COME ON, DIP SHIT! TAKE YOUR BEST SHOT! YOU'RE DYING TODAY!
YOU BROKE MY FUCKING NOSE, YOU SON OF A BITCH! I'LL KILL YOU!!
RACE! PLEASE...

LOOK OUT! YOU'RE GETTING TOO CLOSE TO THE EDGE!
I'LL KILL YOU! I'LL KILL YOU!
OW!

GIMME THAT STICK SO I CAN... OOF! LOOK OUT!
WEEX!

OH, MY GOD! HE-HE FELL OVER! HE-HE'S DEAD! AND IT'S ALL MY FAULT! I SHOULD'VE...
DAMN! HOW COULD I HAVE... THE HEAT? I DON'T... NO, WAIT! HE'S OK! HE'S OK!!
21

WELL, IT HAPPENED. THAT GEEK WON'T GRAB MY BUNS AGAIN. HE BROKE HIS PINCHING ARM. ANYWAY, THIS IS IT, HOPEY. HERE'S WHERE I FIND OUT IF WE'RE TO BE WIPED OFF THE MAP, OR IF SANCHO SAN JO REALLY WANTS TO SAVE THAT PITO. I JUST WANNA GO HOME. NOW!

I RETIRED TO MY HUT WITH THAT NAUSEATING FEELING OF IMPENDING DOOM. I DON'T KNOW WHAT I WAS GOING TO DO. SO I SAT STARING AT THE WALL. THEN CAME A KNOCK ON MY WALL.

WELL, LATELY, I HAVE BEEN HEARING ALL THESE STORIES ABOUT MISTER SAN JO BEING THIS LUNATIC AND THAT US BEING HERE IS A BIG, BIG JOKE! THAT THERE REALLY IS NO REASON FOR US TO BE HERE! THAT...

WELL, YOU'RE RIGHT ABOUT THAT. WHEN I WAS DOWN THERE SAVING HIS SON, I FOUND A LARGE HOLE AT THE BOTTOM OF THE SHIP! AND...

IT STARTED GETTING DARK ALL AROUND US. AT FIRST I THOUGHT THE SUN WAS GOING DOWN. IT GOT DARKER... AND DARKER...

AND THEN RACE STARTED FADING WITH EVERYTHING ELSE. I GUESS I WAS PASSING OUT. DAMN IT, SOMEBODY UP THERE MUST HATE ME.

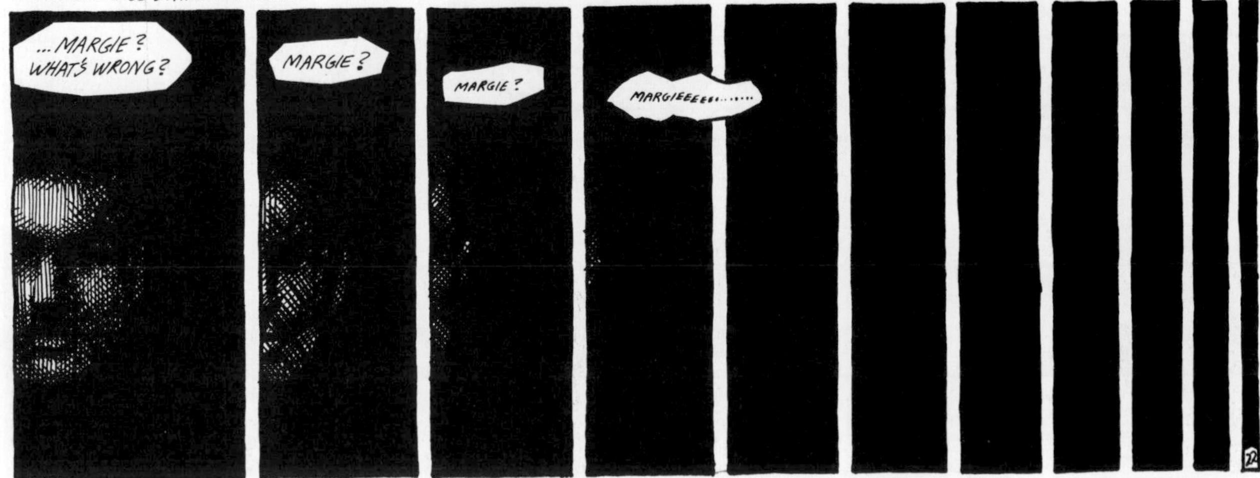

BUT THEN I STARTED COMING OUT OF IT REALLY FAST. BUT RACE WASN'T THERE ANYMORE. ONLY THE FUNNY MASKS HANGING IN MY HUT. CUCUY...

AND THEN I REALIZE THAT I'M IN BED WITH ALL THE WINDOWS COVERED, I'M DRIPPING WITH SWEAT BECAUSE I HAVE A THOUSAND DEGREE TEMPERATURE, MY HUT SMELLS LIKE RUBBING ALCOHOL, AND THERE ARE SERIOUS MEN OUTSIDE DISCUSSING SERIOUS MATTERS. MY CONCLUSION IS THAT I ATE SOMETHING THAT DIDN'T AGREE WITH ME.

TSE TSE! HAVE YOU FOUND OUT WHAT IT IS MARGIE HAS?
YES SIR, MISTER RACE! SHE GOT MOE TOWNE FEVER! I THINK SHE GOT IT FROM A PLANT!

THAT'S EXACTLY WHAT IT WAS! THE OTHER DAY A FLOWER HAD EXPLODED IN MY FACE, BUT I DIDN'T THINK IT WAS SERIOUS, EVEN THOUGH I GOT SOME SHIT IN MY EYES.

IS IT VERY SERIOUS? I MEAN... COULD IT BE FATAL?
I'M SORRY, DUKE, BUT ALL I CAN TELL YOU NOW IS SHE'S TO REMAIN IN THAT HUT TILL THE FEVER IS BROKEN! AND THAT COULD MEAN THREE TO FOUR DAYS! ALL WE CAN DO NOW IS WAIT! ONLY TSE TSE AND I CAN GO NEAR HER SINCE WE'VE ALREADY HAD THE FEVER!

OH, GREAT! BECAUSE OF ME WE'LL PROBABLY ALL BE DEAD IN A FEW DAYS. WE COULD HAVE ALL BEEN SUN BATHING IN OXNARD VERY SOON. INSTEAD, WE'LL PROBABLY FRY ON A BIG, BIG ROCK IN THE ZHATO JUNGLE.

BECAUSE OF MY FEVER, MY AWFUL DREAMS OF THE SATURN STILLETTO HAVE TURNED INTO NIGHTMARES. THE DAMN THING JUST WON'T LEAVE ME ALONE. IT'S SPOOKY.

SQUAD LEADER TO SADIE ONE, TWO, THREE, AND FOUR! NEXT STOP: ZHATO!

DAY 31-32

SORRY I HAVEN'T WRITTEN YOU IN A WHILE, BUT THE PAST WEEK HAS BEEN OFF THE DEEP END. MY FEVER RAN SO HIGH I COULDN'T LIFT MY ARMS, MY INSIDES FELT LIKE THEY WERE ON FIRE, MY SKIN FELT LIKE A MILLION NEEDLES WERE POKING INTO ME, MY EYES WERE ALMOST GONE, MY FINGERNAILS TURNED PURPLE AND I GREW THESE GROSS, GIGANTIC, GREEN FEVER BLISTERS ALL OVER MY FACE AND CHEST. I WAS A MESS. I COULD TELL I WAS FADING FAST, BUT TSE TSE AND RENA WOULD ALWAYS BE THERE TO LET ME KNOW I WAS STILL AROUND TO MEET THE SOON-TO-BE WRATH OF SAN JO.

YOU MUST HAVE STRENGTH, MARGARET! WE HAVE SENT FOR THE TOP MEDICINE DOCTOR IN WHOLE COUNTRY!
I-I DON'T KNOW IF-IF I CAN... I...

I... TSE TSE... AM I DEAD YET? PLEASE... IF I'M NOT... LET ME. BUT IT... IT WILL BE OK... I... I'LL STILL BE HERE... IN SPIRIT... BECAUSE, YOU KNOW... I... HOPEY... YEAH? NO... DON'T TAKE MY BIKE... THE CHAIN IM ZYDE DUH LID... LIDLL HOUTH... TAKE... BIKE... DUH... SADURN STILLEDO... IT... IT'S FIN... UHH...

I HEAR THIS GUY THEY'RE BRINGING IN IS A REAL WITCH DOCTOR! YOU DON'T SUPPOSE HE MIGHT PUT A CURSE ON US BECAUSE WE'RE BUGGIN' HIM, DO YA?
NAW! HE'LL PUT A CURSE ON YOU 'CAUSE YOU WERE BORN WITHOUT A BRAIN!
YOU DON'T SUPPOSE SHE'S REALLY DYING?

RELAX, BOYS! SHE'S IN GOOD HANDS! I HEAR DOCTOR NUMURA MUMURA IS THE BEST! HE'S WORLD FAMOUS FOR THIS OPERATION! ONLY HE CAN HANDLE THIS SICKNESS!
WHAT'S HE GONNA DO, TOMMY GUN IT OUT OF HER?

I WAS SO DELIRIOUS THAT ALL I REMEMBER WAS A BIG, BIG SHADOW COME INTO MY HUT AND IT STARTED PAINTING THE WALLS. AND THEN IT STARTED TO SMELL LIKE OLD, MOLDY TORTILLAS. I THOUGHT FOR SURE I WAS BEING PICKED UP TO GO TO THE OL' BARRIO IN THE SKY.

JUST THEN, ALL THE THINGS IN THE ROOM STARTED SLAMMING LIKE CRAZY. I THOUGHT THAT WAS MY GOING AWAY PARTY. I SCREAMED.

THAT WAS WHEN I STARTED TO REALLY GET SCARED. EVERYTHING STARTED TO GET DULL, AND THEN CAME THE KOOKY PATTERNS. BUT THE THING TO TOP IT ALL OFF WAS THE MARCHING DOUGHNUTS.

IT SEEMED LIKE FOREVER, AND JUST WHEN I WAS READY TO CASH IT IN, I COULD HEAR A WOMAN CRYING. THEN ALL OF A SUDDEN I GOT REALLY COLD. AND THE CRY GOT LOUDER, AND I GOT COLDER. AND THE CLOSER THE CRYING GOT, THE COLDER I GOT.

END OF PART IV

MECHANICS PART 5

JAIME 82

DAY 33-36

WITH MY SICKNESS ALL GONE, I WOKE UP TODAY FEELING LIKE I COULD FLY. TSE TSE TOLD ME I SLEPT THREE WHOLE DAYS. SHE ALSO TOLD ME THAT IT WASN'T MOE TOWNE FEVER I HAD. IT WAS THE VAN SCOY FLU, WHICH IS WORSE. SHE SAID IT WAS A MIRACLE I LIVED THROUGH IT. MUST BE THE CHICANA BLOOD. ANYWAY, I WON'T BE SHOWING MY FACE TO ANYBODY TILL THESE UGLY MONSTER BUMPS GO AWAY. I TRULY LOOK LIKE A BEAST FROM THE HAUNTED DAIRY. HOW EMBARRASSING, HAH? EARLIER TODAY I HEARD THE MEN TALKING ABOUT THAT DAMN SHIP AGAIN. THEY WANT TO VENTURE INSIDE. THEY'LL BE SORRY IF THEY DO.

THE BOYS ARE IN ZHATO RIGHT NOW! THEY'RE...
OH, GOOD! BECAUSE I'VE GOT A VERY FUNNY FEELING ABOUT THAT SHIP...

WHEN I WAS RAGING WITH FEVER, I HAD THESE REALLY CRAZY DREAMS ABOUT ME GOING DOWN INTO THE SHIP ALL ALONE! AND THE FURTHER DOWN I WENT, THE MORE I GOT THIS STRANGE FEELING, AS IF SOMETHING ALIVE WAS DOWN THERE WAITING! OR EVEN THE SHIP ITSELF... LIKE IT WAS ALIVE, WAITING TO SWALLOW ME! YOU CAN FEEL IT, TOO! I KNOW YOU DO! YOU DO... DON'T YOU...?

WELL, YOU DON'T HAVE TO WORRY! NO ONE WILL BE GOING DOWN THERE! THE WHOLE JOB HAS BEEN CALLED OFF! SAN JO HAS HAD THE WHOLE PROJECT DROPPED! KAPUT!
THEN, WE CAN GO HOME NOW?

"NOT FOR AWHILE! THE BOYS ARE IN ZHATO BECAUSE RACE WAS ARRESTED FOR BEATING THE HELL OUT OF PEDERO RODRIGUEZ SAN JO! DUKE AND YAX WENT ALONG TO ACT AS HIS DEFENSE! I SHUDDER TO THINK HOW THAT TRIAL IS TURNING OUT! POOR RACE."

SHOULDN'T WE TAKE THE CHOPPER AND GET TO THEM RIGHT AWAY?
NO GOOD! WHEN SAN JO ENDED THE JOB, HE TOOK AWAY ALL HIS TOYS, TOO!

"HE TOOK AWAY EVERYTHING HE SUPPLIED YOU WITH! INCLUDING THE CHOPPER, FOOD, TOOLS, ETC... ALL THAT'S LEFT IS TSE TSE, YOU, ME AND THE LOCALS! THEY ALREADY AGREED TO SHARE THEIR FOOD WITH US IF WE HELP WITH THE CHORES. AT LEAST SAN JO HAD THE DECENCY TO LEAVE THESE POOR PEOPLE ALONE.

"WHILE YOU SLEPT THOSE PAST THREE DAYS, THAT SCREWBALL SAN JO HAD A NEWSTEAM FLOWN OVER TO COVER 'THE STORY OF THE YEAR!' BUT THAT ENDED WHEN THE GOOD OL' DINOSAUR ATE THE CAMERA."

SO YOU BETTER GET USED TO THIS PLACE, BECAUSE WE CAN'T LEAVE TILL RACE IS OUT OF THE CLINK! AND THAT'S GOING TO BE A LONG TIME! JUST US, THAT DINOSAUR, AND...
...AND THE MOUTH OF HELL...?
YEAH...

BERNIE... (SIGH)
26

DAY 37

ANOTHER DAY PASSED AND THE BOYS STILL HAVEN'T RETURNED, AND SAN JO HASN'T YET LOWERED THE BIG ONE ON US. ALL DAY LONG RENA AND TSE TSE WORK WITH THE NATIVES WHILE I LIE HERE WAITING TO LOOK LIKE A HUMAN BEING AGAIN.

DAY 38 STILL WAITING FOR THE BOYS TO RETURN, MY BLISTERS FINALLY DISAPPEARED AND I CAME OUT.

PLEASE, RENA? I'M DYING TO HEAR ALL ABOUT YOUR WRESTLING CAREER! AND THEN LIKE, WHAT HAPPENED AFTER...

WELL, OK! I USUALLY DON'T LIKE TO GET INTO IT, BUT SEEING YOU'RE A FAN OF THE SPORT...

"I WAS FOURTEEN AND SERVING IN THE P.P.S. JUNIOR HARD CORPS WHEN I STARTED TO ENJOY GOING TO THE MATCHES. MY FAVORITE WAS THE WOMEN'S CHAMPION, TIGER ROSA. I'D FOLLOW HER EVERYWHERE SHE'D GRAPPLE. SOON, I STARTED DREAMING ABOUT US AS TAG TEAM PARTNERS. THAT WAS WHEN I DECIDED TO ASK HER TO TRAIN ME.

"SHE AGREED, AND IN SIX MONTHS I BECAME A PRO! AND GIRL, WAS I HOT! I WON EVERY ONE OF MY MATCHES AND WAS NAMED ROOKIE OF THE YEAR. I WAS TEARING ALL THE OLD LOUD MOUTHS APART.

"BUT I SHOULD HAVE REALIZED IT WAS A SCAM WHEN TIGER FINALLY ASKED ME TO BE HER PARTNER. THE CONTRACT'S FINE PRINT SAID I COULD ONLY WRESTLE ALONGSIDE HER. SO, FOR A FULL YEAR I WASTED MY TALENT STANDING BY AS TIGER TOOK ALL THE GLORY. SEE, BEING CHAMP, SHE HAD A LOT OF MONEY POWER. ENOUGH TO KEEP ME OUT OF THE SPOTLIGHT. SHE KNEW I WAS STAR MATERIAL, AND SHE ALSO KNEW I'D STEAL HER TITLE SOON ENOUGH. HER CONTRACT MADE SURE I WAS PUT ASIDE. BUT SOON, MY CONTRACT SOMEHOW GOT TERMINATED, AND I WAS READY TO DESTROY HER. BUT, AS ALWAYS, THERE WAS A CATCH.

"A NOBODY WASN'T ALLOWED TO SHOOT FOR THE WORLD TITLE! BUT THAT DIDN'T STOP ME. I HAD TO TAKE ON ALL THE BIGGIES BEFORE I COULD GET MY HANDS ON TIGER. FIRST, I MADE FORMER CHAMP, BAD MONTANA JANE EAT SHIT. THEN I BEAT THE STATE CHAMP, ANN AUSTIN. IT'S TOO BAD BECAUSE SHE WAS A GOOD FRIEND. FINALLY, I MADE THE NATIONAL CHAMPION, FAT, OLD MARIA BRAVO PLEAD FOR MERCY. GIRL, I WAS ON FIRE!

"SO FINALLY WHEN I GOT A CHANCE AT THE WORLD TITLE, ROSA NEVER KNEW WHAT HIT HER. IT TOOK A LONG TIME, BUT IT WAS WORTH IT. I WAS NOW QUEEN RENA OF THE LADY WRESTLERS. AND BEING CHAMP WAS FUN. CHALLENGERS CAME IN ALL FORMS. MY BIGGIES WERE AGAINST MAD MALA, SULTRY SIRENA, THE BLACK WIDOW, WHO I UNMASKED, AND KITTY KATZ, THE HOT NEWCOMER I WAS SUPPOSED TO WATCH OUT FOR. HELL, IT LASTED FIVE MINUTES. I WHIPPED 'EM ALL!

"I WAS INVINCIBLE! FOR TEN YEARS NOBODY COULD BEAT ME! VERY FEW EVEN CAME CLOSE. I WAS GETTING BORED...

"SO THEN I DECIDED TO DO TAG TEAMING AGAIN. MY PARTNER WAS A NEWCOMER NAMED VICKI GLORI. AND SURE ENOUGH, WE RIPPED AND QUICKLY BECAME THE NEW WORLD TAG TEAM CHAMPS.

"FOUR YEARS WE WERE UNDEFEATED, UNTIL ONE NIGHT WHEN WE WRESTLED THE VICIOUS HOGG SISTERS. I WAS IN TROUBLE. BOTH THOSE FAT BITCHES WERE STOMPING THE SHIT OUT OF ME. I CRIED AND CRIED OUT FOR HELP FROM VICKI. BUT WHEN I LOOKED UP, I SAW HER STARING AT ME BACKING AWAY SHAKING HER HEAD LIKE A DAMN COWARD. AND AFTER I WAS PLASTERED, PINNED, AND LOST OUR BELTS TO THOSE ELEPHANTS, VICKI CAME BACK TO THE RING TO HELP ME UP. I PASTED HER A COUPLE AND FLUNG HER OUT OF THE RING. I'LL NEVER KNOW WHY SHE EVER DID THAT, BUT FROM THEN ON, WE'VE BEEN GREAT ENEMIES. SHE TRIED TO STEAL MY TITLE SEVERAL TIMES, AND SEVERAL TIMES SHE ALMOST DID. BUT NOT BY WRESTLING ALONE. SHE BEGAN TO USE ILLICIT MEANS TO PREVAIL. I MEAN, SHE WAS DIRTY. SHE KICKED, PUNCHED, GAUGED, CHOKED, PULLED HAIR, ANYTHING TO WIN. SHE BECAME MERCILESS.
"BUT, AS ALWAYS I CAME BACK AT THE END TO WHIP THE BUNS OFF HER. UNTIL ONE DAY...

"THAT ONE DAY, TEN YEARS AGO IN NEW KEOPS. IT WAS THE VERY FIRST WRESTLING MATCH TELEVISED VIA SATELLITE. IT WAS SHOWN IN THIRTY DIFFERENT COUNTRIES AROUND THE WORLD. TARZAN GOVENDER CALLED IT, 'THE MATCH OF THE CENTURY.' IT WAS WILD..."
OH OH! VICKI HAS RENA IN REAL TROUBLE NOW!

I REMEMBER THAT DAY, WHEN SHE FINALLY BEAT YOU! I SAW IT WHEN...
SAW IT?! HAH! WHERE?! HOW OLD WERE YOU?!

I SAW IT ON TV! I REMEMBER, IT WAS MY BIRTHDAY! I HAD JUST TURNED EIGHT!
EIGHT?! YOU'RE BLIND WHEN YOU'RE A LITTLE KID! AND TV DIDN'T SHOW WHAT REALLY HAPPENED! I WAS CHEATED! SHE USED THE DAMN ROPES! I YELLED, "ROPES, ROPES!" BUT WE HAD A DEAF REF! SHE USED THE ROPES, I TELL YA!

SHE USED THE ROPES... SHE USED THE DAMN ROPES! SHE USED THE GOD DAMN FUCKING SHITTY ROPES!

B-BUT WASN'T THERE SOMETHING ABOUT A REMATCH? I DON'T CLEARLY REMEMBER, BUT THEY SAID THAT YOU NEVER CAME OUT OF YOUR DRESSING ROOM, AND THAT YOU SKIPPED TOWN BECAUSE YOU TURNED YELLOW!
ARE YOU KIDDING? I WAS KIDNAPPED FROM MY ROOM AND TAKEN TO WAR TORN ZYMBODIA! THEY LOVED MY WRESTLING SO MUCH THAT THE DICK DICTATORS OF DURIA PAN MADE ME QUEEN! I LATER TURNED ON THEM AND JOINED THE BLACK FIST LIBERATION ARMY! I WAS ITCHING TO GET BACK TO THE RING, BUT I WAS JUST TOO BUSY!
"THEN THAT'S WHEN I MET CAPTAIN BERNIE CARBO! WE WERE GOING TO RULE THE WORLD TOGETHER IN HIS SATURN STILLETTO. BUT, WHEN HIS SHIP WAS LOST, I THOUGHT IT WAS ALL OVER. YOU KNOW, THERE'S NEVER BEEN ANYONE SINCE.

WAR
NOW
COME ON! LET'S GO GET SOME BEER!
PERVERT SAYS: "ITS HERE! EVACUATE
WAR COME SOON
GET OUT!
HELP!
SPLIT!!
29

AND IZZY, I BROUGHT THE MASK YOU WANTED SO YOU CAN DO SOME OF THAT WEIRD MAGIC YOU'RE ALWAYS CLAIMING YOU DO! I HOPE YOU DON'T MIND IF I GOT ONE AS CLOSE TO YOUR LIKNESS AS POSSIBLE!

HM, NOW I KNOW WHO I CAN PUT MY FIRST SPELL ON!

MECHANICS 6
YOU WIMMINS IS CRAZY! TOROMBOLO GET YOU BUT GOOD!
HEAR THAT, RENA? COME ON! WHAT'S IT GOING TO PROVE BY GOING DOWN THERE?

NOW, MARGARET! WE'VE ALREADY GONE THROUGH THIS BEFORE! WE'RE JUST GOING TO MAKE SURE THIS OLD EYE SORE REALLY IS DEAD!

BUT, WHAT IF SOMETHING IS STILL DOWN THERE? LIKE, SOMETHING EVIL?
DON'T WORRY! IF I NEED YOUR HELP, I'LL HOLLER ON THE OL' RADIO!

WELL, WHAT ABOUT AIR? THEY TOOK ALL THE GAS MASKS! YOU...
TSK! SHE IN TROUBLE!
THERE'S A BIG DRAFT THAT SEEMS TO TRAVEL THROUGH THE SHIP! 'BYE, MOM! DON'T WAIT UP TOO LATE FOR ME!

SHIT, DUKE! YOU HAD TO OPEN YOUR BIG FUCKING MOUTH! I WOULD HAVE BEEN OUT BY NOW! BUT, NOOO... YOU HAD TO TAKE MY CASE TO A HIGHER COURT! OH, I DESERVE MUCH BETTER... SHEEIT... WHAT THE HELL GAVE YOU THE IDEA YOUR MECHANIC KNOW-HOW WOULD MAKE YOU A GOOD LAWYER ANYWAY?
OYE... YOU RAND RACE? YEAH, YOU ARE...
32

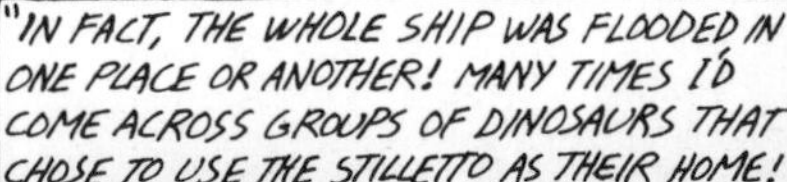

"I EVEN RAN INTO A FEW OLD FRIENDS, BUT NOWHERE IN THE SHIP COULD I FIND BERNIE CARBO'S BODY... FORTUNATELY...

"AT FIRST I ALMOST WANTED THAT SHIP TO SWALLOW ME UP. BUT, YOU KNOW, THE DEEPER I WENT DOWN INTO IT, THE MORE I GOT THE FEELING I WAS THE ONLY THREAT IN THE WHOLE DAMN THING. I SOON REALIZED I HAD ABSOLUTELY NOTHING TO FEAR...

"THEN I KNEW IT WAS TIME TO LEAVE WHEN I ACCIDENTLY OPENED THE WRONG HATCH! WHATEVER WAS DOWN THERE IS NOW PART OF THE WORLD'S LARGEST AQUARIUM! HELL, THERE NEVER WAS ANY MONSTER DOWN THERE..."

BUMP BAM BOO
THERE'S YOUR DAMN MONSTER!
AIEEE!!

HE'S HERE! TOROMBOLO! NO! MARGARET! WHERE YOU GOING?!
I GOTS TO KNOW!

NO, MARGARET! IT'S TOROMBOLO! AND HE BE ANGRY AT US! WE'S HAS TO RUN, OR WE DIE!
OH MY GO— NO, IT'S NOT TOROMBOLO... IT'S...

IT'S WORSE! IT'S... IT'S... SANJO!

...WELL, YOU COULD PRETEND YOU DROPPED YOUR KEYS RIGHT NEXT TO MY CELL!
SO YOU CAN ESCAPE? FEH!

ESCAPE? NOW, WHY WOULD I WANT TO...
¡ALTO!
KIKILIN...

OYE, KIKI... I MEAN LIKE, WHAT'S SHAKIN'?
AY KARAY...
34

I HOPE YOU REALIZE I'M IN DEEPER TROUBLE THAN EVER NOW!

WE CAN WORRY ABOUT THAT LATER! RIGHT NOW WE HAVE TO SAVE MY BEST FRIEND FROM CERTAIN DOOM!

IS THIS NOT FUN, MARGARET? NOW THAT YOU TOLD ME THOSE BIG BOMBS ARE NOT TOROMBOLO, I NOT BE SCARED NO MORE!
WELL, START! THIS IS WORSE!

LET'S HOPE THE WHOLE PLACE ISN'T A GODDAMN VACANT LOT YET!
OR A CRATER!
OR... A CREVASSE...?
WHAT'S THAT UP AHEAD?
SEXCH

LOOK!
OH, SHIT! MORTARS! LET'S STEP ON IT!

DAMN YOU, SAN JO! I'LL GET YOU FOR THIS! IF I EVER GET OUT OF THIS ONE, I'M COMING AFTER YOU!
SAN JO BIGGER'N TOROMBOLO, HUH? RENA TITAÑON, LOOK!
EEEK

IT'S GOTTA BE THE BOYS! AND JUST IN TIME, TOO! GRAB ALL THE STUFF!
THE GROUND'S MOVING!

SHIT! THE WHOLE THING'S SINKING! HURRY, RENA! WHERE'S MARGIE?
I DON'T KNOW! SHE WAS RIGHT BEHIND ME!

GRAB ON! WE CAN'T LAND THIS THING! AND WHERE THE HELL IS MARGIEEE?!
HERE I AM!
36

HEY! WAIT FOR ME! EVERY-THING'S SINKING!
NEVER MIND! JUST GRAB HOLD!
COME ON, MARGIE! YOU'RE ALMOST THERE!
URK
GOT YOU!
WOW! THAT'S THE STUFF COMICS ARE MADE OF!
EEK! SOMEBODY TURN THE PAGE! YOU CAN SEE MY PANTIES!
37

DOWN IT WENT. DOWN IT ALL WENT. THE DINOSAUR, THE PAIN IN THE ASS SATURN STILLETO, ALL THOSE FEARS I HAD THAT PAST MONTH, ALL OF IT. IT WAS KINDA LIKE TURNING THE HANDLE AND FLUSHING THIS BIG, BIG TOILET KNOWN AS MY HEAD. I FELT SO RELIEVED. BUT IT WASN'T OVER YET.

WE FINALLY REACHED THE OUTSKIRTS OF ZHATO WHEN SOME SOLDIERS TOOK AWAY OUR CHOPPER AND WE HAD TO WALK. AFTER A WHILE WE REACHED THE TOWN ONLY TO FIND IT A FUCKING WRECK. PEOPLE WERE RUNNING ALL OVER THE PLACE LAUGHING, CRYING, LOOTING, DANCING, FIGHTING, WHATEVER THEY COULD THINK OF. I GUESS IT WAS WAR. PENNY DIDN'T CARE, RENA LOVED IT AND I WAS SCARED OUT OF MY SHIT. IT WAS KIND OF EXCITING, THOUGH, WHEN WE SAW THEM BRING DOWN THE STATUE OF SAN JO THEY HAD IN A PARK.

MR. RACE! WE REGRET TO INFORM YOU THAT SANCHO SAN JO AND HIS ENTIRE FAMILY HAVE FLED THE COUNTRY AND ARE NOWHERE TO BE FOUND. HE TOOK WITH HIM HIS PRIVATE DOCUMENTS, SO ACCORDING TO LAW, YOU AND YOUR COLLEAGUES CANNOT BE PAID UNTIL HE IS LOCATED. BUT, YOU'LL BE HAPPY TO HEAR YOUR SENTENCE HAS BEEN COMMUTED. SINCE WE CANNOT LOCATE THE PLAINTIFFS WE CANNOT HAVE A CASE! CONGRADULATIONS, MR. RACE!

SO, ALL ALONG THE PEOPLE OF ZYMBODIA PLANNED TO DESTROY THEIR SELF APPOINTED LEADER. AND RENA, WHOM THEY CALL "LA TOÑA," WAS BEHIND THE WHOLE THING. WHAT A WOMAN. SHE SHOWS THE PEOPLE HOW TO THINK FREE THEN MOVES ON. WILD.

WE LEFT TSE TSE AT THE ORPHANAGE IN EL PICASON, WHERE SHE LIVES WITH TWENTY OTHER KIDS. I PROMISED TO GO BACK AND VISIT HER IF SHE TOLD ME HER REAL NAME. IT'S ROSA COLORES ARRIAGA BANUELOS. I PROMISED TSE TSE I'D WRITE HER.

THE PLANE WILL TAKE YOU STRAIGHT TO HYMEH AIRPORT IN TURO! THEN YOU'RE HOME FREE!
THANKS, RENA! WHERE WILL YOU GO NOW?
I STILL HAVE SOME UNFINISHED BUSINESS HERE IN ZHATO, THEN I'M GOING TO MANO VIEJO!
'BYE, RENA! AND I HOPE YOU FIND YOUR CAPTAIN BERNIE CARBO!
THANK YOU! AND DON'T FORGET TO TELL YOUR AUNT VICKI I WANT THAT REMATCH!
YUP, SHE KNEW ALL ALONG I WAS VICKI GLORI'S NIECE! I GUESS YOU JUST CAN'T FOOL RENA TITAÑON! I HOPE I SEE HER AGAIN SOMEDAY! SHE'S REALLY SOMETHING!
SHE SOUNDS LIKE SOME KIND OF GODDESS!
YEAH, KINDA! AND SAN JO, THE SATURN STILLETTO, THE LIZARD, EVEN PENNY, ALL LIKE TOROMBOLO WERE KINDA LIKE GODS, TOO!
IT'S KINDA WEIRD, Y'KNOW? AT FIRST, RACE WAS KIND OF LIKE A GOD OR IDOL WHEN I MET HIM!
HE'S JUST A MAN!
EXACTLY! AND BY MY EXPERIENCES I REALIZED THAT ALL THESE GODS I CAME ACROSS WERE JUST FLESH LIKE ME, OR WERE JUST FLAT OUT FEARS TO BEGIN WITH...
EITHER GOOD OR BAD, IN MY MIND...
OH, OH! HERE COMES THE PUNCH LINE...
I-I DON'T KNOW! IN MY MIND IT WAS KINDA LIKE THE DAY THE GODS CAME DOWN AND DESTROYED EACH OTHER!
MAGGOT, YOU'RE A REAL NUT!
I KNOW! I LOVE YOU GUYS, TOO!
WELCOME BACK, DEAR MAGGIE!
THE WAR IN ZHATO STILL RAGES ON...
39

I DON'T GET IT, CARBO! TEN YEARS IN THIS PIT OF SLIME AND YOU CAN STILL SMILE?
1/82-10/92
free
R19-5171
SUSPICION
DAILY GLIBERÓ
INVASION HALT!
SAN JO GUNNED DOWN ON STREET
TITAÑON STARTS N
REVOLUTION IN MANO VI
WOMAN EA
APPLE PIE
FIN

hey hopey
HEY'S FOR HORSES, ASS BITE!
JAIME 85

HEY, HOPEY! WHERE YOU OFF TO, GIRL?
NUNYA.

NUNYA?
NUNYA BUSINESS.

HEY, HOPEY! MOM'S IN TOWN. SHE WANTS TO SEE YOU.
WHAT'S SHE WANNA DO? SHOW OFF HER NEW BOY-FRIEND?

YOU MET HIM ALREADY?
I DON'T HAVE TO MEET HIM, IF I KNOW OUR MOTHER...

HE'S BLOND, MUSTACHE, ONE EYEBROW, BLUE EYES, WEARS HIS SPORT SHIRTS TWO SIZES TOO SMALL, RIGHT?
WRONG. GREEN EYES.

WELL, I'M GLAD TO SEE MOM'S MADE A BIG CHANGE IN HER LIFE.
HEY, I NOTICED YOU HAVEN'T BEEN RAISING TOO MUCH HELL NOW THAT YOUR LOVER MAGGIE'S BEEN GONE.
BOXERS FACES

WHAT'S THE MATTER, CASANOVA? JEALOUS BECAUSE YOU CAN'T GET INTO HER LITTLE PANTIES?
SHEEIT! SHE'S JUST SCARED I MIGHT CRIPPLE HER.

DON'T WORRY, JOEY. YOU STILL HAVE ALL THOSE THIRTEEN YEAR OLDS WAITING IN LINE.
BUT THEY'RE NOT MAGGIE, MAN! HOW COME YOU NEVER SET ME UP WITH HER?
1

I DUNNO, JOEY. I DON'T THINK YOU'RE MAGGIE'S TYPE. SHE KINDA LIKES HER MEN RUGGED, YOU KNOW WHAT I MEAN?
SHE LIKES THAT SPEEDY CHOLO, HUH?
EL SANTO

WELL, YEAH. SHE LIKES 'EM A LITTLE OLDER, TOO.
SHE STILL STUCK ON THAT MECHANIC DUDE? GOD, WHAT A DIPSHIT!

BUT THEN, SHE LIKES 'EM TO TREAT HER REAL TENDERLIKE. REAL NICE...

...AND THEN SHE LETS 'EM TIE HER UP TO BEAT HER WITH A HOT WHEEL TRACK!

BUT, YOU JUST SCREW 'EM AND THEN HANG 'EM OUT TO DRY. WHAT THE HELL IS THAT? NO SELF RESPECTING GIRL WANTS THAT KINDA SHIT!
HUH! YOU'D KNOW, 'CAUSE ALL YOU GO OUT WITH IS GIRLS. WHAT THE HELL IS THAT?

MY BROTHER. MY POOR LITTLE BROTHER. MAYBE SOMEDAY YOU'LL SEE THINGS MY WAY...
HUH? I AIN'T GONNA TURN GAY!

IF YOU THINK I'M EVER GONNA BECOME A FAG... YOU'RE REALLY STUPID!
I MEANT YOU'LL ACCEPT THINGS FOR WHAT THEY ARE! NOW I'M NOT SO SURE!

I MEAN, JUST 'CAUSE ME AND MAGGIE LIVE TOGETHER AND SLEEP IN THE SAME BED DOESN'T MEAN ANYTHING. JUST 'CAUSE WE HOLD HANDS WHILE WALKING DOWN THE STREET DOESN'T MEAN SHIT!
BUT, YOU LIKE HER...

SURE, I LIKE MAGGIE, STUPID! SINCE WHEN CAN'T A GIRL LIKE ANOTHER GIRL?
NO. I MEAN, YOU WANNA HAVE HER FOR LUNCH. YOU WANNA DRINK HER THIGHS...
2

YOU'RE GETTING REAL ANNOYING, NOW...
C'MON, HOPEY! YOU'RE NOT FOOLING ANYBODY! EVERYBODY KNOWS ABOUT YOU AND MAGGIE!
LITTER

OH, YEAH, MISS RONA? WHAT ARE THEY SAYING?
WELL, THAT YOU TWO ARE... YOU KNOW, GOING OUT.

OH, HORRORS! WILL I EVER LIVE IT DOWN? GET LOST, WILL YA?
AW, WHY DONT YOU JUST COME OUT AND ADMIT IT? YOU ARE A LESBO!
RODDY PIPER
EL SANTO
LITTER

GET AWAY FROM ME! I DONT WANNA TALK TO YOU NO MORE! YOU'RE HOPELESS!
AND YOU ARE SPOILING MAGGIE'S CHANCE TO BE WITH A REAL MAN!

I SAID GET OUTA HERE, YOU ASSHOLE!
HEY! THOSE HURT! OUCH!
KLAK
KLAK
KLAK

NOW, ARE WE GONNA QUIT ACTING LIKE THE ALL POWERFUL SHIT HEAD, OR DO I PASTE YOU SOME IN THE EYES?
OK, OK! I GIVE UP! STOP!

SO, ARE YOU GONNA GO SEE MOM OR DO I HAVE TO BRAVE IT ALL BY MYSELF?
I'D RATHER SURF THE SAN ANDREAS FAULT.
PURO WESTSIDE
SORANO
LOCOS
CHUY

CAN'T YOU SEE, JOEY? ME AND MOM ARE ON THE OUTS RIGHT NOW. KAPUT!
YEAH, SHE STILL GIVES ME SHIT FOR LIVING WITH DAD. BUT THAT'S ONLY LIKE NOW, WHEN SHE GETS A NEW HUNK.

I'VE GOT A BETTER IDEA, JOEY. WHY DON'T WE PICK UP A SIX PACK AND READ MY LATEST LETTER FROM MAGGIE. MAYBE SHE PUTS IN A GOOD WORD FOR YOU TODAY.
YOU BUY.
END

JAIME 82-83

Maggie vs MANIAKK

THE MECHANIC WITH: HOPEY • GIGGLES GALDRE • VENETIA VENDETTA • PENNY CENTURY

HOW CUTE. LOOK AT PENNY AND HER SILLY COMIC BOOKS.

SILLY IS RIGHT! PENNY, ARE YOU GOING TO SIT THERE ALL DAY READING THOSE THINGS? THERE'S MORE IMPORTANT THINGS IN LIFE, YOU KNOW!

I'M HIP. I'D GIVE ANYTHING TO BE A SUPER HERO.

1

WHEN I WAS A LITTLE GIRL, I SAW COMRADE 7 NAB SOME CROOKS. SINCE THEN, I'VE BEEN THE PRESIDENT OF HER FAN CLUB.
I HAVE AN AUTOGRAPH FROM ROCK MAN.
THAT'S NOTHING! I USED TO GO OUT WITH RAT MAN BEFORE HE WAS PUT IN THE SLAMMER FOR LIFE!
MAGGIE WAS A SUPER HERO ONCE.

YEAH, HE USED TO TAKE ME TO... A WHAT? A SUPER HERO!?!
YOU WERE, MAGGIE? YOU?

NOW'S YOUR CHANCE, MAG. THEY'VE BEEN TALKING SHIT ALL AFTERNOON. GO 'HEAD, TELL 'EM HOW YOU BECAME A SUPER HERO.
WHEN? OH, YEAH. THEN...

YOU, MAGGOT? DON'T MAKE ME LAUGH! WHO WERE YOU? RUMP WOMAN? BUTT ANGEL? ATOM ASS? BUTTOX, THE...
GO ON. QUIT TEASING US, MAGGIE. WE'RE SERIOUS.
YOU TELL 'EM, MAG.

R-REALLY, MAGGIE?
HONEST.
OH, YEAH? TELL US ABOUT IT THEN!

"WELL, IT STARTED WHEN I GOT MY FIRST SOLO MECHANICS JOB. I HAD TO FIX A HIGHLY DELICATE MAEYAMESE MINI TRANSPORTER.
YAWN
TOP SECRET

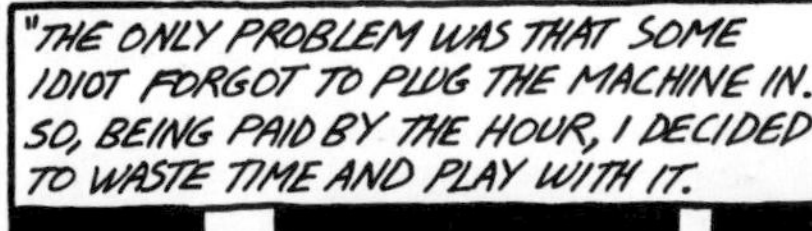
"THE ONLY PROBLEM WAS THAT SOME IDIOT FORGOT TO PLUG THE MACHINE IN. SO, BEING PAID BY THE HOUR, I DECIDED TO WASTE TIME AND PLAY WITH IT.

"IT WAS LOADS OF FUN, LIKE, TRANSPORTING LITTLE ODDS AND ENDS ACROSS THE WORLD AND GETTING BACK EVEN ODDER ENDS. BUT THEN IT WENT A LITTLE TOO FAR...
2

TO BE CONTINUED--

PART 2
ULTIMAX
OH, EXCUSE ME. I MUST HAVE THE WRONG ROOM! I'M LOOKING FOR... OH, MY... YOU'RE ULTIMAX?
OOH... AN ANGEL! AN' SHE KNOWS YA, UL!
YEH, YEH, IT'S ME. MAKE IT FAST, THEN SPLIT. I DON'T LIKE VISITORS.

DON'T TELL ME. YOU NEED MY HELP TO SAVE THE WORLD. WELL, YOU CAME TO THE WRONG GUY. DON'T DO THAT CRIMEFIGHTING SHIT NO MORE. WHY DON'T YOU GET SOMEONE LIKE THE ABOVENGERS, OR THE BESTEST LEAGUE OF ARMENIA, OR...
BUT... WELL... UM...

YOU'RE THE ONLY SUPER HERO WHO CAN WITHSTAND MANIAKK'S DEATH BOLTS.
MANIAKK? NO! IT COULDN'T BE! I SENT HIM INTO THE NINTH DIMENSION YEARS AGO!

YOU DID SAY MANIAKK! HOW DID HE ESCAPE? HOW? HOW?
WELL, Y'SEE, IT STARTED WHEN I WAS FIXING A BROKEN M-MINI TRANSPORTER AND, Y'SEE...

IT'S NOT YOUR FAULT! I FIGURED SCIENCE WOULD FIND A WAY INTO OTHER DIMENSIONS SOONER OR LATER! COME, WE HAVEN'T A MOMENT TO LOSE! I THINK I STILL REMEMBER THE INGREDIENTS TO... AHH...
THIS IS ULTIMAX??

THIS CONCOCTION I NOW HOLD IN MY HAND IS THE THING THAT COMPLETELY CHANGED THE LIFE OF A YOUNG, NAIVE SCIENTIST MANY YEARS AGO.
OOTAH...

SO STAND BACK AND WITNESS THE ULTIMATE, MOST AWSOME SPECTACLE YOUR EYES COULD EVER WITNESS.
YOU'RE KIDDING.
BEHOLD...
YOU'RE NOT KIDDING?
4

HOW COULD YOU EVER HAVE DOUBTED ME? HM?
WHO? ME?

GO AHEAD, TOUCH IT. SEE? IT PROVES YOU'RE NOT DREAMING. IT'S THE REAL ME, ALL RIGHT. AND NOW, IF YOU'LL EXCUSE ME, I'M OFF TO END MANIAKK'S REIGN OF TERROR.
GO, MAN, GO.

OH, WOE... I-I CAN'T DO IT! I JUST REMEMBERED THE REASON I QUIT THE BUSINESS IN THE FIRST PLACE! IF YOU'LL NOTICE, MY BACK UP DOESN'T SEEM TO BE HERE!
YOUR LOYAL SIDEKICK, GO-GO GIRL. WHERE IS SHE?

SHE LEFT ME! SHE SOMEHOW GOT SUPER POWERS AND TURNED BAD ON ME! SHE BECAME DEMONA, THE MOST POWERFUL WOMAN ON THIS WORLD!

WITHOUT HER I'M NOTHING! YOU SEE, GO-GO GIRL WASN'T JUST A KICK ON THE SIDE! SHE WAS ALSO MY GET UP AND GO! SHE WAS MY SOUL... MY INSPIRATION... SHE GAVE ME CONFIDENCE TO KICK ASS! WITHOUT HER I-I'M NO GOOD, I... I... YOU...
H-HEY! YOU'RE GO-GO GIRL!
WHAT?!?

PLEASE? BE GO-GO GIRL FOR JUST ONE HOUR! I'LL GET YOU A COSTUME AND THEN WE CAN...
BUT... I CAN'T FIGHT! I DON'T HAVE ANY SUPER POWERS, OR...

YOU WON'T HAVE TO FIGHT! JUST STAND THERE AND LOOK GOOD! BESIDES, IT'LL BE A GOOD EXPERIENCE FOR YOU! JUST THINK, WHEN ALL YOUR FRIENDS SEE YOU! I MEAN, NOT EVERYONE CAN BE A REAL SUPER HERO FOR FREE NOWADAYS! WHAT DO YOU SAY?
DUH...

YOU'RE LOOKING REALLY TIP-TOP TODAY, GO-GO GIRL. READY FOR SOME ACTION?
UM... SURE. ONLY, HOW DID GO-GO GIRL FIGHT IN THIS THING?

YOU KNOW, I FEEL STRONGER ALREADY.
OOH! DO YOU FEEL A DRAFT?
5

TO BE CONTINUED--

PART 3 WHEN TITANS CRASH!!

UM... ULTIMAX? I'M SORRY TO BOTHER YOU, BUT DON'T YOU THINK YOU SHOULD START LOOKING FOR MANIAKK LIKE YOU PROMISED?

SURE, SURE, SURE. FIRST, LET ME CHECK ON OUR BOOKING FOR VEGAS, RENO, AND SALT LAKE CITY.

WHAT'S THE MATTER? WHY ARE YOU JUST STANDING HERE? I THOUGHT YOU WERE BACK TO NORMAL.
WELL, HEH. GO-GO GIRL ALWAYS STARTS THE BATTLE OFF WITH A DROPKICK OR SOMETHING.

HEED ME, MORTAL! BEFORE THIS DAY IS DONE, YOUR WORLD AS YOU KNOW IT WILL REEL UNTO MY SUPREME RULE! AND MY WILL, WILL BE DONE!!
YOU KNOW THIS WON'T LAST, YOU RABID FIEND!

I TOLD YOU NEVER TO CALL ME RABID!!

FFTOOM
OH, ARE YOU ALL RIGHT? DID HE HURT YOU?
ARE YOU KIDDING? THAT WAS JUST A LIGHT SHOW! BUT, SINCE I'M A MEMBER OF THE S.H.G. (SUPER HERO GUILD), I HAVE TO MAKE THIS FIGHT LOOK GOOD! MANIAKK HAS NO IMAGINATION! WITH HIS POWERS HE COULD RULE THE WORLD! HE JUST DOESN'T KNOW HOW!

BUT NOW THE LUNACY ENDS! I MUST PUT AN END TO MANIAKK'S SICK PLOY BEFORE ANY MORE LIVES ARE THREATENED! THINGS MAY GET BLOODY! WISH ME LUCK!
BREAK A LEG?

"FISTS FLEW, BOLTS BASHED, BUILDINGS BROKE, AND AFTER ABOUT TEN MINUTES, IT STARTED TO SLOW DOWN..."
THIS IS HORRIBLE! THEY... WAIT! ULTIMAX IS WINNING! HE...
¡POM!
POW
SOK
ZZAPPP
BIFF
TISH
BTHOK
BIM
BAM
BEM
BUM

YOU DID IT! YOU BEAT HIM! YOU WON!
DUH... YEAH... I DID, DIDN'T I? UH... WHERE ARE YOU?
"MANIAKK WAS SENT BACK TO THE NINTH DIMENSION."

THEN AFTER IT WAS ALL OVER, HE GAVE ME A BIG KISS AND LEFT. AND... THAT WAS THAT.
WOW!
BULL!
(CHOKE)
8

OH, BEBEH.

NOW, I DON'T WANT TO SEE YOU OR YOUR GANG HANGING AROUND HERE AGAIN. GOT THAT?

L-LOUD AND CLEAR, ATOMA!

EEYAGHHH! WE'RE SORRY WE'RE AIR HEADS! HAVE MERCEEEE!

FIN

STORY AND ART - JAIME MANIAKK'S DIALOGUE - MARIO HERNANDEZ 1982-83

LOCAS TAMBIEN

HI. WHERE ARE YOU GUYS GOING?
COMING TO SEE YOU. WE JUST GOT BACK FROM IZZY'S. WE HAD TO LEAVE BECAUSE SHE STARTED TO TALK ABOUT HER CEILING AGAIN.
AND THOSE FLIES...
SHE SAYS THAT THE FLIES UP THERE ARE REALLY RIGHT SIDE UP AND THAT THE REST OF US ARE UPSIDE DOWN. DO YOU THINK THAT'S TRUE?
DAFFY, YOU'RE THE ONLY PERSON IN THE WORLD WHO'S DUMBER THAN 'OL MAGGIE HERE.
HMF! CAN WE GO NOW?
MAG, DO YOU THINK ONE BOX OF SNICKERS IS ENOUGH? OOH, LOOK! SPACE WARRIOR STICK ONS! THESE'LL LOOK GREAT ON MY JACKET.
HMM...
HEY, LOOK! I THINK THE NATIONAL BLABBER HAS THAT PICTURE OF ME AND RACE WHEN WE GOT BACK FROM ZYMBODIA. WOULDN'T THAT BE FUNNY IF THEY SAID WE WERE GOING OUT OR SOMETHING?
HILARIOUS. LEMME SEE.
VIDA LOCA
BY GUM, YOU'RE RIGHT, MAG. THEY EVEN MADE YOU UP TO LOOK LIKE THAT TV STAR, LAVANA LAVERNE. OH, NO, THERE YOU ARE. YEP...
OK, OK, WHAT DOES IT SAY?
"LAVANA LAVERNE AND PROSOLAR MECHANIC RAND RACE HAVE BEEN SEEING A LOT OF EACH OTHER LATELY, SO I WOULDN'T BE SURPRISED IF THEY TIED THE KNOT REAL SOON." POOR RACE. THE GUY IS TRAPPED IN HIGH SOCIETY.
I'LL BET HE LOVES IT, TOO! GOD, REMIND ME NEVER TO LOOK IN ONE OF THOSE AGAIN.
FOODMART
YOU DON'T BELIEVE THAT ARTICLE, DO YOU? BY THE WAY, HOW ARE YOU AND RACE ANY WAY? I MEAN, DOES HE EVEN LIKE YOU?
SHOOT, I DON'T KNOW. SOMETIMES HE'LL REALLY COME ON TO ME, AND OTHER TIMES HE DOESN'T EVEN KNOW I'M ALIVE.
MAYBE HE DOESN'T KNOW WHAT HE WANTS. MAYBE HE'S CRAZY AS YOU ARE. MAYBE I DON'T EVEN KNOW WHAT THE HELL I'M TALKING ABOUT.
AND MAYBE WE SHOULD DROP THE SUBJECT, BEFORE I START CRYING.
MAY I HELP YOU?
VIDA LOCA
HI, PENNY. HOW LONG HAVE YOU BEEN WORKING HERE?
TWO DAYS. BUT, GUESS WHAT? I'M BEING FIRED ALREADY.
VIDA LOCA
THE MANAGER TRIED TO POKE ME IN THE STORE ROOM AND HIS WIFE SAW AND THEY BLAMED ME.
MEN ARE THE WORST. WHO NEEDS 'EM?
THEY THINK THEY CAN PUSH US WOMEN AROUND. WHEN THEY NEED US, OH, THEY TREAT US SO GOOD. BUT WHEN THEY DON'T, THEY TOSS US AWAY LIKE AN OLD RAG. WELL, I'M NOT STANDING FOR IT. THE DOGS WILL FALL...
THERE GOES SPEEDY.
OH, GOD, I HOPE HE COMES BACK THIS WAY. HE'S SO CUTE.
FIN
LA CHOTA VS ROY COWBOY THE CRUSTY KID
BY THE WORST '83
PICHO BEL TRINCHIS!
PAW! MENTO IL NOZ VEX! SAL TRINCHIS.
GINN TOOB NO SEMAYAN TOOB YI.
TOX!
CHEM!
B-BEDDO BIM BUM DEL TRINCHIS.
ENG

100 ROOMS

PART 1

HEY, VICKI! THIS GIRL WANTS TO TALK TO YOU! SHE SAYS SHE'S YOUR NIECE. SHOULD I THROW HER OUT?
NO, IT'S OK. SAY, SHRIMP! WATCHA DOON? SAY HI TO MY NIECE, GIRLS.
(GRUNT) PLEASED TO MEET... YIIII!
HOWDY, NIECE.

YOU DIDN'T COME ALL THIS WAY DOWN-TOWN JUST TO TELL ME THAT, DIDJA?
WELL, NO. I JUST HAPPENED TO BE NEAR AND DECIDED TO HEAR HOW THINGS ARE WITH YOU.
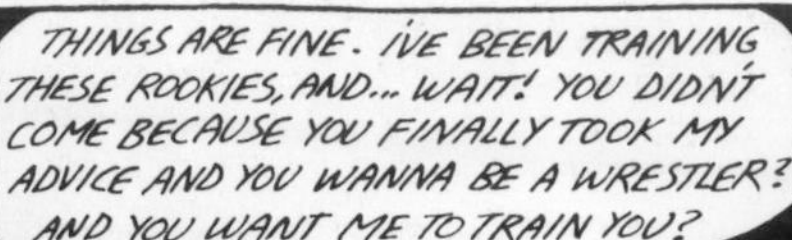
THINGS ARE FINE. I'VE BEEN TRAINING THESE ROOKIES, AND... WAIT! YOU DIDN'T COME BECAUSE YOU FINALLY TOOK MY ADVICE AND YOU WANNA BE A WRESTLER? AND YOU WANT ME TO TRAIN YOU?

WHO, ME? UH, WELL... NO... Y'SEE... I COULDN'T...
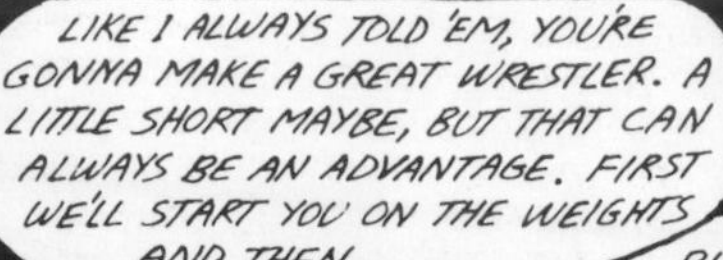
LIKE I ALWAYS TOLD 'EM, YOU'RE GONNA MAKE A GREAT WRESTLER. A LITTLE SHORT MAYBE, BUT THAT CAN ALWAYS BE AN ADVANTAGE. FIRST WE'LL START YOU ON THE WEIGHTS AND THEN...

BUT THAT'S NOT WHY I CAME, TIA.

OK. THEN WHY DID YOU COME, KIDDO?
WELL.. UM... I... I WAS WONDERING IF YOU COULD... WELL, THAT IS... IF I COULD HAVE A LOAN OF FIFTY DOL...

I TAKE IT SHE SAID NO.

I JUST GOTTA GET AHOLD OF FIFTY BUCKS, HOPEY.
YOU SHOULD TAKE UP LUCHA LIBRE, MAG. THEN YOU COULD GIVE ALL YOUR OPPONENTS "THE FLYING SITDOWN."
VIDA LOCA

SHIT, I COULDN'T BE A WRESTLER. I DON'T THINK I COULD STAND LIVING WITH A SCARRED FOREHEAD, LET ALONE SHOWING OFF CELLULITE TO A CROWD OF THOUSANDS.
WHY NOT? YOU DO TO ME.
EL SANTO
=MAX=

HELP ME THINK, HOPEY! WHO OWES ME MONEY?
I DO. BUT LITTLE TONY HAS IT. HE OWES ME LOTS MORE.
VIDA LOCA

WELL, MAYBE WE CAN FIND HIM, BREAK HIS LEGS, THEN...
YOU KIDDING? EVERY TIME THAT KID GETS AHOLD OF CASH, HE SPENDS IT ALL ON HIS SKATEBOARD. THAT THING IS BEGINNING TO LOOK LIKE A CAR.
3

WHAT ABOUT THAT RICH PRIEST YOU TOLD ME ABOUT THAT USED TO BUY YOU THINGS WHEN YOU WERE LITTLE, GOING TO THAT CATHOLIC SCHOOL?
BROTHER BORIS? UGH! WHAT ABOUT HIM?
HE'S STILL AT THE CHURCH, ISN'T HE? MAYBE YOU COULD...
SORRY. HE'S IN JAIL FOR MOLESTING LITTLE GIRLS AT THE SCHOOL.
SPEAKING OF MOLESTERS, WHAT ABOUT DEL CHIMNEY? HE'S A SLOB, BUT HE'S ALWAYS HAD CASH STASHED AWAY SOMEWHERE. MAYBE WE COULD...
WE COULD... IF HE WASN'T DEAD.
VIDA LOCA
CHIMNEY IS DEAD? OH, GEE...
YEAH. JOEY AND HIS BUDDIES FOUND HIM IN HIS HOUSE NAILED TO THE WALL. HE HAD A LOT OF ENEMIES, Y'KNOW?
EL LOUIE LOUIE XIII
MY GOD... HE WAS THE FIRST GUY TO EVER PUT HIS TONGUE IN MY MOUTH. I GARGLED FOR DAYS.
I WOULDN'T FEEL TOO BAD, THOUGH. HE ALWAYS SAID HE WAS THE SAVIOR.
NO, I'M SERIOUS, HOPEY. DEL WAS NICE TO ME, REALLY! HE TAUGHT ME A LOT OF THINGS.
I'LL BET HE TAUGHT YOU A LOT OF THINGS. ROWRRR!
VIDA LOCA
HOW COME YOU DIDN'T LIKE HIM?
HUH? I DID, I GUESS. WHEN HE WASN'T FLYING OFF THE DEEP END...
YOU JUST DIDN'T UNDERSTAND HIM. SOMETIMES HE REMINDED ME A LOT OF MY DAD.
YEAH, A NO GOOD WOMANIZER.
OH, GREAT! WE HAD TO COME THIS WAY. OH, THE PAIN...
WHAT THE... OH, I SEE...
4

THERE THEY ARE. BLACK STEEL TOED BOMBER BOOTS. ON SALE FOR ONLY FORTY-EIGHT FIFTY, AND THEY JUST HAPPEN TO BE YOUR SIZE.
OH, HOPEY. LOOK AT THEM! I JUST GOTTA HAVE 'EM OR I'LL DIE!
SALE
40%

YOU'RE REALLY CHOKED UP ABOUT THIS. HOW COME?
YOU DON'T UNDERSTAND. IF I CAN'T GET THEM, DAFFY WILL WHEN SHE GETS BACK FROM HER TRIP WHO KNOWS WHEN...

...THEN SHE'LL RUSH OVER TO OUR HOUSE, PARADE 'EM OFF FOR US, AND TALK ABOUT WHAT A GREAT BUY THEY WERE. IT NEVER FAILS WHEN I WANNA BUY SOMETHING REAL BAD.
SO WHAT? SHE'S YOUR FRIEND...

...I'M SURE SHE'LL LET YOU BORROW 'EM ONCE IN A WHILE. DAFFY'S A GOOD KID.
OH, KA KA! YOU HAVE AN ANSWER FOR EVERYTHING, DON'T YOU?

OH! NOW, HEY, WAIT! HOPEY? I'M SORRY, I DIDN'T MEAN...
OH, MAGGOT. FOR CRYING OUT LOUD. I'M NOT LEAVING...
HEY, SPEEDY!

¡OYE, ESPERANZITA! WHAT ARE YOU CRAZY BROADS UP TO NOW? YOU GONNA ROB THAT STORE, OR WHAT?
OR WHAT. ANY OF YOU GUYS GOT FIFTY BONES YOU COULD LEND MAGGIE?

FIFTY BONES?! ¿POR QUE?
FOR WHAT SHE'S DROOLING AT IN THAT WINDOW.

AREN'T THOSE JUST ABOUT THE NEATEST BOOTS YOU'VE EVER SEEN?
SHEEIT... THEY LOOK LIKE CHALUPAS.
¡CHALUPAS CHICHARROÑES! HAW!

HEY! DON'T FUCK AROUND! YOU ASKED US! OUCH!
HMF! WHAT DO YOU KNOW ABOUT FASHION?

THAT'S FASHION? IT LOOKS MORE LIKE HORROR MOVIE PROPS! HAW!
YEAH? WELL, AT LEAST I DON'T ENDANGER MY LIFE IN THAT BOMB!

GOD, HE'S SO CUTE IT'S SCARY, HOPEY!
YEAH, WELL, THAT STILL DOESN'T GET YOU FIFTY DOLLARS.
MENUDO

OH, YEAH. I ALMOST FORGOT ABOUT THAT FOR A SECOND. SHOOT...
WHAT YOU NEED IS SOME KIND OF SHORT, QUICK JOB, OR...
VIDA LOCA

WAIT A MINUTE! I KNOW, FIRST WE'LL DRESS YOU IN SOMETHING REALLY DARING. SOMETHING THAT SHOWS OFF YOUR BUTT REAL GOOD. THEN WE'LL STAND YOU ON THIS CORNER...
?

...AND THE FIRST RICH FARTASS THAT COMES ALONG, YOU SAY TO HIM: "HEYYY, BIG BOY... IS THAT A BAZOOKA IN YOUR POCKET OR ARE YA JUST GLAD TA SEE ME...?"
FORGET IT!

HI, GIRLS. WHAT'S NEW?
HI, PENNY.
HI.

IS SOMETHING BUGGING YOU, BABY DOLL?
YEAH. YOU WOULDN'T HAPPEN TO HAVE FIFTY DOLLARS YOU COULD LEND ME, WOULD YOU?
MAGGIE WANTS TO BUY SOME FRIED PIG SKIN CANOES.

REALLY? WELL, I DON'T HAVE IT, BUT I KNOW WHO DOES...
REALLY? WHO?
VIDA

HAVE YOU EVER HEARD OF H.R. COSTIGAN?
YOU MEAN THE MULTI BULTI BILLIONAIRE? WHO HASN'T?
YOU KNOW H.R. COSTIGAN?
VROOMM
VROOMM
VROOMM
VROOMM
VROOMM
6

SURE! WE'VE BEEN GOOD FRIENDS FOR A FEW YEARS NOW. HE LIKES TO SPEND HIS MONEY ON ME AND I LET HIM.
DO YOU THINK HE'D LEND ME THE MONEY?
ARE YOU KIDDING? WITH THOSE BUNS?

IF I ASKED HIM NICELY ENOUGH. COME ON, WE'LL CALL HIM RIGHT NOW.
I DON'T WANNA IMPOSE... I MEAN...
IMPOSE! IMPOSE! THIS SOUNDS INTERESTING.

NO PROBLEM. CHECK IT OUT. HE GAVE ME THIS SPECIAL PHONE SO I CAN REACH HIM ANYWHERE IN THE WORLD. I CAN EVEN REACH HIM ON THE TOILET, AND VICE VERSA.
HOLY HOT LINE, BAT GUT!

HERV, DARLING? IT'S ME. YES, I'M JUST FINE. I HAVE A GIRL FRIEND WHO IS IN NEED OF A FAVOR AND, OH... REALLY? UH HUH... YOU DON'T SAY...
THIS IS SO EMBARRASSING.

I FEEL SO BAD ABOUT THIS, HOPEY. WHAT IF WE CAUGHT HIM IN THE MIDDLE OF SELLING A COUNTRY OR SOMETHING LIKE THAT?
THANKS, DARLING. SHE'LL BE GLAD TO HEAR IT. BYE BYE.

WHAT DID HE SAY?
HE WON'T BE BACK FOR A FEW WEEKS. I CAUGHT HIM IN THE MIDDLE OF SELLING A COUNTRY OR SOMETHING LIKE THAT.
CALL ME URI.
BUT, GET THIS...
VIDA LOCA

HE SAID WE CAN STAY AS GUESTS IN HIS HOME IN BADGEPORT UNTIL HE GETS BACK FROM EL CABALLO.
THAT GUY LIVES IN A FUCKING PALACE.
WHAT DID HE SAY ABOUT THE LOAN?

I DIDN'T HAVE A CHANCE TO ASK HIM. YOU TWO GO ON AND PACK YOUR BRAS. ASK IZZY IF SHE WANTS TO COME, TOO. TONIGHT, WE FLY.
WHAT THE HELL? IT SURE BEATS TV.

RELAX, MAG. IT'S GONNA BE A SWELL THREE WEEKS.
I GUESS I COULD ASK HIM WHEN HE GETS BACK, HUH?
Z
7

END OF PART 1

PART 2

WELCOME TO COSTIGAN MANOR WEST. I AM WEBSTER, YOUR HEAD SERVANT.

DIG THE CRAZY HOTEL. WHERE DO WE SIGN IN?

THIS PLACE IS PERFECT FOR A GIG.

ARE YOU KIDDING?

I CAME ACROSS THE LAUNDRY ROOM THIS MORNING. I COULD'VE SWORN IT WAS A BEER VAT. IT WAS PRODIGIOUS.
PRODIGIOUS? LET'S SEE YOU TRY TO SPELL THAT.
T-H-A-T?
L-O-A-D-E-D. DEAL ME IN, GIRLS.
OXNARD

DON'T YOU LIKE YOUR OWN ROOM?
YOU KNOW IT'S HARD FOR ME TO SLEEP ALONE. MAN, THIS FOOD IS GOOD. ¿QUIERES?

NO, THANKS. BOY, I'VE NEVER SEEN YOU EAT THIS MUCH FOOD BEFORE.
I'VE NEVER SEEN THIS MUCH FOOD BEFORE. I'M JUST TAKING ADVANTAGE OF MR. COSTIGAN'S HOSPITALITY.

GREAT! I'M GONNA LOVE SLEEPING IN THE SAME BED WITH THE FOOD YEAR BLIMP.
⁝BURP⁝ THANKS A LOT. EXCUSE ME WHILE I GO TO THE HEAD.

SHALL I HAVE 'EM SEND YOU UP A COW THIS TIME?
IF YOU'RE ASLEEP BY THE TIME I GET BACK, REMEMBER NOT TO HOG THE BED.

THAT WAS NO BATHROOM, THAT WAS A ROMAN BATH. HMM... NOW WHICH WAY IS OUR ROOM?

NOPE. NOT IN HERE.
9

:WHEW: I MUST HAVE CHECKED OVER A HUNDRED ROOMS AND I STILL HAVEN'T FOUND IT. WELL, I'LL FIND IT IN THE MORNING. I'M TOO POOPED. I'LL JUST PLOP INTO ONE OF THESE EMPTY BEDROOMS.

DAMN! EVERY ROOM IS A BALLROOM. YOU COULD HOLD A FUNNY CAR SHOW IN ONE OF THESE. HOW BORING THAT WOULD BE, THOUGH.

AND I'LL BET THE CLOSETS ARE AIRPLANE HANGARS...

SHH...
!

WHAT ARE YOU DOING?! STOP! I'LL CALL THE COPS...
QUIET...

HELP! HOPEY! HELP!
OH, FOR... C'MERE...

NOW, ARE YOU GONNA KEEP QUIET OR DO I HAVE TO GET TOUGH?
OK...

HELP!
AW, FOR THE LOVE A GOD...

MAGGIE'S BEEN GONE FOR OVER AN HOUR. I WONDER IF THE TOILETS HERE ARE ALSO SO BIG THAT SHE WAS SUCKED IN WHEN SHE FLUSHED IT.
10

MAN, THIS PLACE REALLY BECOMES A TOMB AFTER DARK, DOESN'T IT?
YES, MA'AM.

IZZY'S RIGHT. THIS IS A HOTEL. THERE'S PEOPLE OCCUPYING THESE ROOMS. KINDA SPOOKY... AHH, HERE WE ARE...

SAY, IZZY. HAVE YOU SEEN MAGGIE?
WHY DON'T YOU ASK HIM?

GAAA!
FUNNY, THAT'S WHAT HE SAID, TOO.

W-WHA' HOPPEN? IS HE D-D-D-D-D...
AS A DOOR NAIL. PLEASE DON'T ASK ME HOW...

I WAS JUST SITTING HERE WHILE HE WAS TAKING HOURS TELLING ME WHAT GREAT ARCHITECTURE THIS HOUSE HAS, WHEN BEING THE POLITE PERSON I AM, I ASKED HIM TO LEAVE. WHEN HE KEPT ON I TOLD HIM TO DROP DEAD...
AND...?
...HE DID.

TALK ABOUT LOYAL SERVICE.
YEAH, WELL NOW, WHAT ARE WE GONNA DO WITH HIM?

WHAT DO YOU MEAN "WE"? CALL ROOM SERVICE OR SOMETHING. I'M NOT STICKING AROUND TO SEE THEM PICK UP THE LAUNDRY.
SOME FRIEND YOU ARE...

CORPSES EVEN!
SHEEIT!
11

YES, MA'AM! THE ESTATE CORONER'S OFFICE WILL SEND SOMEONE RIGHT BY TO PICK UP THE BODY. YES, MA'AM...

GET THAT, ETHEL. A CORPSE IN ONE OF THE ROOMS. I TOLD YOU THIS WAS A NUTHOUSE.
YOU CAN SAY THAT AGAIN. YES? OPERATOR. HELLO? WHAT? I'M SORRY, I CAN'T HEAR YOU...

MFF MXL VPP!
I'M SORRY, SIR. I DON'T UNDERSTAND WHAT YOU'RE SAYING.

OUR BUTLERS AND MAIDS ALL SPEAK TEN DIFFERENT LANGUAGES. PERHAPS IF YOU WOULD LIKE TO... HELLO? HELLO?
CRAZY FOREIGNERS.
SMACK
MAD

THAT WAS REALLY DUMB.

LOOK! I DON'T WANT TO HURT YOU. I JUST DON'T WANT YOU TO GIVE ME AWAY. THEY MUST NOT KNOW I'M HERE. DON'T YOU SEE?

I'M GOING TO TAKE YOUR GAG OFF NOW. PROMISE ME YOU WON'T SCREAM. PLEASE? LOOK, IF I WAS GOING TO DO ANYTHING TO YOU IT WOULD HAVE BEEN DONE DAYS AGO. I MEAN, YOU BEING A BEAUTIFUL YOUNG WOMAN... I MEAN, IT'S HARD TO... Y-YOU KNOW...

GOOD GIRL...

12

END OF PART II

PART 3

ANY OF YOU SEEN MAGGIE LATELY?
NOT ME.
I WONDER WHAT THE POOR PEOPLE ARE DOING RIGHT NOW?

I'M TELLING YOU, IZZY. THIS PLACE GIVES ME THE CREEPS. NOW MAGGIE WON'T EVEN COME OUT TO TALK TO US, WHEREVER SHE IS.
IT'S A MADHOUSE, Y'KNOW...
WE'RE SLOWLY BEING DRIVEN INSANE. MAGGIE MUST'VE BEEN THE FIRST TO SNAP, THE POOR DEAR. SHE'S PROBABLY UP IN THERE PLOTTING TO KILL US IN OUR BEDS.
OR WORSE, CUTTING OUT PAPER DOLLS.
URP
THANKS FOR HAVING ALL THAT FOOD SENT UP. I HAVEN'T EATEN LIKE THAT SINCE THE BEAVERS WON THE PENNANT.
GLAD YOU LIKED IT. CASEY...?
NOW THAT YOU HAVE A FULL STOMACH, WHAT ARE YOU...
THERE'S SOMETHING BOTHERING YOU. IT'S YOUR FRIENDS, ISN'T IT? WHY DON'T YOU GO OUT AND BE WITH THEM? YOU'RE NOT MY PRISONER ANY MORE.
I'M SCARED. I WOULDN'T KNOW WHAT TO TELL 'EM WITHOUT TELLING 'EM ABOUT YOU.
WELL, YOU'RE GONNA HAVE TO DO SOMETHING SOON OR THEY'RE GONNA HAVE A SEARCH PARTY COMING AFTER YOU.
O-OK. I'LL GO OUT. TOMORROW. SHIT! I WISH I WAS LIKE YOU, A LONER. YOU DON'T HAVE TO WORRY ABOUT ANYBODY TELLING YOU WHAT TO DO. LIVE WITHOUT RESPONSIBILITIES, HAVING NO ONE TO CARE FOR BUT YOURSELF...
IT DON'T MAKE SENSE! SHE CAN'T BE UP THERE JUST EATING!
WHY NOT? I'VE SEEN MAGGIE DO SOME WEIRD THINGS.
BUT SHE WON'T EVEN COME OUT TO TALK TO US.
MAYBE SHE WAS KIDNAPPED.
C'MON! BE SERIOUS, ISABEL!
HELL, I DUNNO! MAYBE SHE'S PISSED OFF AT US!
15

YEAH? DO YOU THINK MAYBE I WENT TOO FAR BY SAYING SHE WAS FAT?
WHO KNOWS WITH MAGGIE? SAY, CAN WE GET OUT OF THIS HERE SWEAT BOX NOW?

GIRL, STOP FOR A SECOND AND LOOK AT WHAT YOU'RE DOING. I MEAN, WHO IS THIS GUY?

HE KNOCKS YOU DOWN, TIES YOU UP, TELLS YOU TO TRUST HIM, AND ALL ON THE SAME DAY, YOU MAKE LOVE TO HIM.

I MEAN, LOOK AT HIM. HE'S A BUM! HE HASN'T BATHED OR CHANGED HIS CLOTHES IN TEN YEARS. HE'S... HE'S MISSING TEETH! HE...

IT'S OK. I'M MISSING TEETH, TOO.

WHEN WE SEE HER, SHE'S GONNA PRETEND NOTHING HAPPENED AND THEN SHE'LL SAY, "HI, GUYS! WHATCHA DOON?" THEN I'M JUST GONNA HAVE TO KICK HER ASS UP AND DOWN THE STAIRS.
YOU'RE NOT GOING TO DO ANYTHING.

HUH?
YOU'RE GOING TO PRETEND NOTHING HAPPENED OR I WILL KICK YOUR ASS UP AND DOWN THE STAIRS!

IZZY, DON'T START GIVING ME YOUR SHIT...
DON'T YOU THINK YOU'VE GIVEN MAGGIE ENOUGH SHIT FOR A YEAR? GIVE HER A REST, HUH?

OH, COME ON! I'VE BEEN CALLED WORST THINGS THAN THE FOOD YEAR BLIMP, BUT IT NEVER...
CRAPAZOLA! QUIT ACTING LIKE A KID! IT'S MORE THAN THAT AND YOU KNOW IT!
16

YOU'RE CRAZY.
THAT'S THE FIRST LOGICAL THING YOU'VE SAID ALL DAY.

...AND THERE I WAS, STANDING BEFORE THE OL' KING OF DRUSSIA HIMSELF, WITH HIS BIG BEARD AND STOMACH TO MATCH...
GEE, HOW EXCITING! THEN WHAT HAPPENED?

THEY PUSHED ME ASIDE. FOR ALL THEY KNEW, I WAS JUST A BUM.
DO YOU REALLY THINK YOU COULD BE THE TRUE HEIR TO THE THRONE OF DRUSSIA?

WELL, I HAVE THE BIRTHMARK AND I WAS RAISED IN AN ORPHAN'S HOME NOT REMEMBERING WHO MY PARENTS WERE. MAN, I'LL NEVER FORGET ALL THE SHIT I GOT. ONE OF THESE DAYS I'LL SHOW THOSE BIG SHOTS...
WHY ARE YOU HIDING IN THIS HOUSE ANYWAY?

I WANT COSTIGAN. THE BIG SHOT OF ALL BIG SHOTS. I WANT TO SHOW HIM JUST WHO THIS BUM REALLY IS. I KNOW HE'S NOT HERE RIGHT NOW, BUT I'LL WAIT. AS LONG AS IT TAKES I'LL STILL WAIT.
MY!

YOUR MAJESTY. I AM YOUR SLAVE. DO WITH ME WHAT YOU WILL.
ANYTHING I WANT, EH?

STRAP ME TO THE SIDE OF A MAD BULL. BEAT ME WITH A HOT WHEEL TRACK. CALL ME A SLUT! CALL ME A BITCH! CALL ME A COP!
VERY WELL, MY WORTHLESS SERVANT...

GO OUT AND SEE YOUR FRIENDS! RIGHT NOW, BEFORE THEY FORGET WHO YOU ARE! YOU DON'T HAVE TO TELL THEM ABOUT ME! JUST GO SEE THEM!
OH, ALL RIGHT!

I'LL JUST TELL 'EM THAT I GOT LOST. NAW, TOO CORNY. I'LL TELL 'EM THAT I WAS KIDNAPPED BY... NAW. I KNOW... I CAUGHT MOE TOWNE FEVER AND HAD TO BE QUARANTINED. YEAH, THAT'S IT.
17

HOWDY, STRANGER! AH HAVEN'T SEEN YOU AROUND THESE HERE PARTS FOR ABOUT A WEEK!
HI, HOPEY. I GOT LOST. WHAT ARE YOU DOING?

JUST MAKING MYSELF A REAL SNACK. MY STOMACH ISN'T USED TO THE MENU HERE SO I MADE 'EM GO OUT AND GET ME ALL THIS JUNK. HELP YOURSELF.
NO, THANKS ANYWAY.

COSTIGAN REALLY HAS THESE SERVANTS TRAINED TO DO ANYTHING YOU TELL 'EM.
YOU CAN SAY THAT AGAIN. WAS THAT A SIREN?

UM... HOPEY? I'VE BEEN MEANING TO TE... UH... ASK YOU, ARE YOU... UM... HAVING A GOOD TIME HERE...?
WHY DO YOU ASK THAT? (WHERE'S THAT SALT?)
GROANN...

WELL, UM... I'M ASKING BECAUSE, IF YOU DON'T... UH...
ISABEL! BOY, YOU SOUND LIKE YOU'VE BEEN HAVING A BALL! WHERE YOU GOING?
HOME!

YOU DON'T LIKE IT HERE, IZZY?
I CAN'T STAND IT. IT'S TOO FUCKING BIG!

THE CEILING'S WAY TOO DAMN HIGH. I DON'T EVEN COME CLOSE. IT DRIVES ME NUTSO BEING SO FAR FROM IT. I MISS ALL THE FLIES...
POOR BABY.
18

END OF PART III

PART 4

LOOK AT ALL THE PEOPLE! COSTIGAN SURE KNOWS HOW TO THROW A PARTY, HUH? LOOK, THERE'S DEREK CINEMA.

I DON'T CARE WHAT ANYONE SAYS, I STILL DON'T THINK YOU LOOK ANYTHING LIKE HIM.

WELL, UM... INSTEAD OF A DRINK, HOW ABOUT...
ATTACK AND BE A DESTROYER. I'M GONNA CHECK ON SOME OF OUR GUESTS.

SOMETIMES I REALLY WORRY ABOUT THAT GIRL. POOR MAG.
HI! MY NAME IS GELLEX

WHAT DID YOU SAY?
I SAID ONE OF THESE DAYS SHE'S GONNA DRIVE HERSELF CRAZIER THAN SHE ALREADY IS AND TAKE US ALL WITH HER.

THAT'S RIGHT, BOYS. WHEN YOU HAVE SOMEONE LIKE RAND RACE WORKING FOR YOU, YOU KNOW YOUR MACHINES ARE IN THE FINEST HANDS.
BRAVO, COSTIGAN! BUT, WHEN DO WE GET TO SEE... MEET PENELOPE?
YEH...

OH, (AHEM) WELL... I THINK SHE'S SHOWING MY NEPHEW HAROLD AROUND SOMEWHERE.
PENNY'S HERE?

HEY, SOMEONE SWIPED MY SOLID GOLD LIGHTER!
WHAT ARE YOU LOOKING AT ME FOR, BUDDY?

I WONDER WHERE PENNY'S BEEN ALL NIGHT.
I'M SORRY, MISS, BUT YOU CAN'T DANCE IN HERE...

THESE ITEMS ARE VERY VALUABLE AND YOU MIGHT... LOOK OUT!
CRASH!
OOP! SPOKE TOO SOON...

HOPITA! HOWZA GIRL? WHERE'S MY BABY?
SHE'S EATING, PENELOPE. SHE'S GOT A CASE OF THE GUILTS RIGHT NOW.
21

DOES SHE SHTILL TINK WE'RE MAD ABOUT THAT HIDE 'N' SEEK BIT?
IT'S REALLY EATING HER UP, THE POOR THING.

HELL, IF SHE WANTS TO GO TO BED WITH SOME GUY, CROOK OR NO CROOK, IT'S REALLY NONE OF OUR GOD-DAMN BUSINESS, RIGHT?
RIGHT...

AND IF SHE WANTS TO MARRY HIM AND GO AWAY FOREVER, WHO ARE WE TO STOP HER, RIGHT?
RIGHT...

SAY, DOLL. YOU LEFT ME ALL ALONE BACK THERE.
GET LOST, YOU FUCKING CREEP!
UH... YOU HEARD THE LADY, MISTER...

OUTA MY WAY, WIMP. C'MERE!
LEGGO!

SAY, BUDDY. WE WANT NO TROUBLE, SEE?
BUTT OUT!
PUT ME DOWN, YA BIG APE!

MY GOODNESS! WHAT IS ALL THE COMMOTION?
I THINK SOMEBODY'S FIGHTING.

THAT GORILLA'LL KILL THAT GUY!
WHO CARES? IT'S ONLY RAND RACE. C'MON, HARRY.
OOF!
POW
SOK
BAM
22

THE BOUNCERS FINALLY KICKED HIM OUT... WHERE'S PENNY?
WENT FOR A WALK. SO, YOU'RE RAND RACE?
YES. DO I KNOW YOU?
I'M HOPEY. YOU KNOW, PENNY'S AND MAGGIE'S FRIEND...?
YES, YES! HOPPY! MARGIE'S TOLD ME SO MUCH ABOUT YOU!
AND YOU'RE GLAD TO SEE ME?
PENNY. WHAT WAS GOING ON OVER THERE?
NOT TOO MUCH. I HEAR YOU'RE STILL DOWN ON YOURSELF FOR HIDING OUT ON US.
WELL... I REALLY SHOULD HAVE TOLD YOU ABOUT... IS HOPEY MAD?
NAW. IN FACT, SHE'S WORRIED ABOUT YOU. HEY, DID YOU STILL WANNA TALK TO COSTIGAN?
I DON'T THINK SO. I FEEL KINDA SILLY...
NONSENSE! COME ON, I'LL EVEN INTRODUCE YOU AS MY SISTER.
WAIT! HOLD IT! LOOK!
WUZZAT? WUZ WRONG?
LOOK WHO'S STANDING NEXT TO COSTIGAN...
I KNOW. DEMOÑA, THE MOST POWERFUL WOMAN IN THE WORLD.
I THOUGHT SHE WAS A BAD GUY.
SHE IS, BUT SHE NEEDS MONEY, SO COSTIGAN'S HIRED HER AS HIS OWN PERSONAL BODYGUARD. MAN, IF ATOMA WERE HERE, SHE'D...
23

IMAGINE IF SHE TURNS ON HIM.
THEN THAT'S WHEN SHE COMES IN. LOOK, OV' YONDER...

OOH! ITS HER! COMRADE 7! AREN'T YOU THE PRESIDENT OF HER FAN CLUB?
I ALSO INVITED HER TO THIS PARTY TO KEEP AN EYE ON THAT BITCH.

LET'S GO ASK COSTIGAN FOR YOUR FIFTY BONES NOW...
NO... UH... WAIT! LEMME GO TO THE POWDER ROOM FIRST! YOU KNOW... HEH... I'LL BE RIGHT BACK.

DAMN! I FORGOT THIS ALL STARTED BECAUSE I WAS CRYING OVER A PAIR OF LOUSY BOOTS.

GULP
MAN, I'M TELLING YOU... IF IT ISN'T ONE THING, IT'S ANOTHER, Y'KNOW?
YEH...

I MEAN, I'M TRYIN' TA MAKE AN HONEST LIVING, Y'KNOW? AN' SOME PEOPLE JUST LIKE TA FUCK THINGS UP BY SHOWIN' UP ALLA TIME.
I KNOW WHAT YOU MEAN. MY EX SHOWED UP TONIGHT.

BUT, MY MAMA ALWAYS TOLD ME TO FACE MY PROBLEMS, SO...
...I THINK I'LL GO SMASH IN HER DAMN COMMUNIST FACE.
SAY, MAYBE I SHOULD DO THAT TO HARRY.
GIVE HIM ONE FOR ME. I WAS HIS SECOND WIFE.

"FACE YOUR PROBLEMS." SHEESH! MINE ARE PRACTICALLY HITTING ME IN THE FACE.
24

YOU THINK SOMEONE IS TRYING TO GET YOU? WHAT YOU NEED IS PROTECTION, MR. COSTIGAN.
DON'T WORRY. I HAVE THE BEST BODYGUARD IN THE WORLD. SHE'S IN THE LADY'S ROOM RIGHT NOW...
BUT, HOW CAN YOU? SHE'S...
I KNOW WHAT YOU'RE GOING TO SAY. I ALSO DIDN'T TRUST HER AT FIRST...
...BUT SCHWARTZ HERE FINALLY CONVINCED ME TO HIRE HER. DEMOÑA CAN DO SOME REALLY FASCINATING THINGS, AND SCHWARTZ HAS ALWAYS GIVEN ME GOOD ADVICE.
THANK YOU, SIR.
AND WHAT AM I HERE FOR, TO LOOK AT?
NOW, PENNY... BE REASONABLE! BUSINESS IS BUSINESS!
AND TO THINK, YOUR NEW TAN WOULD HAVE MATCHED COMRADE SEVEN'S CAPE. TSK!
DEMOÑA. WE HAVE REASON TO BELIEVE SOMEONE IS OUT TO "GET" MR. COSTIGAN. KEEP AN EXTRA EYE OUT, HM?
SEZ YOU, FOUR EYES. YOU AIN'T MY BOSS.
LISTEN, I WAS SENT BY COSTIGAN HIMSELF TO TELL YOU...
NO. YOU LISTEN, FUCK FACE. I TAKE ORDERS FROM NO ONE BUT HORN HOOK HIMSELF, SO YOU CAN TAKE A FLYING SHIT ON A GUILLOTINE! GOT THAT?
IF YOU'LL EXCUSE ME, HOPPY. I'M GOING TO TRY TO FIND MARGIE. IT'S BEEN NICE MEETING YOU.
HMM... GOOD LUCK.
OH, OH, HOPEY. WHAT'S THIS? YOU'VE ACTUALLY BECOME A JEALOUS BITCH. YOU BETTER WATCH YOURSELF. HM...
THERE'S MAG. I'LL BE EXTRA NICE TO HER. I'LL LEAD HER TO RACE. SHE'LL LIKE THAT.
25
END OF PART IV

PART 5

HOPEEE! WHERE ARE WE GOING?

I'M TAKING YOU TO MEET 'OL' WHAT'S HIS NAME...

YEAH, GO AHEAD! WALK AWAY! I DON'T NEED THIS SHIT, EITHER!

AND IF YOU'RE GONNA KICK MY ASS, YOU BETTER MAKE IT A GOOD ONE, 'CAUSE AFTER TONIGHT, YOU'RE NOT GONNA HAVE THE CHANCE.

SHIT! NOW WHY DID I HAVE TO DO THAT?
MADAME?

WHY DO I KEEP MAKING THINGS WORSE? IT'S NOT HER FAULT THAT IM MISERABLE. GOD, IM THE WORST...
MADAME?

I SAW YOU STANDING ALL ALONE AND WAS WONDERING IF I COULD HAVE THIS DANCE?
YOU?!

IT IS YOU! CASEY, YOU MADE IT!
PLEASE, CALL ME BARON GIFFS OF ORIENTAR.

IT IS YOU, ISN'T IT?
'COURSE. YOU DIDN'T THINK FOR A MINUTE THAT THEY COULD EVER KEEP ME AWAY FROM YOU, DIDJA?
NO, I GUESS I DIDN'T.

HOW ROMANTIC. THE BARON HAS ASKED THAT LOVELY GIRL TO DANCE.
WHERE IS ORIENTAR?
NEAR LA BREA I THINK.

DAMN! I DON'T KNOW WHAT TO DO ANY MORE, CASEY. PLEASE, TELL ME WHAT I SHOULD DO...
WELL... I WAS GOING TO ASK YOU...
27

MAGGIE, WILL YOU...
MY APOLOGIES, BARON, BUT MR. COSTIGAN WOULD LIKE TO MEET YOU.
HERE'S YOUR CHANCE, CASEY.

AH, BARON GIFFS. I'M PLEASED TO MEET YOU. DEMONA?
!
YESSUH, MASSUH.

WE HAVE REASON TO BELIEVE THAT SOMEONE IS OUT TO "GET" ME, BARON. IF THAT'S WHO YOU REALLY ARE...
CASEY!

IS IT TRUE? ARE YOU REALLY AN ASSASSIN?
NO WAY! THESE GUYS ARE NUTS!
I'M SORRY, MISS, BUT YOU SHOULD HAVE REALIZED WITH WHO YOU WERE DEALING.

BEING SEEN HIDING IN MY HOME FOR THE PAST MONTH IS WHAT FINALLY CONVINCED US. YOU KNOW WHAT TO DO, MY DEAR.
RIGHTO. DON'T WORRY, BARON, THIS WILL ONLY HURT FOR A MINUTE.
YOU'RE MAKING A MISTAKE!

¡LA CAUSA!
EEK!
YAAAA

WILL YOU PEOPLE PLEASE STOP YELLING? IT MAKES ME VERY NERVOUS.
EEYOW

GET OUT OF MY WAY! YOU'RE BLOCKING MY AIM.
28

WHEEEE
SHIT! I WAS TRYING FOR THE MIDDLE ONE.

DEMOÑA! CONTROL THE CROWD! GO LOOK FOR THE ASSASSIN! SHE MAY COME BACK!
ME?! WHY?! THIS IS FUN.

THAT'S IT! YOU'RE FIRED! I'M GOING TO FIND COMRADE 7! MAYBE SHE NEEDS A JOB.
FINE. YOU DO THAT. THEN MAYBE ME AN' HER CAN GO A COUPLA ROUNDS.

WHEE! JUST LIKE CHIMNEY'S USED TO BE... WHERE YOU GOING, HOPITA?
AS FAR FROM THIS HOUSE AS POSSIBLE.

WHAT ABOUT MAGGIE? OH, DO YOU THINK SHE'S GONNA RUN OFF WITH THAT BIG GUY AFTER ALL? DO YOU THINK SHE'S...
BLOWING IT? YEAH, STRAIGHT THROUGH HER ASS HOLE.

DON'T BE MAD AT HER, HOPEY. SHE'S CONFUSED RIGHT NOW...
LOOK, SHE TOLD ME HERSELF HE REMINDS HER SO MUCH OF HER DAD!

HER DAD IS SHIT, PENNY! HE'S A GHOUL! HE LEFT THE WIFE AND KIDS FOR A WHORE!
DO YOU THINK THIS GUY WILL DO THE SAME TO MAGGIE?

AAH, I DON'T KNOW WHAT I THINK ANY MORE. LET THE CUNT GO WITH HIM. IT'LL SERVE HER RIGHT!
MAYBE YOU SHOULD GO FIND HER BEFORE IT'S TOO LATE.

THAT'S JUST WHAT I'M GONNA DO. I HAVE A FEW PARTING WORDS FOR THE LITTLE SNIT.
ATTA GIRL.
29

'TIS MORNING...
EXCUSE ME, PLEASE. THANK YOU!
OOF!
HEY!
EXCUSE ME. HAVE YOU SEEN A GIRL, ABOUT MY SIZE... BLACK SCARECROW HAIRCUT... WAITER'S JACKET...
SORRY MISS. HAVEN'T SEEN HER...
MAGGIE.

CASEY! I THOUGHT THEY... YOU'RE...
YEAH, I'M GOING. I GOTTA GET TO THE DOCKS IN AN HOUR TO CATCH A FREIGHTER HEADED FOR POMONOLA. I JUST CAME TO ASK YOU AGAIN...
?

THAT'S RIGHT. WHAT WAS IT?
IF...IF YOU'LL COME WITH ME. I REALLY WANT YOU TO...

COME WITH YOU? BUT...
MAGGIE, I'M SO TIRED... TIRED OF RUNNING... TIRED OF BEING ALONE... I GOTTA STOP...

COME WITH ME... PLEASE... I LOVE YOU...
YOU... I-I CAN'T... NOT NOW. Y'SEE, I'VE BEEN THINKING... ABOUT THINGS... ABOUT MYSELF...

MAYBE I COULD RUN AWAY WITH YOU FIVE YEARS FROM NOW, BUT NOT RIGHT NOW...

RIGHT NOW THERE'S NO ONE I'D RATHER SPEND MY LIFE WITH THAN MY FRIEND HOPEY. I WISH SHE WAS HERE THIS VERY MINUTE.
30

BUT, I'M AFRAID I MAY HAVE BLOWN THAT SKY HIGH. NOW, I DON'T KNOW IF SHE'LL EVER COME BACK. I DON'T... KNOW...

I'LL SEE YOU IN FIVE YEARS.
YEAH...

WOW. NOW THAT'S WHAT I CALL AN EXIT.
H-HOPEY?

OH, HOPEY, HOPEY, HOPEY! I'M SORRY FOR EVERYTHING! FORGIVE ME...
YOU HAVE NOTHING TO BE SORRY ABOUT. IT SEEMS I'M THE ONE WHO SHOULD BE SORRY.

DID YOU HEAR...?
EVERY WORD. C'MON, MAGGIE. LET'S GET PACKED AND GO HOME.

I SAW DAFFY TODAY. SHE WORE A BRAND NEW PAIR OF BOOTS SHE GOT ON SALE FOR FORTY-EIGHT FIFTY.
OH? GOOD NIGHT, HOPEY.
GOOD MORNING, MAGGIE.
LOCAS TAMBIEN · 100 ROOMS · BY JAIME '83-'86
FIN

LOCAS STARRING
hopey
WITH HER FRIENDS MAGGIE AND IZZY
JAIME IN '83, HOME BOY!
EEK!
YOU GUYS HAVE BEEN COLORING YOUR HAIR! WHY DIDN'T YOU TELL ME? I... WHAT'S WRONG WITH HOPEY?
THE POOR CHILD IS SICK. SHE'S REALLY SUFFERING.
(GROAN) DYING'S MORE LIKE IT.
LUCHA
BRE
TITANON
VS
LA PANTERA NEGRA
RENA TITAÑON
CHAMPION OF THE WORLDS
BATTALION OF SAINTS
MAGGIE + HOPEY + SPEEDY + DANY
MINOR THREAT
WORLD CHAMPION
VICKI GLORI
BATS
1

THAT'S CRAZY! HOPEY'S NEVER BEEN SICK A DAY IN HER LIFE.
WELL, SHE'S NOT EXACTLY SICK. IT'S MORE LIKE A DEEP, DEEP STATE OF DEPRESSION.
DEEP DEEP... DEEP...

HOW DID THIS EVER COME ABOUT?
EASY. COME BY THE WINDOW.

SEE THAT BUILDING OVER THERE?
MOAN...
THE NEW ONE? THEY FINALLY FINISHED PUTTING IT UP. SO WHAT?

LOOK CLOSER AND OBSERVE THE BIG, WHITE, CLEAN WALL IN FRONT OF IT.
MOOAANNNNN
OH, NOW I GET IT.

HOPEY. I THOUGHT THOSE DAYS WERE OVER.
SO DID I, BUT I GOT THE FEVER AGAIN...
...SPRAY CAN FEVERRR
2

YEARS AGO ANYTIME ANYBODY PUT UP A NEW WHITE WALL OR JUST REDID THEIR OLD WALLS WHITE, WELL, HOPEY'S ALWAYS HAD A THING FOR WHITE SURFACES. SHE NEVER MISSED ONE...

THIS WENT ON FOR QUITE A WHILE, TILL OFFICER SADO STARTED CATCHING ON TO HER SHENANIGANS. HELL, HOPEY ONLY SIGNED EVERY ONE OF HER WORKS...

I NEED ONE MORE NOTCH TO MAKE SERGEANT, YA LITTLE FREAK.
WE DON'T NEED NO STINKIN' BADGES, MAN!
LA HOPEY

HOPEY WAS FINALLY CAUGHT AFTER A RECORD OF NINETY-EIGHT MASTERPIECES AND HAD TO PROMISE HER MOTHER, AND HERSELF SHE WOULD NEVER DO IT AGAIN. SHE THOUGHT SHE WAS CURED. TILL NOW...

YOU TINK YOU PIRDY SMARD, EH?
I ASSURE YOU, MRS. GLASS, HOPEY IS NOT GOING TO PRISON.

DAMN THAT WALL! IT BECKONS! MAN, IT BECKONS! IT'S SAYING, "COME AND GET ME, AHAB!"
ADOBE DICK! THE GREAT WHITE WALL!
CALL ME FISHMAEL.

HOLD IT, IZZY. THIS IS ALL WRONG. YOU AND I ARE SUPPOSED TO BE THE MISERABLE ONES IN THIS COMIC, NOT HOPEY.
YOU'RE RIGHT. WE CAN'T LET THIS HAPPEN OR WE'D HAVE TO CHANGE OUR TITLE TO "MANIC DEPRESSANTS ON PARADE." MAGGOT, WE MUST ACT NOW!

OK, THE STREET'S BUSY DAY AND NIGHT SO YOU'LL HAVE TO DO IT IN FRONT OF ALL THESE CARS. NOW WE JUST GOTTA DO SOMETHING ABOUT OFFICER SADO.
ARE YOU KIDDING? THE ASSHOLE STILL HAS A TWENTY-FOUR HOUR RADAR ESPECIALLY DESIGNED FOR ME!

HUERO'S HAVING A BIG, BIG PARTY FRIDAY NIGHT. THAT SHOULD KEEP SADO OCCUPIED FOR A WHILE.
ESTA BIEN. YOU'RE ALL SET, HOPEY.
I THINK I'M GONNA CRY.
3

NOW, WHAT COLOR PAINT SHOULD YOU USE?
ANYTHING BUT (UGH) GOLD.
HOW ABOUT GREEN?
PUSH

NAW, SHE SHOULD USE SOMETHING BRIGHT, LIKE RED.
GREEN'S BRIGHT. RED'S TOO COMMON.

GREEN'S TOO DULL! RED!
RED'S TOO COMMON! GREEN!

RED!
GREEN!

RED! GREEN!
BLACK!

I GOT THE BLACK PAINT, BUT I HAD TO PAY A GUY TO GET IT FOR ME 'CAUSE I DIDN'T HAVE AN I.D. THEN HE SAID HE'D GIVE ME MY MONEY BACK IF I'D... OOH... I HOPE THIS IS ALL WORTH IT.
DON'T WORRY, MAG. IT IS.

FRIDAY NIGHT...
IZZY, WHY ARE WE WAITING AROUND SO LONG? I COULDA FINISHED THAT WALL HOURS AGO.
WE'RE WAITING FOR MAGGIE'S CALL. SHE'S AT HUERO'S PARTY SO SHE CAN LET US KNOW WHEN SADO SHOWS TO BREAK IT UP.
PHONE
4

IZZY! I'M GETTING ITCHY!
BIG GLUP
OK, OK! THIS GUY'S DONE. I'LL CALL MAGGIE TO SEE WHAT'S GOING ON. DO YOU HAVE A DIME?

HALLO? HEY, IZZY. MAGGIE? YAH, OK... HOLD ON...

SPEEDY! IT'S YOUR SISTER. SHE WANTS MAGGIE.
WELL, DON'T TELL ME. SHE'S BEEN IN THE BATHROOM FOR ALMOST AN HOUR.

HEY, MAGGIE! OPEN UP! IZZY'S ON THE PHONE!
WAIT. MAYBE THE DOOR'S UNLOCKED.

HA! CHECK HER OUT...
DON'T LAUGH, MALO! SHE'S MY COUSIN! HELP HER UP!

KNOCKED OUT, HUH? TOO MUCH TEQUILA, HUH? NO, THAT'S OK. JUST TAKE CARE OF HER, OK? THANKS, LICHA. 'BYE.

THAT MAGGIE. ONE OF THESE DAYS SHE'S GONNA WIND UP... HOPEY? HEY! WAIT UP!
PHONE
5

IF YOU WANT SOMETHING DONE RIGHT, YOU GOTTA DO IT YOURSELF.
HEY, C'MON... WE TRIED...

NO NAZI ASSHOLE COP IS GONNA SCARE ME AWAY! NEITHER IS SOME ASSHOLE WALL!
HARPOON THAT MOTHER, SISTER. I'M DUCKING OUT OF SIGHT.

PLEASE, PLEASE, NO COPS. JAIL IS THE WORST. I REMEMBER ON MY EIGHTEENTH BIRTHDAY I WAS ARRESTED FOR URINATING IN PUBLIC, AND THEY PUT ME INTO A CELL WITH TWO MEAN SOUTHSIDE BAD GIRLS WHO SLICED ME UP WITH RAZOR BLADES. I VOWED I'D NEVER GO THERE AGAIN.
HMMM...

I DON'T BELIEVE IT! NO COPS! IT LOOKS LIKE WE'RE GOING TO HAVE A MASTERPIECE ON OUR HANDS AFTER ALL! WAIT! SHE'S NOT WRITING! HOPEY! WHAT'S WRONG?!?!
YOU WON'T BELIEVE THIS, BUT...

...I DON'T KNOW WHAT TO WRITE.

NOW I THINK I'M HAVING A CASE OF DEJA VU...

OK. PUT THAT CAN DOWN, YA LITTLE FREAK.
...AND ESP...
6

WHEN WILL YOU EVER LEARN? I'VE GOT YOU WIRED. I KNEW YOU'D BE BACK SOONER OR LATER.
OH, BOY... HOPEY'S HAD IT NOW...
AND YOU, IZZY... AREN'T YOU KINDA OLD TO BE HANGING AROUND MUNCHKINS?
ACH!
WHERE'S YOUR GIRLFRIEND TONIGHT, HOPEY? DID SHE LEAVE YOU FOR ANOTHER WOMAN? IS THE WICKED WITCH OF THE EAST HERE YOUR NEW LAY?
WHAT'S IT TO YOU, YA SHIT FACED COCK WALLOPER!
I WOULDN'T BE SUR-PRISED. EGAD! WHAT ZOO DID YOU TWO ESCAPE FROM ANYWAY?
HOPEY...
HA HA HA! THAT'S FUNNY, SADO! BURN ANY CROSSES LATELY? HOW ARE THINGS DOWN AT THE THIRD REICH?
WHAT? NO SMART-ASS REMARKS? YOU KNOW, I'VE GOT ENOUGH ON YOU TO TAKE YOU IN, AND SINCE YOU'RE OVER EIGHTEEN NOW, YOU WON'T BE GOING TO JUVIE WHERE MOMMY CAN PICK YOU UP ANY MORE.
AH, GO FUCK YOURSELF, ASSHOLE!
HOPEY... PLEASE, DON'T...
WELL? WHAT DO YOU HAVE TO SAY FOR YOURSELF, YA LITTLE FREAK?
FUCK!!
HOPEY! NO...
7

I CAN'T BELIEVE I ACTUALLY DID IT.
YOU CAN SAY THAT AGAIN.
I GOT MYSELF THROWN IN JAIL BECAUSE I PAINTED SERGEANT SADO'S FACE TO MATCH HIS UNIFORM.
SPEEDY WAS ACTUALLY WAITING FOR ME WHEN I GOT TO THE PARTY.
IZZY WOULDN'T TALK TO ME THE WHOLE TIME WE WERE IN THE CELL.
NOT EVEN BIG BOOBS BLANCA RIZO WAS THERE TO DISTRACT HIM.
MEANWHILE, THERE ARE FOUR MEAN SOUTHSIDE BAD GIRLS JUST WAITING TO SLICE US UP WITH RAZOR BLADES.
IT WAS PERFECT. I HAD HIM ALONE WITH ME IN THE BEDROOM, BUT WHAT HAPPENED?
MEANWHILE, SOME JIVE ASSHOLE SPRAY PAINTS MY WALL... IN GOLD PAINT!
I DRANK TOO MUCH TEQUILA AND PASSED OUT IN THE BATHROOM.
YOU REALLY KNOW YOU'VE LOST IT WHEN...
...YOU DON'T GET OUT OF BED FOR TWO WEEKS.
IT'S A COKE, MAN!
END

LOOK, THE WAY I SEE IT, WE'RE DOING HIM A FAVOR BY BEING IN THIS STRIP. AND HE HAS TREATED YOU PRETTY ROTTEN LATELY.

YEAH, I AM GETTING KINDA TIRED OF GOING THROUGH A LOT OF SHIT WHILE HE GETS ALL THE GLORY.

YOU KNOW, THAT IS A GREAT IDEA! IF WE FIRED HIM WE COULD GET A WHOLE TEAM TO DO OUR STORIES! A SEPARATE WRITER, PENCILLER, INKER, AND LETTERER!

YEAH, WE COULD...

I STILL SAY YOU'RE WASTING OUR TIME ON THIS. YOU'VE FAILED THREE TIMES ALREADY.
JUST GIVE ME TWO WEEKS! TWO MORE WEEKS! YOU'LL SEE...

OK, LET'S SAY YOU COULD. DOT, THE GUY'S A MECHANIC.
NOT JUST ANY MECHANIC, FRANCO! A PROSOLAR MECHANIC! THE YO...
IS THERE A DIFFERENCE?
THE YOUNGEST PRO MECH EVER, AND IS HE SOMETHING, BOY! HUNK CITY!
EDITOR

I'M TELLING YOU RIGHT NOW, THIS GUY'S GONNA MAKE EVERYONE FORGET DEREK CINEMA SO FAST! JUST YOU WAIT, FRANCO BOY...

HM, SEEMS TO ME YOU WANT SOME-THING MORE OUT OF THIS THAN AN INTERVIEW.
FRANCO, YOU KNOW ME BETTER THAN THAT.

OK. I MAY BE CRAZY, BUT... TWO WEEKS! TOPS!
YOU WON'T REGRET THIS, SWEETIE.
EDITOR

DEREK CINEMA, DETECTIVE IS OUT. RAND RACE, PROSOLAR MECHANIC IS IN.
1

MECHANICS

HI HO HI HO
IT'S BACK TO WORK WE GO
BEEN WEEKS AND WEEKS
SINCE I'VE SEEN RACE
HI HO HI HO

HEY, RACE. HERE SHE COMES.
GOOD OL' MARGIE, LATE AS USUAL. IT'S SURE GONNA BE GREAT WORKING WITH HER AGAIN.

HEY, GUYS!
HEY, YOURSELF. IT'S BEEN AWHILE, MARGIE.
HI.

HOW'VE YOU BEEN KEEPING? UH...
JUST FINE. YOU KNOW WHAT?

WHAT'S THAT?
I FORGOT I DON'T KNOW HOW TO STOP ONE OF THESE THINGS!

JUST KEEP SLOWING DOWN TILL YOU COME TO A STOP!
NO! I FELL OFF LAST TIME, REMEMBER? AND THE TIME BEFORE THAT...

OH, YEAH. OK, TELL YOU WHAT! COME THIS WAY, I'LL YANK YOU OFF, AND YAX WILL STOP THE BIKE!
WHO? ME?
OK, HERE I COME!
3

GOTCHA! GO GET 'EM, YAX!
OOG! CAN'T HOLD IT!

RUNAWAY HOVER BIKE!
OH, OH. IT'S HEADED FOR... DUKE!
WHADDAYA WANT?

OUCH.
IT WAS NICE KNOWING YOU GUYS.
YAAAA
CLUNK
TINKLE
THUMP

I MIGHT HAVE KNOWN!
H-HI, DUKEY.

YEAH, YEAH, LITTLE GIRL. NOW THAT WE'RE ALL HERE, CAN WE GET SOME WORK DONE?
AYE AYE, SIR!
BINGO.
4

HEY, RACE! SOMEONE OUT HERE TO SEE YOU!
I'LL BET I KNOW WHO, TOO. OK, MARGIE, TAKE A BREAK. I'LL BE RIGHT BACK.

ABOUT WHAT?
BEATS ME.

IF YOU'LL EXCUSE ME, I HAVE WORK TO DO.
OK, SOREHEAD! CAN I AT LEAST HANG AROUND AND WATCH YOU GUYS IN ACTION?

SUIT YOURSELF.
THANK YOU.

S'MATTER, RACE? STRIKE OUT?
MUMBLE MUMBLE
SO TELL ME, SON. WHAT'S IT LIKE WORKING WITH RAND RACE? I HEAR HE CAN REALLY BE A BIG...
HUH? WHAT?

HEY! I KNOW WHAT YOU'RE UP TO! BUT IT WON'T WORK...
TUT TUT! YOU JUST TAKE CARE OF YOUR BUSINESS OVER THERE AND WE'LL TAKE CARE OF OURS OVER HERE, HM?

WHAT ABOUT YOU, HONEY? ARE YOU HIS GIRLFRIEND, OR WHAT?
WHO, ME? I... UH... HUH?
6

I MEAN, HAS HE EVER TRIED TO... YOU KNOW...
WE'RE FRIENDS, BUT, I DON'T...
DON'T LISTEN, MARGIE! LIES I TELL YOU! ALL LIES!
RACE! WATCH IT, YOU'RE...
JEEZ, I'M GETTING NOWHERE WITH THESE GRUNTS AND GROANS. MIGHT AS WELL JUST...
OOPS
BONK!
OOF!
YOU KNOW, YOU SHOULD BE A LOT MORE CAREFUL.
LOOK, I'M REALLY SORRY ABOUT THIS...
SO, THERE IS A SOFT SIDE TO YOU, HM, MR. RACE?
MAYBE I'LL BE ABLE TO GET THAT INTERVIEW, AFTER ALL, YES?
HA, WE'LL SEE...
HI, MAG. HOW WAS YOUR FIRST DAY BACK AT WORK?
CAN WE CHANGE THE SUBJECT, PLEASE?
7

WHAT'S WRONG? DID YOU GET FIRED OR DID RACE FIND A NEW GIRLFRIEND?
A SNOOPY, FLIRTY REPORTER BITCH, THAT'S WHAT!
OOH, NASTY...
SHE HANGS AROUND WORK AIMING TO GET AN INTERVIEW WITH RACE, AND HE'S ENJOYING EVERY MINUTE! MAN, JUST WHEN I...
MARGARITA, TELÉFONO.
THANK YOU, MRS. LOPEZ.
MAGGIE REALLY LIKES RACE, DOESN'T SHE?
YEAH, BUT SO DO A LOT OF OTHER LOVE-CRAZED FEMALES. SHE BETTER DO SOMETHING WHILE SHE HAS THE CHANCE, OR...
EEEEEEEE
THAT WAS EITHER RACE ON THE PHONE OR A RED HOT POKER.
THAT WAS RACE! WE'RE GOING TO RIO FRIO! WE HAVE A JOB THERE! RIO FRIO! RIO FRIO!
I'VE BEEN THERE WITH MR. COSTIGAN. VERRRRY ROMANTIC.
AND THE BEST PART IS, IT'S ME AND RACE, AND RACE AND ME, TOGETHER IN RIO FRIO!
:SIGH: OUR LITTLE GIRL IS GROWING UP MORE AND MORE EVERY DAY.
HAVE YOU EVER BEEN TO RIO FRIO?
NOPE. FIRST TIME.
GHOST STORIES
END OF PART I

MECHANICS PART TWO

JAIME 84

HEY HOPEY! YOU GOT A LETTER FROM MAGGIE!
BAM BAM BAM
WHA'D YOU SA--
E WEEX!
THUMP

SO THIS IS WHY YOU HAVEN'T BEEN PRACTICING WITH YOUR BAND LATELY. YOU'VE GONE INTO THE WRECKING BUSINESS.
SQUEEK

PAINTING, TOO? WHY THE SUDDEN INTEREST IN MODERN ART?
HEEYAAA

IF YOU MUST KNOW, I'M TRYING TO SURPRISE MAGGIE BY FIXING UP THIS DUMP BEFORE SHE GETS BACK FROM RIO FRIO.
FIX UP OR BUST UP?

WELL, I ADMIT IT DOESN'T LOOK TOO HOT RIGHT NOW, BUT...
FORGET IT FOR A SECOND. OPEN THE LETTER...

FROM MAGGIE?! DAMN IT, PENNY! WHY DON'T YOU EVER TELL ME THESE THINGS?
WELL... DUH... GEE...
2

DEAR HOPEY AND GANG,

ALOHA! OR AS THEY SAY HERE IN FUNNY, SUNNY, RIO FRIO... KAMANA-WANALEYA! MAN, THEY SURE DON'T WASTE TIME HERE, I TELL YA. ONCE YOU STEP OFF THE PLANE, ≈CACHOING≈ YOU'RE ENGAGED OR SOMETHING. BUT YOU DON'T HAVE TO WORRY ABOUT THIS ONE, JACK. I'VE GOT MY EYE ON SOMETHING A LITTLE CLOSER TO HOME, AND HIS INITIALS ARE RANDALL RACE. TELL PENNY I KNOW THAT HE'S JUST A MACHO CREEP AND I JUST LIKE HIM BECAUSE HE'S A PROSOLAR MECHANIC. WELL, MAYBE, MAYBE NOT. WE SHALL SOON SEE.

ANYWAY, THIS JOB WE'RE ON CALLS FOR ONLY TWO MECHANICS. A PRO MECH AND (KAFF KAFF) HIS ASSISTANT. THAT'S RIGHT, BOYS AND GIRLS. IT'S JUST RACE AND I LET LOOSE IN THIS STRANGE, STRANGE, EXOTIC LAND. OH, HOW WILL WE EVER MANAGE?

WELL, TO TELL YOU THE TRUTH I HAVEN'T REALLY SEEN MUCH OF THE STUD SINCE WE GOT HERE. HE'S BEEN OFF TALKING JOB (AS USUAL), SO I'VE JUST BEEN HANGING AROUND THE BEACH GETTING FAT LIKE ALL THE OTHER LAME TOURISTS. BUT, MY TIME SHALL COME, BABY.

LOVE YOU,
MAGGIE

DR. BEAKY, THIS IS MY ASSISTANT, MARGIE CHAS...

OH, I KNOW, I KNOW... AH YES, MS. CHASCARRILLO. SO TINY, SO... I AM MOST DELIGHTED TO MEET YOU. RACE HAS SPOKEN OFTEN OF YOU.

ALL GOOD I HOPE. HEH...

CHEPAN! THE ISLE OF GREAT HISTORY! THOUSANDS OF YEARS AGO THE BLASCANS FLED TO THE ISLAND TO ESCAPE THE TYRANTS THAT RULED BLASCANIA (RIO FRIO). YOU KNOW, WITH ALL MY MONEY KEEPING THAT SINKING ISLAND AFLOAT, THOSE UNGRATEFULS STILL WANT ME DEAD. JUST WAIT TILL THAT BIG ONE COMES, BOY... AND WHEN THEY COME RUNNING TO ME...
YOU KNOW, I REALLY HATE TO BE PUSHY, BUT...

EXACTLY WHAT KIND OF WORK WILL WE BE DOING FOR YOU, DR. BEAKY?
ROBOTS, MY BOY! ROBOTS! A MILLION OF 'EM...
YEO!
SLAM!

MARGIE! ARE YOU ALL RIGHT?
OH, MY...
WHOA... YEAH, I THINK SO.

WHAT HAPPENED? DID YOU SLIP, OR...
NO. IT FELT MORE LIKE I WAS THROWN.
CHINESS!

MUST I PUNISH YOU OVER AND OVER BEFORE YOU FINALLY UNDERSTAND? HM?
HM?
NO, DR. BEAKY, I'M ALL RIGHT! YOU DON'T HAVE TO...

A THOUSAND APOLOGIES, MISS CHASCARRILLO. I'LL MAKE SURE IT NEVER HAPPENS AGAIN. MY MAN ON THE ISLAND WILL FILL YOU IN ON THE DETAILS OF YOUR JOB. NOW, IF YOU'LL EXCUSE ME, IT'S TIME FOR MY MEDICINE. GOOD DAY.

WELL, MS. WINKS. YOU NOW HAVE PERMISSION BY DR. BEAKY TO ENTER CHEPAN.
THANK YOU. IS THERE A PHONE I CAN USE?
THERE'S ONE OUT IN THE HALL.
5

FRANCO? IT'S DOT. YEAH, I'M IN FRIO RIO AND... RIO FRIO, WHATEVER... AND I GOT PASSAGE TO THE ISLAND... YEAH, CHEPAN. THAT'S WHERE RACE IS WORKING. YEAH...

NO, SMART GUY, HE DOESN'T KNOW I'M HERE... YET. OH, GOTTA GO NOW, FRANCO. THERE'S A DOZEN GORGEOUS BLASCAN HUNKS BREATHING DOWN MY BACK JUST WAITING TO JUMP THIS BOD. UH HUH. WHO? RACE? NO WAY! OK, BYE BYE, SWEETIE.

THAT FRANCO'S GOT SOME KINDA IMAGINATION. ALL I WANT FROM RACE IS AN INTERVIEW, AND I'M GETTING IT, EVEN IF IT KILLS ME.

HEY, MARGIE! WASN'T THIS A GREAT IDEA RENTING THIS SMALL TUG TO TAKE TO THE ISLAND INSTEAD OF THE STANDARD LINER?
YEAH. SWELL, RACE.
MAN, DO I FEEL GREAT!
GROWL!
JEEP

STILL THINKING ABOUT THE INCIDENT IN DR. BEAKY'S OFFICE?
DOES HE ALWAYS TREAT HUMAN BEINGS LIKE ANIMALS? NOT THAT THAT SHOULD EVEN HAPPEN TO TEN DOGS...

AW, I KNOW BEAKY'S A SCREW BALL, BUT LET'S JUST FORGET ALL THAT RIGHT NOW. LOOK, WE HAVE ALL THIS NICENESS. NO NOISE... NO MACHINES... NO BOSSES... NO NOSEY REPORTER DOWN MY NECK...
WELL, THAT'S A STEP IN THE RIGHT DIRECTION.
OK, RACE...
HEY, BOSS!

JOE, I TOLD YOU NOT TO CALL ME BOSS! JUST CALL ME RACE!
OK, BOSS. BUT HERE COME THOSE COAST GUARDERS AN' THEY LOOK KINDA HUNGRY!
I'LL SLIP BELOW IF YOU DON'T MIND.
6

I'M AFRAID YOU'LL HAVE TO COME OUT TOPSIDE... MADAME. POR FAVOR...
OK, OK! JUST A SECOND, HUH? CHEE...

EVERYTHING IS IN ORDER, MR. RACE. HAVE A NICE STAY IN CHEPAN.
THANK YOU.

WHA'D I TELL YA? THERE AIN'T NOTHING THAT CAN RUIN MY EUDAEMONIA RIGHT NOW!
YOUR WHAT?
WE REACH SHORE IN TEN MINUTES, BOSS!

OK, FOR THE NEXT TEN MINUTES I'M GONNA BE LIFELESS. I'M NOT GONNA MOVE AN INCH. BE NUMB... JUST RELAX... NO NOISE... NO MACHINES... NOBODY...
SWELL.

YOU CALL IT AN ISLAND AGAIN AN' WE WHIP YOUR BUTT SOME MORE!
LA TOÑA
YOU'VE GOT YOUR INSTRUCTIONS I TRUST? GOOD. IT'S JUST AROUND THIS CORNER.
LOW LIFE DISHRAG!
REMEMBER, IT'S ONLY AN ISLAND FROM THE WATER!
7

JUST GO TO IT, AND IF YOU HAVE ANY QUESTIONS JUST ASK FOR BENSO.
WE'LL DO THAT, THANKS.
8

DAMN THAT BEAKY! HE'S ALWAYS PULLING SHIT LIKE THIS! THIS IS THE REASON I ALWAYS TAKE MY BUSINESS TO COSTIGAN!
WHAT ARE YOU TALKING ABOUT?

HE STICKS US IN THIS STINKING WAREHOUSE WITH A BUNCH OF ROTTING ROBOTS JUST SO HE CAN CALL UP COSTIGAN AND TELL HIM HE HAS ME WORKING FOR HIM!
DID HE HIRE US JUST FOR THAT?

OF COURSE HE DID! AND COSTIGAN'S NOT SO INNOCENT EITHER! MAN, I CAN SEE THEM RIGHT NOW QUARRELING OVER WHO'S GOT MORE BASEBALL CARDS!
ARE YOU MAD?

WHAT'S IT LOOK LIKE, GODDAMN IT!
JUST ASKING.

YOO HOO
NAW...

THIS CAN'T BE HAPPENING...
WELL, WELL, WELL, WELL, WELL... NOW ISN'T THIS A COINKYDINKY! FANCY MEETING YOU HERE, MR. RACE! HOW'S THE OL' FIX-IT BUSINESS?

YOU KNOW, HERE I WAS ALL ALONE IN THIS STRANGE LAND, AND YOU COME ALONG. MY, MY! THEY MUST LOVE ME IN HEAVEN! LOOKIT YOU! MHMM! BOY! SMALL WORLD, HUH?
I GOTTA GET BACK TO WORK. SO LONG. NICE TALKING TO YA.
9

NO, DON'T GO! SINCE YOU'RE HERE, HOW ABOUT THAT INTERVIEW I'VE BEEN ASKING YOU SO NICELY FOR?
OH, CHRIST...

WHAT DO I HAVE TO DO TO GET IT THROUGH YOUR DINGY BLONDE HEAD THAT I DON'T WANT YOU NEAR ME? READ-MY-LIPS: I-DON'T-WANT-YOU-NEAR-ME! GET OUTA HERE!

SPLIT!
O-OK!

YOU ASSHOLE, FRANCO. YOU WERE RIGHT. COULD IT BE THAT I'M ACTUALLY FALLING IN LOVE? DOT, WHAT HAVE YOU DONE?

MAN, WHAT'S WRONG WITH ME? I'M COMING UNGLUED! I...
MARGIE!

MARGIE? YOU STILL HERE?
YEAH. I... UH... WAS JUST ABOUT TO GET TO WORK.

LOOK, MARGIE, I'M SORRY I ACTED THE WAY I DID. I JUST GET SICK OF ALL THIS BUSINESS BULL. I'M REALLY SORRY YOU WERE TRAPPED IN MY EXPLOSION.
THAT'S OK. I UNDERSTAND. THE PRESSURES AND ALL...

YOU DON'T KNOW HOW MUCH BETTER THAT MAKES ME FEEL. I JUST HOPE DOT WILL BE AS UNDERSTANDING AS YOU ARE. I BETTER FIND HER BEFORE...
WHO?!

HELL, DON'T ASK ME!
END OF PART II

24T
JAIME 84
I READ A LETTER FROM A FRIEND OF MINE TODAY.
OH?
SHE WROTE FROM RIO FRIO.
OH.
SHE SAYS SHE SAW YOU THERE.
HOW NICE.
SHE SAW YOU IN A TAXI...
MHMM...
...WITH A WOMAN IN RED.
MY SECRETARY.
HERV!
WELL, WHAT THE HELL AM I SUPPOSED TO SAY? OK, YOU GOT ME! OK! WHO ARE YOU, MY WIFE?
I JUST LOVE IT WHEN HE DOES THAT.
END

MECHANICS

PART THREE

SO FAR:

RACE AND MAGGIE ARE IN RIO FRIO HIRED TO FIX ROBOTS ON THE NEARBY ISLE OF CHEPAN AND REPORTER DOT WINKS HAS COME TO VISIT.

JAIME 84

I SWEAR! NOTHING EVER GOES RIGHT FOR THIS JUNKY BAND!
GOT A TICKET? HEY! I SAID, YOU GOT A TICKET?
SHE'S PLAYING TONIGHT! LEAVE HER ALONE, ASSHOLE!
YEAH! LET HER GO!
HEY! I'M IN THE BAND, TOO! LEMME IN!
LIAR!
MADDOG'S
IT'S COOL, MAN. SHE IS PLAYING TONIGHT.

MONICA! WHAT'S GOING ON? PEOPLE ARE TELLING ME THAT...
OH, YOU MEAN ABOUT MAGGIE? THAT THE POOR THING'S DEAD?
EXIT

WHAT DID YOU SAY?
MONICA! HOW COME WE'RE NOT PLAYING TONIGHT?
BECAUSE ZERO'S SICK, TERRY.
APE SEX

HEY! DON'T START TALKING YOUR SHIT ABOUT MAGGIE! I KNOW YOU HATE HER BUTT, BUT THAT...
BUTT BUTT?
WHY? WHAT DID I SAY?
ZERO'S NOT SICK! I JUST TALKED TO HIM ON THE PHONE! HE WANTS TO KNOW WHY WE'RE NOT PLAYING!

YOU SAID THE POOR THING IS DEAD!
WE'RE NOT PLAYING BECAUSE THEY SAID THERE WERE TOO MANY BANDS PLAYING ALREADY.
BULL SHIT, MONICA!

YOU SAID MAGGIE IS DEAD!
I SAID THAT?
MONICA, IF YOU DON'T WANT TO PLAY TONIGHT, WHY DIDN'T YOU JUST SAY SO IN THE FIRST PLACE!
2

YOU SAID THAT! WHY?
WHY WOULD I SAY THAT? MAGGIE'S NOT EVEN HERE!
I QUIT THIS FUCKING BAND, I SWEAR!
WHAT? AGAIN?

SHE'S WORKING WITH RAND RACE IN RIO FRIO, ISN'T SHE? HAS SHE WRITTEN YOU LATELY, HOPEY? HOPEY?
WHY IS HOPEY SO UPTIGHT?
IZZY ORTIZ HAD AN ACCIDENT AT HOPEY'S PLACE AND ALMOST DIED. SHE GAVE HOPEY QUITE A SCARE.

SO, AGAIN I'D LIKE TO APOLOGIZE FOR ALL THE TROUBLE I'VE CAUSED YOU, AND SO WE CAN BE FRIENDS I'M GOING TO FORGET ABOUT THIS INTERVIEW BUSINESS, OK?
I MEAN, WHO NEEDS A HUNDRED DOLLAR BONUS, ANYWAY? NOT ME, BOY!
AND WHO CARES ABOUT ALL THOSE MILLIONS OF FANS WHO CRAVE THE TRUE STORY OF RAND RACE'S LIFE AS AN EVER POPULAR PRO MECH?
TRYING TO MAKE ME FEEL LIKE A HEEL, DOT? IT'S WORKING.

HM, I DON'T MEAN TO. IT'S JUST THAT YOU'RE THROWING AWAY A LOT HERE. YOU KNOW, WITH MY COLUMN, I COULD MAKE YOU VERY FAMOUS. WITH YOUR LOOKS YOU COULD EASILY BECOME THE NEXT DEREK CI...
HELL, I HAVE A HARD ENOUGH TIME JUST KEEPING UP WORK! I HAVE BOSSES WHO KEEP WOMEN AS PETS, I HAVE ASSISTANTS WHO CLOBBER ME WITH ROBOT LIMBS... THEN DISAPPEAR!

BY THE WAY, WHERE IS YOUR LITTLE PARTNER THIS MORNING?
AW, SHE SAID SHE WAS ILL OR SOMETHING. YOU KNOW, BY THE LUMP ON MY HEAD, I'M BEGINNING TO BELIEVE SHE REALLY IS... MENTALLY!
3

I THINK THE POOR KID HAS A CRUSH ON YOU. DON'T YOU LIKE HER?
OF COURSE I DO! MARGIE AND I GET ALONG JUST FINE. SHE'S THE FINEST HUMAN BEING YOU COULD EVER KNOW! BUT I DON'T WANT TO MESS THAT UP!

I DON'T WANT THIS TO TURN OUT LIKE THE LAST TIME! THERE'S THIS GIRL NAMED PENNY. MAN, SHE WAS IT. THE CHURCHIEST OF ALL LA FEMMES. THE... WE USED TO GO OUT A WHILE BACK. I LOVED PENNY SO MUCH, BUT SOMEHOW, I DON'T KNOW HOW... I HURT HER. REAL BAD. SO BAD, THAT I CAN NEVER SPEAK TO HER AGAIN. I DON'T KNOW... SHE HATES ME...

AND MARGIE... I'M AFRAID I MIGHT HURT HER THE SAME WAY. I COULD NEVER HURT MARGIE. SHE'S SO... OH, I'M SORRY. I MUST SOUND LIKE A SOAP OPERA.
WHICH ONE?, RACE, YOU CAN'T KEEP PUTTING YOURSELF DOWN LIKE THIS OR YOU'LL GO NUTS!

LOOK, HOW ABOUT LUNCH? I'M BUYING.
SWELL. STILL FISHING FOR THAT INTERVIEW, EH? HA HA!

STUPID! RETARDED! FAT! YES, YOU!

MARGARITA LUISA CHASCARRILLO! YOU'VE GOTTA BE THE BIGGEST FUCKING JERK WITH A HORSE'S ASS EVER TO BE PUT ON THIS PLANET! YOU THINK YOU CAN JUST HIDE IN YOUR ROOM AFTER WHAT YOU DID TO RACE? MAN, IF YOU DON'T DO SOMETHING AND DO SOMETHING FAST YOU MIGHT AS WELL JUST STAY IN THIS HOTEL FOREVER! ARE YOU LISTENING TO ME? YES, YOU!

HMM... IT WOULD BE KINDA BORING STAYING IN HERE FOR THE REST OF MY LIFE. WHAT AM I SO AFRAID OF ANYWAY? IT'S NOT LIKE HE'LL HIT ME BACK. SHEESH!
OR WILL HE? WHAT IF THAT BONK ON THE HEAD MADE HIM KILL-CRAZED OR... OOH...
4

THANKS FOR THE SWELL GET WELL GIFTS, GUYS. BUT YOU REALLY SHOULDN'T HAVE...
THAT'S OK, IZZY. I SEE YOU'RE RECOVERING NICELY.

YEAH, I FEEL GREAT! THOSE CHOCOLATE M&M'S YOU GOT ME REALLY DID THE TRICK.
YEAH. I FIGURED THE GREEN ONES WOULD HAVE MADE YOU SICKER.
WHERE'S YOUR LOUD ROOMMATE? HAVING MOUTH SURGERY?

OH, SHE DIED LAST NIGHT. IT WAS SAD BECAUSE SHE WAS ALREADY DEAD TEN MINUTES BEFORE ANYBODY CAME TO CHECK ON HER. THE POOR WOMAN HAD AN INCURABLE VIRUS YOU CAN ONLY GET IN THE PALO PALO REGIONS. HAS SOMETHING TO DO WITH THEIR MULES, I DON'T KNOW...
ISN'T THAT AROUND WHERE MAGGIE IS WORKING?
: ULP :

WHAT'S WRONG, HOPEY? YOU SICK OR SOMETHING?
I GOTTA CALL MAGGIE.

PERHAPS MS. TITAÑON WOULD ENJOY ANOTHER FRUIT COCKTAIL?
NO, NO, THIS IS FINE, THANK YOU VERY MUCH.
RENA...

I DON'T KNOW WHAT TO DO. THE PEOPLE ON MY ISLAND ARE STARTING TO THREATEN ME NOW! I WANT TO AVOID ANY UNNECESSARY BLOODSHED. YOU KNOW...
MAYBE IF YOU COULD TALK TO THEM. THEN MAYBE...
LOOK, BEAKY. THEIR MIND IS ALREADY MADE UP. THEY WANT THEIR COUNTRY BACK FROM YOU AND THEY'LL STOP AT NOTHING TO GET IT.
5

BAH! I GIVE THOSE ISLANDERS EVERYTHING THEY NEED AND WHAT DOES IT GET ME? A BIG KNIFE IN MY BACK! WELL, WE SHALL SEE...
A FRIEND OF MINE TELLS ME YOU HAVE RAND RACE AND HIS ASSISTANT WORK-ING FOR YOU ON THE I... CHEPAN.

YES, BUT THEY HAVE NOTHING TO DO WITH THE MATTER AT HAND! I WANT YOU TO TELL THOSE ISLANDERS THAT...
I HAVEN'T SEEN MARGARET AND RACE SINCE ZHATO. MAYBE I'LL DROP IN ON THEM... WITH YOUR PERMISSION OF COURSE, DOCTOR BEAKY...
PHONE, DOCTOR...

YES, YES! GO ON! HELLO? WHO IS THIS?
THANK YOU. AND BEAKY, IT'S ONLY AN ISLAND FROM THE WATER. REMEMBER THAT, OR YOU'VE GOT MORE TROUBLE FROM THEM THAN YOU EXPECTED.

I'M SORRY, DOCTOR BEAKY, BUT THE REBELS ON CHEPAN HAVE INFORMED ME THAT IF YOU DON'T START NEGOTIATIONS WITH THEM CON-CERNING THE ISLAND SOON, THEY'RE GOING TO HAVE TO..."RESORT TO DRAS-TIC MEASURES."
HAH?!

OH, THEY WILL, WILL THEY? WELL, YOU TELL THEM I'M CALLING THEIR BLUFF! THEY DON'T SCARE ME ONE BIT! LISTEN! I'M LAUGHING!
HA-HA-HA!
AT ONCE, DOCTOR.
CLICK!

THOSE BASTARDS ARE RUINING EVERY-THING! HOW EMBARRASSING. THEY ACTUALLY HATE ME. I CAN ONLY IMAGINE WHAT COS-TIGAN IS GOING TO SAY. I'LL NEVER BE ABLE TO SHOW MY FACE AT ONE OF HIS SHINDIGS AGAIN. OH, WOE IS ME...

YOU KNOW, YOU'RE RIGHT? I THINK I'VE BEEN WORKING MYSELF TOO HARD. ALL THOSE MACHINES HAVE REALLY GOTTEN TO ME.
WHAT YOU NEED IS REST AND RELAXATION. AND I THINK I HAVE JUST THE THING FOR YOU...
6

...BUT THE RATS AND BUGS ARE USING MY HOTEL ROOM FOR A CONVENTION, SOOO... YOUR HOTEL WILL HAVE TO DO.
I SEE...

YOU STILL WANT THAT INTERVIEW, MS. WINKS?
I THOUGHT YOU'D NEVER ASK, MISTER RACE.

OK, NO MORE PUSSYFOOTIN' AROUND HERE, GIRLY, YOU'VE GOT WORK TO DO! THERE ARE ROBOTS THAT NEED FIXING. I HOPE RACE HAS COOLED OFF BY NOW...
MISS CHASCARRILLO? THERE IS A PHONE CALL FOR YOU DOWNSTAIRS!
KNOCK! KNOCK!

I'M FIRED, RIGHT?
DID HE OR SHE SAY WHO IS CALLING?
NO. IT IS A YOUNG LADY... LONG DISTANCE.

REET!

HELLO? YES? HOPEY? IS THAT YOU? HELLO?

YEAH, IT TOOK ME ALL DAY TO GET AHOLD OF YOU! YOU SOUND LIKE YOU'RE ALL RIGHT! YOU'RE NOT... NO, NOTHING! EVERYTHING OK OVER THERE IN ROMANCE LAND? EVERYTHING'S FINE HERE. IZZY HAD AN ACCIDENT BUT SHE'S OK NOW. HEY, WAIT'LL YOU SEE THE WAY I FIXED UP OUR PLACE! HUH? UH, WHY DID I CALL...?
LEMME TALK NEXT.

LA TOÑA! THAT VULTURE BEAKY WON'T LISTEN TO REASON! ALL WE WANT IS OUR HOME! PERHAPS IF YOU COULD PERSUADE HIM...
FLACO, PLEASE! I'M IN RIO FRIO ON VACATION, NOT TO FIGHT. AND I CAME TO CHEPAN TO SEE SOME FRIENDS, THAT'S ALL. I'M SURE YOU AND BEAKY CAN WORK YOUR DIFFERENCES IN A CIVILIZED MANNER. JUST KEEP A LEVEL HEAD, EH?
7

YEAH, OK. BIG MAN. YEH... DID YOU DO IT TO PROVE SOMETHING, OR WHAT? LIKE, THAT YOU'RE STILL ALL MAN, OR JUST BECAUSE YOU PLAIN ENJOYED IT? DID YOU DO IT BECAUSE IT'S SO HARD FOR YOU TO EVEN ASK MARGIE TO PASS YOU A WRENCH? MAN, IF SHE FINDS OUT ABOUT THIS, ABOUT ME AND DOT... MARGIE REALLY LIKES YOU A LOT, YA BIG COWARD!

WAIT, WHAT AM I AFRAID OF? SO WHAT IF I GO TO BED WITH THIS WOMAN? I DON'T OWE MARGIE ANYTHING! SHE'S MY ASSISTANT MECHANIC, NOT MY GIRLFRIEND! SO WHAT IF SHE HAPPENS TO BE NICE... SWEET... SOFT... AND THINKS I'M THE GREATEST THING SINCE SEEDLESS WATERMELON.

WELL, I BETTER SIGN OFF NOW, HOPITA. HOW ARE YOU EVER GONNA PAY THIS PHONE BILL?
DON'T HAVE TO! DAFFY GOT A NEW CREDIT CARD NUMBER FROM HER DAD. THE OTHER DAY WE CALLED ZHATO AND TALKED TO THEIR NEWEST PRESIDENT.

WELL, IT WAS NICE OF YOU TO CALL, HOPEY. UH HUH. THANKS. I MISS YOU. BYE BYE.

NOW I FEEL LIKE A MILLION BUCKS! I DON'T EVEN MIND GOING UP TO RACE AND APOLOGIZING RIGHT TO HIS FACE! I JUST MIGHT HAVE TO GIVE A GREAT, BIG KISS TO THAT BUMP ON HIS HEAD. I THINK I SAW A LIGHT ON IN HIS ROOM.

SEE? I TOLD YOU THERE'S NOTHING TO WORRY ABOUT, ESPERANZITA.
I SUPPOSE YOU'RE RIGHT, PENNY.
8

BOO BOO! LOOK! I GUESS THERE'S NO WORK FOR US TOMORROW, HUH?
GOOD. THANKS TO THOSE REBELS NOW I CAN TAKE MY KIDS TO THE FAIR IN THE MORNING.
HUH! YOU THINK THEY'LL HAVE A FAIR NOW WITH ALL THIS RACKET?

NOW MAYBE BEAKY WILL HAVE TO LISTEN TO US, EH? JUST REMEMBER, NO LIVES ARE TO BE JEOPARDIZED HERE! THESE ARE JUST SCARE TACTICS AGAINST DOCTOR BEAKY.
WOW! WOTTA SHOW!

DOCTOR BEAKY! THERE WAS AN ACCI-DENT AT ONE OF YOUR FACTORIES IN CHE-PAN! IT SEEMS...
ACCIDENT, MY CORNS! WHY ARE THEY DOING THIS TO ME? I DONT WANT A FIGHT! OHH...

IT WAS GREAT LAST NIGHT, DOT. NOW I, UH, HAVE TO GO SEE ABOUT WORK. I'LL BE RIGHT BACK.
OK, SWEETY.

RACE! I WAS JUST COMING UP TO... OH.
M-MARGIE!! WHAT A... NICE SURPRISE!
OUCH! S'CUSE ME. HI.

Y-YOU WERE COMING UP TO SEE ME? TALK TO ME? TELL ME TO GO TO HELL? SKIN ME ALIVE?
NO. YES. I JUST CAME UP TO TELL YOU I'M GOING BACK TO THE ROBOT WAREHOUSE TO MAKE UP FOR THE DAYS I CALLED IN SICK. OK, BOSS?

WAIT! I'LL GO WITH YOU IF YOU'LL JUST WAIT A SECOND. I JUST...
NO. I CAN MANAGE, THANK YOU, BOSS. I'LL SEE YOU THERE LATER.
9

MARGIE! PLEASE DON'T... MARGIE!
ONE MORE THING, BOSS. IT'S MAGGIE. NOT MARGIE. MAG-GIE! MAG-GIE! NOT MAR-GIE! MAG-GIE! MAGGIE! MAGGIE!
PHONE CALL FOR YOU DOWNSTAIRS, MR. RACE!
?

WAIT! PLEASE! DON'T BE MA... YES, HELLO?
RACE? BEAKY. I MUST TALK WITH YOU. URGENT. MY OFFICE. NOW. PLEASE!

SO, DID I BLOW IT, OR WHAT? YOU TOLD ME YOU WEREN'T GOING OUT WITH LITTLE MISS FROWN!
I'M NOT... YOU DIDN'T... IT'S NOT YOUR FAULT, DOT. MAGGIE'S JUST... WELL... I GOTTA GO SEE DOCTOR BEAKY. IT'S NOTHING... REALLY!
SLAM!

FACE IT, CHICK. HE JUST DOESN'T GO FOR CHUNKY MEXICAN GIRLS, THAT'S ALL. THAT GIVES YOU NO RIGHT TO ACT THE FOO' IN FRONT OF EVERY-BODY.
WE'RE REACHING SHORE NOW, BOSS LADY!

YOU JUST GOTTA TAKE THESE THINGS IN STRIDE. YOU GOTTA BE STRONG, LIKE...
RENA TITAÑON?
MARGARET, DEAR! IT'S SO NICE TO SEE YOU AGAIN!
RUBE'S

HOW'VE YOU BEEN, GIRL? HAVE YOU LANDED THAT RAND RACE YET? WHERE IS THE STUD BY THE WAY?
OH, HE'S AROUND. IN HIS HOTEL ROOM IN RIO FRIO, I GUESS.

NOW, MARGARET! DON'T TELL ME THAT BOY IS STILL BREAKING YOUR LITTLE HEART...
NO WAY! I'VE FORGOTTEN RACE. HE'S NOT WORTH IT.
10

REALLY? THEN WHAT ARE THE TEARS FOR MARGARET? I KNOW IT'S NOT BECAUSE YOU'RE SO EXCITED TO SEE ME. COME ON, YOU NEED A BIG SHOULDER TO CRY ON, HON?

HOPEY SURE LOOKS HAPPIER TODAY.
SHE TALKED TO MAGGIE ON THE PHONE FROM RIO FRIO LAST NIGHT. I GUESS ALL THOSE HINTS OF MAGGIE BEING DEAD WERE ALL COINCIDENCE.
I WONDER...
DOA
MISSILES OF OCTOBER

CALM DOWN, BEAKY! WHAT'RE YOU TRYING TO TELL ME?
THE ISLANDERS ARE DESTROYING MY FACTORIES AND WAREHOUSES IN CHEPAN ONE BY ONE! WHO KNOWS WHAT THEY'LL TRY NEXT?

LATEST REPORT, DOCTOR BEAKY. THEY JUST BOMBED ANOTHER ON THE SOUTH COAST.
VERY WELL. I WANTED TO AVOID THIS, BUT THEY LEAVE ME NO ALTERNATIVE. GET ME GENERAL MATAPOLAS ON THE PHONE. WE'LL HAVE TO PLACE CHEPAN UNDER ARREST. HAS ANYONE BEEN HURT IN THE EXPLOSIONS?

NOT YET, SIR. THEY'VE ALL BEEN EMPTY OR CONDEMNED BUILDINGS THUS FAR. IF YOU ASK ME, THEY ARE ONLY TRYING TO SCARE YOU.
BEAKY! MY ASSISTANT MAGGIE HAS GONE TO THE ROBOT WAREHOUSE.
OH, YES... AND RENA TITAÑON WAS GOING TO MEET YOU THERE ALSO.

RENA TITAÑON, TOO? WE'VE GOT TO WARN THEM BEFORE...
ALL COMMUNICATION HAS BEEN CUT OFF TO THE MAINLAND! I'LL SEND SOMEONE TO...
FORGET IT! I'LL GO!

YES, BOSS! I TOOK HER THERE MYSELF. SHE WAS ON HER WAY TO THE ROBOT WAREHOUSE YOU WORK AT. I DUNNO, I DON'T THINK IT'S TOO GOOD AN IDEA TO GO INTO CHEPAN RIGHT NOW. I SAW SOME BOMBS GOING OFF ON LAND.
YOU CAN TURN BACK AS SOON AS YOU DROP ME OFF ON LAND.

OH OH! IT'S THOSE RIO FRIO COAST GUARDERS AGAIN, BOSS, AND THEY LOOK MADDER THAN THE LAST TIME.
SHIT! STALL THEM FOR ME, WILL YOU?
11

I'LL TAKE YOUR WORD THAT THERE'S NO ONE ELSE ON BOARD, JOE. BUT I'M AFRAID YOU CAN'T DOCK IN CHEPAN TO-DAY. THINGS HAVE GOTTEN HAIRY BETWEEN DOCTOR BEA-KY AND THE PEOPLE ON THE ISLAND.
HEY! COME ON, LESTER. IT'S ONLY AN ISLAND FROM THE WATER.
DAMN CHEPAN LOCAL.

THERE GOES ANOTHER BUILDING! LUCKILY THE BLAST DIDN'T COME FROM THE DIRECTION OF THE ROBOT WAREHOUSE. I HOPE MAGGIE AND RENA DECIDED TO EAT OUT INSTEAD OF GOING THERE.

MISTER RACE! HELLO! REMEMBER ME? I'M BENSO FROM THE WAREHOUSE!
BENSO! HAVE YOU SEEN MAGGIE, MY ASSISTANT?

SURE. I DROVE HER TO THE ROBOT PLACE. SHE WAS WITH THAT CHAMPION WRESTLER LADY... WHAT'S HER NAME AGAIN?
I NEED TO BORROW YOUR RIDE!

SORRY, MISTER RACE, BUT IT JUST KONKED OUT. I DON'T KNOW WHAT'S WRONG WITH IT.
CRACKED ENGINE BLOCK! NEVER MIND! HEY, YOU!

THIS IS FORTY-FOUR. POSTPONE THE DEMOLISION OF THE ROBOT WAREHOUSE. THERE ARE INNOCENTS INSIDE. WAIT TILL THEY'RE OUT AND SAFELY AWAY.
TOO LATE, FORTY-FOUR. THE PRO-CEDURE IS UNDER WAY AT THIS MOMENT.

I'M NOT GOING NEAR ANY FACTORIES OR WAREHOUSES TODAY, MY MAN. THEY'RE ALL JINXED! I'M AFRAID YOU'RE ON YOUR OWN. MAY GOD GO WITH YOU, FRIEND.
THANKS ANYWAY!
12

DAMN! THERE GOES ANOTHER ONE! THEY'RE GOING UP ONE EVERY TEN MINUTES NOW!
PUFF
PUFF

THE STREETS ARE BARE! LET'S HOPE THAT'S BECAUSE IT HASN'T HAPPENED... YET!
PUFF
PUFF
PUF

MY INSIDES ARE ON FIRE... BUT I CAN'T STOP... GOTTA WARN 'EM... GOTTA RUN... SO TIRED, THOUGH...
PUFF
PUFF
PUF
P

I WONDER WHAT'S WITH ALL THE FIRE-WORKS. MUST BE SOME KIND OF HOLIDAY.
MARGARET, YOU'RE JUST BEING SILLY! IT'S NOT WORTH PUTTING YOURSELF THROUGH ALL THIS AGONY! EVERYTHING WILL BE ALL RIGHT, IF YOU ONLY LET IT.
YEAH, WELL... LOOK DOWN THIS PIT. IT LEADS TO THE SE-WER TUNNELS UNDER-GROUND...

WE THROW ALL THE LEFT OVER, USELESS JUNK DOWN THERE. YOU KNOW, ROBOT PARTS, THINGS LIKE THAT. IT ALL WASHES OUT TO SEA EVENTUALLY, I GUESS. IT WOULD SEEM LIKE THE PERFECT SOLUTION, DON'T YOU THINK, RENA?
GREAT! NOW YOU'VE GONE FROM SILLY TO RIDICULOUS. DON'T YOU EVEN THINK OF JUMP-ING IN OR I'LL THROW YOU IN MYSELF!

NO, I WAS JUST KIDDING. DON'T WORRY ABOUT ME, RENA. I'LL BE FINE. I JUST HAVE TO CRACK A FEW STALE JOKES ONCE IN A WHILE JUST SO I WON'T DRIVE MYSELF CRAZY.
?

MARGARET? DO SOME OF THESE ROBOTS EVER TURN THEMSELVES ON?
NOT UNLESS THEY'RE IN LOVE WITH THEMSELVES. HAR HAR! NO, THEY ALL HAVE TO BE TURNED ON BY AN ELECTRONIC KEY, WHY?
13

END OF PART THREE

PART FOUR
JAIME 84
ZOBENINA HOSPITAL IN CHEPAN...
RACE! YOU'RE AWAKE! HOW ARE YOU FEELING, M'BOY?
BETTER. WHAT'S THE WORD, DOCTOR BEAKY?
1

IT'S REALLY WONDERFUL! THINGS ARE LOOKING UP. THE ENTIRE ISLAND IS CRAWLING WITH GENERAL MATAPOLAS' MEN KEEPING EVERYTHING UNDER CONTROL AND SEARCHING FOR THE TROUBLEMAKERS WHO STARTED THIS WHOLE BOMBING BUSINESS. THEY SHOULDN'T BE TOO HARD TO FIND, I'M SURE.
WELL, UH... I MEANT THE ROBOT WAREHOUSE. MAGGIE AND RENA...?

OH, THAT. NO, NO BODIES HAVE BEEN FOUND IN THE WRECKAGE YET. NOW, RACE, ONCE AGAIN: ARE YOU CERTAIN THEY WERE IN THE WAREHOUSE AT THE TIME OF THE BLAST?
I DON'T KNOW. IT'S ALMOST BEEN A DAY SINCE THE EXPLOSION AND THEY'RE NOWHERE TO BE FOUND. WHERE ELSE COULD THEY BE? TELL ME THAT!

BE CALM. WE'RE NOT PRONOUNCING ANYONE DEAD TILL WE FIND OUT FOR SURE WHAT HAS HAPPENED TO THOSE TWO.
...AND DOT, DID YOU GIVE HER PERMISSION TO COME TO CHEPAN?

THAT, I'M AFRAID I COULDN'T DO, RACE. DOT WINKS IS A REPORTER, AND IF THERE IS ONE THING THIS SITUATION DOES NOT NEED RIGHT NOW IS A SNOOPY...
SHE'S A CELEBRITY COLUMNIST AND ALSO MY FRIEND.

A REPORTER IS A REPORTER. DO YOU KNOW WHAT COULD HAPPEN TO ME IF SOMETHING LIKE THIS HITS THE INTERNATIONAL PRESS?? I CAN SEE THE HEADLINE NOW..."TITAÑON DEAD, BEAKY TO BLAME!"
OH, WE COULDN'T HAVE THAT.

I MUST HAVE BEEN GOOFY TO THINK RAND RACE WOULD FALL FOR THIS BROAD. THE WHOLE TIME WE WERE LOVE MAKING HE HAD HIS MIND ON THAT TEENY BOPPER. RIGHT NOW HE'S PROBABLY IN CHEPAN FUCKING HER LITTLE BRAINS OUT AND SHE'S FORGIVING HIM. OH WELL, WHY NOT? I WOULD, TOO. HE'S RAND RACE, AIN'T HE?

I BETTER GET PACKED. I GOT A PLANE TO CATCH IN A COUPLE OF HOURS. DON'T KNOW WHY I'M HURRYING, THOUGH. I PROBABLY WON'T HAVE MY JOB WHEN I GET BACK, SINCE I DIDN'T GET "THE DEFINITIVE RACE INTERVIEW." HM, I COULD WRITE ABOUT "THE NIGHT I SEDUCED A PRO MECH IN RIO FRIO JUST TO GET A STUPID INTERVIEW," OR HOW ABOUT "I FELL IN LOVE WITH A JERK." GAD, STOP! STORY OF MY LIFE. JEEZ...
2

LA TOÑA

ARE YOU SURE YOU SAW TWO WOMEN IN THE WAREHOUSE WHEN YOU PLANTED THE EXPLOSIVES?
I'M POSITIVE! ONE OF THEM CAME AFTER ME! I-I GOT SCARED...

...SO I RAN...
...BEFORE YOU COULD DEACTIVATE THE EXPLOSIVES. ARGHH! NOW BEAKY'S NOT ONLY AFTER OUR NECKS BUT OUR DICKS AS WELL!
YOU CAN SAY THAT AGAIN! HE HAS SOLDIERS BREATHING DOWN OUR NECKS! WE CAN'T STAY HERE MUCH LONGER.

DO YOU THINK THEY COULD HAVE GOTTEN OUT BEFORE...
WHERE WILL WE GO NOW?
I DON'T KNOW! I DIDN'T LOOK BACK, BUT I HEARD THE EXPLOSION...
WELL, WE CAN'T USE THE SEWERS. THEY HAVE BEEN SEALED OFF FOR YEARS NOW.

ARE YOU STILL THERE, RENA?
I'M STILL HERE.

WHY DO WE KEEP WALKING? I'M HUNGRY.
DON'T TALK. YOU'RE DELIRIOUS.

HOW LONG HAS IT BEEN?
OH, ABOUT TWENTY HOURS.

TWENTY HOURS? IT SEEMS MORE LIKE TWENTY DAYS!
MHMM. DON'T DRAG YOUR FEET.
MEANWHILE, OH, ABOUT TWENTY HOURS AGO...
3

HOOIEEE LO'D!
WHO'DA BELIEVED IT IN A MILLION YEARS THAT THIS OLD BOD COULD STILL MOVE FAST ENOUGH TO SAVE OUR NECKS! WE'RE MOSTLY LUCKY WE HAD THIS PIT TO DIVE INTO OR ELSE THAT BOMB WOULD'VE GOTTEN US BUT GOOD!
LOOKS LIKE THE WRECKAGE FROM THE BLAST SEALED OUR WAY OUT OF HERE. WE'LL NEVER BE ABLE TO CLEAR IT. TOO BAD. AS LONG AS WE'RE ALIVE, RIGHT, KID?
MY HEAD FEELS LIKE IT'S ON FIRE...

OH, IT'S NOTHING, REALLY. BLOOD MOSTLY. YOU'LL BE FINE. DO YOU HURT ANYWHERE ELSE, MARGARET?
NO, BUT EVERYTHING'S GETTING DARKER BY THE MINUTE. I THINK I'M GOING BLIND, RENA.

NO, THAT'S JUST THE FIRES GOING OUT. WE'RE GOING TO HAVE TO FIND SOME OTHER FORM OF LIGHT. I DON'T THINK FIRE WILL LAST TOO WELL IN THIS THIN AIR.
WELL, IF THERE'S A MINER AMONG THIS SCRAP OF ROBOTS WE MIGHT HAVE SOME KINDA LIGHT.

A MINOR OR A MINER? WHAT'S A...
HERE'S ONE. THEY'RE USED FOR WORKING IN VERY DEEP MINE SHAFTS WHERE THERE'S VERY LITTLE OXYGEN.

SEE? THEIR HEADS CAN BE REMOVED AND USED AS SPOTLIGHTS.
I KNEW THERE WAS MORE TO YOU THAN JUST A CUTE FACE.

WELL, WE BETTER GET GOING. WHERE DO YOU THINK THAT TUNNEL IS GOING TO LEAD US?
TUNNEL? WHY? AREN'T WE GONNA WAIT FOR SOMEONE TO COME RESCUE US? HUH?
4

ARE YOU SERIOUS? WE'LL STARVE BY THE TIME ANYONE FIGURES OUT WE'RE EVEN DOWN HERE, LET ALONE CLEARS THAT WRECKAGE UP THERE. THAT IS, IF WE DON'T SUFFOCATE FIRST.
BUT, SOMEONE WILL...

THE ONLY WAY WE'LL FIND A WAY OUT OF THIS SEWER IS TO START WALKING. MAYBE THE AIR WILL GET CLEARER AS WE GO. ARE YOU WITH ME, KIDDO?
BUT, JUST WAIT, RENA. SOMEONE MIGHT...

OK. SUIT YOURSELF.
WAIT FOR ME!

AH, GENERAL MATAPOLAS. YOU'VE DONE AN EXCELLENT JOB OF BRINGING ORDER BACK TO CHEPAN.
THANK YOU, DOCTOR. WE'LL HAVE THOSE REBELS UNDER ARREST IN NO TIME.

I KNOW YOU WILL. I... HEY! WHO LET THOSE CAMERAS ON MY ISLAND?
AH, DOCTOR BEAKY! TELL ME, IS IT TRUE THAT RENA TITAÑON WAS KILLED IN THE WAREHOUSE EXPLOSION HERE? SOME LOCALS WERE TELLING ME THAT...

GENERAL! ARREST THESE NEWSPEOPLE! CONFISCATE THEIR VIDEO EQUIPMENT!
YOU CAN'T SILENCE US, BEAKY! WE ALREADY SENT OUT A WIRE! THE WORLD WILL HEAR OF THIS!

NOW THEY DID IT! NOW ALL THOSE BIGGIES ARE GONNA LAUGH ME OUT OF SOCIETY! CHUDE BALLOONE, PEDERO SAN JO, H.R. COSTIGAN... ESPECIALLY COSTIGAN!

HERV!
5

HERV? HERV R. COSTIGAN! WHERE DID YOU GO?
IN HERE, PENNY.

WHAT ARE YOU DOING? DON'T YOU WANT TO SWIM ANY MORE?
NOT NOW. SOMETHING HAS HAPPENED IN CHEPAN. I JUST WANT TO HEAR WHAT THEY HAVE TO SAY AND I'LL BE RIGHT OUT. THAT'S BEAKY'S TERRITORY, YOU KNOW.

MY FRIEND IS WORKING IN CHEPAN.
...ACCORDING TO REPORTS, IT IS ALMOST CERTAIN THAT TITAÑON ALONG WITH A FRIEND WAS IN THE WARE-HOUSE AT THE TIME OF THE EXPLOSION...
SHH...

THE FRIEND WITH TITAÑON IN THE WARE-HOUSE IS BELIEVED TO BE THE ASSISTANT OF PROSOLAR MECHANIC RAND RACE. WE HAVEN'T BEEN ABLE TO TALK WITH MISTER RACE AT THIS TIME...
NO WAY...

I REPEAT: IT IS STILL NOT CLEAR IF IN FACT RENA TITAÑON WAS KILLED IN A TERRORIST ATTACK ON A WAREHOUSE IN CHEPAN. STAY TUNED FOR FURTHER DEVELOPMENTS...
TITAÑON, DEAD? NOW AIN'T THAT A KICK IN THE HEAD? ON BEAKY'S ISLAND YET. HAR!
NO! THEY SAID IT'S STILL UNCER-TAIN, DIDN'T THEY?

WELL, YEAH, IT'S STILL NOT CLEAR YET. BUT IF IT IS, I'LL BET BEAKY'S ALREADY CHEWED RIGHT PAST HIS NAILS UP TO HIS KNUCKLES. COME ON, LET'S GO SWIMMING.
I CAN'T! I HAVE TO SEE WHAT'S GOING ON. OH, MAG...

MISTER RACE. YOU REALLY SHOULDN'T BE UP AND OUT OF BED TILL YOU'VE FULLY RECOVERED...
WAIT A SEC. WHAT'S THAT LITTLE GUY SCREAMING ABOUT?
HOSPITAL CHEPAN
ZOBENINA
6

HEY, BENSO! WHAT'S THAT FELLOW BABBLING ABOUT?
IT'S NOW CONFIRMED, MR. RACE...

...HE SAW THE TWO WOMEN IN THE WAREHOUSE BEFORE-- I'M SORRY, MR. RACE!

...THERE'S A NEW DEVELOPMENT ON THE WAREHOUSE EXPLOSION IN CHEPAN...
GENERAL MATAPOLAS!!!
NEWS

EXCUSE ME, BUT IS YOUR NAME DOT WINKS?
YEAH, BUT I CAN'T STOP TO CHAT. I GOT A PLANE TO CATCH.
RIO FRIO AIRLINES

AND YOU ARE A REPORTER, ARE YOU NOT, MS. WINKS?
YES, BUT...
COME WITH US, PLEASE. YOU ARE UNDER ARREST.

HEY! WHAT GIVES? THIS IS A JOKE, RIGHT, GUYS? RIGHT?
THIS WAY, PLEASE...

R-R-RENA TITAÑON...??
THAT'S IT. WE'RE BEAKY'S DINNER NOW...
GULP
SOB

YEOW!
RENA TITAÑON, HAH? HAH?!
VICKI'S GYM FOR WOMEN WRESTLERS
NO GUYS ALLOWED
VICKI'S GYM →
7

SAY IT AGAIN! WHO IS THE GREATEST WRESTLER IN THE WORLD? HAH?
RENAAAH! I MEAN, YOU ARE, VICKI! VICKI GLORI!!

I'M SO GOD DAMN SICK OF HEARING THAT NAME! I HATE RENA TITAÑON! I'M THE GREATEST WRESTLER THAT EVER LIVED! NOT HER!!
WELL, YOU ARE NOW ANYWAY, VICKI.

WHAT DO YOU MEAN BY THAT CRACK, CASH?
LISTEN...
...NO BODIES HAVE BEEN FOUND, BUT A WITNESS NOW CLAIMS HE SAW TITAÑON AND THE MECHANIC IN THE WAREHOUSE MINUTES BEFORE THE EXPLOSION...

CAN YOU BELIEVE IT? QUEEN RENA, DEAD? WHADAYA MAKE OF IT, VICKI? HEY, VICKI! WHERE YA GOIN'?
I NEED A SHOWER. I'LL SEE YOU GUYS IN THE MORNING.

A WITNESS CLAIMS HE SAW RENA TITAÑON AND RAND RACE'S ASSISTANT MECH ACTUALLY DIE IN A TERRORIST'S ATTACK ON A ROBOT WAREHOUSE IN CHEPAN. OFFICIALS ARE STILL UNCERTAIN WHAT THE REASON FOR THE ATTACK WAS. MS. TITAÑON WAS FORTY-EIGHT.
TITANON

...SO, THIS MECHANIC WAS A FRIEND OF YOURS, PENELOPE?
YES... A VERY CLOSE FRIEND...

MAY I MAKE A LONG DISTANCE CALL BACK HOME, HERV? CERTAIN PEOPLE MIGHT NOT HAVE HEARD THE REPORT.
SURE. I'LL GET YOU A DIRECT LINE.
8

YOU CALL THAT A PICTURE? C'MON, HOPEY! TRY KICKING IT OR SOMETHING. I'M MISSING MY SOAP.
HOLD YOUR HORMONES, WILL YOU? I ALMOST GOT IT...
YOU WATCH SOAPS, IZZY? YOU'RE THE LAST PERSON I'D IMAGINE WATCHING A SOAP OPERA.

I CAN'T HELP IT. I GOT HOOKED WHILE I WAS LAID UP IN THE HOSPITAL.
IF MAGGIE WERE HERE, SHE'D HAVE IT FIXED IN NO TIME.
WELL, SHE'S NOT HERE. SO WE'LL JUST HAVE TO DO WITHOUT, HUH?

HOW ABOUT IF WE GIVE HER ANOTHER CALL ON MY FATHER'S CREDIT CARD?
THE PHONE DOESN'T WORK. BUT THERE'S A PAY PHONE ON THE CORNER.

UGH! FORGET IT. YOU'RE NOT GETTING ME OUT IN THIS RAIN.
I WONDER IF MAGGIE HAS HER NEW TAN BY NOW.
YOU MEAN HEAT RASH...

♫ A HAND FOR EACH HAND WAS PLANNED FOR THE WORLD... ♫

♫ ...WHY DON'T MY FINGERS REACH... ♫
MARGARET. IF YOU DON'T STOP SINGING THAT SONG THIS VERY SECOND, I'M GOING TO DROWN YOU. ¿COMPRENDE?

YEAH, WELL YOU JUST DON'T KNOW GOOD SINGING WHEN YOU... HEY, ARE WE SINKING?
THE WATER'S RISEN. I HADN'T NOTICED IT BEFORE. THERE'S MORE WATER COMING THROUGH!
9

THE CURRENT'S GOTTEN A LOT STRONGER, TOO...
WOOP!
MARGARET! GRAB ON TO ME!

HANG AROUND MY NECK AND WHATEVER YOU DO, DON'T LET GO OF THAT LIGHT!

WHO FLUSHED THE DAMN TOILET ANYWAY?
GLUB!
RENA! LOOK! ON THE CEILING!

DAMN, YOU'VE GOT GOOD EYES, GIRL! HOLD ON TIGHT! WE JUST MAY HAVE FOUND OUR WAY OUT OF HERE.

NOPE. ANOTHER TUNNEL. AT LEAST THIS ONE HASN'T ANY WATER AT ALL. LOOKS LIKE IT'S BEEN DRY FOR A LONG WHILE.
OOPS!

OH, GREAT! THERE GOES OUR ONLY LIGHT SOURCE! I THOUGHT I TOLD YOU TO HOLD ON TIGHT TO THAT THING!
I...I...I WAS HOLDING ON TO YOU.

WELL, NO USE CRYING OVER BURNT TOAST. WE'LL JUST HAVE TO FEEL OUR WAY OUT OF HERE.
I'M SORRY, RENA.

DON'T WORRY ABOUT IT. THE AIR'S A LOT CLEANER IN THIS TUNNEL.
OUCH!

DID YOU HURT YOURSELF, MARGARET?
NO. DID YOU?

NO.
THEN WHY DID YOU SAY OUCH?
SHE DIDN'T. I DID. WOULD YOU MIND GETTING OFF MY HAND?
END of PART 4

PART FIVE

STORY THUS FAR: WORD HAS GOTTEN OUT THAT RENA AND MAGGIE HAVE BEEN KILLED IN A WAREHOUSE EXPLOSION (WE KNOW BETTER) AND A PARANOID BEAKY IS BECOMING A REAL GHOUL.

IN THE MORNING I HAVE TO TAKE A BUS TO MONTOYA TO BE WITH MAGGIE'S MOM AND RELATIVES. I'M REALLY LOOKING FORWARD TO THAT. CHRIST...
OK. I'LL GO SEE HOPEY.
NIXON

I MIGHT AS WELL GO SEE HER NOW. THE SOONER THE BETTER I SUPPOSE... I'LL SEE YOU LATER, ISABEL.
DIOS TE CUIDE, PENNY.

DAMN! AFTER THIS I MAY NEVER WALK AGAIN! HOW ARE YOU DOING, MARGARET?
GEE, I DUNNO. IT'S CRAZY, BUT... I DON'T KNOW IF IT'S BECAUSE WE'VE BEEN IN THE PITCH BLACK FOR SO LONG OR IF MY MIND'S FINALLY GONE, BUT...
BUT, WHAT, SEÑORITA? WHAT...?

I-I THINK I CAN SEE YOU GUYS. YEAH... AM I CRAZY OR WHAT?
NO! YOU'RE NOT! I CAN SEE YOU, TOO!
HOORAY! THERE MUST BE AN OPENING SOMEWHERE AHEAD, LADIES! C'MON!

I DON'T GET IT, JOE. WHY ARE YOU TAKING ME TO THE WAREHOUSE THIS LATE AT NIGHT?
IT'S VERY IMPORTANT, MISTER RACE. IT'S ABOUT YOUR ASSISTANT AND LA TOÑA.

LET ME GET THIS STRAIGHT, JOE. YOU THINK THEY STILL MAY BE ALIVE BECAUSE THEY FELL INTO THE WASTE PIT THAT LEADS TO THE SEWERS? THAT'S QUITE A LONG SHOT THERE, JOE.
WELL, THAT DOES EXPLAIN THE UNFOUND BODIES, DOESN'T IT?

BUT, LOOK! THE SEWER'S BEEN FLOODED. EVEN IF THEY DID SURVIVE THE BLAST, I DON'T THINK THEY COULD HAVE...
WELL, THAT'S A CHANCE WE HAVE TO TAKE, ISN'T IT?
2

HOLD IT! I'M CONFUSED. A FEW DAYS AGO YOU WERE ONLY OUR TRANSPORTATION TO AND FROM CHEPAN, BUT NOW... WHY ARE YOU DOING THIS?
OK, I MIGHT AS WELL TELL YOU...

I'M SORT OF PARTLY RESPONSIBLE FOR WHAT HAS HAPPENED. I WAS WORKING WITH THE TERRORISTS WHO BLEW UP THE ROBOT WAREHOUSE...

IT WAS AN ACCIDENT! BELIEVE ME, NO ONE WAS SUPPOSED TO GET HURT! IT WAS ONLY TO SHOW DOCTOR BEAKY THAT WE THE PEOPLE OF CHEPAN CANNOT BE PUSHED AROUND...

"THEY WERE ONLY DESTROYING EMPTY BUILDINGS THAT WERE OWNED BY BEAKY. HECK, THOSE TERRORISTS ARE JUST A HANDFUL OF COLLEGE STUDENTS WHO WERE TIRED OF BEAKY AND HIS WEALTH AND WHO JUST HAPPENED TO GET A HOLD OF SOME EXPLOSIVES. I HELPED THEM BECAUSE I KNEW IT WAS A GOOD CAUSE..."
JED

SO, IF YOU THINK THIS IS SOME WILD-GOOSE CHASE, YOU CAN WALK AWAY RIGHT NOW. BUT IF YOU CAN IMAGINE THE TWO WOMEN SOMEWHERE OUT THERE ALIVE AND BREATHING, CRYING OUT FOR HELP, THEN YOU CAN MEET ME AT THE ROCKET HANGERS IN THE MORNING AT SIX. THINK ABOUT IT.

AW, WHAT THE HELL HAPPENED? WHERE DID WE GO WRONG?
RENA! I CAN'T SEE YOU GUYS ANY MORE!

I... CAN'T UNDERSTAND IT. FOR A FEW MINUTES THERE, WE COULD ACTUALLY SEE... THEN...
OH, KAKA!

DON'T CRY, MARGARET. WE'RE NOT FINISHED YET. WE'LL GET OUT OF HERE...
C'MON, LADIES. WE'LL SLEEP IT OFF. WE CAN START AGAIN IN A FEW HOURS.

Z
Z
SHIT... WE'RE NEVER GETTING OUT OF HERE... MAYBE THIS TUNNEL IS LEADING US TO HELL...
MAYBE... ZZZ
3

WHAT A DAY THIS HAS BEEN. IT STILL FEELS LIKE A DREAM. I DON'T THINK I COULD EVER LAST ANOTHER LIKE IT.

TWO O'CLOCK. DIDN'T REALIZE IT WAS SO LATE. HOPEY'S PROBABLY NOT EVEN UP. WAIT, THE DOOR'S BEEN LEFT OPEN.

HOPEY? ARE YOU UP?

HOPEY? IT'S ME PENNY. ARE YOU...
11

THEN, IT'S TRUE?

Z

MARGARET!
WHADDAYA WANT?

MARGARET! COME ON! COME ON OUT!
RENA? WHAT...?
4

ISN'T IT WONDERFUL? EVERYTHING WENT DARK AGAIN IN THE TUNNEL BECAUSE THE SUN WENT DOWN! WE WERE ONLY YARDS FROM THE OPENING THE WHOLE TIME!
THEN WE'RE OUT? WE'RE REALLY OUT? ZOWIE!!
BUT, RENA... WHERE IS THAT MAN?
HE WENT RIGHT ON THROUGH. HE LIVES IN THERE, REMEMBER?
GEE, I DIDN'T EVEN GET HIS NAME OR ANY-THING. WHAT DID HE LOOK LIKE?
WHO CARES? I REALLY THINK WE SHOULD BE GOING, MARGARET.
BUT... OH, ALL RIGHT. WHERE ARE WE, ANYWAY?
I'M NOT SURE...
...BUT I DON'T THINK WE'RE OUT OF THESE WOODS YET, KIDDO.
5

RIO FRIO...
... AND THE WAREHOUSE BLEW SKY HIGH WITH THE WOMEN STILL INSIDE, AND RAND RACE IS IN THE HOSPITAL RECOVERING FROM MINOR BURNS...
NO WONDER I NEVER HEARD FROM HIM AGAIN! THE WHOLE TIME HE WAS... AND HIS GIRLFRIEND... BOY, DO I FEEL SHITTY!
AND NOW ALL JOURNALISTS ARE BEING THROWN IN JAIL. THAT BEAKY'S GONE TOO FAR!
DOT WINKS! SOME MAN HAS PAID YOUR BAIL!
BH + DP
LOIS WAS NEAR
TWO QUESTIONS: WHO'S THE GUY THAT SPRUNG ME? WHAT'S HE LOOK LIKE? I WANT TO THANK HIM IN PERSON.
IT'S ME, DOT.
I HEARD ABOUT THE AWFUL THINGS THAT HAVE HAPPENED TO YOU. I DON'T KNOW WHAT TO SAY.
IT TOOK ME ALL NIGHT TO FIND YOU. ARE YOU OK?
YOU'VE JUST BEEN THROUGH HELL AND YOU ASK ME IF I'M OK? RACE...
DOT. I NEED YOU TO COME WITH ME. I'LL EXPLAIN IT TO YOU ON THE WAY.
ABOUT WHAT TIME WOULD YOU SAY IT IS RIGHT NOW?
OH, I'D SAY ABOUT SIX OR SEVEN AM...
IT'S FUNNY. I RARELY EVER SEE THIS TIME OF DAY. I USUALLY SLEEP TILL ABOUT NOON.
BY THAT TIME YOU'VE COMPLETELY MISSED THE BEST PART OF THE DAY. OOH...
6

RENA? ARE YOU OK? YOU'VE BEEN...
FORGET IT, I'M FINE.
RENA, IT'S OK TO GET TIRED. THE HEAT GETS TO ALL OF US.
I SAID, I'M FINE! REALLY!
JUST A TWITCH...
MAYBE IT'S FROM BEING BODY SLAMMED ALL YOUR LIFE.
I'LL BODY SLAM YOU IN A MINUTE...
DOCTOR BEAKY HAS ORDERED THAT ALL ROCKETS STAY GROUNDED BUT THAT CARGO SHIP. IT DELIVERS FOOD AND MEDICAL SUPPLIES TO VILLAGES THROUGHOUT OUTER CHEPAN.
IT'S OK, KATO. THEY'RE MY EXTRA CREW FOR THIS MONTH'S RUN. WE HAVE A BIG LOAD TODAY. LOTS OF VILLAGES TO COVER, YOU KNOW.
THANKS, CARLOS. I OWE YOU ONE.
YEAH, SHUT UP AND GET IN. WE'RE ALREADY IN ENOUGH TROUBLE HAVING THAT...THAT WOMAN ON BOARD. I HAVE A VERY HORNY CREW, YOU KNOW.
TELL US ABOUT IT, EL CAPITAN HORN.
YEESH! SOMETIMES I WONDER WHY I'M EVEN DOING THIS.
YOU'RE TELLING ME. I KINDA PICTURED MYSELF ON A PLANE RIGHT NOW HEADED FOR HOME FORGETTING THERE EVER WAS A RIO FRIO OR A CHEPAN.
7

YEAH... I'M REALLY SORRY ABOUT THIS. I REALLY SHOULDN'T HAVE MADE YOU COME ALONG. THIS IS MY PROBLEM AND I...
HEY, IF I DIDN'T WANT TO COME, I WOULDN'T BE HERE.

BUT, THIS ALL SEEMS SO HOPELESS! IT'S A BILLION TO ONE SHOT...
REMEMBER WHAT JOE SAID? PEOPLE HAVE BEEN KNOWN TO LIVE IN THOSE TUNNELS FOR LONG PERIODS OF TIME. SO THERE'S STILL THAT CHANCE.

YOU'RE INCREDIBLE. WHAT WOULD I DO WITHOUT YOU, DOT?
I KNOW, I KNOW...

QUINA CHASCARRILLO'S HOME IN MONTOYA...
SPEEDY'S JUST A LITTLE DRUNK, IZZY. WE'LL TAKE CARE OF HIM.
OK, THANKS, LICHA.
HEY! DON'T TALK TO THAT BITCH IN THERE! SHE USED THE ROPES TO WIN THE BELT FROM TITAÑON, MAN!

SORRY ABOUT MY BROTHER. NOW, AS I WAS SAYING... I'M REALLY A BIG FAN OF YOURS. I WATCH YOU WRESTLE ON TV ALL THE TIME. I REALLY ENJOY YOUR ATOMIC PILEDRIVER.
YEAH, WELL, WE CAN'T TALK ABOUT THAT RIGHT NOW. I'M IN MOURNING FOR TWO PEOPLE, Y'KNOW...

FIRST, I HEAR ABOUT QUEEN RENA... THEN ALL OF A SUDDEN I HEAR THAT MY LITTLE NIECE WAS WITH HER IN THE HOOPLA.
I REALIZE YOU MUST BE IN REAL PAIN.
8

DAMN STRAIGHT! RENA TITAÑON TAUGHT ME EVERYTHING I KNOW. AND IN OUR FUEDING DAYS, THERE WAS ONLY ONE GAL WHO COULD SEND ME FLYING OVER THAT TOP ROPE O THOSE HUNDRED TIMES. SHE WAS THE GREATEST...

...SO, IN HER (AND SHRIMP'S) HONOR, VICKI GLORI, CHAMPION OF CHAMPIONS IS, Y'ALL HEARD IT HERE FIRST, IS GOING CLEAN. NO KICKING, NO BITING, NO GOUGING, NO MORE ATOMIC PILEDRIVER!
THIS CALLS FOR A DRINK, CHAMP.

HELLO, HOPEY. HOW ARE YOU?
HELLO.
HI. LET'S GO TO THE RESTROOM, TERRY.

THIS PLUMBING, I SWEAR... HOW ARE YOU DOING, HOPEY? ARE YOU FEELING BETTER?
I'M FINE, I'M FINE! I'M JUST GOING CRAZY STAYING ALONE IN THAT APARTMENT. IZZY OFFERED TO LET ME MOVE IN WITH HER. I'M THINKING ABOUT IT...
JOE

HMF! I OFFERED YOU THE SAME DEAL, BUT... WHAT ABOUT YOU AND I, HOPEY? YOU THINK NOW THAT... YOU KNOW...
YOU AND I COULD NEVER BE AS CLOSE AS WE ONCE WERE, TERRY. YOU COULD NEVER HANDLE IT WHEN THE SHIT CAME DOWN.
AXEL
SHIT
PISS
WINNIE THE KA KA HEAD
JOE
HANGIN' HOOV
FLAG FLAG

YEAH? WELL, WHAT ABOUT MAGGIE? SHE WAS NEVER YOUR TYPE AND YOU KNOW IT!
OH, OH, OH! AND YOU WERE? YOU... AGHHH! NEVER MIND!
STRAP ON DICKS
APE SEX
SUCKS

YOU JUST HAD HER AROUND BECAUSE SHE'D DO ANYTHING YOU'D FUCKING WANT HER TO!
PUT A BIG LOAD OF SHIT IN YOUR MOUTH AND CHOKE ON IT, WILL YOU, TERRY?

HELLO, HOPEY. HOW ARE YOU?
HELLO.
AH, SHADDAP!
TSK! POOR HOPEY.
9

THAT'S A HORSE?
SHHH... YES, THAT'S A HORSE. DON'T SCARE IT, NOW. IT'S OUR TRIP HOME.

WE'RE NOT GONNA RIDE THAT POOR, DESTROYED THING, ARE WE? HE CAN BARELY HOLD HIMSELF UP LET ALONE CARRY OUR FAT ASSES.
QUIET... HERE, BOY... GIRL...?

THERE HE GOES, RENA! GET HIM!
FRAM DAMN IT!

HEH! SORRY 'BOUT THAT. I GUESS I GOT A LITTLE EXCITED...
IF YOU DON'T SHUT UP I'M GONNA RIDE YOU HOME!

10

GO, RENA, GO!
RIDE 'EM, COWGIRL!
WAHOOO!

RENA!

WHAT HAPPENED? WHA...
YOU SLIPPED AND FELL, RENA. BUT THAT'S OK, 'CAUSE NOW IT'S MY TURN!

HERE, HORSEY! HERE, HORSEY HORSEY...

WHERE YOU GOIN', YOU LITTLE HOSS, YOU?

AHA! THERE YOU ARE...

YEOW!
11

HEY, RENA! WHAT DO YOU THINK OF THE TRADE I MADE FOR MY SHIRT AND PANTS? NEAT, HUH?

VERY NICE, MARGARET, BUT WE BETTER BE OFF NOW. WE WANT TO BE AS FAR AWAY FROM HERE AS POSSIBLE BY NIGHTFALL.

THEY DON'T TAKE TOO KINDLY TO THE WHITE SKIN AROUND HERE, KIDDO. THEY'D JUST AS SOON CUT YOUR WHITE COLORED BREASTS OFF BEFORE...
G'WAN!
OK! OK! YOU WANNA GO HAVE DINNER WITH 'EM? FINE! YOU GO ON AHEAD! ME, I'M GOING TO FIND MYSELF A NICE TREE TO SLEEP ON TOP OF! OK?
YOU DON'T HAVE TO GET NASTY ABOUT IT.
WHAT THE HELL'S WRONG WITH YOU, ANYWAY?
SAY! WHAT GOES ON DOWN THERE? CAN'T YOU SEE I'M TRYING TO SLEEP?
HOW CAN YOU SLEEP WHEN THE TERRORISTS HAVE BEEN FOUND...
...AND BEAKY'S GOING TO HAVE THEM EXECUTED!
WE MUST STOP HIM NOW!
LOOK, CARLOS! THERE'S SOMEONE DOWN THERE!
YEAH, JOE. THAT'S LUTHOR. C'MON, BOYS! WE'RE BREAKING FOR LUNCH!
SO, LUTHOR. WHAT'S BEEN HAPPENING SINCE THE LAST TIME WE STOPPED BY, EH?
STILL HANGIN' AROUND THE OL' TUNNELS. AND YOU WOULDN'T BELIEVE WHAT I FOUND IN THERE THE OTHER DAY...
DON'T TELL ME... A BEAUTIFUL WOMAN, RIGHT, YOU HORNY OL' BASTARD?

NO! TWO, COUNT 'EM, TWO BEAUTIFUL WOMEN! YEP...
HO HO! STILL THE OLD STORYTELLER, EH, LUTHOR?
!

!
HEY, YOU!!
YIIII!
!

SAY! WHAT'S THAT GUY DOING, MAN?
WAIT! IT'S OK...

I SWEAR I DIDN'T TOUCH 'EM! DON'T TAKE ME TO BEAKY! I DIDN'T KNOW THEY WERE HIS GIRLS! HONEST!
WE'RE NOT WITH BEAKY! JUST TELL ME ABOUT THE WOMEN!

I DON'T KNOW WHERE THEY ARE! AS SOON AS THEY FOUND THEIR WAY OUT OF THE TUNNELS THEY TOOK OFF! I SWEAR I DIDN'T TOUCH 'EM! I-I TRIED TO, BUT SHE SLUGGED ME! I SWEAR IT! WOTTA PUNCH...

DO YOU KNOW WHAT THIS MEANS?! THEY'RE ALIVE! JOE WAS RIGHT! THEY'RE ACTUALLY ALIVE!
THA'S WHAT THE MAN SAID, HE DID!

MMMMMM...

I CAN'T BELIEVE IT! YOU WERE RIGHT, JOE! YOU WERE RIGHT!
WE'RE ON THE RIGHT TRACK NOW, BOY!

*
OH, CHRIST...
* WHISTLED TO THE TUNE OF SUKIYAKI — BY KYU SAKAMOTO
14

I STILL THINK SLEEPING IN A TREE IS PRETTY SILLY. WILD ANIMALS, MY... AAAA!
WHAT THE...

VERY FUNNY, MARGARET. YOU'LL WOW 'EM ON THE MOON.
NO, NO! THAT SHADOW SCARED ME! THAT... RENA! LOOK!

IT'S A RESCUE SHIP!
A CARGO SHIP MORE LIKE IT. I WONDER WHAT IT'S DOING OUT HERE.

WHO CARES WHY IT'S HERE! IT'S HERE! C'MON, RENA! IT'S NOT MOVING VERY FAST! MAYBE WE CAN CATCH IT!
I'M COMING, MARGARET! OOF...
HURRY, DUKE! WE CAN JUST MAKE THE FREIGHT!
I'M (PUFF) TRYING! HOW DO YOU (GASP) DO IT, RENA?

WELL, WHADDAYA KNOW? IT ACTUALLY FIT THROUGH THE DOOR. THANKS, GUYS.
OOF! THAT'S OK! THANKS FOR HELPING ME PUT IT DOWN, HUH, JOEY?!
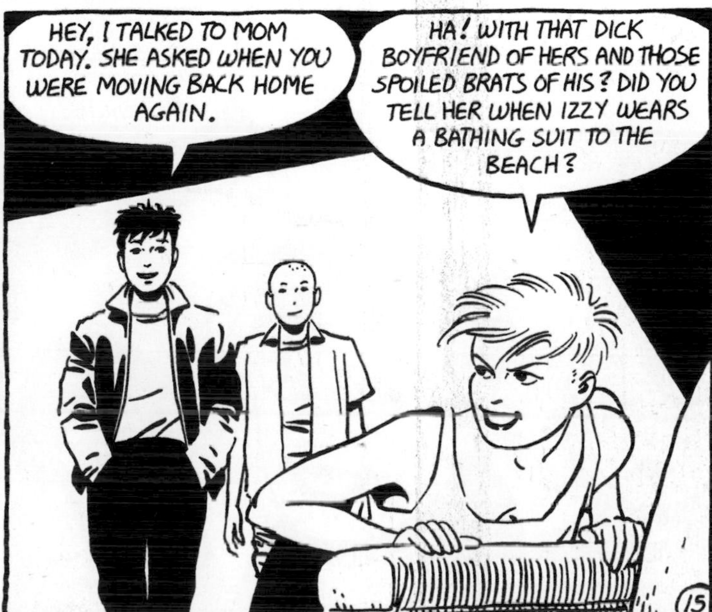
HEY, I TALKED TO MOM TODAY. SHE ASKED WHEN YOU WERE MOVING BACK HOME AGAIN.
HA! WITH THAT DICK BOYFRIEND OF HERS AND THOSE SPOILED BRATS OF HIS? DID YOU TELL HER WHEN IZZY WEARS A BATHING SUIT TO THE BEACH?
15

HEH... YEAH... WELL, WE GOTTA GET GOING NOW...
WAIT! THERE'S SOME BEER IN THE REFRIGERATOR. YOU WANNA WATCH TV OR SOMETHING?
HEY!

UH, NO. WE BETTER GO. MAYBE YOU SHOULD REST OR SOMETHING. THANKS ANYWAY.
OK... SEE YA.
HEY! I WANTED A BEER, MAN!

BUT YOU HATE YOUR MOTHER, HOPEY! I DON'T GET IT! AND YOUR HAIR...
DAFFY. I'LL BE BACK IN A FEW DAYS.

IT'S NOT LIKE I'M GOING TO LIVE THERE FOR GOOD. I HAVEN'T LOST ALL MY MARBLES... YET. BUT I DO NEED A VACATION FROM THIS CRAZED TOWN AND IT'S INHABITANTS. AT LEAST MY MOM'S BEEN NUTS ALL HER LIFE. NOT JUST RECENTLY...
DON'T LET YOUR MOTHER'S NEW BOY-FRIEND RAPE YOU, EH, HOPITA?

(SNIFF) I WISH MAGGIE WAS HERE AND EVERYTHING WAS BACK TO NORMAL.
SO DO I. THEN MAYBE EVERYBODY WOULD STOP ACTING SO SERIOUS.
TO BE CONCLUDED NEXT ISSUE

MECHANICS

PART 6

84 JAIME 85

BUT, CARLOS! WE STILL HAVEN'T FOUND THE LOST WOMEN YET. COULDN'T WE GO JUST A LITTLE FURTHER?
I'M SORRY, JOE. I ALREADY HAVE MY NECK ON THE LINE JUST BRINGING YOU THIS FAR.

BESIDES, I'M GETTING REAL TIRED OF LOOKING FOR A COUPLE OF DEAD BROADS!
HEY, NOW WAIT A MINUTE, BUDDY...
NO! YOU WAIT A MINUTE, BUDDY...
RACE! WATCH OUT!

WELL, WELL... I GUESS BY NOW PEOPLE HAVE COME TO THE CONCLUSION THAT I'M DEAD, EH?
WHAT... WHAT DO YOU MEAN?
LA
TON

WELL, FIGURE IT OUT, MARGARET. IT'S BEEN, WHAT, THREE OR FOUR DAYS SINCE THAT WAREHOUSE INCIDENT. I'M SURE WE MUST BE CORPSES IN THEIR MINDS BY NOW...
BUT... I MEAN... HOPEY... MY MOM... RACE... THEY ALL... OH, MY GOD...

NOW WHAT ARE YOU DOING?
MAYBE THEY HAVE A PHONE SOMEWHERE... OH, GEE...
2

AW, C'MON, MONICA! DON'T LEAVE! WE CAN PRACTICE WITH-OUT A BASS TILL HOPEY GETS HERE.
HOPEY'S NOT COMING, ZERO. SHE WENT TO STAY AT HER MOM'S FOR A FEW DAYS.
THE POOR THING. SHE EVEN DYED HER HAIR BACK TO BLACK FOR THE VISIT...

REALLY? THAT'S NOT LIKE HER. WHEN SHE USED TO VISIT HER MOM SHE'D USUALLY GET EIGHT MOHAWKS OR CARVE HIEROGLYPHICS IN HER HEAD JUST TO PISS HER OFF.
I DON'T GET IT, EITHER, TERRY. I GUESS MAGGIE'S DEATH AFFECTED HER MORE THAN EVEN SHE THOUGHT.
YOU CHICKS ARE NUTS! C'MON! WE CAN PRACTICE WITH-OUT A BASS!

...THE WINNAH AND STILL CHAMPEEN... VICKI GLORI!
LISTEN TO THIS... VICKI ACTUALLY CHANGED THE "VICIOUS" IN HER NAME TO "VIVACIOUS" AND EVEN GAVE UP THE NOTORIOUS ATOMIC PILEDRIVER!
¡ES MUY INCREÍBLE!
THA'S NOTHIN'! SHE EVEN TURNED ON ME, HER PARTNER LAST WEEK AS I WAS STRANGLING ANGEL SWABODA!
WRESTLING NEWS

WOW!

WHAT THE HELL ARE YOU DOING?!
YOU WENT TOO FAR, BUDDY! NOW YOU'RE GONNA DIE!

LET'S SEE HOW YOU LIKE BEING HIT FROM BEHIND, BUSTER!
HEY, BITCH!
3

HEY! WHO'S DRIVING THIS THING?
I THOUGHT YOU WERE!
OH, SHIT...

CRUNCH!

HEY! C'MON, GUYS! ENOUGH ALREADY!
OOF!

OW!
OK, THAT DOES IT! NOW I'M REALLY MAD... OOF!

OH OH.
OH OH.

DAMN IT, RACE! COULDN'T YOU JUST LEAVE IT TO ME? DON'T YOU TRUST ME? I HAD MEN SEARCHING FOR THE WOMEN ALL ALONG.
HAVE YOU FOUND THEM YET, DOCTOR BEAKY?
4

WELL, NO, BUT BY THE CLUES YOU'VE GIVEN ME, MY BOYS SHOULD FIND THEM WELL BEFORE MORNING. I PROMISE...

NOW, IF YOU'LL EXCUSE ME, MY BABIES AND I MUST LEAVE THIS PLACE. THE PEOPLE HAVE GOTTEN OUT OF CONTROL. IT'S MUCH TOO DANGEROUS FOR ME NOW...
WHY DON'T YOU JUST RELEASE THE TERRORISTS?

WELL, HEH... I CAN'T. YOU SEE, THEY WERE EXECUTED THIS MORNING...

HALP!!
JOE! NO! STOP!

HEY!

KRAK
THAT'S ENOUGH, BABIES.
YEOW!
BLAMM!
OOF!
WHUN
TINKLE!

I'M SORRY, RACE! I MUST LEAVE NOW!
WHOOP WHOOP!
JOE! WE BETTER SPLIT, TOO! THERE'S GONNA BE A LOT OF BLOOD!
NO! YOU GO!

THIS IS MY HOME, REMEMBER? MY LIFE. I HAVE TO STAY AND FIGHT FOR THE HOMELAND.
I DON'T KNOW WHAT TO SAY, JOE.
WE'LL NEVER FORGET YOU. AND DON'T WORRY, WE'LL FIND THOSE LOST WOMEN.
5

PHONE? TELEPHONE? CALL?
I THINK HE'S TRYING TO TELL YOU HE HAS NO PHONE, MARGARET.

SHIT! WHAT'LL I DO NOW?
JUST RELAX A BIT, GIRL. WE'LL GET YOU HOME TO YOUR HOPEY AND YOUR MOMMY REAL SOON...
‹HEY, YOU! GET UP FROM THERE!›

‹YOU TRAMPS CAN'T SIT THERE! I RUN A CLEAN PUB HERE!›
YEAH, YEAH! GO AHEAD, CALL A COP. JUST TAKE YOUR TIME, EH? I NEED AT LEAST EIGHTY HOURS OF SLEEP...

RENA. I THINK HE MEANS IT.
WELL, GOOD. THE COTS IN JAIL HAVE GOTTA BE MORE COMFORTABLE THAN THESE THINGS...

FIFTY SAYS THOSE LOST WOMEN ARE ROTTING DEAD IN THOSE FUCKING SEWERS.
YOU'RE ON. WE'LL BE BACK. THERE'S SOMETHING GOING ON IN THAT BAR.
TAKE IT EASY, GRAMPS. CAN'T YOUR LOCAL POLICE HANDLE THIS?
LA TOÑA XXX
LA TOÑA XXX
LA TOÑA XXX
6

OK, WHAT'S GOING ON IN HERE?
HUH! EMPTY. MUSTA HEARD US COMING AND SPLIT OUT THE BACK WAY.
GET BACK HERE.

THOSE SOLDIERS SEEM TO BE SEARCHING FOR US, MARGARET.
THEN SHOULDN'T WE SURRENDER OURSELVES TO THEM?

WELL, SORT OF. YOU'RE GOING TO SURRENDER YOURSELF. ME, I'M GOING THAT-A-WAY.
B-BUT, WHY? I MEAN, WE'RE SAVED...

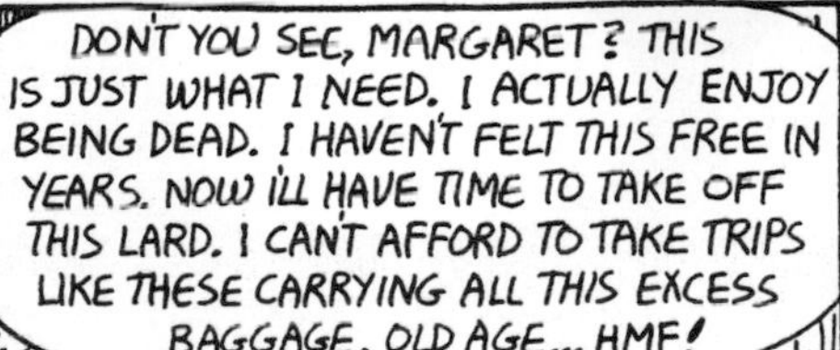
DON'T YOU SEE, MARGARET? THIS IS JUST WHAT I NEED. I ACTUALLY ENJOY BEING DEAD. I HAVEN'T FELT THIS FREE IN YEARS. NOW I'LL HAVE TIME TO TAKE OFF THIS LARD. I CAN'T AFFORD TO TAKE TRIPS LIKE THESE CARRYING ALL THIS EXCESS BAGGAGE. OLD AGE... HMF!

YOU, ON THE OTHER HAND, DESERVE A CIGAR FOR THE WAY YOU HANDLED YOURSELF. YOU ACTED LIKE A REAL PRO. YOU SHOULD BE REAL PROUD.
BUT, RENA... I NEVER COULD'VE SURVIVED WITHOUT YOU... I CAN'T...

WHAT I WANT YOU TO DO IS WALK UP TO THOSE SOLDIERS AND INTRODUCE YOURSELF TO THEM. WELL, GO ON...
I DON'T KNOW IF I CAN, RENA. I...

YOU CAN DO IT, MARGARET. YOU'RE A BIG GIRL NOW. REMEMBER THAT...
BUT, RENA... RENA!

SEE YOU IN THE FUNNY PAPERS, KIDDO!
RENA! COME BACK HERE, DAMN YOU!

RENA!

RACE,

IN CASE YOU WERE WORRYING ABOUT ME, I'M FINE. I RAN INTO A LITTLE TROUBLE (YOU MAY HAVE HEARD ABOUT IT) AND I COULDN'T CONTACT YOU TILL NOW. I JUST WANTED TO TELL YOU THAT I WON'T BE COMING BACK TO WORK FOR YOU AGAIN. IF I'M ALREADY FIRED, I UNDERSTAND. I'M SORRY I COULDN'T TELL YOU IN PERSON, BUT THEY'RE FLYING ME HOME TONIGHT FROM APEL AIRFORCE BASE.

AGAIN, I'M SORRY IF I'VE CAUSED ANY TROUBLE. IT WAS REALLY NICE WORKING FOR YOU, AND PLEASE SAY BYE TO DUKE AND YAX FOR ME AND ANYONE ELSE I FORGOT, OK?

LOVE,
MAGGIE

HERV! WHAT'S GOING ON? ARE YOU ACTUALLY...
YES, PENELOPE. I'M GOING TO BUY CHEPAN FROM DOCTOR BEAKY.

YES, I THINK IT'S A GREAT INVESTMENT, AND THE MAN IS PRACTICALLY GIVING IT TO ME, SO I'D BE A FOOL NOT TO. TUT TUT! LET ME FINISH...
TAP TAP

BEFORE YOU CLOBBER ME BECAUSE YOU THINK I'M A COLD HEARTED GHOUL, I THINK YOU'LL BE THRILLED TO HEAR THAT YOUR MECHANIC FRIEND FROM CHEPAN HAS BEEN FOUND ALIVE AND WELL...

HERV, OH HERV! I ALWAYS FELT DEEP DOWN INSIDE... OH, MY BABY IS ALIVE!
I SUPPOSE YOU'LL WANT TO SEE HIM RIGHT AWAY, HM?

WELL, NATURALLY, I... HUH?
HE'S A VERY CLOSE FRIEND, ISN'T HE? WHAT IS HE, SOME HIGH SCHOOL FLAME, OR WHAT?

NOT THE HORNS! PLEASE, PENNY! NOT THE HORNS!

DAMN IT! I HAVE EVERY RIGHT TO BE JEALOUS! JEEZ...
THIS "HIGH SCHOOL FLAME" JUST HAPPENS TO BE A GIRLFRIEND OF MINE FROM BACK HOME! MY FRIEND MAGGIE, HERV! MY GOOD FRIEND!

HOW YOU EVER GOT TO BE THE RICHEST MAN IN THE UNIVERSE IS BEYOND ME. EXCUSE ME, I HAVE TO GET HOME RIGHT AWAY.
FAN CLUB
9

LOOK, YOU IGNORANT ASSHOLE! SEE THIS PRESSCARD? THAT MEANS I CAN GO OUT THERE WITH ALL THOSE OTHER PEOPLE WITH PRESS CARDS! GET IT?
I'M SORRY. IT IS OUT OF MY HANDS. YOU'LL HAVE TO ASK THAT MAN OVER THERE.
HEY, YOU! C'MERE!

HE'S NOT HERE. I WAS HOPING MAYBE... SHOOT...
LOUDER INTO THE MIKE, PLEASE, MS. CHASCARRILLO. YOU'RE ON THE AIR...
WHAT ABOUT RENA TITAÑON, MS. CHASCARRILLO, PLEASE...

AS I TOLD THOSE ARMY GUYS, RENA AND I SPLIT UP HOURS BEFORE I ARRIVED AT THE VILLAGE. SO, THERE! I GOTTA GET ON MY PLANE NOW, OK? I WANNA GO HOME...

WHERE'D SHE GO, DOT? I DON'T SEE HER! WHERE'S MAGGIE?
MAYBE SHE'S ALREADY BOARDED HER PLANE.

THE GIRL ON THE NEWS? SHE ALREADY BOARDED. YEAH, THERE GOES HER PLANE NOW.

10

...THERE'S MORE TROUBLE IN CHEPAN. HR COSTIGAN SAYS HE'S STILL INTERESTED IN BUYING THE ISLAND, BUT LOCALS WHO HAVE TAKEN OVER THE ISLAND SAY THEY WANT IT FOR FREE, SINCE IT IS THEIR HOME AFTER ALL. WE'RE ALL STILL WAITING FOR A WORD FROM DOCTOR BEAKY...
MY WORD?? HA HA HA HA HA HA LET 'EM SWEAT! ESPECIALLY YOU, COSTIGAN!

HEH... YES, MY LITTLE MACHI AND MY LITTLE CHINESS... THEY'RE NOT GOING TO HURT US ANY MORE. LET THEM CUT EACH OTHER'S THROATS... LEAVE US BE, HM?

WHAT DO YOU BABIES THINK OF ALL THIS? YOU NEVER SPEAK. YOU'RE SO INNOCENT, SO NAIVE ABOUT THIS CRAZY, SCREWED UP WORLD. ALL YOU EVER WANT TO DO IS PROTECT AND COMFORT YOUR DADDY...

THAT'S WHY I LOVE MY LITTLE... BABIES... I...

M-MY THROAT! AGHH! WHAT HAVE YOU DONE, YOU LITTLE MONSTER?! I'LL KILL YOU!
YAGHHHH!

YAGHHHHHHH
11

HI, IZZY! HI, DAFFY! I'M HOME! AND BOY, DO I HAVE A STORY TO TELL YOU! THE ABSOLUTE WORST...
HOPEY! WE'VE BEEN WAITING AND WAITING...

OK, I'LL IGNORE THE FACT THAT AS SOON AS I GOT TO MY MOM'S HOUSE, SHE CALLS ME A GUTTER SLUT! AND I'LL ALSO IGNORE THAT THOSE BRATS OF HER BOYFRIEND'S HAVE BECOME HEAD BANGING PARTY GLADIATORS AND THOUGHT MY HAIRCUT WAS "RAD"...
HOPEY! WE...

...BUT I WILL NOT IGNORE THE FACT THAT WHILE WE WERE ALONE IN THE HOUSE, THAT FUCKING GHOUL OF A BOYFRIEND ACTUALLY TRIED TO FUCKING RAPE ME! I SHIT YOU NOT! MY MOM'S BOYFRIEND...
OH, MY...
HOPEEE!!

AND IF THAT DON'T BEAT ALL, WHEN I RAT ON THE GUY (WHO NATURALLY PLAYS DUMB) MY SCREWBALL MOM ACTUALLY TAKES HIS SIDE OF THE STORY! THEN I KNEW IT WAS TIME TO DISOWN THE SNIVELING CUNT AND COME HOME! WOTTA PAIR! OOH... I SHOULD GO BACK AND SHOOT HIS BALLS OFF! THEN HER TITS... DAFFY!?!?
MAGGIE'S OK!

HUH? WHAT...?
IT'S TRUE, HOPE. OUR BABY IS COMING HOME.

READ HEARTBREA SOU
LAS MUJERES PERDIDAS
THE LOST WOMEN
BY JAIME 83-84
THE END

RAD-RADICAL

HEY, THANKS FOR BUYING US BEER, IZZY! I'LL TELL THE FAMILY YOU SAID HI, EH?

YEAH, SURE. JUST DON'T LEAVE YOUR EMPTIES ON MY LAWN, HUH?

SOLD
REALTY
R19-1234

1242

LOCOS

POR JAIME LOCO DE SCXCH '84

HERMANA/SISTER

GABACHA/WHITE GIRL MAS CHIQUITOS/VERY YOUNG CHILDREN HUERA/LIGHT SKINNED GIRL CHUCAS/MEX. AMER. GIRLS TAMBIEN/ALSO

THAT WAS WHEN SHE STARTED CHANGING HER WAYS. MY DAD ALWAYS WANTED HER TO BE A TEACHER, BUT SHE WANTED TO BE A MYSTERY WRITER. MAN, THOSE TWO DROVE US ALL CRAZY ARGUING TILL THE MIDDLE OF THE NIGHT ALMOST EVERY NIGHT. IZZY WAS THE FIRST PERSON I EVER HEARD TELL MY DAD TO FUCK OFF AND GET AWAY WITH IT.
¿DE VERAS? AT WHAT TIME WAS THIS?

"WELL, THAT WAS WHEN MAGGIE MOVED BACK. HER FAMILIA HAD TO MOVE TO CADEZZA THREE YEARS BEFORE 'CAUSE HER DAD WORKED THERE AND THEY ONLY SAW HIM ON WEEKENDS. SOON, HER MOM FOUND OUT THE OLD MAN WAS BONING ANOTHER BROAD IN CADEZZA THE WHOLE TIME, SO SHE MOVED BACK HERE WITH THE NIÑOS.
...SHE EVEN PUT LITTLE MARGARITA TO WORK DOWN AT SAL'S GARAGE!
HMF! GOOD FOR HER! I HAD TO SUPPORT SIX, TOO, WHEN MY JUSTO DIED DRUNK! I SENT THEM ALL OUT TO WORK IN THE FIELDS...

"AND MAGGIE, ≡WHEW≡ TURNED INTO A FINE OL' THIRTEEN YEAR OLD IN THOSE THREE YEARS SHE WAS GONE, BUT I WAS TOO FUCKIN' STUPID TO KNOW IT! I WAS ELEVEN, AND TO ME, MOST OF THE CHICKS STILL HAD COOTIES. HA! 'MEMBER COOTIES, 'EY?"

YEAH, SHE WAS BACK, AND THAT'S WHEN IZZY INTRODUCED HER TO HER LITTLE PUNKER FRIEND HOPEY.

THAT'S WHEN EVERYTHING WENT PSYCHO, EH? THOSE WEIRDO CHICKS TURNED IZZY MUY LOCA?

"THAT'S WHAT EVERYBODY SAYS. BUT I THINK SHE LOST HER MIND WHEN SHE GOT MARRIED TO THAT WHITE DUDE JACK RUEBENS. HE WAS HER ENGLISH TEACHER IN COLLEGE. EVERYONE KNEW THAT MARRIAGE WOULDNT LAST. SHIT, THE FUCKER WAS ONLY TWICE AS OLD AS SHE WAS.

"AND WOULDN'T YOU KNOW IT, THEY WERE DIVORCED A YEAR LATER. I COULD TELL IZZY WAS BUMMED ABOUT IT BUT SHE NEVER TRIED TO SHOW IT. SHE JUST KEPT ON WITH HER WRITING. BUT SHE DIDNT WRITE MYSTERY STUFF NO MORE. SHE STARTED WRITING ABOUT SHIT LIKE... DEAD BABIES AND DANCING SKELETONS, YEH.
3

¿DE VERAS?/ REALLY? NIÑOS/ CHILDREN

"SHE WROTE UNDER HER MARRIED NAME ISABEL RUEBENS, AND BELIEVE IT OR NOT, SHE EVEN GOT SOME OF THAT SHIT PUBLISHED, 'EY. THEN SHE WENT TO MEXICO. WE ONLY GOT ONE POSTCARD FROM HER, SO WE FIGGERED SHE MIGHT NOT COME BACK AT ALL. BUT WE SAW HER AT MY DAD'S WAKE, AND SHE SCARED THE FUCKING SHIT OUT OF EVERYBODY THERE!

SO, (KAFF) WHAT DOES OUR SHAMEFUL (KAFF) DAUGHTER HAVE TO SAY, WOMAN?
TO
JUANA ORTIZ
MOM,
I'LL COME HOME WHEN YOU RID OF THE VERMIN
—TILL THEN, I LOVE YOU

"SHE LOOKED HALF DEAD, AND STARTED DRESSING LIKE A BORRACHO, LIKE SHE DIDN'T CARE ABOUT NOTHING NO MORE. BEFORE MEXICO SHE WOULDA NEVER GONE OUT IN A TORE UP ROBE AN' SLIPPERS, NO MATTER HOW BAD THINGS GOT!"

"YOU THINK MAYBE SOMETHING HAPPENED IN MEXICO, 'EY?"
BUFFIES
SWEET CEREAL
VATO GOLD

"I DUNNO, MAYBE. 'CAUSE NOW SHE'S MUY TRASTORNADO! SHE TAKES WALKS AROUND THE BARRIO IN THE MIDDLE OF THE NIGHT, AND SCARES ALL THE NEIGHBORS TO HELL. IT'S LIKE, SHE'S UNA VAMPIRA OR SOMETHING, YOU KNOW?

"NOW ALL THE KIDS AROUND HERE CALL HER THE WITCH LADY. I DON'T THINK THEY'RE TOO FAR FROM THE TRUTH, EITHER. IT'S KIND OF EMBARRASSING SOMETIMES, YOU KNOW?"

HA HA! SINCE WHEN DO YOU CARE ABOUT WHAT ANYBODY SAYS, PEDRO LIBRE?
HEY, I'LL KILL ANYBODY WHO MESSES WITH MY FAMILY! ESPECIALLY WITH MY SISTER...

...'CAUSE, YOU KNOW, I FEEL KINDA SORRY FOR HER. I DUNNO...
END

BORRACHO/DRUNKARD   TRASTORNADO/CRAZY, DISTURBING   PEDRO LIBRE/LIBERATED

YOUNG LOCAS

BY JAIME "HIT MAN" HERNANDEZ 85

POOR MAGGIE WAS REALLY HATING LIFE AT THE AGE OF THIRTEEN. SHE WAS SCARED TO DEATH OF BOYS. ESPECIALLY THE OLDER ONES WHO WERE JUST ITCHING TO GET INTO HER PANTS. THINGS WEREN'T TOO COOL WITH HER FAMILY EITHER. HER MOTHER AND THE KIDS MOVED OUT OF TOWN BUT LEFT MAGGIE TO LIVE WITH HER AUNT VICKI, SO SHE COULD STILL WORK DOWN AT SAL'S GARAGE (WHICH SHE HATED DOING BECAUSE IT WAS TAKING UP SO MUCH OF HER TIME). THEN, ONE RAINY AFTERNOON IN BARRIO HUERTA, HOPPERS 13...

YOU NEVER HANG OUT ANY MORE, MAGGIE. EVERYBODY THINKS YOU DON'T LIKE 'EM ANY MORE.

IT'S NOT THAT! IT'S JUST THAT AFTER SCHOOL I GOTTA GO STRAIGHT TO WORK, THEN STRAIGHT HOME TO DO HOME-WORK!

POOR LITTLE MAGGIE.
ALREADY AN OUTCAST AT THE TENDER AGE OF THIRTEEN.
SHE COULD HAVE KEPT ON BEING A MECHANIC, WHICH WASN'T REALLY SO BAD BECAUSE LEARNING TO FIX THINGS WAS KIND OF EXCITING TO HER.
BUT AT THE SAME TIME, SHE WAS LOSING A LOT OF FRIENDS.
NO, HER FRIENDS CAME FIRST.
IT WAS TIME TO QUIT.

BUT THEN THERE WERE HARVEY AND LOUIS DOWN AT THE GARAGE. NOW, THESE WERE SWELL GUYS. THEY TAUGHT MARGARITA ALL THEY KNEW ABOUT FIXING THINGS.
BY THE WAY, IT WAS LOUIS WHO GAVE YOUNG MARGARITA HER MORE POPULAR MONIKER.
=BH=
Louis

HEY, MAGGIE, YOU LITTLE SWEET THING.
HI, LOUIS. WHERE'S HARVEY? I GOTTA TALK TO HIM.

SOMEBODY CALL MY NAME? MAGGIE! I BEEN WAITIN' FOR YOU!
I GOTTA TALK TO YOU ABOUT SOMETHING, HARVEY.

NOT TILL I SHOW YOU SOMETHIN' OUT BACK. I'LL BET YOU THINK BY NOW YOU IS PURTY GOOD AT FIXIN' CARS AN' TOASTERS AN' TV'S AN' THINGS...

HOW'D YA LIKE TO HANDLE ONE OF THEM SUCKERS?
FOOTAH...
Carmen

SOME FOREIGN DUDE LEFT IT HERE TO SEE IF WE COULD FIND OUT WHAT'S WRONG WITH IT. WHADDAYA THINK, GIRL? THINK WE CAN HANDLE IT?
UH... SURE! SURE WE COULD! YEAH!
2

THIS WOULD SURELY BRING A BIG CHANGE IN MAGGIE'S LIFE. AND LITTLE DID EVERYONE KNOW, THE WORST WAS YET TO COME.

SUPER HEROES SUCK

WHAT THE FUCK ARE YOU LOOKING AT?

END

HI! I'M ROY COWBOY! AND I'D LIKE YOU TO MEET SIX FRIENDS OF MINE! THEY ARE THE WOMEN OF TOMORROW TODAY! THEY ARE WILD! THEY ARE CRAZY! THEY ARE...
LOCAS
BY JAIME "KING OF THE HUSTLE" HERNANDEZ 84-85

MARGARITA LUISA CHASCARRILLO

ESPERANZA LETICIA GLASS
HUGE • GROTH
APE SEX
+VOID+
ANGELIQUE P
WEIRDOS
ZAP COMIX

ISABEL MARIA ORTIZ RUEBENS

DAPHNE MATSUMOTO

THERESA LEEANNE DOWNE

BEATRÍZ GARCIA
1

MAGPIE!

WHAZZAT? OH, KA KA...

RRIPPPPPPP

best of the

FOR SHAME, MAGGOT. THAT'S THE THIRD PAIR YOU'VE DESTROYED IN THE PAST MONTH. YOU BETTER STOP EATING ALL THEM TACOS.
I KNOW, BUT WHEN I GET DEPRESSED, I EAT. MY LAST GOOD PAIR, TOO. SHOOT...
SAINT
APE SEX APR 18

YOU GET ANY MORE DEPRESSED AND YOU'LL START FLOATING AWAY. RELAX, MAG. LIFE'S NOT THAT TOUGH.
THAT'S WHAT YOU THINK! YOU DON'T HAVE TO WORK AT VANDY'S ON FRIDAY NIGHTS AFTER THE HIGH SCHOOL FOOTBALL GAMES. BLEHHH...
2

AND DON'T START BUGGING ME ABOUT RETURNING TO MY MECHANIC JOB, 'CAUSE I WON'T GO BACK AND THAT'S THAT!
OK OK, I JUST WANNA SHOW YOU SOMETHING. CHECK IT OUT, I JUST GOT BACK FROM LITTLE TONY'S...
TROGGS
I CAN'T CONTROL MYSELF

WOW! WHA'D YOU DO? ROB HIM? BEAT HIM UP?
NAW! THAT LITTLE FUCKER'S OWED ME FOR THE LONGEST TIME. WHERE'S IZZY? SHE STILL SLEEPING?

YEAH. SHE WAS UP ALL NIGHT AGAIN HOWLING AT THE MOON.
GOOD. I DON'T WANT HER TO KNOW I HAVE THIS. IT'S TIME ME AN' YOU HAD NEW CLOTHES!

I DUNNO, MAG. I KINDA THOUGHT THAT CRAZY DRESS WAS REALLY YOU.
HA HA! THAT DRESS WASN'T MADE WITH THOSE SIDE HOLES. I RIPPED IT TRYING IT ON! OINK! OINK!
THRIFT SHOP

OOH, LOOK! PUNKERS SHOPPING THE THRIFT STORES! THEY'RE SO COOL...
EAT SHIT AND DIE, FUCK NUTS!
ASSHOLES.
RAD MAMA

HEY, WASN'T THAT SELF-APPOINTED PUNK QUEEN, JULIE WREE? IN A FOUR BY?
YEAH, SHE'S A PHONEY LIKE ALL THOSE RICH WESTENDERS. BUT, THAT'S OK. ME AN' TERRY WILL KICK HER CANDY ASS WHEN OUR BAND PLAYS AT MADDOG'S FRIDAY NIGHT. HEY, YOU'LL FINALLY GET TO SEE US PLAY.
5

I HOPE YOU GO ON AFTER ELEVEN. REMEMBER, I WORK FRIDAY NIGHTS.
THEN, QUIT! YOU JUST GOTTA SEE US BEFORE WE BOOT MONICA. SHE'S A GAS TO WATCH PERFORM.
‹AH, NOW THAT'S MORE LIKE IT!›
TOCO'S

WHAT ARE YOU BABBLING ABOUT NOW, CHUCHO?
‹WHAT'S MORE LIKE IT?›
‹YOUR SKIRT! A WOMAN SHOULD ALWAYS WEAR A SKIRT OR A DRESS. YOU WON'T FIND A HUSBAND BY WEARING MEN'S CLOTHES.›
TOCO'S

‹SEE? LOOK AT YOU. LONELY AND REJECTED BECAUSE...›
SORRY, CHUCHO MAN! I DON'T LISTEN TO OLD SHIT EATING DRUNKS!
BE NICE.

IT'S OK, MAG. CHUCHO DOESN'T UNDERSTAND ENGLISH. ONLY ESPAÑOL, RIGHT, CHUCHO YOU OLD PATHETIC HEAP?
NO, BUT HIS FRIENDS DO.

CHUCHO! MAGGIE'S REALLY WEARING A SKIRT BECAUSE SHE BLEW A HOLE IN HER...
‹NEVER MIND!›
¿QUE DICE?

THIS IS PROBABLY THE WORST BURRITO I'VE EVER TASTED IN MY WHOLE LIFE.
OOH, LOOK. THERE GOES YOUR GOOD BUDDY, SERGEANT SADO.
MEXICAN FOOD
LOCO

THAT BUTT FUCK ASSHOLE SADO! WHEN I SAY RUN, MAG, YOU RUN, OK?
WHATCHA GONNA DO?
4

‹SPANISH›

WHAT DO YOU THINK? RUN!
¡AI, DIOS MIO!

DID I HIT HIM? DID I HIT HIM?
SHEESH! ALMOST!
AKO

I STILL GOT ANOTHER BOTTLE! WAIT HERE...
HE'S GONE, HOPEY! CALM DOWN!

YOU'RE GONNA GET INTO REAL TROUBLE ONE OF THESE DAYS, YOU KNOW THAT?
WHY? JUST 'CAUSE I'M TRYING TO HAVE FUN IN THIS BORING, STUPID, FUCKED UP TOWN?

AT LEAST YOU GET TO TAKE TRIPS AROUND THE WORLD. I HAVE TO STAY HERE AND ROT WITH THE REST OF THESE CORPSES. IT'S DRIVING ME OUT OF MY UGLY FUCKING MIND, MAN!
HAMBONE FUNNIES

OH, NOW DON'T START POUTING, MAG. I WAS JUST KIDDING.
I WASN'T GONNA START POUTING.
YOU TWO!

DID YOU SEE THE DING DONG WHO HIT MY NEW CAR WITH A BOTTLE? HE'S GONNA PAY! NO ONE GETS AWAY WITH THAT!
NO HABLO INGLES, SEÑOR.

GOD DAMN WETBACK ILLITERATES.
<NICE SHOT, HOPE.>
<SOME SHOT. I MISSED HIS HEAD.>
5

WE'RE GONNA HAVE TO START FINDING A NEW PLACE TO LIVE, MAG. I DON'T THINK IZZY'S GONNA LET US STAY AT HER PLACE MUCH LONGER.
IF ONLY WE COULD AFFORD A PLACE.
CLOSED
MANDATE

NOW, WHAT AM I SUPPOSED TO DO WITH THIS? I CAN'T TAKE IT LIKE THIS NOW, CAN I ?
OF COURSE NOT, MA'AM. I'LL GET YOU ANOTHER CASE RIGHT AWAY.
MOXALI

HMF!
WHEW! MY BREAK COULDN'T COME AT A BETTER TIME. COME ON, LET'S GO DOWN TO THE CAFETERIA.
SHE THINKS THAT STUFF'S GONNA HELP?

SO, IZZY'S FINALLY KICKING YOU GUYS OUT FOR GOOD?
NOT YET. WE FIGURED WE'D STAY ONE STEP AHEAD OF HER BOOT.

I DON'T KNOW, HOPE. PAUL'S BEEN LIVING AT MY PLACE FOR THE PAST WEEK AND IT MIGHT BE A LITTLE TOO CROWDED FOR ALL OF US.

I MEAN, I COULD HAVE ROOM FOR ONE MORE, BUT WE COULDN'T LEAVE ANYONE OUT, YOU KNOW WHAT I MEAN?
LOUD AND CLEAR...
OK, TERRY. WE GET THE HINT.

MAN, WHAT A BITCH! WHY DOES SHE HATE ME SO DAMN MUCH?
CAN'TCHA SEE, MAG? YOU STOLE AWAY THE HEART OF HER FAVORITE GIRL FRIEND.

SO THAT'S WHAT'S BEEN STICKING UP HER ASS. IT'S NOT MY FAULT I'M SO GOD DAMN IRRESISTABLE.
I THINK MODEST IS THE WORD YOU'RE LOOKING FOR.
7

BUT, GUY... THINGS LIKE THIS JUST HAPPEN, Y'KNOW? IT'S NOBODY'S FAULT, REALLY. WHY'S SHE GOTTA CARRY SUCH A GRUDGE?
BE HAPPY SHE DOESN'T CARRY ONE AGAINST YOU LIKE PENNY DOES AGAINST RANDY RACE.
41

I KNOW. WHY DOESNT PENNY JUST LEAVE RACE ALONE? SHE HATED HIS GUTS FROM THE BEGINNING, BUT USED HIM 'CAUSE HE'S A PROSOLAR MECHANIC, I BET.
THAT'S NOT WHAT I HEARD.

ACTUALLY, PENNY WAS REALLY CRAZY ABOUT HIM... TILL HE GOT HER PREGNANT THEN SPLIT ON HER.
OH, WHO TOLD YOU THAT LIE?
SUPER FREAK

PENNY TOLD ME HERSELF.
AND AS USUAL I'M ALWAYS THE LAST TO HEAR... I DON'T BELIEVE IT! H R COSTIGAN PROBABLY DID THAT TO HER AND SHE BLAMED RACE!

HOW WOULD YOU KNOW? MAN, YOU'D DEFEND THAT GUY TO THE DEATH, NO MATTER WHAT HE DOES.
WHAT ABOUT YOU? YOU'D STICK UP FOR STUCK UP TERRY IF SHE CUT YOUR EYES OUT!

AT LEAST SHE'S NOT JUST SOME MACHO FUCK I'M AFTER.
OH, ISN'T SHE? I CAN IMAGINE WHAT GOES ON WHILE I'M AWAY!

WELL, SHIT, MAG! WHAT THE HELL AM I SUPPOSED TO DO WHILE YOU'RE AWAY? LOCK MYSELF UP AND WAIT FOR YOU TO COME HOME? I'VE GOT A LIFE TO LIVE AND IT DOESN'T ONLY CENTER AROUND YOU! BUDDHA HELP ME IF IT DID!

I GOTTA GO TO WORK NOW.
8

LET ME GET THIS STRAIGHT, MIJA. IF YOU DO MOVE OUT OF HERE, YOU AND HOPEY WON'T GET A PLACE TOGETHER? HOW COME? YOU GUYS BEEN FIGHTING AGAIN? HOW DID YOU DECIDE...
WELL, THIS IS SORTA MY IDEA. HOPEY DOESN'T KNOW YET...

SO, WHAT IS THIS MIRACLE THAT FINALLY SEPARATES THE DREADED TAG-TEAM OF TERROR AFTER THESE WILD, KILL CRAZED YEARS?
IT'S NO JOKE. I DUNNO... IT SEEMS LIKE EVER SINCE I GOT BACK FROM CHEPAN, HOPEY'S BEEN ACTING... WELL, DIFFERENT.

REALLY? IN WHAT WAY?
I DON'T THINK SHE LIKES... WANTS TO BE AROUND ME TOO MUCH ANY MORE. MAYBE IT'S ME, I DUNNO.

MAYBE IT IS YOU. MAYBE YOUR EXPERIENCE IN CHEPAN CAUSED YOU TO START SEEING THINGS IN A DIFFERENT PERSPECTIVE. MAYBE THIS KIND OF LIFE DOESN'T RELATE TO YOU ANY MORE.
HUH? NO WAY! I LIKE YOU GUYS MORE THAN EVER BEFORE!

IT'S JUST THAT HOPEY'S GONE REALLY LOCA LATELY. SHE'S DOING THE KINDS OF THINGS SHE DID WHEN I FIRST MET HER.
YOU KNOW, WHEN WE ALL HEARD ON THE NEWS THAT YOU WERE KILLED IN CHEPAN...

...THAT STORY REALLY KICKED OUR ASSES, BUT GOOD! ALL EXCEPT HOPEY. SHE TOOK IT REAL WELL. SHE NEVER CRIED OR LOST HER COOL. SHE FELT THAT LIFE SHOULD GO ON, EVEN WITHOUT YOU. BUT, STILL IT SCARED HER. SHE GOT A BAD CASE OF LONLINESS, EMPTINESS, AND WORST OF ALL... RESPONSIBILITY.

YOU KNOW, I THINK FOR THE FIRST TIME IN HOPITA'S LIFE, SHE THOUGHT ABOUT THE NEXT DAY.
WELL, AT LEAST IT MADE HER THINK ABOUT OTHERS FOR ONCE. BUT, SOMEONE HAD TO DIE FIRST.
9

BUT WHEN WE FOUND OUT YOU WERE OK, I'LL NEVER FORGET THOSE TEARS POURING DOWN HOPEY'S FACE. SHE WANTED TO STRANGLE THAT FIRST NEWSWOMAN LIKE CRAZY! SHE EVEN WENT TO THE TV STATION AND ALMOST GOT HERSELF ARRESTED.

SO, YOU SEE WHAT I'M TRYING TO SAY? I THINK HOPEY'S JUST REALLY EMBARRASSED BY THE WHOLE THING AND DOESN'T KNOW YET HOW TO SHOW YOU HOW MUCH SHE REALLY APPRECIATES HAVING YOU BACK.
SHE DID THAT 'CAUSE OF ME, HUH?

SO, DON'T MOVE AWAY FROM EACH OTHER, MIJA. I THINK THIS IS A TIME WHERE YOU NEED EACH OTHER THE MOST.
YOU'VE ALWAYS KNOWN WHAT TO SAY, IZZY. NOW, I'M THE ONE THAT'S EMBARRASSED. WHAT DO I DO NOW?
HOPPERS
=13=

WELL, I WOULDN'T WORRY TOO MUCH ABOUT THAT. I KNOW THAT ANY MINUTE NOW, WE'RE GOING TO HEAR A VERY LOUD...
HEY MAGGOT!
!

DAFFY'S GOT A BRAND SPANKING NEW 280 ZXYZ AND WE'RE GONNA GIVE YOU A RIDE TO WORK!
OK, I'LL BE RIGHT OUT.

OOTAH...
YOU'RE WELCOME, MARGARITA. NOW JUST GO TO WORK, EH?

OK. AND THANKS FOR LETTING US STILL LIVE WITH YOU IN THIS HOUSE. SO LONG, IZZY!
HEY! NOW, WAIT A MINUTE...
SLAM
END

I DON'T WANNA GO TO WORK! I HATE WORK! WORK HATES ME!
GOOD. THEN QUIT SO YOU CAN WATCH US PLAY TONIGHT.
MAGGIE MIJA? CAN I ASK YOU A FAVOR?

I HAVE TO GO TO THE DOCTOR BUT MY CAR WON'T START. COULD YOU BE A SWEETHEART AND SEE WHAT'S WRONG WITH IT?
WHY DON'T YOU JUST DRIVE IT OFF A CLIFF AND PUT IT OUT OF OUR MISERY?
OH, IZZY! I'VE LOOKED AND LOOKED AT IT, AND HOPEY'S RIGHT! IT'S JUST NOT WORTH FIXING ALL THE TIME!

TELL YOU WHAT. YOU START IT, YOU CAN HAVE IT.
REALLY? SERIOUS? NO LIE?
EEK! JUST THINK, MAG! WE CAN FINALLY GO PLACES OUT OF TOWN WITHOUT THE BUS!

ON ONE CONDITION! YOU LET ME TAKE IT TO THE DOCTOR FOR ONE FINAL HURRAH.
DEAL!
I'LL GET YOUR TOOLS, MAG.

UGH! WHAT A MESS! HOW LONG HAVE YOU HAD THIS TANK, ISABEL?
I GOT IT TEN YEARS AGO FROM MY COUSIN CHEPA FOR SEVENTY-FIVE DOLLARS.
HEY! YOU CAN SEE THROUGH TO THE STREET IN HERE! AIR CONDITIONING, HUH?
1

REMEMBER THOSE LONG TRIPS WE USED TO TAKE WITH THE TIRES DOWN TO THE THREADS? SIGH...
I THINK SHE'S GONNA CRY...
THERE, THAT SHOULD HOLD IT FOR AWHILE. TAKE HER AWAY, IZZY!
MOTT

¡GRACIAS, MIJA! I'LL BE BACK TO SIGN THE PINK SLIP OVER TO YOU!
IF YOU WANNA ADD ANOTHER NAME TO THAT SLIP, IT'S OK WITH ME!
OH, KA KA! I FORGOT ABOUT WORK! I BETTER HURRY!

Y'KNOW, MAG? AS I WATCHED YOU DANCE THROUGH THAT CAR WITH YOUR EYES CLOSED, I CAME TO THE CONCLUSION THAT YOUR LIFE BELONGS IN MACHINES, NOT IN BURGERS.
DON'T START! I DON'T WANNA BE A PROSOLAR BANANA ANY MORE!

FUCK PROBONER MECHANDICKS! WHAT ABOUT SAL'S GARAGE? I'M SURE HARVEY AND LOUIS WOULD BE GLAD TO HIRE YOU BACK.
I DUNNO...

WELL, HOW ABOUT STARTING YOUR OWN BUSINESS? PEOPLE ARE ALWAYS BUGGING YOU TO FIX ONE THING OR ANOTHER FOR 'EM. YOU COULD START CHARGING 'EM.
I GOTTA GO TO WORK NOW.

TSK! IS THAT ALL YOU CAN EVER SAY?

IZZY! THAT WAS QUICK! DID THE DOCTOR SAY TO FORGET IT AND GIVE UP?
NO. YOU KNOW THAT BRICK WALL ON THE CORNER OF COOPER AND FIRST?
2

I SHOULD. THAT WAS MY FAVORITE WALL TO WRITE ON. ISN'T THAT SPOOKY THE SMOKEY'S WALL?
YEAH, WELL, MAGGIE'S NEW CAR IS SITTING HALFWAY THROUGH IT RIGHT NOW. I GUESS I FORGOT TO TELL HER THE BRAKES NEEDED A LITTLE FIXING, TAMBIÉN.

OH, MY... ARE YOU OK?
I DUNNO. MY SHOULDER HURTS A LITTLE. I SUPPOSE I SHOULD CALL AND CANCEL MY DOCTOR'S APPOINTMENT. IT'S TOO LATE TO GO NOW.

WHAT ABOUT THE CAR?
AH, IT'S OK! IT DOESN'T LOOK ANY WORSE THAN IT DID BEFORE.

I MEAN, WHAT ARE YOU GONNA DO ABOUT IT?
WELL, I WAS KINDA HOPING YOU WOULD HELP ME PICK IT UP BEFORE THE COPS DO.

CAN'T! I'M EXPECTING TERRY ANY MINUTE NOW. WE GOTTA GET TO THE CLUB EARLY. THEY'RE ACTUALLY GIVING OUR BAND A SOUND CHECK TONIGHT.
HUH! THEY MUST THINK YOU'RE IMPROVING, EH?

REMEMBER, YOU GOTTA GET THAT CAR BACK BEFORE MAGGIE GETS HOME.
DON'T WORRY! I'LL JUST HAVE SPEEDY FETCH IT. I DON'T EVEN WANT TO GO NEAR THAT DEATHTRAP!

BUT FIRST, A NAP...

IZZY SOUNDED PISSED. HAVE YOU AND MAGGIE FOUND A NEW PLACE TO LIVE YET?
NOPE.
3

HOPEY, I KNOW YOU THINK I WON'T LET YOU MOVE INTO MY PLACE BECAUSE OF MAGGIE, BUT I REALLY DON'T HAVE ANY ROOM.
I KNOW YOU DON'T, WHY?

OH, IT'S NOTHING. I WAS JUST... NEVER MIND.
YOU'RE ONE IN A MILLION, ALL RIGHT, TERRY!

WHY? WHY DID YOU SAY THAT? WHAT DID YOU MEAN BY THAT, HOPEY?
NOTHING! NEVER MIND! FORGET IT!

WILL WONDERS NEVER CEASE? THEY LET ME OFF AT EIGHT SO NOW I CAN FINALLY SEE HOPEY'S BAND. THEY GO ON ABOUT TEN OR ELEVEN, SO THAT GIVES ME TIME TO GO HOME, CHANGE, THEN COME BACK IN MY NEW CARRO.
VANDY'S

NINE FIFTEEN. THAT WAS QUICKER THAN I THOUGHT. MIGHT AS WELL GO HANG OUT BEFORE HOPEY'S BAND GOES ON. BESIDES, I HAVEN'T SEEN THE CROWD AT MADDOGS FOR A FEW MONTHS. WORK DOES THAT TO YOU, Y'KNOW...

THE CAR'S NOT HERE. IZZY MUST BE STILL USING IT. I HOPE SHE LEAVES ME SOME GAS.
Z

OOI, THE CLUB IS ONLY A HALF HOUR WALK AWAY, BUT I DON'T THINK I WANT TO TAKE THAT WALK ALL BY MYSELF. HEH!
MAGGIE!

W-WHO SAID THAT?
ME, SPEEDY! C'MERE JUST A SECOND!
4

CARRO- CAR

WHERE YOU GOING RIGHT NOW, MAGGIE?
I'M ON MY WAY TO MADDOGS TO SEE HOPEY'S BAND PLAY. COULD YOU GIVE ME A RIDE?

YEAH? HOPEY? OK, BUT FIRST, KICK BACK. I HAVEN'T SEEN YOU FOR AWHILE. YOU WANT A BEER?
YEAH, OK. I'LL HAVE JUST ONE, THEN I GOTTA GO.

YAY HOPEEE!
AW, YOU GUYS SUCK!
MISSILES OF OCTOBER SUCKS!
DON'T WORRY 'BOUT IT! APE SEX IS ON NEXT, DINGLE BERRY!
YAY!
EXIT
...YOU HAVE A WONDERFUL GUITAR PLAYING STYLE. EVEN THOUGH I DON'T PARTICULARLY LIKE THE REST OF YOUR BAND, I THINK YOU HAVE A WONDERFUL GUITAR PLAYING...
THANK YOU.

HEY, TERRY! HAVE YOU SEEN MAGGIE?
NO, WAS SHE SUPPOSED TO COME?
HOPEY!

IZZY BELLE!
IS MAGGIE HERE? I THINK I SLEPT TOO LONG...
I THINK YOU'RE GREAT, BUT YOUR BAND STINKS.
JAKE

YOU WANT ANOTHER BEER, MAGGIE?
NO, IF I HAVE A FOURTH ONE I MIGHT...OH, SHIT! IT'S TWELVE THIRTY!
5

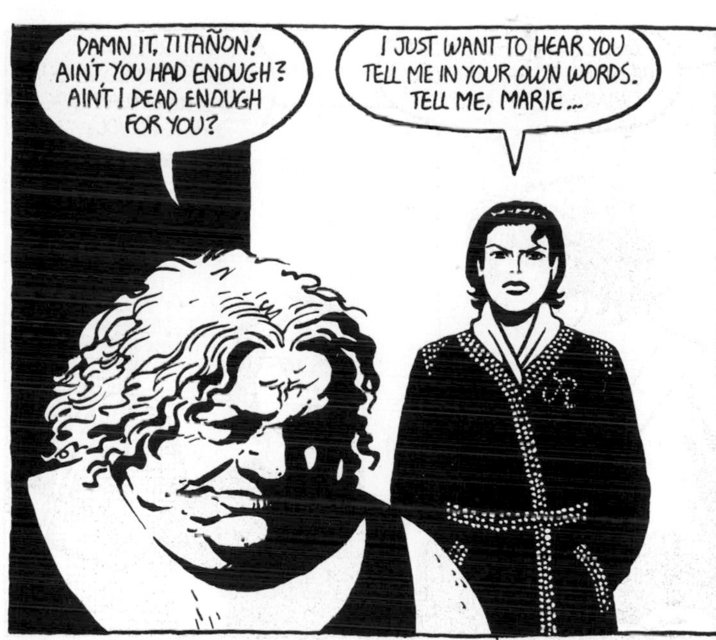
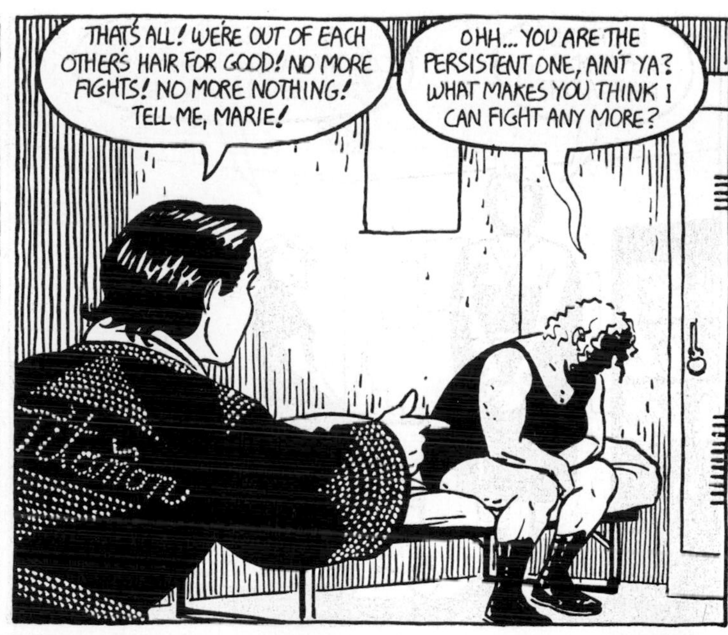
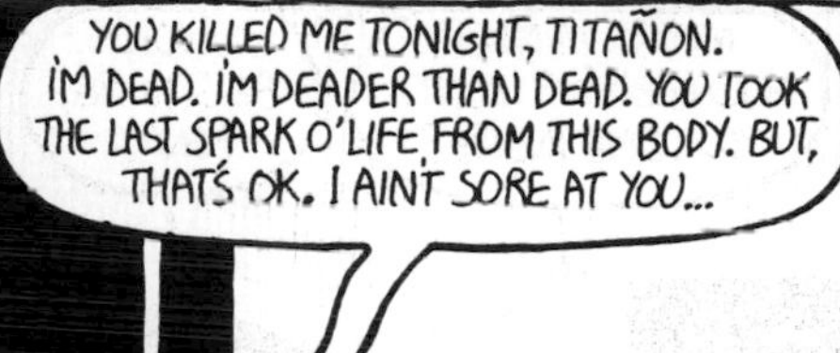
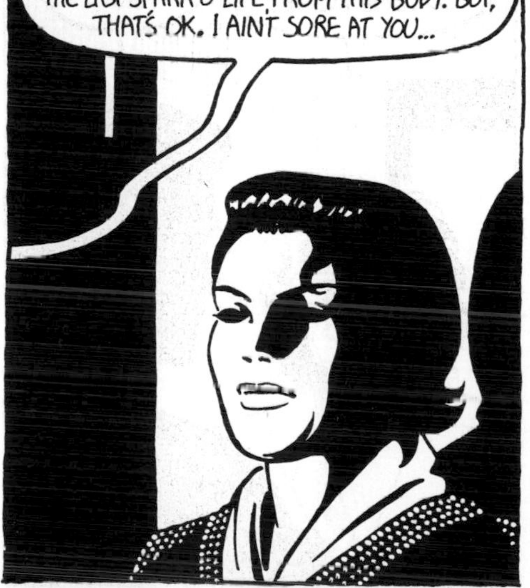

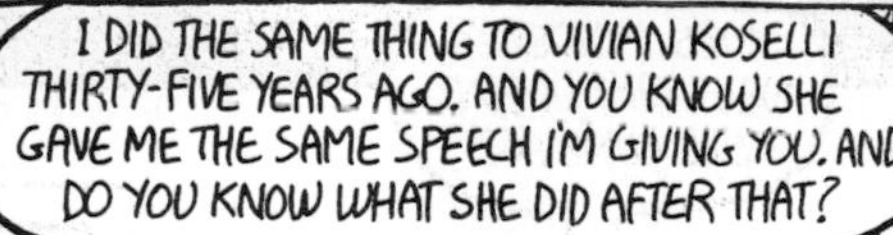
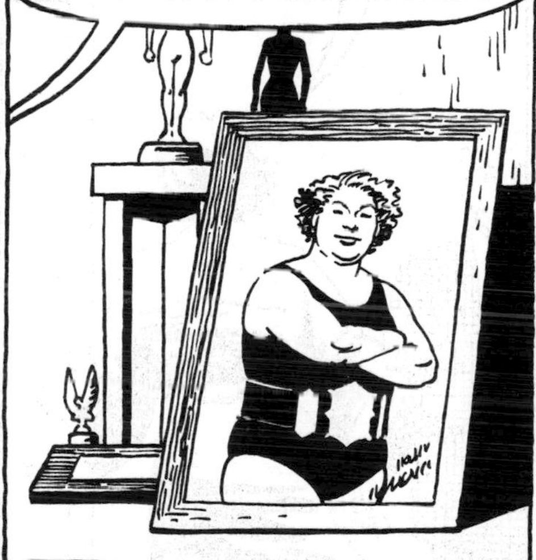

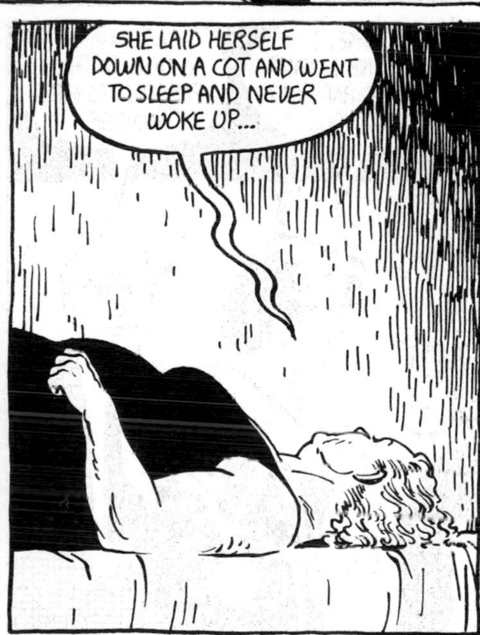
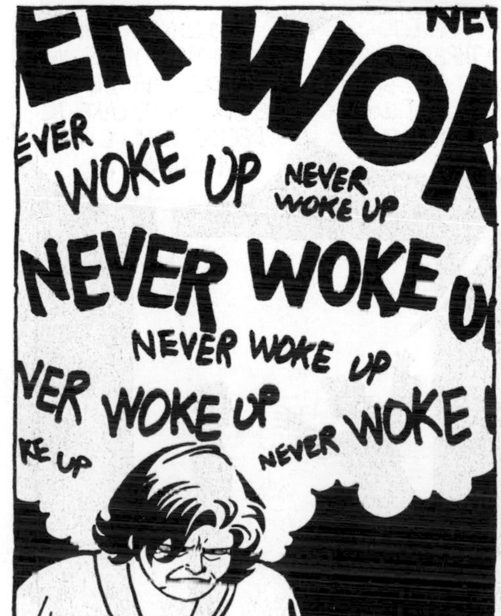
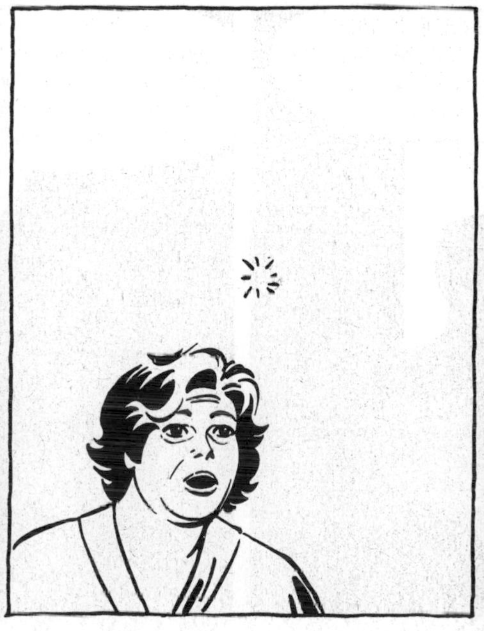

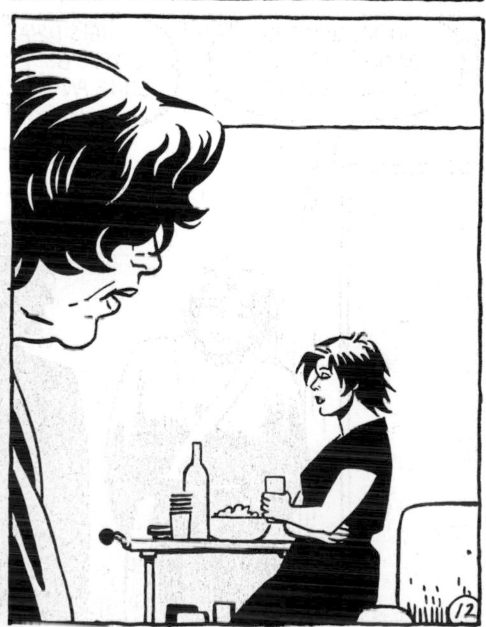

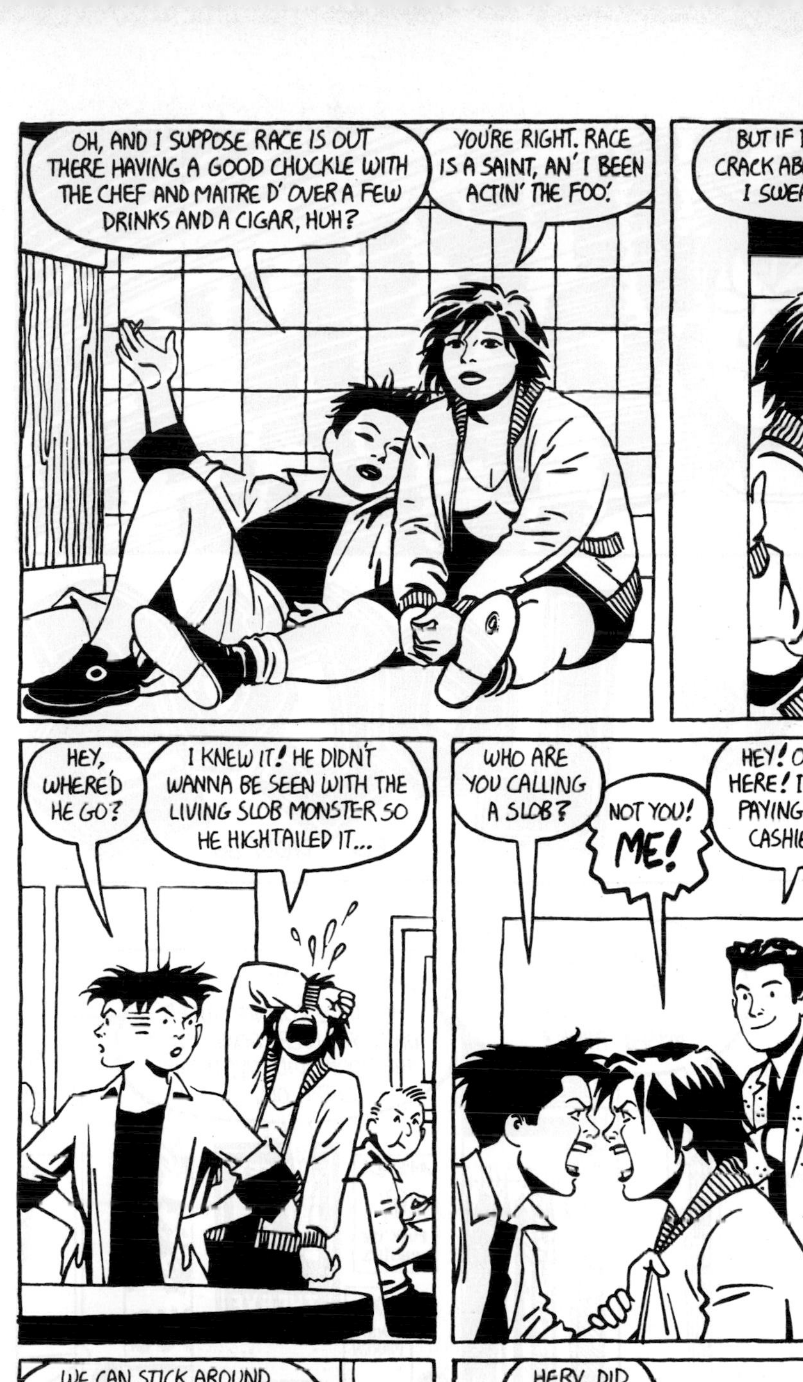
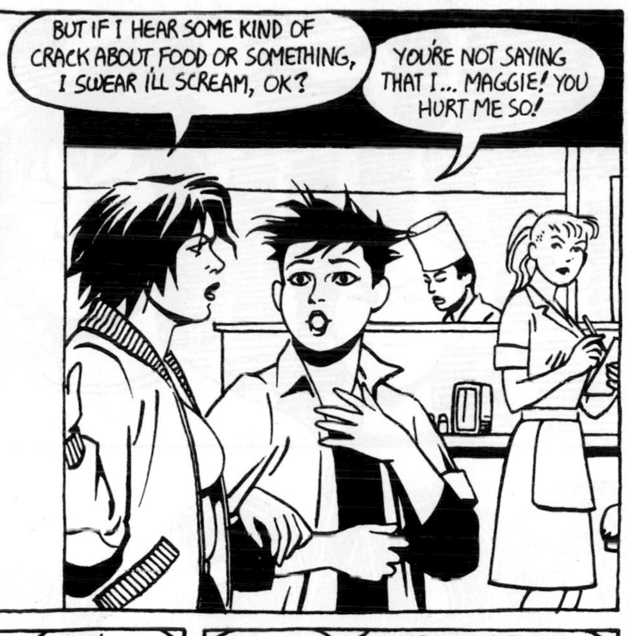
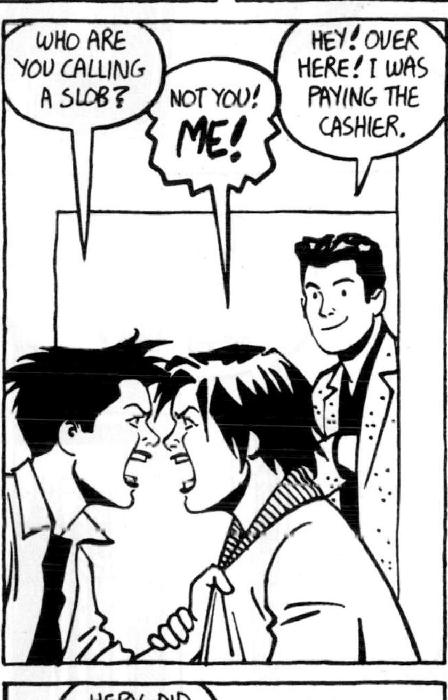
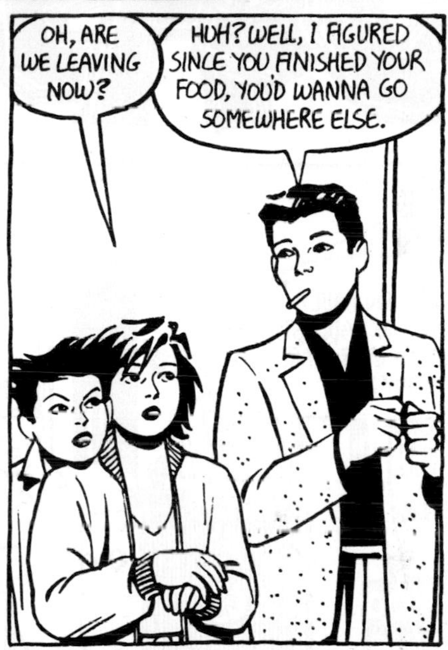
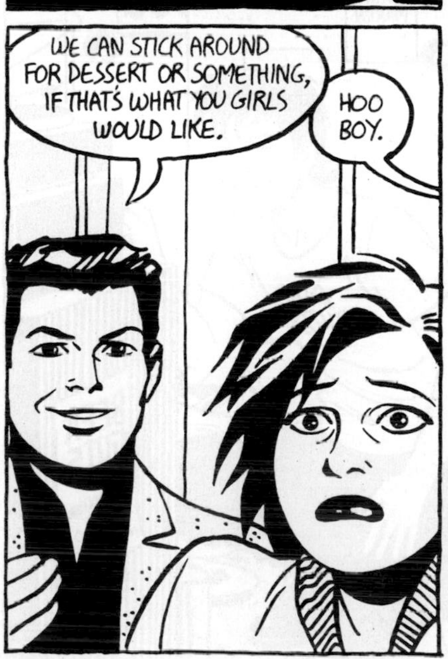
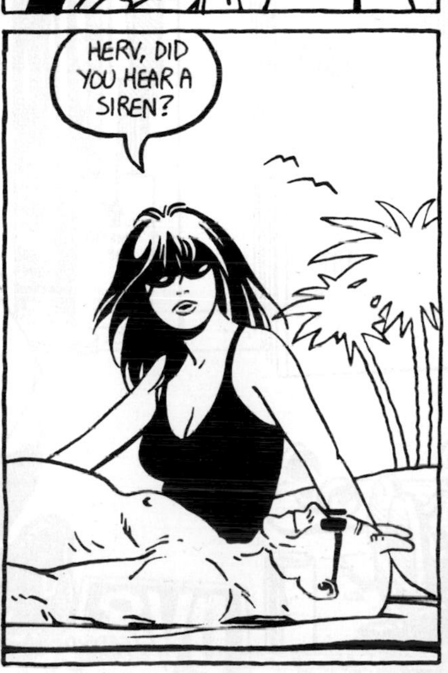
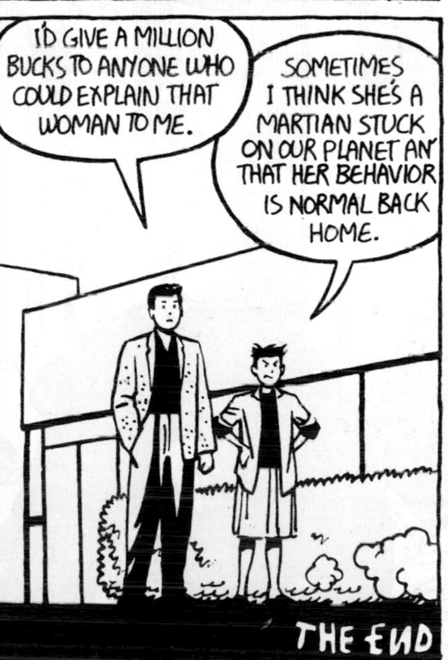

GEE, LOOK AT 'EM GO! ARE ROYAL DON AND RENA LOVERS?
YOU MIGHT SAY IT WAS A MATCH MADE IN HEAVEN. THEY FIGHT LIKE CATS AND DOGS!
HAR! HAR!
¡SERIO, MANUEL!

"ACTUALLY, DON ASKED RENA OUT WHEN SHE WAS IN HER EARLY TWENTIES AND HAD JUST WON THE LADIES TITLE FROM TIGER ROSA. SHE WASN'T GOOD ENOUGH FOR THE ROYAL ONE BEFORE THEN."
"AND WAS HE FURIOUS WHEN SHE TURNED HIM DOWN!"

"BUT, AFTER DON FINALLY PROVED HIS LOVE FOR HER, THEY WENT TOGETHER FOR SEVERAL YEARS. DUKE AND I WOULD DOUBLE DATE WITH THEM OCCASIONALLY."
"BUT, WHAT ABOUT BERNIE CARBO? I THOUGHT..."
"OH, NO. RENA AND BERNIE HAPPENED YEARS AFTER. ABOUT TEN YEARS AFTER."

THAT'S ALMOST AS LONG AS IT TOOK YOU TO MARRY ME!
THAT'S IT! BRING IT UP IN FRONT OF THE KID!
UH OH. THAT'S MY EXIT.

SO, I WONDER IF MAYBE ROYAL DON GOT RENA PREGNANT AND... NO, NO, NO! TIA VICKI WAS JUST TALKING HER USUAL BULLSHIT.

I THINK.

ANY WORD ON BERNIE CARBO, BABY?
NO. I THINK I'VE LOST TRACK OF HIM FOR GOOD.
8

HE'S PROBABLY LIVING BEHIND SOME PUB SOMEWHERE IN ZHATO, WITH ALL THE DRINK AND WOMEN HE CAN CARRY.

HEY, I KNOW! WHY DON'T YOU AND I GO OUT DANCING TONIGHT?
SORRY, DON. I'M EXPECTING A SPECIAL GUEST TONIGHT.

DAMN IT, WOMAN! YOU DO THIS BECAUSE YOU KNOW IT DRIVES ME UP THE WALL! WHO IS THIS GUY?
YOU KNOW THIS YOUNG MAN VERY WELL, DON.

OK, OK! I'LL BE SEEING YOU! GOTTA GO!
COWARD.

HOW CAN YOU TAKE ALL THAT SHIT FROM THE AUDIENCE? I COULDN'T STAND IT MYSELF.
WE'RE USED TO IT. RENA'S HAD TO PUT UP WITH IT HER WHOLE CAREER. I'M SURE SHE'S HEARD WORSE.

BUT, WHEN RENA WAS CHAMPION, SHE WAS LIKE, THE GOOD GUY, Y'KNOW?
IT DOESN'T MATTER. ALL FEMALE GRAPPLERS ARE TREATED SHITTY, VILLAIN OR NOT.

I MEAN, HAVEN'T YOU EVER BEEN WALKING DOWN THE STREET AND A CARLOAD OF GUYS DRIVES BY AND SHOUTS ALL KINDS OF STUPID, OBNOXIOUS SHIT?
YEAH, I GET IT. AND FOR A GIRL WHO FIGHTS IN A RING FOR A LIVING, IT'S A HUNDRED TIMES WORSE, HUH?

WELL, SURE! SO ANY TIME YOU FEEL YOU'RE HAVING IT TOUGH, THINK OF RENA, QUEEN OF THE RING. EVERYBODY'S GAL.
9

I'D LIKE TO STICK AROUND LONGER, RENA, BUT I GOTTA GO SEE MY KID. HE'S ALREADY LEARNING TO WORRY.
OK, BYE BYE, PEPPER. AND TELL YOUR MAMA ROSA NOT TO WORRY ANY. WE'LL GET THOSE BELTS, ALL RIGHT.

I KNEW I RECOGNIZED HER! SHE'S ROSA RICO'S KID, EH? LAST TIME I SAW HER, SHE WAS ONLY FOUR. AND NOW SHE'S YOUR TAG TEAM PARTNER! HOO HOO! WOTTA WORLD!
WHO'S ROSA RICO?
AKA "LA PANTERA NEGRA." SHE WAS ONE OF MY TOUGHEST RIVALS IN MY CHAMPION DAYS. YOU SEE THIS SCAR ON MY INNER THIGH?

ONE NIGHT ROSA FORGOT TO TAKE HER EARRINGS OFF FOR OUR MATCH, SO WHEN I SLAPPED THE HEAD SCISSORS ON HER...
OUCH! YOU POOR THING!

YOU MEAN POOR ROSA! HER WHOLE EAR WAS NEARLY CUT OFF.
YEOW!
YEAH, BOY! THOSE WERE SOME BATTLES!

AND JUST RECENTLY ROSA AND PEPPER HELD THE TAG TEAM BELTS TILL THOSE SUGAR TWINS CAME ALONG. I TEAMED WITH PEPPER AS A FAVOR TO ROSA TO GET THEM BACK.
BUT, WHAT ABOUT ROSA?

OH, KID. THEY BEAT ROSA SO BAD SHE WAS HOSPITALIZED FOR WEEKS. DAMN IT! WHY DIDN'T ANYONE HAVE THE HEART TO TELL HER SHE'S TOO... OLD TO... WRESTLE?
JUST BE HAPPY SHE DIDN'T END UP LIKE BULL MA...
RALPH!

WHA'D I SAY?
DON'T YOU KNOW EVERY TIME YOU OPEN YOUR MOUTH TONS OF TURDS COME OUT?
???
10

WHAT WAS IT? FIFTEEN YEARS AGO? THIS ONE WAS GONNA FINISH IT FOR GOOD. REMEMBER, MARIE?
WOULD YOU LOOK AT THAT? MARIE'S OUT LIKE A LIGHT AND THE REF HAS CALLED FOR THE BELL, BUT LOOK AT RENA! THE CHAMP DOESN'T WANT TO LET GO!

WHAT A MIGHTY DISPLAY OF STRENGTH FROM THE CHAMPION. BULL MARIE SAID THIS WOULD BE HER LAST ONE, AND I HATE TO SAY IT, BUT RENA MADE SURE MARIE WOULD KEEP HER WORD. WOW!
TELL ME, MARIE! TELL ME NOW!

BUT YOU GOTTA HAND IT TO MARIE. NOT MANY WOULD TAKE ON A PRIME CHAMPION AT THE AGE OF FIFTY-FIVE! AND SO WE SAY, SO LONG, MARIE. WE'LL MISS YOU.
I WANNA HEAR IT NOW, MARIE! TELL ME NOW, MARIE!
FOR CORN'S SAKE, GET HER OUTA HERE, WILL YA?

WHAT DO YOU WANT? SHE DOESN'T WANT TO SEE ANYBODY! ESPECIALLY YOU, QUEENIE!
SHE WANTS TO SEE ME, ALL RIGHT.

I'M SORRY, MARIE. SHE WOULDN'T TAKE NO FOR AN ANSWER...
GET OUTA HERE.

SHE MEANS YOU, FAT HEAD!
SCRAM!
SLAM!
11

DAMN IT, TITAÑON! AIN'T YOU HAD ENOUGH? AIN'T I DEAD ENOUGH FOR YOU?
I JUST WANT TO HEAR YOU TELL ME IN YOUR OWN WORDS. TELL ME, MARIE...

THAT'S ALL! WE'RE OUT OF EACH OTHER'S HAIR FOR GOOD! NO MORE FIGHTS! NO MORE NOTHING! TELL ME, MARIE!
OHH... YOU ARE THE PERSISTENT ONE, AIN'T YA? WHAT MAKES YOU THINK I CAN FIGHT ANY MORE?
Titañon

YOU KILLED ME TONIGHT, TITAÑON. I'M DEAD. I'M DEADER THAN DEAD. YOU TOOK THE LAST SPARK O' LIFE FROM THIS BODY. BUT, THAT'S OK. I AIN'T SORE AT YOU...

I DID THE SAME THING TO VIVIAN KOSELLI THIRTY-FIVE YEARS AGO. AND YOU KNOW SHE GAVE ME THE SAME SPEECH I'M GIVING YOU. AND DO YOU KNOW WHAT SHE DID AFTER THAT?

SHE LAID HERSELF DOWN ON A COT AND WENT TO SLEEP AND NEVER WOKE UP...

ER WOR
NEV
EVER WOKE UP
NEVER WOKE UP
NEVER WOKE U
NEVER WOKE UP
VER WOKE UP
NEVER WOKE
KE UP

12

WHERE DID EVERYBODY GO, MARGARET.
OH, THEY ALL WENT TO CONGRATULATE TIA VICKI. SHE JUST BEAT LA VIBORA.

OH, WELL. THEN SHALL WE DRINK TO HER VICTORY, MARGARET? NO?
HEY, QUEENIE. THERE'S SOMEONE OUT HERE WHO WANTS TO TALK TO YOU.

NO, DUKE. I DON'T THINK I WANT TO TALK TO ANYBODY RIGHT NOW.
YOU'LL WANT TO TALK TO THIS PERSON. IT'S MRS. MINDER.

MRS. MINDER?? WELL, WHY DOESN'T SHE COME IN?

M-MRS. MINDER. HOW ARE YOU? WON'T YOU COME INSIDE?
I WON'T BE STAYING, RENA.

OH, YOU WON'T BE, STAYING? UM... ISN'T ANTONIO WITH YOU?
THAT'S WHAT I CAME TO TALK TO YOU ABOUT. I WON'T BE BRINGING LITTLE ANTONIO BY TO SEE YOU TONIGHT, RENA.

WHAT DO YOU MEAN? I HAVE TO LEAVE FOR ZYMBODIA IN THREE HOURS! I DON'T KNOW HOW LONG IT WILL BE TILL I'LL BE BACK IN THE STATES! JUST WHO DO YOU THINK YOU ARE THAT YOU CAN...
AS LONG AS THE AGREEMENT YOU SIGNED STILL HOLDS THAT THE CHILD REMAINS IN MY CARE, I'LL DECIDE WHAT HE CAN AND CANNOT DO.
13

WHEN I WITNESSED YOUR DISPLAY OUT THERE TONIGHT. THE WAY YOU PARADED YOURSELF ABOUT AS THOSE PEOPLE SHOUTED THOSE FOUL NAMES AT YOU. AND YOUR GOADING AND... AND...

WELL, I MADE UP MY MIND RIGHT THEN THAT AS LONG AS YOU KEEP UP THIS... THIS... LIFESTYLE, I WILL KEEP ANTONIO AS FAR FROM YOU AS POSSIBLE.
DOES HE EVEN KNOW ABOUT THIS?

IF YOU MEAN DOES HE KNOW I WON'T LET YOU SEE HIM, YES, IT WAS DISCUSSED.
I'D PLASTER YOU ACROSS THE HALL BUT YOU'D PROBABLY TELL ANTONIO THAT... NEVER MIND.

OH, SO NOW I CAN'T EVEN BE RELATED TO VICKI GLORI WITHOUT RENA TITAÑON TURNING INTO A FULL ON BITCH! AND I CAN'T EVEN THINK ABOUT RENA TITAÑON WITHOUT VICKI GLORI--MY WONDERFUL FRIENDS...
BLEH!

I'M SO FUCKING TIRED OF THIS SHIT! OLD LADIES PLAYING JUNIOR HIGH SCHOOL GAMES. WELL, THAT'S IT, BUBBA! IT ENDS RIGHT NOW!

HEY, LITTLE GIRL! WHAT ABOUT THAT TIA OF YOURS?
DUKE, DOES RENA HAVE ANY CHILDREN?

HMM...

NO, LITTLE GIRL. I DON'T THINK SO.
END

those wild and mixed up
LOCAS
IF I OUTGROW ANOTHER PAIR OF JEANS, SOMEONE'S GETTING SUED.

DON'T WORRY, MAG! I'D STILL LOVE YOU IF YOU LOOKED LIKE ME!
HOPEY, DON'T! AW, SHOOT...
PPY HOUR
POP!

THAT DOES IT! I'LL NEVER WEAR ANOTHER PAIR OF PANTS AS LONG AS I LIVE!
THEN THIS IS GONNA MAKE QUITE A COMICAL SITUATION, BECAUSE HERE COMES RAND RACE.

VERY FU... HUH?!
NO KIDDING. HE JUST DROVE UP RIGHT NOW.

OH MY GOD! IT IS HIM! WHAT THE HELL IS HE DOING HERE?
PROBABLY TO SEE YOU, MAGGOT.

STALL HIM TILL I'M OUT OF THE COUNTRY! SEE YOU LATER, HOPEY! I'LL WRITE YOU!
AW, C'MON, MAG. DON'T BE A COWARD. THIS SHOULD BE A GOOD ONE.

YES? MAY I HELP YOU?
UH, YES YOU CAN. DOES MAGGIE CHASCARRILLO LIVE HERE BY ANY CHANCE?

WELL, I'M NOT SURE, EXACTLY. THAT ALL DEPENDS...
HEY!
RACE! WHAT A SURPRISE! HOW ARE YOU?
MAGGIE!

IT TOOK ME AWHILE TO FIND YOU, Y'KNOW?
K-REALLY? WHAT BRINGS YOU WAY OUT HERE?
HI. I'M HER PAL, POKEY.

I WANTED TO SEE YOU. WE NEVER REALLY SAID GOOD BYE WHEN YOU QUIT WORKING FOR ME. CAN I TAKE YOU TO LUNCH OR SOMETHING?
SURE, I GUESS SO.
ME AN' DUMBY HERE ARE SWELL PALS.

YOU CAN COME ALSO, POKEY.
CHEE, THANKS.
YEAH, BUT FIRST LET ME AN' POKEY FIX OUR FACES.

OH GOD, HOPEY! WHY DID HE HAVE TO COME NOW THAT I'M SUCH A WALRUS AND MY HAIR'S ALL ...WHAT AM I GONNA DO?
MISTER MEXICO
YOU'RE GONNA LET HIM TAKE US TO LUNCH, THAT'S WHAT! THERE'S ABSOLUTELY NO FOOD IN THIS HOUSE AND I'M STARVED!

BUT- BUT WHAT IF WHILE WE'RE EATING AND TALKING, I LOSE CONTROL AND START ATTACKING MY FOOD LIKE THE DREADED MONSTER WOMAN?
JUST KEEP COOL, MAG. I'LL KICK YOU IF YOU GET OUTTA LINE.
520'S
WORMS UNDER ARRES
2

I MEAN, ALL OF A SUDDEN YOU WERE ON A PLANE HEADED FOR HOME WITHOUT EVEN... WELL, YOU DID LEAVE A NOTE, BUT I DUNNO, I STILL GET THE FEELING IT WAS SOMETHING I DID.
OH, NO, NO! IT WASN'T YOU, RACE! IT WAS ME, REALLY!

I MEAN, I THOUGHT WE HAD BECOME CLOSE ENOUGH FRIENDS WHERE WE COULD, YOU KNOW, TALK IT OVER IF SOMETHING WASN'T RIGHT, OR... YOU KNOW...
YEAH, REAL CLOSE FRIENDS. ¿TU SAVES?
GULP

I REMEMBER YOU NOW. I MET YOU AT THAT HUGE PARTY AT H.R. COSTIGAN'S... AND YOUR NAME'S NOT POKEY!
NO, IT'S SNEEZY...

YEAH, AND OUR CONVERSATION WENT JUST LIKE THIS ONE! YOU NEVER GAVE ME A STRAIGHT--
!

HOPEY, MY LIPSTICK IS SMEARED. WILL YOU HELP ME FIX IT IN THE LADY'S ROOM, PLEASE?
DO I HAVE A CHOICE?
THEM

GET BACK HERE, YOU COWARD!
NO, HOPEY, PLEASE! LEMME GO!

KICK BACK, MAG. CAN'T YOU SEE HE WANTS TO MAKE UP AND BE FRIENDS? WHO KNOWS, MAYBE BEFORE THE NIGHT IS OVER, HE'LL EVEN PROPOSE!
LET'S FACE IT! I'M THE BIG, FAT, FAT, FAT "BEFORE" WOMAN IN THE DIET ADS!
3

OH, AND I SUPPOSE RACE IS OUT THERE HAVING A GOOD CHUCKLE WITH THE CHEF AND MAITRE D' OVER A FEW DRINKS AND A CIGAR, HUH?
YOU'RE RIGHT. RACE IS A SAINT, AN' I BEEN ACTIN' THE FOO'.
BUT IF I HEAR SOME KIND OF CRACK ABOUT FOOD OR SOMETHING, I SWEAR I'LL SCREAM, OK?
YOU'RE NOT SAYING THAT I... MAGGIE! YOU HURT ME SO!
HEY, WHERE'D HE GO?
I KNEW IT! HE DIDN'T WANNA BE SEEN WITH THE LIVING SLOB MONSTER SO HE HIGHTAILED IT...
WHO ARE YOU CALLING A SLOB?
NOT YOU! ME!
HEY! OVER HERE! I WAS PAYING THE CASHIER.
OH, ARE WE LEAVING NOW?
HUH? WELL, I FIGURED SINCE YOU FINISHED YOUR FOOD, YOU'D WANNA GO SOMEWHERE ELSE.
WE CAN STICK AROUND FOR DESSERT OR SOMETHING, IF THAT'S WHAT YOU GIRLS WOULD LIKE.
HOO BOY.
HERV, DID YOU HEAR A SIREN?
I'D GIVE A MILLION BUCKS TO ANYONE WHO COULD EXPLAIN THAT WOMAN TO ME.
SOMETIMES I THINK SHE'S A MARTIAN STUCK ON OUR PLANET AN' THAT HER BEHAVIOR IS NORMAL BACK HOME.
THE END

LOCAS vs LOCOS
BIG DADDY 86
THAT'S PROBABLY THE FUCKIN' RADDEST SONG I'VE EVER HEARD IN MY LIFE.
HEY! WHY DON'T YOU GUYS TURN THAT SHIT DOWN? I CAN BARELY HEAR MYSELF THINK!
HEY, DAD! CONNIE CALLED WHILE YOU WERE GONE. CLOSE THE DOOR, WILL YA? THANKS. LATER ON.
OCTOBER
HOUR
DR. KNOW
ILL REPUTE
AGRESSION
OXNARD NEW YEARS EVE
APE SEX
OCT 10 MADDOGS
KEEP OUT
FUCK THE WINGTIPS
DOA
QUINN MARTIN
THE AXE
THIS SIDE UP
DOG GUTS
BEER GUTS
LOS FRONTERA
APR 10
MADDOGS
LEADSIDE
1

MAN, IF I EVER TALKED TO MY DAD THAT WAY, HE'D COME AFTER ME WITH A FUCKIN' HAMMER.
JOEY, PUT ON THAT APE SEX ALBUM. BUT JUST PLAY THE THIRD SONG ON SIDE ONE.
SINCE WHEN DO YOU LISTEN TO APE SEX, TONY?
ZERO GRAVITY LEFT IT AT MY HOUSE. THERE'S ONLY ONE SONG ON IT THAT THRASHES, THOUGH.
DON'T LISTEN TO THIS HEAVY METALLER. PLAY THE WHOLE THING.
I WOULD IF I HAD IT HERE. MY SISTER HAS IT, THE BITCH!
I HAVEN'T SEEN YOUR SISTER FOR A WHILE. DOES SHE STILL LIVE WITH THAT GIRL WITH THE BIG BUTT?
MAGGIE? YEAH, BUT SHE'S ALL FAT AN' SHIT NOW!
AAH, SHE AIN'T THAT BIG. JUST 'CAUSE TONY'S INTO THOSE SUN BLEACHED BLONDE TWIGS WITH MAN FACES!
METALLICA
REMEMBER WHEN SHE WOULD WEAR THOSE REALLY TIGHT SKI PANTS?
YEAH, HER THIGHS WOULD STICK OUT A MILE IN THE FRONT AND HER ASS TWO MILES OUT THE BACK. SHE'S STILL SECOND ONLY TO PAM ROSSI.
NOW WE'RE TALKING HUNDREDS OF MILES, BOY. LEAGUES!
FUCK, WE SHOULD GO GET MY RECORD FROM HOPEY. I HAVEN'T EVEN BEEN ABLE TO HEAR IT. I'LL GIVE YOU A BUCK FOR GAS IF YOU DRIVE, DOYLE.
SURE, I'D LIKE TO SEE WHAT THOSE GIRLS HAVE BEEN UP TO, ANYWAY.
WELL, ONE OF 'EM'S UP TO ABOUT FOUR HUNDRED, LATELY.
DOG BUTTS
METALLICA
AND BOY, AM I GLAD YOU CAN'T COME WITH US! IZZY'S STILL PISSED OFF AT YOU FOR BREAKING HER REFRIGERATOR!
AAH, I COULDN'T FIT IN HER HOUSE, ANYWAY! MAGGIE LIVES THERE, REMEMBER?
2

SHIT, I DON'T CARE WHAT ANYONE SAYS. TO ME, MAGGIE'S STILL THE BEST... BUT WOULDN'T YOU KNOW IT, SHE STILL SEES ME AS HOPEY'S LITTLE BROTHER.
LIFE IS TOUGH, MAN.

YEAH, BUT I'LL SHOW HER. I HAVE MY LITTLE BROTHER RIGHT HERE JUST WAITING...
LITTLE IS RIGHT... HEY, ARE WE JUST GONNA WALK RIGHT IN?
5506

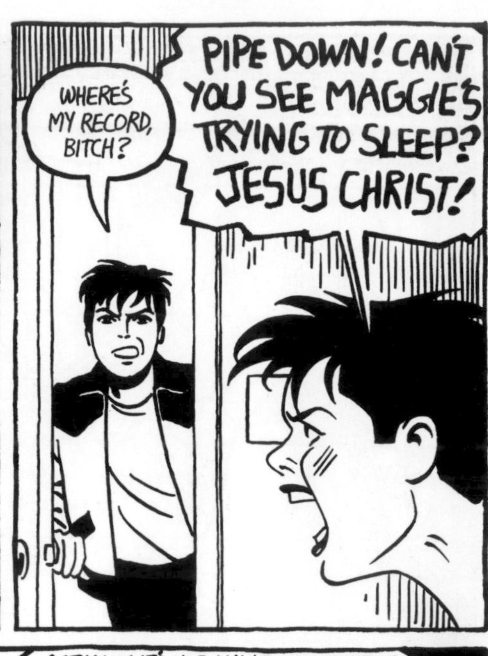
WHERE'S MY RECORD, BITCH?
PIPE DOWN! CAN'T YOU SEE MAGGIE'S TRYING TO SLEEP? JESUS CHRIST!

IN THE DAY? WHAT'S SHE DOING, TAKING AFTER IZZY THE WITCH LADY?
HER BAD FOOT KEPT US UP AGAIN LAST NIGHT SO I FINALLY MADE HER DRIVE TO EMERGENCY AT FOUR IN THE MORNING. LOCO SPIDER SALAS WAS THERE. SOMEONE STUCK HIM WITH A RUSTED SCREWDRIVER BEHIND RAY'S LIQUOR.
SEX 1·2·3
TARZAN

AW, POOR BABY. SO, WHAT'S WRONG WITH HER FOOT?
ACTUALLY, IT'S HER ANKLE. SHE HURT IT WHEN SHE WAS LITTLE AND NEVER TREATED IT RIGHT. SO, ONCE IN A WHILE, IT ACTS UPON HER... MOVE, EGGHEAD!

HEY, ARE YOU PACKING? DON'T TELL ME IZZY FINALLY GAVE YOU AN' MAGGIE HER POINTED SHOE.
YOU KIDDIN'? WE ALL GOTTA BE OUTTA HERE BY TOMORROW. I SURE WISH THEY WOULDA TOLD US SOONER. I'LL BE DAMNED IF I KNOW WHERE WE'RE LIVING NOW.

DOES THAT MEAN MY RECORD IS IN ONE OF THESE BOXES?
NO, IT'S AT DAFFY'S. HEY, DOYLE! WHEN WE FIND OUT WHERE WE'RE TAKING THIS JUNK, DO YOU THINK YOU COULD HAUL SOME OF IT IN YOUR TRUCK?
SURE, I GUESS SO.
LOS BVKIS
DENNIS THE MENACE
3

DAFFY?! WHO GAVE YOU THE RIGHT TO LEND OUT MY RECORD?
SHE SAID SHE'D TAKE GOOD CARE OF IT.

AW, SHIT! YOU STILL HAD NO RIGHT! COME ON, DOYLE. LET'S GO TO DAFFY'S.
TALK TO YOU LATER, HOPEY.
OK.

I CAN'T BELIEVE WHAT A DREAM YOU ARE RIGHT NOW.

GUESS WHAT, IZZY. WE'VE GOT IT NARROWED DOWN TO TWO PLACES WE'RE NOT LIVING.
OH, HOPEY. I'M SURE YOUR MOTHERS WOULD LOVE TO HAVE THEIR DARLING DAUGHTERS BACK WITH THEM.

WHAT ABOUT MAGGIE'S AUNT?
NO WAY! MAGGIE'S NOT EVEN GOING NEAR THAT LADY FOR AT LEAST A YEAR! DIDN'T YOU HEAR? VICKI GLORI LOST HER CROWN LAST NIGHT.

W-WHA...? REALLY? THEN RENA TITAÑON IS CHAMPION AGAIN?
NAW, IT WAS SOME RUSSIAN LADY NAMED SULKA OR SOMETHING LIKE THAT. SHE USED THE ROPES, I THINK.

WOW. THAT'S THE KIND OF SHIT YOU JUST NEVER THINK ABOUT, Y'KNOW?
WELL, SHE AIN'T DEAD.

IT GETS YOU RIGHT BETWEEN THE EYES WHEN YOU LEAST EXPECT IT.
WHAT DOES? ISABEL, ARE YOU ALL RIGHT?
4

SHE NO HOME!
SHE NO HOME!
TEE HEE! DAPHNE TOOK ALL HER RECORDS OVER TO TOM TOM'S HOUSE BEFORE MY DADDY GETS HOME TO THROW THEM OUT.
TEEN GROOVE

SHIT! IS THIS THE SAME TOM TOM THEY CALL "SHE-MAN"? I DON'T EVEN KNOW WHERE THE FUCK SHE LIVES!
I DO. YOU GOT THAT BUCK FOR GAS?

DID YOU HEAR? THE GIRLS ARE KICKED OUT OF THEIR HOUSE. ISN'T IT AWFUL?
NAW, THEY'LL BE FINE. HOPEY'S ALWAYS GOT 'EM OUT OF TROUBLE. SHE'S THE CRAFTY ONE.
YEAH, HER AN' MAGGIE ARE SO COOL. GIMME A BREAK! THOSE TWO OLD LADIES MUST HAVE YOU BRAINWASHED!

I FORGOT. TO TOM TOM, ANYONE OVER EIGHTEEN IS OLD AND WASHED UP.
OH, HERE COMES DOYLE BLACK AND JOEY GLASS. MAYBE THEY CAN BUY US SOME BEER. DOYLE IS OVER TWENTY-ONE, ISN'T HE?
YEAH. I'LL BE RIGHT BACK.

EVERYBODY OUT OF MY ROOM, RIGHT NOW! THAT MEANS YOU TOO, GOO GOO!
JOEY GLASS IS HERE.

OH, THAT WAS YOUR RECORD, JOEY? I'M SORRY. I LENT IT TO TERRY DOWNE!
AW, SHHH... LOOKING FOR TERRY IS LIKE LOOKING FOR A GOOD COMIC BOOK!
KICK BACK FOR AWHILE, JOE. I'M GONNA GO BUY 'EM SOME BEER RIGHT NOW.
5

YOU'VE NEVER BEEN IN MY HOUSE, HAVE YOU, JOEY?
NO, I DIDN'T KNOW YOU WERE RICH. WELL, YOUR PARENTS, ANYWAY.

YOU KNOW, I WAS JUST THINKING THAT... WELL, NOW THAT YOU'RE HERE, WE COULD G-GO UP TO MY ROOM...
I WAS JUST NOTICING ALL THE GOLF TROPHIES. MY DAD GOLFS...

...AND THEN MAYBE WE COULD... I MEAN, NOW THAT WE HAVE THE CHANCE... I MEAN, I REALLY LIKE YOU AND, WELL, YOU ONCE SAID THAT...
YOU GUYS EVEN HAVE A POOL? MAN, WHAT DOES YOUR DAD DO BESIDES GOLF?

UH, THEN, NO... MAYBE WE SHOULDN'T, BECAUSE YOU KNOW, ALL THESE PEOPLE AND...
HUH? DID YOU SAY SOMETHING, KID?

T-THEY'RE MY MOTHER'S TROPHIES...
OH, THA'S COOL. HEY, DOYLE! LET'S GO SEE IF WE CAN FIND TERRY!
WHY DON'T YOU CALL FIRST, MAN?

SHE AIN'T GOT A PHONE. COME ON, MAN! I WANT MY RECORD!
AND I WANT MY BUCK!
KID.

WHAT'S WRONG, JOE? COULDN'T YOU TELL HOW BAD TOM TOM WANTS YOU?
I KNOW, I KNOW. I ACTED LIKE A REAL SHIT, DIDN'T I?

YEAH, IT AIN'T LIKE YOU TO PASS UP SOMETHING LIKE THAT. TOM TOM AIN'T SO BAD. IN FACT, SHE'S KINDA CUTE...
SURE, SHE'S CUTE! BUT, YOU DON'T REALIZE THAT THAT GIRL IS HOPEY WHEN HOPEY WAS SIXTEEN! IT WOULD BE LIKE SCREWING MY OWN SISTER, MAN! CHILLS UPON CHILLS...
6

YOU JUST GONNA SIT THERE ALL DAY, OR WHAT?

HEY, IZZY! WHERE DO YOU WANT... WHAT'S WRONG?
I DON'T FEEL LIKE PACKING BOXES ANY MORE.

SOME PEOPLE WERE BORN OUT OF THEIR MIND. ME, I HAD TO LEARN IT THE HARD WAY!

TERRY'S LIVE-IN BOYFRIEND SAID SHE'S DOWN AT THEIR BAND'S PRACTICE PAD. LET'S HURRY BEFORE SHE LEAVES OR SOMETHING.
(SIGH) I SUPPOSE I'LL NEVER GET THAT BUCK FOR GAS, HUH?
TELEPHONE

TERRY? SHE JUST LEFT TO TALK TO HOPEY. WHA'D YOU WANT HER FOR, ANYWAY?
WE BELIEVE SHE HAS JOEY'S APE SEX RECORD, ZERO.
BAM BAM

THE APE SEX ALBUM? SHE LENT IT TO ME. IF I'DA KNOWN...
AH, OUR JOURNEY ENDS...
WAIT A... YOU DIDN'T HAPPEN TO LEND IT TO... NAW... NO WAY...

WHERE THE HELL IS THAT DOYLE? I CAN'T MOVE ALL THIS SHIT WITH ALL THESE ZOMBIES LYING AROUND... ZAT HIM?
BEEP BEE

HI, TERRY. WHATCHA DOIN' HERE?
SOMEONE TOLD ME YOU WERE BEING EVICTED. I HAD TO SEE IT FOR MYSELF.
7

DAMN STRAIGHT! I DON'T KNOW WHAT WE'RE GONNA DO. IZZY WON'T EVEN WANT US NEAR HER NEW HOUSE.
SHE ALREADY HAS A NEW PLACE, HUH? TELL YOU WHAT...
6605

PAUL'S GOING TO FRANCE FOR TWO WEEKS. WHY DON'T YOU STAY AT MY PLACE TILL YOU FIGURE OUT WHAT YOU'RE GOING TO DO.
HAR DE HAR HAR. YOU KNOW I CAN'T LEAVE MAGGIE OUT IN THE COLD LIKE THAT.

I SWEAR, SOMETIMES YOU CAN BE SO...
WELL, OF COURSE I MEANT MAGGIE CAN COME, TOO!

REALLY?
I KNOW IT SOUNDS ODD OF ME, BUT I'VE REALIZED HOW SILLY I'VE BEEN. I CAN'T GO ON LIKE I DO ABOUT MAGGIE. IT'S ONLY BUILDING UP A WALL BETWEEN US. KEEPING US APART...

TERRY, I'VE ALWAYS KNOWN YOU TO BE ONE SLY BITCH...
NOW NOW, HOPEY. WE'RE ALL GOING TO BE FRIENDS FROM NOW ON.

FUCKING SHIT! HERE I WANNA STRANGLE TONY 'CAUSE HE HAD MY RECORD THE WHOLE TIME AND YOU RUN OUTTA GAS!
I RUN OUT...? IF YOU WOULDA JUST PULLED YOUR HEAD OUT AND GAVE ME THE LOUSY DOLLAR, THIS WOULD HAVE NEVER HAPPENED!

OH, WELL. TOM TOM'S HOUSE IS ONLY A COUPLE OF BLOCKS FROM HERE. MAYBE WE CAN SIPHON FROM HER LAWN MOWER OR SOMETHING.
HEY, DOYLE, WAIT! WE CAN'T GO BACK TO TOM TOM'S! THAT GIRL WANTS ME DEAD LIKE, RIGHT AWAY!
ESTATE ESTATES
8

THAT'S RIGHT. YOU BROKE HER HEART. OK, YOU STAY HERE. I'LL SEE WHAT I CAN DO ABOUT GETTING SOME GAS.
HURRY BACK.

DOYLE! DID SHE SAY ANYTHING?
SHE ASKED ME WHAT HAPPENED TO MY FRIEND, THAT'S ALL.

SHIT, I KNEW IT. I'M THE WORST, HUH?
AH, YOU'LL GET OVER IT. SO WILL SHE. SHE CALLED YOU MY FRIEND, DIDN'T SHE? C'MON, LET'S GET TO A GAS STATION. I PROMISED YOUR SISTER I'D HELP HER MOVE.

HELP HER MOVE? AREN'T YOU GONNA HELP ME FIND TONY? I'M GONNA KILL THAT ASSHOLE!
SEE? YOU'VE FORGOTTEN THE OL' SHE-MAN ALREADY. OK, I'LL HELP YOU FIND TONY IF YOU GIVE ME TWENTY DOLLARS FOR GAS.

MUCHISIMAS GRACIAS, MUCHACHOS. ¿NO MAS NO PEGUEN ARRIBA DE LA PUERTA, EH?
¡AI, ISABEL! ¡MIS MANOS!
¡AI CARAI!
ISABEL'S GOING TO LIVE IN THAT HOUSE ALL ALONE? IT LOOKS SORT OF CREEPY.
IZZY'S LOVED THIS HOUSE FOR YEARS. MRS. GALINDO, THE OLD LADY WHO LIVED HERE TOLD IZZY SHE'D GIVE IT TO HER WHEN SHE'D PASS AWAY. AND BY GOLLY SHE DID...
9

PENNY CENTURY USED TO STAY HERE WHENEVER SHE WAS IN TOWN, AND WE USED TO GET DRUNK AND EVERYTHING IN THE BACK. MRS. GALINDO DIDN'T MIND. SHE USED TO CHUG DOWN THAT NIGHT TRAIN ALL DAY LONG, PENNY WOULD TELL US.

PENNY ALSO SAID THAT THE OLD PLACE WAS SUPPOSED TO BE HAUNTED. I THINK THAT'S WHY IZZY WANTED TO MOVE HERE SO BAD. SO SHE COULD TALK WITH HER OWN KIND ONCE IN AWHILE.
THAT'S RIDICULOUS. YOU DON'T BELIEVE ALL THAT HAUNTED GARBAGE, DO YOU?

I'LL TELL YOU ONE THING: IF FLIES START GATHERING ON THE CEILING OF THIS HOUSE, I'LL BELIEVE YOU AND MAGGIE WOULD GET MARRIED.
OH, HAVE YOU TALKED TO MAGGIE ABOUT OUR DEALIE?

YES, I DID. AND TO TELL YOU THE TRUTH, I DON'T KNOW EXACTLY WHAT HER ANSWER WAS. I THINK SHE SAID YES, BUT SHE KINDA JUST BOBBLED HER HEAD AROUND, LOOKING DOWN A LOT, SHRUGGING HER SHOULDERS... YOU KNOW, THE WHOLE BIT.

HOW ABOUT IF I TALK TO HER? MAYBE I CAN CONVINCE HER THAT I'M SINCERE ABOUT THIS, AND THAT...
...YOU WANT TO JUMP MY BONES. OR IS IT MAGGIE'S BONES? OOH, TERRY! I'M JEALOUS NOW.

DAMN YOU, HOPEY! WHY DO YOU ALWAYS MAKE IT LIKE I'M THIS EVIL WITCH OUT TO RUIN EVERY... WHAT ARE YOU DOING?! STOP IT!
BUT, I THOUGHT WE WERE FRIENDS FROM NOW ON, THERESA...

C'MON, I'M SORRY, TERRY. LET'S SHAKE AND BE FRIENDS. OR WOULD YOU RATHER KISS AND MAKE UP? HUH?
GET AWAY FROM ME! I NEVER WANT TO SEE YOUR FACE OR YOUR FAT FRIEND'S FAT FACE IN MY APARTMENT EVER! I'VE HAD IT WITH YOU!
END

LOCAS
8:01 AM
JAIME 86

HELLO, DAFFY? YEAH, UH, WHY DON'T YOU GO TO THE BEACH WITHOUT ME. I HAVE A LOT OF THINGS I HAVE TO DO TODAY. YEAH, SORRY 'BOUT THAT. OK, BYE.

UP AND AT 'EM, HOPELESS! C'MON, DOYLE'S GONNA BE HERE SOON, SO WE CAN MOVE THE REST OF OUR JUNK.
DOYLE ISN'T SUPPOSED TO BE HERE FOR ANOTHER THREE HOURS...

WELL THEN, LET'S GO TO BREAKFAST. C'MON, I FEEL LIKE I JUST GOTTA GET OUT AND DO SOMETHING!
NO WONDER. YOU ONLY SLEPT THROUGH YESTERDAY. DOESN'T YOUR FOOT STILL HURT?

NOPE! I'M CHIPPER THAN A CHIPPENDALE'S DANCER NOW, BOY!
AND ALMOST AS MACHO. HEY, ARE THOSE NEW BOOTS?

YEAH, NEAT, HUH? THEY'RE REAL, GENUINE WRESTLING BOOTS.
I THOUGHT YOU TOLD ME THOSE KIND WERE IMPOSSIBLE TO FIND.
1

THEY ARE. RENA TITAÑON SENT 'EM. I FORGOT ALL ABOUT IT. IT WAS WHEN ME AN' HER WERE STUCK IN THE CHEPAN DESERT. MAN, WAS I GETTING ON HER NERVES FAST...
HUH? 'XPLAIN.
I'M HUNGRY.
SHUT UP AND HAVE SOME ROOTS.
SEE L+R #'S 6-11 "LAS MUJERES PERDIDAS" - STUPID

MAN, WHAT A CRAB. WERE YOU LIKE THIS IN THE RING, TOO?
YOU SAW ME. YOU TELL ME.

WELL, I ONLY SAW YOU THAT ONE TIME ON TV AGAINST MY TIA VICKI YEARS AGO... HEY, HOW COME ONLY WRESTLERS GET TO WEAR THOSE COOL BOOTS? I THINK THOSE ARE THE COOLEST BOOTS IN THE WHOLE WORLD...

IF I HAD A PAIR OF THOSE, I'D REALLY...
TELL YOU WHAT. YOU KEEP YOUR TRAP SHUT TILL WE'RE OUT OF ALL THIS, AND I'LL SEND YOU A PAIR, JUST YOUR SIZE! SPECIAL DELIVERY! DEAL?
NATURALLY, I NEVER SHUT UP FOR A MINUTE, BUT SHE SENT 'EM ANYWAY.
TONTA.

I CAN IMAGINE WHAT DAFFY'LL SAY WHEN SHE SEES 'EM. "OH, I LOVE THEM..."
"...WHERE DID YOU GET THEM? I WANT SOME." MAN, I SWEAR, SOMETIMES...

SO, ARE WE GOING TO BREAKFAST, OR WHAT?
NO, YOU GO AHEAD. I ATE LAST WEEK.

YOU'RE NO FUN. I'M GONNA GO SEE WHAT THE WORLD LOOKS LIKE WITH THE SHADOWS ON THE OPPOSITE SIDE OF IT.
DO ME A FAVOR WHILE YOU'RE AT IT. SEE WHAT THE FRONT BUMPER OF A MOVING TRUCK LOOKS LIKE.
2

I SURE COULD GO FOR SOME CANDY RIGHT NOW. I THINK I'LL WALK DOWN TO THE LIQUOR STORE TO PASS THE TIME. TOO BAD YELLOW MARSHMALLOW PEEPS AREN'T IN SEASON.

FOOTAH! IN FRONT OF THE LIQUOR STORE. IT'S BIG BOOBS BLANCA RIZO! THAT GIRL'S BEEN AFTER ME SINCE NINTH GRADE. I'D BE DEAD BY NOW IF MY COUSIN LICHA WASN'T THE HEAD OF THE BADDEST CHUCA GANG AROUND. ¡QUE VIVA LAS WIDOWS!
ATO'S GOLD
$5.25
NO PARKING

IT'S KINDA FUNNY. IT ALL STARTED 'CAUSE THE GUYS SHE LIKED ALWAYS LIKED ME BETTER. THEN WHEN SHE GOT HOT ON SPEEDY ORTIZ, WELL... WAIT A MINUTE! WHO'S THAT SHE'S TALKING TO??

SPEAK OF THE DEVIL. HE USED TO TELL ME HE DOESN'T EVEN LIKE HER, THE DICK!
THE WINANS

OH OH OH! PUT ON A LITTLE FAT AND THE RATS JUMP SHIP, HUH? NO, I GET IT. A LITTLE FAT'S OK. IT ALL DEPENDS ON WHERE YOU PUT IT. SHEEIT!

LISTEN TO ME. THE GUY'S SITTING THERE MERELY TALKING TO THIS GIRL AND I START SHARPENING THE OL' CLAWS. SPEEDY'S MY CHILDHOOD FRIEND, FOR CHRISSAKE.

I'LL JUST STAB HIM IN THE BALLS THE NEXT TIME HE TRIES TO COME ON TO ME.
3

LOCAS
11:47AM

MAGNUM
J.H. 86

MONDAY I GOT FRIDAY ON MY MIND...
OK, DOYLE. BEFORE WE DROP ALL THIS STUFF OFF AT TERRY'S, WE WANT YOU TO MAKE A LEFT TURN ON CROWN ROAD.
TERRY'S?! HEY, GOLDEN VOICE! DIDN'T YOU TELL ME THAT LAST NIGHT TERRY BOOTED YOU TWO FROM HER PLACE BECAUSE HOPEY PISSED HER OFF?

YEP, I DID AND SHE DID. SO THIS MORNING OL' HOPITA HAD A LITTLE ASS SMOOCHING TO DO.
WHAT DO YOU MEAN A LITTLE? MAN, THAT SHIT'S EMBARRASSING AS HELL!
OK, SO WHY ARE WE GOING INTO CROWN ROAD? YOU GONNA GANG RAPE ME?

YOU WISH, BOY. NO, THAT'S WHERE WE UNLOAD THE SLEEPER SOFA.
YOU'RE GONNA JUNK IT? IT DON'T LOOK TOO BAD TO ME.
WE'RE NOT GONNA JUNK IT. WE'RE GONNA CREMATE IT!

DAMN, THIS THING'S HEAVY! WHY CAN'T YOU JUST CREMATE AN OLD TEDDY BEAR?
¡AI! ¡PICAS!
OOF!

UGH! IT FEELS LIKE YOU GIRLS AREN'T EVEN LIFTING...
OH, DID YOU WANT US TO LIFT? LIFT, HOPE.
WHAT DO YOU THINK I'VE BEEN TRYING TO DO?

YOW!

DIDN'T YOU KNOW THESE SOFA BEDS WEIGH TEN TIMES MORE THAN A REGULAR SOFA?
WE GOT IT ON THE TRUCK ALL RIGHT.
THERE WERE TWO OTHER GUYS HELPING LOAD, MAGGOT.

I HATE TO BE RUDE BUT, WHY DON'T YOU SAY A FEW LAST WORDS, THEN SHOOT IT IN THE HEAD, SO WE CAN GET GOING. DON'T YOU HAVE TO BE AT ANOTHER WAKE TODAY?
THAT'S RIGHT. MRS. GALINDO'S WAKE.
WANNA COME WITH US, DOYLE? LOADS OF LAUGHS!

HA HA! NO, I'D REALLY LIKE TO, BUT I HAVE TO MEET SOMEONE IN AN HOUR.
AW, YOU'RE NOT LEAVING US FOR A TALL, RICH, BLUE EYED BLONDE CAREER WOMAN WITH ENORMOUS BREASTS, ARE YOU, DOYLE?
DOYLE, I'M JEALOUS.

C'MAN, YOU THINK I'D CHOOSE ANYONE OVER MY TWO MOST FAVORITE, INTELLIGENT, BEAUTIFUL, HAPPENIN' WOMEN?
IT WON'T TAKE HIM VERY LONG TO CHANGE HIS MIND IF HE SEES PENNY CENTURY AT THE WAKE, HUH?
5

LOCAS
1:28 PM
EL PUMA
86

I HAVEN'T SEEN PENNY SINCE SHE MARRIED COSTIGAN MONTHS AGO. IT'S FUNNY...
WHO KNOWS HOW MANY DRUGS ARE HOLDING UP THAT BODY.

I KNOW, IT'S SO SAD. SHE AND COSTIGAN NEVER EVEN SEE EACH OTHER. SHE'S BEEN SCREWING HER DRUG BUDDIES, COSTIGAN'S SERVANTS.
PENNY WILL ALWAYS FIGURE A WAY TO SCREW SOMETHING. HER OWN LIFE MOST OF THE TIME.

THE OTHER DAY I RAN INTO PENNY'S OLD ROOMMATE, DOLORES MANTEGAS, AND WE GOT TO TALKING ABOUT PENNY'S RELATIONSHIP WITH RAND RACE. SHE SAID IT'S TRUE THAT RACE KNOCKED HER UP.
THEN WHAT DID PENNY DO? ABORT?

APPARENTLY, YEAH. DOLORES SAID THAT'S WHAT REALLY FUCKED PENNY UP IN THE HEAD. SHIT, IF SHE THINKS ONE'S BAD, SHE SHOULD GO FOR THREE LIKE IZZY.
BUT STILL, HOW COULD RACE DO SUCH A THING AND RUN OUT ON HER?
DEDDEN MORTUARY

OH, YEAH. DOLORES ALSO SAID THAT OL' RACE DOESN'T EVEN KNOW SHE EVER WAS PREGNANT. PENNY WAS SO UPSET, THAT SHE SPLIT ON HIM WITHOUT EXPLANATION.
NO WONDER HE'S STILL WHIPPED ON... OH, HERE SHE COMES.
6

SO TELL ME, BABIES. HOW IS IT LIVING IN THE GALINDO MANSION? AIN'T IT WOW?
WE DON'T KNOW. IZZY WON'T LET US LIVE WITH HER.
YEAH, SO WE'RE STAYING WITH TERRY DOWNE UNTIL WE CAN FIND A PLACE OF OUR OWN.

WELL, I GUESS IT'S GOOD THAT YOU DON'T. THE PLACE IS HAUNTED, Y'KNOW?
SO, I'VE HEARD. IZZY SHOULD HAVE A BALL.
I CAN ONLY IMAGINE THOSE ALL NIGHT POKER PARTIES.

NO, I'M SERIOUS! I COULD SPEND THE WHOLE DAY TELLING YOU ABOUT THINGS THAT HAVE HAPPENED THERE. I THINK MRS. GALINDO (GOD REST HER SOUL) ATTRACTED CRAZY THINGS LIKE THAT. WOO...

LIKE ONE TIME I ASKED HER IF SHE WAS AFRAID OF GHOSTS AND SHE SAID, "NO WAY! ANY GHOST THAT WILL SHARE HIS HOUSE IS WELCOME TO SHARE MY BOTTLE OF NIGHT TRAIN." RIGHT THEN I SWEAR SOMETHING CRAWLED INTO THE BOTTLE AND CHUGGED AWAY!
MUST BE SOME PRETTY PARTYIN' SPOOKS.

YEAH, WOW... MAGGIE, HAVE YOU BEEN SEEING RAND RACE LATELY?
HA HA! NOT LATELY, PENELOPE.

OH. THERE'S SOMETHING I THINK I SHOULD TELL HIM, BUT, I CAN'T SEEM TO FIND HIM, I DUNNO...
WELL, I READ IN THE PAPER THAT HE'S BACK WORKING AT LILLIAN ELLISON'S AIR BASE JUST OUTSIDE TOWN. MY OLD PASS CARD IS STILL GOOD. YOU CAN HAVE IT AND SAY YOU'RE ME.
!

THAT WAS REAL SWELL OF YOU, MAG.
WELL, I FIGURE THAT OL' PASS CARD WILL DO HER A LOT BETTER THAN IT EVER DID ME.
7

LOCAS
2:50PM

LET'S GO INTO MIKE'S MUSIC. I GOTTA PICK UP SOME BASS PICKS.
LOOK WHO'S GOING IN. ISN'T THAT HENRY WHO USED TO BE IN CATECHISM THIRTEEN? DIDN'T HE TEACH TERRY HOW TO PLAY GUITAR?
1228
1226
MIKE'S MU
SALE
EL CONEJO LOCO 86

HEY, WHAT'S UP? HOW'S THE OL' BAND GETTING ALONG?
GREAT, MAN. WE GOT A WHOLE EIGHT SONGS DOWN NOW.

THA'S COOL. LEAST YOU'RE GETTIN' THERE. WHAT ARE YOU GUYS CALLED AGAIN?
'SOUL TRAIN LINE.'
HUH? WHAT EVER HAPPENED TO 'TIVOLI NIGHTS?'

THAT WAS TWO WEEKS AGO, MAG. I'LL BET YOU DIDN'T EVEN KNOW THAT BEFORE THAT WE WERE 'THE RONKIES.'
WHY DO YOU GUYS ALWAYS CHANGE YOUR NAME? I STILL LIKE 'MISSILES OF OCTOBER' BETTER.

I REALLY LIKE THE WAY YOU DO THAT CRAZY VERSION OF "TWO FACES HAVE I."
YEAH, WE... HUH? WHAT SONG IS THAT?

YOU KNOW, THE ONE WHERE MONICA SINGS WITH JUST THE DRUMS ON SOME PARTS.
IS THAT WHAT IT'S CALLED? THIS WHOLE TIME, I THOUGHT IT WAS, "DO VASES HAVE EYES?"
8

LOCAS
3:12 PM
JED 86

...AND I COULD BARELY HOLD BACK MY LAUGHTER 'CAUSE THIS GUY THOUGHT HE WAS MY MAN RON JEREMY. HE ACTUALLY WANTED TO TAKE ON ME, MONICA AND OL' TERRY RIGHT THEN AND THERE! BUT POOR ZERO WOULD ONLY BE ABLE TO WATCH...
OH, GOD. CHECK IT OUT, HOPEY. SOME JERK NEEDED TWO PARKING SPACES SO NO ONE WOULD SCRATCH HIS PRECIOUS CAR.

SHIT! THIS PISSES ME OFF SO BAD! DOESN'T THIS ASSHOLE KNOW HE'S ONLY ASKING FOR IT A HUNDRED FOLD?
REMEMBER WHAT WE USED TO DO IN THESE SITUATIONS?
HHHUNK

YEAH, BUT WE DON'T HAVE ANY SPRAY PAINT. NEVERTHELESS, I'VE ALWAYS THOUGHT A SIMPLE, ORDINARY HOUSE KEY ADDED MORE FLAVOR TO THIS PARTICULAR SITUATION. DO YOU NOT AGREE?
OH BOY. I NEVER COULD STAND THE SOUND OF A SHOVEL SCRAPING ON THE SIDEWALK.

TAKE THAT, YOU FUCKER...
OOH, WAIT. IT LOOKS LIKE THIS CAR HAS ONE OF THEM... WHAT DO YOU CALL 'EM? ONE OF THEM... OH...

WEEEEE-WOOP
ONE OF THEM!!

SOMETIMES YOU GOTTA WATCH OUT FOR THOSE MOTION DETECTOR ALARMS, HOPE.
9

LOCAS
3:57 PM
SID 86

WHAT'S THE RUSH, MAG? YOU HAVE A WHOLE HOUR BEFORE WORK AND IT'S ONLY A FIVE MINUTE DRIVE, AINT IT?
YOU'RE FORGETTING, WE DON'T LIVE ONLY A FIVE MINUTE DRIVE AWAY ANY MORE.

OH, THAT'S RIGHT. OH, WELL, THEN YOU'RE GONNA MISS THE FUN OF UNPACKING ALL OUR SHIT.
OH, DARN THEM SOCKS, MAN.

IT'S A GOOD THING WE'RE HERE ONLY TWO WEEKS, SO I ONLY HAVE TO UNPACK A FEW... WAIT A MINUTE. THIS AIN'T OUR BOX. WHAT THE...?
HOW LONG... BEFORE YOU REALIZE I'M STRANGE...

JACKPOT.
THE SECRETS OF LIFE AND DEATH
VOL. 5
BY
DR. ISABEL ORTIZ RUEBENS

IT'S WONDERFUL. I DON'T REMEMBER THE LAST TIME A SHOWERHEAD DID WHAT I ASKED IT TO. WHAT'S WRONG?
CHECKITOUT, MAG! WE GOTONEOFIZZY'S BOXES BY MISTAKEANDLOOKWHATWAS INIT! WOWEEE!

HEY, THAT'S ONE OF HER SECRET DIARIES. YOU DIDN'T OPEN IT, DID YOU?
WHAT DO YA MEAN? OF COURSE I DID! I ALREADY FINISHED A CHAPTER. THIS IS PRICELESS SHIT!
10

HEY, WHERE YOU GOING? AREN'T YOU GONNA READ ME SOME?
I THOUGHT YOU HAD TO GO TO WORK?

AW, COME ON HOPEY! DON'T FUCK AROUND!
YOU GOTTA KISS MY BUTT FIRST.

OKOK! OUCH! HEY, WHERE'D YOU GET MUSCLES?
MAKIN' THEM FRENCH FRIES AIN'T NO SISSY SHIT, CHICK!

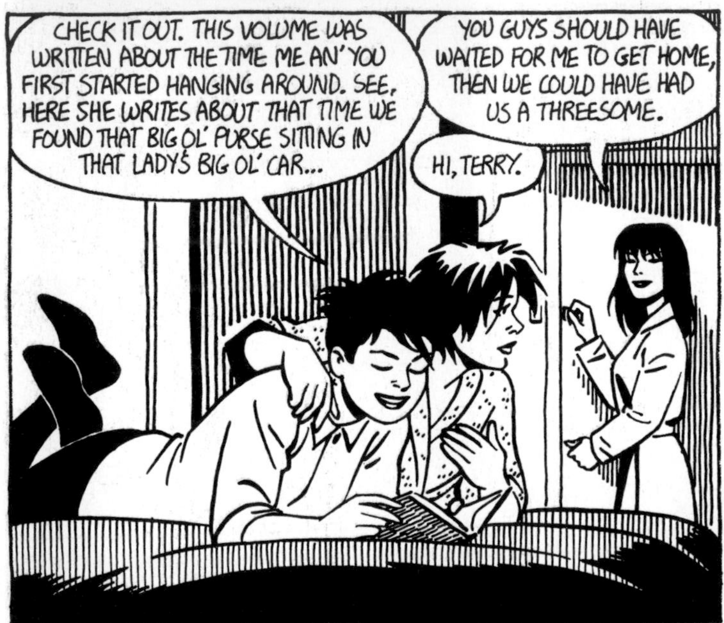
CHECK IT OUT. THIS VOLUME WAS WRITTEN ABOUT THE TIME ME AN' YOU FIRST STARTED HANGING AROUND. SEE, HERE SHE WRITES ABOUT THAT TIME WE FOUND THAT BIG OL' PURSE SITTING IN THAT LADY'S BIG OL' CAR...
YOU GUYS SHOULD HAVE WAITED FOR ME TO GET HOME, THEN WE COULD HAVE HAD US A THREESOME.
HI, TERRY.

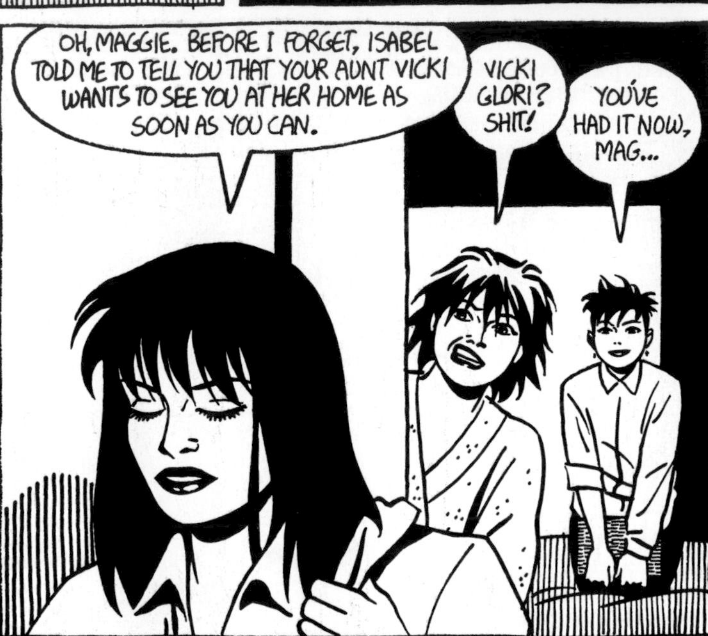
OH, MAGGIE. BEFORE I FORGET, ISABEL TOLD ME TO TELL YOU THAT YOUR AUNT VICKI WANTS TO SEE YOU AT HER HOME AS SOON AS YOU CAN.
VICKI GLORI? SHIT!
YOU'VE HAD IT NOW, MAG...

NO, THIS IS SERIOUS SHIT. SHE'S REALLY CRAZY. AND SHE JUST LOST HER WRESTLING TITLE THE OTHER DAY. WHO KNOWS WHAT KIND OF CONDITION SHE'S IN RIGHT NOW...
IT'S TRUE, Y'KNOW...

ONE TIME SHE CHASED ME AN' DEL CHIMNEY OUT OF HER HOUSE AND DOWN THE STREET WHEN MAGGIE USED TO LIVE WITH HER.
I'LL GO AND SEE HER AFTER WORK. SHOOT, MAN...

IT'S BEEN NICE KNOWING YOU, GIRLS.
REMEMBER, MAG. IF SHE TRIES ANYTHING, RAKE THE EYES.
11

MESKIN/MEXICAN

LOCAS
10:10 PM

HI, SHRIMP! COME ON IN! FOR A MINUTE THERE I THOUGHT YOU DIDN'T GET MY MESSAGE.
YEP! I GOT IT AND HERE I AM, TIA! HEH!
SOMETHING'S FUNNY. SHE'S NOT ACTING LIKE SOMEONE WHO RECENTLY LOST HER TITLE.
SANTO 86

YOU WANT ANYTHING TO DRINK? I GOT SOME OF THAT BEER YOU REALLY LIKE.
OK, THANKS.
OFFERING ME A DRINK EVEN. SHE WANTS SOMETHING FROM ME. I CAN TELL.

I WON'T WASTE YOUR TIME, SHRIMP. I JUST CALLED YOU OVER BECAUSE I GOTTA ASK YOU A BIG, BIG, BIG FAVOR...
ASK AWAY.
I KNEW IT! HERE IT COMES! SHE'S GONNA ASK ME TO HELP HER TRAIN FOR THE BIG REMATCH BY POSING AS A PRACTICE DUMMY. OOG...

AS YOU PROBABLY HAVE ALREADY HEARD, LAST WEEK I LOST MY CHAMPIONSHIP BELT TO STRASKA, THE RUSSIAN WIND, SO I'M REALLY DOWN THESE DAYS. I HELD THAT BELT A LONG TIME, Y'KNOW?
UH HUH.
GRUNT!
13

YOUR WITCH FRIEND TOLD ME YOU'RE HAVING A TOUGH TIME FINDING A PLACE TO LIVE, AND I'D LIKE TO HELP YOU OUT. HOW WOULD YOU LIKE TO MOVE IN HERE WITH ME?
OH, MY GOD! WHAT DID I DO TO DESERVE THIS?
WHO, ME?

SO I FEEL I SHOULDN'T BE ALONE RIGHT NOW. I NEED SOMEONE HERE I CAN TALK TO. AT LEAST TILL I CAN GET THAT REMATCH...
BUT, ME? I MEAN...

ANOTHER REASON IS BECAUSE I'M SICK AND TIRED OF TELLING MY CRAZY SISTER-IN-LAW LIES THAT HER DAUGHTER STILL LIVES WITH ME AND NOT WITH SOME LITTLE DYKE.
MOM STILL BELIEVES THAT, HUH? WOW, SHE IS CRAZY.

AND I STILL CAN'T SEE WHY SHE'D MAKE YOU LIVE APART FROM YOUR BROTHERS AND SISTERS. LEGITIMATE OR NOT, YOU'RE STILL HER GOD DAMN DAUGHTER.
WELL, DAD GAVE HER A LOTTA SHIT WHEN I WAS BORN, AN' MOM'S NEVER BEEN ALL THERE, Y'KNOW? I DUNNO, IT'S WEIRD...

LOOK, SHRIMP. I DON'T WANNA PUSH YOU INTO ANYTHING. LORD KNOWS YOU'VE HAD ENOUGH OF THAT, BUT I REALLY DO NEED YOU HERE RIGHT NOW. LOOK, I WON'T PICK ON YOU. I WON'T EVEN BITCH ABOUT YOU PLAYING YOUR MUSIC TOO LOUD.
PLEASE, MAGGIE...?
SURE, ALL RIGHT, TIA.

GREAT, SHRIMP. YOU'LL SEE, BEFORE YOU KNOW IT, I'LL BE THE OWNER OF THAT BELT ONCE AGAIN, AND YOU CAN WEAR IT ANY TIME YOU WANT.
HUFF!
OK, TIA. BUT I GOTTA GO NOW.

OK, MOVE YOUR JUNK IN ANYTIME. TONIGHT IF YOU WANT.
I'LL BRING IT ALL BY IN THE MORNING. LATER.

NOW I KNOW WHAT I INHERITED FROM MY MOM. I MUST BE NUTS!
14

LOCAS
11:15 PM
COOL BREEZE 86
MAGPIE! I THOUGHT YOU'D BE OUT LONGER. DID YOUR AUNT PICK A FIGHT WITH YOU, OR WHAT?
NO, WORSE. LEMME USE THE BATHROOM FIRST, THEN I'LL TELL YOU ALL ABOUT IT.

SO THAT'S IT. I TOLD HER I'D STAY WITH HER ONLY SO SHE'D GET OFF MY BACK.
THAT'S FUNNY. HOW COME IF YOUR AUNT IS MEXICAN, SHE SPEAKS WITH THAT TEXAS ACCENT?

WELL, WHEN SHE FIRST BROKE INTO WRESTLING, SHE CALLED HERSELF "COWGIRL VICKI LANE." LATER SHE DROPPED THE "COWGIRL" ANGLE, BUT THE ACCENT STAYED. SHEEE!... SHE'S REALLY DONE IT THIS TIME.
KICK BACK, MAG. YOU'LL GET YOUR SHIT TOMORROW.

I MEAN, THIS SHIT'S ONLY TEMPORARY. IN A MONTH OR TWO FROM NOW, ME AN' YOU WILL HAVE OUR OWN PLACE LIKE BEFORE.
YEAH, WITH ALL THAT CASH WE MAKE. ARE THESE YOUR CIGARETTES?

Y'KNOW, THE WAY I SEE IT, WE'RE GONNA KEEP GETTING FUCKED AROUND TILL WE'RE GONNA HAVE TO GIVE IN AND MARRY SOME BRAIN SURGEONS, OR SOMETHING.
TSK! THAT'S JUST LIKE YOU, MAG. IF YOU WERE ON FIRE RIGHT NOW, YOU'D GO OUT AND BUY A GALLON OF KEROSENE.
15

J'GGED/JUGGED (PRONOUNCED JIGGED)

"THAT WAS THAT. THERE WAS NOTHING LEFT FOR ME HERE. I HAD NO OTHER CHOICE BUT TO GO TO MEXICO."
V
THE SECRETS OF LIFE AND DEATH
VOL: 5
ISABEL ORTIZ R
LOCAS JAIME 86

"THE END... FOR NOW." FUCKING IZZY. WOULDN'T YOU KNOW SHE'D PUT ALL THAT SHIT ABOUT HER IN MEXICO IN A WHOLE OTHER VOLUME.

YOU KNOW WHAT THIS MEANS, TERRY? NOW I'M GONNA HAVE TO SNEAK INTO HER HOUSE AND STEAL THE SIXTH VOLUME. SHEEIT...
WHAT THE HELL IS THAT YOU'RE READING ANYWAY, HOPE?

IF YOU WOULDA LISTENED TO ME THE FIRST SIX TIMES, YOU'D KNOW THIS IS ONE OF IZZY'S DIARIES. YOU KNOW, WHERE SHE WRITES ABOUT THINGS LIKE, WHEN ME AN' YOU LIVED AT DEL CHIMNEY'S...
NOW, WHY IN THE WORLD WOULD ANYONE WANT TO WRITE ABOUT DEL CHIMNEY?
CALL MY FRIEND 'RUDE' AGAIN, BITCH! I DARE YOU...
HERE, CUNT! YOU FORGOT YOUR OTHER SHOE!
STOP
1

DID YOU GUYS SEE TERRY FLATTEN THAT JULIE WREE CHICK? KILLER!
YEAH, I WISH I HAD A GOOD LOOKING GIRL WITH A GREAT RIGHT CROSS TO JUMP AT THE SNAP OF MY FINGER.
HOPEY'LL BE REWARDING HER TONIGHT. THEY LET ME WATCH ONE TIME.

IZZY'S NOT EVEN HOME, HOPEY. WE CAME ALL THIS WAY FOR NOTHING.
NO, WE DIDN'T. LOOK, TERRY...
LOMA

SEE THAT GIRL RIGHT THERE? THE SHORTER ONE? I HATE HER.
HOW COME?
'CAUSE SHE'S A BITCH.

LOOK AT THAT LITTLE SNIT. IF SHE WASN'T WITH THAT GIRL, I'D...
WELL, SHIT! I CAN HANDLE THE BIGGER ONE. WELL, MAYBE...

NO WAY, TERRY! YOU WANNA DIE, OR WHAT? REMEMBER, THAT'S THE CHUCA WHO KICKED DEL'S ASS UP AND DOWN THE STREET WITH A CHICKEN WIRE FENCE.
OH.

GOD, I KNOW WHAT YOU MEAN ABOUT THAT LITTLE SNIT, HOPEY. LOOK AT HER, ACTING ALL HOT SHIT JUST BECAUSE SHE HAS ALL THAT BACK UP. PEOPLE LIKE THAT DESERVE A GOOD, HEALTHY ASS BEATING.

LOOK, HOPEY! SHE'S COMING BACK THIS WAY, AND SHE'S ALONE!
2

GO AHEAD, HOPEY. KICK HER ASS NOW. I'LL BE BEHIND YOU. YOU CAN DO IT...

HI, MAGGIE. HOW ARE YOU? REMEMBER ME? I'M HOPEY, ISABEL'S FRIEND.
!
HI.

NICE SEEING YOU AGAIN. BYE BYE NOW.
YOU... FUCKING... BITCH...

I KNOW WHAT YOU'RE DOING. YOU DID THAT JUST TO GET AT ME! YOU'RE ALWAYS TRYING TO MAKE ME LOOK LIKE SHIT! YOU KNOW WHAT YOU ARE...?

HEY, MAGGIE! WAIT UP!

I DON'T GET IT, IZZY. NOW ALL OF A SUDDEN SHE'S BEING REAL NICE TO ME AND EVERYTHING. DO YOU THINK SHE REALLY WANTS TO BE FRIENDS OR IS SHE JUST BULLSHITTING?
OH, I DON'T KNOW, MIJA. I CAN'T TALK RIGHT NOW. I HAVE TO GET ALL THESE WEDDING INVITES OUT RIGHT AWAY.

DAMN! THOSE MOTHS ARE EXTRA CRAZY TONIGHT. WAIT, THOSE AREN'T MOTHS. SOMEONE'S THROWING ROCKS AT MY WINDOW. IF IT'S THOSE BRATS NEXT DOOR, I SWEAR I'LL...
TAK!
TAK
3

WHO'S OUT THERE?
IT'S ME, HOPEY! REMEMBER? THE OTHER DAY I ASKED YOU IF YOU'D WANNA GO TO A PARTY.

IT'S AT DEL CHIMNEY'S HOUSE. HE SAYS HE KNOWS YOU.
WELL, OK. BUT I GOTTA SNEAK OUT. MY TIA DOESN'T LIKE ME STAYING OUT LATE ON SCHOOL NIGHTS.

SO HOW THE HELL DO YOU HAPPEN TO KNOW A CREEP LIKE DEL?
I USED TO ALWAYS GO OVER WITH MY COUSIN LICHA TO SCORE DRUGS FROM HIM. BUT I HAVEN'T BEEN OVER SINCE SHE BEAT HIM WITH A CHICKEN WIRE FENCE. SHE CAN BE MEAN...

HEY, HOPEY! TERRY'S LOOKING FOR YOU.
HI.
WHO'S THAT, HOPEY? FINALLY PICKING ON SOMEONE YOUR OWN SIZE?
FUCK YOU, DOYLE! COME ON, MAG.
GROWING TIRED OF THIS USELESS SITU

YEAH, I'VE SEEN YOU IN SCHOOL. YOU KNOW RAY DOMINGUEZ? HE'S OUR HOME BOY.
YEAH, I KNOW HIM.
YEAH, SOMETIMES WE GET TO HOLD UP THE WALL WITH ALL THE CHOLOS AT LUNCH.

I DON'T SEE WHAT YOU'RE SO PISSED OFF ABOUT, TERRY. SHE'S JUST SOME CHOLA FRIEND OF IZZY'S. IT'S NO BIG DEAL. C'MAN...
WELL FUCK, HOPEY. I NEVER PULL THIS SHIT ON YOU...
Suck me raw, Del
MANDO PANDO
4

I MEAN, I TRY TO BE COOL TO YOU AND EVERYTHING, HOPEY...
OH GOD, TERRY! STOP! I CAN FEEL THEM BURRITOS COMING UP LIKE CHINGA!

ONE NIGHT LATER...
A MECHANIC? NO KIDDING? LIKE CARS AN' STUFF?
MOSTLY.

MAN, I COULDN'T DO ANYTHING LIKE THAT. BUT, I CAN ALMOST PLAY "LOUIE LOUIE" ON BASS. TERRY CAN PLAY IT ALL THE WAY THROUGH ON GUITAR.
YOU GUYS REALLY LIVE HERE IN THIS CLOSET?

YEAH, BUT ONLY 'CAUSE ME AN' TERRY WON'T LET DEL TAKE US TO BED.
YOU ALMOST DID.
YOU GUYS RAN AWAY FROM HOME, OR DID YOU GET KICKED OUT?

I LEFT 'CAUSE MY MOM HATES ME. BUT THAT'S COOL, 'CAUSE I HATE HER WORSE. WHY DO YOU ASK?
'CAUSE MY TIA IS DRIVING ME NUTSO! I GOTTA GET OUTTA THAT HOUSE, FAST!
WHAT IS A TEE-AH?

AN' YOU DON'T EVEN BOTHER COMING HOME ON WEEKENDS! AN' WHAT'S ALL THIS SHIT ON YOUR FACE? AN' THOSE CLOTHES! I CAN'T TELL WHETHER YOU'RE A GOD DAMN WHORE OR A GOD DAMN BUM!
HOW 'BOUT A TRAMP? NO, JUS' KIDDING.
BING BON
KNO
KNOCK
KNO

W-WAIT! I'LL GET THAT, TIA. IT'S PROBABLY FOR ME.
OH NO YOU DON'T! I'M GONNA SEE WHAT KINDA GUTTER TRASH YOU'VE BEEN HANGIN' AROUND WITH...
KNO
K
5

HI. MAGGIE IN?

AND WHAT THE HELL ARE YOU SUPPOSED TO BE? I KNOW IT AIN'T HUMAN...
WELL, HAR DE HAR HAR...

GOSH, MAGGIE. I'VE ALWAYS WONDERED WHAT THE BOTTOM OF KING KONG'S SHORTS LOOK LIKE, AN' THIS WHOLE TIME...

I GOTTA ADMIT I WAS PRETTY SCARED WHEN SHE LIFTED ME OVER HER HEAD. MAGGIE SHOULDA GOT AN AWARD FOR PLAYING POCAHONTAS THE WAY SHE DID...
AND NOW SHE'S BACK LIVING WITH THAT WOMAN. FATE SURE HAS A WEIRD SENSE OF HUMOR.

BULLSHIT! TWO PAIRS DOES NOT BEAT THREE OF A KIND!
NO, BUT FOUR KNUCKLES DOES.
END

FLASHBACK MANIA
PSST! HEY, MAGGOT.
MMM... WHAT'S WRONG, HOPEY?

I WAS JUST THINKING. WHAT IF ONE MORNING WE WOKE UP AND I LOOKED EXACTLY, SCAR FOR SCAR, LIKE CHUCK CONNORS?
I... HUH?

WHAT WOULD YOU DO?
WHA...SPUT! NOTHING! GO TO SLEEP!!

OH, WELL. I WAS JUST WONDERING, THA'S ALL.
CHUCK CONNORS. SHEE...
LOCO 86

A date with Hopey
Prince 86-87

HI. YOU DON'T KNOW ME, BUT MY NAME'S HENRY, AND I DIDN'T ALWAYS LOOK LIKE A SLOB. NO, A FEW YEARS AGO I LOOKED LIKE THIS PICTURE. NO KIDDING.

LOUIS

"IN THE SUMMERTIME ME AND SOME FRIENDS USED TO HANG OUT AT A PLACE CALLED 'CHIMNEY'S ISLAND OF LOST SOULS.' IT WAS ACTUALLY A HOUSE IN THE MIDDLE OF A MEXICAN NEIGHBORHOOD THE LOCALS CALL 'HOPPERS.' I THINK THEY CALL IT THAT BECAUSE THE CHOLOS PUT HYDRAULICS IN THEIR LOWRIDER CARS TO MAKE THEM HOP.

?
YAY!
POW!
OW!
WAH!

"ANYWAY, THIS ISLAND WAS A PRETTY COOL PLACE TO HANG AROUND. ALL KINDS OF WEIRDOS AND LOWLIFES COULD PLAY THEMSELVES AND NOT HAVE TO WORRY ABOUT IMPRESSING ANYBODY. ONE COULD ALSO CRASH THERE A NIGHT OR TWO IF HE HAD NOWHERE ELSE TO GO. AND THAT IS WHERE I MET THESE CHICKS NAMED HOPEY AND MAGGIE.

?
JED

"I NEVER THOUGHT I COULD BE SUCH GOOD FRIENDS WITH GIRLS, TO TELL YOU THE TRUTH. I'VE ALWAYS HAD TROUBLE WITH THEM IN ONE WAY OR ANOTHER. MAYBE IT'S THE GIRLS I HUNG OUT WITH, MAYBE IT'S ME, I DON'T KNOW. BUT I REALLY, HONESTLY LIKED HOPEY AND MAGGIE, AND I BELIEVE THEY REALLY, HONESTLY LIKED ME. COOL, HUH?

"WELL, AFTER AWHILE I HAD TO STOP HANGING AROUND DEL'S ISLAND BECAUSE MY STUPID BUDDIES (WHO SUPPLIED OUR TRANSPORTATION) GOT TOO DRUNK AND OUT OF HAND ONE NIGHT AND WERE ALMOST KILLED BY A GANG OF CHOLOS DOWN THE STREET. I NEVER EVEN GOT TO SAY GOOD-BYE TO HOPEY AND MAGGIE. BUMMER.

1

"THE ONLY TIME I'D GET TO SEE THOSE GIRLS AGAIN WOULD BE AT ONE OF THE LOCAL GIGS. THEY'D BE RUNNING AROUND STARTING FIGHTS WITH LONG HAIRS AND LETTING THEIR GUY FRIENDS FINISH THEM.

"I NEVER GOT TO SAY ANYTHING MORE THAN HI TO THEM, THOUGH. THEY WERE TOO BUSY PLAYING 'HOT, SNOTTY NOSED PUNK CHICKS' AND PRETENDING THEY WERE IN LOVE WITH EACH OTHER. I THEN FIGURED THEY ONLY HUNG OUT WITH ME BECAUSE THEY NEEDED SOMEONE TO FEED THEIR EGOS.

"ONCE SCHOOL STARTED, PARTYING AND GOING TO GIGS DIED DOWN AND LIFE BECAME BORING AGAIN. THEN, ONE NIGHT I MET HOPEY AND MAGGIE ON MY SIDE OF TOWN IN A BOWLING ALLEY BUYING RUBBERS IN THE MEN'S BATHROOM. IT WAS MY TURN TO SHINE THEM ON.
SLOW JOE BLOW

"BUT WOULDN'T YOU KNOW IT, THEY WERE ABSOLUTE ANGELS, JUST LIKE AT CHIMNEY'S ISLAND. I TOLD 'EM WHAT SNOBS THEY WERE BEING EARLIER AND THEY QUICKLY APOLOGIZED. I'VE ALWAYS BEEN A SUCKER FOR SOULFUL EYES AND POUTY LIPS. ESPECIALLY ON PRETTY GIRLS. I GUESS WE WERE BEST FRIENDS AGAIN.

"THAT NIGHT TURNED OUT GREAT. THE THREE OF US GOT DRUNK AND WALKED THE STREETS FOR HOURS, DOING NOTHING, YET EVERYTHING. WHEN IT WAS TIME TO CASH IT IN, WE EXCHANGED NUMBERS. BUT, LIKE A STUPID DRUNK, I LOST THEIRS BEFORE I EVEN GOT HOME.

"WEEKS PASSED, AND NO WORD FROM THE GIRLS. I SORT OF FELT LIKE A SUCKER AGAIN. THEN I GET A CALL FROM HOPEY AND WE'RE PALS AGAIN. THOUGH, THIS TIME SHE DIDN'T STOP CALLING. AFTER AWHILE, WE LIVED TOGETHER ON THE PHONE. THEN, I KNEW HOPEY WAS TRUE BLUE.
I THOUGHT I TOLD YOU KIDS NOT TO PLAY ON THAT ONE!
2

"PRETTY SOON I BOUGHT A CAR FOR THREE HUNDRED BUCKS AND HOPEY AND MAGGIE GOT THEIR OWN APARTMENT TOGETHER IN HOPPERS, SO I WAS OVER THERE EIGHT NIGHTS OUT OF THE WEEK. IT WAS GREAT. I MEAN, WE WERE ALL THESE GREAT FRIENDS, Y'KNOW?
431-451

"AFTER AWHILE, MAGGIE COULDN'T HANG AROUND BECAUSE OF BOY-FRIEND PROBLEMS, OR WHATEVER. I HAD THIS FEELING ROMANCE WOULD SOMEHOW BREAK UP OUR LITTLE THREESOME. BUT I FIGURED, THAT'S LIFE, I GUESS.

"PRETTY SOON HOPEY AND I WOULD MEET AT GIGS AND HANG OUT TO-GETHER THE WHOLE NIGHT. THAT'S WHEN IT HIT ME LIKE A SLEDGEHAMMER. YEP, I FELL IN LOVE WITH THIS GIRL. MAN, I COULDN'T HELP MYSELF.

"SO ONE NIGHT I ASKED HOPEY TO BE MY OFFICIAL GIRLFRIEND. WELL, FOR HOURS SHE TRIED EVERY TRICK TO DODGE THE ISSUE AND I DON'T QUITE REMEMBER IF SHE EVEN ANSWERED. ALL I KNEW WAS THAT I WANTED HER BAD. I GUESS THAT'S WHY THEY SAY LOVE IS BLIND, Y'THINK?

"THE NEXT NIGHT I WAS SUPPOSED TO MEET HER AT SOME CORNER FOR OUR FIRST OFFICIAL 'DATE' AND THEN WE'D TAKE IT FROM THERE. I SHOULD HAVE REALIZED WHAT KIND OF 'DATE' IT WOULD BE WHEN I SAW MAGGIE WAITING WITH HER.

"I COULDN'T BELIEVE HOW COLD AND DISTANT HOPEY ACTED TOWARD ME. LIKE SHE HARDLY KNEW ME. WELL, AFTER THE MISERABLE NIGHT ENDED, PISSED OFF AND HURT, I CONFRONTED HOPEY ALONE. SHE PLAYED DUMB, AND WE PARTED NOT EXACTLY FRIENDS.
3

"THE NEXT MORNING WAS LIKE I WOKE UP FROM A WEIRD DREAM. ALL OF A SUDDEN THERE I WAS IN MY BED. NO MORE HOPEY, NO MORE MAGGIE, NO MORE HANGING OUT. IT WAS BACK TO HOW IT WAS BEFORE I EVER MET THEM. STRANGE.

"IT TOOK ME DAYS TO FIGURE OUT WHAT HAPPENED TO OUR FRIENDSHIP. I GUESS THERE'S JUST SOME PEOPLE WHO YOU SHOULD NOT GET TOO CLOSE TO IF YOU WANNA KEEP 'EM, HUH? BUT, I WAS IN LOVE, MAN!

"THREE WEEKS AFTER THAT FATEFUL NIGHT, HOPEY CALLS ME. WE TALKED AND TALKED LIKE NOTHING HAPPENED. IT WASN'T THE SAME. SHE NEVER CALLED AGAIN AFTER THAT.

"I SAW HER ABOUT SIX MONTHS AFTER THAT WHILE LEAVING AN APE SEX GIG. SHE WAS YELLING AT THE GUY WHO RUNS THE DOOR. SHE DIDN'T SEE ME, AND I COULDN'T BUILD UP THE COURAGE TO WALK UP AND TALK TO HER. THAT WAS MY LAST PUNK GIG."
APE
SEX

IT'S BEEN A FEW YEARS AND SOMETIMES I WANNA PICK UP THAT PHONE AND GIVE HOPEY A CALL, BUT I DON'T KNOW IF SHE'S STILL THERE, OR WHAT. I STILL CAN'T BELIEVE WHAT A GOOD THING WE HAD GOING...

The end

TWO DOLLAR DRESS... RATTY HAIR... COMBAT BOOTS... HEAVY DATE, SHRIMP?

WHY DON'T YOU SHUT YOUR PIG FACE?

NINA/GODMOTHER

HOW WAS YOUR TRIP TO NEW MEXICO, IZZY? DID YOU DO A LOT OF INDIAN STUFF?
NOT REALLY. I WAS SICK THE WHOLE TWO WEEKS.
AND DO YOU KNOW WHO ELSE IS BACK?

CAN YOU BELIEVE IT? ONE HUNDRED AND SIX IN THE SHADE AND I CAUGHT A COLD.
CHIVITA DOMINGUEZ'S BOY, RAY. HE WAS GOING TO A UNIVERSITY BACK EAST THE PAST FEW YEARS.
OOH...

SO, TELL ME, MIJA. WHAT KIND OF SHENANIGANS DID YOU AND HOPITA COOK UP WHILE I WAS GONE?
I'D APPRECIATE IT IF WE DIDN'T DISCUSS HER RIGHT NOW.

SO, ARE YOU GIRLS GOING TO LET ME UNPACK, OR WHAT?
AW, WE'LL LEAVE BEFORE HE GETS BACK. FIRST, YOU GOTTA TELL US ALL ABOUT YOUR HONEYMOON!
BUT LEAVE OUT THE BEDROOM STUFF. THAT SHIT'S OBVIOUS...
PLINK
PLANK
PLUNK
PLONK
PLINK
PLONK

WELL, FRANCE WAS OK. DON'T TELL JACK, BUT I STILL WOULD HAVE RATHER GONE TO MEXICO.
ME AN' HOPEY ALMOST WENT TO TIJUANA YESTERDAY.

YEAH, DEL WANTED US TO SMUGGLE SOME DOPE FOR HIM OUTTA THERE...
BUT, WE CHICKENED OUT AT THE LAST MINUTE.

WHAT DO YOU MEAN "WE"? YOU CHICKENED OUT!
SO DID YOU!
OK! PARTY'S OVER! I HAVE TO UNPACK! NOW!
3

OYE, MAGGIE. WHAT ARE YOU DOING STANDING OVER HERE BY YOURSELF?
I'M LOOKING FOR MY SISTER, SPEEDY. WHAT ARE YOU DRINKING?

VATO'S GOLD FROM THE KEG. IT'S ALL FOAM, THOUGH. HEY, HOW COME I HAVEN'T SEEN YOU HANGING AROUND?
I DUNNO. I'VE BEEN LIVING WITH MY AUNT LATELY.

WAY OUT THERE? NO WONDER I DON'T GET TO SEE YOU. I'VE KINDA MISSED YOU, Y'KNOW?
SPEEDY...

WHAT'S WRONG?
NOTHING. I JUST WANNA FIND MY SISTER.

FUCKIN' B-- YOU'RE REAL HARD TO FIGURE OUT AT TIMES, YOU KNOW THAT?
YEAH, ME TOO.
FUCKING BASTARD! YOU NEVER WANTED ME BEFORE!
!

WHERE YOU GOING, YOU LITTLE PEARL YOU?
ESTHER BABIES! I WAS LOOKING ALL OVER FOR YOU!
4

YEAH, THAT'S MOM ALL RIGHT! SHE'S ALL GLAMOUR NOW 'CAUSE SHE GOT A JOB AT THE UNEMPLOYMENT OFFICE.
NO KIDDING? SO, HOW IS LIFE IN MONTOYA, LATELY? OR SHOULD I SAY, "DAIRYTOWN"?
CAMARGO
40

KINDA DEAD. IT ISN'T HALF AS COOL AS HOPPERS. AT LEAST YOU HAVE CUTE GUYS HERE.
YEAH, BUT AS ALL THINGS GO, YOU NEVER KNOW WHICH ONES ARE GONNA BE TRULY NICE.

YEAH? HOW ABOUT THE GUY WITH THE ONE EYEBROW YOU WERE TALKING TO?
OH, SURE. SPEEDY WILL SHOW YOU A GREAT TIME. FIRST, HE'LL SHOW YOU HIS FAVORITE TATTOOS...

TATTOOS, HUH? YOU THINK HE'LL SHOW THEM TO ME? HUH, PERLITA?
OH, STOP, ESTHER! HE'S... ESTHER!

SHIT...

WHAT WERE YOU TRYING TO DO, FINISH THAT KEG ALL BY YOURSELF?
YEAH, I WAS HOPING I'D DROWN MYSELF AFTER A WHILE, SO THEN I'D... NEVER MIND.

SO, HOW LONG WILL HOPEY BE GONE?
TWO WHOLE FUCKING MONTHS! CAN YOU BELIEVE THAT SHIT?
URP
¡PERLITA! MAGGIE!
5

IF YOU TALK TO MOM, TELL HER I'M GETTING A RIDE HOME LATER ON, OK?
OK...

MIJA, WHY DON'T YOU COME INSIDE AND LIE DOWN FOR AWHILE. YOU LOOK TIRED.
NO, I'M ALL RIGHT, IZZY. IT'S JUST KINDA WEIRD BEING BUZZED IN THE DAYTIME, Y'KNOW...

YOU'RE SURE YOU'RE ALL RIGHT?
I'M FINE. SEE YOU LATER, ISABEL.

FAT

6

SPARX
½ OF
SALE

REALLY, JULIE? THEY ACTUALLY WENT ON TOUR WITH THE 40 THIEVES? HOW?
I THINK TERRY KNOWS THE GUITAR PLAYER.
THAT'S WAY TOO WEIRD!

BUT TERRY'S BAND IS SO BAD! THEY'RE GOING TO BOMB LIKE REAL TERRIBLE!
I ONLY HOPE THEIR VAN HITS HEAD ON WITH A TRAIN... WHILE TERRY AND HOPEY ARE IN THE DRIVER'S SEAT!
I WONDER IF THEY TOOK-- OH.

NOT VERY BITCHIN' WITHOUT YOUR BACK UP, ARE YOU?
GUESS NOT.

WHY ARE YOU GUYS WALKING SO FAST?
7

MAGGIE?! AIN'T YA SUPPOSED TO BE WORKIN' RIGHT NOW?
I QUIT YESTERDAY, DANITA. NONE OF THAT SPINNIN' SHAKES SHIT FOR ME NO MORE.

REALLY? DID YA KNOW THAT I QUIT, TOO?
UH UH! WHEN?
JUS' NOW. I GOT BETTER THINGS TO DO. LIKE GETTING LIQUOR FOR US BOTH. WE'RE CELEBRATIN'!

HOW MUCH MONEY DO WE HAVE?
WAIT! LEMME SEE... THREE... FOUR BUCKS!
THAT'LL GET US TWO BOTTLES OF OLD BARN OWL.
OR A TWELVER OF VATO'S!
OR A CASE OF BLITZEN-MEISTER!

NOW MUST WE WAIT FOR SOMEBODY WHO IS OLD ENOUGH TO BUY FOR US?
I AIN'T GONNA ASK NO CHOLOS OR CRIPS THIS TIME!
HERE COMES YOUR FRIEND HOPEY, DAFFY. SHE'S OLD ENOUGH TO BUY, ISN'T SHE?

MAGGIE! I THOUGHT YOU WENT ON TOUR WITH HOPEY'S BAND!
CAN ONE OF YOU BUY BEER FOR US?
I'M NOT TWENTY-ONE YET.
ME NEITHER. SAY...
RAY'S

AW, SHEEIT... YOU AIN'T REALLY NO INDIAN. I SEE THAT NOW!
OH, WAIT. IF McNUTTY'S WORKING, HE'LL PROBABLY SELL TO ME.
WE'RE LUCKY! HE IS WORKING TODAY!
8

DANG! HOW WAS I SUPPOSED TO KNOW McNUTTY HAS A TWIN BROTHER?
WHAT DO WE DO NOW?
YOU ALL IS CRAZY! GIMME THAT MONEY! I'LL GET US SOME LIQUOR!

HEY, THIS ISN'T THE KIND OF BEER WE WANTED!
THE COLT?
IT'S FINE, IT'S FINE! THANK YOU VERY MUCH! BYE MAGGIE!
CHEE, MAGGIE! WHERE DO YOU FIND 'EM?
HEY, DANITA...

I COULDN'T TELL, BUT, THAT GUY WHO BOUGHT THE BEER...
BLANDINA DOMINGUEZ'S BROTHER, RAY. I THOUGHT HE DIED...

HEY, DOYLET PAPER! YOU CRUSTY POOR WHITE TRASH PIECE O' SHIT!

HEY, RAY D. ATE HER! YOU GREASY WETBACK SHIT MONGER!

YOU'RE A HARD MAN TO FIND. YOUR FAMILY HAD ME RUNNING IN CIRCLES.
I TOLD 'EM TO WAKE ME WHEN YOU CAME BY. THEY DIDN'T TELL ME SHIT, SO I WENT TO THE LIQUOR STORE FOR A MINUTE. SORRY, MAN...

'S COOL. AT LEAST THEY GOT TO WARN ME ABOUT WHAT A SCHOLAR YOU ARE NOW.
HA! BOY, HAVE I GOT A STORY TO TELL YOU...
9

STILL CAN'T GET OVER THAT VATO WITH THE HAIRCUT.
AW, C'MON. YOU'RE NOT GONNA TELL ME YOU'VE NEVER SEEN SOMEONE WITH A MOHAWK.

HAVEN'T YOU EVER SEEN THOSE GUYS LIKE ON TV, MOVIES AN' COMICS AN' SHIT LIKE THAT? THEY ALWAYS MAKE 'EM REAL BAD ASSES...
THAT VATO DIDN'T SEEM LIKE NO BAD ASS TO ME.

WELL, JUST 'CAUSE SOME GUY WEARS A MOHAWK DOESN'T MAKE HIM A BAD ASS.
SO, THEN TV AN' ALL THEM OTHERS ARE FULLA SHIT, HUH?

OF COURSE THEY ARE! THERE AIN'T NO ESCAPE FOR THESE POOR KIDS...
FUCK THE POOR KIDS! WHAT ABOUT ALL THEM DEAD INDIANS?

HOW DO YOU THINK THEY'D FEEL IF THEY SAW SILLY OL' WHITE MAN WALKIN' AROUND IN INDIAN 'DOS?
ON A VIDEO YET!

WANNA KNOW SOMETHING, DANITA? I USED TO THINK YOU WERE... WELL, DIDN'T HAVE MUCH TO SAY. BUT, NOW...
PEOPLE ALWAYS THINK THAT ABOUT ME. BUT I CAN BE SMART SOMETIMES.

THEN YOU'D HAVE A BALL TALKING TO OL' CHUCHO OVER THERE. EVERY TIME ME ANY MY FRIEND HOPEY PASS HIM HE ALWAYS HAS SOMETHING NEW AND INTERESTING TO SAY.
SO LET'S SEE WHAT HE HAS TO SAY TODAY.
10

HE ONLY SPEAKS SPANISH, SO I'LL TRY TO TRANSLATE FOR YOU.
HEY CHUCHO!
HE'S ALSO HARD OF HEARING.
SO AM I... NOW.

<SO, I SEE YOU HAVE REPLACED THE GIRL WHO PRETENDS TO BE A MAN.>
<THAT'S ME, CHUCHO. CAN'T MAKE UP MY MIND WHO I WANNA BE SEEN WITH.>

<YOU KNOW, YOU CAN LAUGH, BUT DURING ALL THAT LAUGHTER ALL THOSE MEN THAT ARE SO IMPORTANT TO YOUR LIFE ARE SLOWLY SLIPPING AWAY.>
OH, HORRORS! WHAT EVER SHALL I DO WITHOUT MY MAN?

<LITTLE DO YOU KNOW THAT RIGHT NOW SOME BEST FRIEND OR EVEN A RELATIVE IS SCOOPING THEM UP RIGHT BEHIND YOUR BACK.>
<THEN, I'D BETTER GO STRAIGHT TO HIM AND DEMAND THAT HE BEAT ME RAW WITH THAT HOT WHEELTRACK TILL I BLEED, HUH?>

<JUST REMEMBER WHAT I SAID.>
<SURE, JUST LIKE THE TIME I WAS GONNA MARRY YOUR GRANDSON. RIGHT, CHUCHO?>

WHA'D HE SAY, MAGGIE? IT SOUNDED REAL FUNNY...

MAGGIE...?
HUH? NOTHING. I WAS JUST... LET'S GO CELEBRATE QUITTING OUR JOBS.
11

OOH, REET!

I DIDN'T KNOW YOU'RE A MAMA, DANITA. I CAN'T BELIEVE WHAT A DREAM HE IS!
DO YOU LIKE YOUR MARGARITA WITH TEQUILA, OR YOUR TEQUILA WITH MARGARITA MIX?

...AN' I'LL BE DANCIN' ON A PONY KEG...

KA-POW!
LOOK AT THAT BUTT! I'LL BET I COULD BALANCE THIS DRINK ON IT NO SWEAT, BOY!
OH, YEAH? I'LL BET I COULD SERVE BREAKFAST ON YOURS. SAY, WE'RE OUTTA STUFF!

LOOKS LIKE WE'LL HAVE TO DRINK THIS SHIT STRAIGHT.
LET 'ER POUR, ELEANOR BICUSPIDOR.

DANG, DANITA! I CAN'T GET OVER IT! JUS' LOOK AT YOU, WOMAN!
WHA'S WRONG?

I MEAN, YOU'RE ALL WOMAN! I'LL BET MEN WEAR THEIR BEST SUITS TO WATCH YOU WALK DOWN THE STREET.
12

MAGGIE, COULD I ASK YOU A QUESTION, BUT PROMISE YOU WON'T GET MAD?
GO'HEAD THEN, FRED.
9:48

I DON'T MEAN THIS BAD, BUT... ARE YOU A FAG?
HEE HEE HEE YA HA HA HA HA HA HA HA HA!

AW, YOU AIN'T! I JUS' THOUGHT...
OH, YEAH? YOU KNOW WHAT I DID A COUPLA WEEKS AGO, AND LIKED?

I MADE LOVE TO MY BEST FRIEND HOPEY, AND IT WASN'T THE FIRST TIME NEITHER...
HEY, I DIDN'T MEAN NOTHIN'. I JUS' ASKED...

BUT, YOU DON'T UNDERSTAND. I DON'T THINK I COULD DO IT WITH JUST ANY GIRL OTHER THAN HOPEY. WELL, I NEVER REALLY TRIED, BUT... I DUNNO, I CAN'T EXPLAIN IT...

SEE, HOPEY'S LIKE... WELL, SHE'S REALLY A BITCH SOMETIMES... MOST OF THE TIME... BUT, SHE'S THE ONLY PERSON WHO... SEE, EVERYBODY ALWAYS TELLS ME SHE'S THIS AN' THAT, AND THAT I SHOULD... I SHOULD...

NOW SHE'S GONE ON TOUR WITH TERRY... FUCK IT...

WHO EVER TOLD YOU YOU COULD CUT HAIR OUGHTA BE SHOT!
RELAX, MAGGOT! YOU GET WAY TOO EMOTIONAL AT TIMES.
34
13

I SUPPOSE TERRY SAID THAT, TOO?
AS A MATTER OF FACT, SHE DID, MAGGOT.

WHAT DID YOU WRITE? LEMME DO SOME!
AH, LET'S GO. THAT CEMENT IS DRY ALREADY.
WET CEMENT

GOD, THIS DAY IS SO BORING! WE SHOULD GO MEET SOME GUYS OR SOMETHING.
GUYS?

YEAH! DON'T TELL ME MEETING GUYS AIN'T THE "PUNK" THING TO DO.
THUTHUTHU THUTHUTHUTHU... AWRIGHT, AWRIGHT!

OK, SO LET'S GO MEET SOME "GUYS".
OH, SHUT... HEY, LOOKIT, HOKEY!

SEE THAT GUY? THAT'S RAY DOMINGUEZ. HE'S MY BOYFRIEND.
THAT GUY?

WELL, SHOOT! THEN DON'T YA THINK IT'S TIME FOR A FEW INTRODUCTIONS?
WAIT! NO, HOPEY! DON'T SAY ANYTHING TO HIM...

HE'S NOT MY REAL BOYFRIEND. WE JUST KINDA... AH, SHIT! I'M DEAD!
♫

C'MON, I AIN'T PLAYIN', MAGGIE! YOU GOTTA GO LIKE, RIGHT NOW!
14

WHA...? WHAT TIME IS IT?
THREE-THIRTY. C'MON, MY DADDY'S HOME AND HE'S DRUNK AND PISSED OFF AS HELL.

OK, OK! NO NEED TO PUSH! I'M LEAVING ALREADY, DANITA!
SHH... NOT THE DOOR. THE WINDOW. CAN'T LET HIM KNOW YOU'RE HERE.

SORRY, MAGGIE. SEE YOU LATER, HUH?
OK...

!
OOF!

WHO THE HELL PUT THE GROUND RIGHT HERE?

HOW DO YA LIKE THAT? THREE-THIRTY IN THE MORNING AN' MY BED IS FIFTEEN MILES AWAY AN' I AIN'T GOT MY RIDE. I BETTER GET GOING...

GEE, I WONDER IF DANITA REALLY KICKED ME OUT OF HER HOUSE 'CAUSE I SAID SOMETHING RUDE. MAN, I ALWAYS DO THIS! GET TOO DRUNK AND THEN... C'MON, CHICK! WAKE UP!
15

ONE TIME TO SOBER ME UP, RAY DOMINGUEZ MADE ME RUN THROUGH THE SPRINKLERS.

I CAN'T REMEMBER IF IT EVER WORKED, THOUGH.

NOW THAT I THINK OF IT, HE DID IT JUST TO MAKE A FOOL OF ME.
BRRRRR! WHAT THE HELL DID I DO WITH MY SHIRT?

FUCKIN' RAY. THE THREE YEARS YOU WERE AWAY, YOU WEREN'T EVEN IN SCHOOL? WHAT DID YOUR PARENTS SAY ABOUT THAT?
THEY STILL DON'T KNOW, DOYLE MAN. THEY THINK I WAS OUT MAKING SOMETHING OF MYSELF. IT'S BULLSHIT, MAN.
DODODONUTS

SO WHAT THE HELL DID YOU DO FOR THREE YEARS?
WORKED. PAINTED. HAD PASSIONATE LOVE AFFAIRS WITH CRAZED WOMEN ARTISTS. GOTTA TELL YA, IT WAS SURE A FAR CRY FROM LIFE IN HOPPERS.

PASSIONATE LOVE AFFAIRS, HUH? MAKES ME WONDER WHY YOU'D WANNA COME BACK.
MOM'S TORTILLAS. I DUNNO...

I'M STILL NOT SURE IF I'M STICKING AROUND. THERE'S NOT MUCH TO DO IN THIS TOWN. I'M SURPRISED YOU HAVEN'T TRIED TO LEAVE.
!

16

HI, DOYLE.
HEY, MAGGIE. SMALL WORLD. YOU REMEMBER RAY?
HOW YA DOIN'?

WE WERE JUST SPLITTIN'. YOU NEED A RIDE SOMEWHERE, MAGGIE?
OH, NO. I HAVE MY CAR JUST AROUND THE CORNER. THANKS ANYWAY, GUYS.

OK, THEN WE'LL SEE YOU, HUH?
BYE.

GOTTA HAND IT TO YOU, DOYLE MAN. YOU'VE ALWAYS HAD, WELL... UNIQUE FRIENDS.
YEAH, WELL I GUESS MAGGIE DOES LOOK A LOT DIFFERENT FROM THE LAST TIME YOU SAW HER.

WAIT A MINUTE! THAT WASN'T MAGGIE CHASCARRILLO...
YEAH. WHAT A STRANGE PLACE TO MEET HER AGAIN, HUH?

NO SHIT. YOU KNOW PEOPLE USED TO SAY SHE AND I WENT OUT. HELL, I HARDLY KNEW HER.
THOSE HIGH SCHOOL RUMORS, HUH? SHEE...

HEY, ARE YOU RAY?
YEAH.
VH13

I'M REAL GOOD FRIENDS IN SCHOOL WITH YOUR SISTER BUNDINA, AN' SHE TOLD ME ALL ABOUT YOU, DUDE.
BLANDINA.
VH13
17

WHATEVER. I JUST THOUGHT I'D SAY HI. IT'S REALLY NICE TO MEET YOU. BYE.
LATER.

I HATE YOU.
WHY? HE'S A DREAM, MAGGOT.
EL LOCO SPIDER

SO HE'S ALWAYS HATED MY GUTS. SO I STARTED THAT STUPID RUMOR JUST 'CAUSE I LIKED HIM. LIKE I LIKED RACE... AND SPEEDY...

I WONDER WHAT WOULD HAPPEN IF I SAT HERE LIKE THIS FOR THE REST OF MY LIFE.

HOPEY LOVES MAGG

DO YOU THINK THEY FOUND OUT AND ARE CALLING THE COPS?
WHY DO YOU THINK WE'RE RUNNING? HURRY IT UP, MAGGOT!
LIQUOR
QUOR

BUT... DIDN'T DEL KICK YOU AND TERRY OUT?
HE WENT TO SAN FRANCISCO! GET IN!

WHEW! ALL THAT FOR A LOUSY PACK OF CIGARETTES.
WHAT DO YOU MEAN? I GOT GUM, TOO!

YOU KNOW I'M STILL MAD AT YOU FOR WHAT YOU DID.
I TOLD YOU I DIDN'T TELL HIM ANYTHING ABOUT YOU! WHY DON'T YOU BELIEVE ME?
18

GOD, ALL I DID WAS TELL THE JERK I KNOW HIS SISTER, WHO I CAN'T EVEN STAND...
OK, I BELIEVE YOU...

EEYAAAHHHH! THAT'S WHY I LOVE YOU SO MUCH! YOU ARE SUCH A WEIRDO!
HEY! DON'T GRAB MY BOOBS! HEY, STOP! HOPEY!

HOPEY! WHAT ARE YOU...?

DON'T BUMP THE WALL!
IT'S NOT ME. DEL MUST HAVE BROUGHT BACK A FRIEND FROM FRISCO.
WEIRDOS
TEEN IDLES

ARE YOU MAD?
NO, JUST...

WOULDN'T YOU KNOW IT, MOM GAVE ME HER CAR KEY INSTEAD OF HER HOUSE KEY. I DON'T DARE WAKE HER AT FIVE IN THE MORNING.

I GUESS IT'S BACK TO SLEEPING IN A CAR. I WAS HOPING I'D NEVER HAVE TO DO THAT AGAIN...
OH, JESUS...
IZZY, THAT FUCKIN' BITCH... SOME FRIEND... SHEEIT...
19

WHAT KIND OF FRIEND WON'T EVEN LET YOU BORROW THEIR COUCH FOR ONE LOUSY, STINKIN' NIGHT?
SHIT--- FUCK--- PISS---

HEY, C'MON. WHY DON'T YOU LET ME TAKE YOU HOME?

THANKS.
HEY, WHAT ARE YOU DOING TOMORROW? OR SHOULD I SAY, THIS MORNING?

OK. WELL, MAYBE I'LL SEE YOU AROUND, HUH?

SHE CAN'T COME TO THE PHONE. SHE'S RUNNIN' A VERY HIGH TEMPERATURE. THESE KIDS, I TELL YA...
THE END

HAPPY HOUR
NO CLASH, SEX PISTOLS OR THE RAMONES IN 1987!
JERUSALEM CRICKETS
THE DIRT CLODS
THRAS
WEEKEND SURF PARTY!!!
40 THIEVES
BEERGUTS • LA LLORONA
ACTIVE THOUGHTS • RADDD
come + Support the cause!!!
hippie
JPA PARK • SAT 10 • 1 PM
$5 w/FLYER $7 WITHOUT $100 HIPPIES
JAIME 1987
APE SEX
BLAST
BYOB

SOMEWHERE ABOUT TWO THOUSAND MILES FROM HOME...
GASS
67
80
U HAUL
1

DID YOU CALL HER?
NO, I WAS GETTING CIGARETTES.

TWO WEEKS ON THE ROAD AND YOU STILL HAVEN'T CALLED HER. SHE MUST BE MIGHTY SORE BY NOW.
I DIDN'T WANNA LEAVE HER BEHIND. YOU HIPPIES WANTED TO LEAVE AT FOUR O'CLOCK IN THE MORNING.

ALL YOU HAD TO DO WAS TELL HER WE WERE LEAVING EARLIER THAN PLANNED.
OH, SO NOW IT'S MY FAULT SHE COULDN'T COME.

IT'S NOBODY'S FAULT. ALL I'M SAYING IS THAT YOU SHOULD CALL HER AND EXPLAIN IT TO HER. I'M SURE SHE'LL UNDERSTAND.
WHY DON'T YOU CALL HER AND EXPLAIN IT TO HER?

JESUS CHRIST. IF I'D HAVE KNOWN YOU WERE AFRAID OF HER...
YEAH, YOU KNOW EVERYTHING, DON'T YOU?

WHAT ARE THESE GUYS CALLED AGAIN?
LA LLORONA. THEY'RE TOURING WITH THE 40 THIEVES.
OH, WELL. AT LEAST THEY LOOK NICE ON STAGE.
2

I CAN'T BELIEVE WE ACTUALLY GOT PAID TODAY. NOW WE CAN EAT.
WE SHOULD SAVE MOST OF THIS MONEY IN CASE THE CAR BREAKS DOWN.
FUCK THE CAR! LET'S GET A MOTEL TONIGHT! I'LL JUST DIE IF I HAVE TO SLEEP IN THAT DEATHTRAP OR ON SOMEONE'S COLD FLOOR ANOTHER NIGHT STRAIGHT!

NO WAY! WE CAN'T TAKE A CHANCE ON THE CAR FUCKING UP!
C'MON, ZERO! JUST ONE LOUSY MOTEL ROOM...
WE WOULDN'T BE IN THIS BIND IF MAGGIE THE MECHANIC WAS WITH US.

YEAH, HOW COME SHE DIDN'T COME AFTER ALL?
DON'T YOU FUCKERS LOOK AT ME! I MEAN IT!
LET'S GET A MOTEL ROOM!

MMM... SORT OF MAKES YOU FORGET YOU'RE A MILLION MILES FROM HOME.

HEY! YOU SPILLED ALL THE FUCKIN' WINE, YOU ASSHOLE!
WELL, WHY DID YOU PUT IT WHERE I'D TRIP OVER IT?
!!!
3

ZERO, WHO ARE THESE PEOPLE?
CHECK IT OUT. THIS GUY CRACKS ME UP.
LOCAL SCENE MAKERS. I DIDN'T KNOW THIS STATE GREW PUNKS.

HEY, WHY DON'T YOU PEOPLE PARTY SOMEWHERE ELSE? SOME OF US HAVE TO DRIVE TWO HUNDRED MILES IN THE MORNING.
LET'S GO. IT'S A RERUN, ANYWAY.

ROCK STARS.
I KNOW. TSK!
HEY, KID. I'LL GIVE YOU MY LAST CIGARETTE IF YOU MAKE A PHONE CALL FOR ME.
NYEH! I DON'T SMOKE.
PHONE

I'LL GIVE YOU THE REST OF MY BEER, THEN...
NYEH! I DON'T DRINK.

C'MON! JUST MAKE THIS CALL FOR ME. THERE'S THIS REALLY HOT CHICK IN CALIFORNIA THAT...
CALIFORNIA?? DOUBLE NYEH!

TAKE THE BEER ANYWAY, YOU FUCKIN' STRAIGHTEDGE FAGGOT!

DID YOU...?
SHUT UP.
APE SEX
4

SIX FLAGS OVER HARDCORE SHORES

SO, WE'RE KICKED OFF TONIGHT'S SHOW. IT'S NOT THE FIRST TIME, ZERO.
BUT THAT MAKES OUR NEXT GIG IN THREE DAYS. WHAT ARE WE GONNA DO FOR MONEY TILL THEN?
OK, THEN, WHAT DO YOU SUGGEST?

I SAY FUCK IT, AND LET'S GO HOME.
I GUESS THAT'S ALL WE CAN DO.
LUCKY DOG. NOW YOU DON'T HAVE TO CALL MAGGIE.
YOU KNOW WHERE TO PUT THIS...

OH, WELL. I WAS SORT OF LOOKING FORWARD TO WATCHING THE SUN RISE OVER THE OCEAN.
I'D RATHER SEE MY OWN BED RISE OVER THE OCEAN.

OH, C'MON, TERRY. YOU HAD FUN AND DON'T DENY IT.
OH, YES. I ESPECIALLY LOVED ALL THAT BOOING...

IT SURE BEAT SELLING COSMETICS AT MONTY'S.
FOR YOUR INFORMATION, LITTLE ONE, I QUIT THAT JOB SO I COULD GO ON THIS FUCKING TOUR!
5

YOU WOULDA ROTTED IN THAT FUCKING JOB ANYWAY.
LISTEN YOU...
OH, PLEASE! MUST YOU TWO CONSTANTLY QUARREL SO?

I SWEAR, IT'S LIKE TRAVELING WITH A BUNCH OF JERUSALEM CRICKETS.
A BUNCH OF WHATS??
YOU CAN TALK, MONICA...
HEY, LISTEN UP! I GOT US A GIG FOR TOMORROW!
U HAU

SATAN'S LAW NEED AN OPENING BAND AND THEY'LL GUARANTEE AT LEAST A HUNDRED BUCKS.
THEY'RE SPEED METAL, ZERO!
SO WHAT? WE CAN INSULT THEIR FANS.

YEAH, TERRY. WHERE'S THAT ROCK 'N' ROLL SPIRIT YOU OL' JERUSALEM CRICKET?
OK, THAT MEANS YOU HAVE TO CALL THE MAGPIE! AND I MEAN TONIGHT!
I JUST MAY SEE THAT SUN RISE OVER THAT OCEAN AFTER ALL.

IF YOU WERE REALLY HARD CORE, YOU'D HAVE THROWN A FULL BOTTLE.
EXIT

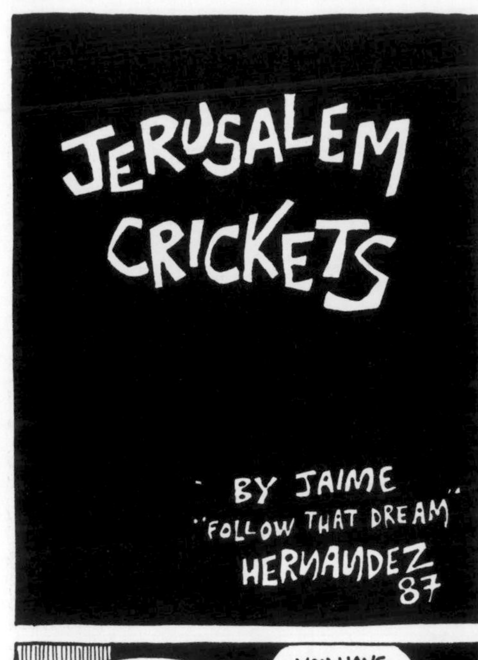
JERUSALEM CRICKETS
BY JAIME
"FOLLOW THAT DREAM"
HERNANDEZ
87

TERRY, I GOTTA HELP LOAD UP OUR SHIT!
IT CAN WAIT. COME ON.

YOU HAVE A CHOICE. TELEPHONE OR LETTER.
LETTER.

WHY ARE YOU SO ANXIOUS FOR ME TO WRITE THE MAGPIE? YOU HATE HER!
YOU HAVE TO CLEAR MY GOOD NAME, LOVE...
YFM

I JUST KNOW SHE THINKS I'M THE ONE RESPONSIBLE FOR LEAVING HER BEHIND ON THIS TOUR.
I KNEW IT WAS MORE THAN JUST THINKING OF MAGGIE...

I AM THINKING OF MAGGIE. SHE STILL MUST BE HEARTBROKEN WITHOUT A WORD FROM YOU YET.
SURE, SURE, OK.

DAMN! HOW DOES ANYONE START ONE OF THESE THINGS?
"DEAREST MAGPIE...

"SORRY I COULDN'T GET IN TOUCH WITH YOU EARLIER, BUT THIS PAST MONTH HAS BEEN VERY HECTIC FOR OUR BAND...
HOW DO YOU SPELL "HECTIC"?

"BY THE WAY, WE'RE ALSO SORRY YOU COULDN'T COME WITH US, BUT WE HAD TO GET AN EARLY START, AND YOU..."
SHE'S NOT GONNA BUY THAT!

IT'S THE TRUTH!
SO? COULDN'T I TELL HER WE GOT HIJACKED AND RAPED BY A BUNCH OF GUYS THAT LOOKED LIKE ED SULLIVAN?

"WE DIDN'T WANT TO WAKE YOU KNOWING HOW YOU LOVE YOUR SLEEP SO MUCH..."
HOW DO YOU KNOW THAT?

I DON'T KNOW THAT. YOU KNOW THAT!
HOW CAN YOU MAKE ME WRITE THAT IF YOU DON'T EVEN KNOW IT TO BE TRUE?

LOOK, DON'T TAKE ME LITERALLY! I'M JUST TRYING TO GIVE YOU AN IDEA OF WHAT TO WRITE!
OK, WHAT ELSE?

OH, I DON'T KNOW. TELL HER ABOUT PLACES AND BANDS WE'VE SEEN, I GUESS...
...AND THAT IT'S NOT YOUR FAULT...

THAT'S NOT FAIR. I'M REALLY TRYING TO BE NICE TO MAGGIE, BUT YOU WON'T GIVE ME A CHANCE.
OK, QUIET. I KNOW HOW TO FINISH THIS LETTER NOW.

"HUGS AND KISSES, HOPITA." THERE.

"P.S. TERRY HAS LOST EIGHT POUNDS WHILE ON TOUR."
AHA!
XAIME 87

VIDA LOCA

THE DEATH OF SPEEDY ORTIZ

JAIME 87

SO, HEY, MAGGIE. WHEN IS YOUR SISTER COMING FOR ANOTHER VISIT?

HOW SHOULD I KNOW? YOU TALK TO HER MORE THAN I DO, SPEEDY.

I GUESS THAT GUY REALLY LIKES THAT GIRL, HUH, 'LITOS?
SPEEDY? LIKE A FIEND, RAY! HE'S ALWAYS LIKE THIS WHEN IT COMES TO BROADS, 'EY.

OH, WELL. SO MUCH FOR FINDING JOBS TODAY.
SORRY I WASN'T MUCH FUN TODAY, DANITA. MAYBE WE CAN TRY AGAIN TOMORROW, HUH?
J. CASAS XIII

SOUNDS GOOD. AN' DON'T BE SO HARD ON THAT SPEEDY VATO, OK, MAGGIE?
SO, WHO'S BEING HARD?

HMF! WHAT'S WRONG WITH TRYING TO PROTECT YOUR BABY SISTER FROM A FATE WORSE THAN DEATH? TEENAGE PREGNANCY!

IT'S A DAMN GOOD THING FOR THEM THAT THEY LIVE EIGHTY MILES AWAY FROM EACH OTHER.

TOOK YOU LONG ENOUGH, PERLITA. I'VE BEEN WAITING FOR YOU.
HUH?!

E-ESTHER BABIES?! WHAT ARE YOU DOING HERE?
I'M LIVING WITH YOU AND TIA ON WEEKENDS FROM NOW ON. PRETTY COOL, HUH?
2

SIMÓN/OF COURSE!

I DUNNO, 'LITOS. TO TELL YOU THE TRUTH, THERE'S NOT MUCH FOR ME TO DO HERE.

IT MAY BE FINE FOR YOU GUYS, BUT-- WHAT?

THOSE WERE DAIRYTOWN BOYS, HOLMES!
WHAT THE FUCK ARE THEY DOING HERE?
SHIT!
THAT'S WHY I GOTTA GET OUTTA THIS FUCKED UP PLACE, MAN!

I'M SO FUCKING SICK AND TIRED OF ALL THIS MADDOGGING AND TERRITORY SHIT! YOU CAN'T EVEN WALK DOWN YOUR OWN STREET WITHOUT LOOKING OVER YOUR GOD DAMN SHOULDER! IT'S... IT GETS YOU NOWHERE BUT IN THE HOSPITAL OR THE FUCKING CEMETERY, MAN!

THOSE FUCKERS BETTER NOT COME BACK THIS WAY IF THEY KNOW WHAT'S GOOD FOR THEM, 'EY!
MY COUSIN'S GOT A PIECE IN HIS TRUNK. I THINK HE'S HOME RIGHT NOW, HOLMES.

BLANCA! YOUR TABLE!
I'LL SEE YOU LATER, SPEEDY? SOON?
CATCH YOU LATER, BLANCA.
EL GALLO
RESTAURANTE
PARKING ONLY
4

PIECE/GUN

GUY, BLANCA. THAT WAS PRETTY DANGEROUS. SOMEONE COULD HAVE WALKED IN.
SHIT, THEY CAN FIRE ME. I DON'T CARE...
BLANCA!

...'CAUSE NOW I KNOW FOR SURE THAT HE DOES LOVE ME AND NOT THAT MAGGIE CHASCARRILLO.
I ENVY YOU, GIRL. I WOULDN'T MIND GETTING IN THE SACK WITH THAT ONE MYSELF.
HEY!

YOU JUST TRY TO GET NEAR HIM, CHIVITA!
I WAS JUST KIDDI... ¡AIII, NO! ¡CABRONA!

MAGGIE CHASCARRILLO? SINCE WHEN?
EVER SINCE I DROVE HER HOME THAT MORNING, I GUESS...

SO, WHAT'S HOLDING YOU BACK?
A JEALOUS BLOOD THIRSTY BOYFRIEND, THAT'S WHAT!

OH, YEAH. THOSE HOPPERS LOCOS CAN GET PRETTY LOCO. YOU OUGHTA KNOW...
DAMN STRAIGHT! I GREW UP WITH A LOT OF THOSE GUYS AND I STILL GOTTA WATCH WHAT I SAY TO THEM.

YOU DON'T FEEL MUCH BETTER, DO YA, SPEEDY?
YEAH, YOU'RE REALLY GIVING US GUYS A BAD NAME.
5

GUESS WHO!
WHAT THE FU...?!

HEY, DON'T GET EXCITED. IT'S ONLY ME.
YOU SHOULDN'T BE DOING THINGS LIKE THAT.

GOD DAMN, SHRIMP! YOU'RE DEAD NOW.
OH OH. WHAT'S CRAWLING UP THE GREAT VICKI'S ASS TODAY?
NEAT STUFF

UM...TIA? YOU WERE LOOKING FOR ME?
WHAT THE HELL ARE YOU DOING HERE, SHRIMP?

UM...WELL, I WAS LOOKING FOR A JOB TODAY BUT...WELL, I'M GONNA TRY AGAIN TOMORROW.
WELL, IF YOU'RE HERE, THEN SOME ASSHOLE WHO'S GONNA DIE A HORRIBLE DEATH STOLE MY CAR!

OH. ESTHER TOOK IT. UH... I THINK.
DAMN IT, SHRIMP! I CAN'T KEEP TRACK OF YOU BOTH! IT'S GONNA BE UP TO YOU TO KEEP YOUR SISTER IN LINE WHILE SHE'S HERE!
6

YOU'RE MAD AT ME.
I JUST WANNA KNOW, THAT'S ALL!

THE ANSWER'S NO. WELL, I DID HAVE, BUT HE'S A JERK AND WE BROKE UP, AND THAT'S ALL. HONEST, SPEEDY...

...SO NOW I'M A BABY SITTER! I SWEAR, THAT GIRL IS GONNA CRASH... HARD!
OH. AND I THOUGHT IT WAS HOPITA THAT WAS THE CAUSE OF THIS WEEK'S ULCER.

MIJA, I DON'T KNOW WHAT HAS HAPPENED BETWEEN MY BROTHER AND YOU THESE PAST FEW YEARS, BUT IF YOU WANT MY ADVICE (WHICH YOU PROBABLY DON'T), JUST STAY GOOD FRIENDS. YOU TWO WERE SUCH GOOD PALS AS BABIES.
I'M AFRAID YOU MISSED THAT NAIL'S HEAD THIS TIME, ISABEL. ME AND SPEEDY? HO HO!

POW! RIGHT ON THE HEAD, WITHOUT EVEN LOOKING!
I HAVEN'T SAID A NON JEALOUS WORD SINCE THOSE TWO HAVE BEEN TOGETHER. I MUST BE A REAL DRAG TO BE AROUND LATELY.

SPEEDY'S RIDE. IT'S TIME YOU WERE REALLY SUPER NICE TO THEM, FATSO.

HI, GUYS! WHATCHA ALL DOIN'?
PERLA, YOU'RE A RAT.

YOU TOLD TIA I TOOK HER CAR!
I HAD TO! SHE THOUGHT SOMEBODY STOLE IT AND SHE WAS GONNA CALL THE COPS!
?
7

SO I THOUGHT IF THEY WOULDA FOUND YOU, AND SINCE IT'S NOT YOUR CAR...
OH, RIGHT, MAG-GIE! YOU JUST DON'T WANT ME HERE AND YOU KNOW IT!

...THEN I'LL STRETCH HER TONGUE OUT WITH FISH HOOKS AND SPRINKLE RED ANTS ON IT. AND HIM...? HOO BOY!

HOW COME YOU AN' MAGGIE GOTTA FIGHT?
SHE HATES ME! SHE'S ALWAYS HATED ME SINCE WE WERE LITTLE!

IT'S HER OWN FAULT THAT SHE ALWAYS LOOKS SO SLOPPY. SHE COULD MEET MORE GUYS IF SHE'D JUST DRESS UP A LITTLE MORE. SHE...

I'M THE WORST, HUH?

I GUESS SOME OF US WERE BORN TO BE KINGS! LOOK AT YOU GUYS! IT AIN'T EVEN NOON YET!
THIS IS STILL LAST NIGHT'S DRUNK, HOME BOY.
TWO CASES, 'EY!
WE HAVEN'T GONE TO SLEEP YET, DUDE.

LAST NIGHT WE WENT UP TO DAIRYTOWN TO SEE IF THEY WANTED ANY SHIT WITH US.
...AND WE GOT CHASED OUT! THREE FUCKING CARS ON OUR ASS, 'EY!
SHIT, I STILL SAY WE COULDA TOOK 'EM.
8

WHY DON'T YOU GUYS GET SOME JOBS INSTEAD OF HANGING AROUND STREET CORNERS?
HEY! IT SMILES! HE MUSTA FORGAVE HER!
LOOKS LIKE HE FORGAVE HER ALL NIGHT!

YOU'RE LOOKING AT A NEW MAN, HOLMES. THINGS ARE LOOKING UP...
AT THE HEAD OF MY PITO? HERE, SUCK ON THIS.
HOW 'BOUT YOU RAY? GRAB ONE...
WHAT THE HELL...

...AND I KNOW YOU WERE ONLY TRYING TO HELP ME... YOU KNOW, ABOUT THE CAR. I'M SORRY, PERLITA.
THA'S OK.

HEY, WHY DON'T YOU AN' ME GO OUT AN' DO STUFF TODAY? YOU COULD SHOW ME STUFF FROM OUR OLD NEIGHBORHOOD.
OK, I'LL EVEN TAKE YOU BY THE HOUSE YOU USED TO BE AFRAID OF. SPEEDY'S SISTER LIVES THERE NOW...
YOU CAN'T BE SISTERS. WHERE'S THE CLAWING AND YOWLING?

IF YOU TWO ARE GOING OUT, WHY DON'T YOU TAKE MY CAR? I DONT NEED IT TILL FIVE.
THANKS, TIA! I'LL DRIVE, PERLITA!

YOU FEELING OK?
GO, BEFORE I CHANGE MY MIND.

SO WHO'S GONNA GET THE NEXT CASE?
NO HURRY. THE LIQUOR STORE DOESN'T CLOSE FOR ANOTHER TEN OR TWELVE HOURS.
9

GIMME ANOTHER... WHOA!
HA! RAY'S ALL FUCKED UP, 'EY!
AT LEAST HE AIN'T LIKE THOSE TWO LIGHTWEIGHTS WHO HAD TO GO BEDDY BYE.

FUCK YEAH! ME AN' RAY USED TO ALWAYS GO ON THOSE MARATHON DRUNKS. ¿QUE NO?
YOU BETTER FUCKIN' BELIEVE IT, MAN!
BEEP
BEEP
WHO THE F... WELL, EXCUSE ME, GENTLEMEN.

TSK! DRUNK SO EARLY IN THE DAY.
WHAT'S GOING ON? HOW COME YOU GOT YOUR AUNT'S CAR?

SHE'S LETTING HER FAVORITE NIECES USE IT TODAY. LET'S GO FOR A QUICK SPIN. MAGGIE'S VISITING SOMEONE DOWN THE STREET.
YOU GUYS ARE BUDDIES AGAIN?

CAN YOU BELIEVE THAT FUCKER...?
WHAT'S WRONG? THAT'S HIS WOMAN, 'EY.

THAT'S WHAT I MEAN, MAN! ME AND YOU MAY HAVE BEEN FUCK UPS WHEN WE WERE YOUNGER, BUT WE NEVER FUCKED OVER ANY WOMEN LIKE THAT GUY!
WHAT THE FUCK ARE YOU TALKING ABOUT, MAN?

REMEMBER WHEN ME, YOU, MANDO, LOUIS AND BIG EDDIE STOLE THAT KEG AND THEN WE MET THOSE GIRLS FROM DAIRYTOWN...
COURSE I DO! BIG EDDIE MARRIED ONE OF THEM. YOU WERE IN HIS WEDDING.
10

END OF PART ONE

VIDALOCA 2

THE DEATH OF SPEEDY ORTIZ

1 20 84

JAINAS/GIRLS

YOU KNOW, I'VE BEEN SEEING YOUR SISTER EVERY WEEKEND FOR A MONTH, AND NOW ALL WE EVER DO IS FIGHT. IT'S FUCKED.
YOU THINK MAYBE IT'S NOT GONNA LAST?

AH, I'VE THOUGHT ABOUT THAT. BUT I CAN'T EVEN BEGIN TO MENTION BREAKING UP WITHOUT HER FREAKING OUT.
YOU KNOW, I REALLY LIKE HER A LOT. IT'S JUST THAT... I CAN'T TALK TO HER LIKE I CAN WITH YOU...

ACTUALLY, I CAN'T TALK TO ANYBODY THE WAY I CAN WITH YOU. I PROBABLY TELL YOU MORE SHIT ABOUT ME THAN I'VE EVER TOLD MY OWN FAMILY.

I DUNNO, I JUST THOUGHT YOU SHOULD KNOW THAT...

I THINK I BETTER GET THE HELL OUTTA HERE BEFORE I RAPE YOU.

MEKOS
SMOKE JOKES
3

LIFTED RANFLAS/CARS WITH HYDRAULICS

THERE'S MORE JURA HERE THAN HUMAN BEINGS! DON'T YOU EVEN TAKE THAT THING OUTTA THERE!
FUCK, MAN. YOU DON'T KNOW HOW IT IS...
COOL IT ANYWAY, CARLOS.

WHAT HAPPENED, 'LITOS?
AH, THEY'RE NO MORE THAN FIFTEEN YEARS OLD! ALL DRESSED IN THEIR SILLY NEW WAVE SHORTS...

HA! YOU SHOULDA SEEN 'EM WHEN I SAID I'D SPANK 'EM ALL AN' TAKE AWAY THEIR SKATEBOARDS.
HEY, OLD MAN!

¡CR-RINK!
VATO'S GOLD

TELL THAT FUCKIN' SPEEDY TO LEAVE ROJO'S WOMAN ALONE OR ELSE!
DAIRYTOWN!
DAIRYTOWN!

NOW SEE WHAT YOU DID?
I NEVER SAID WHO THE OTHER GIRL WAS, DID I?
SHE WOULDN'T REALLY CUT ME BALD, WOULD SHE?
WOULD SHE?
BAM

JURA/POLICE

OK, MAGGIE. I'LL SEE YOU LATER. AND THANKS...
'S OK. BYE.
5

MONTOYA / DAIRYTOWN

YOU'RE DEAD! DEAD!
SPEEDY! DON'T START ANYTHING! LET ME TALK TO ESTHER FIRST!

GET OUT OF MY FUCKIN' WAY! WHAT DO YOU KNOW ANYWAY, WITH ALL YOUR PUNKER FAG SHIT!
ALL RIGHT! THEN GET YOURSELF KILLED, YOU STUPID, MACHO PEESASHIT!

THE BEST ONE MINUTE, THE WORST THE NEXT. BUT, OF COURSE, HOW COULD I EVER ACCUSE YOU OF BEING HUMAN?
WOM
XIII
CHUY LOCO
RCN

IT BETTER NOT BE YOU, BITCH. LICHA DE LAS WIDOWS' COUSIN OR NOT, THIS TIME I SWEAR, I'LL KILL YOU.

I'M A NEW MAN... AW, DON'T TELL ME THOSE GUYS WENT AND...
YOU KNOW 'LITOS. THE DUDE'S VIDA LOCA ALL THE WAY.
LOANS

JUST LET ME GET MY PIECE OUTTA YOUR TRUNK!
I GOT A BLADE, 'EY!
YOU GUYS AFRAID TO GO TOE TO TOE WITH A BUNCH OF KIDS, OR WHAT?
7

THIS IS ALL MY FAULT, YOU KNOW...

I HAD TO GO AND BEG MY MOTHER FOR A SISTER.

!

WHAT ARE YOU GUYS DOING HERE?
WE'RE WAITING FOR ESTHER.

LIKE HELL, YOU ARE! YOU GUYS HAVE FUCKING NERVE TO COME HERE AFTER WHAT YOU DID! GET OUTTA HERE BEFORE I CALL THE COPS!
HEY, RELAX, CHICK...
WHAT'S GOING ON HERE?

GET OUT, ASSHOLE! NOW!
I NEVER HIT A GIRL BEFORE...
...BUT YOU'RE THINKING OF IT, HUH, BOZO?
!

LISTEN. HOW ABOUT IF YOU HIT ME INSTEAD, AND THEN MY NIECE CAN FINALLY SEE HOW TWO GROWN MEN CAN FIT INTO AN ASPIRIN BOTTLE.
AW, LET'S GO, MAN.
8

THROW PLEITO/FIGHT

WHAT DID I TELL YOU, MAN? HER WHOLE FAMILIA'S LOCO! I DON'T KNOW WHAT TO DO WITH HER, MAN.
I HEAR WHAT YOU'RE SAYING, ROJO.
Montoya 35
San Jose 110
101 North

I'M WONDERING IF I SHOULD JUST LET HER GO. I'M GETTING SICK OF THIS HIGH SCHOOL SHIT.
WHO THE FUCK IS SHINING THEIR BRIGHTS?

BUMP!

WHAT THE FUCK ARE THEY DOING?!

KRUMP!

¿HOPPERS, Y QUE, PUTAS?
¡G#@*!

NEXT TIME I'LL SHOOT THE FUCKERS.
VERY VERY HIGH (YOU PICK THE DRUG)

FOPPIN' AN' ROCKIN'
OW!
THUMP!
RATA-TATA-TAT!
Y'ALL!
OOH!
10

THUMP!
CLA
BUMP!
FREAK!
FUNKY!
UH!

GRAMMA! TIO SPEEDY FELL ASLEEP IN HIS CAR AGAIN!

WHY DON'T YOU JUST PUT YOUR BED IN THERE AND MOVE IN, MENSO?

YEAH, SHE'S HERE, BUT YOU AIN'T GONNA TALK TO HER. NO, YOU AIN'T TALKIN' TO HER, NEITHER. YOU DON'T WASTE TIME, DO YA, GUY?

CLICK!
FUCK ALL O' YOU, THEN.

THUS BEGINETH THE FALL OF THE MIGHTY LOVER.

El Gallo
RESTAURANT
11

WOOPED/ TOTALLY IN LOVE

END OF PART TWO

SEE, YOU'RE TALKING ABOUT THE OLD WIDOWS! NOWADAYS, WE AS A GROUP DO THINGS TO HELP THE BARRIO, NOT HURT IT. WE PUT ON DANCES, CAR WASHES...
RAZA
UNIT

AND WE'VE BEEN TALKING WITH THE ALL-GIRL CAR CLUBS IN DAIRYTOWN AND THEY'VE AGREED TO HELP STOP THIS LATEST HOPPERS/DAIRYTOWN WAR BEFORE IT HEATS UP ANY MORE...
GOOD JOB, LICHA...

I DON'T KNOW WHERE HE IS, LICHA! NO ONE'S SEEN HIM SINCE HE BEAT UP HIS BEST FRIEND YESTERDAY MORNING!
WHAT ABOUT ESTHER? MAYBE SHE KNOWS...
SORANO CULTURAL CENTER

NO, THANKS. ME AN' ESTHER AREN'T EXACTLY BUDDIES RIGHT NOW. BESIDES...
YOU HAVE TO, MAGGIE, OR SOMEONE MIGHT END UP WITH A BULLET IN HIS HEAD! MOST LIKELY SPEEDY ORTIZ!

BUT, SHE'S ON A BUS RIGHT NOW HEADED FOR HOME, LICHA. I SWEAR TO YOU...
THEN LET'S GO SEE IF IZZY KNOWS WHERE HE IS, EH?

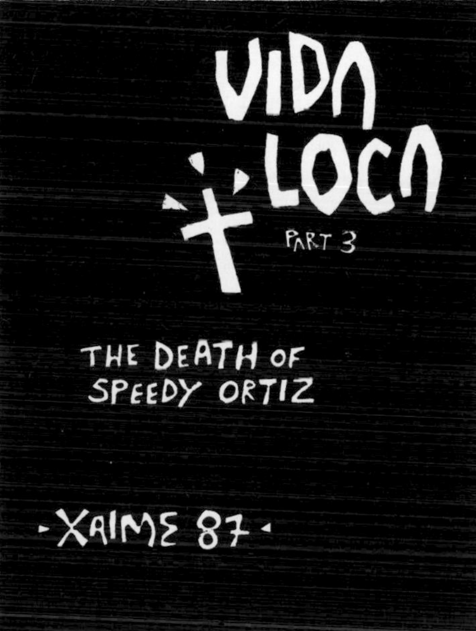
VIDA LOCA
PART 3
THE DEATH OF SPEEDY ORTIZ
·XAIME 87·

CLICK
WHHHHIIIRRR
1

I CAN'T WAIT FOREVER FOR YOU TO WAKE UP.
I WAS JUST GETTING UP RIGHT NOW, MA...
WWA
WHIRRRRR

I THOUGHT YOU WERE GOING TO LOOK FOR AN APARTMENT TODAY.
DOYLE HAD TO WORK, I THINK...

SO, IN THE MEANTIME YOU'VE BEEN HANGING OUT WITH JUANA ORTIZ'S BOY EULALIO, EH?
IS THAT THE ONE THEY CALL SPEEDY? NOT REALLY. WHY?

AI, THAT BOY. THE NIGHT BEFORE LAST HE BANGED UP HIS CAR AND TOLD HER HE DIDN'T CARE...
HOW'D HE DO THAT?

PTCH! DRUNK, WHAT ELSE? ALL OF HER KIDS ARE LIKE THAT...
EXCUSE ME A MINUTE, MA...

BUENOS DIAS, MUCHACHITAS. MY, WE LOOK LOVELY THIS FINE MORNING.
IT'S NOT MORNING ANY MORE, RAY. AND IT'S HOTTER THAN A...
HAVE YOU SEEN SPEEDY ORTIZ?

MAN, THAT GUY'S POPULAR LATELY. WHA'D HE DO, STRIKE GOLD IN HIS BACKYARD?
RAY, THIS IS SERIOUS. COME ON, MAGGIE.
BYE, RAY.
2

MONTOYA/DAIRYTOWN

SHEESH! DOESN'T ANYBODY HAVE A SENSE OF HUMOR AROUND HERE ANY MORE?
AH, SHE WAS BORN WITHOUT A SENSE OF HUMOR.

HOW ABOUT YOU? HOW COME I ONLY SEE YOU SMILE ONCE IN A BLUE MOON?
I'M TRYING...

THERE YOU GO. I DON'T THINK YOU REALIZE WHAT A NICE SMILE YOU HAVE.
OW!

W-WHAT HAPPENED, MAGGIE?
YOU KICKED MY TOE, THAT'S WHAT!

HEY, I'M SORRY! I DIDN'T MEAN TO! I...
I KNOW. I DIDN'T MEAN TO YELL...

SCREEEE
EEEEEE!

'LITOS! ARE YOU FUCKIN' CRAZY, MAN?!
I'M NOT THE ONE SITTING IN THE MIDDLE OF THE STREET.
YOU SCARED THE...
?!?
Y QUE

I NEED YOU TO COME WITH ME, RAY. THE SHIT'S HITTING THE FAN...
BUT... MAGGIE?
IF YOU GENTLEMEN WILL EXCUSE ME, I THINK I'VE JUST SEEN A GHOST.
4

ESTHER, YOU SHIT! DO YOU REALIZE WHAT YOU'RE DOING BY STILL BEING HERE?
I DON'T CARE, PERLITA. I LOVE HIM AND I WANNA SEE, HIM AND YOU CAN'T STOP ME!
CHIV

YEAH, I LOVE HIM! DID YOU EVER THINK OF THAT? NO, OF COURSE NOT! NONE OF YOU DID! YOU WERE ALL TOO WORRIED ABOUT YOUR OWN PROBLEMS! YOU NEVER EVEN ASKED HOW I FELT!

SHOOT, I KNOW IT'S ALL OVER BETWEEN ME AN' HIM, BUT I'M NOT LEAVING TILL I SEE HIM AT LEAST ONE LAST TIME. AND THERE'S ONE LAST THING I WANNA SAY TO YOU, PERLITA...

...THINK OF ALL THE GUYS YOU'VE LOVED AND LOST, AND THEN REMEMBER...

HEY, YOU.
5

SOMEONE TELLS ME SOME GIRL NAMED CHASCARRILLO HAS BEEN HITTING ON MY BOYFRIEND. ARE YOU HER?
ME? I...

DIDN'T YOU KNOW HE ALREADY HAS A GIRL-FRIEND? HUH, BITCH? HUH? HUH?
YEAH, BITCH!
HEY, DON'T PUSH...
BLANCA!

I-I'M A CHASCARRILLO TOO, 'MEMBER?

HEY!
?

YEOW!
BUMP!
BAM!
OPEN THIS... DOOR!
HEY!

?!?
HOW MANY TIMES HAVE I TOLD YOU PEOPLE NOT TO LOITER AROUND MY RESTROOMS? NOW TAKE OFF!
WE WERE JUST DOING OUR MAKE UP...
GUY...
6

DAMN CHOLOS.
?!?!

P-PERLITA?

=CHUCHO JOTO=
NOBODY HERE BUT US BEACHED WHALES...

OH, PERLITA...
OHH... WHAT A SISSY. SHE HIT ME WITH AN OPEN PALM...

I'VE BEEN AFRAID OF NOTHING SINCE THE NINTH GRADE...
I'M SORRY, PERLITA! I'LL LEAVE NOW, AND I WON'T COME BACK! JUST PLEASE FORGIVE ME!

I SHOULDA CALLED HER OUT AGES AGO...
{ SOB }
MAGGIE! ESTHER?? WHAT...?

BLANCA?
NO!
YES!

WILL YOU EVER LEARN?!
WAH! STOP YELLING AT ME!
?!
7

STOP BEING SO NEGATIVE. SAY SOMETHING POSITIVE. OK, SOMETHING POSITIVE...

WHY WAS HE THE ONLY ONE IN THE FAMILY BORN WITH THOSE BEAUTIFUL EYEBROWS?
WHAP
WHAP

OH, MY GOD, PLEASE... THIS CAN'T BE HAPPENING...

WE JUST WANNA KNOW WHERE HE IS, 'LITOS.
CAN'T YOU FUCKERS SEE THAT WE GOTTA STICK TOGETHER? ESPECIALLY RIGHT NOW...
WHY DON'T YOU TELL SPEEDY THAT? HE'S THE ONE FUCKING UP HIS OWN HOMEYS!
HIS BEST COMPA, 'EY! MY BROTHER!
HE'S A FUCKIN' BACK STABBER...
CORONA

POP!

YOU WANNA FUCK WITH SPEEDY? YOU FUCK WITH ME FIRST!
OK, 'LITOS. THAT DID IT...

YOU BLEW IT, MAN. YOU AND SPEEDY ARE ON YOUR OWN NOW...
8

WHAP!
WHAP!
WHAP!
WHA

ISABEL, I COULD HEAR YOU ALL THE WAY FROM MY... AI...

EVERYTHING'S FINE... NOTHING'S FINE... AND LIFE GOES CHUGGIN' ON LIKE A SEVENTY-FOUR CHEVY VEGA...
ANDROGYNOUS

HAVE YOU EVER GONE TO BED AT NIGHT, AND EVERYTHING WAS FINE? THERE WAS NOT A SAFER PLACE IN THE WORLD... LIFE WAS SIMPLY BEAUTIFUL... BEAUTIFUL...
ISABEL, I THINK YOU BETTER GET DOWN...

THEN JUST ONE NIGHT LATER, IN THE SAME SITUATION, NOTHING IS FINE. NOT EVEN TWENTY LOCKS ON YOUR DOORS AND WINDOWS CAN SAVE YOU FROM THE HORRORS OF THIS COLD, VICIOUS WORLD... INSECURITY RUNS WILD... HOW THE HELL CAN ANYONE SURVIVE?
C'MON...
ANDROGYNOUS

EVERY NIGHT WE HEAR THE SIRENS, THE POPS... FIRE CRACKERS? BOX CARS COUPLING AT THE TRAIN STATION? FARM SHOTS IN THE FIELDS? GUN SHOTS? ARE WE EVER CERTAIN? DO WE EVEN CHECK? NO...
ANDROGYNOUS

NO, WE'RE JUST GLAD IT SOUNDS A MILE AWAY AND NOT DOWN OUR STREET. AH, LIFE GOES CHUGGIN' ON... LIKE A GOD DAMN SEVENTY-FOUR CHEVY VEGA...
YOU GET SOME SLEE... GET OUTSIDE! I'LL BE RIGHT OUT!
9

DO YOU KNOW THAT THE LAST TIME SHE CLEARED HER CEILING WAS WHEN MRS. GALINDO DIED?
AND BEFORE THAT SHE THOUGHT LITTLE MAGGIE WAS... ONE OF THESE DAYS THE MEN IN THE WHITE COATS ARE GONNA...
DON'T YOU EVEN THINK IT! YOUR OWN COUSIN...

I DON'T KNOW WHAT GOOD KICKING IN CAR DOORS IS GONNA DO...
IT STOPS ME FROM KICKING IN PEOPLE'S FACES.

WHAT THE FUCK WENT WRONG, RAY? THIS KINDA SHIT WOULDA NEVER HAPPENED WITH OUR OLD HOMEYS! WE NEVER FUCKED WITH EACH OTHER!
WELL, THESE ARE NEW KIDS. IT'S DIFFERENT NOW, 'LITOS.

JUST LOOK AT YOU, MAN! YOU'RE ALMOST THIRTY, AND YOUR GIRLFRIEND'S GONNA HAVE YOUR KID ANY DAY NOW. DON'T YOU THINK IT'S TIME YOU SLOWED DOWN JUST A LITTLE?
I'M TRYING, MAN! BUT I CAN'T! I CAN'T!

I DUNNO, IT'S LIKE THIS IS MY LAST DAY OF SUMMER VACATION AN' I GOTTA DO SOMETHING BEFORE SCHOOL STARTS. YOU KNOW, LIKE, GO OUT IN A BLAZE O' GLORY...
HEY! ANY OF YOU VATOS SPEEDY?

SHIT! I'M SPEEDY, MAN! WHAT THE FUCK DO YOU WANT?
WAIT, 'LITOS...
I GOT A MESSAGE FROM ROJO...
10

BAM
AH, SHIT!!
BAM

'LITOS! 'LITOS!
SCREEEE

OH, FUCK... DID I SAY BLAZE O' GLORY?
CALL A FUCKING AMBULANCE, MAN!

TELL MR. CARRANZA THAT HIS GRANDSON WILL PULL THROUGH, BUT I'M AFRAID WE CAN'T SAVE HIS EYE, AND IT'LL BE AWHILE BEFORE WE KNOW IF THE BULLET DID ANY DAMAGE TO HIS BRAIN.

DIDN'T I TELL YOU IT TAKES MUCH MORE TO KEEP THAT CRAZY BOY DOWN?
RAY, YOU'RE SO... YOU ALWAYS SEEM TO KEEP YOUR WITS...
COMING THROUGH!

WHAT IDIOT'S CAR IS BLOCKING THE EMERGENCY ENTRANCE?
NEVER MIND. THIS WAY...
11

THAT WAS BLANCA RIZO, MAN!
THOSE DAIRYTOWN FUCKERS DON'T QUIT!
WAS THAT SOMEONE YOU KNOW?
S-SOMEONE I KNOW...?
LET'S GO SEE IF CARLOS STILL HAS HIS COUSIN'S PIECE, 'EY!

IT DOESN'T MATTER ANY MORE. THEY'RE ALL GOING TO KILL THEMSELVES AND THEN IT WILL BE ALL OVER...

WHY ARE YOU THE ONLY SANE PERSON HERE?

ARE YOU MAGGIE?
YES...?

SOMEONE NAMED SPEEDY (?) WANTS TO SEE YOU OUTSIDE.
SPEEDY?!

SPEEDY?
RIGHT HERE, MAGGIE...
12

OH, SPEEDY! WHERE HAVE YOU BEEN? EVERYBODY'S BEEN GOING CRAZY LOOKING FOR YOU! POOR 'LITOS. IT'S SO TERRIBLE, BUT HE'S GONNA BE OK...
I KNOW. I JUST HAD TO SEE YOU.

...AND BLANCA. OH, BLANCA. SHE DIDN'T MEAN IT. SHE JUST WANTED YOU SO BAD AND SHE THOUGHT YOU WANTED HER...
I KNOW, I KNOW. IT'S OK...

AND ESTHER WANTED TO SEE YOU SO BAD...
UH HUH...

DON'T YOU EVEN CARE?
AW, MAGGIE. WHAT DO YOU THINK?

I'VE JUST ABOUT FUCKED OVER EVERYBODY THAT EVER MEANT ANYTHING TO ME. YOU'RE ALL I'VE GOT LEFT...

A-AND IF I EVER LOST YOU, I DON'T KNOW WHAT I'D DO. I NEED YOU, MAGGIE. I NEED YOU BAD...

I NEVER REALLY WANTED ESTHER, OR BLANCA, OR... YOU'RE THE ONE I'VE WANTED FOR A LONG OL' TIME. YOU KNEW THAT. YOU DID...

PLEASE, MAGGIE... KEEP ME GOING... ONLY YOU CAN DO IT FOR ME. I... I-I LOVE YOU...
OH, STOP IT, WILL YOU?!
13

DON'T YOU DARE PUT THIS ON ME! DAMN YOU, SPEEDY! AREN'T YOU GUYS ALL SICK AND TIRED OF WATCHING ME MAKE AN ALL-STAR ASS OF MYSELF? AREN'T YOU? I AM!

I DON'T WANT TO WANT YOU ANY MORE, SPEEDY. I DON'T WANT TO WANT RAND RACE ANY MORE. I CAN'T... I CAN'T DO IT ANY MORE. IT HURTS TOO MUCH...

EMERGENCY

ISN'T THAT THAT ORTIZ KID'S CAR?
YEAH, WHAT'S HE UP TO SO LATE, OR SHOULD I SAY SO EARLY?

SAY, BUDDY! YOU CAN'T PARK HERE! C'MON, LET'S GO! MOVE IT, BAH-TOE...

BAH-TOE/VATO

AW, JEEZ... JERRY, GET ON THE RADIO...
WHAT'S UP?
14

HEY, IZZY! WAKE UP...
HUH? WHAT?

SPEEDY? WHAT ARE YOU DOING HERE?
SHHH... IT'S OK...

I JUST WANTED TO TELL YOU THAT EVERYTHING'S GONNA BE ALL RIGHT FROM NOW ON, AND NOT TO WORRY ABOUT ME...
SPEEDY, THIS IS CRAZY. DO YOU KNOW WHAT TIME IT IS?

HOLD ON A MINUTE. LET ME OPEN THE SHADE...

15

I STILL CAN'T BELIEVE BIG EDDIE GOT MARRIED, 'LITOS.
I KNOW, CAN YOU BELIEVE THAT SHIT?
(FUCKIN' DAIRYTOWN PUSSIES...)
IS THAT ANY WAY FOR A BEST MAN TO TALK?
AI, MAGGIE MIJA! COME FIX MY HEART, SINCE YOU'RE THE ONE THAT BROKE IT! YOU TOO, LETTY!
OOH, MANDO! WE'RE GONNA TELL YOUR GIRLFRIEND!

THOSE CHICKS GO TO YOUR SCHOOL, RAY?
YEAH. FRESHMEN, I THINK.
"FRESHMEN, I THINK." SHEEIT, PUSSY'S PUSSY! RIGHT, LOUIS?
(DAIRYTOWN, MY ASS...)
YOU KNOW IT, HOME BOY. CHECK IT OUT...

BIG EDDIE'S LITTLE BROTHER AN' HIS FRIEND. I SWEAR ALL THOSE GUYS EVER DO IS RUN.
HEY, "SPEEDY"! WHERE YOU GOING, "SPEEDY"?
YOU TOO, "LEADSIDE"!

HEY, YOU STUPID DRUNKS! GIVE US SOME BEER!
YEAH!
GROW SOME DICKS FIRST!
SCRAM, WEENIES!

SO, THE BIG, BAD SENIOR IS TOO COOL TO HANG OUT WITH FRESH-MEN, OR WHAT?
I DIDN'T SAY THAT! I DON'T EVEN KNOW THOSE CHICKS!

DON'T LIE, RAY! JUST 'CAUSE YOU'RE GETTING AN ART SCHOLARSHIP!
WELL, YOU KNOW HOW HIGH SCHOOL GIRLS THINK OF COLLEGE MEN...
QUIET, MAN. 'LITOS IS MAKING A TOAST...
XAIME 87

THE NIGHT APE SEX CAME HOME TO PLAY

XAIME 87

YOU GOT ANY SPARE CHANGE? I GOTTA TAKE A BUS HOME AFTER THIS.

GOLLY, KIKO! WHERE IS EVERYBODY? I DON'T KNOW ANY OF THESE PEOPLE.

OF COURSE NOT, DAFFY. PUT A LOCAL BAND ON A REAL LABEL AND YOU AUTOMATICALLY ATTRACT MILLIONS OF GEEKS.

APE SEX

SOLD OUT

<JAPANESE>

NO! READ MY LIPS! NO!
YOU'RE AN ASSHOLE, CID.
NEW HAIRCUT, CID?
WHO LET YOU HIDE IN HER HOUSE WHEN THE POLICE WERE AFTER YOUR ASS?

HE'S RIGHT, YOU KNOW. IT WAS IZZY THAT LET HIM HIDE IN HER HOUSE.
DOESN'T HE LOOK WEIRD WITH HAIR?
SO, WHAT ARE WE GOING TO DO NOW?

YOU GIRLS WANT TO GO SEE DOYLE'S NEW APARTMENT? HE AND HIS FRIEND ARE MOVING IN TONIGHT...
HIS MEXICAN FRIEND?

YES. IT'S NOT TOO FAR FROM HERE.
AT LEAST WE CAN DRINK THERE. AND IF WE ARE LUCKY, WE JUST MAY CATCH DOYLE WITH HIS PANTS DOWN!

MAYBE YOU GUYS SHOULD GO WITHOUT ME...
HOW COME??
BAM
BO

LEMME GO, MAN! LEMME GO!

COME ON! I'LL TAKE ALL YOU JERKS ON!
ONE STAGE DIVE! ONE STAGE DIVE!
JOEY! TONY!
GO NOTANS
2

THIRTEEN BUCKS! SEATS! JOCKS! YUPPIES! GESTAPO!
AND BEFORE THEY HAD SOME ZANY COLLEGE BAND DOING ZEPPLIN SONGS! SHEE...
WHA'D YOU GUYS EXPECT? YOU DON'T EVEN LIKE APE SEX, TONY.
NOMAD
I LIKE THAT THIRD SONG ON SIDE ONE, "IN BED WITH THE LIGHTS ON." AS SOON AS THEY STARTED PLAYING IT, ME AN' JOEY STARTED A PIT...
BY THE WAY, MAGGIE. YOU GOT SOME LETTERS FROM HOPEY. SHE SENT 'EM TO MY HOUSE.
SQUEAK
HOW LONG HAVE THESE BEEN COMING?
A FEW WEEKS. I DUNNO...
OH, AND I SUPPOSE YOU COULDN'T START GIVING THEM TO ME A FEW WEEKS AGO!
AND I SUPPOSE THEY OPENED UP BY THEMSELVES!
WELL, I WAS KINDA HOPING YOU'D COME OVER TO MY HOUSE AND PICK THEM UP IN PERSON.
CLICK
OH, GROW UP, JOEY!
GROW UP!
SO, DO WE HIT UP DOYLE'S NEW PLACE, OR WHAT?
I DON'T WANT TO GO IF MAGGIE CAN'T...
WHY CAN'T YOU GO?
I DON'T THINK HIS ROOMMATE LIKES ME, THAT'S ALL. YOU GUYS CAN GO...
THAT HOMEBOY? WHAT IS HE, AN ASSHOLE? ARE WE GONNA HAVE TO KICK HIS HEAD IN?
KICK WHOSE HEAD IN??
LOOK, IT'S NO BIG DEAL! I JUST DON'T WANNA GO, THAT'S ALL!
3

OK, MAGGIE. BUT IF THIS ROOMMATE SAYS ANYTHING OUT OF LINE, HE'S A CORPSE!
YOU'RE A REAL IDIOT, JOEY! DID YOU KNOW THAT?
IDIOT!

YOU MEAN, SHE LIKES THIS GUY??
IT WAS ONLY WRITTEN ON HER FACE! THAT GIRL COULDN'T HIDE HER FEELINGS IF HER LIFE DEPENDED ON IT!
GO HOMAN

NO SHIT? SHE REALLY SAID THAT?
YEAH, SHE THINKS YOU WANNA RUN HER OVER WITH A STEAM ROLLER.
SHE'S WRONG?

OF COURSE SHE IS! I MEAN, WHY WOULD I HATE HER? I HAVEN'T EVEN SEEN HER SINCE THAT HOSPITAL THING...
WELL, ACTUALLY, SHE REALLY DIDN'T COME BECAUSE SHE WENT TO MADDOG'S TO SHOW OFF SOME LETTERS FROM HER...
...LOVER! MY AHEM SISTER.

MAGGIE'S RIGHT. YOU ARE A REAL IDIOT, JOEY.
WOULD A REAL IDIOT FIGURE OUT THAT HOMEBOY HAS THE HOTS FOR HER AS WELL? IT'S WRITTEN ON HIS CIGARETTE.
XAIME 87

JERRY SLUM and the CRICKETTES

E.T. 87

NAME: CHARLES JOSEPH GRAVETTE
INSTRUMENT: DRUMS
LIFELONG AMBITION: TO MEET JOHN BONHAM

NAME: ESPERANZA LETICIA GLASS
INSTRUMENT: BASS
LIFELONG AMBITION: TO DANCE THROUGH THE SOUL TRAIN LINE

NAME: MONICA MIRANDA ZANDINSKI
INSTRUMENT: VOCALS
LIFELONG AMBITION: TO BE ELVIS (1970 UP)

NAME: THERESA LEEANNE DOWNE
INSTRUMENT: GUITAR, VOCALS
LIFELONG AMBITION: TO BE IN A GOOD BAND

SO, YOU QUIT FOR GOOD THIS TIME? C'MON, TERRY...
I'M SERIOUS! I REFUSE TO PLAY WITH YOU INCOMPETENTS ANY LONGER!

AND IF YOU LET THAT BITCH MONICA NEAR ME, I'LL...
YOU'RE THE ONE BEING THE BITCH.

WHAT DID YOU SAY? I'LL KICK YOUR LITTLE ASS RIGHT NOW!
FUCK YOU, TERRY! FUCK YOU!

BOMG!
WHAT THE...?
BREAK 'EM UP! THEY'RE FUCKING UP MY DRUMS!
BANG!
CRASH!
BIO RAD

BITCH! CUNT! WHORE! TUNA!
OK, HOPEY! KNOCK IT OFF!
AH, SHIT, MAN! LOOK AT MY DRUMS!

THEY'RE ALL RIGHT, ZERO. I'LL STILL BUY THEM OFF YOU.
YOU'RE SELLING YOUR... YOU WERE GONNA QUIT THIS WHOLE TIME? YOU ASSHOLE...
FUCK YOU, BITCH! I'M GOIN' HOME...

HEY, TEX. CAN I HAVE THE CASH NOW? I GOTTA GET THE TRAIN TICKETS FOR TOMORROW MORNING. ME AN' MONICA ARE GONNA...
YOU AND MONICA?? WHY, ZERO? 'CAUSE SHE'S THE ONLY ONE OF US THAT WILL SUCK THAT TEENIE WEENIE ANTEATER YOU CALL A COCK?

YOU HEAR HOW SHE IS? I SWEAR I'M GONNA KILL HER...
I THINK YOU SHOULD COOL IT, GIRL...
MIND YOUR OWN GOD DAMN BUSINESS, FUCKIN' NIGGER!
FORTY THIEVES

I'M GONNA IGNORE THAT ONE BECAUSE I KNOW YOU'RE UPSET...
OH, YOU KNOW I DIDN'T MEAN... I JUST...
OK!

SLAM!
AND I HEARD YOU CALIFORNIANS WERE LAID BACK.
SHE CALLED YOU A FUCKING NIGGER...

DIE, YOU DEMONS OF HELL...
2

YOU KNOW, YOU COULD HAVE SOLD THEM AND BOUGHT A TRAIN TICKET, TOO...
SHIT, I'D HAVE TO PAY SOMEONE TO TAKE 'EM.

I JUST CAME BY TO TELL YOU THAT TERRY JOINED THE FORTY THIEVES FOR THE REST OF THE TOUR, AND THEY'RE LEAVING THE CAR TO YOU...
OH, JOY. IT'S BEEN BROKEN DOWN FOR A WEEK. DAMN, WHERE'S A MECHANIC WHEN YOU NEED ONE?

COLE

KAFF
KAFF
KAFF
KAFF
KAFF
KAFF

OOTAH! IF I SPEND ONE MORE NIGHT IN THIS THING, I'M SERIOUSLY GONNA TURN INTO HANK QUINLAN'S TWIN!
YOU GOT AN EXTRA BACK SEAT IN THERE?
KAFF KAFF

WHAT HAPPENED, TEXAS? YOU RUN AWAY FROM THE BATSHELDER HOTEL, OR WHAT?
PIGS RAIDED IT. I THINK I WAS THE ONLY ONE THAT GOT OUT... MINUS MY DRUMS!
3

SO, YOU GOING HOME, OR WHAT?
NO ROOM. BUT I AIN'T STAYING HERE, EITHER. THIS PLACE GETS TO YOU AFTER AWHILE.

HAVE YOU EVER THOUGHT OF GOING TO CALIFORNIA?
SURE. WITH WHAT MONEY?

OH, GOD... I SWORE TO MYSELF I'D NEVER HAVE TO DO THIS...

HELLO, MOM? THIS IS HOPEY. HEY, GUESS WHERE I'M CALLIN' FROM...
PHONE

CAN YOU LEND A BROTHER THIRTY-SEVEN CENTS?
I'M BROKE, SORRY, MAN.

COME ON... YOU KNOW HOW IT IS. YOU'RE A BROTHER...
REALLY, MAN. I AIN'T EVEN GOT A DIME.

OK, MAN. YOU DON'T HAVE TO SWEAR...
I KNEW I SHOULDN'T HAVE... SHE'S SUCH A BITCH!
NO LUCK, HUH?

YOU EVER SLEEP IN A STATION WAGON? THERE'S A TRICK TO IT, Y'KNOW... SNIFF
MY MIND IS WIDE OPEN, HOPEY.
XAIME 87

A Mess of Skin...

JAWBONE 87

GAY. HUH! DO I FEEL LIKE I JUST SWAM OVER...

OH, I DUNNO. MOST OF MAGGIE'S "FRIENDS" THAT I'VE SEEN DIDN'T LOOK LIKE GIRLS TO ME, RAY.

HEY, BOXHEAD! WHAT'S GOIN' ON?
NOT MUCH, MAN. WE BEAT UP SOME JOCKS AND THEY SAID THEY'RE COMIN' BACK WITH REINFORCEMENTS. WE'RE JUST WAITIN'...

HEY, RAY. SINCE WE'RE HERE, YOU WANT TO GO IN AND TALK TO MAGGIE, OR... NO?
SO, I'M A PATHETIC HEAP. HEY, WHAT DOES YOUR GIRLFRIEND DO WHERE SHE HAS TO WORK SO LATE AT NIGHT?

WHERE'S YOUR GIRLFRIEND, RAY? WE ALL COULDA GONE OUT AFTER MY LAST SHOW AND DONE SOME REAL RUDE STUFF.
I DON'T HAVE A GIRL-FRIEND...

NO GIRLFRIEND? THEN WHAT DO YOU DO FOR SNATCH? YOU HANG AROUND THE STROLL, OR WHAT?
I JUST DON'T HAVE A GIRLFRIEND RIGHT NOW...
LILY... JUST IGNORE HER, RAY. I ALWAYS DO...

OR DO YOU PREFER YOUNG MEN, HUH, PABLO?
NO, I DON'T.

WELL, YOU NEVER CAN TELL WITH THE KINDA CROWD I'VE SEEN DOYLE HANG OUT WITH. RIGHT, BABY?
KNOCK IT OFF...

AW, TAKE A JOKE ONCE IN AWHILE! THIS IS MY LAST SHOW TONIGHT AND I HATE TO DANCE FOR ANGRY PUPPIES.
PUPPIES, THAT'S US.
ANGRY ONES.
2

DOYLE WENT TO THE HEAD, BUT HE SAW THE WHOLE DANCE...
WHAT DO YOU WANT ME TO DO ABOUT IT?

NOW I KNOW WHY DOYLE NEVER TOLD ME ABOUT YOU. YOU'RE A REAL GOOD LOOKING GUY...
THANKS.

...AND YOU'RE AN ARTIST, TOO...
WELL, I'M NOT REALLY AN ARTIST ARTIST. I JUST LIKE TO PAINT NOW AND THEN. UH...

WHAT KIND OF BULL-SHIT IS THAT? NOT AN ARTIST ARTIST...
HEY, DON'T START GETTING SORE, RAUL...
LOOK, ALL I SAID WAS...
RAY!
THEY REALLY HAVE STICKY OL' BATHROOMS HERE...

YOU GOING, RAY?
BYE, RAY! I'LL MAKE DOYLE BRING YOU BY MY PLACE ONE OF THESE DAYS. WE'LL ALL HAVE A REAL HUMDINGER...

Bumper's
TOPLESS
WEEK!
LILY RIVERA

SHIT! IF I DON'T DO IT NOW, I'LL NEVER DO IT...
STOP
SCREEEEEE-
3

SHIT! THEY CALLED OUT THE NATIONAL GUARD!
MADDOG

WHO, HOPEY? NAW, SHE WAS, BUT THE COPS CLEARED THE PLACE OUT.
MAGGIE YOU MEAN...
MAGGIE, HOPEY, DAFFY, SNEEZY... I CAN NEVER TELL 'EM APART, MAN...
HEY, SPLIT, MAN! COME ON...

ARE THEY STILL THERE?
I DON'T HEAR ANY-THING.
40 THIEFS
.2MAN.

WHAT WILL I DO? THEY CAN GET ME FOR CURFEW.
WE'LL MAKE A BREAK FOR THE BACK DOOR.
BABY DAPHNE!
I HATE JOEY GLASS

I DON'T THINK THERE'D BE ANY COPS IN THE ALLEY...
HEY!

≡SOB≡ THEY'RE GOING TO PUT US IN JAIL, I KNOW IT!
WAIT! THERE'S... DOYLE!!
???

HOME, JAMES! ON THE DOUBLE! HURRY, DAFFY! I THINK THEY'RE COMING!
BUT... BUT...
4

GUY, DAFFY! YOU SHOULD HAVE SEEN YOUR FACE WHEN THAT COP CALLED US...
MAGGIE, THIS IS NOT DOYLE...

HUH??
THIS IS NOT DOYLE.

IS THAT WHAT MY FACE LOOKED LIKE??

YOU COULD UNDERSTAND HOPEY'S WRIT-ING? I STILL CAN'T!
WELL, NO. I JUST THOUGHT SHE WAS BEING POETIC...
IF YOU WERE A PILL
I'D TAKE A HANDFUL AT MY WILL

MAGGIE, THERE'S JOEY AND THOSE GUYS. WE CAN GO NOW.
MY CAR'S STILL OVER AT MADDOG'S.
I'LL TAKE HER TO HER CAR... IF YOU WANT.

MAGGIE...
HE'LL TAKE ME TO MY CAR, DAFFY.

WELL... OK. I'LL CALL YOU TOMORROW... IN THE MORNING?
OK.
5

CLINK!
CHLOK!
CLICK!

white Power
SMF
SPLIT wet backs
TRESE

ALL THIS AND PENNY, TOO...

...A MILLION MILES FROM HOME

HYMEH 87

THIS BUS RIDE USED UP THE REST OF OUR CASH. THIS BETTER BE GOOD.
DON'T WORRY, TEXAS. IT'S SMOOTH SAILING FROM HERE ON IN, BOY.

WHY DIDN'T YOU JUST COME WITH THE TOUR LIKE EVERY-BODY ELSE?
'CAUSE WE'RE GUESTS OF MRS. H.R. COSTIGAN HERSELF, SMART GUY!

SHE DID, HUH? YA DON'T SAY. WELL, I'LL BE...
...A DICK BRAINED ASS BITE.

HOKAY! THE TRAM WILL TAKE YOU RIGHT UP TO THE FRONT DOOR.
COME, TEXAS.

MORE YOYOS. I WONDER WHAT GOES ON IN THAT HOUSE.
I'D RATHER NOT KNOW MYSELF.

HEY, WEBSTER. REMEMBER ME? HUH, WEBSTER?
OF COURSE.
HOPEEE

COME ON UP! HURRY! WE'RE PLAYING!
WHY, I'D RECOGNIZE THOSE BOOBS ANYWHERE.
2

MMM... YOUR CHEEK IS LIKE ICE!
WHATCHA PLAYIN,' PENNY? AEROBIC VIDEOS ON PARADE?

AIN'T IT FAB? I JUST HAD THE POKER ROOM TURNED INTO X AVENUE, ATOMICA'S FAVORITE HANGOUT. YOU WANNA SEE A PERFORMANCE?
IS IT FREE?
ROY'S

OK, YOU VILLIANOUS SCUM! BREAK'S OVER! IT'S TIME TO IMPRESS SOME FRIENDS OF MINE!
SHIT. HERE WE GO AGAIN, GUYS.
OH, WELL. IT'S A LIVING, HUH?
LIVING, HE SAYS.

THIS TIME YOU JUST ROBBED THE JEWELRY STORE. NOW, WHO'S LEADING IN THIS SHINDIG?
GO AHEAD, TED. YOU REALLY MAKE A GREAT LEADER.
M-ME?
GO, TED!

HALT, RATMAN!
OH, MOTHER! HERE IT COMES!

TAKE THAT!
Y-YOU MEAN, THAT'S IT? I JUST FALL DOWN THIS TIME?

OH NO! PLEASE! NOT THE WINDOW!
WE'RE WAITING.
3

GO FOR IT, TED! IT'S GOTTA BE WORTH THE THOUSAND BUCKS WE'RE GONNA GET!
THAT'S WHAT YOU THINK!
AT LEAST IT'S ON THE FIRST FLOOR THIS TIME.

CRASHH

YOU OK, TED?
I THINK I SWALLOWED SOME GLASS. AKK!
YOU! BLACK BASHER !!!

ZZASP!
WHY DO I ALWAYS GET THE "BRICK WALL"?
USMC

REMEMBER, ZACK! A THOUSAND SMACKERS...
KEEP REMINDING ME...

AAAAAAH

YOU DON'T SUPPOSE SHE'S STARTED USING REAL BRICKS, DO YA?
YOO HOO! APOLLO!
GULP

I-I DON'T UNDERSTAND THIS POWER YOU HAVE OVER ME. YOU'RE CONTROLLING MY EMOTIONS SOMEHOW AND I CAN'T FIGHT IT...
?

Y-YOU'RE MAKING ME WANT YOU BADLY! I MUST OBEY! I MUST! AND-AND THEN ALL OF A SUDDEN...
SAY, THIS ISN'T BAD...
4

...BOOBY TRAP!
EEEEEE

THOUSAND OR NO THOUSAND... I QUIT!
ME, TOO! YOU'RE NUTS, LADY!
ONCE AGAIN, GOOD TRIUMPHS OVER EVIL...

ARE ALL YOUR FRIENDS LIKE HER?
ONLY MY CLOSEST FRIENDS.

YOU CAN'T FIND GOOD HELP NOWADAYS. YOU GUYS EATEN?
EATEN? WHAT'S THAT?
I THINK THAT'S SOMETHING NORMAL FOLKS DO ABOUT THREE TIMES A DAY.

YOU KNOW, I WAS THINKING OF TURNING THIS ROOM INTO THE PLANET BLOTOS.
WHERE'S YOUR HORNED HUSBAND?

I DUNNO, HAVEN'T SEEN HIM FOR MONTHS. C'MON, TELL THE TRUTH. HOW DO YOU THINK THIS ROOM WOULD LOOK WITH BLUE CRATERS?

WHO'S SHE TRYING TO FOOL? SHE'S BEEN LIKE THIS EVER SINCE SHE MARRIED THAT HORNY GHOUL.
I THOUGHT YOU SAID SHE'S ALWAYS BEEN CRAZY.

WELL, SURE! BUT A DIFFERENT KINDA CRAZY! NOW THERE'S KIND OF A FUCKNESS TO HER CRAZY. SHE AIN'T HAPPY HERE. NO FUCKIN' WAY...
YOU'D KNOW MORE THAN ME.
5

TIA THREATENED TO BUY ME A WIG, HOPEY. WHAT'LL I DO?
EASY... MOVE OUT, MAGGOT!
YOO HOO!

BOY, AM I BUSHED! SELLING FLOWERS ON BUSY STREET CORNERS IS NO FUN! BE GLAD YOU BABIES DON'T HAVE TO DO IT!

Y'KNOW, I'VE BEEN DYING TO GET TO NEW KEOPS, BUT YOU NEED MONEY FOR THAT AND MONEY I DON'T GOT!
WOW.
BUMMER.

WELL, NO REST FOR THE WEARY. I'LL TALK TO YOU BABIES LATER, OK?
SEE YA.
BYE.

WHO-THE-HELL-WAS-THAT??
WHO?? WHAT THE HELL WAS THAT?

...MY EYES ARE STILL CURLY AND MY HAIR IS STILL BLUE, WHY DON'T YOU LOVE ME LIKE YOU USED TO DO...

HI, MAGGIE! GOING TO WORK I SEE! CATCH YOU LATER, OK?
?!?

...AND THEN SHE STARTS RAMBLING ON ABOUT THE CRAZIEST THINGS...
WHO, PENNY?
VARRIO
6

IS THAT HER NAME? YOU KNOW HER?
ACTUALLY, HER NAME'S BEATRÍZ, BUT ME AN' IZZY CALL HER PENNY TENTIARY. GET IT? 'CAUSE SHE'S SO KOOKY...
D.T.
VARRIO HOPERS
13

¡MENSA! A PENITENTIARY IS FOR CROOKS, NOT FOR CRAZY PEOPLE!
SO? WE CALL HER THAT ANYWAY. SHE'S BEEN HANGING OUT AT IZZY'S THE LAST COUPLE OF NIGHTS. WHAT A NUT...

WE'RE GOING OVER AGAIN TONIGHT. YOU SHOULD SNEAK OUT AND COME.
ARE YOU SURE I'LL FIT? FOUR'S A CROWD, Y'KNOW.
HOPERS

WELL, LISTEN TO YOU! DO I DETECT A LITTLE JEALOUSY, MI QUERIDA?
NOPE. YOU GUYS ARE JUST FUCKED.

YOU ARE! YOU ARE JEALOUS! JEALOUS, JEALOUS, JEALOUS...
I AM NOT! YOU'RE FUCKED! FUCKED, FUCKED, FUCKED!
HEY, ARE YOU GUYS REALLY FIGHTING?

WELL, IF IT AIN'T PENNY OF THE CENTURY.
THAT'S TENTIARY! JEALOUS, JEALOUS, JEALOUS...
PENNY CENTURY! THAT'S SO CUTE!

DON'T YOU THINK I LOOK LIKE A PENNY CENTURY?
JEALOUS, JEALOUS, JEALOUS, JEALOUS...
ONCE MORE! SAY IT ONCE MORE!

WHEN MY HAIR IS THIS COLOR I'LL BE PENNY CENTURY, AND WHEN IT'S NORMAL, I'LL BE BEATRÍZ GARCIA. OR IS THAT JUST WAY TOO DUMB?
JEA-- OW! BITCH!
I WARNED YOU... YEOW!

YOU GUYS AREN'T REALLY FIGHTING.
RRARRRR!
HISSSS!
ROWRRR!
FFFT!
7

DON'T YOU EVER SLEEP?
HI, HOPEY! I'M JUST CUTTING OUT STUFF FOR MY SCRAPBOOK.

YOU SURE THAT'S WISE? SOME OF THESE BOOKS LOOK REAL ANCIENT...
I SUPPOSE THEY ARE. THIS ONE'S A FIRST EDITION. IT'S GOT SOME GREAT LINES IN IT THAT WILL FIT NICELY ALONGSIDE MY PICTURES.
MOBY DICK

IF YOUR HUSBAND COULD SEE YOU NOW.
PTCH! NOT EVEN WITH HIS GLASSES ON, BABY!

LAST WEEK I DROVE THREE OF HIS ROLLS ROYCES INTO THE POOL AND WHEN I CALLED AND TOLD HIM ABOUT IT, HE SAID, "OH, YOU'VE BEEN SWIMMING, DEAR?"
WOTTA LIFE!

I'LL BET IF YOU BURNED THIS PALACE DOWN, HE'D SAY "OH, WELL... AT LEAST I HAVE THREE MORE."
YEAH...

OH, BEFORE I FORGET. COULD YOU GIVE SOMETHING TO MAGGIE FOR ME WHEN YOU SEE HER?
IF I SEE HER. WHAT IS IT?

MAGGIE'S PASS CARD TO LILLIAN ELLISON'S AIR BASE IN PT. MAGOO.
REMEMBER? SHE GAVE IT TO ME WHEN I HAD TO SEE RAND RACE ABOUT SOMETHING.
8

J'G/JUG (PRONOUNCED JIG)

SHE OPENED UP THE CLOSET, AND THERE HE WAS, ALL...

...!//!
OK, HOW DID YOU FIND ME?

WHAT THE FUCK, PENNY? WHY'D YOU CHICKEN OUT?
I DIDN'T CHICKEN OUT. I'M GOING...

...BUT FIRST I'M GONNA STICK AROUND FOR A WEEK OR TWO AND SPY ON THE OLD BOY. WATCH HIM SQUIRM...
YOU MEAN YOU'RE REALLY SAFE IN HERE? THEY WON'T EVER FIND YOU?
MA

NO WAY! HERV'S NEVER EVEN SEEN THIS WING OF THE HOUSE!
WELL, TEX. IT LOOKS LIKE WE CAN STAY AFTER ALL.
AAH, YOU TWO, I SWEAR...

OK, SO WE'RE HERE! WHAT THE HELL ARE WE GONNA DO IN THIS ROOM FOR TWO WEEKS?

HEY, I THINK HIS HEART HAS STOPPED.
LET'S GIVE HIM A FEW MORE MINUTES.
THAT'S ALL FOLKS!

IN THE VALLEY of the POLAR BEARS
RIC FLAIR SINGS 'STYLIN' 'N' PROFILIN'
XAIME THE FREAK 88
1

SHRIMP! WAKE UP!

WAKE UP AND LOOK WHAT I GOT BACK...
WHAT YOU GOT BA...?

TIA?! OH MY GOD! WHAT ARE YOU DOING HERE? SHIT!
I LIVE HERE. LOOK, SHRIMP...

GOD DAMN, TIA! YOU WEREN'T SUPPOSED TO BE BACK UNTIL TOMORROW!
WHEN YOU STOP ACTING LIKE A RETARD, COME DOWNSTAIRS. I'VE GOTTA TALK TO YOU.
SEX
OCT 10

I GUESS I SHOULD GO, HUH?
NO, NO! PLEASE! STAY! I PROMISE I'LL BE RIGHT BACK! DON'T LEAVE! PLEASE?

OH, SHIT...
A COUPLE OF YOUR FRIENDS JUST RAN OUT THE BACK DOOR.

I'M GLAD YOU WON YOUR CHAMPIONSHIP BELT BACK.
AIN'T IT THE TRUTH? THIS TIME IT'S STAYING WITH ITS RIGHTFUL OWNER, AND THAT'S WHAT I WANNA TALK TO YOU ABOUT...
2

IS THE COAST CLEAR, DAFFY?
I'M NOT SURE, TOM TOM.

LET'S GO OUT THE BACK WAY IN CASE THEY'RE IN THE FRONT ROOM.

MAGGIE?! WHERE IS YOUR AUNT?
SHE STEPPED OUT AWHILE.

NO SCARS, NO BRUISES. WHAT DID SHE DO? WHAT DID SHE SAY?
BELIEVE IT OR NOT, SHE OFFERED ME A JOB.

HUH?!
SERIOUS. SHE'S STARTING A NATIONWIDE WRESTLING TOUR TOMORROW AND SHE WANTS ME TO GO ALONG. I DON'T KNOW WHAT I GOTTA DO, BUT SHE SAYS I'LL MAKE REAL GOOD MONEY.

SHE SAID, "I'M DOING THIS FOR YOU, SHRIMPO, BECAUSE I'M MOVING OUTTA STATE AFTER THIS TOUR AND I WOULDN'T WANNA LEAVE YOU OUT IN THE COLD. Y'ALL UNDERSTAND WHAT I'M SAYING?

"THIS WAY YOU CAN AFFORD TO GO LIVE WITH YOUR DYKE GIRLFRIEND BACK EAST, OR AFTER WHAT I JUST SAW IN YOUR BED, WITH YOUR BOYFRIEND. YOU HAVE UNTIL LATE AFTERNOON TO THINK ABOUT IT...

"...SO GET OFF YOUR FAT ASS AND CLEAN THIS GOD DAMNED HOUSE BEFORE I RETURN!"
3

WELL, THAT'S THAT. I GUESS I SHOULD PACK NOW. I CAN'T AFFORD TO STAY HERE.

OOH, WHEEE! HOW COME YOU NEVER WEAR YOUR WRESTLING BOOTS ANY MORE?
SHIT, TIA WOULD SKIN ME ALIVE IF SHE KNEW I HAD THOSE. QUEEN RENA GAVE 'EM TO ME AND... WELL, I TOLD YOU ABOUT THOSE TWO...

OH, BUT THEY'RE TOO PRETTY TO SIT IN A CLOSET! IF THEY WERE MINE, I'D WEAR THEM ALL THE TIME!
I'LL GIVE 'EM TO YOU FOR YOUR LEATHER.
?

MY JACKET?! NO WAY! AS MUCH AS I LOVE THOSE BOOTS, I COULD NEVER GIVE THIS UP!
MIKE, THE SINGER OF "BLAMED YOUTH" GAVE IT TO HER!
OH, YEAH. HOW'D IT GO BETWEEN YOU AN' HIM, DAFF?

I DON'T KNOW. HE WAS WITH GOO GOO LAST NIGHT.
I TOLD YOU HE WAS A POLAR BEAR.
A WHAT?!
C.O.C.

A POLAR BEAR. SO CUTE AND CUDDLY IN HIS CAGE BUT WHEN YOU WANT TO GET CLOSE ENOUGH TO CUDDLE HIM HE TEARS YOU APART AND SWALLOWS YOU WHOLE.
TSK! GUY! HE'S NOT LIKE THAT...
HE'S RAD!

HE'S LIKE, SO INTENSE ON STAGE! LIKE FUCKIN'...
SO INTENSE...
AND HE KNOWS JELLO...
SO RAD...
HE KNEW DARBY...
OOH...
4

I'M REALLY GLAD YOU DECIDED TO COME ALONG, SHRIMP.
I DIDN'T HAVE MUCH OF A CHOICE, DID I?

WHAT DID YOUR BOYFRIEND SAY?
HE SAYS I'M GONNA PICK HOPEY WHEN I GET BACK.
UNIGHTED ERRLINES

WELL, I'M SURE Y'ALL WILL MAKE THE RIGHT DECISION.
OH, YOU THINK SO, HUH?
REGENCY

TAKE IT EASY THE REST OF THE DAY, SHRIMP. I'LL FILL YOU IN ON WHAT YOU GOTTA DO AFTER I MAKE A FEW TV ANNOUNCEMENTS.
TAKE YOUR TIME.

LET ME GET THIS STRAIGHT, VICKI. YOU WANT TO "INSURE" YOUR WORLD CHAMPIONSHIP BELT? WELL, THAT'S QUITE AN ODD REQUEST AND I'M NOT SURE THE W.W.W. BOARD IS GOING TO GO ALONG WITH THAT.
SNORT
WHY NOT??
PAY TV
Welcome to the Regency Hotel

Y'ALL SEEM TO FORGET THAT I COME FROM A LONG LINE OF TEXAS OIL BARONS AND I CAN MATCH ANY PRICE THEY THROW AT ME...
BUT, YOU DON'T UNDERSTAND, VICKI. I DON'T THINK YOU CAN INSURE A TITLE!

YOU'RE ALSO FORGETTING THAT I'M CHAMPION OF THE WORLD, AND IF I WANT TO BRING MY OWN PERSONAL ACCOUNTANT TO MEET WITH THE BOARD NEXT WEEK, SOMEBODY BETTER LET ME!
LET'S GO TO THE RING...

BUT, TIA. I DON'T KNOW ANYTHING ABOUT ACCOUNTING OR ANYTHING LIKE THAT! OUCH!
YOU WON'T HAVE TO. JUST SIT THERE AN' LOOK REAL SERIOUS.
5

I'M SORRY, BUT THERE ARE JUST SO MANY KNOTS...
GRUNT! COULDN'T I JUST TIE IT UP?
AIN'T NO ACCOUNTANT EVER LOOKED LIKE NO CAVEMAN.

I LOOK LIKE A DAMN FOOL.
IT'S AN IMPROVEMENT. NOW, REMEMBER TO STAND THERE SILENT LIKE YOUR SHIT DON'T STINK...
LET'S GO, VICKI!

THE BOARD REFUSED TO MEET WITH YOU? WELL, YOU MUST ADMIT, IT WAS AN ODD REQUEST!
THERE'S NOTHING WRONG WITH WANTING TO INSURE MY BELT, AN' Y'ALL KNOW IT!

THEY'RE ONLY DOING THIS 'CAUSE THEY'RE STILL SORE AT HOW I RECAPTURED THIS BELT, BY PUTTING THAT SISSY INDIAN OUT OF WRESTLING FOR SIX MONTHS! I'M TELLIN' YA, IT AIN'T MY FAULT THEIR NECKS BREAK LIKE PENCILS!

Y'ALL LISTEN HERE, MISTER W.W.W. PRESIDENT AND BOARD MEMBERS! I AM GOING TO CONTINUE TO HOSPITALIZE EVERY OPPONENT UNTIL Y'ALL AGREE TO MEET WITH MS. MAGGIE AN' ME ON THIS MATTER. WE'LL BE WAITIN'...

HEY, I GUESS NOW YOU CAN CALL YOUR FRIENDS BACK HOME AN' TELL 'EM TO WATCH YOU ON TV.
YOU THINK I WANT THEM TO SEE ME LOOKING LIKE THIS?
HEY, BO! AIN'T YOU GOT SOMETHIN' TO DO RIGHT NOW?

WHAT'S WRONG WITH YOU? I THOUGHT YOU WERE THE ONE THAT CAME UP WITH THAT POLAR BEAR THEORY...
WELL, SHIT, TIA! YOU GOTTA FEED 'EM TO FIND 'EM! BESIDES, IT AIN'T LIKE I WAS INVITING THE GUY OVER TO MY PLACE FOR COCKTAILS!
6

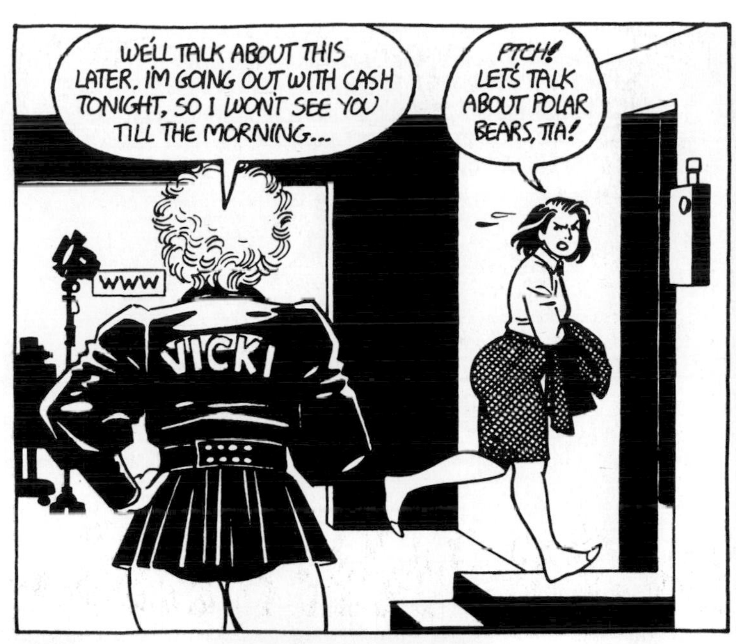
WE'LL TALK ABOUT THIS LATER. I'M GOING OUT WITH CASH TONIGHT, SO I WON'T SEE YOU TILL THE MORNING...
PTCH! LET'S TALK ABOUT POLAR BEARS, TIA!
WWW
VICKI

YOU GUYS WILL GET IT ON CHANNEL FIVE AT NINE, YOUR TIME, SO DON'T GET TOO SCARED WHEN YOU SEE A FAT, BLOATED MONSTER INVADE YOUR TV SCREEN.
WHICH REMINDS ME. HOPEY CALLED EARLIER.

SHE DID?! GUY! WHEN? WHAT DID SHE SAY??
SHE RAGGED ABOUT YOUR TIA'S ANSWERING MACHINE THEN THE OPERATOR CUT US OFF.

YEAH... IT'S SO STUPID... SHE GOT ME THIS YUPPIE SUIT AND THIS YUPPIE HAIRCUT AND STOOD ME IN FRONT OF A CAMERA, AND... GOD, IT WAS SO STUPID...

YEAH? HA! CAN'T WAIT TO SEE IT. SO... THEN I'LL SEE YOU WHEN YOU GET BACK, HUH? OK, SEE YA...

I'M GONNA KILL THIS HOPEY PERSON...
HUH? WE KEEPING YOU UP, RAY?

JMMM...
7

THE GUYS WERE ONLY KIDDING ABOUT THAT VICKI LA MOMMA JAZZ...
(PUFF PUFF) THEY SHOULDN'T JOKE LIKE THAT, CASH.
JOBS
LIGHT

SOMEBODY'S GOTTA FEEL SORRY FOR THAT KID! I HAD TO TAKE HER IN YEARS AGO BECAUSE HER PARENTS HAD THE BALLS TO USE HER AS THEIR EXCUSE FOR BREAKING UP! JEEZ, I TOLD QUINA NOT TO MARRY MY BROTHER! HE AIN'T THE KIND THAT SHOULD EVER MARRY! BUT SHE WAS STUPID...
REGENCY

AN' I REALLY TRIED TO BE MORE THAN JUST AN AUNT TO THE SHRIMP IN THOSE TOUGH TIMES, BUT I DON'T THINK SHE EVER APPRECIATED IT...

EVEN NOW SHE RESENTS EVERYTHING I TRY TO DO FOR HER! HELL, NOBODY'S PERFECT! I AIN'T NO MOTHER! I'M A WRESTLER!
YEAH, BUT SHE AIN'T NO WRESTLER.

(SIGH) OK, I'LL TRY TO BE EASIER ON HER...
HUH? NOW? WHAT ABOUT OUR LITTLE AFTER HOURS DIP IN MY WATER BED, BABY?

HEY, SHRIMP! YOU UP?
IT'S OPEN.

I WAS THINKIN', SHRIMP. IF YOU WANT, TOMORROW WE COULD... WHAT THE HELL DID YOU DO TO YOUR HAIR??
I PUT SOAP IN IT. I'M DONE PLAYING YUPPIE ACCOUNTANT, Y'KNOW...
8

YEOW! TIA, YOU'RE BREAKING MY ARM!
STINKIN' BRAT! I'LL TELL YOU WHEN I'M DONE WITH YOU!

I GOT SOAP IN MY EYEEEEEE!
YOU WANNA ACT LIKE A BRAT, YOU MIGHT AS WELL BE TREATED LIKE ONE!

EVERY GOD DAMN TIME... WHAT AM I GONNA DO WITH YOU?!?
FIRE ME!

OH, NO YOU DON'T! YOU LISTEN AND, YOU LISTEN GOOD! FROM NOW ON, YOU'RE GONNA DO EXACTLY WHAT I TELL YOU TO DO, OR ELSE! DO-YOU-UNDERSTAND?!
HEIL HITLER.

TONIGHT
WWW WRESTLING
MAIN EVENT
WORLD CHAMPIONSHIP
VICKI GLORI VS CANDYCANE LAINE
TAG TEAM CHAMPIONSHIP
THE FOUR HORSEMEN VS JIM, ELMER, LUKE & JUNIOR
EL SANTO VS EL BOMBO
MOOLAH VS MANGLER
BLASSIE VS TOLOS
GOLIATH VS TONY ROME
LOS BROS VS LOS MEDICOS

NOW, RELAX OUT THERE, SHRIMP. JUST DO LIKE YOU DID ON TV.
YES SIR.
VICKI GLORI VS RITA CORTEZ
MULKEYS VS BROOKS & RIZZ
ISMAEL VS NIKI
BOLO VS THE APE
OXNARD AUDITORIUM
9

VICKI! YOU'RE A PIG!
OINK OINK!
KEEP WALKING, GIRL.
SHOULDN'T YOU BE LEADING THE WAY?
OINK OINK!
EVENT STAFF

NGHH!
ALL RIGHT! LET'S CUT THE CLOWNING, SHRIMPO...

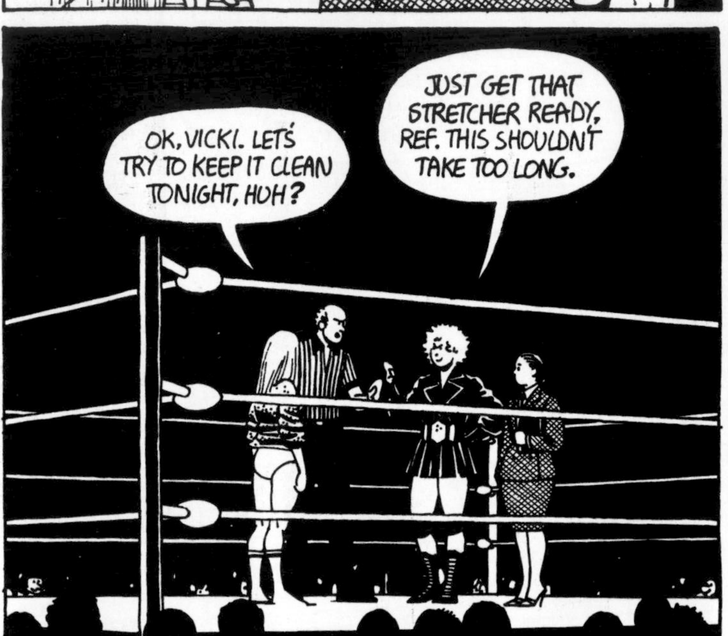
OK, VICKI. LET'S TRY TO KEEP IT CLEAN TONIGHT, HUH?
JUST GET THAT STRETCHER READY, REF. THIS SHOULDN'T TAKE TOO LONG.

YOU DID GOOD, SHRIMP. NOW STAND OVER THERE, AN' IF YOU'RE SPAT ON, TRY TO IGNORE IT.
I'VE BEEN SPAT ON BY EXPERTS.

BING BING!
AH, SHIT!
CHRIST! NOW WHAT?

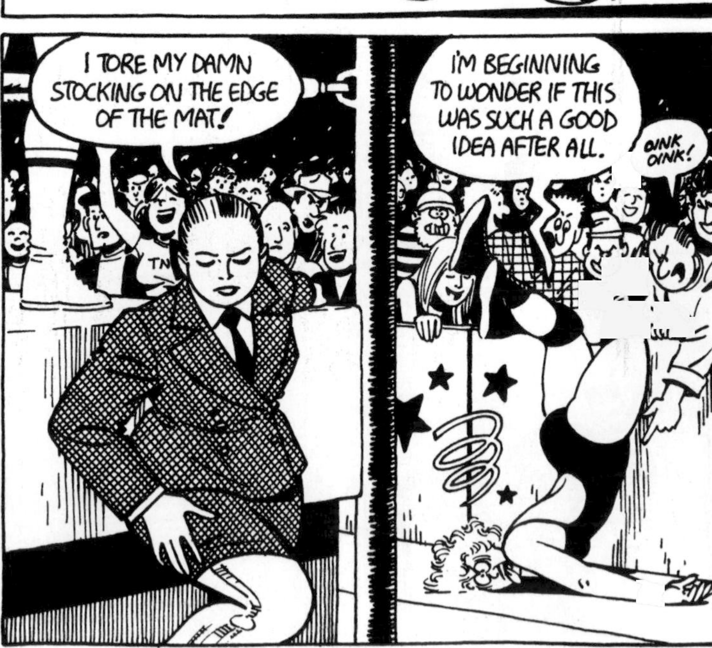
I TORE MY DAMN STOCKING ON THE EDGE OF THE MAT!
I'M BEGINNING TO WONDER IF THIS WAS SUCH A GOOD IDEA AFTER ALL.
OINK OINK!

END OF PART I

In the Valley of the Polar Bears

Part 2

BY JAIME "THE SPINKS JINX" HERNANDEZ 88

ONE LOW BLOW, TWO BODY SLAMS, AND ONE ATOMIC PILEDRIVER LATER...
I KNOW Y'ALL IS OUT THERE WATCHIN', W.W.W. BOARD AN' I KNOW Y'ALL DON'T LIKE WHAT Y'ALL JUST SAW, BUT Y'ALL KNOW WHAT Y'ALL CAN DO TO STOP IT!

I'M TELLIN' YA, VICKI! YOU BROKE HER DAMN COLLAR BONE!
YOU CAN'T PIN THIS ON ME! IF THAT TWERP LEARNED TO FALL RIGHT IN THE FIRST PLACE, THIS WOULDN'T HAVE HAPPENED!
A REAL HUMANITARIAN, AIN'T SHE?

C'MON, VICKI! YOU KNOW THE SHRIMP AIN'T HAPPY. WHY DON'T YOU SEND HER HOME?
WHY DON'T YOU GUYS LET ME WORRY ABOUT THE SHRIMP, OK?
WWW

NOT HAPPY... I'LL SHOW YOU WHO'S NOT HAPPY!
EIGHT YEARS AND YOU STILL HAVEN'T BUSTED THAT BRONC, CASH BABY?
YOU AIN'T A WHISTLIN' DIXIE...

2

PRINCESS WARFEATHER, CANDYCANE LAINE, BLANCHE DE LA BOOM, MRS. T., AND NOW MONTANA JANE! WHEN DOES IT ALL END, VICKI?
IT NEVER ENDS! I'M TOO FAR GONE, MEL! I'M OUTTA CONTROL!

I DON'T EVEN WANNA INSURE MY TITLE ANY MORE! I DON'T HAVE TO! AT THE RATE I'M GOING, I'LL NEVER LOSE THIS BELT! PRETTY SOON THERE'LL BE NO ONE LEFT TO CHALLENGE ME FOR IT!
MOO HOO HOO HA HA HA HAAA!
CACKLE CACKLE!

VICKI, THE BOARD SAYS IF YOU KEEP THIS UP, THEY'RE GONNA STRIP YOU OF YOUR TITLE, AND THEY AIN'T KIDDING.
I CAN'T HELP IT, CASH! EVERYTIME I SEE HER FROWNING FACE, I GO APE SHIT! SHE'S DRIVING ME NUTSO!

THEN I GUESS IT'S TIME YOU SENT HER HOME...
BULLSHIT! EVERYBODY KNOWS THAT SINCE I STARTED THIS ACCOUNTANT BIT, I'VE BEEN THE ONE SELLING OUT ALL THE ARENAS! NOT EVEN YOU HEADLINE OVER ME ANY MORE!

I GET THE FEELING THAT'S NOT THE REAL REASON YOU'RE NOT SENDING HER HOME.
NO IT AINT...

YOU'D THINK THAT JUST ONCE SHE'D APPRECIATE WHAT I DO FOR...
3

SLAM!
I ALWAYS KNEW THERE WAS A HEART TRAPPED IN THERE SOMEWHERE. AT LAST I FOUND THE ONE THING THAT WILL SET IT FREE...

HI.
HI. HOW DO YOU LIKE YOUR JOB SO FAR?

I DUNNO, IT'S ALL RIGHT. IT'S KINDA FUN, BUT I DON'T THINK TIA'S TOO HAPPY WITH ME. I GUESS I DON'T DO A VERY GOOD SNOB.
YOU JUST KEEP DOING IT THE WAY YOU DO IT. I'LL HANDLE YOUR TIA.

VICKI GLORI'S REIGN OF TERROR HAS GOT TO END, AND I BELIEVE I'M THE ONLY ONE WITH THE SPEED, THE AGILITY, THE STAMINA, AND THE STRENGTH TO DO IT...
PEPPER MARTINEZ!

I KNOW PEPPER. SHE WAS RENA'S PARTNER.
SHRIMP, I'D APPRECIATE IT IF YOU DIDN'T TALK TO HER UNTIL AFTER I BEAT HER ASS INTO THE GROUND.

HUH? I CAN'T EVEN SAY HI?
NOT EVEN HI, SHRIMP.

YOU THINK JUST BECAUSE YOU'RE MY BOSS IN THAT RING, YOU CAN...
919
I DON'T WANT YOU BEFRIENDING MY RIVALS, AND THAT'S THAT!
4

916-999
THAT'S IT. THAT'S REALLY IT. I CAN'T TAKE THIS SHIT NO MORE.
WAIT, KID. LISTEN TO ME FOR A SECOND...

SHE SAID THAT, HUH? SO WHAT AM I SUPPOSED TO DO, FEEL SORRY FOR HER WHEN SHE BREAKS MY ARM? SHEEE...
AW, DON'T GIVE UP! SHE NEEDS YOU!
WW

HELL, I NEED YOU...

"...SO DON'T JUDGE HER TOO HARSHLY. SHE REALLY DOES CARE ABOUT YOU, Y'KNOW."

MY GOD, I KNOW I'M GONNA REGRET THIS...

WRESTLING
FRI - ROY COWBOY IN "FU
SAT - LOS BUKI

I WAS EASY ON THOSE OTHER SAPS COMPARED TO WHAT I'M GONNA DO TO THAT FAT MONSTER! SHE'S GONNA WISH SHE NEVER LEFT PUERTO RICO!

SOMEONE MUSTA DROPPED HER ON HER HEAD WHEN SHE WAS LITTLE 'CAUSE SHE AIN'T PLAYIN' WITH A FULL DECK! WHAT I'M GONNA DO TO HER, NONE OF HER TEXAS MILLIONS WILL BE ABLE TO REPAIR!
WW
5

GIVE 'EM HELL TONIGHT, VICKI.
THANKS.

YOU READY?
YEAH.

KAWHAM!!
OOF!

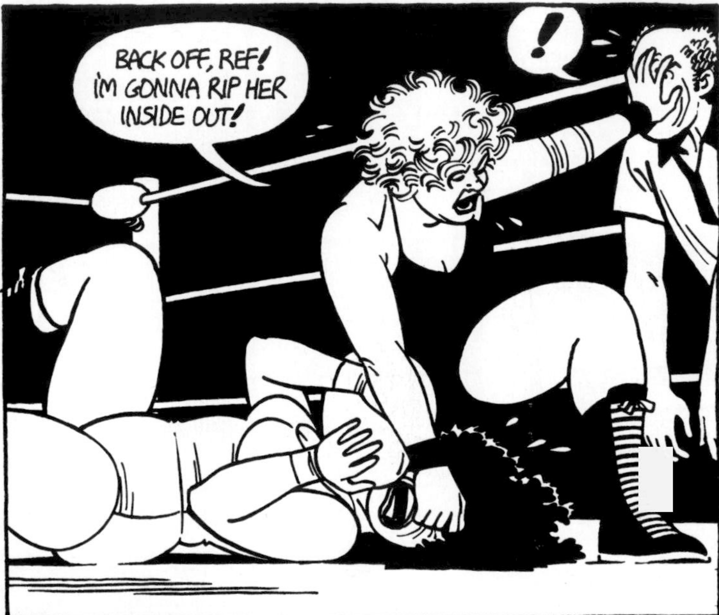
BACK OFF, REF! I'M GONNA RIP HER INSIDE OUT!
!

PLEASE, SOMEONE RUN IN AND KNOCK TIA OUT WITH A CHAIR OR SHOOT HER IN THE HEAD OR SOMETHING! SHE'S OUTTA CONTROL AND IT'S ALL BECAUSE OF ME!

BONK!
GASP! PEPPER!
6

OH, MY GOD! SHE'S REALLY OUT! PEPPER...
AHA!

OF ALL THE BACKSTABBIN'...
GET THE HELL OUTTA HERE, SHRIMP! SCAT! ¡PRONTO!

I'LL GET YOU FOR THIS, YOU LITTLE SHIT!

OH GOD-OH GOD-OH GOD... I-I-I REALLY DID IT... SHE-SHE-SHE REALLY WANTED TO-TO-TO KI-I-ILL ME-E-E...

I KNOW! I-I'LL HOP A TRAIN AND SEND FOR MY STUFF LATER... EEP!
CLICK!

WELL, SHRIMP. YOU DID IT. YOU ACTUALLY FIGURED A WAY WHERE I'D HAVE TO FIRE YOU. PRETTY DARN CLEVER...
B-BUT, TIA. I DIDN'T MEAN TO... I DON'T WANNA BE FIRED...

WELL, TOUGH! THOUSANDS OF FANS SAW YOU TURN ON ME. I HAD TO MAKE A T.V. ANNOUNCE-MENT STATING THAT YOU WERE OUT TO STEAL MY MONEY ALL ALONG. AS MUCH AS I'D LIKE TO, IT'S TOO LATE TO CHANGE NOW.
BUT...
7

LOS DIABLOS BLANCOS
HELLO? DIRK? I WANT YOU TO CHANGE ONE OF THE PLANE TICKETS FOR THE ATLANTA GIG TO L.A. INSTEAD. NO FLIGHT UNTIL TOMORROW MORNING? THAT'S OK...

DOYLE! I'M BORED, MAN!
THEN CLEAN YOUR HALF OF THE APARTMENT LIKE YOU SAID YOU WOULD!
MOISES TRESE

SO, THAT'S THE SINGER OF "BLAMED YOUTH" EVERYBODY'S BEEN TALKING ABOUT...
YEAH, KING POLAR BEAR HIMSELF. MAKES JOEY GLASS SEEM LIKE A SAINT.

IT MAKES ME SAD THAT DAFFY HAS TO LEARN THE HARD WAY LIKE THE REST OF US.
YOU MAKE IT SOUND LIKE THERE'S NO ALTERNATIVE FOR YOU GIRLS.
YOUTH

WELL, YOU TELL ME: WHERE DO ALL THE GOOD ONES HANG OUT?
WELL, I CAN'T SPEAK FOR MYSELF, BUT MY ROOMMATE'S AS GOOD AS THEY COME NOWADAYS. THE BOY'S OOZING WITH RESPECT FOR HIS GIRLFRIEND...

SO, HE'S THE EXCEPTION TO THE RULE...
...BUT HE WAS ALSO LUCKY NOT TO BE IGNORED BY HER AS JUST "A NICE GUY, BUT..."
8

OH, SO MOST OF US ASK TO BE TREATED LIKE SHIT, HUH? AND EVERYBODY TALKS ABOUT WHAT A NICE GUY YOU ARE...
YOU KIDDING? NICE GUYS GET SHITTED ON.

BUT THERE ARE EXCEPTIONS TO THE RULE, RIGHT? GIVE ME A BREAK...
OF COURSE THAT'S IF YOU WANNA KEEP FOLLOWING THEM BOGUS RULES.

RAY'S GONNA HAVE TO BE REALLY SOMETHING TO FILL IN HOPEY'S SHOES LIKE HE IS...
THERE'S BEEN OTHERS BESIDES HOPEY...
APE SEX

HO HO! THOSE GUYS COULDN'T EVEN LICK HOPEY'S SHOE PRINTS! SHE HAS A SPELL ON MAGGIE THAT NOT EVEN THAT CHOLO WHO WAS KILLED COULD MATCH!
I DUNNO, I THINK A LOT OF THAT HOPEY MAGIC'S FADED SINCE RAY'S COME AROUND.

MR. KNOW-IT-ALL. MAGGIE'S ONLY WITH HIM BECAUSE HOPEY DESERTED HER WHEN THE BAND WENT ON TOUR.
FUNNY, THAT'S WHAT HE SAID. AH, BUT WE'LL SEE.

YES, WE WILL SEE...
DOYLE, WHAT TIME IS IT?
FIVE MINUTES LATER THAN THE LAST TIME YOU ASKED ME. WHAT'S UP?
APE SEX

I PROMISED TO PICK UP MAGGIE AT THE AIRPORT AT FOUR. I'M GOING TO ASK HER BOYFRIEND IF HE'D LIKE TO GREET HER. WOULD YOU LIKE TO COME, AS WELL?
MR. KNOW-IT-ALL STRIKES AGAIN. SHALL WE GO?
9

HEY, JUST BECAUSE THE PIG LADY FIRED YOU DOESN'T MEAN YOU HAVE TO QUIT THIS BIZ ALTOGETHER! WHY DON'T YOU COME WITH US ON OUR EAST COAST TOUR?

I ADMIT, IT WON'T BE JETS, HOTELS AND LIMOS, BUT IT'LL BE A GAS ALL THE SAME! WE'RE HITTING MOST BIG CITIES, AND...

OK, MAGGIE. I KNOW HOW YOU FEEL. YOU HAVE A SAFE TRIP HOME, Y'HEAR?
THANKS, PEPPER...

NOW, BE SURE TO GET TO THE AIRPORT PLENTY EARLY SO YOU DON'T MISS YOUR PLANE. I WON'T BE AROUND TO FIX IT IF YOU SCREW UP...
TIA? COULDN'T I JUST...

NOW DON'T START AGAIN WITH THAT PHONEY BULL ABOUT HOW YOU WANT TO BE WITH ME! YOU GOT WHAT YOU WANTED, SO KNOCK IT OFF, ALREADY!
IT-IT'S NOT PHONEY BULL...

LOOK, LET'S NOT FIGHT ABOUT THIS, SHRIMP. IT'S PERFECT FOR YOU NOW. THE FINAL SALE ON MY HOUSE AIN'T FOR A FEW MONTHS, SO YOU CAN LIVE IN IT UNTIL YOU FIX YOURSELF UP, AND SINCE I'M MOVING TO TEXAS AFTER THIS TOUR, YOU WON'T EVER HAVE TO SEE ME AGAIN. AIN'T THAT GREAT?
IT'S-NOT-PHONEY-BULL.

OH, IT'S NOT, HUH? YOU THINK I NEVER KNEW ABOUT YOU AND YOUR LITTLE DYKE FRIEND LAUGHING AND CURSING ME BEHIND MY BACK? NEVER ONCE IN YOUR GOD DAMN LIFE DID YOU APPRECIATE ANYTHING I DID FOR YOU! I WAS ALWAYS SOME MONSTER TO YOU! HA! TALK ABOUT CALLING THE KETTLE BLACK!
OK...OK, THEN SO BE IT, SOVIET...
10

I'M NOT GOING HOME AFTER ALL...
YES, YOU ARE...
NO, I'M NOT! I'M HEADING EAST WITH PEPPER AN' I'M GONNA FIND HOPEY, AN' I'M GONNA MARRY HER, SEE...
!?!

...AN' ONE OF US IS GONNA GROW A WEENIE AN' WE'RE GONNA HAVE BABIES AN' WE'RE GONNA NAME 'EM RENA AN' WHO-EVER ELSE YOU HATE JUST BECAUSE YOU HATE 'EM! Y'ALL HEAR WHAT I'M SAYING?
SO DO IT, SHRIMP! SEE IF I CARE!

SURE I WAS SERIOUS. BUT ARE YOU? THAT'S A BIG EAST COAST OUT THERE AND IT'S A BIGGER CHANCE YOU WON'T FIND YOUR FRIEND.
IT'S A CHANCE I'D RATHER TAKE. I DON'T WANNA TURN BACK NOW.
PHON

OK, MAGGIE. WE'RE GLAD TO HAVE YOU ALONG. AND FOR YOUR SAKE, I HOPE YOU MADE THE RIGHT DECISION.
GOD, I HOPE SO, TOO, PEPPER.
PHONE

WHAT DO YOU MEAN SHE'S NOT COMING HOME AFTER ALL?
RAY JUST TALKED TO HER ON THE PHONE. SHE'S GOING EAST WITH SOME PEOPLE. SHE SOUNDED UPSET...
MR. KNOW-IT-ALL STRIKES OUT AGAIN.
APE SEX

DOESN'T PROVE A DAMN THING...
YOU JUST DON'T WANT TO ADMIT YOU COULD BE WRONG ABOUT THE MAGPIE!
RAY THINKS SHE'S GOING TO LOOK FOR HOPEY.
11

HOO HOO! STRIKE FOUR, SEÑOR KNOW-IT-ALL!
C'MAN! THE BOY'S DELIRIOUS WITH GRIEF! HE DOESN'T KNOW WHAT HE THINKS RIGHT NOW!

BAW!

M-MAGGIE'S GONE AWAY TO BE WITH HOPEY AND SHE'S NEVER COMING BACK! AND MIKE TOOK HIS JACKET BACK AND HE'S NEVER COMING BACK EITHER! OH, KI KI! I JUST WANT TO DIE!!

ASK HER REFEREE! ASK HER!
YEOWCH

A MILLION CLUBS, A MILLION BANDS, AND WHO KNOWS HOW MANY TIMES THEY'VE CHANGED THEIR NAME SINCE.
YO' WINNAH, PEPPERRRRRR MARTINEZ!
BOO!
CLAP CLAP
Z Z Z
DEVIL MASAMI
#1
HILLBILLY JAIME

ANY LUCK?
A FEW MAYBES. BO SAID HE'LL TAKE ME BY A FEW CLUBS AFTER HIS MATCH.

I PROMISE, THIS IS THE LAST STOP OF THE NIGHT...
S'OK...
12

MAYBE THEY WERE CALLED "BUTT PRETZELS" AT THE TIME. "PARTS UNKNOWN"? "THE JACKSONS"?
THE ONLY BAND WITH A LOTTA CHICKS THAT HAS PLAYED HERE RECENTLY WAS THAT BLACK GROUP "THE KLANSMEN".

CAN WE TRY JUST ONE MORE PLACE? I PROMISE, THIS WILL BE THE LAST ONE. I'LL BUY YOU A BEER. PLEEZE?
SURE.

"THE BLACK MARTIANS"? "THE SOUL PATROL"? "ABDOMINAL STRETCH"? "SONS OF BTO"? "UNCLE PETE AND LOUISE"?
SORRY.

"THE JEEPS"? "LOS COCHINOS DEL NORTE"? UH, "ALISON WONDERLAND"?
WHAT WAS THAT LAST NAME AGAIN?

"STUPID FAT CHICKS THAT WASTE EVERYBODY'S TIME"? THOUGHT NOT.

MY GOD. I'M SORRY, BO. BUT YOU'D THINK THEY WOULD HAVE PLAYED AT LEAST ONE OF THOSE PLACES. THEY...
THROW IT! I DARE YOU...
VIDA LOCA

THAT'S MY SWEATSHIRT, YOU CROOK!
GAKKK
!?
13

I LENT THAT SWEATSHIRT TO MY GIRLFRIEND! WHERE DID YOU GET IT?
YOU BETTER ANSWER HER, MAN. THAT'S BO BUNYAN WITH HER, SO SHE MUST BE A WRESTLER, TOO.
I FOUND IT IN AN OLD JUNKED CAR! I CAN EVEN SHOW YOU...

OH, GOD. HOW COULD I BE SO STUPID? TO ACTUALLY BELIEVE THAT THEY'D STILL BE TOGETHER AS A BAND (OR STILL FRIENDS FOR THAT MATTER) AFTER ALL THIS TIME... FEH!
HEY, BO. DO YOU SIGN?

...AND SHE DIDN'T EVEN BOTHER TO COME HOME OR TO CALL, OR... JUST THOSE STUPID LETTERS THAT MAKE ABSOLUTELY NO SENSE AT ALL! AH, BUT WHO CARES? SHE'S HAVING FUN SOMEWHERE AS I SIT HERE WITH MY FINGER UP MY ASS...

I'M SORRY, BO. I PROMISED YOU I WOULDN'T BORE YOU WITH MY PATHETIC LIFE STORY. YOU WANT ANOTHER BEER? I'LL HAVE ONE IF YOU WILL. JUST ONE MORE? I PROMISE I'LL CHANGE THE SUBJECT.

NO, BUT SERIOUS! YOU TEACH ME HOW TO DO THE FIGURE FOUR LEG LOCK AN' I'LL TEACH YOU... I'LL TEACH YOU HOW TO REBUILD A TRACTOR. A TOASTER?
I'D BREAK YOUR LEG.

NAW, YOU WOULDN'T! I GOT GOOD, STRONG LEGS! PEOPLE HAVE TOLD ME I'D GIVE KILLER HEAD SCISSORS. NO, BUT SERIOUS...
WE BETTER HEAD BACK.

HOPEY USED TO LIKE MY LEGS. BEFORE I GOT FAT ANYWAY...
WE BETTER HEAD BACK.
14

HOW DO YOU LIKE THEM MUSHROOMS? SHE DIDN'T WANNA BE SEEN WITH A BIG, FAT MONSTER ANY MORE SO SHE HIGHTAILED IT! WHAT A CHICKENSHIT...

!?!

YOU'RE NOT GONNA PILEDRIVE ME, ARE YOU?

THERE YOU ARE, YOU BASTARD!
BASTARD!

LAST NIGHT AT MADDOG'S YOU PICKED A FIGHT WITH MIKE, DIDN'T YOU?
DON'T DENY IT, DOYLE!
I AIN'T DENYING IT. I WOULDA KILLED THE FUCKER, TOO, IF THE BOUNCERS DIDN'T BREAK IT UP...
XXX

SEE? SEE? NOW MIKE WON'T TALK TO ME BECAUSE HE THINKS I SENT DOYLE AFTER HIM!
YOU'RE SUCH A MAN, DOYLE...

WHY CAN'T YOU JUST LEAVE HER ALONE? WHY DO YOU ALWAYS HAVE TO...
GOD DAMN... GET OUT OF MY FUCKING FACE, SHE-MAN!

SHE'LL GET OVER IT. DAFFY, I MEAN...
ASK ME IF I GIVE A SHIT...
15

Ring
Ring
Ring
Ring

NOW WHERE THE HELL WOULD YOU BE AT SEVEN O'CLOCK IN THE MORNING?

I'LL TRY AGAIN WHEN WE REACH BLOSSOM CITY.
WHAT HAPPENED TO YOUR HAIR?

YEAH, AND IT GETS WILDER! NOT ONLY DID THE BOARD STRIP VICKI OF HER TITLE, BUT THEY ALSO BOOTED HER OUT OF THE WHOLE W.W.W. FOR GOOD.
IT AIN'T FAIR! I'VE BEEN DREAMING OF THIS REMATCH FOR WEEKS!

THEY CAN'T BOOT HER BEFORE I'VE HAD A SECOND CRACK AT HER. YOU AND I ARE GOING DOWN TO THE ARENA TO TALK TO SOMEBODY... ANYBODY!
OK, BUT AFTER SHE BROKE BIG KAT BROWN'S LEG, TOOK OUT TWO REFEREES AND BLINDED THE ANNOUNCER, WHAT WOULD YOU HAVE DONE?

THEY'VE ALWAYS HAD IT IN FOR ME, CASH. EVERYBODY KNOWS BIG KAT BROWN WEARS HER COWBOY BOOTS WAY TOO DAMN SMALL...
YEAH, THEY'RE SCUM. IT'S A GOOD THING YOU'RE OUT OF THERE...

SO, WHAT DO YOU THINK I SHOULD DO? THE JAPAN CIRCUIT? MEXICO?
I CAN'T TELL YOU WHAT TO DO, BABY, BUT AS FAR AS THIS OL' BOY'S CONCERNED, I'M GETTING OUT FOR GOOD.
16

YOU, CASH? BUT YOU STILL HAVE A GOOD THING GOING HERE.
THIRTY YEARS OF A GOOD THING IS MORE THAN ENOUGH FOR ME, BABE.

IT'S TIME I STARTED THINKING ABOUT THE REST OF MY LIFE, WHILE I STILL CAN THINK. YOU KNOW, MAYBE BUY A RANCH AND RAISE A FAMILY. I KNOW IT SOUNDS FUNNY AT MY AGE, BUT I NEVER HAD TIME FOR ANY OF THAT STUFF...

I'VE ALWAYS WANTED A FAMILY I COULD REALLY CALL MY OWN. YOU KNOW WHAT I MEAN, BABE?
YEAH... YOU'RE A NUT.

YOU EVER BEEN TO THE ZOO?
SURE. I WENT TO JUNGLELAND WHEN I WAS REAL LITTLE. BUT ALL I REMEMBER WAS DRINKING WATER FROM THE LION'S MOUTH.
STER

I LIKE THE POLAR BEARS. I COULD SIT ALL DAY WATCHIN' EM.
I KNOW ALL ABOUT POLAR BEARS, BELIEVE ME...

ONE TIME I SAW ONE PLAYING WITH A KEG.
SEEMS FITTING SOMEHOW.

SHOULDN'T YOU BE AT THE ARENA RIGHT NOW?
I BROUGHT YOU HERE TO RELAX. SOMEONE LIKE YOU SHOULD RELAX MORE OFTEN.

ARE YOU RELAXING YET?
NGHHH...
17

A POLAR BEAR. SO CUTE AND CUDDLY IN HIS CAGE BUT WHEN YOU WANT TO GET CLOSE ENOUGH TO CUDDLE HIM HE TEARS YOU APART AND SWALLOWS YOU WHOLE.
TSK! GUY! HE'S NOT LIKE THAT...
HE'S RAD!

THEY'RE ALL RIGHT IF PEOPLE JUST LEAVE 'EM ALONE...

I SWEAR... I SWEAR I'LL NEVER RUN OFF LIKE I DID EVER AGAIN... I KNOW WHAT I HAVE NOW... I'LL NEVER LEAVE YOU...

NEVER NEVER...

HEY, SHRIMP! WAKE UP! C'MON, SHRIMP!
AW, SHHH

GOD DAMN, TIA! WHY DO YOU ALWAYS DO THIS TO ME?
HEY, RELAX, SHRIMP! WAKE UP!
18

T-T-TIA...? WHAT...?
WHAT ARE YOU CRYING ABOUT, SHRIMP? LOOK AT YOU, YOU'RE SWEATING LIKE A DAMN PIG...

OH, YEAH... THAT'S RIGHT. I WASN'T FEELING WELL, SO I MADE BO BRING ME BACK TO THE HOTEL AND... WHOA...
SHRIMP, I GOTTA BE IN VEGAS IN ONE HOUR, SO... UM, AREN'T YOU GONNA ASK ME WHAT I'M DOING HERE?

WELL, THE THOUGHT HAD CROSSED MY MIND. LOSING YOUR BELT AND ALL THAT... I FIGURED YOU'D BE UP FOR MURDER ONE BY NOW...
I'M... MARRYING CASH.

HO! WAIT! HOLD ON A SECOND! I MUST BE STILL SLEEPING...
LOOK, SHRIMP! I WAS HOPING TO COME HERE AND... BUT IF YOU WANNA BE NASTY, LET'S JUST FORGET IT, OK?

GUY, I WAS JUST KIDDING. WHAT DO YOU WANT ME TO SAY?
THAT YOU'RE HAPPY FOR ME! I DON'T DO SOMETHING LIKE THIS EVERY-DAY, Y'KNOW!

WELL, OF COURSE I'M HAPPY FOR YOU, TIA.
OH, THANKS, SHRIMP! THAT'S JUST WHAT I HAD TO HEAR! UM...

I'M PRETTY DARN NERVOUS ABOUT THE WHOLE THING, AND I DON'T THINK I COULD GO THROUGH WITH IT IF I DIDN'T HAVE YOUR BLESSING, Y'KNOW?
UH HUH.
UM...
19

OOH, DAFFY! WHERE'D YOU GET THOSE BOOTS?
SHE BOUGHT 'EM OFF MAGGIE! THEY'RE REAL WRESTLING BOOTS! THEY'RE SO COOL!
HI, DOYLE! HI, KIKO!
1776

HI, MAGGIE. WHAT HAVE YOU GOT THERE?
IT'S A POSTCARD FROM MY TIA. SHE'S HONEYMOONING/WRESTLING IN JAPAN RIGHT NOW.
YOU GOT THAT HUGE OL' HOUSE ALL TO YOURSELF NOW, HUH?

YEAH. FOR A FEW MONTHS ANYWAY.
SO, WHAT HAPPENS AFTER THOSE FEW MONTHS?

OH, I DUNNO. WHATEVER HAPPENS HAPPENS, I GUESS.
I MEAN, ARE YOU GOING OUT LOOKING FOR HOPEY AGAIN?

ASK ME NO QUESTIONS AND I'LL TELL YOU NO LIES.

THE POOR MAGPIE. BUT I GUESS SHE WOULDN'T BE HAPPY IF SHE WASN'T GOING AROUND IN CIRCLES, HUH?
OH, I DUNNO. SHE MAY BE COMING TO THE END OF HER WHIRLPOOL VERY SOON...

MISTER KNOW-IT-ALL...
the END

SOMEWHERE ON MY BODY, IF YOU LOOK REAL CLOSE...
1776

...YOU'LL FIND YOU...

...YOU'LL FIND Y...
!?!
WHAP!

WISEGUY.
I GOT ANOTHER ONE, SO IF YOU DON'T WANT THE OTHER CHEEK ZAPPED, YOU'LL GET BACK ON THAT STOOL THERE.
ZOXL SHOES

COULDN'T YOU WAIT UNTIL I LOST A FEW MORE POUNDS? LIKE MAYBE TWENTY YEARS?
MHMM...

SHIT, I PUT 'EM ON INSIDE OUT AGAIN. RAY, DO YOU REMEMBER ME WHEN I WAS SKINNY?
YEAH. BORING, SHAPELESS, LIFELESS... HEAD UP, PLEASE.
1

OK, THEN HOW'S THIS FOR A POSE?
WATCH IT OR I WILL PAINT YOU LIKE THAT.

OK, THEN HOW ABOUT THIS ONE?
PLEASE...

OR THIS ONE?
AM I GONNA HAVE TO SPANK YOU?

DID YOUR GIRLFRIENDS BACK EAST GIVE YOU A HARD TIME WHEN YOU ASKED THEM TO POSE FOR YOU?
NEVER ASKED 'EM TO.

NEVER? I'M THE FIRST ONE? HOW COME?
I DUNNO.

KNOK!
KNOK!
KNOK!
DANITA'S BACK WITH THE FOOD! TEN MINUTE BREAK!

HOW'S THE PAINTIN' COMIN'?
YEAH, HOW...? IS THAT ALL YOU'VE DONE SO FAR?
HEY, WE AIN'T USING A CAMERA HERE. THESE THINGS TAKE TIME.
2

AW, RAY! I CAN'T SIT ON A STOOL FOR SIXTEEN HUNDRED HOURS! I GET ALL SQUIRMY AND ANTSY AND FIDGETY AND...
NO SHIT, HUH?
I'LL POSE FOR YOU AN' I WON'T MOVE A MUSCLE.

YEAH! PAINT HER, RAY! LOOK, SHE'S GOT WAY MORE CHARACTER THAN ME. SEE?
LOOK WHO'S CALLING WHO A CHARACTER.
HOKAY, GET ON THE STOOL.

WELL, SHIT. IF MAGGIE WON'T POSE, I GOT THE SECOND BEST THING HERE. ACTUALLY I'VE WANTED TO PAINT DANITA FOR A LONG TIME...

I'D SURE LIKE TO DO A FULL BODY PORTRAIT. ACTUALLY I'D LOVE TO DO AN "ODALISQUE" OF MAGGIE, BUT I'D MOST LIKELY GET SLAPPED OR LAUGHED AT FOR JUST MENTIONING IT.

WHAT AM I SAYING? I DON'T EVEN DRAW WELL ENOUGH TO CAPTURE SOMETHING LIKE THAT. COME TO THINK OF IT, A CAMERA COULDN'T DO SOMEONE LIKE DANITA LINCOLN JUSTICE.

YEP, THAT'S WHY I DRAW THE WAY I DRAW, PAINT THE WAY I PAINT. BECAUSE I CAN'T DRAW. I CAN'T PAINT. LOOK AT ALL THIS GODDAMN PRETENTIOUS BULLSHIT! PHONEY, NO GOOD GARBAGE...
3

"OH, DO IT LIKE PICASSO. DO IT LIKE KLEE." AND I DON'T EVEN KNOW WHY! SHIT, THOSE GUYS KNEW WHY THEY DID IT. THEY HAD TO! THOSE WEREN'T JUST KOOKY NEW WAVE LINES AND COLORS JUST SO THEY COULD ADVERTISE JOGGING SHOES ON MTV! THEY LEARNED HOW TO DRAW BEFORE THEY KNEW HOW TO REALLY DRAW! DIDN'T THEY?

O-OR MAYBE ALL THAT BACKGROUND SHIT DIDN'T MATTER IN THE LONG RUN! I MEAN, MAYBE THEY DIDN'T GIVE A SHIT! MAYBE IT DOES ALL COME FROM THE INSIDE OF US... YEAH... YEAH...

AFTER ALL, ART IS ART. ART FOR ART'S SAKE. BEAUTY IS IN THE EYE OF THE BEHOLDER. DAMN THE TORPEDOS! FUCK 'EM IF THEY CAN'T TAKE A JOKE AND ALL THAT SHIT! YEAH, I CAN DRAW AND I CAN PAINT ANYTHING I FUCKING WANT!

GUY, RAY! HER BOOBS AREN'T THAT BIG!
HUH? NO, IT'S NOT... IT'S NOT FINISHED...
LEMME SEE!

WOW! LOOKIT ME! I LOOK LIKE LUBA, QUEEN OF WOMEN! ARGHHH!
MORE LIKE BOOBA, QUEEN OF THE BALLOON WOMEN!
...IT'S ONLY SKETCHED... I-I WAS GONNA FIX IT...

IF I WAS REALLY THAT BIG I'D HAVE TO HIRE MUSCLEMEN TO HOLD 'EM UP WHILE I WALK!
YOU'D ALSO NEED TO CARRY AROUND WITH YOU A RADAR SCOPE SO YOU CAN SEE WHERE YOU'RE STEPPING! HOO HOO!

YOU THINK YOU SHOULD GO UP AN' APOLOGIZE NOW?
WHY? HE NEVER DRAWS ME LIKE THAT.
VH
THE END

TERRY? WELL, SHE'S GREAT. SHE'S BEAUTIFUL, SHE'S TALENTED, SHE'S VERY INTELLIGENT... AND IF SHE EVER FLICKS ANOTHER CIGARETTE AT ME, I SWEAR I'LL BUST HER FUCKING FACE.

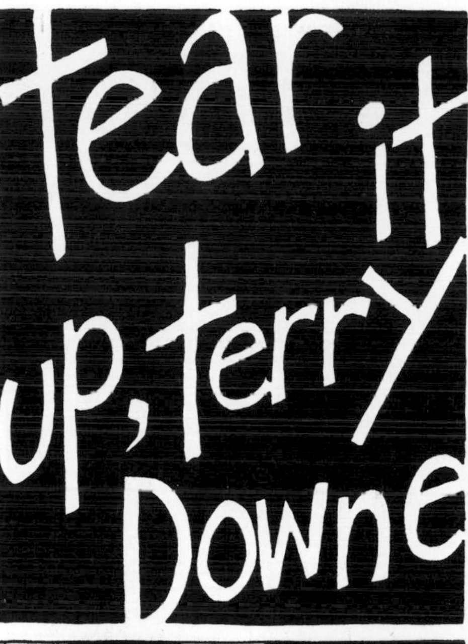
tear it up, terry Downe

bison Club
I'M A CLICHE
Plugz
Sex pis
DEVO
PUNK

STEVIE TV! SEE YOU BROUGHT YOUR SHADOW ALONG...
HUH?
3.00

TERRY.
the GERMS
=X=

YOU CAN'T KEEP FOLLOWING ME. I'M GETTING MARRIED SOON, AND...
MY STEP FATHER HATES ME...
DISCO SUCKS
DESTRO
THE DAMNED
-X-
ZEROS
"X"
THE EYES EAT

WHAT ARE WE DOING HERE? I HATE MEXICANS.
THAT'S SOMETHING YOU'RE GOING TO HAVE TO GET OVER RIGHT AWAY...
hell
HOPPERS 13

TERRY, THIS IS DEL CHIMNEY. HE'LL TAKE CARE OF YOU NOW.
YOU'RE VERY PRETTY, TERRY.

HUFF HUFF HUFF
LAUGH AT ME! YAWN! DO SOMETHING, BITCH! YOU'RE DRIVIN' ME NUTS!
HUFF HUFF HUFF
GO DEL, GO. HYUK!
1

TERRY DOWNE. HA! SHE'S GREAT! SHE SITS THERE WITH THAT "YOU'RE BORING ME" LOOK ON HER FACE WHILE SHE HOLDS HER CIGARETTE AS THOUGH SHE WERE WADING IN WATER UP TO HER NECK. PEOPLE FIND THAT ANNOYING BUT, I DUNNO, I FIND IT ALL PART OF HER CHARM...

YEAH, ME AN' HOPE USED TO BE BEST FRIENDS. BUT THAT WAS BEFORE SHE STARTED GETTING WEIRD. I CAN'T TALK TO HER ANY MORE...
I KNOW WHAT YOU MEAN, JULIE...
ALGEBRA

TAKE THAT SEAT BEHIND GLASS. AND IF YOU WANT TO STAY IN THIS CLASS, YOU'LL TAKE OFF THAT HAT.
LOOKS LIKE HOPE'S FOUND A NEW FRIEND.
WHAT A COUPLE.

LOOKS LIKE SHE WAS RUN OVER BY A DAMN LAWN MOWER...
DEVO...
SNORT
MATH 6

ESPERANZA? YOU MAY COME IN NOW. I HAVE YOUR THERAPIST ON THE PHONE...
THANK YOU.
INCIPAL
L FRIET

YOU BETTER BE DRESSED OUT TOMORROW, DOWNE, OR YOU'RE RUNNING LAPS FOR A WEEK. I MEAN IT...

...B-BUT, WHERE DO YOU GO WHEN YOU RUN AWAY FROM HOME?
WHY? WHAT'S IT TO YOU?
GLASS

AND IF YOU WANNA COME WITH ME, YOU MAKE LOVE TO ME AND NOBODY ELSE. HAVE YOU EVER MADE LOVE TO A WOMAN BEFORE? HAVE YOU EVER MADE LOVE TO A MAN BEFORE? HUH, HOPELESS?

WHAT ARE WE DOING HERE? I HATE MEXICANS.
THAT'S SOMETHING YOU'RE GOING TO HAVE TO GET OVER RIGHT AWAY...
hell
2

ESPERANZA. WHAT A BEAUTIFUL NAME. DID TERRY EVER TELL YOU HOW MUCH I LOVE MEXICANS?
I'M COLOMBIAN AND SCOTTISH...

JUST TRY AND STICK THAT IN HER, YOU FAT FUCK, AND I SWEAR YOU'LL NEVER USE IT AGAIN!
YOU'RE GETTING A BIG MOUTH, TERRY...
MOM
DAD

IF I EVER HEAR THAT YOU'VE BEEN WITH SOMEONE ELSE, I SWEAR I'LL...
O-OK...

MAN, I TRY TO BE NICE, Y'KNOW? BUT WHEN I WALK UP TO SAY HI, SHE LOOKS AT ME LIKE HER SHIT DON'T STINK AND SAYS SOMETHING LIKE "YOU FARTED." IN FRONT OF EVERYBODY! AND I DIDN'T! I SWEAR IT! MAN, Y'KNOW...?

IF I EVER HEAR THAT YOU'VE BEEN WITH SOMEONE ELSE, I SWEAR I'LL...
O-OK...
FESTER

SHAMPOO

HI, JULIE WREE! 'MEMBER, WE USED TO BE BEST FRIENDS?

AW, DON'T LET NOBODY TELL YOU NOTHIN'. TERRY'S COOL. PEOPLE JUST DON'T UNDERSTAND HER LIKE WE DO. HER LEADS RIVAL MIKE'S...
AH, SHE'S ALL RIGHT.
THEE 40 THIEVES

3

TERRY? WHY, WHAT DO YOU WANNA HEAR? THAT SHE'S WARM, SENSITIVE AND COMPASSIONATE? SORRY, CHARLIE...

MONTY'S
TERRY
SALE 1/2
SALE

INRI

STEVIE TV! IT'S BEEN YEARS. HOW'S LIFE IN LONDON?
HEY, BARB.
THERE SHE IS...
BOMBER BOOTS

TERRY, THERE'S SOMEONE HERE WHO WANTS TO SAY HELLO TO YOU...

HONEY...? WHAT HAPPENED IN THERE?
GOD DAMN CIGARETTE...
OPEN
=BIG YO=

TERRY DOWNE. WELL, I DON'T KNOW HER THAT WELL. BUT, ONE TIME WE HAD LUNCH AND I FOUND HER TO BE VERY NICE. I HAVE HEARD TERRIBLE STORIES, BUT I DON'T LISTEN. I KNOW I HAD LUNCH WITH A GOOD CHRISTIAN.
MONTY'S

TEAR IT UP, TERRY DOWNE.
I BEG YOUR PARDON...
XAIMO 1988

the adventures of maggie the mechanic
OK, I'M READY...
GREAT, MAGGIE. LET'S GO.
COPYRIGHT © JAIME HERNANDEZ 1988

HOW COULD HE HAVE FALLEN THIS FAR DOWN AND STILL BE ALIVE, RACE?
THESE THINGS ARE BUILT TO ABSORB SHOCK, I GUESS.

AND THERE SHE IS. YOU CUT WHILE I APPLY OXYGEN.
ARE WE IN TIME?

HIS SHELL IS SO THICK. IT'S CUTTING TOO SLOW...
WATCH IT! YOU'RE THROWING SPARKS TOO CLOSE TO THE...

FOOF!
1

WELL, IT'S ABOUT TIME! I COULD HAVE SUFFOCATED IN HERE, Y'KNOW!
YOU NEVER LOOKED BETTER, DUKE. HOW DO YOU FEEL?

I DUNNO, MY LEG SMARTS. NNG! YES, RIGHT THERE, LITTLE GIRL...
HAVE YOU OUTTA HERE IN A JIFFY, DUKEY BOY.

NOW, DON'T HESITATE GETTING YOUR BUTTS OUTTA HERE. I HEARD SOMETHING CRAWLING AROUND HERE EARLIER.
L-LIKE WHAT?

WEEEHONK!
GREEEEEE

AW, LOOK. IT WAS JUST A BABY ONE.
IT SURE SOUNDED BIG TO ME.

OH, YEAH, RIGHT! I'M SURE! RAZZZZ!
MAGGIE THE MECHANIC
XAIME 88

RRRRRRRRRR RRRRRRRRRRRRRRR

RRRRRRRRRRRRRRR

RRRRRRRRR

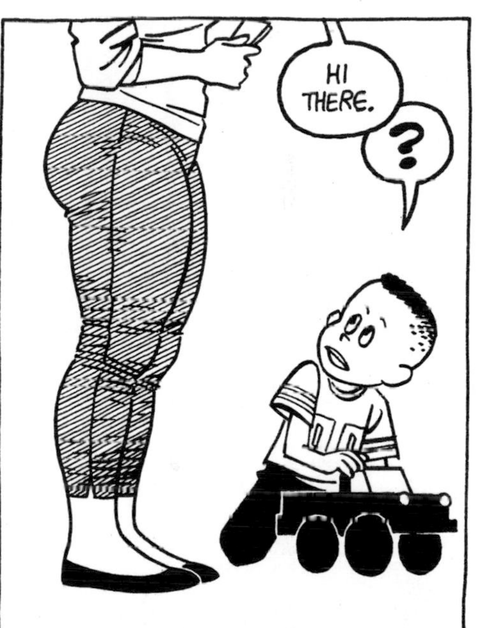
HI THERE.
?

AREN'T YOU DANITA LINCOLN'S BOY? HOW OLD ARE YOU NOW?
BABY ELIAS!

WHATCHA DOIN', BOY? YOUR MOM'S WAITIN'! MAN, ARE YOU IN TROUBLE!
BYE.
NO, I AINT! YOU ARE!
1

NINETY-THREE MILLION MILES FROM THE SUN

...AND COUNTING

BY the FAKE Santa CLAUS 88

2

UNITED STATES POST O
MADDOG'S
MAGGIE.
?
MAGGIE.
MAGGIE.
MAGGIE.
MAGGIE! COME ON IN! IT'S ME DAFFY!
...AND ME ITSUKI!
OH MY GOD! I THOUGHT THE JOINT WAS HAUNTED!
YOU KNOW, IT'S SO WEIRD. WE HAVEN'T SEEN YOU SINCE THIS PLACE BURNED DOWN.
THAT'S RIGHT...
YEAH, AND DID YOU KNOW IT'S EXACTLY TWO YEARS AGO TONIGHT SINCE THE FIRE?
BIG DEAL.
BIG FUCKIN' DEAL.
IS IT TRUE THAT BOXHEAD AND WOLFIE FIREBOMBED THIS PLACE BECAUSE THEY GOT RID OF SLAM NIGHT?
NO. EL CID FELL ASLEEP IN THE BACK WITH A LIT CIGARETTE. NOW HE'S BACK AT THE DESPERADO AND ALL HE HAS TO DO TO KEEP PEOPLE AWAY FROM THE BACK DOOR IS RAISE HIS ARMS AND MAKE MONSTER SOUNDS.
GET DOWN!
GET DOWN!
3

SO, HAVE YOU HEARD HOW PENNY COSTIGAN IS DOING?
PENNY? NO, NOT FOR AWHILE, ANYWAY...
THEN YOU HAVEN'T HEARD ABOUT HER ACCIDENT?

ACCIDENT? NO, WHEN?
TWO DAYS AGO! SHE WAS FLYING INTO TOWN AND HER JET CRASHLANDED...
...NOW SHE'S AT ST. ANTHONY'S WITH NEARLY EVERY BONE IN HER BODY BROKEN! IT WAS IN ALL THE PAPERS!

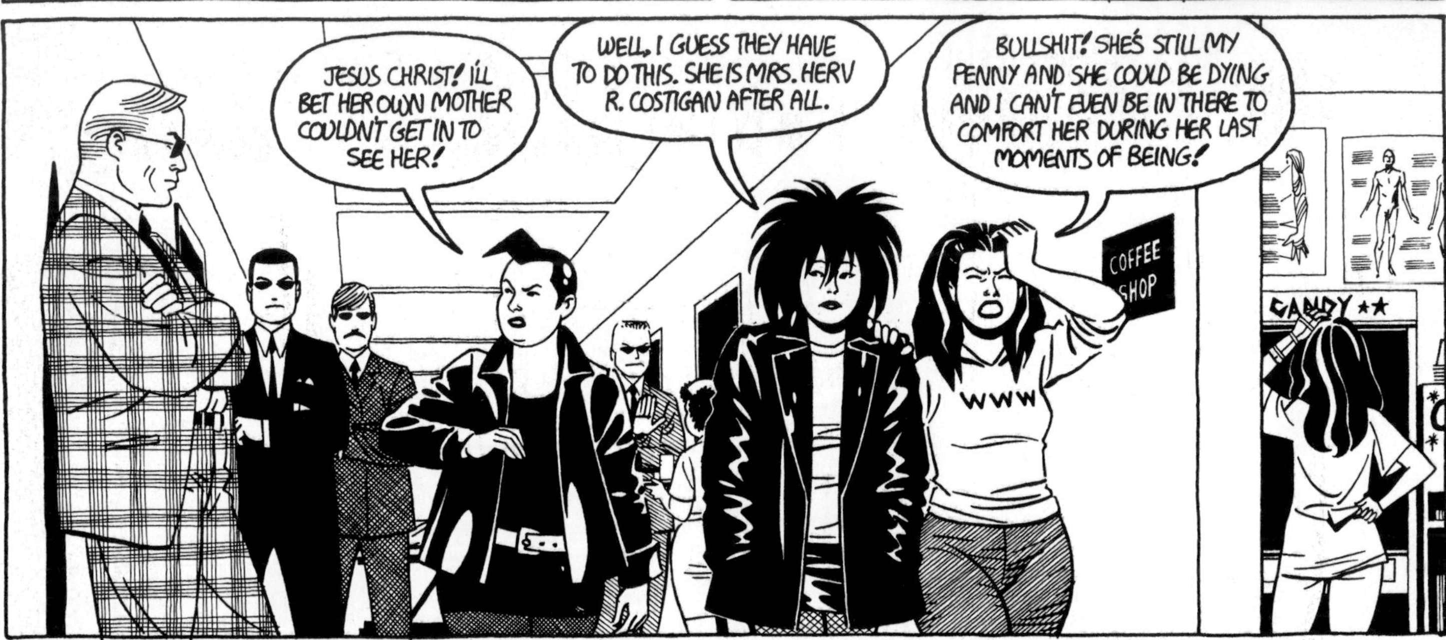
JESUS CHRIST! I'LL BET HER OWN MOTHER COULDN'T GET IN TO SEE HER!
WELL, I GUESS THEY HAVE TO DO THIS. SHE IS MRS. HERV R. COSTIGAN AFTER ALL.
BULLSHIT! SHE'S STILL MY PENNY AND SHE COULD BE DYING AND I CAN'T EVEN BE IN THERE TO COMFORT HER DURING HER LAST MOMENTS OF BEING!
COFFEE SHOP
CANDY

HER FINAL WORD MAY PERTAIN TO SOME LONG LOST SECRET THAT IS TIED TO HER INNOCENT CHILDHOOD THAT ONLY I'D KNOW ABOUT!
THEN THEY CAN MAKE A MOVIE OUT OF IT, HUH?
CANDY

AHH, BUT IF I KNOW PENNY, HER FINAL WORD WOULD BE SOMETHING LIKE...
ANYBODY GOT CHANGE FOR A DOLLAR?

I KNEW IT!! I KNEW IT!!!
MAGGIE! WHAT ARE YOU DOING HERE? ARE YOU SICK?
4

PLEASE, COME STAY WITH ME, MAGGIE! I HAVEN'T SEEN YOU IN SO LONG AND YOU HAVE TO SEE MY NEW BABY AND EVERYTHING...
WELL, YOU KNOW IT'S NOT THAT EASY FOR THOSE OF US WHO HAVE TO WORK FOR OUR MONEY TO JUST GET UP AND GO LIKE THAT.
WWW

DON'T TELL ME YOU'RE STILL RUNNING THAT PHOTO-COPY MACHINE FOR THAT OL' INSURANCE COMPANY!
OK, I WON'T TELL YOU...

MAGGIE, YOU SAID YOU WERE GOING TO DO THAT JOB FOR ONLY TWO WEEKS! IT'S NOW GOING ON TWO YEARS!
SO WHAT? IT'S A JOB. I GET PAID...
WWW

I CAN'T BELIEVE WHAT I'M HEARING! THIS ISN'T MY BABY DOLL TALKING! WHAT HAVE YOU BEEN UP TO IN THE LAST TWO YEARS?
NOT MUCH...

SEE? THAT'S WHY YOU HAVE TO COME STAY WITH ME! YOU HAVE TO GET THAT CIRCULATION GOING! BELIEVE ME, MAGGIE! I'M DOING YOU A BIG FAVOR!
WELL, I'LL GO IF RAY CAN GO, TOO.

...AND RIGHT THEN HER FACE GOES SERIOUS AND SHE SAYS, "OH. ARE YOU STILL SEEING HIM?"
DOESN'T LIKE ME, HUH?

OH, IT'S NOT YOU PERSONALLY. IT'S... WELL, SHE STILL LIVES BY AN OLD BOGUS DREAM THAT SOMEDAY HOPEY AND I WOULD GET MARRIED AND LIVE HAPPILY EVER AFTER.
THEN WHY AM I GOING? I CAN'T STAY ANYWHERE I'M NOT WELCOME.
5

OH, PENNY'S ALL RIGHT. SHE JUST HAS TO ACCEPT THE FACT THAT WE'RE ALL DIFFERENT PEOPLE NOW...
OK, THEN COUNT ME IN...

HEY, AND MAYBE YOU CAN SEE HOPEY AFTER ALL THIS TIME. SHE LIVES NEAR BADGEPORT, DOESN'T SHE?
I DON'T KNOW ANY MORE...

NOBODY I KNOW HAS HEARD FROM HER IN OVER A YEAR. SO YOU CAN IMAGINE THE RUMORS THAT HAVE BEEN SPREADING AROUND...

"HOPEY'S BROTHER JOEY HEARD THAT SHE MOVED TO TEXAS AND JOINED A METAL BAND...

"SOMEONE ELSE HEARD THAT SHE FELL IN WITH AN ART CROWD AND SHE NOW EXPRESSES HERSELF IN CHICAGO...

"BUT THE BEST ONE I'VE HEARD YET IS THAT SHE'S MARRIED, PREGNANT AND LIVES IN ALASKA..."

DON'T YOU THINK YOU'D WANT TO KNOW THE TRUTH?
NAH...

WHY NOT?
I JUST THINK IT'S BETTER THAT I DON'T KNOW WHERE SHE IS...

OK.
YOU BROUGHT IT UP.
6

HI, WEBSTER. DO YOU HAVE MY FRIEND'S ROOM ALL READY?
YES, MRS. COSTIGAN. BUT, WHERE...?
THEY WENT LOOKING FOR THE HEAD. TEN TO ONE THE FOOLS ARE LOST.

NOW, LET'S SEE IF I REMEMBER... WHILE LOOKING FOR A BATHROOM, ALWAYS FOLLOW ONE OR TWO SIMPLE BUT IMPORTANT RULES. ONE: GO WITH SOMEONE WHO KNOWS THEIR WAY AROUND. JMMM...
MAGGIE, PLEASE! I'M ABOUT TO PASS OUT...

...BUT IF YOU CAN'T DO THAT, FOLLOW RULE NUMBER TWO...
I'M AFRAID I CAN'T WAIT FOR RULE NUMBER TWO. THE FIRST ROOM I COME ACROSS WILL HAVE TO BE THE UNFORTUNATE FLOOD VICTIM.

OOSH...

DID YOU KNOW THERE ARE PEOPLE INHABITING THESE ROOMS?
RAY, YOU DIDN'T...

NOT YET I DIDN'T. SO, I'M AFRAID A DARK CORNER WILL HAVE TO DO...
BOMBS AWAY...
7

I CAN'T BELIEVE YOU GUYS GOT LOST. DIDN'T YOU REMEMBER THE BATHROOM RULES?
I COULDN'T REMEMBER RULE NUMBER TWO.

"ALWAYS FOLLOW THE HALLWAY LAMPS THAT MATCH IN COLOR." C'MON, YOU SHOULD HAVE THAT EMBEDDED IN YOUR BRAIN AFTER WHAT HAPPENED TO YOU THE FIRST TIME.
YOU DON'T HAVE TO REMIND ME, Y'KNOW.

WERE YOU REALLY GONNA RUN AWAY WITH CASEY?
I CAME A LOT CLOSER THAN ANYONE SUSPECTED.

WOULD YOU DO IT NOW IF YOU HAD THE CHANCE?
I'M NOT GOING TO ANSWER THAT! GUY, PENNY...

WELL, I'M GONNA GET SOME LUNCH. DO YOU WANT SOME?
IN A MINUTE.

S'MATTER? YOU DON'T LIKE AIRPLANE FOOD, OR WHAT?
OH. HI, HOW YA DOIN'?

MMM... WHAT MIGHT WE HAVE HERE? CHILIBURGERS, SUGAR POPS AND BEER. MY FAVORITE...
?
CORN POPS
8

HUM HUM HUMM...

CASEY...
TOLD YOU I'D SEE YOU IN FIVE YEARS. HOW ABOUT IT, MAGGIE?

EEEEE

ZAW!
<EMIL! WAKE UP! GET YOUR GUN! IT'S A PROWLER! I TOLD YOU THIS PLACE WAS A NUTHOUSE! EMIL!>
HEY, NOW WAIT...

WELL, THE FACE LOOKS SORT OF FAMILIAR...
PENNY, IF YOU TELL RAY, I SWEAR...
9

EXCUSE ME, RAY, BUT CAN YOU HELP ME FOR A MINUTE?
UH... WHAT IS IT?

COULD YOU TELL ME IF MY SEAMS ARE STRAIGHT?

WELL, ARE THEY, OR AREN'T THEY?

♫

♫

CA-CA-CABLE, MA'AM?

SO, YOU GUYS ARE LEAVING? UH... TOGETHER?
YEAH, AND I THINK IT'S BEST THAT WE LEAVE AS SOON AS POSSIBLE.

BUT, THIS IS SILLY! CASEY WAS NEVER HERE!
THAT DOESN'T MATTER! THE ONLY PERSON I HAD ON MY MIND BEFORE I CAME HERE WAS RAY AND I WAS HAPPY! IF I STAY HERE ANY LONGER, WHO KNOWS WHO ELSE I'LL START IMAGINING HIDING INSIDE CLOSETS!
10

(SIGH) OK... IT WAS REALLY NICE HAVING YOU HERE JUST THE SAME. I'LL TELL HOPEY YOU SAID HI...

Y-YOU'VE TALKED TO HER LATELY?
UH... WELL, YEAH. ABOUT TWO WEEKS AGO...

I WAS JUST WALKING DOWN THE STREET AND SHE JUST KINDA SAID HI...

I CAN'T LIE TO YOU, MAGGIE! I DID SEE HER TWO WEEKS AGO... BUT IN THE HOSPITAL!
H-HOSPITAL? WHAT HAPPENED TO HER?

MAGGIE, OPEN YOUR EYES! DO I LOOK LIKE I JUST HAD A BABY TWO WEEKS AGO?!?
THEN... THEN... THEN...

I PROMISED HER I WOULDN'T TELL A SOUL. BUT I JUST COULDN'T KEEP IT FROM YOU! HOPEY WAS SO FREAKED OUT BY HER PREGNANCY THAT I TOLD HER I'D TAKE THE BABY AND PRETEND SHE WERE MY OWN AS LONG AS SHE WENT THROUGH WITH THE BIRTH...
PENNY, WHERE IS SHE? PLEASE, I GOTS TO KNOW...

PLEASE, RAY? JUST ONE MORE DAY, AND THEN I PROMISE WE'LL LEAVE.
...OK.
MA...
...TODOS LOS NEGROS TOMAMOS CAFÉ...
11

RELAX, BABY DOLL. THINGS WILL BE JUST FINE.
I-I DUNNO, I CAN'T STOP SHAKING. I MEAN, WHAT IF SHE'S LIKE TANNED NOW WITH A BIG NOSE AND A DEEP VOICE?

NOBODY HERE. COPS RAIDED THE PLACE THIS MORNING AND TOOK IN EVERY LAST ONE OF THEM DRUG ADDICTS. I SAY, GOOD RIDDANCE AND MAY THEY ALL ROT IN JAIL FOREVER!
BRUCE LEE
BRUCE LI
BRUCE LE

6236662-78257
BADGEPORT
6236662-78257

WHERE'D YOU FIND MONEY TO BAIL ME OUT, TEX?
BUT, HOPEY. I JUST GOT HERE. I DIDN'T BAIL YOU OUT...

OHO! NOW I SEE! PENNY'S TITS AT SIXTEEN O'CLOCK! LET'S SNEAK OUT THE BACK WAY OR ELSE SHE'LL BEG US TO STAY AT THE MANSION AGAIN.
THERE IS NO BACK WAY TO THIS PLACE.

THEN WE'LL HIDE IN THE HEAD TILL SHE GETS TIRED OF WAITING AND LEAVES.
WAIT, THIS IS THE WOMEN'S BATHROOM...
12

WE CAN PULL THIS OFF ANYWHERE ELSE, BUT NOT IN A POLICE STATION!
OH, JUST PRETEND YOU'RE BLIND, OR...

G-GO AHEAD, LITTLE HOPEY. DADDY WILL STAND RIGHT HERE WHILE YOU USE THE POTTY...
?!?

OK, PERVERT. OUTSIDE. NOW.
I'M GOING. HOPEY? YOU COMING?

HO... HOPEY! HO...
SHE SAID OUTSIDE, FAT BOY!
YOU GOT HIM, DEE?

AAAH, YOU'RE A HIPPIE!

HI, TEXAS. YOU SEEN HOPEY AROUND?
THERE IS NO MORE TEXAS. THERE IS ONLY THE TURDMAN OF ALAKAZAM...
RICO
SACRELIGIO

YOO HOO, RAY!
WOULD YOU COME OUT HERE FOR A MOMENT, PLEASE?
13

DO YOU REALIZE THAT WE ARE THE LUCKIEST PEOPLE ON EARTH RIGHT NOW?
YEAH? HOW COME?
BECAUSE WE ARE ALLOWED TO WITNESS THE REUNION OF THE GREATEST LOVE IMAGINABLE BETWEEN TWO BEINGS...
NO KIDDING...
POW
SO, WHAT'S THE LATEST ON PUNCH AND JUDY?
THEY'RE STILL KISSING AND MAKING UP SOMEWHERE IN THIS HOUSE.
S'MATTER, BOYS? AIN'T GOT NOTHING TO DO? WISH I COULD HELP YOU...
HOW ABOUT SOME POOL?
SURE.
X AVENUE
14

THOSE TWO MUST HAVE QUITE A RELATIONSHIP. AND I'M NOT TALKING ABOUT MAGGIE BEGGING HOPEY TO HIT HER BACK, BUT HOPEY REFUSING TO HIT BACK.
HUH...

I'VE DREAMT OF THIS DAY FOR A LONG TIME AND I MUST SAY IT'S TURNING OUT EXACTLY AS I PICTURED IT.
...(SIGH)...

KNOK
KNOK

<WHO'S THERE?>

EEEEEEEEEEEEE

YOU GET HER, MAG?
YEAH, SHE RAN OFF LIKE... HEY, TURN IT OFF ALREADY! THIS THING'S HARD TO HANDLE...

HOPEY! YOU TURNED IT THE WRONG WAY!
NEVER COULD TELL MY LEFT FROM MY RIGHT...
15

LOOKS LIKE YOU TWO JUST FELL INTO THE BATHROOM SINK...
SOMETHING LIKE THAT...
WHERE'S RAY?

HE WENT INTO TOWN. SAID HE'D BE BACK SOON.
REALLY? ALONE?
C'MON, MAG! LET'S GO BACK AND SEE IF WE FLOODED THE WHOLE PLACE!

HO HUM...

MY FRIENDS TOLD ME TO HANG OUT WITH ARTISTS. "YOU'LL NEVER HAVE A DULL MOMENT."
NO ONE'S FORCING YOU TO STAY IN...

TSK! WHATEVER HAPPENED TO THAT SHY, ADORABLE HIGH SCHOOL KID I ONCE KNEW?
GRUNT!
16

MISTER JOKER
BIBI
CS + DM

BOZO
2C

WHO IS IT, BABY?
HMMM... I DUNNO. IT WAS PROBABLY ONE OF YOUR GIRLFRIENDS...

BELIEVE ME, WEBSTER. YOU SHOULDA LET THEM GUARD DOGS FINISH ME...

AHH, SHE APPEARS OUT OF NOWHERE, LIKE THE GENTLE BREEZE THAT COOLS MY HEATED BROW.
RAY. WHERE WERE YOU?

OH, I WAS JUST CHECKING OUT MY OLD NEIGHBORHOOD. YOU KNOW, TO SEE IF IT'S STILL THERE...
I MISSED YOU.

YOU AND HOPEY HAVE A LOT OF FUN TODAY?
MHMM...

HEY, MAGGOT! WHERE YOU AT?
17

HEY MA--

SNIFF

YOU OK?
HUH? OH, YEAH... RAY HAS TO GET BACK HOME TO WORK.

YOU'RE NOT GOING WITH HIM?
NOT YET. THERE'S SOMETHING I GOTS TO KNOW FIRST...

PENNY!
?
PLEASE SHOW THEM IN, DEMOÑA.

YOU TOLD MAGGIE THAT YOUR KID WAS MY KID!
SURE I DID. HOW ELSE WAS I GONNA GET YOU TWO TOGETHER AGAIN?
BY THE WAY, YOUR SEAMS ARE CROOKED, PENNY!

OH. YOU KNOW ABOUT THAT...
NO DUH, HUH?
JUST GO TO HELL, PENNY! C'MON, MAG! WE'RE OUTTA HERE...
18

OH NO YOU DON'T! IF YOU WANT THE TRUTH, THEN WE'LL HAVE THE TRUTH! RIGHT, HOPEY...?
PENNY, OUT OF THE WAY...
RIGHT, HOPEY?

GOD DAMN IT, PENNY! UNLOCK THIS DOOR!
I'LL OPEN IT AFTER WE GET A FEW THINGS STRAIGHT...
RIGHT, HOPEY?

I DON'T HEAR ANY MORE SCREAMING. THEY MUSTA PASSED OUT.
THERE'S A TEAR IN MY BEER, CUZ I'M CRYIN' FOR YOU, DEAR...
WEIRDO

I THINK THE LAST TIME I WROTE YOU TEX AND I HAD JUST MOVED IN WITH MARY CHRISTMAS...

"WELL, THAT DIDN'T LAST MORE THAN A FEW WEEKS. ME AN' HER GOT IN A BIG FIGHT AND SHE BOOTED OUR ASSES BACK ON THE STREET. SHE WAS OUR LAST FRIEND IN TOWN, TOO. THANKS TO MY WINNING PERSONALITY...
Costigan INDUSTRIES

"OF COURSE THERE WAS ALWAYS PENNY TO TURN TO, BUT I WAS TOO PROUD TO ACCEPT HER WELCOME MAT. I WAS STILL PISSED AT HER FOR NOT LEAVING HER BUTTHOLE BILLIONAIRE HUSBAND LIKE SHE SAID SHE WOULD. BELIEVE ME, I WAS BECOMING VERY HARD TO LIVE WITH...
19

"WE RAN INTO SOME HIPPIES WHO PROMISED US A PLACE TO STAY IF WE JOINED THEIR BAND. WE WERE BOOTED AFTER OUR FIRST GIG (FOLLOWING TWO PRACTICES) BECAUSE...WELL, I STILL CAN'T STAND GODDAMN HIPPIES! NEVER COULD, NEVER WILL...

"I COULD TELL TEX WAS GETTING REAL TIRED OF PLAYING 'MUSICAL HOUSES,' SO ONE NIGHT, TOTALLY RAGGED OUT, I GIVE HIM THE WORKS. I CALL HIM SPINELESS AND DARE HIM TO GO HOME TO HIS FOLKS. HELL, I NEVER THOUGHT HE'D TAKE ME UP ON IT! HE LEFT ME STANDING IN THE RAIN AT FOUR IN THE MORNING AND DIDN'T LOOK BACK ONCE. WHY DOES THE WORD 'WIMP' DO THAT TO GUYS, ANYWAY?

"SO NOW I'M ALONE, AND I DECIDE TO TRY GETTING HOME. WELL, OL' PENNY'S ON VACATION SOMEWHERE, AND MOM... WELL, RIGHT THEN IT WAS TIME FOR SERIOUS TACTICS. THOSE OTHER LADIES WEREN'T TOO HAPPY ABOUT ME HOGGING THEIR TURF. JEEZ, I ONLY NEEDED ONE CUSTOMER...

"ANYWAY, ME AN' THIS OLD FUCKER WENT DOWN TO THIS OLD HOTEL THAT HIS BROTHER IN LAW OWNED IN THE FIFTIES OR SOME SHIT LIKE THAT. MAN, I HAD HIS WALLET AND WAS OUTTA THERE BEFORE HE COULD UNTIE HIS FIRST SHOE...

"HE HAD JUST ENOUGH CASH TO GET ME TO I-DIDN'T-CARE-WHERE, JUST FAR ENOUGH AWAY FROM THAT SICK OLD CITY...

"IN LINE TO GET MY TRAIN TICKET I DID SOMETHING I HADN'T DONE SINCE KINDERGARTEN. I PASSED OUT. GUESS I SHOULDA USED SOME OF THAT CASH FOR FOOD, HUH?

"ALL I REMEMBER IS THAT STUPID LADY'S VOICE SAYING 'JUST STEP OVER HER! WE'RE IN A HURRY!' OVER AND OVER AND OVER...

"I WAKE UP IN SOME MEDICAL CLINIC WITH A HEADACHE THE SIZE OF ASIA, ALL MY MONEY'S GONE AND TO MAKE MATTERS WORSE, THE DOCTOR TELLS ME THE MAIN REASON I PASSED OUT. HE SAYS I'M PREG-NANT. I SAY HE'S NUTS. HE SAYS I'M OVER THREE MONTHS. I BAWL.

"NEXT I ASK THE QUACK FOR THE NEAREST ABORTION CLINIC, BUT HE TELLS ME I'M TOO FAR INTO MY PREGNANCY. THAT IT WOULD BE WAY TOO DANGEROUS FOR ME. WELL, BY THIS TIME I'M REALLY SCREWED UP, SO I HEAD STRAIGHT FOR THE NEAREST RIVER TO JUMP INTO WHEN ALL OF A SUDDEN I SPOT A FAMILIAR, ROUND SHAPE ON THE OTHER SIDE...

"ME AN' TEX ARE ONCE AGAIN TRAVELLING PARTNERS AND WHEN I TELL HIM OF MY SITUATION, HE ODDLY REPLIES...
HUH, THAT'S FUNNY. SO IS PENNY...

"AND WOULDN'T YOU KNOW WHEN WE GET TO PENNY'S, SHE'S ALL HAPPY AND BUBBLY AND SHE'S STUFFED HALF HER HOUSE WITH BABY STUFF. JUST WHAT I NEEDED TO SEE...
ABC

"ONCE WE COMPARE STORIES AND STOMACHS, IT DOESN'T TAKE ME LONG TO FIGURE OUT SOMETHING PENNY AND TEXAS ALREADY KNOW. THAT WE BOTH GOT POKED ON THE SAME NIGHT, BY THE SAME GUY! DO I HAVE TO SPELL OUT HIS NAME?
HEH!

"IT'S REALLY STUPID, BUT WHEN ME AN' TEX WERE LIVING HERE IN THE MANSION ABOUT A YEAR AGO, ME AN' PENNY USED TO TEASE THE POOR BOY WITH THE GARTERS. YOU KNOW, LIKE ME AN' YOU DID WITH SPOOKY THE SMOKEY...?

"WELL, HEH, ONE NIGHT WE WERE ALL GETTING REALLY FUCKED UP ON EVERYTHING AND ANYTHING AND... WELL, I DON'T REMEMBER MUCH OF THAT NIGHT, BUT PENNY DOES. SHE EVEN TOLD HER HUSBAND ABOUT IT. I GUESS HE WAS JUST HAPPY THAT SOMEBODY WOULD GET HIM A SON. SINCE HE COULDN'T HIMSELF. OLD GOAT...
21

"ANYWAY, ON THE DAY I WENT INTO LABOR, THAT WHOLE TIME I KEPT WONDERING WHAT I WOULD HAVE DONE THAT DAY AT THE RIVER IF OL' TEX WASN'T THERE. MAN, I STILL WONDER ABOUT THAT, BUT NOT AS MUCH AS I DID THAT DAY...

"BY THE WAY, I WASN'T TOO SURPRISED WHEN I MISCARRIED, BUT PENNY TOOK IT LIKE THERE WAS NO LONGER SUCH A THING AS ICE CREAM. SHE EVEN TRIED TO GIVE ME HER BABY THAT SHE HAD TWO DAYS EARLIER, WITH GREAT SUCCESS, I MIGHT ADD. AND THAT WAS TWO MONTHS AGO, NOT TWO WEEKS. I SWEAR..."

ANYWAY, SINCE THEN TEX AND I HAD BEEN LIVING WITH SOME PEOPLE WHO TURNED OUT TO BE MAJOR CRACK MAFIA. THAT'S WHY YOU FOUND ME IN JAIL...

...AND... THAT'S ALL...
I-I'M SORRY...

WHAT ARE YOU SORRY ABOUT? THE KID'S BETTER OFF! CAN YOU IMAGINE ME BEING ITS MOM?! C'MON, MAG...

STODOLA
STODOLA
STODOLA PUMPA-
STODOLA PUMPA-
STODOLA
PUM

YOO HOO! IS EVERYTHING ALL HUNKYDORY?
YES, PENELOPE. EVERYTHING IS ALL HUNKYDORY.
22

WAIT A SEC! WHERE ARE YOU GOING?
HOME.

B-BUT... WHAT ABOUT HOPEY?
I DUNNO. I DIDN'T ASK HER...
WWW

YOU DIDN'T ASK HER...? BUT, I THOUGHT...
PENNY, I'M GOING HOME. RAY'S WAITING FOR ME...

OH, YEAH? AND JUST HOW ARE YOU GONNA DO THAT?
PENNY, PLEASE. PUT ME ON ONE OF YOUR JETS SO I CAN GET AWAY FROM THIS HAUNTED HOUSE.

THERE YOU GO, BLAMING THE HOUSE AGAIN FOR YOUR OWN STUPID INSECURITIES! IF ANYTHING, THIS HOUSE BRINGS OUT THE TRUTH!
PENNY, PLEASE...

NO NO NO! CAN'T YOU SEE? THIS IS HOW IT'S SUPPOSED TO BE! YOU AND HOPEY! HOPEY AND YOU! LIKE THIS! LIKE...
ANYBODY HOME?

PENNY DARLING. YOU LOOK LIKE A BILLION.

HERV, WHAT ARE YOU DOING HERE...?
THE DOC SAYS I HAVE TO TAKE IT EASIER, SO I'LL BE WORKING RIGHT HERE AT HOME FROM NOW ON...
WWW
23

I'LL BE RETIRING NOW, COMRADE EIGHT. DON'T FORGET TO PUT OUT THE CAT.

YOU GUYS COULDA ASKED US TO LEAVE, Y'KNOW.
HR

DON'T WORRY ABOUT IT, MAG. HE'S PROBABLY OUT GETTING THE MAIL OR SOMETHING. YOU CAN TRY CALLING HIM AGAIN WHEN WE GET TO THE CITY.
OK...
TELEPHONE

WE'LL GET INTO TOWN, GET TO THE CAR, YOU'LL FIX THE CAR, AND CALIFORNIA, HERE WE COME. OK, MAG...?
OK...

WHAT'S WRONG?
NOTHING.

WHEW
IS THAT SUN GETTING CLOSER, OR DOES IT JUST SEEM LIKE IT IS?
END

LAS MONJAS ASESINAS

NED THE WINO 89

YOUR BOYFRIEND'S EX-GIRLFRIEND, MAYA.
MAYA?
HOT DAMN! LETS GET OVER THERE, MAG, AND FAST!

MARY SWEETS! YOUR BOYFRIEND'S A GENIUS!
THANKS, BABE. GOT A MINUTE?

THIS IS MAGGIE.
HELLO.
HELLO.

DAMN THAT MARY! I DIDN'T WANNA MEET HER! SHE SAID SHE WANTED TO MEET ME!
AND I THOUGHT TERRY HELD HER CIGS HIGH.

SHE'S A REAL SOCIETY JET SETTER BABE, ISN'T SHE?
AS SOCIETY JET SETTER BABES GO, I GUESS...

I FEEL REALLY FAT RIGHT NOW...
BUT YOU'RE ACTING LIKE THE FAT'S IN YOUR HEAD...
MAGGIE?

I WANT TO APOLOGIZE. I DIDN'T REALIZE WHO YOU WERE WHEN WE WERE INTRODUCED. I'M REALLY HAPPY TO MEET YOU. HOW IS RAY? IS HE DOING WELL?
UH, YEAH. HE'S FINE. HE'S... YEAH, DOING GREAT.

I'M SO GLAD. WELL, I JUST WANTED TO TELL YOU HOW LUCKY YOU ARE TO HAVE SOMEONE LIKE HIM AND TO TELL HIM MAYA SENDS HER LOVE. OK? BYE BYE.
BYE.
WELL NOW...

I'VE SEEN SHIT COME OUT OF THE ASS. I'VE SEEN IT COME OUT OF THE MOUTH. BUT I'VE NEVER SEEN IT COME OUT OF THE EYES, NOSTRILS AND EARS SIMULTANEOUSLY.
YOU DON'T THINK SHE WAS BEING SINCERE? I THOUGHT SHE WAS...

MAGGIE, SOMETIMES YOU CAN BE SO...
OH, C'MON, HOPEY. NOT EVERYBODY CAN BE AS SARCASTIC AND SPITE-FUL AS YOU AND I.

YEP! YOU'RE ABSOLUTELY RIGHT, MAG! BUT NOT EVEN YOU CAN LOAD UP AND PLANT A BOOT UP YOUR OWN BIG FUCKIN' ASS!
!!!

BELOW MY WINDOW LURKS MY HEAD

BY XAIME 1989

WHAT'S THAT? OK, I'LL TALK TO YOU SOON. BYE, MAGGIE...

GLOOM

HEY! HEY!

HEY, RAY! YOU STILL LIVE UP THERE?
YEAH, COME ON UP, DOYLE, YOU BUM!
OIN WASH

LOOKS A HELL OF A LOT BETTER THAN WHEN I LIVED HERE.
IT'S BEEN AWHILE, MAN. WHERE YOU BEEN HIDING YOURSELF?

I'VE BEEN SLEEPING AT THE MISSION LATELY. IT'S BEEN COLD, Y'KNOW...
YOU WANNA STAY HERE? MAGGIE'S STILL AWAY...

NAW, 'S'COOL. BUT I COULD USE A SHOWER...
SURE, SURE! HELP YOURSELF! ANYTHING YOU WANT!

WHAT'S WITH THE HOSPITALITY, MAX?
I'M HAPPY TO SEE YOU! YOU'RE LOOKING AT ONE LONELY SON OF A BITCH!
2

YOU WANNA GO IN FOR A DRINK? I'LL BUY, BILL.
TWIST MY ARM, BOB.
Cocktails

YEAH, LILY'S BEEN ASKING ME TO MOVE BACK IN WITH HER, BUT I DUNNO, I DON'T THINK I'M READY TO MOVE IN WITH ANYBODY RIGHT NOW...
MMM...

GID OUDDA BED, DERE'LL BE NO MO' NAPPIN'...

HI! GRRR...
HI.

ELIAS, C'MERE. DON'T BOTHER THE MEN.

DANITA? WHAT ARE YOU DOING HERE, AND SO LATE?
ELIAS'S DADDY'S IN TOWN AN' I'M AFRAID HE MIGHT TRY TAKIN' HIM AGAIN, SO WE'RE HIDING OUT FOR A FEW DAYS. HE'S A REAL CRAZY MAN...

WELL, YOU CAN'T STAY HERE ALL NIGHT. HERE, TAKE MY KEY. YOU CAN STAY AT MY PLACE AS LONG AS YOU HAVE TO...
THANKS.
BATH
3

I KNEW IT WAS PRETTY MUCH OVER BETWEEN MAGGIE AND ME WHEN SHE AND HOPEY WERE REUNITED. BUT I KEPT MOPING AND HOPING ANYWAY...

THEN ONE DAY I RAN INTO DANITA AND SHE WAS REALLY SAD TO HEAR ABOUT MAGGIE AND ME...

"SHE THEN ASKED ME IF I STILL PAINTED, AND TO CHEER ME UP, OFFERED TO POSE FOR ME. IT WAS NEVER ANY SECRET TO HER HOW MUCH I'VE ALWAYS ADMIRED HER RATHER ROBUST PHYSIQUE. AND HEY, SHE WOULDN'T HAVE TO WORRY ABOUT ME, ALL I HAD ON MY MIND WAS MAGGIE...

"DANITA BECAME A REAL COMFORTING FRIEND AS THE DAYS PASSED. IT WASN'T UNTIL SHE OFFERED TO POSE NUDE THAT I REALIZED SHE WAS INTERESTED IN BEING SOMETHING MORE THAN A COMFORTING FRIEND...

END OF PART ONE

...AND IN THIS CORNER...!
XAIME 89
SO, LIKE, WHO'S DANITA, MAG?
IT DOESN'T REALLY MATTER. NOT ANY MORE IT DOESN'T...
PHONE
1

THE ABSOLUTE GALL!!!
HANG HIM BY HIS BALLS, MAGGIE!
MAYBE DAFFY'S WRONG. SHE'S KNOWN TO GET THINGS MIXED UP, Y'KNOW...
NO, SHE'S RIGHT THIS TIME. RAY'S HAD HIS EYE ON HER BUTT FOR YEARS. ONLY I NEVER THOUGHT...
FISH HOOKS, MAG. USE FISH HOOKS.
SO, I TAKE IT WE'RE NOT GOING OVER TO MAYA'S FOR COFFEE...
YES! YES, WE ARE! AND BOY, WILL HE BE SORRY...
REMEMBER, MAGGIE. THE ONLY GOOD POLAR BEAR IS THE KIND IN A ZOO...
?
...AND SO I TOLD MY SHRINK... HEY, DID YOU EVER SEE THE DEAD BOYS WHEN THEY PLAYED L.A.?
NOT ME. I HATE THAT SONG "TRUCKIN'..."
SO, MAYA. DID RAY EVER YELL AT YOU FOR USING THE WRONG SPONGE TO WASH THE SINK?
I WENT OUT WITH NICK ROT BACK IN SEVENTY-SIX. BUT IT ONLY LASTED A MONTH AS THE JERK DUMPED ME FOR HOLLY WEEN OF THE TOMBS.
DIDN'T THEY DO "WRECK OF THE EDMOND FITZ-GERALD"?
HUH! WHO DID RAY DUMP YOU FOR?
I HATE TO TELL YOU THIS, BUT, I SENT THE BOY ON HIS WAY. HE JUST COULD NOT HANDLE BIG CITY LIFE.
HUH! CAN'T HANDLE SMALL TOWN RELATION-SHIPS TOO WELL, EITHER...
OH, FOR THE LOVE OF CARMEN...
2

ACTUALLY, HE WASN'T HALF AS BAD AS DICK PLASTER. BIG, BAD PUNK ROCK STAR. RAN HOME TO MOMMY JUST AFTER TWO WEEKS OF LIVING WITH ME...
COME ON, MAGGOT! YOU SAID YOU GUYS BROKE UP!
I SAID, AS LONG AS WE'RE APART, HE COULD SEE OTHER GIRLS. THAT'S WHAT I SAID...
JUST WHEN EXACTLY WERE YOU TWO INTO PUNK? I DON'T THINK YOU'VE HEARD OF ANY OF THESE PEOPLE I'VE MENTIONED.
...AND SO HE'S DOING EXACTLY THAT! SO YOU GOT NO RIGHT TO COMPLAIN!
WELL, SHIT! THEN I WANT A PIECE OF THIS DEAL, TOO!
WHAT DOES THAT MEAN?
WELL, I HAVEN'T STUCK AROUND TOWN THIS LONG JUST TO SEE THE TRACTOR PULL.
Y'KNOW, ONCE IN A WHILE YOU'LL COME UP WITH SOMETHING THAT'LL SEND ME WAY OUT TO JUPITER...
IT'S HOT THERE THIS TIME OF YEAR SO YOU WILL HAVE TO DRESS LIGHT. HERE, LET ME HELP YOU...
YOU ANIMAL, YOU.
WOOF.
MMM... AHH... RAY WHO?
!?
3

J'G/JUG (PRONOUNCED JIG)

XAIME 89

BELOW MY WINDOW LURKS MY HEA PART 2
...THEN CORNELIUS STABBED THE GUY IN THE THROAT. THAT'S WHY HE LEFT STOCKTON AN' CAME HERE. I MET HIM AT A PARTY...

ONE TIME HE GOT SO MAD HE WAS GONNA STAB ME. SO RIGHT THEN I TOLD 'IM I WAS PREGNANT. SO HE JUST UP AN' LEFT TOWN...

AN' EVERY ONCE IN AWHILE, HE COMES BACK TO SEE ELIAS. BUT HE'S GETTIN' SCARIER EVERY VISIT. HE BEAT UP MY DADDY LAST TIME...
NOK NOK NO
MAMA, THE DO'...

I'LL GET IT.
DANITA, WAIT...
K NOK
NOK NOK

IT'S ABOUT TIME I FOUND YOU!
SO, YOU FOUND ME. SO WHAT?
HOWARD 99

I JUST CAME TO WARN YOU THAT CORNELIUS IS LOOK-ING FOR YOU...
RAY, DO YOU KNOW RONNIE?
CLIPPERS

OH, YEAH. HE'S A VILLAIN, ALL RIGHT. ONE TIME HE STABBED SOME HOMEBOY WITH A RUSTED SCREW-DRIVER BEHIND RAY'S LIQUOR.
AN' THE COPS NEVER GOT HIM FOR IT, NEITHER.

WELL, YOU REMEMBER WHAT HAPPENED THAT ONE TIME BOZO WAS GOING TO THE COPS...
I DON'T WANNA TALK ABOUT IT.
NOK
NO

HEY, MAN. DON'T YOU THINK YOU SHOULD LOOK THROUGH THE PEEP HOLE FIRST?
SOMEONE PLUGGED IT UP BEFORE I EVER MOVED IN...

JUST WHO THE HELL DO YOU THINK YOU ARE?

RAY, WHO IS IT? IT DON'T SOUND LIKE... RAY...?
BUT... BUT... AW... OK...

IF YOU THINK YOU CAN GO AROUND SEEING OTHER CHICKS WHILE MAGGIE'S AWAY...
NOW WAIT...
WHO THE FUCK IS SHE?
I DUNNO, BUT I HAVE A FEELIN' THIS HAS SOMETHIN' TO DO WITH ME!

HEY, BITCH! IF YOU GOT A BEEF WITH HIM, YOU GOT ONE WITH ME!
SO, THE HARLOT STEPS FORWARD...
ALL RIGHT, ALL RIGHT! KNOCK IT OFF!
NO, LET 'EM GO...
2

ALL RIGHT, MOTHER FUCKER! I KNOW YOU ARE IN THERE! YOU'RE A DEAD MAN!

LOOKIT RAY. ME AN' MY SON COME OVER 'CAUSE WE THINK HE'S ALL LONELY AN' EVERYTHING, BUT CHECK 'IM OUT. PARTYING AN' SHIT...
'LITOS...
FIRE

HOWARD
99

THAT'S THE SAME DUDE THAT SHANKED LIL' SPIDER. THEY NEVER GOT HIM FOR IT, EH?
AN' YOU AIN'T EVEN CALLED THE POLICE? GIRL, EITHER YOU'RE SUPER BRAVE OR SUPER STUPID!
MY DADDY JUS' GOTS ONE EYE.
SO WHAT? MY DADDY GOTS A KNIFE.

Z
I DON'T KNOW WHAT'S WRONG WITH ME! I WAS THE ONE WHO WANTED MAGGIE AND RAY BROKEN UP IN THE FIRST PLACE! YUK!
I GUESS SHE'S REALLY SUPER MAD, HUH?
3

MAD? NAW, I'LL BET BY NOW SHE'S EVEN FORGOTTEN HIS NAME. HATE TO SAY IT, GUY, BUT YOU'RE JUST NO HOPEY.

ANYWAY, I HOPE YOU TWO HAVE A WONDERFUL, LASTING RELATIONSHIP EVEN THOUGH WHAT'S-HIS-NAME WITH THE KNIFE WILL DO EVERYTHING IN HIS POWER TO TRY AND STOP IT.
JUST KIDDING...

WELL, IT'S LATE, SO WE BETTER GET GOING. ELIAS, LET'S GO. GET YOUR JACKET...
AHEM
WE GOIN' HOME NOW?

BABY, I NEVER WANTED TO GET YOU INVOLVED IN THIS. YOU DON'T WANT ANY PART OF MY TROUBLES.
WHY DON'T YOU LET ME DECIDE ON WHAT I WANT AND DON'T WANT.

HEY, DON'T GET MAD. IT'S NOT LIKE I'M GONNA FORGET YOU OR ANYTHING. I'LL BE AROUND. I PROMISE.

C'MON, ELIAS.
CAN WE GO TO CARLOS'S HOUSE TO-MORROW? HE SAID HIS DADDY GOTS JUST ONE EYE...

OFTEN
OF-TEN
OFFEN...
2+2=5
4

WHERE THEY AT?

OK, EDWARDS. DON'T MOVE A MUSCLE OR YOU'RE FUCKING DEAD MEAT...
CLICK!
CLICK!
CLICK!

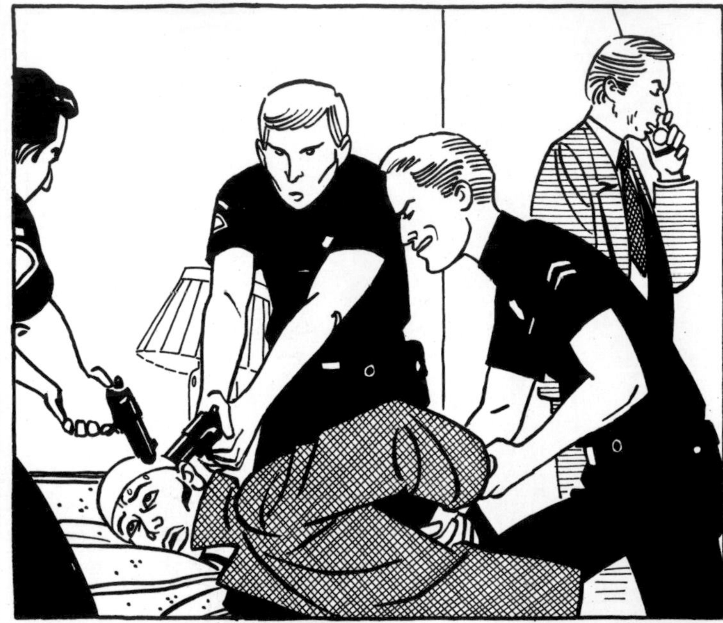

TELL ELIAS HIS DADDY SAID HI.

THE END

LOOK, HOPEY! I FOUND ONE, RIGHT ON THE OL' ORANGE JUICE CARTON.

WHAT...? OH, YEAH. REAL NICE, MAG.

YOU DON'T WANT IT ANY MORE?
NAW, I WOULD IF LIKE, MY STUPID MOM DID IT, BUT NOT IF SOME ASSHOLE IS TRYING TO BE FUNNY.
HAVE YOU SEEN ME?
MATTHEW BUCHER
ESPERANZA GLASS
SUN VALLEY
100% ORANGE JU
YOU THINK SOMEBODY DID IT AS A JOKE? LIKE, WHO? PENNY, MAYBE...?
I DON'T KNOW, BUT I KNOW IT WASN'T MY MOM... WHAT ARE YOU DOING?
I STILL WANT THE PICTURE EVEN IF YOU DON'T. I THINK IT'S REALLY CUTE, JOKE OR NO JOKE.
YEAH, BUT WHAT'S EVERYBODY GONNA DRINK WITH THEIR VODKA NOW, KOOL AID?
OOPS! WELL, I SUPPOSE NOW'S A GOOD TIME TO HEAD ON OVER TO PENNY'S PARTY, DON'T YOU THINK?
YOU GUYS ARE LEAVING? YOU JUST GOT HERE.
HEY, PAT. HOW'S THE BEER VAT?
WELL, THERE'S THIS OTHER PARTY, AND WE KINDA PROMISED...
BITCHIN' KITCHEN, PAT.
THANKS. WHY DON'T YOU GUYS STICK AROUND? MAYA'S COMING...
AND I HOPE SHE BRINGS MORE ORANGE JUICE. HMMM...
I DON'T WANNA WAIT FOR MAYA. LET'S JUST WALK OUT THAT DOOR RIGHT NOW.
UH, MAG. MAYBE WE SHOULD FORGET PENNY'S. I HAVE A FEELING HER PARTY SUCKS BIG TIME.
2

OH, POOTY. SO MUCH FOR US PARTY HOPPING VALKYRIES.
MARY'S CALLING US OVER.
OOG! YOU GO TALK TO HER. SHE'S GOT ROSA WITH HER.
SO? WHAT'S ROSA GONNA DO...?
OH, I SEE...
CAN'T BLAME HER, MAG. THAT IS ONE SEXY, FUCKIN' DRESS.
SO, I DIDN'T KNOW WE WERE STOPPING HERE FIRST, OK?
HEY, MARY CHRISTMAS. HOW'S BUSIMUSS? HEY, ROSA EASTER. HOW'S YOUR SEESTER? HEY JED HALLOWEEN. HOW'S YO' MAMA BEEN?
URP
HOPEY, THIS IS MY BOYFRIEND LEE'S BROTHER LELAND, THE WRITER...
REMEMBER, HOPEY AND MAGGIE ARE STAYING WITH ME AND LEE...
I REMEMBER. THE CALIFORNIA GIRLS...
HEY, MAYA'S HERE.
OH, MY GOD! I KNEW YOU'D BE HERE!
THESE DARLINGS ARE THE LOVES OF MY LIFE! I DON'T KNOW WHAT I'D DO WITHOUT THEM! WHERE'S MAGGIE?
OH, SHE'S STRUTTIN' HER STUFF AROUND HERE SOME-WHERE.
MHMM. THEY CERTAINLY HAVE A WAY OF MAKING YOU WANT TO CUDDLE THEM...
TO CUDDLE? HONEY, I'M TALKING MORE ALONG THE LINES OF PASSIONATE, STEAMY, WHITE HOT SEX! THEY CERTAINLY MADE ME MISS THE OLD DAYS...
YOU...? THE THREE OF YOU?
LEE'S TOLD ME QUITE A BIT ABOUT YOU TWO...
WE LIKE HIM, TOO.
3

WELL, I'LL TELL YOU. MAGGIE WAS A BIT SHY WHEN I JOINED IN BUT THAT LITTLE HOPEY'S A REAL FIREBALL.
MAYA, DID YOU BRING ANY O.J.?

WHAT'S WRONG, BABE? YOU ALL OUT? I CAN GO GET SOME IF YOU WANT.
I'LL GO. I HAVE TO GET CIGARETTES ANYWAY.

HURRY BACK, VERY MARY.
UH HUH.

YES, IT'S AN ACTOR'S WORKSHOP WHERE ONCE IN AWHILE WE'LL ALL SHOW UP AS A CHARACTER FROM ONE OF OUR FAVORITE BOOKS OR PLAYS. AND WERE THEY ALL SURPRISED WHEN I SHOWED UP ONE NIGHT AS CHRISTINE THE CAR...
HA! ONE TIME I BLEW AWAY MY IMPROV GROUP BY DOING DONALD TRUMP IN THE RAW. SOMETIMES YOU HAVE TO LET YOUR PANTS DOWN.

...BUT NOBODY GOT THE REAL JOKE BEHIND IT. THAT IS, I DON'T THINK STEPHEN'S NEWER STUFF IS HALF AS GOOD AS HIS OLDER STUFF.
OBVIOUSLY, YOU'RE INVOLVED WITH PEOPLE RAISED ON T.V. COMEDY. FOR INSTANCE, WHEN I WANTED TO PLAY TOM JOAD PORTRAYED BY GROUCHO MARX.
EXCUSE ME, BUT ARE YOU FRENCH?
NO, MEXICAN.

OH, I'M SO SORRY. EXCUSE US, PLEASE.
THAT'S OK...
HEY, BABE. HOW ABOUT ANOTHER BEER?
GAEL

NO, THANKS. I ALREADY GOT ONE.
URP
I MEANT FOR ME!
HERE YOU ARE, ROSA.

HEY, PAT. IF I WANTED A BEER FROM YOU, I WOULD HAVE ASKED YOU FOR ONE.
YOU'RE IN MY HOUSE NOW, ROSA, SO JUST RELAX.
GAEL
4

MAYBE I SHOULD JUST LEAVE?
DON'T WORRY ABOUT IT. BELIEVE IT OR NOT, SHE ONLY ACTS THIS WAY WHEN SHE'S HOT ON SOMEONE.
PAT! WE GOT ORANGE JUICE!
BOYS

AHH, THAT MARY'S A REAL SWEETHEART. WHERE IS SHE?
SHE DROPPED IT OFF AND HAD TO SPLIT RIGHT AWAY. SHE DIDN'T SAY WHY, THOUGH.
MAY I HELP YOU?
URP!

MARY TELLS ME YOU MET HER WHEN SHE LIVED IN L.A.
YOU'RE FROM CALIFORNIA? I'D LIKE TO VISIT L.A. ONE DAY...

AH, I WAS THERE FOR A WEEK ONCE. ALL I SAW WAS TANNED BODIES FERRARIS, UNREAD SCRIPTS, AND POWER LUNCHES.
WHAT'D YOU DO THERE, TRY TO SELL A SCRIPT?

I DON'T BELIEVE THAT'S ALL THERE IS. I HEAR THERE'S A HUGE GAY COMMUNITY THERE...
I ALSO HEAR A LOT OF THOSE BOYS ARE USING THE GAY SHELTER HANDOUT MONEY FOR TRICKS AND DRUGS.

AND THE PEOPLE WHO GIVE THE MONEY THINK THEY'RE REALLY HELPING OUT THE GAY COMMUNITY...
THAT'S TERRIBLE! YOU...
OH, C'MON! YOU'RE NOT GONNA TELL ME THAT SHIT DOESN'T HAPPEN HERE! JESUS, JUST BECAUSE YOU COULDN'T SELL A FUCKIN' MOVIE SCRIPT...

STUPID ASS HACK! MAKING ME OUT LIKE THE FUCKING AMBASSADOR OF CALIFORNIA...
I LOVE IT WHEN YOU USE BAD WORDS. TELL ME, ARE YOU AND MAGGIE STILL SLEEPING ON MARY'S COLD FLOOR?
5

YEAH, IT'S A LITTLE CRAMPED, BUT...
WHY DON'T ONE OF YOU STAY WITH ME? THAT WAY THINGS WON'T BE TOO CRAMPED...

WELL, WHICH ONE OF US WOULD YOU WANT TO...
HOPEY, WHAT DO I HAVE TO SAY...?

JUST WHAT IS THE STORY ABOUT YOU AND RAY DOMINGUEZ?

YOU NOTICE HOW ALL OF A SUDDEN NOBODY'S TALKING TO US?
I KNOW WHY THEY'RE NOT TALKING TO ME, BUT WHAT DID YOU DO THAT WAS SO TERRIBLE?

I TOLD ROSA I WASN'T INTERESTED. IF I'DA KNOWN IT WAS A CRIME...
I THINK THE DRESS HELPED A LITTLE. OH, WE'RE SUCH SNOTS...
YOU GUYS AREN'T LEAVING, ARE YOU?

I THINK WE BETTER, PAT. YOUR FRIENDS DON'T SEEM TO WANT US HERE ANY MORE.
WELL, I WANT YOU HERE, AND IT'S MY HOUSE...
PAT, PLEASE. I REALLY APPRECIATE ALL YOUR HOSPITALITY BUT, WELL... YOU'RE JUST NOT MY TYPE...

AND WHAT MAKES YOU THINK YOU'RE MY "TYPE"? I WANTED YOU HERE BECAUSE I THOUGHT YOU WERE REAL NICE PEOPLE...
"WANTED"? "THOUGHT"? "WERE"? DOES THAT MEAN...? HEH...
C'MON, MASSIVE MOUTH!
6

JUST HOW MUCH MORE CAN ONE PERSON SUCK? HUH? TELL ME, HOW MUCH MORE?
C'MON, MAG. PAT TOLD YOU SHE UNDERSTOOD...

IT'S NOT JUST THAT! I USED TO THINK I WAS PRETTY UNRESTRAINED BECAUSE I'VE EXPERIENCED J'GGIN' ON BOTH SIDES, BUT WHEN ROSA APPROACHED ME, AND MAYA THE OTHER NIGHT... WELL, I'M REALLY JUST A DOGGONE PRUDE!
WHY, 'CAUSE YOU TURN DOWN PEOPLE YOU DON'T LIKE?

YOU'RE RIGHT...
YOU AIN'T LOOKING AT CHOPPED LIVER HERE, GIRLY GIRL...

I KNOW, I GUESS I JUST HAVE TO BE TOLD ONCE IN A WHILE...
WE AIN'T PLAYIN' TIDDLY WINKS HERE, Y'KNOW.

SO, PENNY INSISTS SHE WASN'T THE ONE WHO PLASTERED MY FACE ALL OVER THOSE CARTONS. I'M BEGINNING TO THINK IT WAS MY STUPID HEAD BROTHER...
UH HUH.
!?
1A

HOPEY, THAT WAS MY BAG.
AND HERE'S MINE. WHAT THE HELL IS GOING ON HERE ANYWAY?
7

'I CAN'T DO ANYTHING' BY X-RAY SPEX

'DEAD END JUSTICE' BY THE RUNAWAYS

YOU KNOW WHAT? I'M GLAD MARY KICKED US OUT OF HER APARTMENT! NOW WE CAN LEAVE THIS CITY OF ASSHOLES.

NO, WAIT! I TAKE THAT BACK! THEY DON'T EVEN RATE AS ASSHOLES! THEY'RE MORE LIKE... LIKE WANNA-BE ASSHOLES!
WANNA-BE WANNA-BE ASSHOLES!

"HEY, BABE. HOW ABOUT ANOTHER BEER?" SHEEIT! I'VE BEEN COME ONTO BY EXPERTS!
SO, WHO WANTS TO FUCK?

MARY, WHAT SAY THE FOUR OF US HEAD ON OVER TO LOIS'S HOUSE?
WHAT? WE CAN'T TAKE THE INCEST TWINS OVER THERE! LOIS HATES STRANGERS! SHE...

WHERE IS IT DID YOU SAY WE'RE GOING?
TO A PARTY. WE CAN GET SOME SPEED THERE.
SO, WHO WANTS TO FUCK? HYUCK!

HE'S TALKING TO YOU...
NO, HE ISN'T. HE'S TALKING TO YOU.
YOU KNOW, THE AZTECS USED TO DO HUMAN SACRIFICES. THE ROMANS THREW CHRISTIANS TO THE LIONS...

THE MORMONS... I THINK IT WAS THE FIRING SQUAD...
SO WHAT?
HE'S ONLY PUTTING YOU INTO THE CORRECT FRAME OF MIND, MI QUERIDA.
FUCK?
YAY!

I SAID, WHO THE HELL WANTS TO FUCK?
NOT I, SAID THE CAT.
NOT I, SAID THE PIG.
NOT I, SAID THE WORM.

I'LL FUCK ANYBODY! DUDES OR CHICKS! STRAIGHT OR GAY! BLACK OR WHITE! THIN OR FAT! CHILDREN! I'LL FUCK CHILDREN! ANIMALS! I'LL EVEN FUCK FUCKIN' ANIMALS!!
ANIMALS?
ANIMALS??
ANIMALS? WHAT KIND OF ANIMALS?

DOGS AND CATS?
WE'LL FUCK LIKE RATS!
WHAT ABOUT A BEAR?
I'LL FUCK HIM IN HIS UNDER-WEAR!
EVEN A DINOSAUR?
I'LL SHOW 'IM WHAT HIS DICK IS FOR!
?!

SO, WHO WANTS TO FUCK?
UH, HOW ABOUT A... A... PLATYPUS?
UH, LOIS. THESE ARE MY FRIENDS.

SO, DID THEY COME TO FUCK, OR TO SUCK?
Bzzz Bzz Bzzzz Bzzz...

WHICH ONE OF YOU IS MAGGIE?
UH... ME...

COME INTO MY BEDROOM, AND QUICK! I AIN'T GOT ALL DAY...
NOW, WAIT...
11

TERRY, WHAT THE FUCK? WHAT DID YOU SAY TO HER?
ENOUGH IS ENOUGH, TERRY. WE SHOULD GET HER OUT OF THERE NOW!
ZIMBA ZAMBA ZIMBLE...

H-HEY, LOOK. I JUST CAME WITH TERRY AND MARY. I'M NOBODY. I-I...
SHUT UP AND TELL ME WHO THAT IS UP THERE ON THE WALL, AND IF YOU'RE WRONG, I'M GONNA FUCK YOU AND ALL YOUR FUCKING FRIENDS TO HELL!

GLORI BEATS TITAÑON 2-3

DRINK UP, BABE! ANY RELATIVE OF VICKI GLORI'S CAN PARTY AT MY HOUSE ANY OL' DAY! SO, YOU THINK MAYBE YOUR AUNT WOULD FUCK SOMEONE LIKE ME...?
I ALWAYS KNEW YOU WEREN'T AS EVIL AS PEOPLE SAY, TERRY.
IT WAS WORTH IT JUST TO WATCH YOU GUYS SQUIRM FOR THOSE MERE MINUTES.

WHERE DID YOU AND TEXAS GO WHEN YOU HAD EVERYBODY MAD AT YOU?
I DUNNO, BUT I'LL TELL YOU RIGHT NOW: I AIN'T GOING BACK TO CALIFORNIA...

AW, PATOOTY! WE GOTTA GO BACK TO PAT'S. I TOOK THE WRONG COAT...
SO WHAT, MAG. IT FEELS PRETTY EXPENSIVE. MAYBE WE CAN SELL IT IF WE HAVE TO.
12

YOUR ORANGE JUICE CARTON PICTURE IS IN THE POCKET OF MINE. I'LL BE RIGHT BACK.
I'LL BE RIGHT HERE.

DUM DE DUMMM... I AIN'T GOING BACK TO CALIFORNIA...

FRENCH? ITALIAN? PERSIAN? INDIAN...?

BRAZILIAN? CUBAN? PUERTO RICAN...?

MEX-I-CAN!
HA
HA
HA

DIDN'T FIND YOUR COAT?
NO.
13

JUST WHEN YOU THINK A CITY IS FULL OF WANNA-BE ASSHOLES, OUT COME THE REAL ASSHOLES. THE RACISTS...
YOU MEAN THOSE TWO ART JERKS? I HEARD THEM. AND AS STUPID AS THEY WERE, I DON'T BELIEVE THEY WERE TRYING TO BE NAZIS...

I'M BETTING IN THEIR "HIP FASHION" WORLD, TO BE MEXICAN JUST ISN'T IN VOGUE AT THE MOMENT...
SO, WHAT'S THE FUCKING DIFFERENCE BETWEEN THAT AND NAZIISM? IT'S STILL A GOOD REASON TO GET AS FAR AWAY FROM HERE AS POSSIBLE!

SO, WHERE ARE WE GONNA GO THAT'S BETTER? IT'S THE SAME SHIT ALL OVER...
OK, THEN DON'T GO BACK TO CALIFORNIA! SHIT, JUST 'CAUSE YOU CAN TURN OFF YOUR "ETHNIC" HALF WHENEVER IT'S GODDAMN CONVENIENT!

HOPE YOU DON'T MIND THAT I LET MYSELF IN, MAYA, BUT MARCEL AND I HAD A REAL RAGER TONIGHT, AND I THINK THIS ONE WAS IT...

GOD, MY LIFE IS SO SCREWED UP. I DON'T KNOW WHAT TO DO. I FEEL LIKE I SHOULD JUST MOVE IN HERE WITH YOU, OR...

WOULD THAT BE ALL RIGHT, MAYA? BECAUSE, I REALLY NEED A FRIEND RIGHT NOW, AND...

ARE YOU LISTENING TO ME AT ALL...?
HAVE YOU SEEN ME?
MATTHEW BUEHER
ESPERANZA GLASS
14

END OF PART I

WHAT'S WITH SUNNY BOY TODAY? OUR SOUP AIN'T GOOD ENOUGH FOR HIM NO MORE?
DON'T YOU KNOW? THIS IS THE DAY HIS GIRLFRIEND COOKS HIM HIS BIRTHDAY BREAKFAST.
WIGWAM BAM
PART 2
JIM HENDERSON 90
1

"DOOWHUTCHYALIKE" - DIGITAL UNDERGROUND

HEY, YOU PUNK ROCKERS. WHICH ONE OF YOU WANTS TO BUY ME A BIRTHDAY DRINK?
OH!
OH, HI, DOYLE...
SMOKE'S

I'M AFRAID WE'LL HAVE TO OWE YOU THAT DRINK. WE'RE RUNNING LATE FOR WORK.
HAPPY BIRTHDAY, DOYLE!

SNIFF...

HEY! ANYBODY ALIVE IN THERE?

LOOKIN' REAL "HIM" TODAY, RAY. BOY...
I LOVE YOU, TOO. HOW'D THE BIRTHDAY BREAKFAST GO?

IT DIDN'T. LILY WAS TOO BUSY HELPING YOUR GIRLFRIEND PREPARE FOR HER OPENING NIGHT AT BUMPER'S.
OH, YEAH...
YOU KNOW, I'D BUY YOU A BIRTHDAY BREAKFAST MYSELF BUT I'M BROKE.

ACTUALLY, A BIRTHDAY SHOWER WOULD SUIT ME A LOT NICER...
WATER HEATER'S BROKEN. FUCKIN' LANDLORD WON'T FIX IT TILL I CATCH UP ON THE RENT. JUST WHEN I LOST MY JOB, TOO...
3

BACHAN- GRANDMOTHER

SO, SHE'S BACK. WHAT'S THE BIG DEAL? DOES SHE HAVE AIDS, OR SOMETHING?
SHE CAME BACK ALONE. THAT'S THE BIG DEAL...

FOURTH FLOOR. LADIE'S HEAD GASKETS... CHILDREN'S HEROIN...

MEN'S ROCKET BRAS...

I HOPE YOU'RE ALL HAPPY. I HOPE YOU'RE ALL JUST...
OW!

EIGHTBALL

WHAT IS IT ABOUT YOU THAT MAYA FINDS SO SPECIAL ANYWAY?
A TONGUE FASTER THAN MUHAMMED ALI AND SWEETER THAN DOLLY PARTON...

... IN THEIR TWENTIES!
SLAM
5

DOESN'T LOOK LIKE THEY'RE HERE ANYMORE. SHIT, AND LILY DOESN'T LEAVE A KEY. YOU WANNA GO SEE IF THEY'RE DOWN AT THE CLUB ALREADY?
WHY, DO THEY HAVE SHOWERS AT BUMPER'S?

MAN, I KNOW HOW YOU FEEL. IF DANITA WAS MY GIRLFRIEND, I WOULDN'T WANT HER TO DO THAT SHIT EITHER. LILY ON THE OTHER HAND, THAT KINDA DANCING IS HER LIFE...
IT'S NOT THAT. DANITA CAN DANCE ALL SHE WANTS...
BWAA

NO, IT'S JUST THAT SHE'S BEEN GIVING ME SHIT BECAUSE HER FOLKS HAVE BEEN GIVING HER SHIT BECAUSE I WON'T MARRY HER. YOU KNOW, ELIAS NEEDS A DADDY AND ALL THAT...
AMIGO...

CAN YOU JUST PICTURE ME AND HER GETTING MARRIED...?
YOU'D HAVE TO LIVE BEHIND RAY'S LIQUOR WITH YOUR BANKROLL...
BWAA BWAAA...

YOU THINK I SHOULD GO ROOT DANITA ON TONIGHT?
HECK, I'M GOING. ER... TO WATCH LILY, THAT IS...

YEAH...
BWAAA...

RELAX. I AIN'T THAT DESPERATE YET...
6

RING!
RING!

CLICK!
♫ NOBODY'S HOOOME... NOBODY'S HOOOME... ♫
BEEEEEP!
DAMN, I THOUGHT YOU'D BE THERE BY NOW...

HOPEY, THIS IS MAYA. I'M GOING STRAIGHT FROM WORK TO LELAND'S PARTY. YOU CAN GO, TOO, BUT IF YOU DON'T WANT TO, THAT'S OK. IT'LL BE PRETTY MUCH THE SAME PEOPLE FROM PAT'S LAST PARTY. OK? GOTTA GO, SWEETIE. BYE.
BEEEEEP!
CLICK!
CLUNK!

HEY, CLYDE! WE STILL HAVEN'T FOUND A SHOWER YET!
I'LL TAKE MY CHANCES, BONNIE. SEE YOU TONIGHT. AT BUMPER'S... MAYBE.
PSST... DOYLE!

HEY, I'M SORRY IF MY MANLY SCENT DOESN'T AGREE WITH YOUR TURNED UP NOSES, BUT IT'S THE ONLY ONE I GOT, SO...
GUY, DOYLE. WE DIDN'T SAY ANYTHING...
SO, WHAT'S THE WORD, DOYLE? DID MAGGIE MOVE BACK IN WITH YOUR FRIEND OR HAVE THEY SPLIT FOR GOOD?

WHAT ARE YOU TALKING ABOUT?
:GASP: THEN THEY HAVE SPLIT FOR GOOD! I WONDER WHERE SHE'S STAYING NOW?
GUY, DOYLE. WE WOULDN'T SAY ANYTHING RUDE ABOUT YOU...

WELL, THEN YOU WANNA KNOW HOW YOU LOVELIES CAN MAKE IT UP TO BIG DADDY?
SORRY, OUR BATHROOM'S BEING RETILED...
YOU CAN USE OUR SHOWER. BUT YOU HAVE TO LEAVE MY HOUSE BEFORE MY PARENTS GET HOME.
7

GOD DAMN IT, MAN! YOU CAN'T LOCK ME OUT OF MY OWN APARTMENT!
WELL, I'M DOING IT. I DON'T UNLOCK THIS DOOR UNTIL YOU'RE CAUGHT UP ON THE RENT...

LOOK, MAN! MY PHONE'S RINGING! HOW THE FUCK AM I SUPPOSED TO ANSWER IT?
..RRING.. ..RING..
THAT'S YOUR PROBLEM. AND I'D APPRECIATE IT IF YOU'D WATCH YOUR LANGUAGE. WE HAVE RESPECTABLE TENNANTS LIVING HERE, YOU KNOW...

C'MON, DANITA! IF RAY HASN'T ANSWERED IN THE LAST TWO HOURS, DON'T YOU THINK HE MIGHT NOT BE THERE?
OH, I WAS JUST CALLING HOME. CHECKIN' ON BABY ELIAS...

YOU CAN'T WORRY ABOUT WHAT YOUR BOYFRIEND THINKS. YOU DO WHAT YOU WANNA DO AND THAT'S IT.
I KNOW, YOU TOLD ME A MILLION TIMES...

AND I AIN'T SAYING IT JUST TO HEAR MYSELF TALK, EITHER. LOOK, YOU CAME TO ME, REMEMBER...?
C'MON, LILY. LAY OFF THE GIRL...
YEAH, I REMEMBER YOU ON YOUR OPENING NIGHT...

OH, YOU MEAN, "OOH, OOH! ARE MY TITS TOO SMALL?"
"OOH, OOH! IS MY CELLULITE SHOWING?"
YOU GUYS WEREN'T EVEN HERE, SO SHUT YER YAPS!
8

SO, ARE YOU GUYS GONNA BE ASSHOLES AND MAKE ME GO TO THIS PARTY ALONE, OR...
I TOLD YOU I'D GO...
I DUNNO IF THEY'LL LET YOU IN, TEX. YOU AIN'T WEARING ALL BLACK.
SACRELIGIOUS

HOW ABOUT YOU, LESTER? ARE YOU COMING OR ARE YOU GONNA RAG ON THOSE PEOPLE FROM WAY OVER HERE?
NAW, I THINK I'M JUST GONNA GO OUT LOOKING FOR A NEW BASS PLAYER.

THANKS FOR THE SHOWER, BLANDINA. BUT, ARE YOU SURE I CAN'T STICK AROUND TO MEET MY FUTURE BROTHER-IN-LAW?
RAY, TSK! HE'S JUST A FRIEND FROM WORK! WE'RE JUST... TSK! WELL, WHAT ABOUT YOU? WHAT ABOUT YOU...?

...DOES MOM KNOW WHAT YOUR GIRLFRIEND IS DOING FOR A LIVING STARTING TONIGHT?
NO, AND I'M NOT GONNA TELL HER, EVEN IF IT'S NOT THAT BIG A DEAL, OK...?

HAVE YOU DECIDED IF YOU'RE GOING TO MARRY HER, OR NOT?
NOPE.

WHAT EVER HAPPENED TO MAGGIE, THE GIRL YOU LIVED WITH FOR A WHILE? EVERYONE FIGURED SHE'D BE THE ONE THAT...
WELL...

DAPHNE, GUESS WHAT? I SAW YOUR FRIEND AGAIN AND SHE WAS BUYING TIGHTS AT THE SOCK STORE!
9

DAPHNE?
SWINGIN' IN THE TREES IN THE JUNGLE, MY FRIENDS, WITH APE SEX... APE SEX!

SWINGIN' IN THE TREES WITH ALL OF MY FRIENDS IN APE SEX...

APE SE... OH, EXCUSE ME...

DAPHNE, DID YOU KNOW SOME GUYS USING OUR SHOWER?
YES, IT'S ONLY DOYLE, NAMI...

DOYLE? THE ONE KIKO USED TO LIKE?
UH HUH.
"THE ONE THAT HANGS ALMOST DOWN TO HIS KNEE?"
I WOULDN'T KNOW...

ANYWAY, I JUST SAW YOUR FRIEND AGAIN DOWN AT THE MALL. I THINK SHE'S STILL THERE...
MAGGIE?
NAMI, COULD YOU DO ME A BIG, BIG FAVOR?

MUST BE A FULL MOON TONIGHT, GUYS. THE HOUSE IS PACKED AND THE TIPS ARE FLOWING LIKE LAVA...
THEY KNOW THIS IS DANITA'S DEBUT...
AW...
THE SEABEES' SHIP CAME IN.
10

BULLSHIT! GO 'HEAD, DANITA. MAKE 'EM CRY FOR THEIR MAMAS.
B-BUT IT AINT MY TURN...
IF YOU'RE STILL NERVOUS, I'LL DO THIS ONE WITH YOU...
LET HER DO IT HERSELF. SHE'LL HAVE TO SOONER OR LATER ANYWAY...

DAPHNE HAD TO GO SEE A FRIEND, SO I'LL BE YOUR SERVANT FROM NOW ON. DO WITH ME WHAT YOU WILL, O MASTER.
THANKS, BUT I'LL BE OUTTA HERE ONCE I'M DRESSED.

SORRY, BUT I'VE ALREADY BEEN IN JAIL ONCE BECAUSE OF A FIFTEEN YEAR OLD...

DON'T WORRY ABOUT A THING, TEX. IF IT SEEMS LIKE THESE PEOPLE HATE YOU, IT'S PROBABLY BECAUSE THEY DO.
ANTONIO!
11

SAN ANTONIO TEXAS! WHAT ARE YOU DOING HERE? HAVE A BEER, YOU FIFI!
HEY, FIFI RICK! YOU STILL PLAYING GUITAR?

OH, HAVE YOU BEEN DESERTED? PLEASE, LET ME BE YOUR OASIS.
HI, MAYA. WHAT'S SHAKIN', BABEH?

=WHEW= I COULDN'T FIND MAGGIE ANYWHERE. I EVEN CHECKED AT ISABEL'S, BUT NOBODY WAS HOME...
I AM NOT FIFTEEN. I'M SIXTEEN...

SHE HAD TO BRING IT UP. SHE JUST HAD TO BRING IT UP...
ROBERT.
1776

AW, FUCK. WHAT AM I DOING? I AIN'T GOT NO MORE APARTMENT.
ROBERT!

HEY, ROBERT!
WHAT...?

THIS IS FOR LORENA, MOTHER FUCKER!
FUCK HIM UP, ESE!
POW!
OOF!
WHAP
WHAP
WHAP
WHAP
12

EEEEEEE! DID I DO IT?
YOU DID IT, GIRL, YOU DID IT!
WHEE!

HEY, HOW ABOUT THAT DANITA? SHE MUSTA HAD ONE HELL OF A TEACHER, HUH? IT'S JUST TOO BAD HER BOYFRIEND'S TOO CHICKENSHIT TO COME WATCH.
RAY HAS A LOT ON HIS MIND LATELY.

PTCH, RIGHT. SO, NOW ARE YOU GOING TO TELL ME THE REAL REASON YOUR SHIRT IS TORN?
THOUGHT I DID...

A FIFTEEN YEAR OLD GIRL TRIED TO SEDUCE YOU IN HER PARENTS' BEDROOM...
THAT'S RIGHT...

YOU SON OF A BITCH! YOU'VE BEEN FIGHTING AGAIN!
BELIEVE WHAT YOU WANT. I'M GONNA GET A BEER...

I COULDN'T BELIEVE IT WHEN I HEARD MAYA TELL MATILDA TO MOVE OUT OF HER HOUSE.
I'D DO THE SAME IF I HAD TO CHOOSE BE-TWEEN MATILDA AND HOPEY.
SO, WHAT HAPPENED TO MAGGIE?

I'M NOT SURE BUT I THINK SHE WENT BACK TO CALIFORNIA.
OH, WHY? WASN'T IT SUNNY ENOUGH FOR HER HERE?
ANYWAY, SINCE WHEN DID MAYA START LIKING LITTLE GIRLS AGAIN?
13

MAYBE SHE'S BEEN VISITING MY MOM...
SPEAKING OF YOUR MOM, HASN'T SHE BEEN LOOKING FOR NEW "SECRETARIES"? MAYBE WE COULD DROP A FEW VALIUMS IN HOPEY'S DRINK AND...
OH, GOD! I CAN'T BELIEVE WHAT I'M HEARING! YOU GUYS ARE SO SICK!

HAHAH
?

HEY, HOPEY! WHERE'S MAGGIE? YOU LOOK NAKED WITHOUT HER.
HI, PAT. HI, ROSA.

HEY, HOPEY! WHERE'S MAGGIE? STILL TRYING TO GET OUT OF THAT DRESS?
TSK!

HEY, HOPEY...
WHAT DO I LOOK LIKE, HER HUSBAND?

I WISH YOU'D GIVE MERCED AND IVAT A CHANCE, SWEETUMS. THEY'RE VERY TALENTED AND ALSO GOOD FRIENDS OF MINE...
I DON'T HAVE TO LIKE ANY ART FAGS I DON'T WANT TO, MAYA.

I STILL DON'T UNDERSTAND WHAT HAPPENED. MAGGIE OVERHEARD THEM CALL HER A SPICK...?
FOR SOME UNKNOWN REASON, THEY THOUGHT IT WAS FUNNY THAT SHE'S MEXICAN AND SHE GOT MAD AT ME BECAUSE SHE THOUGHT I WAS DEFENDING THEM AS RACISTS...
14

... AND THAT'S WHEN SHE SAID "JUST BECAUSE YOU CAN TURN OFF YOUR ETHNIC HALF WHENEVER IT'S CONVENIENT FOR YOU," RIGHT?
RIGHT.

OK, BUT DID SHE MEAN THAT YOU'RE ASHAMED OF YOU'RE ETHNIC ROOTS OR THAT YOU'RE FORTUNATE TO BE ABLE TO HIDE YOUR ETHNICITY AND SHE'S NOT?
I DON'T KNOW...

BY THE WAY, WHAT ARE YOU? I MEAN...
MY DAD IS SCOTTISH-AMERICAN AND MY MOM IS COLOMBIAN. AND IF YOU MAKE A CRACK ABOUT DRUG DEALERS THEN YOU'RE JUST AS BAD AS THOSE TWO ART FAGS...

I SEE. AS IF "FAGS" NEVER HAVE ANYTHING TO WORRY ABOUT.

WHA'D YOU THINK OF THE NEW CHICK?
AH, I DON'T GO FOR ANY OF THAT CHOCOLATE STUFF, MAN...
YOU'RE FUCKIN' NUTS, TOO...
PARTS
SHIT!
Bumper

I TOLD YOU I WOULDN'T PUT UP WITH THIS FIGHTING CRAP, DOYLE!
HEY, I TOLD YOU WHAT HAPPENED! IF YOU DON'T BELIEVE ME, THAT'S YOUR FUCKIN' PROBLEM!
THERE'S THE DUDE, MAN!
HEY!
FLASH!

HEY, ASSHOLE! YOU'VE BEEN FUCKIN' WITH MY GIRL-FRIEND! NAMI'S ALL UPSET AN' CRYIN' AN' SHIT...
DID SHE TELL YOU WHAT I DID, ASSHOLE?
15

MAN, ALL I KNOW IS SHE'S UPSET, AND THAT YOU'RE THE DUDE THAT UPSET HER!
WELL, I SUGGEST YOU GO BACK AND ASK HER, BECAUSE I AIN'T INTO THIS HIGH SCHOOL SHIT.

LET'S GO NOW, MOTHER FUCKER! BOOM!
FUCK HIS ASS UP, EDDIE!
POP!

FUCK HIS ASS UP, EDDIE!

WHUMP! WHUMP!
OOF! OOF!
OK!

OK! OK! OK
BIFF! BIFF!

SO, ANY OF YOU GUYS GOT I.D.?
YOU LITTLE SHITS GET THIS BAREBALLED MOTHER FUCKER OUT OF HERE OR YOU'RE NEXT!
OUT.
OK.. OK... OK...
MAUI

FUCKED 'IM UP...
NOW YOU CAN BITCH AT ME FOR FUCKIN' FIGHTING! OK? OK? OK?
RELAX, DOYLE. HAVE A BEER, MAN. IT'S ALL OVER.
16

HI, HOPEY. ARE YOU LEAVING, TOO? WITHOUT YOUR FRIENDS?
YEAH, I'M JUST WAY TOO POOPED. IT'S LIKE IF SOMEBODY SPIKED MY DRINK...
PARTY

HEY, YOU DON'T HAVE TO HAIL A CAB. I HAVE A CAR. WE CAN TAKE YOU TO MAYA'S.
OH, THAT'S RIGHT. I LIVE THERE...
SUDS

YOU DIDN'T REALLY...
NO!

IT'S TRUE, KIKO. NAMI HAS SEEN HER TWICE ALREADY...

NO, JUST MAGGIE. I DON'T KNOW, THAT'S WHY I'VE BEEN LOOKING FOR HER. IT'S LIKE A REAL MYSTERY...
A REAL MYSTERY...

WELL, IF I SEE HER, I'LL LET YOU KNOW. OH, YOU'LL BE IN TOWN FOR CHRISTMAS? GOODY! OK, I'LL SEE YOU THEN, KIKO. BYE.
DAPHNE, WHY ARE GUYS SO STUPID?

IF ANYONE IS STUPID, YOU ARE! WHY DID YOU TELL YOUR BOYFRIEND DOYLE WAS HERE TAKING A SHOWER?
BECAUSE, IT'S THE TRUTH! AND EDDIE BRAVO'S NOT MY BOYFRIEND. WE JUST GO OUT SOMETIMES...
17

BUT, WHAT IF THEY FIND DOYLE? HE WAS IN JAIL, YOU KNOW...
HE WAS?? WAS THIS REAL JAIL OR OVERNIGHT JAIL? DID HE LIKE, KILL SOMEBODY, OR...?

NAN TUCKER IS YOUR MOM? "AMERICA'S NUMBER ONE FAVORITE COMEDIENNE"? "MY GAL NAN"? "NAN'S WORLD"? "WHERE'S NAN"?
SURE. YOU WANT TO MEET HER?

SURE, ANYTHING. JUST WAKE ME WHEN WE GET THERE...

SIT BACK, RELAX AND LEAVE THE DRIVING TO US, OL' GIRL...

MATTHEW BUCHER
ESPERANZA GLASS
HAVE YOU

HOW ABOUT THAT? LET'S GIVE A BIG HAND TO OUR NEWEST SWEET SENSATION... DA-NI-TAAA...
18

YOUR BOYFRIEND STILL HASN'T SHOWED, DANITA?
PTCH!

GUYS ARE THE WORST. IF THEY AIN'T THINKIN' WITH THEIR DICKS, THEY'RE THINKIN' WITH THEIR FISTS.
DOYLE?

IT'S REALLY TOO BAD HE DIDN'T STICK AROUND. I WANTED TO GIVE HIM A SPECIAL BIRTHDAY KISS.
THAT'S RIGHT. IT WAS HIS BIRTHDAY TODAY...

RAY SAID YOU WERE GONNA DO SOMETHIN' SPECIAL FOR HIM...
OOH, YOU WANNA TELL US WHAT YOU DID, OR DO WE HAVE TO READ ALL ABOUT IT LATER IN THE ENQUIRER?

SHIT, I'M OUTTA HERE. TELL MELINDA I COULDN'T DO MY LAST SHOW. TELL HER I'M HAVING MY PERIOD OR SOMETHING.
OOH...
SOMEONE FORGOT SOMEONE'S BIRTHDAY...

OH, HI, MELINDA. LILY TOLD US TO TELL YOU...
DANITA, I JUST SAW YOUR BOYFRIEND. HE'S OUTSIDE...
WELL, HE'S A LITTLE LATE, AIN'T HE?

THE THINGS YOU GOTTA DO TO KEEP A CHICK HAPPY...
...AND THEY THOUGHT I WAS SOME GUY NAMED ROBERT WHO GOT SOMEONE'S SISTER PREGNANT...
Bumper's
TOPLESS
19

END OF PART 2

WWB P3

PART 3

WIGWAM BAM

FANCY DAN 90-91

LOOK, MIJA! I JUST WANT TO DROP OFF THESE MILK CARTONS AND THEN WE CAN GO! IT WON'T TAKE A MINUTE...
NO, MAMA, NO!

ALL RIGHT THEN! GO WAIT FOR ME AT TIA JUANA'S AND TELL DAVID THAT SOMEONE'S GETTING IT TONIGHT!

LAURA THE RAT.

DID YOU SEE THE WITCH LADY, LALO?
YEAH, BUT YOU SAID SHE LOOKED LIKE FREDDY K'UEGER.
CORTEZ
55

ARE YOU REALLY GETTIN' IT TONIGHT, DAVID?
TSK! LET'S GO SEE THE KITTENS I WAS TELLIN' YOU ABOUT...
55

HEY, KID. SHOW THIS GUY ALL THOSE KITTENS YOU FOUND IN YOUR BACKYARD.
CAN'T. MAMA SAID NOT TO GO BACK THERE.
55

C'MON! YOU SHOWED 'EM TO ME YESTERDAY.
OK, BUT JUST A SMALL PEEK.
HEY, KID! IT SOUNDS LIKE THERE'S A FIGHT IN YOUR HOUSE!
55
2

CHECK THIS OUT. THEY'RE SMALLER THAN RATS.
I WANNA SEE THE FIGHT.

SEE? THEY...

MMMFGHHHH...

WHAT DO YOU THINK YOU'RE DOIN'?
LOOK, MAMA. IT'S RAY...

ELIAS, I THOUGHT I TOLD YOU TO KEEP AWAY FROM THE SHED! GET IN THAT HOUSE RIGHT NOW!
B-BUT, HOW COME HE'S IN THERE, MAMA?

HE'S JUST SLEEPIN'! NOW, C'MON...
B-BUT HOW COME HIS FACE IS LIKE THAT? HOW COME, MAMA?
HEY, I'M OK, LITTLE GUY. SEE? I JUST HAD AN ACCIDENT...

...SEE, I JUST NEED TO GET SOME MONEY SO I CAN PAY THE RENT SO I CAN SLEEP IN MY OWN APARTMENT AGAIN...
GO INSIDE NOW, ELIAS. I'LL BE THERE IN A MINUTE...
3

HOW'S YOUR FACE, BABY?
AH, IT'S OK. THOSE FUCKERS MOSTLY TRIED TO CAVE IN MY RIBS. BUT, POOR ELIAS, I MUST HAVE BEEN QUITE A SIGHT WHEN HE OPENED THAT SHED DOOR...

I KNOW. HE'S BEEN REAL NERVOUS LATELY. BUT WHO CAN BLAME HIM WITH ALL THAT FUSSIN' AN' FIGHTIN' GOIN' ON IN THE HOUSE ALL DAY LONG. HIS WEE MIND CAN ONLY TAKE SO MUCH...
WHICH BRINGS UP OUR NEXT TOPIC...

OK, YES. I'LL TAKE OVER YOUR APARTMENT. IT'D BE GOOD FOR ELIAS, I GUESS...
BELIEVE ME, THAT LITTLE PLACE IS PERFECT FOR YOU TWO...

US TWO? AN' WHERE DO YOU THINK YOU'RE GOIN'...?
WHO, ME? AW, I CAN'T...

WE AIN'T THROWIN' YOU OUT IN THE STREET AN' THAT'S THAT...
NGHHH...

IT'S TRUE, LAURA! WE SAW HIM SLEEPIN' IN THE SHED AN' HE LOOKED JUST LIKE FREDDY KUEGER!
AN' THERE WAS A FIGHT IN THE HOUSE...
NO!

JUST COME OUT AN' TAKE A LOOK...
NO!
LOOK, DAVID! THERE HE IS!
4

HEY, FREDDY K'UEGER!

I SAID, WHAT ARE THE MILK CARTONS FOR ANYWAY, A SCHOOL ART PROJECT?

REMEMBER IN SECOND GRADE WHEN WE HAD TO BRING BEANS TO MAKE MOSAICS AND PITO HERRERA THOUGHT WE WERE GOING TO MAKE FRIJOLES Y SOPA DE ARROZ?
ISABEL...?

OH, I'M SORRY, CHEPA. SOMEONE TOLD ME THAT MAGGIE IS BACK IN TOWN AND I THOUGHT I HEARD HER CAR...
IF SHE STILL HAS THAT CAR YOU GAVE HER, YOU COULD HEAR THAT THING ALL THE WAY FROM TEXAS.

REMEMBER WHEN IT USED TO BE THE OFFICIAL WIDOWS GANGBANG RIDE? WE DIDN'T GET TOO MANY DATES IN THOSE DAYS, DID WE?
WELL, WE WERE SCARIER THAN MOST OF THE GUYS!

YEAH, I TRY TO TELL THOSE DOCTORS ABOUT OUR DAYS IN THE WIDOWS, BUT... I-I DON'T KNOW, SOMETIMES I THINK THEY BELONG IN THERE MORE THAN WE DO. THEN I THINK... I DON'T KNOW...
OH, SHOOT. I GOTTA GO...

YOU SHOW THEM DOCTORS WHO'S BOSS AND HAVE FUN WITH YOUR SCHOOL ART PROJECT, OK, ISABEL? I'LL SEE YOU...
OK, CHEPA. I'LL SEE YOU...
5

HAVE YOU SEEN ME?
HAVE YOU SEEN ME?
HAVE YOU SEEN ME?
HAVE YOU SEEN ME?
HAVE YOU SEEN ME?
HAVE YOU SEEN ME?
HAVE YOU SEEN ME?

I DON'T KNOW IF I'M READY TO MOVE IN WITH HER, LITOS. I FEEL LIKE SUCH A LEECH...
JUST DON'T LET HER TELL YOU WHAT TO DO, RAY. 'CAUSE NEXT THING YOU KNOW, SHE'LL FORCE YOU TO MARRY HER. LOOK AT ME. Y'KNOW, WOMEN AN' THEIR FUCKIN' SECURITY...

SO, WHO WERE THE VATOS THAT FUCKED YOU UP, 'EY?
AH, JUST A BUNCH OF PUNKS...
6

MAYATE - BLACK PERSON FILERO - BLADE

YOU ALWAYS END UP WITH THESE LOSERS! CORNELIUS EDWARDS WAS NEVER MAN ENOUGH TO BE A FATHER TO ELIAS. RONNIE HOWARD WILL ALWAYS BE A CLOWN. AND THIS RAY, I DON'T KNOW WHAT THE HELL HE IS! LOOK AT THIS...

IS THAT SUPPOSED TO BE YOU?? I MEAN, COME ON! THAT MESKIN IS DEGRADING YOU! HE DOESN'T SEE YOU FOR YOURSELF! HE'S JUST ANOTHER FOOL IN THE AUDIENCE!

HONG

OH, HI, BABES.

I WAS HOPING YOU WEREN'T HERE YET. THE PLACE IS KINDA BEAT TO SHIT, AS YOU CAN SEE. HEH...

I GOTTA GO BUY SOME MAKE UP FOR WORK TONIGHT. YOU NEED ANYTHING?
NO MORE FOR ME, THANKS. I'M DRIVIN'...
8

ZIPPY SAM
SOUPY GOOEY
ICKY ZOOIE...
ALE
1/2 O
SALE

SALE

HI.
HI! I DIDN'T KNOW YOU WORK HERE.

SO, DAFFY. HAS MAGGIE COME BY TO SEE YOU SINCE SHE'S BEEN BACK?
I ALREADY TOLD YOU NO, ITSUKI.

OH, YEAH? WITH OR WITHOUT HOPEY?

9

Rocco Gi
HOMING P

TRY NOT TO THINK ABOUT IT... TRY NOT TO THINK ABOUT IT...

I DON'T CARE! I'M GLAD WE TOLD HER MAGGIE'S BACK! SHE'S THE ONE THAT STOLE HER BOYFRIEND ANYWAY, REMEMBER?
STOLE WHOSE BOYFRIEND?
ITSUKI...?
Los Earl's

DO YOU THINK MAYBE MAGGIE WON'T SEE ANYONE BECAUSE SHE AND HOPEY HAD A SUPER, BIG FIGHT AND SHE'S WAY TOO UPSET...?
MAYBE SHE JUST DOESN'T CARE TO SEE YOU, DAPHNE. YOU EVER THINK OF THAT?
SYDYS
10

HI, HOPE. HI, MAG. WHO'S YOUR FRIEND?
HI, MARY. HER NAME'S DAFFY.
SHE CAME WITH KIKO BUT KIKO ALREADY LEFT, SO SHE THINKS WE'RE GIVING HER A RIDE BACK.
2S1-AS
GO-GO'S

I'M THINKING WE SHOULD TAKE HER TO LOIS'S AND LEAVE HER THERE. SNORT
YOU GUYS STILL GO THERE? I FIGURED LOIS WOULD BE SICK OF YOU BY NOW.
JUST 'CAUSE SHE KICKED YOU OUT. SNORT

IT WAS GETTING BORING ANYWAY.
SUUURE, MARY. REAL BORING. C'MON, DAFFY! WE'RE GOING TO A PARTY! SNORT
SNORT
POOL

ARE WE REALLY GOING TO LOIS'S? I MEAN, SHE IS GETTING PRETTY TIRED OF US...
I KNOW, BUT WE CAN'T LET MARY KNOW THAT. BESIDES, WE'RE COOL AS LONG AS YOU'RE VICKI GLORI'S NIECE.
GO-GO'S

WHAT THE FUCK DO YOU WANT?
IT'S US, LOIS, AN' WE BROUGHT THE FUCKIN' BEER!
SO, WHO WANTS TO FUCK?
1242
11

WHAT THE FUCK, LOIS? ARE YOU ALONE TONIGHT, OR WHAT? FUCK A DUCK...
SO, LIKE, WHO THE FUCK WANTS TO, Y'KNOW, FUCK?

HEY, WHAT HAPPENED TO YOUR PERSONALLY AUTOGRAPHED REPLICA OF VICKI GLORI'S WORLD CHAMPIONSHIP BELT?
FOUND OUT SHE'S STRAIGHT.

♫ YOU'RE SHIT OUTTA ♫ LUCK WHEN YOU'RE SHIT OUTTA FUCK... ♫ ♫ ♫

WHERE DID LOIS GO, HOPEY?
DUNNO.
SNORT

SNORT

TEE HEE! GIGGLE! SNORT
?!?

SO, I GUESS YOU WERE THE ONLY ONE WITH BALLS ENOUGH TO STICK AROUND AND FUCK, HUH?
12

WHO KNOWS? MAYBE THERE WAS A DEATH IN HER FAMILY AND THAT'S WHY MAGGIE WON'T...
WHY ARE YOU MAKING SUCH A BIG, FAT DEAL ABOUT IT? WHO CARES?

DAFFY HAS ONLY BEEN A CLOSE FRIEND TO THESE GIRLS SINCE YOU WERE ABOUT SIX OR SEVEN YEARS OLD!
NO, NAMI'S RIGHT. WHO CARES? I CERTAINLY DON'T ANY MORE.

AW, DON'T TALK LIKE THAT, DAFFY...
THERE SHE IS!

LOOK, DAPHNE! THERE SHE IS! IT'S YOUR FRIEND! LOOK, DAPHNE, LOOK!

WELL, WHAT ARE YOU WAITING FOR? DON'T LET HER GET AWAY!

THAT'S NOT MAGGIE!
IT'S NOT? THEN WHO IS IT?
?!

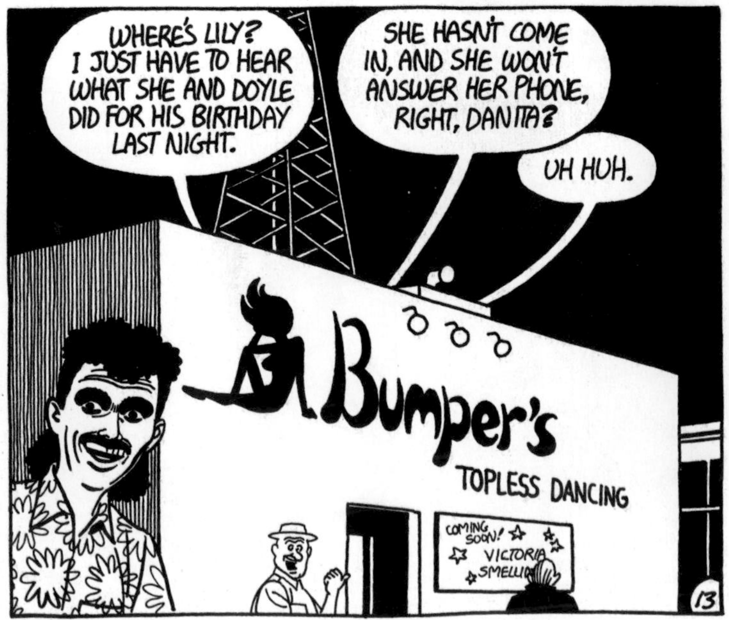
WHERE'S LILY? I JUST HAVE TO HEAR WHAT SHE AND DOYLE DID FOR HIS BIRTHDAY LAST NIGHT.
SHE HASN'T COME IN, AND SHE WON'T ANSWER HER PHONE, RIGHT, DANITA?
UH HUH.
Bumper's
TOPLESS DANCING
COMING SOON! VICTORIA SMELLIO
13

OOH, THEY MUST STILL BE CELEBRATING, YEAH?
FOR ALL WE KNOW, SHE MAY NOT COME IN FOR A WEEK!
DANITA! WHAT'S WITH YOU? YOU'RE ON!
COMIN'...

UH, CLEO? YOU DIDN'T HAPPEN TO SEE IF RAY WAS OUT THERE, OR NOT? NO?
GIRL, I MADE IT A RULE LONG AGO NEVER TO LOOK AT THEIR FACES. SOME GIRLS CAN DO IT, SOME CAN'T. I CAN'T.

SOME GUY TOLD ME I WAS SMART FOR NOT TRYING TO FIGHT OFF MY ATTACKERS. SAID I WOULD'VE GOTTEN IT WORSE IF I DID. THE THING I DIDN'T TELL HIM WAS THAT I DID TRY TO FIGHT THEM OFF. I GAVE THOSE FUCKERS ALL I HAD. TROUBLE IS, THERE WERE THREE OF THEM AND THEY WERE GIVING ME ALL THEY HAD, AND MORE...

AS THEY PUMMELED ME, I FIRST THOUGHT OF BANDAIDS. A FEW SECONDS LATER I THOUGHT OF THE HOSPITAL. A FEW SECONDS MORE AND I'M PICTURING MY TOMBSTONE, WHEN ALL OF A SUDDEN I HEAR A VOICE PLEADING FOR MY LIFE AND EVERYTHING STOPS.

WHEN I LOOK UP WITH MY ONE GOOD EYE TO SEE WHO MY GLORIOUS SAVIOR IS, I FIND IT'S THE SAME GUY WHO THREW THE FIRST PUNCH. IT'S ROBBIE GARCIA.

WHO IS ROBBIE GARCIA, YOU ASK? HE'S ONLY SOME FUCKING KID WHO PLAYS ON THE LITTLE LEAGUE TEAM MY BROTHER COACHES. THESE ASSHOLES WERE NO MORE THAN FIFTEEN FUCKING YEARS OLD...

SO AS I TRY TO PRETEND I DON'T FEEL LIKE I SLEPT WITH A LIVE JACKHAMMER, ROBBIE GOES ON NERVOUSLY APOLOGIZING THAT IT'S ALL A MISTAKE, THEY THOUGHT I WAS SOME-ONE ELSE, BLAH BLAH BLAH... AS IF I'M GONNA KICK HIS ASS. KICK HIS ASS...
14

SHIT, I'M BEGINNING TO WISH ROBBIE'D NEVER RECOGNIZED ME...

BOOM BOOM BAM BOOM BOOM BA

OOM BOOM BAM BOOM BOO

FUCK

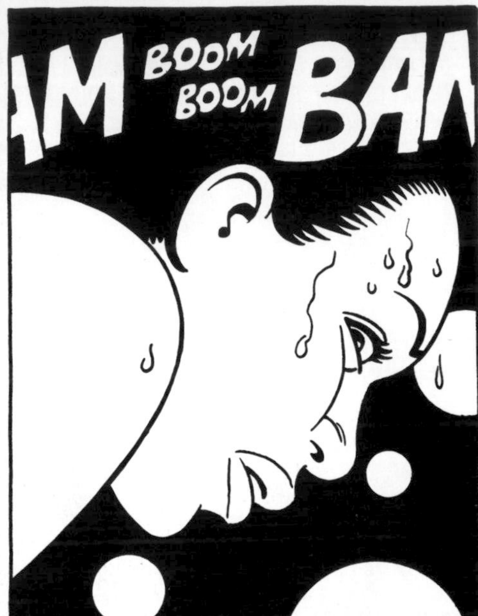
AM BOOM BOOM BAN

FRANCES, WHAT IS HOLDING UP THOSE PIÑA COLADAS?
JUST A MINUTE, MAYA!

YOU ALSO HAVE A PHONE CALL. I THINK IT'S LONG DISTANCE...
LONG DISTANCE? IT BETTER NOT BE MY MOTHER...
15

YES, HELLO? HOPEY? NO, I'M AFRAID I HAVEN'T SEEN HER SINCE THAT PARTY WE ATTENDED LAST NIGHT...

MAGGIE?? WHY, SHE LEFT, OH... FIVE DAYS AGO. YES, I'M SURE...

N ME?
ZA GLASS
FORNIA

I CAN'T UNDERSTAND IT, ISABEL...
HAVE YOU SEEN ME?

DO YOU THINK SOMETHING COULD BE WRONG?
THEY'RE EITHER LYING ON A BEACH IN ALASKA SUCKING ON SLURPEES OR IN A DITCH SUCKING ON THEIR OWN BLOOD...

SOB... SNIFF...
SOB...
GRRRRR... GROARRR...
16

DON'T YOU FUCKIN' MOVE TILL I'M ALL DONE TAKIN' A SHIT!
SNIFF SOB BOO HOO HOO... SOB...

I'M NOT FUCKIN' KIDDIN' NOW, YOU LITTLE SUCK!
OOT!

AHHH... THAT'S WHAT I CALL A LOG...

HEY, C'MON. DON'T CRY. IT'S ALL OVER NOW...
WE WEREN'T GONNA LET NOTHING HAPPEN TO YOU. HONEST...
I JUST WANT TO GO HOME...

DO YOU HAVE ANY MONEY TO TAKE THE BUS HOME?
MY PURSE ONLY HAD TWO DOLLARS IN IT, BUT I LEFT IT AT THAT HOUSE.
WE'LL FIGURE SOMETHING OUT...

I AIN'T LYING! WE REALLY HAVE TO BUY THIS GIRL A BUS TICKET HOME!
WE ONLY NEED ONE MORE DOLLAR AND THAT BUS LEAVES IN TEN MINUTES!
BUS

BYE, DAFFY... AND DON'T FORGET TO TRANSFER!
SEE YOU BACK IN HOPPERS, KIDDO!
17

I WENT BY BUMPER'S BUT THEY SAID YOU ALREADY LEFT. ARE YOU OK?
WHY DO YOU ASK IF I'M OK?

WELL, THEY SEEMED KINDA WORRIED ABOUT YOU, SO I THOUGHT SOMETHING HAPPENED...
NOTHIN' HAPPENED. I JUST FELT LIKE LEAVIN' EARLY...

OK...
RAY, I JUST WANNA KNOW IF YOU'RE STAYIN' OR NOT!

IF I'M STAYING OR NOT...?
I JUST WANNA KNOW, THA'S ALL...

18

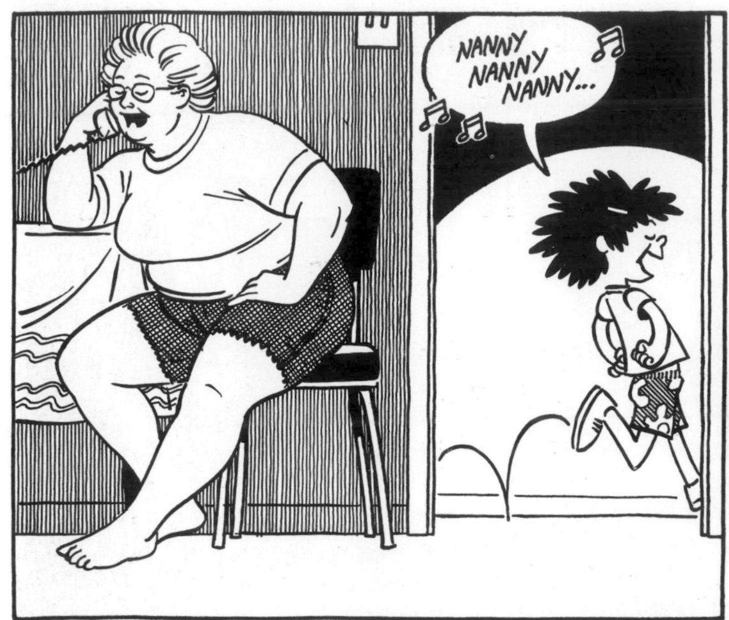

END OF PART III

TWEEEEEEEET
HOLY SH... WHO'S THERE? WHO...?
IT'S THE PHONE, JOEY. YOU WANT ME TO ANSWER IT?
WIGWAM BAM PART FOUR
ΧΛΙΜΣ "BREECHES BUOY" ΗΕRΝΛΝDΕΖ 1991
1

DON'T EVEN TOUCH IT, JANET. WE'RE NOT SUPPOSED TO BE HERE, REMEMBER?
OH, YEAH.
TWEEE
CLIC
WE'RE N
NOW, BUT IF Y
AND NUMBER
TO YOU AS
BEE

REECHARD, I HAF TO TALK TO YOU. EES BEDDY IMPORTANT...
OH, IT'S JUST MOM BUGGING DAD AGAIN.
DOES SHE KNOW YOUR FATHER WAS JUST REMARRIED?

SURE, BUT THAT WON'T STOP HER. AFTER ABOUT FIFTEEN YEARS OF DIVORCE SHE FEELS SHE STILL HAS TO BUG HIM ABOUT THIS AND THAT. "COME FEEX MY TOILET... DERE'S A BOOGLER OUTSIDE MY WEENDOW..."
MAYBE THEY'RE STILL FRIENDS?
BLAH BLAH BLAH BLAH...

BELIEVE ME, JANET, MOM ONLY CALLS WHEN DAD'S GOT A NEW GIRLFRIEND. IN THIS CASE, A NEW WIFE...
HOW SAD.
BLAH BLAH BLAH BLAH YAK BLAH BLAH...

JOEY, IS THAT REALLY YOUR SISTER'S PICTURE ON THAT MILK CARTON?
I TOLD YOU IT WAS. EVERYBODY AND THEIR MOM HAS ONE...
BLAH BLAH YAK BLAH YAK YAK YAK...

WELL, I THINK YOUR MOTHER JUST FOUND OUT ABOUT IT AND SHE DOESN'T SOUND TOO HAPPY...
HUH??
...AN' I KNOW WHO DEED THEES! EET WAS DAT SOMABEETCH TRYING TO BE FONNY!

...AN' WHEN I FIND JOSEPH, I HANG HEEM FROM HEES BOLLS!
WAIT, I DIDN'T PUT HOPEY'S FACE ON ANY MILK CARTON! SHIT, MA...!
2

OK, WOULD ANYONE LIKE TO ADD ANYTHING BEFORE WE CLOSE THIS UP FOR THE DAY?
WHAT ABOUT YOU, ISABEL? YOU HAVEN'T SAID VERY MUCH TODAY.
ARIES

HAVE YOU HEARD FROM MAGGIE AND HOPEY YET?

WOULD YOU LIKE TO TALK MORE ABOUT DAFFY'S OBSESSION WITH MAGGIE AND HOPEY...?

OK... WELL, THAT'S IT FOR TODAY, I GUESS...

...AN' THEN DAVID CREEPED UP TO THE WINDOW AN' HE LOOKED IN AN' ALL THE WALLS IN THE ROOM WERE COVERED WITH PI'TURES, AN' THEY WERE ALL THE SAME PI'TURE!
HEY! DON'T YOU BE TELLIN' BABY ELIAS NO LIES, BOY!
4 Sell $7.00.

BUT, IT'S TRUE! ASK DAVID! AN' THE LADY IN THE PI'TURES LOOKED JUST LIKE FREDDY K'EUGER!
YEAH, AN' SO DID THE MAN IN THE SHACK! BOYYY...
3

ASK THIS KID! HE SAW HIM! HE LIVES IN HIS BACKYARD!
DAT WAS RAY!
CHIQUITA! COME ON, SUGAR. BRING ELIAS.

THAT WAS RAY ASLEEP IN THE SHACK IN BABY ELIAS'S BACK-YARD, HUH, MAMA?
PTCH! I WOULDN'T DOUBT IT.

FOR THE LAST TIME, JOEY, I DID NOT PUT HOPEY ON A MILK CARTON. I MEAN, COME ON. I'M REALLY INSULTED NOW...
SORRY, JULIE. I'M JUST GOING THROUGH MY ADDRESS BOOK CALLING PEOPLE THAT KNOW HER HOPING I'LL FIND SOMETHING...

WELL, I WOULD HAVE BET THAT YOU DID IT. IT SURE SOUNDS LIKE YOUR SPEED...
YEAH, YEAH. THAT'S WHAT EVERYBODY'S SAYING. OK, JULIE. SAY HI TO EVERY-ONE AT CARE UNIT!

OK, WHAT'S THE NEXT NAME, JANET?
WREE WAS IT. MONICA ZANDINSKI IS CROSSED OUT.

YEAH, SHE'S A MAN NOW... MARCO ZANDINSKI.
HEY, HOW COME THERE ARE NO GUYS IN HERE? AND WHY IS THERE A MARK NEXT TO MY NAME?

LOOK, DON'T YOU START BITCHING AT ME, TOO! I'M GETTING ENOUGH OF THAT WHEN MY MOM CATCHES UP WITH ME!
OK, I'M SORRY, JOEY.
4

SHIT! EVER SINCE I WAS A FUCKING KID SHE ALWAYS THOUGHT I DID THINGS JUST TO SPITE HER. SHE NEVER TRUSTED ME... NEVER SAW MY SIDE...
I KNOW, I KNOW, BABY. IT WILL BE ALL RIGHT...

IZZY ORTIZ!
IS WHO ORTIZ?

WELL, WELL. LOOK WHO DECIDED TO COME UP FOR AIR...
HELLO, CLEO.
LFQUES

THAT MUSTA BEEN SOME BIRTHDAY GIFT YOU GAVE DOYLE TO BE TAKING OFF SO MANY DAYS, LILY. SO, NOW YOU HAVE TO FILL US IN ON ALL THE DETAILS.
SHE WAS ABOUT TO TELL US UNTIL YOU INTERRUPTED, CLEO.
LFQUES

GO AHEAD, LILY...
I SWEAR, YOU GUYS... WE FUCKED!
LILY, I COULD DO THAT WITH MY BOYFRIEND EVERY NIGHT...
IF HE COULD GET IT UP THAT OFTEN. WHAT ELSE...?

THEN IN THE MORNING I COOKED HIM CHORIZO AND EGGS...
OH, WELL, CHOREESO AND EGGS, SURE...
HE LOVES CHORIZO AND EGGS.
FORGET HER, LILY. SHE DOESN'T KNOW. WHAT ELSE...?

...AND THEN HE LEFT. JUST LIKE HE ALWAYS DOES. MISTER VAGABOND STREET PERSON TOOK OFF...
AW...
WELL, HOW COULD YOU TOP CHOREESO AND EGGS?
CLEO, JUST SHUT UP, OK?

YOU CAN'T TELL ME T--
...THOUSANDS OF HOMELESS PEOPLE WHO DON'T THINK IT'S COOL OR ROMANTIC TO BE OUT ON THE STREET...
!
!

THOSE WHO NEED A DARK ALLEY CORNER TO SLEEP IN BUT CAN'T BECAUSE THOSE CORNERS ARE TAKEN UP BY PHONEYS LIKE FUCKING DOYLE BLACKBURN!

NAMI, WE GOTTA TALK.
BRA

NAMI...!
TALK ABOUT WHAT, EDDIE? OK, SO, I'M SORRY YOU GOT BEAT UP, BUT I NEVER TOLD YOU TO GO PICK A FIGHT WITH DOYLE BLACKBURN, DID I?

WELL, I JUST FEEL THAT A DUDE ALWAYS PROTECTS HIS GIRLFRIEND, NO MATTER WHAT! I MEAN, ARE YOU MY GIRLFRIEND, OR...?
DOYLE! HI!

MY SISTER DAPHNE SAYS YOU WERE IN JAIL ONCE. WHAT FOR?
FOR AWHILE.

WHERE ARE YOU GOING RIGHT NOW? DO YOU NEED A RIDE SOMEWHERE? WE HAVE EDDIE'S TRUCK HERE.
NAH. I FEEL LIKE WALKING, THANKS...
6

YOU TWO GOTTA TALK.

BLEEP
...THAT'S ALL THE UP-TO-THE-MINUTE NEWS, AND UP TO THE MINUTE THAT'S ALL THE NEWS...
KAK
POOT
KAKA EVENING NEWS WITH LLOYD SNEED

...AN' THEN DAVID PEEKED IN THE WINDOW AN' THEN HE...
THERE'S DAVID!

WE'RE SETTLING THIS WITCH LADY FOOLISHNESS ONCE AND FOR ALL!

YOU'RE SURE THIS IZZY PERSON IS THE ONE BEHIND THE MILK CARTONS, JOEY?
IT MAKES A SHITLOAD OF SENSE. ONE: SHE WAS THE ONE WHO BROUGHT IT TO EVERYONE'S ATTENTION, AND TWO: SHE'S THE ONLY PERSON WEIRD ENOUGH TO PULL SOMETHING LIKE THIS...

BUT, PEOPLE THINK YOU DID IT, JOEY.
WELL, THEY ALL SUCK! OK, JANET. IT'S THE HOUSE WITH THE PICKET FENCE. JUST PULL... HEY, THERE'S DAFFY!

NO ANSWER. DON'T TELL ME SHE WENT BACK TO THE HOSPITAL...
DAFFY!
7

HEY, DAFF! IS THE WITCH LADY IN? I GOTTA TALK TO HER ABOUT THIS MILK CARTON SHIT.
SHE DOESN'T SEEM TO BE HOME. RIGHT NOW, JOEY. WHAT ABOUT THE CARTONS?

SHE DID 'EM, RIGHT? SHE SENT IN HOPEY'S PHOTO AND MADE HER INTO A REAL LIFE MISSING PERSON...
NO, SHE DIDN'T. AS A MATTER OF FACT, SHE TOLD ME SHE WAS SURE YOU DID IT.

TOLDJA!
WHY IS EVERYONE SAYING THAT? SHE'S THE WEIRDO TAPING THEM ALL OVER HER WALLS!
HEY! I'VE JUST HEARD ENOUGH OUT OF YOU...
THIS IS SO EMBARRASSING.

WHAT'S GOING ON, DAVID?
I THINK I JUST WON MY DAY IN COURT.
TSK!

MANAGEMENT
8

SO, WHAT WAS MR. BUMPER'S HAVING A HEART ATTACK OVER THIS TIME, LU?
NOT WHAT. WHOM.
WHOM? SHIT! WHICH ONE OF US IS FIRED? DANITA?

NOBODY'S FIRED. LILY QUIT.
NO SHIT? WHAT A BITCH! SHE DIDN'T EVEN LET US IN ON IT!
WHY WOULD YOU THINK DANITA WAS FIRED?

BECAUSE MR. BUMPER'S DON'T LIKE PEOPLE WHO FLAKE ON HIM...
DANITA DIDN'T FLAKE. SHE'S JUST HAVING BOYFRIEND PROBLEMS.
WHO'S HAVIN' BOYFRIEND PROBLEMS?
HEY...

DANITA DID WHAT, ROCKY?
SHE TOOK YOUR GRANDSON TO WORK WITH HER, AUNTIE. I WONDER HOW SHE'S GOING TO EXPLAIN ALL THOSE NAKED LADIES TO HIM.

EEEEEE!! SHE CAN'T DO THAT TO ME! DO YOU HEAR ME?
MASON HOUSE
FOR WOMEN

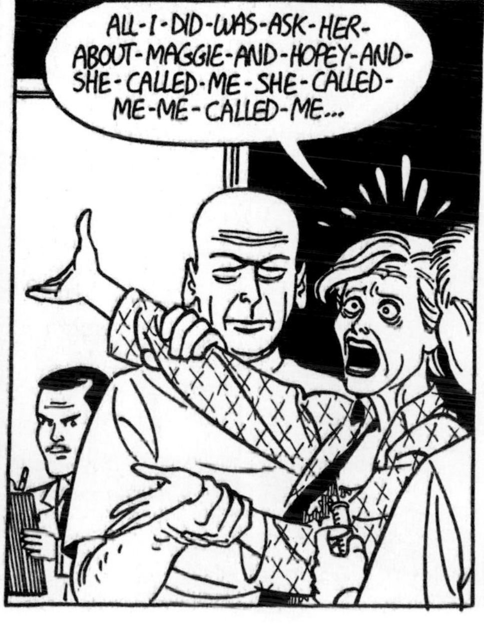
ALL-I-DID-WAS-ASK-HER-ABOUT-MAGGIE-AND-HOPEY-AND-SHE-CALLED-ME-SHE-CALLED-ME-ME-CALLED-ME...

9

WILL WE SEE YOU NEXT WEEK, ISABEL?
I DON'T THINK I'LL BE COMING BACK AT ALL, DOC. I'M JUST WASTING MY TIME HERE, Y'KNOW?

DIDN'T I TELL YOU LONG AGO THAT YOU DON'T BELONG HERE?
YEAH, BUT SOMETIMES IT ONLY TAKES A GOOD NIGHT'S SLEEP TO FIGURE OUT HOW TO JUNK YOUR SEVENTY-FOUR CHEVY VEGA AND START TAKING THE BUS.

ARE WE STAYING AT YOUR FATHER'S AGAIN TONIGHT, JOEY?
NAW, HE AND CONNIE GET BACK TONIGHT FROM THEIR HONEYMOON.
AHEM

¡MOM!
I'VE BEEN LOOKING FOR YOU!
WELL, I HAF WAITED HERE T'REE WHOLE HOURS FOR YOU, JOSEPH...

FOOSH
10

BLEEP
... AN ELEMENT WHICH IS UNKNOWN TO SCIENCE...
B-BUT...
JOHN V. GIRKIN'S "HEAVENS TO BETSY" STARRING DAN MOSSI

JOYCE COPE
ANA BREAD CO.

Bumper's
TOPLESS

FUCK, DOYLE. AFTER TWO FUCKIN' HOURS, I FINALLY CONVINCE MOM I DIDN'T FUCKIN' PUT FUCKIN' HOPEY ON NO FUCKIN' MILK CARTON. AND YET, SHE STILL HAS TO RAG ON ME JUST FOR EXERCISE...
FUNNY, I WOULDA BET MY LAST BEER THAT YOU DID IT, JOE.

YOU FUCKIN' WOULD, YOU...
YOU GUYS BITCHIN' ABOUT WOMEN AGAIN, DOYLE?
HEY, MELINDA. WHAT'S THE LATEST DIRT HANGING OVER BUMPER'S?

DON'T BE FUNNY WITH ME, DOYLE. I AIN'T IN THE MOOD...
HEH, JUST KIDDIN' YA. HEY, I HEARD OL' RAY AND DANITA HAD THE BIG SHOW-DOWN LAST NIGHT...

YOU MEAN, WILL HE BE A MAN AND STAY WITH HER AND THE KID, OR WILL HE BE A MOUSE AND SPLIT?
HEH! I WOULD HAVE WORDED IT A LITTLE DIFFERENTLY, BUT, YEAH. SO, WHAT HAPPENED?
MAN, LOOK AT THAT CHICK GO!

LET'S HEAR IT FOR DANITAAA...
I'M NOT SURE WHAT HAPPENED, BUT IT LOOKS TO ME LIKE YOUR PAL'S A MAN AFTER ALL, DOYLE.
HUH! I WONDER IF HE'LL MAKE ME HIS BEST MAN.
BA BOOM BOOM BAM
CLAP CLAP CLAP

HEH! SO, WHEN DOES LILY GO ON?

BLEEP
¡NET FIRND OM NIPPEN ROY COWBOY! BED BIDDIN MIRKSEN PUDE PESTY... POOT... POOT POOT POOT...
¿PEEN?
PETER THE FREAK

ISABEL,
I'M GOING BACK TO SCHOOL TONIGHT FOR ANOTHER SIX MONTHS AND I WAS WONDERING IF YOU COULD LET ME KNOW IF AND WHEN YOU HEAR ANYTHING CONCERNING MAGGIE AND HOPEY.
SINCERELY,
DAPHNE

12

HAVE YOU SEEN ME?

HAVE YOU SEEN ME?

HOW WAS I SUPPOSED TO KNOW LILY QUIT? SHE NEVER TELLS ME ANYTHING...
HEY, DOYLE!
Ralph Rick's
AUTO PART

HEY, RAY! I HEARD THE BIG NEWS, MAN...
HEY, DID DANITA DANCE ALREADY?
YEAH, SHE FUCKIN' RIPPED, TOO, MAN...

FUCK! I MISSED HER AGAIN! Y'KNOW, I STILL HAVEN'T SEEN HER PERFORM...
SHE'S COOL, MAN. SHE'S THIS BLACK CHICK WITH THESE BIG...
SO, WHEN'S THE WEDDING, RAY? WHO GETS TO HOLD THE SHOTGUN?
Bumper's

WHAT THE FUCK ARE YOU TALKING ABOUT, MAN?
YOU OUGHTA KNOW THAT BUMPER'S IS MERELY A FRONT FOR RONA BARRETT'S HEADQUARTERS. WORD GETS AROUND...
13

CYCLING IS FUN - SHONEN KNIFE

WWW WRESTLING CLASSIC - RENA TITAÑON AND MITZI KUNO VS. THE ROCK SISTERS

WIHSS
FESTER
Tailao
MUKMURO
BMHBMH

HI, FRANCES!
HI, MARY!
HI, LEE!
HI, PAT...
VODKA MARTINI, STRAIGHT UP... WAY AHEAD OF YOU, MAYA.
EXIT

YOU SOUND GIGGLEY TODAY, MAYA DEAR.
THE FUNNIEST THING HAPPENED. I JUST GOT A CALL FROM HOPEY'S MOTHER LOOKING FOR HER DAUGHTER. SHE THOUGHT I WAS RESPONSIBLE FOR THE MILK AND ORANGE JUICE CARTONS.

SO, I TOLD HER TO COMB THE UNITED STATES AND FIND MAGGIE AND SHE'D PROBABLY FIND...
SHE'S NOT WITH MAGGIE...

OH? AND HOW WOULD YOU KNOW THAT, PAT?
BECAUSE SHE WAS JUST HERE FIVE MINUTES AGO WITH JEWEL TUCKER...

SHE WAS...? HOPEY...? WITH... WHAT...?
SURE, DIDN'T FRANCES TELL YOU? SHE'S BEEN STAYING AT JEWEL'S THIS WHOLE TIME.
15

MISS GOLD TAN BIKINI CONTEST FROM MISSION HILLS, CALIFORNIA

TALENT SEARCH STARRING FLEM SCHMEGMY

JOSE MOJICA MARIN'S "AT MIDNIGHT I TAKE YOUR SOUL"

"THE RETURN OF THE BRONTCH LAUNCHERS" STARRING MASA TOBI

"THE OSCARS IN SATICOY" STARRING BAGS DECKER AND EARLY ERB

A LA CAMA CON PORCEL

I.B.B.U.B. TRACK AND FIELD MEET IN QUIT JO, MISSISSIPPI

ADVERTISEMENT

MAN, JEWEL! THIS THING MUST HAVE A MILLION CHANNELS!

YEH...

EEP BLEEP BLEEP BLEEP BLEEP

SHONEN KNIFE

16

END OF PART IV

WIGWAM BAM

by
XAIME
"THE KITTEN NATIVIDAD OF COMICS"
HERNANDEZ
1991

1

AREN'T YOU GONNA GO FIGHT THEM ALL NOW, DOYLE?
IS THAT WHAT YOU WANT ME TO DO, LILY? JUST TELL ME WHAT YOU WANT ME TO DO, 'CAUSE I DON'T KNOW ANY MORE!
ABIERTO
OPEN

I DON'T CARE! I JUST WANT YOU TO PICK UP YOUR STUFF AND GET IT OUT OF MY HOUSE AND MY LIFE!
GIVE ME THE KEY THEN...
RETTICK U. LE
RETTICK U. LE
1242
SSW=

I'LL BRING IT RIGHT BACK.
NO, YOU WON'T! LEAVE IT BEHIND THE PORCH LIGHT! I DON'T EVEN WANT TO SEE YOUR FACE ANY MORE!

DO YOU SEE HIM, PATSY? ISN'T DOYLE JUST THE COOLEST...?
I PICTURED HIM KINDA DIFFERENT, NAMI. ARE YOU SURE THAT WASN'T HIS GIRLFRIEND HE WAS JUST TALKING TO?
COCO

HO! DOYLE ISN'T THE KIND OF GUY THAT HAS "GIRLFRIENDS," PATSY VILLA...
THEN WHAT DOES HE NEED WITH YOU...?

I DIDN'T MEAN IT THAT WAY, NA... NAMI!!

LOOK OUT, BOY! HERE COMES THE SCARY PEOPLE FINDER CLUB!
2

C'MON, DAVID! WE MADE A CLUB WHERE WE LOOK FOR SCARY PEOPLE AN' STUFF...
I AIN'T GONNA JOIN NO STUPID CLUB...
HE'S JUST SAYING THAT 'CAUSE HE THOUGHT HE WAS SO SMART 'CAUSE HE WAS RIGHT ABOUT THE MILK CARTONS...

...BUT THEN OUR MOTHER PUNISHED HIM ANYWAY, AN' TOLD HIM TO LEAVE THE WITCH LADY ALONE ANYWAY!
HAHAHAHAHAHAH

GUYS, SORRY I CAN'T JOIN YOUR CLUB, BUT MAYBE YOU CAN JOIN MY CLUB...

...THE SCARY, GHOST, DRUNKER, UFO, WITCH FINDER CLUB!
YEAH!
HEY, WAIT FOR ME!

LLLET'S HEAR IT FOR DA-NI-TAAA...
HEY, RAY, BABY! CHECK YOU OUT! WHAT BRINGS YOU HERE?

I FIGURED YOU AND YOUR MOM WOULD BE UP TO BLOWS BY NOW...
OH, IT WAS NOTHIN'. I JUST TOLD HER THAT IT AIN'T NOBODY'S BUSINESS BUT MY OWN HOW AN' WHERE I WANNA RAISE MY KID.
3

THEN I TOLD HER I'M A RESPONSIBLE ADULT. WELL, SHE DISAGREED ABOUT THE RESPONSIBLE PART, BUT HAD TO AGREE THAT IT'S MY RIGHT...
CHEE, YOU'RE A BIGGER MAN THAN ME.

H-HEY, WAIT! THIS IS STILL YOUR MOM'S YARD, REMEMBER?
I CAN'T HELP IT, BABY. YOU JUST DRIVE THIS WOMAN INSANE SOMETIMES...

DANITA! I'M GOIN' DOWNTOWN FOR A BIT...

WHERE IS THAT GIRL OFF TO NOW? TSK!

I FEEL LIKE I'M IN HIGH SCHOOL AGAIN...
OOCH! YEAH...

YOUR BRUISES AIN'T HEALED YET? YOU SHOULD GO SEE THE DOCTOR, RAY. I'M SERIOUS...
OK. WELL, SEE, DOCTOR LINCOLN. I GOT THIS PAIN, SEE..?

SOME CLUB! WE HAVEN'T SEEN NOT EVEN ONE DRUNKER...
GUESS IT'S TIME FOR THE FINALE, HUH, DAVID?
DAVID, MAMA SAID TO KEEP AWAY FROM THE WITCH LADY'S HOUSE!
WE'RE NOT GOING THERE, AWRIGHT?
SHACK MAN!
55
4

...AN' HE LOOKED JUST LIKE FREDDY K'UEGER, HUH, ELIAS?
DAT WAS RAY AW BEAT UP!
SHHH... READY? IS HE HOME TODAY?

SHUT THAT DOOR!

I'LL KILL THOSE KIDS, I SWEAR...
RELAX, RAY. THEY DIDN'T SEE NOTHIN'...
ELIAS! C'MERE, BABY!

THAT'S ENOUGH RUNNIN' AROUND NOW. GO INSIDE WITH GRANDMA, OK, BABY?
WHATCHA ALL DOIN' IN THERE?
WORKING, LITTLE GUY. JUST WORKING...

OH OH! I'M SUPPOSED TO BE AT WORK RIGHT NOW! CAN YOU TAKE ELIAS BACK TO THE APARTMENT WITH YOU?
SORRY, I GOT A JOB INTERVIEW IN LESS THAN AN HOUR.
MAMA!

STAY WITH GRANDMA, BABY! I'LL SEE YOU EARLY TONIGHT AFTER WORK, OK?

C'MON, NAMI... OK, SO YOU FOLLOW HIM AND YOU FIND OUT WHERE HE LIVES. THEN WHAT?
GO HOME, PATSY...
Box Tops
5

TSK! LUCKY...

OH, WELL. I HEAR B.P.'S IN MONTOYA ALWAYS NEEDS DANCERS...
CAN THEY DO THAT? I MEAN, POOF? JUST LIKE THAT, LU?
Closed out of business

SURE, IT HAPPENED TO ME AT A RESTAURANT I ONCE WORKED AT. NEVER SAW THE OWNER AGAIN OR NOTHING. AND HE WAS MY DAMN BOYFRIEND...
OH, WELL. I KNOW A FEW PEOPLE THAT'LL BE PLEASED ABOUT THIS...
TOPLESS DANCING
COMING SOON!
Foodmart Expre
6

HERE COMES ONE OF 'EM NOW. MY MOM...
HI, MOM.
HI, BABY...
WHERE'S ELIAS?
7

BAW!

THESE ARE THE TIMES WHEN YOU JUST WANNA HOP A TRAIN...
NOW, WAIT A MINUTE, ED. I'VE BEEN TURNED DOWN FROM JOBS BEFORE...

YOU EVER DONE THAT, RAY? JUST LEFT EVERYTHING BEHIND AND DIDN'T GIVE A SHIT...?
BWAAA

LET'S GO, RAY. YOU KNOW YOU WANT TO. YOU CONSIDERED IT THE OTHER DAY, REMEMBER?

HUP!

LET'S GO, RAYYY...
BWA

RAY RAY RAY RAY RAY RAY...

WHERE YOU GOING NOW?
HELL, MY GIRLFRIEND STILL LIKES ME.
8

DOSE WERE DE DAYS...

THESE ARE THE TIMES WHEN YOU JUST WANNA HOP A TRAIN...
POTASH

LET'S HEAR IT FOR DA-NI-TAAAA...

HEY, BA...?

BOO HOO!

OH! I...I DIDN'T MEAN... I'M GOING!
9

DON'T CALL THE COPS, OK? I WON'T BOTHER YOU ANY MORE. YOUR GIRLFRIEND DOESN'T HAVE TO KNOW I WAS HERE...
YOU DON'T HAVE TO GO, NAMI. SHE'S NOT MY GIRLFRIEND...

SHE TOLD ME JUST TODAY THAT SHE DOESN'T EVEN WANT TO SEE MY FACE ANY MORE...

HEH! WE'RE GONNA GET ALONG JUST FINE...

?!?

BUT, WHY WAS IT SUCH A BIG SECRET? WHY WAS I NOT SUPPOSED TO KNOW THAT HOPEY'S STILL IN TOWN, FRANCES?
IT WAS NO SECRET, MAYA! I-I JUST FORGOT TO TELL YOU, THAT'S ALL!
ON DUTY
GOLD TAXI
R19 5171

I'M SORRY, I DON'T MEAN TO KEEP PRESSING ON THIS. IT JUST SEEMED VERY ODD...
THERE'S JEWEL...
10

HOW'VE YOU BEEN, JEWEL?
JUST FINE...

...AND REMEMBER, MAYA. I SAW HER FIRST.

RRRRP
WOO!

WHY DID YOU GUYS STOP? THAT SOUNDED GREAT!
IT SUCKED. ONE OF US WAS PLAYING A TOTALLY DIFFERENT SONG.
DON'T LOOK AT ME, LESTER!
HE'S NOT TALKING ABOUT YOU, FIFI...

YOU SURE YOU DON'T WANNA PLAY BASS, FIFI?
I'M NOT GOING TO PLAY BASS! YOU PLAY BASS!
HEY, TAKE A BREAK, GUYS. YOUR EGOS ARE STARTING TO DRAW SPARKS...

SPEAKING OF SPARKS. WHAT A GOOD FIRE WOULDN'T DO TO THIS PALACE.
THAT'S RIGHT, LESTER. CHOMP THE NIPPLE THAT NOURISHES YOU...
HEY, HEY, BABEH! WHA'S SHAKIN'?
HEY, HOPEY SWEETY SWEET.
11

OH, THAT'S RIGHT. RICH PEOPLE HAVE PROBLEMS, TOO. I KEEP FORGETTING...
TELL US ABOUT IT, SON OF A BRAIN SURGEON AND A LAWYER...
GUITAR WARS!

OUCH! SORRY 'BOUT THAT...
PLEASE, I'M AN INNOCENT BYSTANDER...
COME ON, MAYA. LET'S GET OUT OF THE LINE OF FIRE...

WE'VE BEEN HAVING THE BEST TIME. HOPEY'S THE COOLEST...
ISN'T SHE, THOUGH? SHE'S THE KIND OF PERSON YOU JUST WANT TO PUT INTO YOUR POCKET AND TAKE HOME WITH YOU.
COULDN'T HAVE SAID IT BETTER MYSELF. SIGH...

BUT, YOU KEEP YOUR HANDS OFF, MAYA, BECAUSE I SAW HER F...
ACTUALLY, JEWEL, YOU DIDN'T SEE HER FIRST. HOPEY WAS LIVING WITH ME UNTIL YOU KIDNAPPED HER AND BROUGHT HER HERE, SO I...
SEE, MAYA? THAT'S WHY I DIDN'T TELL YOU HOPEY WAS HERE! YOU'RE SO... SO POSSESSIVE!

I'M SO POSSE...? MY LORD, I CAN'T BELIEVE WE'RE ARGUING OVER HOPEY AS IF SHE WERE A TOY...
YOU KNOW WHAT YOU CAN DO ABOUT IT, MAYA...

WOULD YOU AT LEAST TELL HOPEY WHY I HAD TO LEAVE?
WE'LL TELL HER.

...SNOBBY BITCH THINKS SHE'S QUEEN OF THE WORLD...
12

HERE YOU GUYS ARE. WHERE'S MAYA?
OH, SHE HAD TO LEAVE SUDDENLY. ARE YOU GUYS DONE REHEARSING, HOPEY?

AH, IT'S DUELLING GUITAR SOLOS RIGHT NOW. BLEH...
OH, BY THE WAY, HOPEY. YOU'RE GONNA HAVE TO SLEEP IN THE RED ROOM FROM NOW ON. MY MOTHER GETS BACK LATE TONIGHT.

OH, THAT'S OK. I REALLY SHOULD THINK OF GOING BACK TO THE CITY WITH TEX...
YOU'RE LEAVING...? WHY...?

I CAN'T LEECH OFF YOU GUYS FOREVER. BESIDES...
BUT, YOU'RE NOT...
JEWEL'S MOTHER WILL WANT TO MEET YOU.

THAT'S RIGHT! I TOLD HER ALL ABOUT YOU ON THE PHONE AND SHE'S DYING TO MEET YOU. C'MON, HOPEY. YOU CAN LEAVE TOMORROW...
I GET TO MEET NAN TUCKER?

YOU SHOULDA LET ME WALK YOU HOME. YOU'D BE THERE BY NOW...
SHE'LL BE HERE. SHE HAD TO SNEAK THE CAR OUT...

YOU KNOW, WE GOT OUT OF THERE JUST IN TIME. YOU KNOW WHAT LILY MIGHT HAVE DONE IF SHE FOUND US IN HER APARTMENT?
HONK!
13

SEE YOU LATER, NAMI.
BYE.

PATSY, WHY DO GUYS ALWAYS GOTTA TALK ABOUT THEIR EX-GIRLFRIENDS?
NEVER MIND THAT, NAMI! TELL ME! WAS IT...?

DOWN TO HIS KNEE? NOT EVEN CLOSE! EDDIE BRAVO IS BIGGER THAN THAT!
GUY, I STILL CAN'T BELIEVE YOU DID IT...
Sal's GARAGE

SO, SHE MOVED BACK TO HER MOTHER'S HOUSE, HUH?
THAT'S RIGHT. GO BACK TO START. DO NOT COLLECT.

YOU REALLY CAN'T BLAME DANITA, RAY. IT'S HARD FOR A YOUNG, SINGLE MOTHER TO JUGGLE JOB AND CHILD. THIS WAY HER MOTHER CAN...
... HELP HER? THEN WHAT WAS I HERE FOR?
STOP WHINING, RAY...

YOU'RE A FREE MAN, SO JUST ENJOY IT...
BUT, THIS AIN'T NO GAME TO ME! I COULDN'T SAY "YOU WERE RIGHT, MOM. I CAN'T DO THIS ALONE. I'LL COME HOME. SORRY, RAY. SEE YA!"
THEN YOU SHOULD HAVE AGREED TO MARRY HER...

WHAT DIFFERENCE WOULD THAT HAVE MADE? WHAT DOES MARRIAGE HAVE TO DO WITH ANYTHING????
WELL, IF YOU DON'T KNOW...
OH, THAT'S RIGHT. NOTHING IS RELEVANT UNLESS RAY PROCLAIMS OTHERWISE...
14

MAGGIE...

ARE YOU GONNA TELL ME THE REASON OUR TWO YEARS TOGETHER FIZZLED IS BECAUSE I DIDN'T MARRY YOU? 'CAUSE IF YOU ARE, I NEED A BETTER REASON THAN THAT...
THAT'S ALL, RAY. WE'RE OUT OF HERE.

HELL, I CAN ACCEPT THAT MAYBE YOU DID LOVE HOPEY MORE THAN ME, BUT NOT...NOT... WHY WAS IT REALLY, MAGGIE...?

I WAS A LOUSY LAY? I BORED YOU TO DEATH? WHAT...?

DO WE KNOW HOW TO HAVE A CLUB, OR WHAT?
YEAH, BUT IT WOULDA BEEN MORE PERFECT IF WE COULD SPY ON THE WITCH LADY...
LET'S DO IT NOW!

WAIT A MINUTE, GUYS...
YOUR SISTER WENT INSIDE. SHE WON'T KNOW...
...OR ARE YOU SCARED OF HER?

ALL THE LIGHTS ARE OUT...
THAT MAKES IT WAY MORE SCARIER, HUH?
THEY'RE OUT 'CAUSE NOBODY'S HOME, YOU BRAINS.

I TRIED TO TELL YOU. LAST NIGHT I HEARD MY MOM TALKING TO HER ON THE PHONE. SHE PACKED UP AN' LEFT TOWN...
YOUR MOM TALKED TO THE WITCH LADY?
DOES THAT MEAN YOUR MOM'S A WITCH, TOO?
55

NOBODY'S A WITCH! SHE'S MY MOM'S COUSIN!
I KNEW THAT.
SOME COUSIN.
CORTEZ
55
15

OH, WELL. SO MUCH FOR THE SCARY, GHOST, DRUNKER, UFO, WITCH FINDER CLUB...
WAIT A MINUTE, GUYS. I WANNA SHOW YOU SOME-THING...

YOU JUST GOTTA PROMISE NEVER TO TELL ANYBODY, EVER! ESPECIALLY MY SISTER...
NOT ME.
NOT ME.

IT'S... IT'S...
... THE MILK CARTONS THE WITCH LADY HAD UP IN HER ROOM. I FOUND 'EM IN THE TRASH...
SO WHAT? SHE AIN'T A WITCH, 'MEMBER?

NO, BUT I GOT A FEELING THIS LADY ON HERE MIGHT BE...
R-REALLY, DAVID...?
SHH! SOMEONE'S COMING... HIDE!

THESE ARE THE TIMES WHEN YOU JUST WANNA HOP A TRAIN...

TH-THAT WAS THE SHACK MAN!
AN' WE HID FROM HIM!
DO WE KNOW HOW TO HAVE A CLUB, OR WHAT?

AHH, ANOTHER GREAT DAY IN HOPPERS COMES TO A CLOSE...
YEAH!
STILL, I WONDER WHERE THE WITCH LADY WENT...

GANGWAY! COMING THROUGH, Y'ROADHOG!
10
EAST
16

END OF PART V

I'M SORRY WE DIDN'T HEAR YOU GET IN LAST NIGHT, MS. TUCKER, BUT WELCOME HOME ANYWAY...
THANK YOU, ARACELI. WE'LL HAVE OUR BREAKFAST WHEN JEWEL GETS UP.
WIGWAMBAM PART 6
THE ARTESIAN 91
1

MA...

N... MA...

NO...

GEE, MOM. JUMP HER BONES, WHY DON'T YOU?
SHHH!

HER NAME IS HOPEY AND SHE IS MY GUEST. OK, MOTHER? MY GUEST!
OH, JEWEL. I JUST WANTED TO SEE... YOU KNOW I CARE ABOUT WHAT FRIENDS YOU CHOOSE.

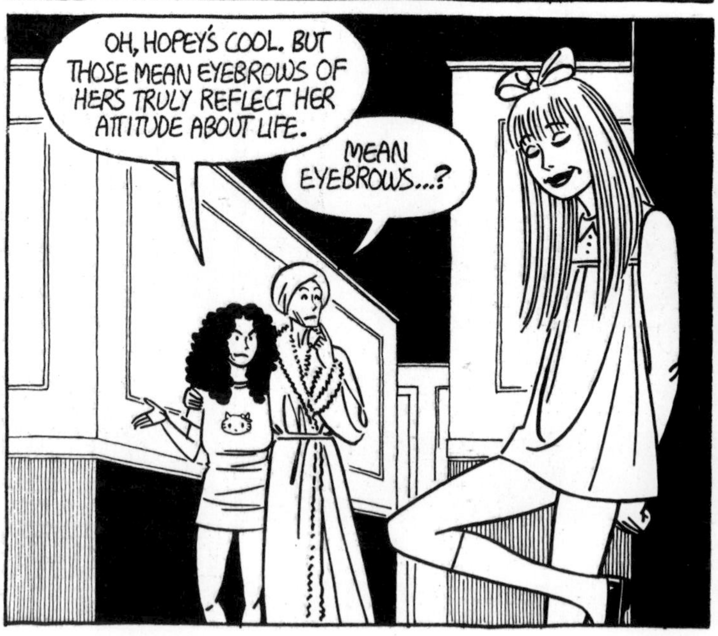
OH, HOPEY'S COOL. BUT THOSE MEAN EYEBROWS OF HERS TRULY REFLECT HER ATTITUDE ABOUT LIFE.
MEAN EYEBROWS...?

WELL, PETE? HOW'S IT LOOK?
NICE.
2

I DON'T MEAN ME, SILLY! MY STOMACH! I'M NOT SHOWING, AM I?
NO, NOT AT ALL, MRS. COSTIGAN.
MEN

LISTEN, BODYGUARD. MY HUSBAND ISN'T HERE, SO YOU DON'T HAVE TO AGREE WITH EVERYTHING I SAY...
WHAT-EVER YOU SAY, MA'AM.

AGHH! I'M GONNA MURDER YOU!
IF YOU THINK THAT'S BEST.
RUNNING AWAY FROM YOUR HUSBAND AGAIN, PENNY?

IZZY BELLE?! WHAT A SURPRISE! WHAT ARE YOU DOING WAY OUT HERE IN THE TULES?
JUST STOPPED TO FILL MY RADIATOR AND, WELL, I'M AFRAID I'M NEVER QUITE AS SURPRISED TO SEE YOU IN UNEXPECTED PLACES AS YOU ARE TO SEE ME.

ISABEL, THIS IS PETE. I'M CARRYING OUR CHILD...
HELLO, PETE...
HOW YA DOIN', ISABEL? NICE TO MEET YOU.

SO, WHERE ARE YOU HEADED? GOING TO GO SEE MAGGIE AND HOPEY?

HMF!
3

OH, YEAH? WELL, WHATEVER HAPPENED TO THE GUY WHO PLAYED MR. JEEVERS ON "NAN'S WORLD"? HE ALSO USED TO HOST "HILLBILLY HIDEAWAY."
JACK "CHEESE" DANKIS. I UNDERSTAND HE NOW DOES LOCAL CARPET COMMERCIALS IN MISSISSIPPI.
SO, WHAT DO YOU WANT TO DO TODAY, HOPE?

NOW, DON'T TRY TO CHANGE THE SUBJECT, HOPEY. YOU WERE A MODEL OR SOMETHING AT ONE TIME, WEREN'T YOU? I CAN TELL...
TRY TO IGNORE IT, HOPEY. SHE DOES THIS TO A LOT OF MY FRIENDS AND IT REALLY DRIVES ME UP THE WALL...

DON'T MIND JEWEL. SHE ALREADY HAD THAT TEMPER WHEN WE ADOPTED HER FROM THAT ALBANIAN ORPHANAGE SOME TWENTY YEARS AGO...
YOU'RE DOING IT AGAIN, MOTHER. YOU'RE TRYING TO TURN HER ON ME. WELL, IT WON'T WORK...
4

WHY DO YOU ALWAYS ACCUSE ME OF... JEWEL, I REALLY DON'T WANT TO ARGUE WITH YOU TODAY...
OH, YEAH? WELL, I'M NOT FINISHED...

CRAZIES IN THE MIND...

DOES YOUR MAMA KNOW YOU SMOKE?
SHIT, HOW OLD DO YOU THINK I AM?

SO, TELL THE TRUTH, ISABEL. DO I LOOK LIKE A MARCO, OR A MONICA WITH A BEARD?
YOU LOOK YAWN! FINE.

YOU MUST BE TIRED FROM ALL THAT DRIVING. YOU REALLY SHOULD STAY THE NIGHT.
WELL, IT IS GETTING LATE...

YEAH, A WOMAN LIKE YOU SHOULDN'T DRIVE THROUGH MISSISSIPPI BACKROADS AT NIGHT. AND I'M TALKING ABOUT THE STATE TROOPERS...
IT'S NOT THAT BAD, MARCO.
YEAH...

END OF PART VI

I WANNA THANK COLE YOUNGER FOR LETTING ME COME ALONG ON THIS TOUR, AND I WANNA THANK YOU PEOPLE FOR COMING OUT TO SUPPORT AIDS RESEARCH...
AIDS MUST DIE!
COLE YOUNGER
RATATATS
TERRY DOWNE
BIG FAT TUBS OF LARD
7PM HANK'S BAR
YAY TERRY!
DO "HOPPERS"!
EX

SOUNDS LIKE THERE ARE PEOPLE HERE FROM L.A.
DO "SPOOKY THE SMOKEY"!

DO "DO VASES HAVE EYES?"

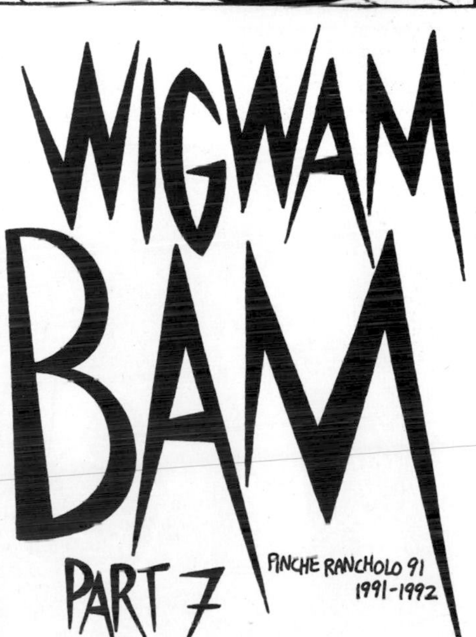
WIGWAM BAM
PART 7
FINCHE RANCHOLO 91
1991-1992

DO VASES HAVE EYES? I WOULD HAVE EXPECTED ONE OF THOSE TWO OTHER CLOWNS, NOT YOU, IZZY.
JUST PASSING THROUGH. HOW'S THE OL' MUSIC CAREER GOING, TERRY?
RANK
DUFUS

IT'S OK. ARE YOU ON YOUR WAY TO SEE HOPEY? GOING TO SEE WHY SHE'S ON THOSE MILK CARTONS? JOEY GLASS CALLED ME THE OTHER DAY ASKING IF IT WAS ME THAT...
I REALLY DIDN'T COME TO TALK ABOUT... GOD, WHAT AM I DOING HERE ANYWAY?

WHAT?
I'M GOING ABOUT THIS WHOLE THING ALL WRONG! OF COURSE YOU'RE GONNA TALK ABOUT... ERT!
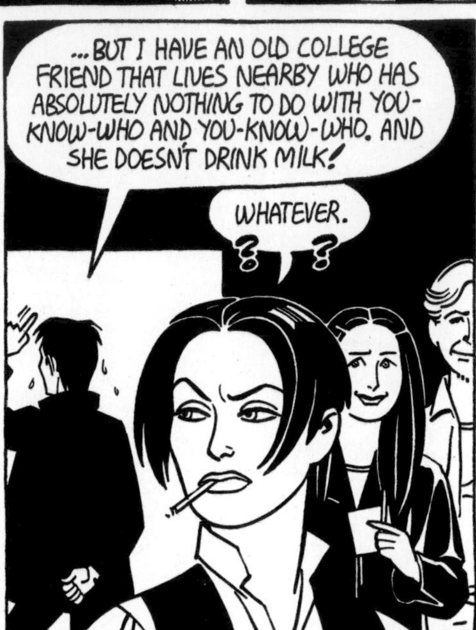
...BUT I HAVE AN OLD COLLEGE FRIEND THAT LIVES NEARBY WHO HAS ABSOLUTELY NOTHING TO DO WITH YOU-KNOW-WHO AND YOU-KNOW-WHO. AND SHE DOESN'T DRINK MILK!
WHATEVER.

COME ON, HOPEY! I WANNA GET TO TALAÓ WHILE FRANCES IS STILL THERE.
JUST ONE MORE MINUTE, JEWEL...

PTCH! WELL, IF YOU'D RATHER WATCH THAT DISGUSTING EXHIBIT THEN MAYBE I'LL GO ALONE...
SEE YOU THERE, JEWEL.

OH OH! DID CRYSTAL GO POOPY AGAIN?
I SOWWY, MOMMY...
2

THEN SOMETIMES I WONDER IF THE PAY IS THAT GOOD.
IT SEEMS KINDA FUN TO ME. YOU WANNA GO GET A DRINK AT TALAÓ?

REMEMBER, I KINDA TOOK AN OATH TO MS. TUCKER THAT I DON'T TALK ABOUT MY JOB, IF YOU KNOW WHAT I MEAN...
DON'T WORRY ABOUT ME, CRYSTAL. MOM... UH, MUM'S THE WORD.

SAY NOPE TO HOPE, AND GAG TO MAG...

I WONDER IF IT'S AN EAST COAST THING NOT TO PUT NUMBERS ON YOUR HOUSE, OR IF I'M JUST SNOWBLIND.
ISABEL! THIS WAY!

I CAN'T BELIEVE IT'S YOU. WHAT'S IT BEEN, THIRTEEN YEARS?
B-B-BARB?

IT'S ME, BUT I GUESS I LOOK SOMEWHAT DIFFERENT TO YOU. I FINALLY GOT RID OF THE DOROTHY HAMMIL HAIRCUT, BUT THEN I ADOPTED HER THIGHS... THREE TIMES OVER, I'M AFRAID...

YOU KNOW, IT'S A REAL FUNNY COINCIDENCE THAT YOU CAME BY BECAUSE I WAS JUST IN YOUR NEIGHBORHOOD OUT IN CALIFORNIA LAST WEEK VISITING, BUT I DIDN'T KNOW HOW TO GET IN TOUCH WITH YOU. YOU'RE NOT LISTED, ARE YOU?
NNNNGHHH...
3

ANYWAY, ISABEL. IT'S A NEW ME. I'M EVEN DRINKING MILK FOR CALCIUM NOW. NO MORE UNHEALTHY ME. NO SIR!
BONK
HAVE YOU SEEN ME?

YOUR BOYFRIEND STILL HASN'T CALLED, DANITA?
NO, AN' I DON'T BLAME HIM, NEITHER. I SHOULDA NEVER MOVED OUT ON HIM LIKE I DID, ROCKY.
Z

OH, HE'LL COME AROUND. YOU AREN'T EXACTLY LIVING IN ALASKA, Y'KNOW.
HUH! GET YOU. YOU HATE RAY...

WELL, ANYTHING'S BETTER THAN THAT EXPLOITIVE STRIP CLUB SCUM, I GUESS...
NOBODY EXPLOITED ME...

I WAS THE ONE IN CHARGE WHEN I WAS UP ON THAT STAGE, NOT THEM! I HAD ALL THOSE MEN CRYIN' FOR THEIR MAMAS!
BOY, DOES THIS GIRL GET THINGS BACKWARDS.
AND NOW THAT IT'S OVER, WHAT ARE YOU GOING TO DO?

WELL, NOW THAT I'VE GAINED ALL THIS NEW CONFIDENCE, AS A STRONG BLACK WOMAN I'M GONNA RAISE MY SON TO BE A STRONG BLACK MAN.
THAT'S WHAT I WANT TO HEAR, DANITA GIRL...

OK! ALL RIGHT! ¡YA! I GIVE! I CONCEDE! YOU GUYS WIN! I CAN'T ESCAPE YOU! I'M ON MY WAY! I'M OUT THE DOOR! JUST PLEASE STOP HAUNTING ME! PLEASE, LORD!!!
4

FUCKIN' SHAME, HUH, DOYLE?
FUCKIN' SHAME, JOE.
Bumpers
Closed out of business

THAT PLACE MUST HAVE MEANT A LOT TO HIM, JOEY...
WELL, SURE, JANET. BUMPER'S WAS HIS HOME AWAY FROM... AH, HIS NEW GIRLFRIEND OUGHTA MAKE HIM FORGET REAL QUICK.

NAMI, DOYLE'S AT THE DOOR.
TSK! WELL, TELL HIM I'M NOT HERE, NOEL!
UCSB

SHE'S NOT HE... HUH?

BLEEP

5

DON'T WORRY ABOUT JEWEL, MAYA. SHE DOESN'T OWN ME, Y'KNOW.
I'D JUST RATHER AVOID ANY ALTER-CATION WITH THAT GIRL, HOPEY.

...BUT I HOPE THIS DOESN'T AFFECT OUR RELATIONSHIP ANY. I'D REALLY LIKE TO REMAIN YOUR FRIEND, NO MATTER WHAT.
WELL, I MAY NEED A FRIEND, IF JEWEL DOESN'T LET ME BACK IN HER HOUSE.

YOU KNOW YOU'RE ALWAYS WELCOME TO COME BACK AND STAY WITH ME, SWEETIE.
WUDDA PAL WUDDA PAL WUDDA PAL...

HEY, DO YOU KNOW WHO SHE LOOKS EXACTLY LIKE...?
IF YOU SAY DEL CHIMNEY, I'LL BELT YOU ONE.

HEY, DON'T GET TESTY, OK? WE'RE ALL FRIENDS HERE.

SHIT, PAT! YOU'D THINK HOPEY CROAKED AND WENT TO HEAVEN! ALL THIS STUPID FUSS OVER A CHICK!
APPARENTLY THE TWO HAVEN'T SEEN EACH OTHER FOR A FEW YEARS, ROSA...

WHERE IS EVERYBODY OFF TO, MAYA?
BACK TO JEWEL'S, I THINK...
URP!
6

YOU WANT ANOTHER VODKA MARTINI?
SIGH LET HER RIP.

I STILL CAN'T BELIEVE IT! I MEAN, LIKE, WHAT ARE YOU DOING HERE?
I CAME TO SEE YOU AND MAGGIE.

THIS IS SO COOL! WHERE ARE YOU STAYING? HOW LONG ARE YOU STAYING? WE GOT SO MUCH TO TALK ABOUT! I MEAN, I'M FREAKIN' OUT!

GEE, I'D REALLY LIKE TO HAVE YOU SPEND THE NIGHT, IZZY, BUT...
NAN! MEET MY FRIEND FROM CALIFORNIA! HER NAME'S ISABEL!
HELLO, WELCOME, ISABEL.

YOU THINK IT'D BE OK IF SHE STAYED THE NIGHT? SHE JUST GOT IN AND...
OF COURSE SHE CAN. ANY FRIEND OF HOPEY'S...
HOPEEE...

WHAT DO YOU THINK YOU'RE DOING? I THOUGHT I JUST TOLD YOU SHE CAN'T STAY...
AN' YOUR MOM SAID SHE COULD...

WELL, I SAY YOU CAN BOTH GET OUT!
TOUGH SHIT, JEWEL. WE'RE YOUR MOTHER'S GUESTS, NOT YOURS.

JUST A MINUTE, GOD DAMN IT.
RING
RING
7

H'LO.
GUESS WHO?

HEY, HEY HEY! WHAT'S HATTENIN'? THIS IS QUITE THE SURPRISE...
I MISS YOU.

HUH!
SO, LIKE, WHAT'S NEW, MAYA?
OH...NOT MUCH. I'M JUST SOOO LONELY, RAY...

YEAH? WELL, YOU SURE CALLED AT THE RIGHT TIME, BECAUSE THINGS AREN'T TOO HAPPENING OVER HERE, EITHER...
OH. ARE YOU HAVING PROBLEMS, SVEETS?

AW, NAW... YEAH... NAW. I DUNNO, IT'S JUST... YOU KNOW, MAYA...
OH, I KNOW... I KNOW...

LET'S HEAR IT FOR DANITAAA...

MY BROTHER'S LYING THROUGH HIS BUNGHOLE. HE PUT ME ON THAT 'OL MILK CARTON SURE AS SHIT. WHO ELSE WOULD DO SOMETHING LIKE THAT?
MAGGIE MAYBE?

FOR A SECOND I THOUGHT YOU MIGHT HAVE DONE IT, AND THEN I THOUGHT IT WAS MY MOM, BUT THEN... BUT THEN, WHO CARES? I'M STILL ALIVE AN' YOU'RE A WITNESS...
WHAT HAPPENED TO MAGGIE?
8

SHIT, I'M STARVED. YOU WANT SOMETHING TO EAT, ISABEL?

WHAT DID YOU DO TO MAGGIE?
THE DAMACHERS

MOM? WHAT'S GOING ON..?
I'M NOT SURE...

WHAT DID YOU DO TO MAGGIE?
NOTHING!
HEY!

WHAT'S THE IDEA OF YELLING IN MY HOUSE AT THREE IN THE MORNING? DON'T YOU KNOW THE PEOPLE THAT LIVE HERE ARE TRYING TO SLEEP?
SORRY.

I DON'T KNOW WHAT THIS IS ALL ABOUT BUT WHATEVER IT IS BETTER TONE DOWN RIGHT NOW OR YOU TWO ARE OUT ON THE STREET TONIGHT! I'M TELLING YOU, I WON'T TAKE IT!
THE DAMACHERS
9

END OF PART VII

MRS. TUCKER IS NOT ENTERTAINING TODAY.

WE DON'T WANT TO SEE MRS. TUCKER. WE'RE FRIENDS OF JEWEL.

JEWEL HAS GONE AWAY FOR THE WEEKEND.

ACTUALLY, WE CAME TO SEE...

HOPEY.

SLAM!

1

BROUGHT TO YOU BY: JAIME "THE WALTER CRONKITE OF PROFESSIONAL WRESTLING" HERNANDEZ 1992

SCREW THAT.
BEHAVE NOW, LITTLE ONE...

EVERYONE IS IN THE PLAYROOM, MADAM.
WHY, THANK YOU, DUDU.

IN THE PLAYROOM, MADAM.

IN THE PLAYROOM, LADIES.

2

BLEEP!
...OK, YOU GOT IT! TAKE IT AWAY, CHARLIE BROWN...
THERE YOU ARE. HI, HOPEY.
HI, BENNY. HI, TWYLA. WHAT BRINGS YOU GUYS HERE?
BLEEP!
BLEEP!
BLEEP!
THE JOHNNY CANALES SHOW

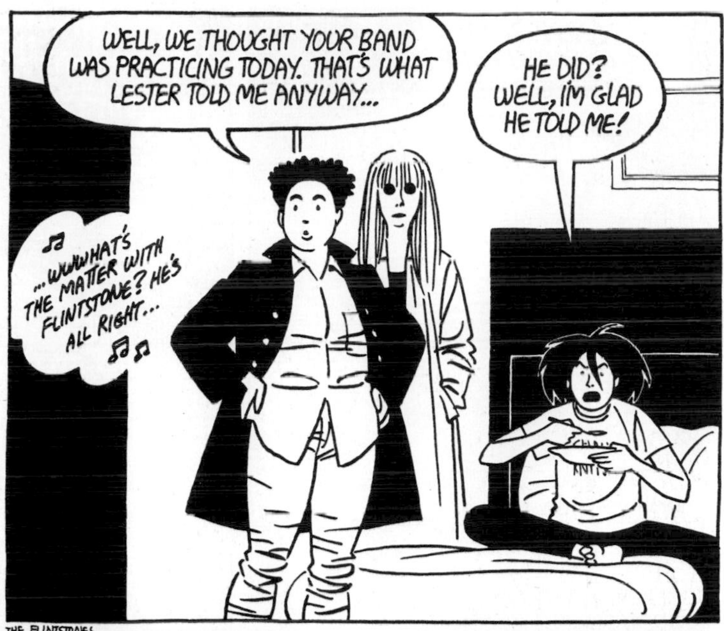
WELL, WE THOUGHT YOUR BAND WAS PRACTICING TODAY. THAT'S WHAT LESTER TOLD ME ANYWAY...
HE DID? WELL, I'M GLAD HE TOLD ME!
...WWWHAT'S THE MATTER WITH THE FLINTSTONE? HE'S ALL RIGHT...
THE FLINTSTONES

SOUNDS LIKE THEY'RE HERE ALL RIGHT, HOPEY.
HEATHENS.
RRRRRRRRRRRRR

RRRRRR

L7

I GOTTA GO GET SOME CIGARETTES.
I GOTTA GET SOME STRINGS OUT OF THE VAN.
SO, HOW'D I DO, LESTER? FIFI? AM I IN...?

I CAN UNDERSTAND THOSE WIMPS, BUT YOU COULD HAVE AT LEAST TOLD ME YOU GOT A NEW BASS PLAYER, TEXAS.
T-THEY WERE JUST TRYING HIM OUT! HE'S NOT FOR SURE... UH, I...
3

YEAH, YEAH, RIGHT. LET'S GO, BENNY, TWYLA.
BUNCHA FUCKIN' WIMPS...

LOOK, WHAT'S THE FUCKIN' DIFFERENCE? YOU DON'T TAKE THIS SHIT SERIOUSLY, ANYWAY! YOU'RE NEVER HERE! IT'S JUST NOT WORTH IT!!!!!
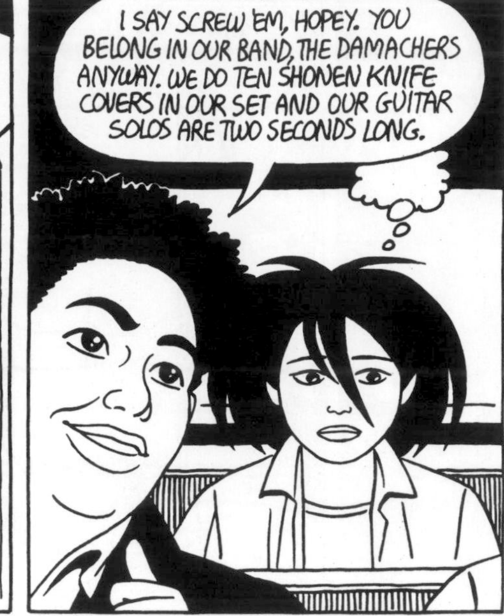
I SAY SCREW 'EM, HOPEY. YOU BELONG IN OUR BAND, THE DAMACHERS ANYWAY. WE DO TEN SHONEN KNIFE COVERS IN OUR SET AND OUR GUITAR SOLOS ARE TWO SECONDS LONG.

I'LL BE RIGHT BACK, LADIES.
BEHAVE NOW, CRYSTAL DARLING.
CcDdEeFfGgHh

HOPEY? I THOUGHT YOU WENT TO EL SWANKOS WITH JEWEL...
NAH.

AND ISABEL? DID SHE LEAVE?
YEAH, THE DAY BEFORE YESTERDAY. SHE HAD TO GET BACK TO...WHATEVER.

YOU KNOW, WE DIDN'T EVEN GET TO CATCH UP ON STUFF. I MEAN, I ONLY HAVEN'T SEEN HER IN WHAT, A MILLION THOUSAND YEARS...

WE DIDN'T TALK ABOUT ME GETTING PREGNANT, OR HER LIVING IN THE NUTHOUSE, OR... WE DIDN'T EVEN GET TO...TALK ABOUT...
4

...WE DIDN'T EVEN GET TO TALK ABOUT SPEEDY...
TSK!

¡SEÑOR CHASCARRILLO! ¿COMO ESTA, USTED?
¿SEÑOR? WHAT EVER HAPPENED TO NACHO, LITTLE IZZY BIZZY?
1242

OK. WHERE IS EVERYBODY, NACHO? I WANTED TO MEET YOUR GIRLS.
OH, THEY ALL WENT SHOPPING WITH THEIR MOTHER. EATING ME OUT OF HOUSE AND HOME, Y'KNOW...
SO, HAVE YOU SEEN MY LITTLE PERLITA?

ACTUALLY, I HAVEN'T SEEN MAGGIE IN AWHILE. SHE HASN'T COME BY HERE LATELY, HAS SHE?
NO, TO TELL YOU THE TRUTH, I DON'T THINK PERLITA'S COMFORTABLE VISITING HERE...

I MEAN, THE GIRLS LOVE HER, SHE LIKES THE GIRLS, BUT... WELL, MY DIVORCE WITH HER MOTHER WAS... YOU KNOW, I DON'T BLAME THEM FOR RESENTING ME. ESPECIALLY PERLITA...
SHE'S ALWAYS TALKED HIGHLY OF YOU, NACHO.
5

BLEEP!
NAN, YOU'RE NOT GOING TO CLOBBER YOUR HUSBAND WITH HIS OWN BAT!
I'D MUCH RATHER BE THE CLOBBERER THAN THE CLOBBEREE, BLANCHE.
HA HA
MY GAL NAN

HAHAHA HAHAHA HAH

SHONEN KNIFE

ZZZAWW!!

JENNY, YOU JUST GOTTA FUCKIN' CALM DOWN OR YOU'LL RUIN THIS GIG FOR ALL OF US!
LOOK, YOU MAY BE INTO THAT SPANKING SHIT, BUT I'M NOT!
HI, HOPEY.
HI, CRYSTAL.
SHONEN KNIFE

IS JENNY GOING OFF AGAIN? THIS'LL TAKE CARE OF HER...
A LITTLE FINGER IN THE PUSSY, BABY?
OH, DON'T! GOD! OH, NOW YOU DID IT! THERE'S NO TURNING BACK! GO AHEAD, FINISH IT!
BABY

GOD DAMN IT! I'M NOT KIDDING! SOMEBODY EAT ME BEFORE I...
NOW!
IS SHE KIDDING ME?
NO, SO YOU BETTER DO IT BEFORE SHE...
OUT OF MY WAY.
SHONEN KNIFE

GO GO, HOPEY!
OH, MY GOD! HAS JENNY THE JET FINALLY MET HER MATCH?
OOH, THIS SHIT'S GETTIN' ME A LITTLE FIRED UP.
SHOOT! SOMEONE'S COMING!

THEY ALL AWAKE YET, DUDU?
THEY'RE JUST FINISHING THEIR NAPS, NOW, SO BE READY IN FIVE MINUTES...
WE'LL BE READY!
SHONEN KNIFE

OH, MAN. NOW MY LITTLE PANTIES ARE ALL SOILED.
OH OH, DER COMMANDANT WON'T STAND FOR THAT.
I KNOW WHERE NAN KEEPS MY EXTRAS. I'LL BE RIGHT BACK. YOU COMING, HOPEY?

SHIT, ON SECOND THOUGHT, THESE AREN'T GONNA FIT THAT BIG OL' CHICK. SHE'S JUST GONNA HAVE TO TELL HER BOSS SHE WENT WEE WEE IN HER PANTTH.
MAN, SHE HAS A WHOLE WARDROBE FOR YOU, CRYS!

YEAH, THIS KID GAME HAS BECOME HER LIFE. IF HER LEGIONS OF FANS ONLY KNEW...
IT'D BE NONE OF THEIR FUCKING BUSINESS. SHE AIN'T DOING ANYTHING WRONG. I THINK IT'S SUPER COOL.
SHONEN KNIFE

ISABEL, WHEN YOU SEE PERLITA, COULD YOU GIVE HER THIS STUFF? THEY'RE THINGS SHE'S LEFT BEHIND EACH TIME SHE'S VISITED.
OK, NACHO.
7

HERE I AM IN TEXAS VISITING DAD AND HIS FAMILY. HOPEY AND HER BAND HAVE BEEN ON THE ROAD FOR OVER TWO MONTHS NOW, SPEEDY'S BEEN DEAD FOR ALMOST TWO WEEKS AND I THINK RAY DOMINGUEZ HATES ME.

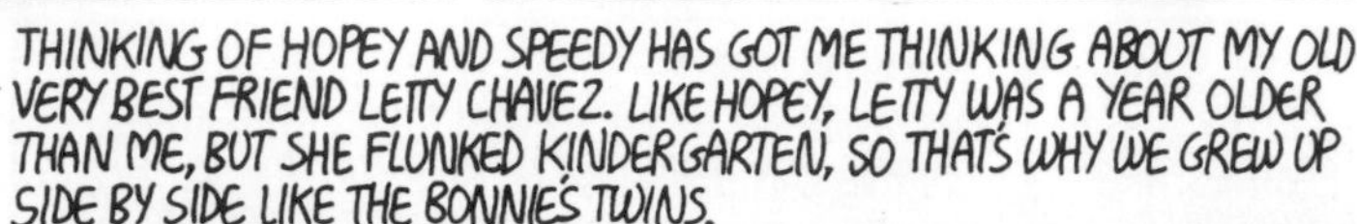

THINKING OF HOPEY AND SPEEDY HAS GOT ME THINKING ABOUT MY OLD VERY BEST FRIEND LETTY CHAVEZ. LIKE HOPEY, LETTY WAS A YEAR OLDER THAN ME, BUT SHE FLUNKED KINDERGARTEN, SO THAT'S WHY WE GREW UP SIDE BY SIDE LIKE THE BONNIE'S TWINS.

THINKING OF LETTY HAS GOT ME THINKING ABOUT HOW INTERESTING I'VE ALWAYS THOUGHT IT WAS THAT ON EVERY FOURTH YEAR CERTAIN RITUALS TAKE PLACE, LIKE, THE PRESIDENTIAL ELECTIONS (BLEH!), THE WINTER AND SUMMER OLYMPICS, FEBRUARY HAS A TWENTY-NINTH DAY (LEAP YEAR) AND LETTY'S BIRTHDAY WHICH FALLS, NATURALLY, ON THAT DAY.

SINCE POOR LETTY ONLY HAD A REAL BIRTHDAY ONCE EVERY FOUR YEARS, WE ALWAYS TRIED TO MAKE THEM REAL SPECIAL. LIKE, ON HER FIRST BIRTHDAY (FOURTH, ACTUALLY), WE ALL WENT TO KNOTT'S BERRY FARM. I WAS ONLY THREE, SO I DON'T REMEMBER MUCH, ONLY THAT THOSE GOD DAMN STATUES, OR WHATEVER THEY WERE, SCARED THE HOLY CRAP OUT OF US YOUNGUNS.

ON HER SECOND (EIGHTH) BIRTHDAY I WOULD SLEEP OVER AT LETTY'S AND WE'D ALL LEAVE EARLY THE NEXT MORNING FOR DISNEYLAND (NO MORE KNOTT'S STATUES FOR US, NO SIR). DISNEYLAND WAS COOL ENOUGH BUT SLEEPING OVER AT LETTY'S WAS ALWAYS TOPS. SHE HAD THE BEST TOYS AND WE ALWAYS SNUCK OUT THESE CRAZY ROCK RECORDS THAT HER BROTHER LIKED (HE HAD A 'FRO) AND PLAYED THEM OVER AND OVER TILL THE WEE HOURS.

ON HER THIRD AND TWELFTH BIRTHDAY, I HAD MOVED AWAY A YEAR BEFORE BUT CAME BACK TO HOPPERS JUST FOR THE OCCASION. WE WERE GONNA DO DISMAL-LAND AGAIN BUT I WAS LOOKING MORE FORWARD TO OUR TRADITIONAL SLUMBER PARTY. BUT WHEN I SAW LETTY WITH HER NEW CHUCA LOOK, I WASN'T SURE IT WOULD BE THE SAME.

BUT IT WAS THE SAME. SHE DIDN'T HAVE AS MANY TOYS AS SHE USED TO, BUT AS I HOPED, SHE STILL SNUCK OUT HER BROTHER'S RECORDS THAT WE DUG SO MUCH. ONE SONG THAT STOOD OUT WAS THIS ONE BY THE SWEET CALLED "WIG-WAM BAM." IT WASN'T THE GREATEST SONG IN THE WORLD, BUT IT WAS OUR SONG. LETTY CALLED IT OUR SECRET ANTHEM.

I DIDN'T KNOW WHY IT WAS SECRET UNTIL I MOVED BACK TO HOPPERS TWO YEARS LATER (WITH MY NEW CHUCA LOOK). NO THIRTEEN YEAR OLD MEXICAN-AMERICAN BAD GIRL LISTENED TO THAT "FAGGY WHITE BOY" MUSIC. THIS RULE SEEMED PRETTY LAME TO ME, BUT I PLAYED ALONG FOR LETTY'S SAKE.

BUT AS TIME ROLLED ON, WE STARTED GETTING MORE INTO SOUL AND DISCO BECAUSE OUR FAVORITE ROCK RECORDS WERE FIVE OR SIX YEARS OLD. THESE WERE OUR "DARK AGES," ONLY LETTY AND I DIDN'T KNOW IT.

THEN, ONE DAY, LETTY LOST HER MIND...

PUNK ROCK?!? LETTY, YOU'RE CRAZY! LOOK AT THIS! ITS STUUUPID!!

I KNOW, BUT JUST LISTEN. DOESN'T IT KINDA SOUND LIKE THAT OLDER STUFF, MAGGIE?

20, 24 HOURS TO GO...

RAMONES ROAD TO RUIN

FOR LETTY'S SAKE, I SAT AND LISTENED...

SO STUPID...

9

"METAL GURU" BY T REX "DEUCE" BY KISS "I WANNA BE SEDATED" BY THE RAMONES

IT ONLY TOOK A WEEKEND TO POSSESS ME AND BEFORE LONG, LETTY AND I HAD A SECRET PUNK ROCK CLUB.

WE DIDN'T EVEN INCLUDE THE FEW DEVO HEADS THAT WENT TO OUR SCHOOL (LITTLE DID I KNOW THAT TWO OF THEM WOULD TURN OUT TO BE DOYLE BLACK[BURN] AND MIKE THE VIET CONG).

I WAS JUST DYING TO KNOW OTHER PEOPLE WHO WERE ALSO INTO THIS MUSIC, SO I WOULD TAG ALONG WITH MY COUSIN LICHA TO DEL CHIMNEY'S WHERE SHE'D SCORE DRUGS. BUT I WAS TOO SCARED OF THESE PEOPLE, SO I'D JUST STARE.

ANYWAY, LETTY NEVER DID REACH HER FOURTH (SIXTEENTH) BIRTHDAY. SHE DIED IN A CAR CRASH TWO YEARS BEFORE. THEY PLAYED "REASONS" BY EARTH, WIND AND FIRE AT HER FUNERAL, BUT I DANCED TO "WIGWAM BAM" ALONE IN MY ROOM, KNOWING LETTY WOULD TOTALLY UNDERSTAND.

WELL, AFTER THAT I WAS SPENDING A LOT OF TIME BY MYSELF, SO IZZY, TRYING TO HELP ME GET OVER LETTY, INTRODUCED ME TO HOPEY. SHE FELT HOPEY AND I WOULD HAVE A LOT IN COMMON (IZZY WAS THE ONLY ONE WHO KNEW LETTY AND I LIKED PUNK). ALL I CAN SAY IS: I HOPE HOPEY NEVER DIES IN A CAR CRASH. LIGHTNING ONLY STRIKES TWICE ONCE, Y'KNOW.

"THE AMERIKAN IN ME" BY THE AVENGERS

I'M SORRY, BUT WE CAN'T WAIT, MRS. GLASS. WE HAVE FOUR OTHER LITTLE GIRLS WHO...
YES, I-I UNDERSTAND, MEESTER DENNIS. TENK YOU...

YOU COULDN' JUS' SMILE FOR DE MAN, ESPERANZA. NO, YOU HAD TO MAKE ME LOOK FOOLEESH...
SALE

MA... MAMA... MA... MAGGIE...
SHONEN KNIFE

WELCOME TO THE ZOO, HOPEY.
THIS IS TOO COOL! EVERY WOMAN FROM TV LAND IS IN THERE!

VAL "BLANCHE" KELLEY, IRIS "MA" RAYMOND, PHYLLIS "DUMBSY" MADDEN...
PSSST!
BAD GIRL!
11

SHHH...
BAD GIRL, LITTLE JENNY! BAD GIRL!
I SAID, WATCH THE CANE!
OH OH. JENNY'S GOING OFF AGAIN.

DO YOU KNOW WHAT MY MOTHER USED TO DO TO ME WHEN I...?
I DON'T GIVE A SHIT, LADY! I'M NOT PLAYING ANY MORE! YOU'RE ALL FUCKING PSYCHO!
NOW, GIRLS. APOLOGIZE TO YOUR MOTHER, JENNY...

AND I DON'T CARE WHO YOU ARE YOU OLD BURNED OUT, SENILE GRINNING SKULL TV FOSSIL!
INSOLENT CHILD!
WHACK!
MRS. WATKINS. YOU...
GET UP, YOUNG ONE, AND I'LL SHOW YOU THE KIND OF THRASHING MY MOTHER USED TO GIVE ME!

OH, SHIT, MS. TUCKER. IS SHE...?
CRYSTAL? WHAT ARE YOU DOING HE...? NO, SHE'S NOT...
INSOLENT LITTLE SCAMP. I OUGHT TO...

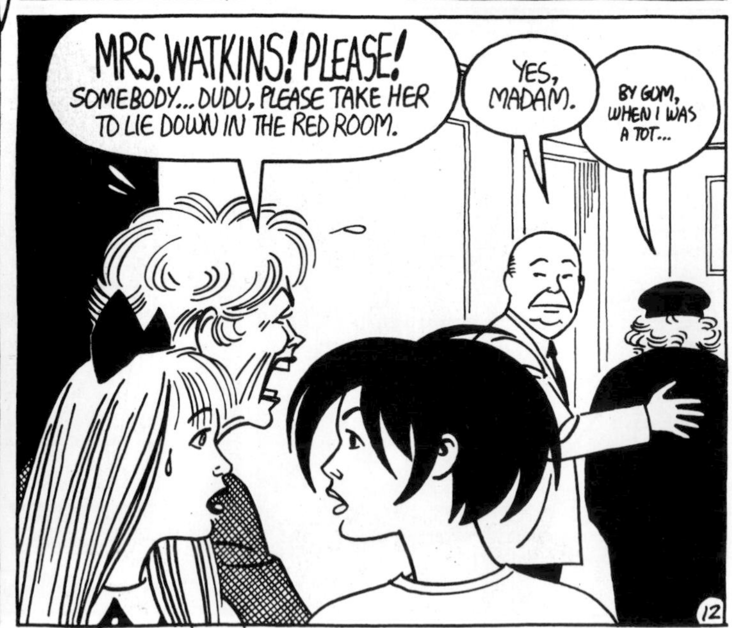
MRS. WATKINS! PLEASE! SOMEBODY... DUDU, PLEASE TAKE HER TO LIE DOWN IN THE RED ROOM.
YES, MADAM.
BY GUM, WHEN I WAS A TOT...
12

WHERE'S NAN?

NAN'S WORLD

I DON'T KNOW. DOES IT MATTER?
GOOD NIGHT, DAFFY.
NO, I GUESS NOT.
GOOD NIGHT, IZZY.
UCL

MAN, I'LL BET JENNY COLLECTS A SHITLOAD OUTTA COURT, HUH, CRYS?
SURE, THAT'S WHAT THOSE OLD BITCHES WOULD LIKE US TO THINK.
$1.50
RNANDO

YOU DON'T THINK THEY'D TRY TO DENY IT. I MEAN, YOU SAW THE AMBULANCE AN'...
ALL I SAW WAS JENNY LAYING THERE LIKE A FUCKIN' CORPSE! YOU SAW IT YOURSELF, AND SO DID NAN...

RELAX, TEXAS. I'LL JUST CALL JEWEL WHEN SHE GETS BACK FROM EL SWANKOS AND WE'LL FIND OUT WHAT REALLY HAPPENED, OK, DUDE?
OK, HOPEY.
KNOCK KNOCK

HOLD ON. THERE'S THE DOOR... ZIP!
TEX, WHY DO YOU EVEN PUT UP WITH ME? I'M JUST ONE SAD, CRAZED STORY AFTER ANOTHER...

I MEAN, I GUESS YOU STICK AROUND 'CAUSE YOU FEEL GUILTY ABOUT ME AND OUR BABY AND... GET THAT... OUR BABY... WHAT A CRACK UP... HEH...

Z Z Z Z Z Z Z Z Z Z Z Z Z Z Z Z Z
14

!

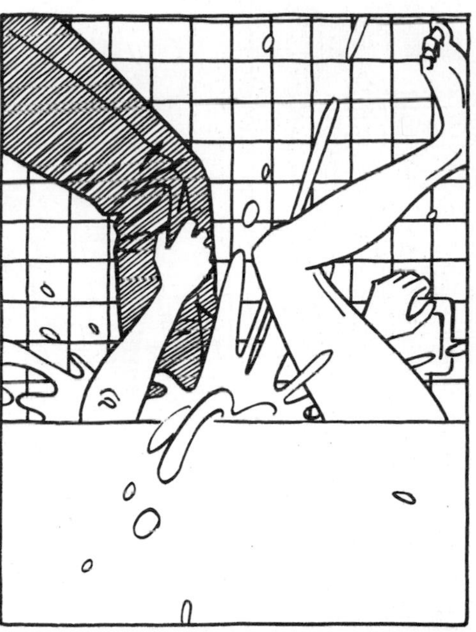

GLUB!
WHA... WHAT THE FUCK ARE YOU DOING?

JUST A REMINDER: THE LADY DOESN'T WANT ANY PUBLICITY, OK? NAN TUCKER'S AN AMERICAN ICON, REMEMBER?

DON'T GET UP.

CHISPA

T-TEX?

EHHH...
15

I JUST DON'T UNDERSTAND THESE KIDS. ANTONIO HAS ALWAYS BEEN SUCH A GOOD BOY.

WHAT KIND OF FRIENDS DOES HE HAVE WHERE THEY ALLOW THIS TO HAPPEN TO MY BABY?
I KNOW, MAMA, I KNOW. SHEEE...

OSPITAL
0605

ENME?

...GONNA MAKE YOU MY MAN...
NAVOR LOPEZ M 1993

YOUR FATHER ASKED ME ABOUT DE MEELK CARTONS TODAY, JOSEPH. I DEEDN'T KNOW WAT TO TELL HEEM...
WHY DIDN'T YOU TELL HIM THE TRUTH, MOM? THAT IT WAS A JOKE...

I DON' KNOW EEF EET'S A JOKE ANY MORE. I GET A STRANGE PHONE CALL THEES MORNING AT SEEX A.M...
SO, WHO WAS IT?

I DON' KNOW. DEY JOST HANG OP...
LOOK, DO YOU WANT ME TO EXPLAIN TO DAD ABOUT THE MILK CARTONS?

MOM...?

OK, OK...
1

IT WAS ME, MOM. I PUT HOPEY'S MUG ON THE MILK CARTONS.
EH?

I PUT HOPEY'S FACE ON THE MILK CARTONS.

YOU TEENK YOU SOOOOOO SMART.

BOY, I WOULDA TOLD HER THAT WEEKS AGO IF I KNEW SHE'D TAKE IT THAT EASY.
...RRRR...

NOW WHAT'S WRONG WITH YOU?
YOU LIED, JOEY! YOU LIED TO YOUR MOTHER! YOU LIED TO ALL YOUR FRIENDS...

C'MON, JANET! YOU KNOW I DIDN'T DO IT! I ONLY TOLD HER I DID SO SHE'LL SLEEP NIGHTS!
I GUESS. IT'S JUST GETTING HARDER TO TELL WHEN YOU'RE LYING OR TELLING THE TRUTH.

OK, THEN YOU GO BACK AND TELL MY MOM I WAS LYING AND THEN YOU GO FIND OUT WHO DID THIS MILK CARTON SHIT, 'CAUSE I'VE HAD IT! I'M OUTTA HERE!
JOEY, I DIDN'T MEAN... COME ON, DON'T BE MAD!
2

hopey monsters
HAVE YOU SEEN ME?
APR 8
w/ BLANK MAGIC AT THE DESPERADO

EXCUSE US, BUT WAS THAT JOEY GLASS YOU WERE TALKING TO?
HOPEY GLASS'S BROTHER JOEY?
UM... YES. IS THAT FLYER YOU GUYS?
YEAH. YOU THINK JOEY WILL BE MAD THAT WE TOTALLY USED HER NAME?

I DON'T... DO YOU KNOW HER?
NOT PERSONALLY, BUT WE USED TO SEE HER BAND "MISSILES OF OCTOBER" WHEN I WAS JUST ELEVEN.
I WAS TEN.
WE USED TO STAND RIGHT IN FRONT AN' YELL YAY HOPEY! SHE WAS OUR GOD!

WE WERE SO CRUSHED WHEN WE HEARD THEY BROKE UP ON TOUR THAT WE PUT A MISSING PERSON REPORT OUT ON HOPEY ON A...
...ON A MILK CARTON.
YEAH, SEE? SIGI'S MOTHER WORKS FOR THE NATIONAL MISSING KIDS CENTER AND WE SNUCK IT IN AS A JOKE.
ALMOST SNUCK IT IN...

WELL, YEAH. BACK THEN WE CHICKENED OUT BUT THEN RECENTLY, FIVE YEARS LATER, SIGI GOT THIS COOL IDEA FOR OUR FIRST RECORD COVER...
TITLED "HAVE YOU SEEN ME?"
YEAH. OH, DID SOMEBODY ALREADY USE THAT IDEA?
3

UM, DO YOU THINK I COULD HAVE ONE OF THOSE FLYERS?
SURE! YOU THINK JOEY WOULD COME TO HEAR US PLAY? WE'LL PUT YOU GUYS ON THE GUEST LIST...

MOM, WHAT'S THE BIG DEAL? I TOLD YOU I DID IT AS A JOKE! C'MON...

BUT, WHY DON'T YOU BELIEVE ME NOW? YOU THOUGHT IT WAS ME AT FIRST...
hopey monsters

FORGET THE CALL AT SIX THIS MORNING! IT WAS A WRONG NUMBER! I'M SURE OF IT, MA...

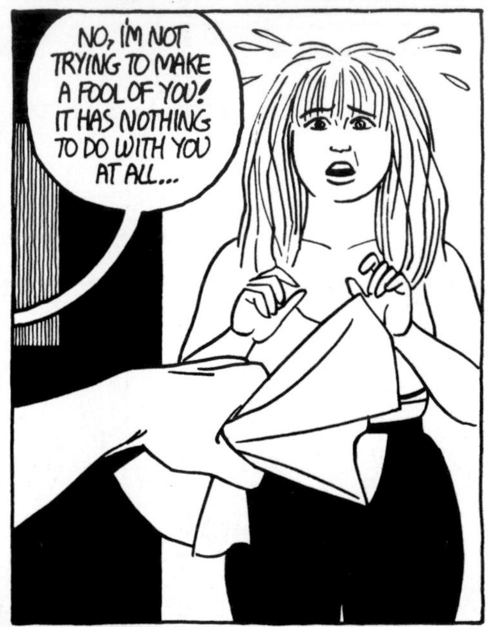
NO, I'M NOT TRYING TO MAKE A FOOL OF YOU! IT HAS NOTHING TO DO WITH YOU AT ALL...

FOR THE THOUSANDTH TIME... MOM! NO...

OK OK! IF I DIDN'T DO IT, WHO DID? HUH?

MA, WILL YOU LISTEN FOR JUST A SECOND? NO, MOM...
XAIME 93

Chester
SQUARE
BE R
WINE
X IME
MOTEL
COIN WASH
1992
MORNING, SARA. HOW'S THE RESTAURANT BUSINESS?
PROBABLY ABOUT THE SAME AS THE MOTEL BUSINESS, ELVA.

SO, HOW'S THE LAUNDROMAT BUSINESS?
PROBABLY ABOUT THE SAME AS THE NEWSSTAND BUSINESS.

THERE SHE IS...
RIGHT ON TIME.

SOMETHING SHOULD BE DONE ABOUT HER.
SO, WHERE'S ALL THAT SECURITY WE PAY FOR?
RIGHT HERE!

AND WHO ARE YOU?
MY FATHER HAS THE FLU, SO I'LL BE IN HIS PLACE TODAY. I'M TITO JR.

WELL... THEN GET TO WORK, TITO JR.
I WON'T LET YOU DOWN, SEÑORAS!

WHO KNOWS, MAYBE HE'LL DO A BETTER JOB THAN TITO SR...
A FROG COULD DO A BETTER JOB THAN...

NOW WHAT?

THIS PLACE IS GOING TO THE DOGS.
TITO JR!

WHAT'S GOING ON?
OH, THE LADY WANTED TO KNOW WHEN THE NEXT BUS COMES.
I'M SURE SHE DID...
2

THOSE GOD DAMN WHORES ARE NOT GOING TO GET AWAY WITH THIS!
SHOULD I CHECK HER OUT, SEÑORA?
WHAT DO YOU THINK, SECURITY OFFICER?

OH!

HEH...

HEH!

3

EXCUSE ME. DO YOU WORK HERE?
UH... YES, OF COURSE! YES...

CAN I GET SOME QUARTERS FOR THE LAUNDRY?
THIS WAY...

THE BUS COMES IN FIVE HOURS.
I KNOW. YOUR SECURITY GUARD TOLD ME...

PRETTY COCKY, ISN'T SHE?
AREN'T THEY ALL?
SARA'S
WASH
MOT

...EL SANTO Y EL CAVERNARIO...
DAVIS INC

SARA, HERE WE COME! BREAK 'EM OUT!
MAN, IS THAT FIRST ONE GONNA TASTE GOOD!

CHUG CHUG CHUG
4

HOW'D YOU LIKE THAT TO SIT ON YOU, EME?
A SLOW AND WONDERFUL DEATH, CHITO.
HM...

WHAT WAS THAT, ENERO?
NOTHING. SHE JUST LOOKS KINDA FAMILIAR, ROSENDO.
¡AI CARAI! EVERYONE LOOKS FAMILIAR TO YOU, ENERO!

SARA'S

DAMN, CHITO. I'M SURE I KNOW THAT GIRL FROM SOMEWHERE.
MUSTA BEEN SOME MOTEL ROOM IN CALIFORNIA.
YOU THINK...?

NAH, SHE AIN'T A WHORE...
WHY DON'T YOU ASK HER AND FIND OUT, ENERO?
ASK WHO?

DON'T YOU GUYS EVER GO HOME TO YOUR WIVES?
NOT WHILE YOU'RE AROUND, RUBY BABY.
HEY, RUBY. WHO'S YOUR FRIEND?

MY FRIE...?

OH OH.
5

I GUESS THEY'RE NOT FRIENDS.
SHIT...

COME ON! LET'S GO! LET'S GO! OUTSIDE!

PICK YOURSELF ANOTHER TOWN, BITCH!

OW! WHAT'D I EVER DO TO YOU??
GET OUT!

WHO ARE YOU?
GET OUT!

GOD DAMN IT! YOU TOUCH ME AGAIN AND I SWEAR I'LL KICK YOUR FUCKING ASS!

OK, WHERE SHOULD I TOUCH YOU, WHORE?

WHEN DOES THAT BUS COME AGAIN?

OH, MAN! BOOM! BOOM! BOOM!
OK OK...
SHIT...
6

AH, YOU GUYS CAN'T TELL ME SHIT, 'CAUSE NONE OF YOU DID ANYTHING TO STOP IT EITHER!
I GOTTA GO.
SARA, ANOTHER ROUND.

WELL, AT LEAST ONE OF YOU CARES ABOUT GOING HOME TO YOUR WIVES AND KIDS.
BEER'S BETTER HERE.

ARE YOU SURE YOU'RE ALL RIGHT?
YEAH. OK IF I TAKE A NAP ON THAT CHAIR TILL THAT BUS COMES?

THE BUS WON'T BE HERE FOR THREE HOURS. MAYBE YOU'LL WANT A ROOM TILL THEN? I'LL ONLY CHARGE YOU HALF.
I'M FINE.

HOW MUCH FOR THAT ROOM, AGAIN?
7

CAN YOU SEND SOMEONE TO WAKE ME A HALF HOUR BEFORE THE BUS COMES?
FOUR-THIRTY. YES.
SHOULD I STICK CLOSE TO HER ROOM?
FORGET HER! DID YOU SEE WHAT THAT OTHER ONE DID AT SARA'S?
HEY, ENERO! YOUR MYSTERY GIRL JUST GOT HERSELF A ROOM!
DON'T WORRY. IT'LL COME BACK TO ME.
WELL, WHILE YOU'RE TRYING TO REMEMBER... SARA! ANOTHER ROUND!
DON'T YOU GUYS EVER GO HOME TO YOUR FAMILIES?
EXCUSE ME, MA'AM, BUT I UNDERSTAND THERE WAS A DISTURBANCE IN HERE EARLIER, AND...
SO? WHAT ARE YOU GOING TO DO?
BUD
WELL, I'M JUST GIVING YOU A WARNING...
AH, GET OUT OF HERE, YOU STINKING COP, BEFORE I... GET OUT!
NICE TRY, OFFICER! YOU ALMOST HAD HER!
HOO! HOO!
SO, CHITO. HAVE YOU HEARD FROM YOUR OLD LADY IN MEXICO?
YEAH, I GOT ANOTHER LITTLE ONE ON THE WAY...
8

ANOTHER ONE? MAN, HOW DO YOU DO IT WHEN YOU'RE OVER HERE AN' SHE'S OVER THERE?
LOTS OF DAYS OFF?
YOU GOT IT, CHARLIE BROWN! SARA!

SO STUPID...

SO FUCKING STUPID... SO GOD DAMN FUCKING STUPID...

STUPID...

SO, HOW OLD ARE YOU, TITO JR?
NINETEEN, SEÑORA.

SO, YOU WANT TO BE A SECURITY OFFICER JUST LIKE YOUR DAD, EH?
I GUESS. NOT MUCH ELSE TO DO...

ARE YOU MARRIED?
NO, SEÑORA.
HAVE A GIRLFRIEND?
NO, SEÑORA.
EVER HAD A GIRLFRIEND?
....
SARA'S
9

WELL, WHEN YOU DO, FIND A GIRL, PROMISE ME YOU'LL STICK TO HER AND NOT END UP LIKE THOSE VIPERS WITH THEIR WHORES.
TITO JR!

ELVA NEEDS YOU. DIDN'T YOU HEAR HER?
I'M GOING.

?!?

WHERE THE HELL AM I...?

OH, THE SEÑORA WENT HOME TO FEED HER FAMILY.
WHAT TIME IS IT?
MARISCO TAM

SIX FORTY-FIVE, A.M.
NINE-THIRTY-SIX.
WHEN DOES THE NEXT BUS COME BY?
NGHHH

OH, THAT'S RIGHT...
10

HOO HOO!

OH, WELL. TWO DOWN, THREE TO GO...
IT'S OK, SARA! MINE AN' ENERO'S FAMILIES ARE BACK IN MEXICO AN' EME'S WIFE LEFT HIS SORRY ASS...
TSK!

BUT, SERIOUS, CHITO. YOU SHOULD BE WITH YOUR WIFE WHEN SHE HAS HER BABY, MAN...
WE ALREADY GOT FOUR. SHE KNOWS HOW TO DO IT BY NOW, EME...

NAW, NAW, MAN! 'CAUSE LOOK AT ME! I DID JUST WHAT YOU'RE DOING, AN'...
I GOT IT! YEAH! HEY...

AW, GET OFF ME, MAN! YOU DON'T KNOW HOW IT IS...
NO, NO! I REMEMBER NOW! LISTEN...

HA HA HA HA

FUCKIN' SLOBS... THINK I'M SOME KINDA WHORE, HUH?

OH, IF YOU FUCKERS ONLY KNEW WHAT YOU'RE MISSING...OH, MAN...

OK...OK...
11

COME AN' GET IT, YOU FUCKING DORKS...

KNOK! KNOK! KNOK!
EET!

WHO'S THERE?
I JUST WANNA ASK YOU SOMETHING. YOU'RE MAGGIE, RIGHT?

WHO'S ASKING?
I USED TO LIVE IN CALIFORNIA WITH MY BROTHERS. YOU FIXED OUR TRUCK ONCE. YOU'RE A MECHANIC...

THE GUYS ARE OK. THEY JUST WANNA MEET YOU. THEY NEVER MET A GIRL MECHANIC BEFORE. WE JUST WANNA BUY YOU A DRINK.

MAYBE I'LL COME OUT LATER.
OK. WE'LL JUST BE OUT HERE...

ARE YOU STILL HERE?
I-I DON'T KNOW WHEN I'M SUPPOSED TO GET OFF...
12

GO HOME, TITO JR. BUT, FIRST MAKE YOUR FINAL ROUNDS.
YES, SEÑORA.

A NEW LITTLE ONE... ON THE WAY...

YEAH, I REMEMBER YOU...
YEAH. YOU WANT A DRINK?

THE GUYS WOULD BE REALLY EXCITED TO MEET A GIRL MECHANIC ...IF THEY WERE AWAKE...
13

UH... HEH! I... DON'T HAVE ANY MORE MONEY...

WELL, YOU DIDN'T THINK YOU WERE GETTING A FREEBIE, DID YOU?

AW, SHIT! I BLEW IT, DIDN'T I, GUYS?

HEY, SECURITY.

Y-YES, SEÑORA? CAN I HELP YOU?
CAN'T GET MY KEY TO OPEN THE DOOR.
14

THERE YOU ARE, SEÑORA.
YOU OFF?

Y-YEAH, I WAS JUST ABOUT...

JUST RELAX. DON'T WORRY ABOUT A THING...

KNOK! KNOK!

THE BUS WILL BE HERE IN A HALF HOUR, MISS.
THANK YOU.

15

MICRO T. ARCE

MASAMI

THE
END

LA CASA DE NACHO Y QUINA CHASCARRILLO...
ATTABOY, COMPADRE! SHE'S A BEAUTY!
MARGARITA LUISA CHASCARRILLO!
HOME COME HER HEAD IS SO ROUND?
SHE LOOKS LIKE PEANUTS!
ISABEL! CHEPA! GET AWAY FROM THERE!
EVERYBODY OUT! LET THE BABY SLEEP!

VICKI, WHAT ARE YOU GOING TO DO NOW THAT YOU'RE OUT OF HIGH SCHOOL?
WELL...
YOU WANT ME TO TELL THEM?

GATHER AROUND, EVERYBODY! I WANT YOU ALL TO HEAR WHAT MY DAUGHTER WANTS TO DO NOW THAT SHE'S OUT OF HIGH SCHOOL...
PAPA POCHENCHO SPEAKS!
EXCUSE ME...

SHE WANTS TO BE A PROFESSIONAL WRESTLER, JUST LIKE ON TV...
THANKS, POPS.
GASP
HA HA HA!
¡AHUA!
GORGEOUS GEORGE!

YOU WILL NOT BE A WRESTLER.
IT'S TOO LATE. I ALREADY WON SIXTEEN MATCHES, PAPA.

YOU WILL NOT BE A WRESTLER.
I WILL. AND I'LL BE BETTER THAN EL SANTO, BOBO BRAZIL AND RENA TITAÑON COMBINED, EH, MARGARITA?
POOT!
1

Chester
SQUARE
BE R
WING
MOTEL

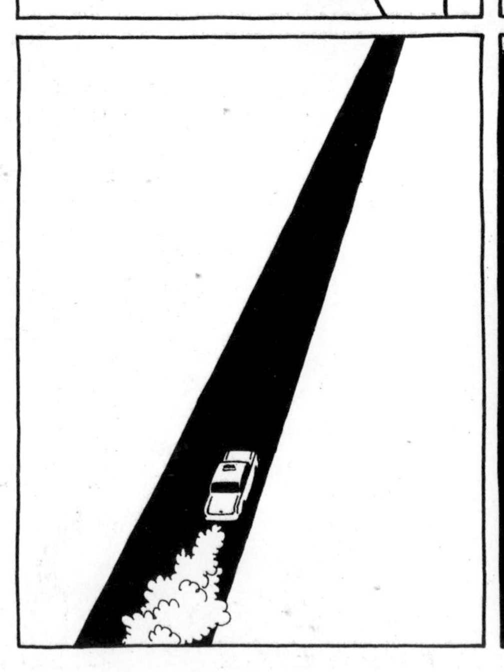

CAMP VICKI
TRESPASSERS WILL
BE BULLDOGGED
SENCILLO 93
2

WHICH ONE'S MY COUSIN, TIA? I HAVEN'T SEEN HER SINCE WE WERE ELEVEN.
THE ONE THAT KEEPS FALLING ON HER EYES INSTEAD OF HER FEET...
C'MON, XOCHITL! MIX IT UP!
OK, TIA... I MEAN... COACH.
CAMP VICKI

TSK! SAME OL' XO. SHE WAS NEVER VERY COORDINATED AS A KID. SHE FELL DOWN ALL THE TIME.
YES, BUT SHE NEVER CRIED.
I THINK I ALMOST GOT HER, COACH!
CAMP VICKI

YOU KNOW, YOU COULD PICK UP A FEW THINGS WHILE YOU'RE HERE, SHRIMP. COULD COME IN HANDY ONE DAY, YA NEVER KNOW...
ANYTIME, XO!
JMMMM...

YAK!
OK, GIRLS... CLAUDIA, THAT'S ENOUGH.

PERLA, YOU LOOK JUST LIKE A WRESTLER!
SO DO YOU, XO... SORT OF.
SO, COACH! HAVE YOU DECIDED WHO GETS TO GO AGAINST GINA FRIDAY NIGHT?
YEAH, XO GOES...
CAMP VI
3

YOU GOT THAT, GINA? XO? BE SURE TO GIVE 'EM AT LEAST TEN MINUTES OF NON-STOP, OK?
OK!
...OK.
WAIT A MINUTE! THAT IS NOT FAIR, COACH!
MOTLEY CRÜE

YOU HAVE A COMPLAINT, CLAUDIA?
EVERYBODY KNOWS I'M THE ONLY ONE HERE GOOD ENOUGH TO TAKE ON GINA! DO I GOTTA TAKE ON THE WHOLE CAMP...?
CAMP VICKI

I'LL PUT YOU AGAINST HEIDI ON THE NEXT CARD...
I KNOW WHAT YOU'RE DOING! YOU'RE BEING RACIST!

I'M WHAT?

I'M WHAT?

SEE? YOU CAN'T EVEN WHIP AN OLD LADY!

SO, ARE YOU TRAINING WITH US TOMORROW, OR WHAT? AINT NO SLOUCHES ALLOWED AT CAMP VICKI, Y'KNOW!
SAY WHAT?
4

LISTEN, ROOKIE. AFTER I KICK YOUR BUTT HERE, HOW ABOUT IF I TEACH YOU A FEW MORE THINGS BACK IN THE LOCKER ROOM, EH?
OH YEAH?

TAKE THAT, YOU FLAMING QUEER.
YO' WINNAH... COWGIRL VICKI LAAAANE!!!

HELL'S BELLS, VICKI! YOU WRESTLED THAT MATCH LIKE IT WAS YOUR LAST!
LAST MATCH FOR PEANUTS.
I DON'T SUPPOSE IT'S 'CAUSE YOU HEARD WHO'S IN THE BUILDING TONIGHT, VICK...

RENA TITAÑON?? HERE??
AND RUMOR HAS IT SHE'S LOOKING FOR A TAG PARTNER, RIGHT, VICK?
LANE, COME IN MY OFFICE.
COMIN', MR. BAIN!
CLICK

HAVE A SEAT, VICKI.
Y'SIR.

DROP THE COWBOY SHIT, CHANGE YOUR HAIR COLOR, CHANGE YOUR LAST NAME, CHANGE EVERYTHING...
YOU'RE IN THE BIG TIME NOW, KID. RIGHT, RENA?
5

CAMP VICKI

CAMP VICKI

CAMP VICKI

WHAT'S THIS GONNA HELP ME DO, OUTRUN ANY ATTACKER?
CAMP VICKI

YOU GOTTA BE THE WORST BUNCHA NANCYS I EVER HAD THE DISPLEASURE OF TRAINING.
NONE OF YOU WOULD LAST TWO MINUTES WITH THE LADIES OF MY DAY.

WHEN RENA AND I HELD THOSE TAG BELTS WE HAD THE MEANEST, TOUGHEST OPPONENTS THIS SIDE OF...
I'LL BET THOSE OPPONENTS HATED RENA FOR HOGGING BOTH THE TAG AND WORLD BELT...
WELL, SURE, BUT NONE OF 'EM COULD BEAT HER FOR 'EM EITHER!
COACH
CAMP VICKI

TO ANOTHER CHAMPIONSHIP YEAR, EH, QUEENIE?
ONLY SEVEN MORE YEARS AND WE BREAK THE ELEVEN YEAR TAG RECORD HELD BY ITZY AND BITZY KAZINAFEK BACK IN '57...
THERE THEY ARE! THE TIGRESSES THAT TOSSED OUR BUTTS UP AND DOWN THAT RING TONIGHT!
WE TOAST YOU, TIGRESSESS-ESSES!

WHY DON'T YOU GUYS GET THE HELL OUTTA HERE BEFORE YOU FORCE US TO DO IT AGAIN!
LISTEN, SWEETIE. WE AIN'T IN THE RING NO MORE, SO WHY DON'T WE JUST KISS AND MAKE UP?

VICKI, WHAT THE HELL IS WRONG WITH YOU? DON'T YOU KNOW WHEN YOU'RE BEING COMMENDED?
DON'T YOU KNOW WHEN YOU'RE BEING COME ONTO TO?

LOOK AT THAT DISGUSTING... I'M SO SICK OF IT! LET ME OUTTA HERE!

IS RENA COMIN' WITH US, VICKI?
NAW, SHE'S TURNIN' IN EARLY... AGAIN!

SO, WHO THE HELL'S HER BOYFRIEND? SOME MYSTERY MAN...?
BEATS ME. I'VE KNOWN HER FOR FIVE YEARS AND I'VE NEVER KNOWN HER TO...
OH, GOD...
7

FRIDAY NIGHT...
YAK!

GEE, XO. I DIDN'T MEAN TO...
COACH SAID NEVER TO APOLOGIZE FOR WINNING, GINA. REMEMBER...
WHAT DO YOU GUYS DO FOR EXCITEMENT IN THIS TOWN?
MAX THE IRON MAN

THE BELLE AIRE HOTEL. THIS IS WHERE THE WRESTLERS STAY WHEN THEY'RE IN TOWN, RIGHT, GINA?
RIGHT.
HEY, IS THAT EL SICODELICO, OR IS IT MICRO SICODELICO?

THEY'RE PREPARING YOU TO BE THE NEXT TEXAS CHAMPION AND YOU'RE ONLY EIGHTEEN? I THINK THAT'S SO COOL, GINA.
YEAH, BUT THAT MEANS FOR THE NEXT MONTH I GOTTA WOOP XO'S BUTT UP AND DOWN THE STATE OF TEXAS...

I DUNNO, ME AN' XO GOT INTO WRESTLING 'CAUSE WE WERE GONNA BE A TAG TEAM, NOT OPPONENTS! I DON'T WANNA WOOP HER! I-I LOVE HER WAY TOO MUCH, PERLA...

WHAT? WHAT'S WRONG WITH THAT?

OH.
8

MY GOD! THIS PROFESSION HAS BEEN OVERRUN BY QUEERS! EVERYBODY'S A QUEER!
EVEN MY OWN PARTNER, THE LIVING LEGEND HERSELF, QUEEN RENA. SHE MUST BE! ALL THE SIGNS ARE THERE!
SO, WHAT DO I DO? DO I STAY AND BASK IN ALL THIS GLORY, OR DO I QUIT, GO SINGLE AND START BACK AT THE BOTTOM AGAIN??
AND WHAT ABOUT THESE HOGG SISTERS? ARE THEY? DO I WANNA CONTINUE TO WRESTLE QUEER OPPONENTS??
...OR DO I QUIT THE ONE SPORT I'VE LOVED SINCE I WAS SIX?
DO... I... WAN'...?
DON' WAN'... NO MO'... NO... NO MO'...
THE WINNERS AND NEW LADIES TAG TEAM CHAMPIONS... THE HOGG SISTERS!!!
9

RELAX, GINA. I PROMISE I WON'T TELL XO WHAT YOU SAID.
WHOOSH!
YOU BETTER NOT, OR I SWEAR I'LL PILEDRIVE YOU OFF THE ROOF, PERLA.

AS BUFFED AS YOU ARE, GINA, YOU COULD PILEDRIVE HAYSTACK CALHOUN. CHECK IT OUT...
NOW YOU'RE MAKING FUN OF ME, PERLA.

NO NO NO... LISTEN, YOU EVER BEEN TO CHESTER SQUARE?
STOPPED BY TO BUY A SODA ONCE OR TWICE. WHY?

WELL, THERE'S THIS REAL BITCH OF A WHORE THERE...
PROSTITUTE.
PROS... OK...

WELL... NO, WAIT! OK, SINCE YOU TOLD ME A SECRET, I'M GONNA TELL YOU ONE, OK...?
OK.

DOWN AT CHESTER SQUARE THERE'S LIKE, THIS BOY OF A SECURITY GUARD THAT I LIKE, SORTA TOOK TO BED WITH ME...
THAT'S THE SECRET?

NO NO NO... AN' I TOOK MONEY FOR IT... HYAK!
OHHH... THAT'S THE SECRET.

NO NO NO... THE REAL SECRET IS THAT I REALLY DIDN'T FEEL BAD ABOUT DOING IT. LIKE IT WAS NO BIG DEAL.

I'M A WHORE, GINA.
TROLLOP, FLOOZY, HARLOT, DOXY, COCETTE, CHIPPIE...
PROSTITUTE.
10

RENA'S WILLING TO FORGET EVERYTHING THAT HAPPENED THAT NIGHT, VICKI.
SO, WHY DON'T Y'ALL MAKE UP AN' GET THOSE TAG BELTS BACK?
AFTER WHAT SHE DID HERE? NO WAY...
OK, HAVE FUN WRESTLING BACK AT THE ELK'S LODGE IN HUERTA, CALIFORNIA WHERE YOU CAME FROM...
YOU PEOPLE DON'T GET IT, DO YA? I WANT HER WORLD BELT!
OH, GOOD NIGHT!
VICKI, RENA'S WORLD BELT AIN'T JUST ANY WORLD BELT. IT IS THE WOOOOORLD BELT...
HOW DO YOU EXPECT TO GET A SHOT AT HER SO FAST?
WATCH ME.
11

...AND THEN YOU COULD GET THAT WH... PROS-TITUTE IN A BOSTON CRAB AND THEN I COULD GRAB A CHAIR AN'...
I CAN DO THAT.
YOU GUYS READY TO GO? ALL THESE GUYS CARE ABOUT IS NEXT WEEK'S CARD.

XO, WE WANNA GO TO CHESTER SQUARE.
WE CAN'T, PERLA. ME AN' GINA SHOULDA BEEN IN BED BY ELEVEN.

SAME OL' CRAZY PERLA. IF TIA FINDS OUT WE'RE NOT IN BED...
I AIN'T ONE OF HER RASSLERS. I'M GOING TO CHESTER SQUARE.

TAKE ME TO THE BELLE AIRE...

12

NEED A CAB, MISS?
PLEASE.

CAMP VICKI
TRESPASSERS WILL BE BULLDOGGED

I'M GONNA LET HER WIN TOMORROW NIGHT.
13

...THREE!
UNBELIEVABLE, TARZAN GOVENDER! AFTER SIXTEEN YEARS WE NOW HAVE A NEW LADIES CHAMPION!
BUT, LOOK! VICKI HAS HER FEET ON THE ROPES UNBEKNOWNST TO THE REFEREE!

I HOPE YOU REALIZE YOU ARE NOW THE MOST HATED WOMAN IN THE WORLD, VICKI.
IF I GOTTA, I GOTTA.
BE CAREFUL WITH THE REMATCH. RENA NEVER LETS ANYONE GET AWAY WITH ANYTHING TWICE.
YEAH, YEAH. SCRAM. I VANT TO BE ALONE.
WORLD

UH... SOMEONE TO SEE YOU, VICK.
RENA?
VICKI.

WELL WELL. TO WHOM DO I OWE THE HONOR OF THIS GRAND VISIT?
I JUST CAME BY TO WISH YOU LUCK WITH YOUR NEW TITLE.

YOU AIN'T SORE?
NOPE.
YOU DON'T WANT A REMATCH?
NOT YET.
OK, I GIVE.
I'M IN LOVE, YOU DOPE!

YOU'D EASILY GIVE UP A CHANCE TO GET YOUR TITLE BACK FOR A LOUSY LOVE AFFAIR? HOO BOY!
LET ME EXPLAIN SOMETHING TO YOU...
14

I'VE BEEN IN THIS PROFESSION SINCE I WAS FOURTEEN. I WON THE WORLD TITLE WHEN I WAS TWENTY-TWO. I HELD THAT TITLE FOR SIXTEEN YEARS. FOR TWENTY-FOUR YEARS ALL I HAD ON MY MIND WAS WRESTLING, WRESTLING, WRESTLING...
SO YOU TOLD ME, TOLD ME, TOLD ME...

LET'S PUT IT THIS WAY: IT'S NOT EVERYDAY A FELLA COMES INTO MY LIFE THAT I CAN'T BEAT UP...
WAIT, YOU DID SAY FELLA...?

BY THE WAY, I SHOULD REALLY PASTE YOU A GOOD ONE FOR THAT RUMOR YOU'VE BEEN SPREADING ABOUT MY SEXUAL PREFERENCE.
OK, SO YOU AIN'T QUEER! HOW WAS I TO KNOW? EVERYBODY AND THEIR MOTHER IS QUEER NOW-ADAYS!

YOU'RE PATHETIC, YOU KNOW THAT?
I'M PATHETIC?? YOU'RE THE ONE WHO CAN'T EVEN HOLD A MAN AND A WORLD TITLE AT THE SAME TIME!

I'M ALSO PREGNANT, DAMN IT.
BINGO!
PATHETIC, TITLELESS AND PREGNANT!

HAVE FUN WITH YOUR TITLE, VICKI... WHILE YOU STILL GOT IT...
15

BUT- BUT DIDN'T RENA EVER TRY TO GET HER TITLE BACK AFTER THAT?
NO. AFTER SHE HAD HER KID SHE GOT WRAPPED UP IN INTERNATIONAL AFFAIRS AND ALL THAT KINDA STUFF...
BUT, WAIT, TIA. TELL ME AGAIN ABOUT YOUR TITLE REIGN...
LOOK, SHRIMP. I'D LOVE TO TELL YOU MY LIFE STORY BUT I GOTTA LOOK IN ON GINA AN' XO'S MATCH.
CAMP VICKI
YAK!
EXCUSE US A MINUTE, SHRIMP.
CAMP VICKI
GINA.
PERLA.
CAMP VICKI
SO, YOU DID IT...
YEP.
CAMP VICKI
YOU KNOW YOU BLEW YOUR CHANCE AT THE TEXAS TITLE.
YEP.
CAMP VICKI
XO REALLY MEANS THAT MUCH TO YOU, HUH?
YEP.
CAMP VICKI
YOU KNOW, SOME SAY YOU SHOULD NEVER FALL IN LOVE WITH YOUR BEST FRIEND.
HMF.
CAMP VICKI
...THE WINNER AND NEW TEXAS WOMEN'S CHAMPION... CLAUDIA CASEY!
THE END

PERLA AND BEATRÍZ
MR. Z.D. 93

EXCUSE ME A MINUTE, WILL YOU, FELLAS?
BUT OF COURSE, MRS. COSTIGAN.
BY ALL MEANS, MRS. COSTIGAN.
HEP!

A PENNY CENTURY FOR YOUR THOUGHTS, QUERIDA?
DO ALL YOUR PARTIES HAVE JUST OLD GUYS?

MAGGIE, YOU NEED CHEERING UP, PENNY STYLE.
BUT, I DON'T FEEL LIKE WATCHING BENNY HILL!

SO, WHAT'S YOUR NEW BODY-GUARD'S NAME?
I DON'T KNOW YET. HE DOESN'T SPEAK A WORD OF ENGLISH OR SPANISH.
79
MUJERCITA

SO, TELL ME IF I'M WRONG, BUT ISN'T YOUR OLD BODYGUARD PETE THE FATHER OF YOUR UPCOMING CHILD?
YES. BUT AS YOU CAN SEE, PETE'S NO LONGER WITH US.
1

THEN, HE REALLY HIGHTAILED IT...?
PTCH! I SENT HIM BACK TO HIS WIFE AND KIDS. HERV'S GONNA PLAY THE DADDY WHETHER HE LIKES IT OR NOT, THE OLD GOAT...

TELL THE TRUTH. DID YOU PLAN TO GIVE CLARITA A MEXICAN/BLACK SISTER OR BROTHER JUST LIKE HER?
ONCE YOU'VE HAD BLACK YOU'RE NEVER GOIN' BACK.

IS TWO GONNA BE IT, OR..?
ARE YOU KIDDING? I'M GONNA HAVE SO MANY KIDS THE NAME CENTURY'S GONNA BECOME IT'S OWN RACE!
SO, I HOPE YOU BROUGHT A CAMERA 'CAUSE THIS IS THE LAST TIME YOU'LL EVER SEE ME LIKE THIS...

IN ABOUT A MONTH, MY BELLY'S GONNA SWELL UP SO BIG I'M GONNA LOOK LIKE JACKIE GLEASON ON A GOOD DAY. THEN, AFTER MY BABY'S BORN, IT'S EVERY MAN FOR HIMSELF...
OH, YOU STILL GOT SEVERAL GOOD SVELTE YEARS IN YOU, QUERIDA.

NOPE. NO MORE WORKING OUT FOR ME. I'VE HAD IT. I'M GONNA LET MYSELF GET SO FAT YOU'RE NOT GONNA RECOGNIZE ME...
YOU THINK HERV'S STILL GONNA WANT YOU?

ARE YOU KIDDING? HERV ONCE TOLD ME HE'D STILL WANT ME IF I SOMEHOW ENDED UP LOOKING LIKE SHEMP.
OH, YEAH. HE ONLY TOLD YOU THAT 'CAUSE YOU LOOK LIKE YOU!
2

YOU GUYS WILL NEVER GIVE HERV A BREAK. NONE OF YOU EVEN CAME TO OUR WEDDING...
NONE OF US WERE INVITED TO YOUR WEDDING!

YOU'RE RIGHT. THAT WAS JUST A REAL FUCKED UP TIME IN MY LIFE. I ONLY MARRIED HERV 'CAUSE I THOUGHT IT WOULD MAKE THINGS NORMAL, BUT IF IT WEREN'T FOR MY BABIES... AND YOU GUYS...
PENNY, YOU DON'T HAVE TO... I HAVE AN IDEA...

COME ON, PENNY. LET ME CHEER YOU UP, MAGGIE STYLE.
HESBY HIGH SCHOOL
PRO WRESTLING
SAT NITE
HOMECOMING FRI

MAGGIE, YOUR COUSIN DOESN'T LOOK LIKE SHE'S WIN-NING VERY GOOD.
YEAH, BUT SHE LOSES A LOT BETTER SINCE SHE TURNED HEEL.

THAT'S IT? SHE WAS ROOKED! THE UMPIRE DIDN'T COUNT ALL THE WAY UP TO TEN!
LET'S GO MEET HER IN THE BACK AND SEE WHAT'S GOING ON TONIGHT.

GREAT MATCH, XO. YOU WOULDA WON IF SHE DIDN'T BEAT YOU.
PERLA, YOU LOOK LIKE YOU'RE READY TO HIT UP THE TOWN. SURE WISH I COULD GO WITH YOU...
3

MARIO AND THE KIDS ARE BACK FROM MEXICO SO I GOTTA BE A GOOD GIRL AND GO BACK TO BEING A PART-TIME HOUSEWIFE.
WELL, OK. TELL 'EM I SAID HI AND ALL THAT...
WHAT WAS THAT NAME SHE CALLED YOU?
PERLA. THAT'S WHAT PEOPLE CALL ME WHO KNEW ME WAY BACK WHEN.
OK, I KNOW YOU GET MAGGIE FROM MARGARITA, BUT HOW DO YOU GET PERLA FROM MAGGIE?
PTCH! MAGGIE WAS A JOKE NAME LOUIS FROM SAL'S GARAGE GAVE ME THAT IZZY THOUGHT WAS CUTE AND IT JUST KINDA STUCK...
POPCORN $25
HOT DOG 30
SOFT DRINKS 80
YOU MEAN, ALL THIS TIME YOU LET US CALL YOU MAGGIE AND YOU HATED IT?
OH, IT'S OK FOR YOU GUYS. I GOT USED TO IT...
MAGGIE'S FOR SKINNY SHORT HAIRED PUNK CHICKS WHO HAVE A KNACK FOR FIXING MACHINES.
WELL, DANG! I'M CALLING YOU PERLA FROM NOW ON.
SO, SHOULD I PREFER TO BE CALLED BEATRIZ?
COME TO THINK OF IT, YOU DON'T LOOK LIKE A MAGPIE ANY MORE, PERLITA...
BUT, YOU'LL ALWAYS LOOK LIKE A PENNY CENTURY, FATTY OR NO FATTY, BEATRIZITA.
END

EASTER HUNT
XAIME 93

HI.
HI.
DOA

A MAP!
OH!

APRUL FOOL! HAR! HAR!
APRIL
1
CALENDAR

THERE'S HOOK!
YEAH, DE BUM!
DOA

FIRE ONE!
DOA

1

WHAT DID YOU DO TO MY SON?
WHAP!
DOA
LET'S BUILD SOMETHING!
DOA
DOA
2

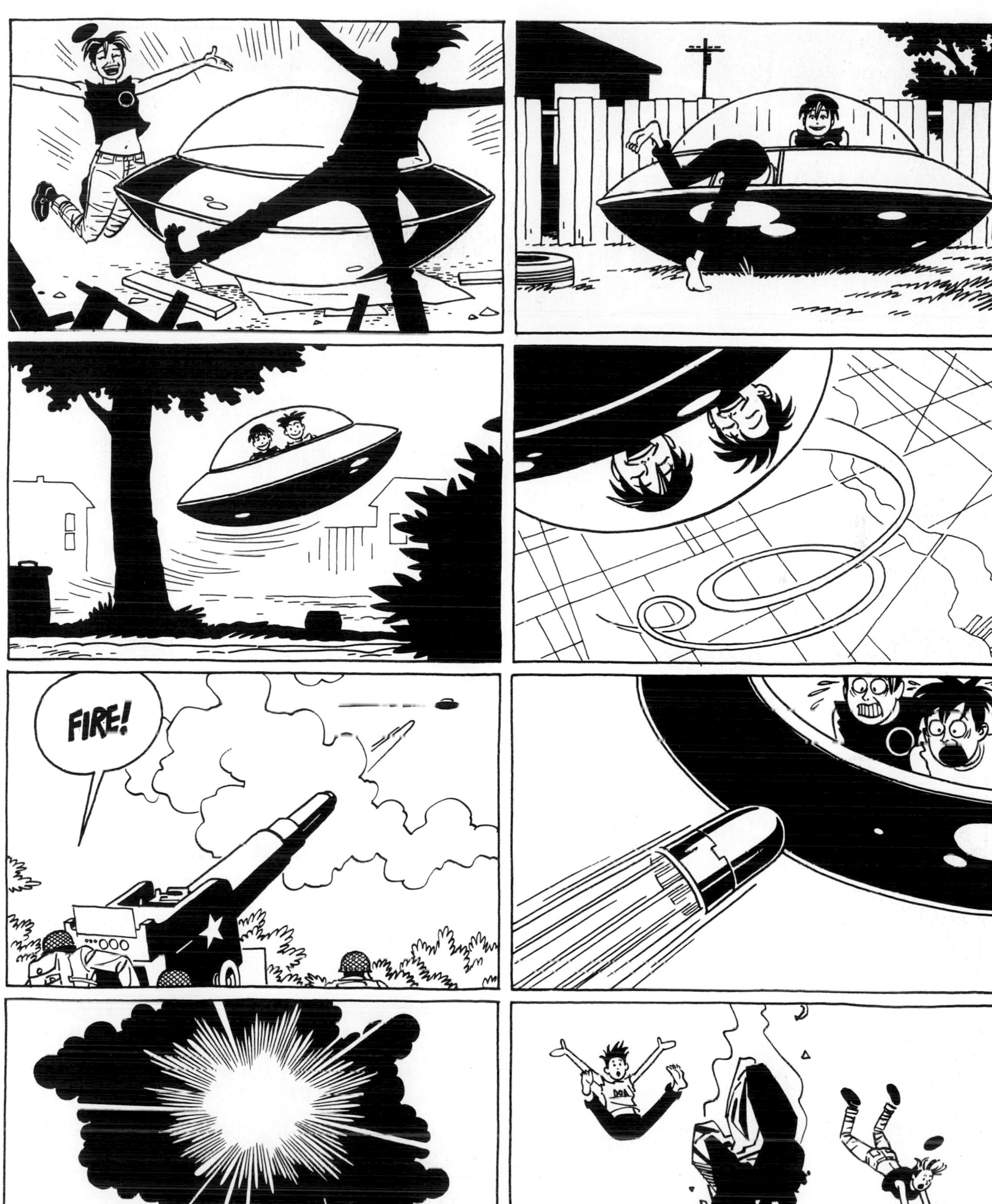
FIRE!
DOA
3

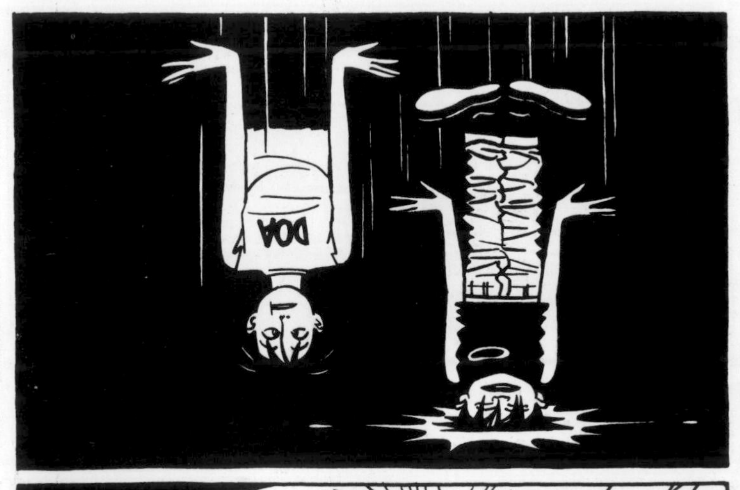

BAM BAM BAM BAM BAM BAM BAM BAM
BAM BAM BAM BAM BAM BAM BAM BAM BAM BAM BAM BAM
BAM BAM BAM BAM BAM BAM
BAM BAM BAM BAM BAM BAM BAM BAM BAM BAM BAM BAM
BAM BAM BAM BAM BAM BAM BAM BAM 4

DOA

MPHGHHH!
DOA

DOA
CHILINDRINA

HELP!

CHOMP!

HEE HEE!

LET'S GO ON AN EASTER HUNT!
5

WE GOT A LOT!
YES!
DOA

Let's Eat!

AHH...
YES, AHH...
DOA

HI!
HI!
DOA

DOA

THE END
WRITTEN AND ORIGINALLY DRAWN BY BETO SOMETIME AROUND 1967
DRAWN BY XAIME IN 1993

MAGGIE THE MECHANIC
OR
PERLA THE PROSTITUTE
LIL JOTITO
93

PENNY, LUZ AND I ARE DOING LUNCH AT FRITO'S, WHERE THE FOOD DOESN'T BITE BACK LIKE HERE. SEE YOU IN A BIT...
I WANNA GO TO LUNCH, TOO, PERLA! LUCKY DUCKS!

CRASH
HOLD ON A MINUTE, LUZ...

LOOKED TO ME LIKE YOU GOT FIRED ON PURPOSE...
I DIDN'T WANNA MISS LUNCH.
YOU LASTED EXACTLY TWO HOURS AND THREE MINUTES ON THIS JOB. THAT'S GOTTA BE SOME KINDA RECORD...
EAT

YOU ALREADY GOT YOUR WAGES, TOO. HOW MUCH?
A FIVE, NINE ONES AND LOTSA CHANGE!
YOU ACT LIKE YOU'VE NEVER SEEN MONEY BEFORE.
RIT

ACTUALLY, PENNY LITERALLY HAS NOT SEEN ANY CASH FOR QUITE A FEW YEARS. THEN, YOU WOULDN'T EITHER IF YOU WERE MARRIED TO HERV R. COSTIGAN.
A REAL TIGHTWAD, HUH?
I FORGOT LINCOLN'S ON THE FIVE...
1

WELL, NOT EXACTLY. HE JUST DOESN'T LET HER HANDLE CASH. I MEAN, SHE GETS ANYTHING SHE WANTS...
IF SHE GETS ANYTHING SHE WANTS, HOW COME SHE HAS TO WORK IN A CAFÉ FOR MINIMUM WAGE?
SO, THIS MUST BE MRS. LINCOLN ON THE ONE...
YEAH, PENNY! WHAT ARE YOU DOING HERE? WHAT AM I DOING HERE? WE DON'T NEED NO STINKIN' MINIMUM WAGE WAITRESS JOBS, DO WE?
HECK NO! WE'RE GOING BOWLING!
TSK! THEY'LL BE BACK.
JOB HUNTING WAS NEVER QUITE CHRISTMAS FOR ME, PENNY.
READ WHAT I CIRCLED AT THE BOTTOM AND TELL ME WHAT YOU THINK...
"MECHANIC WANTED." HA HA! VERY FUNNY, PENNY.
WHAT IS SO FUNNY ABOUT YOU APPLYING FOR A JOB YOU'RE QUALIFIED FOR? DAMN IT, PERLA! YOU'RE MAGGIE THE MECHANIC, REMEMBER?
WELL, MAG. PENNY'S RIGHT. RUNNING FROM YOUR PAST JUST DOESN'T CUT IT ANY MORE.
BUT YOU CAN STILL KICK HER IN HER BIG TITS JUST FOR SAYING IT.
BUT, WHAT AM I SO WORRIED ABOUT? IT'S JUST ANOTHER JOB, WHETHER I LAND IT, OR NOT.
IT'S NOT LIKE RAND RACE IS ON THE OTHER SIDE OF THAT DOOR WAITING TO BUST OPEN OLD WOUNDS.
BUT, YOU NEVER KNOW...
2

WHAT THE FUCKING HELL IS THIS GOD DAMN BULLSHIT? YOU TELL THIS FUCKING BROAD TO GO BACK TO HER GOD DAMN KITCHEN! THIS AIN'T NO GOD DAMN MOTHER FUCKING TEA PARTY!

YES SIR!

IF RAND RACE WAS GIVING OUT THE JOB I WOULDA LANDED IT JUST LIKE THAT.

PERLA, ARE YOU GONNA CHECK OUT THAT OTHER ME-CHANIC JOB I CIRCLED?

IT'S NICE OF YOU TO COME ALONG, GINA, BUT YOU REALLY DIDN'T HAVE TO. REALLY...
YOUR FRIEND PENNY SAID I SHOULD MAKE SURE YOU DON'T BACK OUT.
GARAGE

SOME FRIENDS I GOT THAT THINK I CAN'T HANDLE SHIT ON MY OWN.
<HEY, ENERO. LOOK AT WHO'S HERE.>
<HEY, I TOLD YOU FUCKERS SHE'S A MECHANIC.>

PETRA, THAT WETBACK KEEPS CIRCLING. SHOULD I SEND HIM ON HIS UGLY WAY?
TAKE A CIGAR BREAK, GINA. I KNOW HIM...

H-HI. YOU COME FOR DE JOB, TOO?
YEAH, KIND OF A WEIRD PLACE FOR A FLOOZY, EH?

WELL, I DIDN'T GET THE JOB, BUT I DID GET SORT OF A DATE.
SORT OF A DATE? I HOPE THAT DOESN'T MEAN WHAT I THINK IT MEANS, PERLA.

HE'LL PROBABLY JUST TAKE ME DRINKING SOMEWHERE AND MAYBE THERE'LL BE A LITTLE JIGGIN' TO TOP THINGS OFF. IS THAT WHAT YOU THINK IT MEANS?
PERLA, I NEVER REALIZED... I MEAN, YOU REALLY DO GIVE SEX FOR MONEY?
Bend
4

<SPANISH>

GUY, GINA! THAT WAS ONLY THAT ONE TIME! I'LL NEVER DO IT AGAIN!
OH, THEN IT WAS REALLY JUST THAT ONE TIME...?

WELL, ACTUALLY, THAT WAS THE SECOND TIME. NOT THAT IT'S ANYBODY'S BUSINESS...
PERLA! I'M JUST TRYING TO HELP YOU! WHEN WAS THIS?
MURPHY

"OH, NOT LONG AGO, REALLY. I WAS ON THE EAST COAST. I JUST BROKE UP WITH MY GIRLFRIEND, LIKE, FOR GOOD. I WAS IN A BUS STATION WITHOUT ENOUGH MONEY TO GET HOME TO CALIFORNIA...

"I WAS SO DISTRAUGHT THAT I STILL HAD ON THIS CRAZY DRESS I WORE TO A PARTY EARLIER THAT NIGHT, SO I GUESS I STUCK OUT LIKE A SORE THUMB. NOW, I SAID SORE, NOT WHORE. STILL...

THREE HUNDRED BUCKS.
FINE.

5

"I REMEMBERED HOW MY GIRLFRIEND ONE TIME, POSING AS A CALL GIRL, TRICKED SOME OLD GUY OUT OF HIS WALLET. SO I WENT WITH THIS GUY TO HIS HOTEL. BUT UNLIKE HER, I WENT THROUGH WITH IT. I GUESS IN A CRAZY WAY, I WAS DOING IT TO SPITE HER. ANYWAY, THE GUY KEPT HIS WORD ON THE THREE HUNDRED. HE EVEN GAVE ME AN EXTRA TWENTY FOR THE CAB BACK TO THE BUS STATION...

"I TOOK A BUS AND GOT OFF IN THE NEXT STATE, AND THE FIRST THING I DID WAS GET RID OF THAT CRAZY DRESS AND I GOT A NEW DRESS AND A NEW HAIRSTYLE. I WANTED TO FORGET ANYTHING THAT HAD TO DO WITH MY GIRLFRIEND."

BUT THEN, MY NEW DRESS WASN'T ANY LESS CRAZY. YOU'VE SEEN IT, MY BLACK ONE...?
SO, WHO IS RAND RACE?

I TOLD YOU, HE'S A MECHANIC GUY I USED TO WORK FOR.
YOU ALSO MENTIONED THIS GIRLFRIEND...

YES, GINA. I HAD A GIRLFRIEND. SHE WAS MY CHICK. I WAS HER SAUCE. WE WERE IN LOVE, BUT THAT'S OVER NOW, OK?
OK, BUT...

I WANT TO BE YOUR GIRL-FRIEND.

TIME FOR WORK!
6

OH OH.

AHH...

WELL...

MORNING, BOYS! HOW COME YOU GUYS ARENT WORKING?
WE DON'T KNOW WHAT TO DO.
WE NEED YOU TO BRIEF US, BOSS.

WHAT THE HELL ARE WE RUNNING HERE, YOU BUNCHA LAZY...
YOU! YOU'RE LATE!
SORRY, BOSS...
DDT

OH, RACE...
ARE YOU GOING TO HAVE TO REPRIMAND ME, BOSS LADY?
HOLD IT!

SCRAM, CREEPO! SHE'S MY GAL!
NOW, WAIT... MAGGIE, WHAT IS THIS?
GULP!
7

MAGGIE, WHERE ARE YOU GOING?
SHIT SHIT SHIT...

BAW!
HEY, LOOK OUT FOR THAT PIN!

¡BLAMO!

SO, GIANT GINA'S CRAZY ABOUT YOU, HUH? IS THAT WHAT YOU'RE SO UPSET ABOUT?
I'M NOT UPSET ABOUT THAT! I MEAN, I'M NOT UPSET...

...OR ARE YOU UPSET ABOUT WHAT'S ON THAT PAGE YOU KEEP READING OVER AND OVER AGAIN?
PENNY, I'M NOT... IT'S NO BIG DEAL...
NATIONAL BLABBER

AH, SO...
ISN'T THAT WILD? AND SHE'S FAT, TO BOOT!
BIG SHOT MECHANIC RAND RACE TO WED LAWYER GOLDMAN
AMOS DUNCAN A.Y.S.

AND ALL THIS TIME I WRECKED MYSELF THINKING HE LIKED WOMEN THAT... THAT LOOKED LIKE YOU!
YEAH, AND THAT FUCKER ALWAYS TOLD ME THAT HE'D ONLY MARRY ME!
END

IT'S NOT THAT BIG A DEAL

BEEP! BEEP!
¡PERLITA!
TEXAS
WTS TM1

OH. HELLO...
HELLO. ESTHER, RIGHT? I'M GINA...

THANKS FOR PICKING ME UP, BUT I THOUGHT MY SISTER...
WE'RE GOING TO PICK UP PERLA RIGHT NOW. AS WELL AS YOUR COUSIN XOCHITL AND HER HUSBAND MARIO.

SORRY, BUT YOU'RE GONNA HAVE TO GO GET THEM YOURSELF BECAUSE I'M UNDERAGE...
Cocktails
PHONE

ESTHER! IT'S ME, XO! WELCOME TO TEXAS!

ARE WE GLAD YOU GUYS CAME WHEN YOU DID. PERLA HANGS OUT AT THE CREEPIEST PLACES.
SO, WHERE IS PERLA?
SHE WANTS US TO MEET HER AT THE BELLE AIRE HOTEL INSTEAD. THE WRESTLERS MUST BE IN TOWN TONIGHT.
2

WE'RE NOT SAYING ANOTHER WORD TILL YOU EXPLAIN THE SUDDEN MARYLIN MONROE LOOK, XO...
ME AN' GINA WERE GONNA TAG TEAM AS "THE BLONDE BOMBSHELLS" BUT ONE OF US CHICKENED OUT OF BLEACHING HER HAIR...GINA?
I TOLD YOU, COACH WANTS TO KEEP ME AS A BABY FACE INDIAN...
I CAN JUST SEE IT NOW: PRINCESS TÉCNICA, THE MEXICAN APACHE VERSUS GORGEOUS GEORGIA, LA RUDA...

BABY FACE AND TÉCNICA/GOOD GUY RUDA/BAD GUY

THIS IS SO COOL, BABIES. YOU'RE GONNA BE MARRIED IN JUST ONE MONTH AND YOU CAME ALL THE WAY FROM CALIFORNIO JUST TO HAVE A FINAL FLING WITH YOUR LOVABLE SISTER...
OH OH. CHECK IT OUT, PERLA...
THOSE GIRLS ARE GONNA FIGHT RIGHT NOW AN' IT'S OVER SOME GUY, I BET.
OH OH. YOU MEAN EVERY GUY IN THIS CLUB WHERE THIS PARTICULAR GIRL IS CONCERNED.
HOW DO YOU LIKE THAT? IT'S NOT MY FAULT THEIR MEN DON'T WANNA DANCE WITH THEM!
HI, PERLA. WHATCHA DOON?
HI, PENNY. SHALL WE STEP OUTSIDE FOR A MINUTE?
LEAVING? WE JUST GOT HERE!
WOULD YOU RATHER WALK OUT OR BE THROWN OUT?
BY WHO?
DON'T MAKE A SCENE, LADIES. LET'S JUST GO.
THEY CAN'T KICK HER OUT JUST FOR DANCING. WE OUGHTA GO BACK AN' WOOP ALL THEIR WET-BACK ASSES, XO. ME AN' YOU...
LIGHTEN UP ON THE DRINKS, GINA, OR YOU MIGHT END UP WOOPING ALL OUR ASSES.
SO, WHAT NOW? DO WE JUST CALL IT A NIGHT?
ARE YOU KIDDING? YOUR NIGHT WITH THE GIRLS HAS JUST STARTED!
WHICH BRINGS US TO THE QUESTION OF WHAT I'M DOING HERE.
YOU'RE JUST THE DRIVER, SO DRIVE, DRIVER, DRIVE!
4

WE SHOULD GO TO CHESTER SQUARE. THEN WE COULD REALLY WOOP SOME ASS...
CHESTER SQUARE?? I LOVE CHESTER SQUARE!
LOOK, IF YOU DON'T COME UP WITH SOMETHING SOON, I'M DRIVING HOME.

DRIVER, WE WANNA GO TO THE SQUARE.
YOU GUYS REALLY WANNA GO THERE? I DIDN'T KNOW THAT PLACE STILL EXISTED...
THE SQUARE! THE SQUARE! THE SQUARE!

THIS PLACE IS A FUCKING DUMP! ARE YOU SURE IT'S STILL OPEN?
PERLA'S SPENT SOME TIME HERE RECENTLY.
YOU GOT FRIENDS HERE, PERLA?
YOU MIGHT SAY THAT, XO.

HI, SARA! REMEMBER ME? LET'S START 'EM COMING!
UH, WELCOME, FOLKS. WHAT WILL YOU HAVE?

I STILL SAY THIS PLACE ISN'T OPEN, XO.
MUERTE
DRINK YOUR DRINK, DRIVER.
HEY, CHECK IT OUT, PERLA! THIS JUKE BOX HAS "HEY HEY IN THE HAYLOFT"!
WELL, WIND HER UP PENNY.

WHAT'S RUBY SO FIRED UP ABOUT, GUY? YOUR MONEY COUNTERFEIT?
FUCK YOU, TOO, EME. SOMETHING MUST BE GOING ON AT SARA'S.
THIS I GOTTA SEE.
5

"SPACE STATION #5" BY MONTROSE

PERLA, YOU'VE BEEN AVOIDING ME.
I HAVEN'T BEEN AVOIDING YOU, GINA.

PERLA, I TOLD YOU HOW I FEEL ABOUT YOU, BUT YOU HAVEN'T TOLD ME...
I THOUGHT YOU WERE IN LOVE WITH XO. WHAT HAPPENED THERE?

OUCH! HEH!
PAP!

OW! KNOCK IT OFF!
WHOP!

GODDAMN IT! WHY DON'T YOU FUCKING GROW UP?

MOTHER FUCKIN' FUCK FUCK...
PENNY, WHATCHA DOON?
KISSING THE LOVABLE GROUND.
DON'T YOU JUST LOVE THIS PLACE?
7

WHAT IS IT WITH YOU AND CHESTER SQUARE ANYWAY?
DON'T YOU KNOW, PERLA? THIS IS WHERE I WAS RAISED!
I WAS BORN A MILE OR TWO UP THE ROAD!

NO SHIT? AND I ALWAYS THOUGHT YOU WERE A NATIVE OF HOPPERS.
NOT TILL I WAS TWELVE. AND I USED TO WALK WITH MAMA ALMOST EVERY DAY TO CHESTER SQUARE WHEN THEY USED TO HAVE THE MARKET.
SARA'S

UH, PENNY? WHERE ARE WE GOING? IT'S KINDA DARK OUT HERE, Y'KNOW...
DON'T YOU WANNA SEE MY OLD HOUSE? IT'S NOT FAR...

ARE YOU SURE IT'S ONLY A MILE OR TWO? WE'RE WAY THE FUCK OUT HERE...
NOT MUCH FURTHER, BABE.

PENNY, I CAN'T EVEN SEE CHESTER SQUARE ANY MORE.
YOU NOTICE HOW EVERYTHING SEEMS SO FAR WHEN YOU DON'T KNOW WHERE YOU'RE GOING, BUT IT'S MUCH CLOSER WHEN YOU DO KNOW?

SEE? THEY BUILT THIS SHOPPING CENTER CLOSER TO TOWN AFTER I MOVED. THAT'S KINDA WHY CHESTER SQUARE'S ALMOST A GHOST TOWN.
CAN WE SIT A MINUTE? THESE ZAPATOS WEREN'T MADE FOR WALKING MARATHONS.
TICKY

YOU KNOW YOU WANNA ASK WHAT IT IS WITH ME AND THE SQUARE.
I WASN'T GONNA SAY, BUT I OVERHEARD THOSE GUYS SAYING SOME PRETTY RUDE STUFF ABOUT YOU. DIDN'T YOU GO OUT WITH ONE OF THEM?
8

NO, ENERO HAD TO GO BACK TO MEXICO FOR AWHILE... TO HIS WIFE.
OH, YOU KNOW HOW IT IS, PENNY. A GUY DATES A LOT AND HE'S A STUD. A GIRL DATES A LOT AND SHE'S A SLUT. I DON'T LET IT BOTHER ME, THOUGH...
SAY, WHAT DAY IS THIS?

THERE'S THIS GUY I KINDA KNOW, WHO'S AN OLD BUDDY. BO THINKS I'M GOOD. HE TOOK ME TO THE ZOO ONCE. I GUESS HE STILL JUST WANTS TO STAY FRIENDS...
RAND RACE IS GETTING MARRIED AS WE SPEAK.

ESTHER MUST THINK OF ME AS SOME KINDA GUTTER TRASH SOW BY NOW...
WELL, WHY NOT? EVERYBODY ELSE DOES.
SO, WHAT CAN I DO ABOUT IT? I'M JUST ME...
OH, WELL...

IT'S NOT THAT BIG A DEAL...
COPY BOSS

YOU SAY YOU SAW PERLA STEP OUT WITH THAT PENNY GIRL?
YEAH, AND I HOPE THEY GET BACK SOON SO WE CAN GET GOING. YOU KNOW HOW MUCH BABYSITTERS CHARGE?
LUCHA LAGER
MOE
TEQUILA TO KILL YA!
DRINK CLUB
CERVESA MALA

WHAT'S THE MATTER? CAN'T THE BITCH FIGHT HER OWN FIGHTS?
9

DON'T YOU TOUCH ME! SHE DESERVED TO GET HER ASS KICKED! SHE INVADED MY TURF! SHE...

EEEEEEEEEEEE

PENNY, ONE OF THESE DAYS YOU'RE GONNA DO YOUR DISAPPEARING ACT ON THE WRONG PERSON, AND THAT PERSON WON'T BE THERE WHEN YOU RETURN...
...NAMELY ME.

IT'S JUST ME, MAMA.

MAMA, WE GOTTA GET YOU A BETTER PLACE.
BEATRÍZ.

10

YOU NOTICE HOW EVERYTHING SEEMS SO FAR WHEN YOU DON'T KNOW WHERE YOU'RE GOING, BUT IT'S MUCH CLOSER WHEN YOU DO KNOW...?
COIN WASH
199
JETON

HUH! DID EVERY-BODY IN THE WORLD DISAPPEAR?
UH UH. UH UH. UH UH.

I'M SORRY! WE'RE CLOSED! GOOD NIGHT!
DO YOU KNOW WHERE MY FRIENDS WENT?

WHAT THE FUCK IS YOUR PROBLEM?
BOOM!

HM...

¡AI!

YOU-YOU-YOU PEOPLE ARE CRAZY! IT WASN'T MY FAULT! SHE-SHE...

?!?!
PERLA, BACK HERE.
11

ESTHER? YO...?
MY GOD! GINA, WHAT HAPPENED?
I WAS TRYING TO HELP YOU, PERLA...
THIS IDIOT WENT AFTER THAT WHORE OF YOURS AND GOT HERSELF STABBED!
PERLA, THAT WOMAN IS MORE DANGEROUS THAN YOU THINK!

WELL, SHOOT. SHOULD WE GET HER TO A HOSPITAL OR... WHERE'S MARIO?
HE'S GETTING THE CAR. IT'S REALLY NOT SO BAD A CUT. SHE JUST THINKS TIA VICKI'S GONNA GIVE HER HELL...
COACH IS GONNA MURDER ME...
THERE'S MARIO...

YOU GUYS GO ON AHEAD. I HAVE TO WAIT FOR PENNY...
YOU SURE? OK, BUT STAY LOW. THEY MIGHT HAVE CALLED THE COPS.
I'LL WAIT WITH YOU, PERLA.

THERE'S TWO OF 'EM, TITO!
YOU TWO. C'MERE...
COIN WASH
WE'RE JUST WAITING FOR OUR FRIEND...

WE KNOW ALL ABOUT YOU YOUNG LADY, SO I SUGGEST YOU KEEP YOUR FAT TRAP SHUT TILL THE POLICE ARRIVE...
WHAT DO YOU NEED COPS FOR? CAN'T YOU HANDLE TWO WOMEN BY YOURSELF?

HEY, WAIT A MINUTE! WHAT ARE YOU DOING?
DON'T YOU WANNA STRIPSEARCH US TO SEE IF WE STOLE ANYTHING? WELL, LET'S GET IT OVER WITH...

LOOK, DON'T... HEY, WHY DON'T YOU GIRLS JUST GO HOME, OK?
LIKE FATHER, LIKE SON. C'MON, ESTHER...

DIE, YOU SPAWN OF HADES!
WHO'S THIS?
Che's
SQUARE
WHERE'S
IZZA
MALE?

PERLA, DO YOU HATE ME?
WHY? YOU'RE NOT THE ONE THAT HAS FUCKED UP THIS ENTIRE NIGHT.
YOU REALIZE THESE COULD BE FAKE COPS AND WE COULD BE RAPED AND MURDERED AND NO ONE WOULD KNOW?

PERLA...
DO YOU THINK I KILLED SPEEDY?
SOME PEOPLE'D SAY I DESERVED IT, BUT...
WHAT?? NO! WHY...?
1A·12
13

FOR YEARS, CERTAIN PEOPLE MADE ME FEEL LIKE I DID. AND ALL THIS TIME I WAS SO SCARED THAT YOU BELIEVED IT, TOO.
HOW COULD I KILL HIM? I LOVED HIM.
OF COURSE YOU DID, ESTHER BABIES...
LOOK, EVERYTHING'S GONNA BE OK. IN ONE MONTH, YOU'RE GONNA GET MARRIED AND YOU'RE GONNA BE ABLE TO HAVE TONS OF KIDS...
SHIT, I DON'T WANNA GET MARRIED NO MORE.
I THOUGHT ABOUT IT A LONG TIME, BUT AFTER TONIGHT, I DON'T KNOW WHY, BUT I'M CONVINCED...
I DON'T WANNA GO BACK TO DAIRYTOWN EITHER. I HATE THAT PLACE. I'D RATHER JUST STAY HERE IN TEXAS.
BUT...
BUT...
BUT...
PERLA, IT'S NOT THAT BIG A DEAL...
OK...
WHAT ARE YOU IN HERE FOR?
OH, WE KILLED SOME PEOPLE.
YEAH? ME TOO. SHOT 'EM IN THE HEAD. BOOM.
YEAH, YOU SHOULDA SEEN IT. ALL THAT BLOOD...
...ALL TWENTY OF THEM NUNS.
YEP, JUST WENT UP TO 'EM AND POW, BRAINS ALL OVER...
YEAH, BOY, WHAT A MESS. THEN WE CUT OUT THEIR HEARTS...
...THEN WE WENT AN' HAD ICE CREAM.
CACA COMIX
XAIME 03-94

Angelitas
XAIME 94
DAD COULDN'T HAVE PICKED A BETTER DAY FOR A PICNIC. THE SUN WAS SHINING AND EVERYBODY WAS HAPPY 'CAUSE SOON HIS VISITING DAUGHTER ESTHER WAS GOING BACK HOME TO GET MARRIED.

ONLY NOBODY BUT HER SISTER PERLA KNEW THAT ESTHER CHANGED HER MIND ABOUT MARRIAGE BUT WAS TOO SCARED TO TELL EVERYBODY 'CAUSE SHE DIDN'T WANNA SPOIL THE FUN.
YEAH, THAT'S ME. I'M ESTHER. ONE OF DADDY'S LITTLE ANGELS.

I GOT A REALLY HUGE FAMILY THAT SPANS FROM DAIRYTOWN (MONTOYA, CA) TO HOPPERS (HUERTA, CA) TO HERE IN TEXAS, BUT I'LL ONLY BORE YOU WITH THE ONES THAT MADE IT TO THE PICNIC.
BESIDES ME, PERLA AN' DAD, IT WAS BASICALLY THE WRESTLER SIDE OF THE FAMILY. TIA VICKI AN' TIO CASH WITH THEIR ADOPTED BOY FROM JAPAN, HIROSHI, TIO JAKE AN' TIA FINA AN' THEIR DAUGHTER XOCHITL AN' HER FAMILY. IS THAT ENOUGH?

THEN OF COURSE THERE WAS DAD'S NEW FAMILY (HE'S BEEN WITH 'EM THIRTEEN YEARS, BUT YOU KNOW WHAT I MEAN).
THERE WAS MY HALF SISTERS SOFIA AN' MARIBEL, WHO CAN BE REAL BRATS SOMETIMES, AN' HIS WIFE ALEJANDRA.
SNUFFY

ALEJANDRA REALLY BREAKS HER BACK TO BE NICE TO ME AN' PERLA BUT WE STILL DON'T LIKE HER, ACTING LIKE SHE'S ALL YOUNG AN' EVERYTHING (WELL, SHE IS JUST THIRTY-NINE, BUT YOU KNOW WHAT I MEAN).
1

I GOTTA ADMIT, DAD REALLY KNOCKED HIMSELF OUT WITH THIS PARTY. I THINK HE'S BEING EXTRA NICE 'CAUSE HE STILL FEELS GUILTY ABOUT WHAT HE DID TO US AN' MOM.

WHEN I WAS LITTLE I USED TO CRY IN BED AT NIGHT TELLING PERLA HOW I HATED HIM FOR LEAVING, BUT PERLA ALWAYS TRIED TO CONVINCE ME THAT HE STILL LOVED US AN' HOW ONE DAY HE'D RETURN, BUT I DON'T KNOW IF SHE REALLY BELIEVED IT HERSELF.

IT TOOK ME YEARS TO UNDERSTAND THAT SOMETIMES RELATIONSHIPS JUST DON'T WORK OUT. THAT IT'S NOBODY'S FAULT REALLY...

SOMETIMES PEOPLE JUST KINDA DRIFT APART. THERE'S NO DEEP DARK SECRETS INVOLVED...

JUST A CLEAN SPLIT, RIGHT DOWN THE MIDDLE...

AN' THEN SOMETIMES I THINK THERE'S NO SUCH THING AS A CLEAN SPLIT.

2

I MEAN, MAYBE MOM WASN'T TOTALLY INNOCENT HERSELF, BUT I STILL THINK OF ALL THE SHIT SHE'S PUT UP WITH THROUGH THE YEARS. LEFT ALL ALONE TO RAISE A BUNCHA TERRIBLE BRATS.

I CAN'T REALLY INCLUDE PERLA 'CAUSE SHE WAS LEFT IN TIA VICKI'S HANDS AFTER DAD LEFT, BUT ME AN' MY BROTHERS WERE THE DEFINITION OF ROTTEN. NO WONDER MOM'S PSYCHO.

WHEN I USED TO VISIT PERLA IN HOPPERS, I USED TO THINK SHE WAS SUCH A LOSER, BEING ALL PUNK ROCK AN' EVERYTHING...

I JUST NEVER REALIZED THAT SHE WAS ALL ALONE, JUST LIKE MOM.

SHE WAS MAKING HER OWN LIFE WITH NOBODY'S HELP WHILE WE WERE BACK HOME LEECHING OFF OUR MOTHER.

I STARTED TO REALLY SCREW UP BAD. I WAS HANGING OUT WITH A REAL DANGEROUS CROWD AN' THE WORSER I GOT, THE MORE I MISSED MY SISTER WHO ALWAYS CARED ABOUT ME.

SO, HERE I AM. THAT'S WHY I CAN'T MARRY ALVARO. AS NICE AS HE'S ALWAYS BEEN TO ME, HE'S STILL PART OF THAT WORLD I CAN'T GO BACK TO. I JUST HOPE I'M NOT MAKING A BIG MISTAKE.
3

THEN I THINK ABOUT MY LITTLE BROTHERS. MANUEL AN' ANGEL TRY TO PLAY LIKE THEY'RE GANGSTERS. THEY'LL BE IN JAIL OR DEAD BEFORE YOU KNOW IT... JUST FOR PLAYING, TOO.
RUBEN'S NOT INVOLVED IN ANY OF THAT, BUT I THINK HE'S SECRETLY QUEER AN' HE'S GONNA HAVE ONE TOUGH LIFE IF HE STAYS IN DAIRYTOWN.

I ALWAYS WONDER WHAT WOULDA HAPPENED IF DAD STUCK AROUND. WOULD IT BE THE SAME, OR WOULD IT BE TOTALLY DIFFERENT? TOO LATE FOR WOULDA, COULDA, SHOULDAS, I GUESS...

PERLA SAYS I SHOULD TELL DAD LIKE, REAL SOON ABOUT MY BROKEN WEDDING ENGAGEMENT BEFORE IT GETS TOO DEEP.
EASY FOR HER TO SAY.

I SUPPOSE I SHOULD TELL ALVARO REAL SOON, TOO, HUH?

I JUST HOPE HE WON'T WANNA SHOOT ME, OR ANYTHING LIKE THAT.
I'M JUST KIDDING. HONEST.

OH, THIS IS DUMB, BUT ANOTHER SECRET ME AN' PERLA SHARE IS THAT WE WERE IN JAIL JUST THE DAY BEFORE THE PICNIC. IT WAS FOR VAGRANCY AND DISTURBING THE PEACE. CAN YOU BELIEVE IT? THAT'S THE COOL THING I LIKE ABOUT BEING AN ADULT. NOBODY HAS TO KNOW.

TOO BAD IT DOESN'T APPLY TO OUR FIRST SECRET.

I'M STILL AT A REALLY CONFUSED TIME IN MY LIFE, BUT I'M GLAD I'M HERE 'CAUSE I LOVE MY SISTER MORE THAN ANYBODY IN THE WHOLE WORLD AND I HAVE A LOT TO MAKE UP TO HER.
THE END

WE WANT THE WORLD AND WE WANT IT BALD...
BY JAIME "FOLSOM" HERNANDEZ 94
1

THANKS A LOT! WE'RE THE DAMACHERS! STICK AROUND, THE GREENSMEN ARE NEXT!
EXIT
SUPER-SNAZZ

WELL, AT LEAST THIS ONE WAS BETTER THAN UTAH, BENNY... TWYLA?
WELL, SURE, HOPEY. THIS TIME I HAD TO USE TWO HANDS TO COUNT THE PEOPLE IN THE AUDIENCE.

MAYBE SINATRA'S IN TOWN?
IT'S A SCHOOL NIGHT?
THE PLAGUE?
AND I THOUGHT YOU SAID YOU HAVE FRIENDS HERE IN L.A.
BIKINI KILL

WELL, I KNEW TERRY WOULDN'T MAKE IT, BUT I WAS KINDA CERTAIN DAFFY WOULD. JUST ABOUT EVERYBODY ELSE STILL LIVES IN HOPPERS.
OH, YEAH. DO YOU STILL WANT US TO TAKE YOU TO THE BUS STATION IN THE MORNING?

I HAVEN'T SEEN HOPPERS IN ABOUT SIX YEARS. I EVEN MISS MY MOM, IF YOU CAN BELIEVE IT. YOU SURE YOU GUYS DON'T WANNA COME WITH ME?
WHAT? AND MISS THE GRAVELINE TOUR? THE ACKER-MANSION? HOLLYWOOD BOOK AND POSTER??? SORRY, BABE, WE'RE ONLY HERE A DAY, SO YOU'RE ON YOUR OWN!
BUS
HUSBAND DEAD KIDS DEAD PLEASE HELP
2

REMEMBER TO BE BACK BY SEVEN! WE GOTTA BE IN SAN DIEGO BY TEN OR ELEVEN!

Welcome
HUERTA
POPULATION

HOPEY?

I-I'M JANET POLO. YOUR BROTHER'S REAL BUSY SO HE SENT ME TO TAKE YOU AROUND ANYWHERE YOU WANT.
ANY-WHERE I WANT?

SO, YOU'RE JOEY'S GIRL-FRIEND...
WELL, NOT EXACTLY. WE BROKE UP A FEW WEEKS AGO.

BUT HE STILL MAKES YOU DO STUFF FOR HIM. NOTHING'S CHANGED IN THIS TOWN SO FAR, THAT'S FOR DAMN SURE...
I DON'T MIND...

CLICK!
EULALIO ORTIZ
BELOVED SON
1967 1985
3

THEY CALLED HIM SPEEDY 'CAUSE HE ALWAYS SEEMED TO BE RUNNING...
JOEY SAID HE DID A LOT OF RUNNING FROM THAT GUY HIMSELF.

PORFIRIO DIAZ RUBINSKI, AKA DEL CHIMNEY. SELF-PROCLAIMED PUNK GOD CHEATED ONE TOO MANY A DRUG CUSTOMER...
JOEY SAID HE WAS FOUND CRUCIFIED IN HIS HOUSE.

JOEY TOLD YOU A LOT. SO HOW COME YOU GUYS BROKE UP?
HE SAID HE WAS TIRED OF ME.
CLICK!

THE FEELING WASN'T MUTUAL?
WAS HE EVER NICE TO YOU?
NO, I WAS FINE. I MEAN...
CLICK!

WELL, I... SOMETIMES HE'D...
'CAUSE IF I KNOW MY BROTHER, HE USED YOU, MANIPULATED YOU, TOTALLY DEGRADED YOU...
CLICK!

THAT'S WHAT PEOPLE THOUGHT, BUT IT REALLY WASN'T LIKE THAT...
THE ONLY GIRL HE COULD NEVER GET HIS GRIMY PAWS ON WAS THE MAGPIE, AND BOY, DID HE HATE THAT!

HE STILL TALKS ABOUT HER ALL THE TIME. WISHES HE COULD SEE HER...
HE DOESN'T TAP ON HER BEDROOM WINDOW IN THE MIDDLE OF THE NIGHT IN JUST A BLACK SPEEDO?
4

OH, NO. JOEY SAID SHE LIVES IN TEXAS WITH HER DAD OR SOMETHING LIKE THAT.
OH, REALLY? DID YOU EVER GET TO MEET HER?

NO, SHE HASN'T LIVED HERE AS LONG AS I'VE KNOWN OF HER...
THEN, SHE NEVER MADE IT BACK...?

IS THERE ANYWHERE ELSE YOU'D LIKE TO GO, HOPEY?
NOT THAT I CAN THINK OF.

CAN'T GO BY IZZY'S. WE HAD A FIGHT LAST TIME I SAW HER... LOST MY NERVE TO SEE MY MOM... EVERYBODY ELSE MOVED AWAY... MADDOG'S IS A VANDY'S NOW... TACO MIO PUTS BLACK BEANS IN THEIR BURRITOS...
WHAT'S LEFT? I MIGHT AS WELL JUST HEAD BACK EVEN IF IT'S STILL EARLY.
WE COULD JUST SIT AND TALK UNTIL THE BUS COMES.

OK, THEN 'FESS UP. WHAT ARE SOME OF THE THINGS MY BROTHER DID TO YOU?
I DON'T GET IT. YOU MEAN LIKE, MAKING ME RUN ERRANDS FOR HIM?
I MEAN, LIKE, CHAINS, RUBBER, ROPES, COSTUMES, HOT WHEEL TRACKS, CHEERIOS...

WELL, MOST OF THE TIME HE WOULD MAKE ME STAND STILL ON A TABLE WEARING SOMETHING LIKE A FIGURE SKATING OUTFIT WHILE HE'D CIRCLE ME PRETTY MUCH JUST... OBSERVING BEFORE WE'D HAVE SEX.
OH, GOD! DID YOU EVER DO THAT WONDER WOMAN OUTFIT HE HAS IN HIS CLOSET?
WHE THE BEEF?

NO, I OFFERED TO BUT HE SAID HE'S STILL SAVING IT FOR MAGGIE...
YOU OFFERED? MY GOD! WHY?? WHAT DID YOU GET OUT OF THAT?
5

A LOT, ACTUALLY.
REALLY???

IF THERE'S ANYTHING THAT REALLY TURNS ME ON, IT'S SOMEONE GETTING REAL TURNED ON BY ME...
YEAH?

WELL, WHAT WOULD YOU SAY IF I TOLD YOU YOU'VE BEEN TURNING ME ON SINCE I GOT HERE?
WHO, M-ME? YOU...?

SURE. IT MAKES NO DIFFERENCE IF I'M A GIRL. AS LONG AS I'M TURNED ON, SO ARE YOU.
NO, I'M SORRY, BUT... NO, I COULDN'T. NO...

STILL HOT FOR JOEY?
IT'S NOT THAT. IT'S JUST THAT... I'M NOT REALLY...
YES.

RELAX, JANET OL' GAL. MAYBE ONE DAY WE'LL BE SISTERS-IN-LAW. SISTER-IN-LAWS?
I WOULD LIKE THAT. I THINK YOU'RE A VERY NICE PERSON.

HOW WAS YOUR EXCURSION INTO HOMETOWN U.S.A.?
I LEARNED THAT MY BROTHER AND I HAVE TWO THINGS IN COMMON. WE'RE BOTH MANIPULATIVE DOGSHIT PIGS, BUT WE ALSO HAVE EXCELLENT TASTE IN WOMEN.
THE BLASTO

TEXAS
END

Angelitas Dos
THAT GOES UP IN YOUR ROOM, PERLA.
JH 94
ESTHER, WHAT DO YOU THINK?
RENA
trinchis

NOT MUCH OF A WARDROBE, BUT IT'S A START.
THAT'S ALL THE STUFF YOU GOT?

WELL, YEAH. THE REST OF MY STUFF IS STILL BACK IN HOPPERS AT MY EX-BOYFRIEND'S PLACE.
ARE YOU EVER GETTING IT BACK?

I DUNNO, I SUPPOSE I COULD CALL DANITA. MAYBE SHE COULD MAIL THE STUFF TO ME.
WHY WOULD YOU CALL HER? ISN'T SHE THE SAME GIRL THAT STOLE THAT VERY SAME EX-BOYFRIEND FROM YOU?
SHE DIDN'T EXACTLY STEAL HIM...
THAT'S WHAT YOU TOLD XOCHITL LAST WEEK.

THE TRUTH IS, ME AN' RAY WERE ALREADY KINDA BROKEN UP BY THE TIME THEY STARTED GOING OUT.
DANITA'S MY FRIEND, BABIES...
WHATEVER, PERLA...
HOLA.
1

CAN I HELP YOU?
I JOS CAME TO SEE...
PERLA, DEY TOL ME YOU WERE HERE...
ENERO.

WHEN DID YOU GET BACK FROM MEXICO?
TODAY. I...
HOW'S YOUR WIFE?
HEH! SHE'S OK. SO, YOU GOT YOUR OWN PLACE...

WELL, I'LL SEE YOU, OK?
NICE TO MEET YOU.

BOY, ARE YOU MAD.
THIS IS A NEW ME, BABIES.

WHAT'S UP WITH GIANT GINA? IS SHE GONNA MOVE IN WITH US, OR WHAT?
I DIDN'T EVEN BOTHER TO ASK. WE DON'T NEED HER.

WE DON'T NEED HER?? PERLA, WE CAN'T AFFORD THIS PLACE BY OURSELF!
THEN LET'S FIND SOMEBODY ELSE. GINA'S A WEIRDO. SHE'D BE GONE HALF THE TIME, ANYWAY; WRESTLING ON THE ROAD...
2

WELL, ISN'T THAT KINDA GOOD? IT'LL BE LIKE, JUST US TWO, BUT WITH GINA'S PART OF THE RENT...
...AND SHE SAID THE NEXT TIME SHE SEES ME, SHE'S GONNA BEAT THE HOLY SHIT OUT OF ME.

JUST 'CAUSE YOU DON'T WANNA BE HER GIRLFRIEND?
IT'S THE WAY I LET HER DOWN. I'M AN ASSHOLE, ESTHER. I DESERVE ANY KIND OF PUNISHMENT I GET. ATOMIC DROP... DDT...

ESTHER, WOULD YOU THINK ME WEAK IF I WENT TO SEE ENERO?
NO, PERLA.

CAMP V

HELLO?
AMP VICKI

CAMP VICKI
3

PERLA, YOU'RE BACK EARLY.
YEAH.
HELLO.
YOU'RE ALL SET, ESTHER...
OH, HI.
CAMP VICKI

PERLA, THIS IS OUR DOWNSTAIRS NEIGHBOR, SANTIAGO. HE SAID HE USED TO WORK AT THE HAIR AFFAIR WHERE I WORK NOW.
REALLY? COOL.
YEAH. WELL, I HAVE TO GO. IT'S REALLY NICE TO MEET Y'ALL...
CAMP VICKI

I'M SURE GONNA LIKE LIVING HERE! WHAT DO YOU THINK? YUM YUM?
YES YES. BUT NOT FOR YOU. THAT GUY'S QUEER AS A THREE DOLLAR BILL.

OH, JUST 'CAUSE HE CUTS HAIR? I CAN'T BELIEVE YOU'D SAY THAT; JUST 'CAUSE I SAW HIM FIRST...
BELIEVE ME, ESTHER. THEY'RE ALL GAY...
4

PAISA/WETBACK

BUTT SISTERS

TRUST ME, PERLA. THIS IS THE PERFECT MOVE TO RENDER ANY ATTACKER TOTALLY HELPLESS.

XO, NOTHING I DO WILL RENDER GIANT GINA HELPLESS!

MAYBE YOU SHOULD SHOW HER HOW TO GET OUT OF TOWN BY SUNDOWN, HUH, XO?

MAYBE YOU SHOULD SHUT UP BEFORE I TELL YOUR COACH ABOUT ALL OF YOU LOAFING WHEN YOU SHOULD BE TRAINING.

IT RENDERED HER ATTACKER HELP-LESS, ALL RIGHT.
IT WASN'T SUPPOSED TO GO LIKE THAT EXACTLY.
#1 RUDA
LOOK, WHY DON'T YOU JUST FAINT WHEN GINA APPROACHES YOU...
THAT WAY YOU DON'T HAVE TO WATCH HER TEAR YOU APART LIMB FROM LIMB.
TSK!
YEAH, WELL, FUCK YOU, TOO, BITCH!
LOOK, YOU GOT A BIG MOUTH! JUST BECAUSE YOU'RE THE COACH'S NIECE...
I ALSO GOT A BIG FIST FOR YOUR UGLY FACE!
OH OH, BREAK IT UP. COACH IS COMING...
#1 RUDA
TRAINING TIME WAS OVER SEVEN MINUTES AGO.
YES, COACH.
YES, COACH.
YES, COACH.
CAMP VICKI
WAIT A MINUTE, XO. ISN'T IT YOUR TURN TO SWEEP THE GYM?
OK, COACH.
P VICKI
I STILL DON'T SEE WHY WE HAVE TO HIDE FROM OUR OWN TIA EVERY TIME WE COME HERE.
DIDN'T YOU READ THE SIGN OUTSIDE? "TRESPASSERS WILL BE BULLDOGGED"? WELL, THAT NOW INCLUDES FAMILY. SO, YOU AND I ARE TRESPASSERS, BABIES.
IT'S BECAUSE TIA THINKS PERLA'S A BAD INFLUENCE ON GINA'S WRESTLING CAREER. WHY, I COULDN'T TELL YA...
2

YOU WANNA GO OVER THAT MOVE ONE MORE TIME, PERLA?
NO, THANKS, XO. WE, UH, GOTTA GET TO THE TRAIN STATION.
SAY HI... OR DON'T SAY HI TO TIA FOR US, OK?
RUDA
PERLA, I'LL TRY TO TALK TO GINA, BUT WHEN SHE SETS HER MIND ON SOMETHING, IT'S PRETTY HARD TO CHANGE IT.
THANKS A LOT FOR THE INFO, XO...
BYE, XO.
PERLA, DO YOU THINK YOU'RE A BAD INFLUENCE ON GINA 'CAUSE SHE'S IN LOVE WITH YOU?
YEAH. TIA BELIEVES LOVE RUINS WRESTLING CAREERS. QUEEN RENA'S, FOR ONE...
BUT, IF GINA'S BEST FRIEND XO DOESN'T EVEN KNOW SHE'S QUEER...
TIA VICKI KNOWS... OR SUSPECTS. SHE THINKS SHE HAS A NOSE FOR SNIFFING OUT HOMOSEXUALS.
...AND NOW A GIANT HOMOSEXUAL WANTS TO POUND ON MY WIMPY LITTLE BODY.
SHIT, I'M THAT GIRL IN HIGH SCHOOL JUST WAITING FOR BLANCA RIZO TO DO SOMETHING...
THAT'S JUST IT, PERLA! YOU AIN'T IN HIGH SCHOOL NO MORE!
YOU GOTTA GO RIGHT UP TO HER AND TALK IT OVER WOMAN TO WOMAN.
I WAS SORTA HOPING YOU'D ADVISE ME TO FAINT SO I DON'T HAVE TO WATCH HER TEAR ME APART LIMB FROM LIMB.
XAIME 94

son of butt sisters
STOP
AMERICA
L25393263 Y

SEMPER FI
do yourself a favor!
do yourself a favor!

return of the butt sisters
EXPLAIN SOMETHING TO ME, PERLA.
HOW DO YOU GO FROM WRITING TO THIS GIRL IN HOPPERS ASKING HER TO SEND YOUR CLOTHES AN' STUFF YOU LEFT BEHIND TO INVITING HER AND HER SON TO COME LIVE WITH US?
DANITA'S IN TROUBLE AND I'M THE ONLY ONE SHE CAN TURN TO RIGHT NOW, ESTHER.

SO, SHE'D RATHER RUN AWAY THAN FACE HER TROUBLES. I DUNNO, PERLA...
AS I RECALL, DIDN'T YOU KINDA END UP HERE BY RUNNING FROM SOMETHING YOURSELF?
RACK 29 OUT
I WASN'T NO STRIPPER AT NO PLACE CALLED BUMPERS...
TSK! BABIES, WHEN I WAS SEVENTEEN, EVERY PUNK GIRL IN HOPPERS AT LEAST KNEW ABOUT BUMPER'S IF THEY DIDN'T WORK THERE WAITRESSING, OR... YES, STRIPPING!
THE FAKE I.D. BUSINESS BOOMED THAT YEAR...

WELL, KIKO. WE FINALLY GOT THE MAGPIE TO WORK HERE. HOW LONG BEFORE HER TWIN COMES ROLLING IN?
NOT HOPEY, MONICA. SHE SAYS SHE'S JUST GONNA KEEP SWALLOWING HER PRIDE TILL HER MEAGER INHERITANCE RUNS OUT.
THE WAY SHE SPENDS IT, THAT'LL BE IN A COUPLE OF WEEKS.
1

NEVER THOUGHT YOU'D SEE TERRY UP THERE, HUH, MAG?
IF HOPEY ONLY KNEW WHAT SHE'S MISSING.

AND IF ALL THOSE MEN KNEW HOW MUCH SHE'D RATHER BE BLOWING THEIR FACES OFF WITH A BAZOOKA.
I KNOW. WHY DOESN'T SHE JUST QUIT IF SHE HATES IT SO MUCH?
BECAUSE RIGHT NOW THAT IS THE BEST PAYING GIG IN THIS WHOLE TOWN NEXT TO MAYBE MR. BUMPER'S HIMSELF.

I STILL DON'T KNOW HOW YOU GUYS DO IT. IN YOUR OWN TOWN, I MEAN. DON'T YOU HAVE UNCLES OR COUSINS, OR...?
THAT'S WHY YOU GET YOURSELF A WIG, OR SOMETHING.
SINCE I COLORED MY HAIR, MY STEP DAD HASN'T RECOGNIZED ME YET. AND HE'S HERE EVERY NIGHT.

WELL, I HAVE BEEN THINKING OF DOING SOMETHING WITH MY HAIR...
THERE YOU GO...
YOU GUYS WOULD BE MUCH BETTER OFF WITH A WIG, BELIEVE ME...

HOW LONG DOES IT TAKE TO GET YOUR HAIR DONE, ANYWAY?
AND WHY DID SHE GO TO A BEAUTY PARLOR? I COULD HAVE DONE IT TO HER FOR FREE.
SHE'S HERE!
daddy
RUBEN

HI, DAFFY.
HI, HOPEY.
HI, IZZY.
I HATE IT, SO, NO CRACKS, PLEASE.
THANK YOU.
GOOD NIGHT.
2

C'MON, MAG. YOU GOTTA COME HOME SOMETIME. DAFFY THOUGHT YOUR HAIR WAS THE MOST BEAUTIFUL THING SHE'S EVER SEEN. SHE SAYS SHE'S GONNA GO BLEACHED BLONDE ALL 'CAUSE OF YOU!
YES, "BLEACHED BLONDE," NOT "BLEACHED BEAST"!

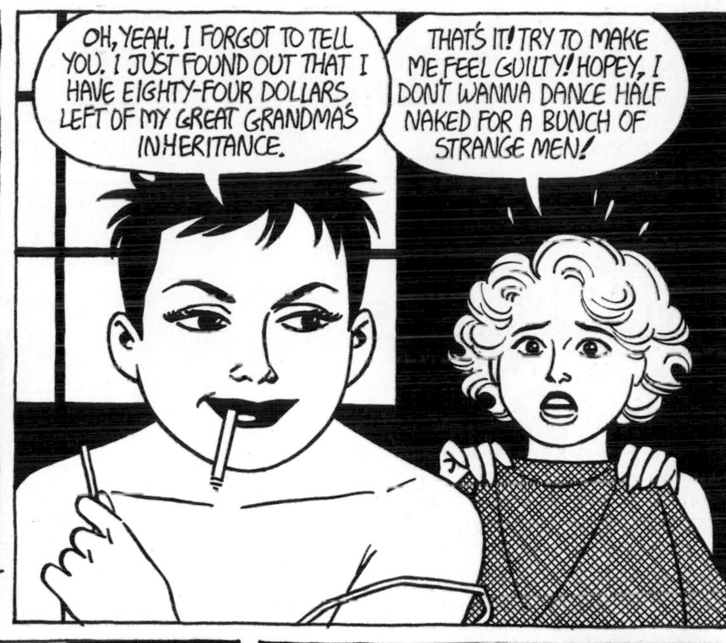
OH, YEAH. I FORGOT TO TELL YOU. I JUST FOUND OUT THAT I HAVE EIGHTY-FOUR DOLLARS LEFT OF MY GREAT GRANDMA'S INHERITANCE.
THAT'S IT! TRY TO MAKE ME FEEL GUILTY! HOPEY, I DON'T WANNA DANCE HALF NAKED FOR A BUNCH OF STRANGE MEN!

I'M NOT ASKING YOU TO! PERSONALLY, I'D RATHER SEE YOU BACK AT SAL'S GARAGE INSTEAD OF THAT OL' CRUMMY DIVE.
SAL'S?? WOULD YOU HIRE ME BACK AFTER ALL MY FUCK UPS?

THEY ALL THOUGHT I QUIT 'CAUSE OF SCHOOL, BUT IT WAS REALLY FOR THEIR SAFETY. I'M JUST A FUCKING JINX...
AT LEAST SPILLING DRINKS IS EXPECTED AT BUMPER'S.
HAVE YOU SPILLED ANY DRINKS?

THIEVES
NO...
HUH.
...BUT, I WILL EVENTUALLY.
HUH.
HUH.

IN OTHER WORDS, MAGGIE IS AN EXCELLENT MECHANIC, BUT SHE CONTINUES TO FUCK UP AT ANY MECHANIC JOB BECAUSE THE BACK OF HER MIND KEEPS TELLING HER A YOUNG WOMAN IS NOT SUPPOSED TO FIX CARS FOR A LIVING...

...AND THEN SHE SAYS IT'S OK IF YOU GO BACK TO SAL'S, 'CAUSE, WELL, I DON'T REMEMBER EXACTLY, BUT, IT'S A REALLY COOL JOB, MAG, AN'...
WHAT ARE YOU TALKING ABOUT? I GOT A JOB...
3

BUT, TO DO WHAT YOU'RE BEST AT... YOU... MAG, IT'S NOT THAT BIG A DEAL!
I KNOW IT'S NOT! SO, WHY DO YOU KEEP MAKING IT ONE?

MAGGIE, I KNOW YOU HAVE THIS PICTURE IN YOUR HEAD OF WHAT IT'S LIKE, BUT REALLY, IT'S NOT... I MEAN, IT'S TRUE, SOME OF THE GIRLS DO GET CAUGHT UP IN SHIT LIKE, HARD DRUGS AN' STUFF...

OTHERS GET INTO CLOSER, MORE INTIMATE ACTIVITIES WITH CUSTOMERS DURING WORK HOURS.
I KNOW YOU'RE TALKING ABOUT ME, MONICA! DON'T TRY TO MAKE ME OUT LIKE SOME FUCKIN' FREAK, OK?

ALL I'M SAYING IS THAT YOU CAN PLAY IT SIMPLE AND TAKE YOUR PAY AND TIPS HOME AT THE END OF THE NIGHT AND THAT'S IT.
IT'S NOT THAT BIG A DEAL.
CAN I STILL THINK ABOUT IT?
LET HER THINK ABOUT IT!

SO, CREAKY. IS IT TRUE? DID YOU REALLY...? ACTUALLY...?
OH, LIKE MONICA HASN'T!
THAT HYPOCRITE HAS WHORED MORE THAN ANY OF US COMBINED! BELIEVE ME, MONICA SAID IT HERSELF, IT'S REALLY NOT THAT BIG A DEAL.

SO, THEY'RE THROWING ALL THIS AT ME AN' MY BRAIN'S GOING ALL OVER THE PLACE AND IT KINDA MAKES SENSE, BUT IT DOESN'T REALLY, AN'...
SO, WHAT ARE YOU GONNA DO?
APE SEX
PONTIAX SCXCH

I DUNNO. 'AN' THEN I'M WONDERING IF I SHOULD CUT THIS OFF. I MEAN, I HATE IT, BUT I MIGHT NEED IT, AN'...
LOOK, EITHER YOU DO IT, OR DON'T DO IT, BUT DO SOMETHING, MAG, 'CAUSE YOU'RE DRIVING ME NUTS!
BONG
4

RAPE SEX

SORRY, TERRY. DID YOU SEE WHERE HOPEY WENT?
SHE WENT HOME TWO HOURS AGO! IT'S ALMOST FIVE IN CASE YOU DIDN'T NOTICE, MAGGIE!

HOPEY, WHEN WE WAKE UP IN THE MORNING, THE FIRST THING YOU TELL ME TO DO, I'LL DO IT. EVEN IF I FIGHT YOU, I'LL DO IT. I PROMISE. THAT IS, AFTER YOU CUT MY HAIR...

RING RING SEVEN A.M.
FRAM DAMN IT! OK! IF I CUT YOUR FUCKIN' HAIR, WILL YOU QUIT PLAYING YOUR SILLY-ASS GAMES AND GO BACK TO BEING A MECHANIC? HUH? TODAY? OK?!!
OK! OK! I'LL DO IT! JUST GET OFF! YEOW!

SO, I DID IT.
I NEVER BECAME A STRIPPER. MONICA ONLY WANTED ME TO SO SHE COULD CHECK ME OUT HERSELF.
I QUIT WAITRESSING AND WENT BACK TO BEING A MECHANIC FOR AWHILE.
BY THAT TIME EVERY DANCER AT BUMPER'S WAS LESBIAN OR BI.
THEY WERE ALL FIRED WHEN IT WAS RUMORED THAT THEY WERE GONNA MURDER MR. BUMPERS AND TURN THE PLACE INTO A FULL ON DYKE OPERATION.
(SIGH...) MY LITTLE HOPEY...

OH. HERE COMES DANITA'S TRAIN.
TRACK 29 SOUTH
5

HI, PERLA. ARE OUR NEW ROOMMATES STILL SOUND ASLEEP?
THE KID IS. DANITA WENT TO SEE SOMEONE ABOUT A JOB. AND NO, I DON'T THINK IT'S A STRIPPER JOB...
I WASN'T...
TSK!
ANYWAY, I SAW GINA.
YOU DID?? D-DID YOU TALK TO HER?
SORT OF. WE WERE BOTH STOPPED AT A RED LIGHT, AN' I SORTA CALLED OVER TO HER AN' ASKED HER IF SHE HAD SOME KINDA BEEF WITH YOU...
YOU DIDN'T! A-AND WHAT'D SHE SAY...?
NOTHING. SHE JUST KINDA GRINNED AN' THEN THE LIGHT TURNED GREEN, AN' SHE WAS GONE.
I'M THAT GIRL IN HIGH SCHOOL...
HI!
HOW DO YA LIKE MY OUTFIT FOR MY NEW JOB?
IT'S... CUTE! IT'S... UM...
WHAT DO YOU DO AT YOUR NEW JOB, DANITA?
GIVE ME TIME, PERLA. I'LL CATCH ON...
ESTHER, DO PEOPLE FAINT FORWARDS, OR BACK?
the end
XAIME 94

Chester
SQUARE
BE R
WINE
X IM
MOTEL

FOR THIRTY-FIVE YEARS THAT SIGN STOOD UNHARMED...
UNTOUCHED...

DAMN WHORES.
DAMN WHORES...

COIN WASH
SARA'S

HEY RUBY!
LONG TIME, NO SEE!
MUCHACHOS.
¡TOMA!

BOY, ARE YOU BRAVE. I THOUGHT YOU WERE BARRED FROM HERE.
TSK! WHAT CAN THOSE OLD BIDDIES DO?
¡AH!
1

HOW DARE YOU COME BACK HERE, AFTER WE TOLD YOU...
I'M NOT DOING ANYTHING, SO SHUT UP AND GET ME A DRINK!

SO, WHAT HAVE I MISSED SINCE I'VE BEEN AWAY, YOU STUDS?
WELL, YOU KNOW...
YOU'RE LOOKING AT IT.
I'LL CALL SECURITY! I WILL...

SECURITY? RIGHT. A COMPLIMENTARY BLOW JOB JUST PUT THAT ONE AWAY FOR THE REST OF THE WEEK.
GASP

GOD DAMN WHORE! WE TOLD YOU WE DON'T WANT YOU HERE ANY MORE AND WE MEAN IT!
¡AI!

OUT! OUT! OUT!
FUCKING HAG...
¡AH!
SNIKT!

WHA

THAT'S IT! CRAWL BACK TO WHERE YOU CAME FROM!
AND IF THAT OTHER WHORE WANTS TO COME BACK AND HAVE THE SAME, YOU TELL HER SHE'S PERFECTLY WELCOME!
2

JOTO/HOMOSEXUAL PIPI/PENIS

SO, ARE YOU GONNA SEE HIM AGAIN?
ARE YOU KIDDING? AFTER HE STUCK HIS PIPI IN SOME GUY'S BUTT?

I NEVER KNOW WHEN TO BELIEVE YOU.
YOU MEAN THERE'S A CHANCE THAT I MAY BE LYING?

AND WHEN YOU'RE DONE WITH THAT, SWEEP THE FRONT...
I WILL.
THEN, DO IT!
LITTLE LUIGI'S

OK, OK. MAN, YOU'D THINK QUEEN ELIZABETH WAS COMING...
POO! THAT QUEEN COULDN'T HOLD A CANDLE TO THIS QUEEN...

YEAH? HEY, IS THIS YOUR QUEEN COMING NOW?
WHO? NO, THAT'S NOT...
?!?

BOODIE

HEY.
HEY, DANITA. YOU OK?
4

I DUNNO. I FEEL KINDA WEAK...
YOU'RE BURNING UP. NO WONDER, YOU HAVEN'T STOPPED SINCE YOU MOVED HERE. YOU GET TO BED RIGHT NOW.
OH, SWEET PEA...

BUT, I GOTTA WORK TONIGHT. MY BOSS IS IN THE MAIN EVENT. HE CALLS ME HIS GOOD LUCK CHARM.
WELL, EL DIABLO BLANCO IS JUST GONNA HAVE TO DO WITHOUT HIS FAVORITE VALET TONIGHT.

WELL, AT LEAST LEMME CALL 'IM, AN' TELL 'IM I CAN'T MAKE IT...
OK, THEN IT'S STRAIGHT TO BED WITH YOU, RIGHT, ELIAS?

ARE YOU SURE YOU DON'T WANT A DOCTOR TO LOOK AT YOU, MISS?
WHAT KIND OF CLIENTELE DO YOU GET IN THIS PLACE?

EVERY-THING OK?
YEAH, BUT I STILL GOTTA GET DOWN TO THE ARENA. HE CAN FIND A REPLACEMENT BUT THEY NEED MY COSTUME.

YOU AIN'T GOING NOWHERE! I CAN GET IT THERE FOR YOU. YOU'RE STAYING IN BED, RIGHT, ELIAS?
WHAT IF HE LIKES THIS NEW GIRL BETTER?

MAN, WHAT'S THIS GUY LOOK LIKE WITHOUT THIS MASK ANYWAY; DENZEL?
NO... JUST LIKE SOME MESKIN MAN, S'ALL...
5

WHAT IF HE LIKES THIS NEW GIRL BETTER?
EL DIABLO BLANCO
OPEN UP. THERE'S SOMEBODY OUT HERE THAT SAYS THEY HAVE A COSTUME FOR SOMEBODY...
EVENT STAFF

UH, HI. I'M DROPPING THIS COSTUME OFF FOR...
OH, YES! GOOD! C'MON, C'MON, C'MON! YOU'RE LATE!
MMMS

BUT, WAIT. DO I JUST GIVE IT TO YOU, OR WHAT...?
WHY? I'M NOT GOING TO WEAR IT. HURRY UP, THE MAIN EVENT IS NEXT.

WELL?
I'M NOT...

OH, I FORGET, YOU'RE NEW...
YOU CHANGE IN THERE. NOW, HURRY! EL DIABLO BLANCO'S WAITING!
GRUNT!

¡HURRA! ¡HURRA!
HMM...
6

FALSE
TRUE
WAIT A MINUTE! MY GOD, WHAT WAS I THINKING???
THERE IT IS!
HEY YOU!

IT'S ABOUT TIME YOU BROUGHT IT. HAND IT OVER, GIRL!
?!
WAIT A MINUTE! DON'T GIVE IT TO HER! I'M WEARING IT TONIGHT!

LEGGO, BITCH! THEY CALLED ME FIRST!
BUT, I WAS HERE FIRST, SO LEGGO!
? ? ? ?
GIRLS! GIRLS! BREAK IT UP!

WHAT'S GOING ON, MORA?
OH, SEÑOR! YOUR VALET CALLED IN SICK, SO I CALLED FOR A REPLACEMENT BUT THEN SO DID EUFEMIO, SO NOW...
...THEN WHO ARE YOU?
I JUST BROUGHT THE COSTUME OVER FOR DANITA...

SO, YOU BROUGHT IT, NOW LEAVE! NO FANS ARE ALLOWED BACKSTAGE!
DON'T PUSH!

DICK!

TSK!
7

ARE YOU ALL RIGHT? YOU'RE NOT HURT?
I'LL LIVE, BUT SOMEBODY OWES ME A NEW COAT.

COME ON INSIDE. I'LL TAKE CARE OF THE RE-PAIRS. YOU'RE SURE THERE'S NOTHING ELSE?
NO, JUST THE COAT.
EVE
STA

BUT, SEÑOR! THE MAIN EVENT...
IT CAN WAIT.
ARE YOU SURE YOU CAN FIX IT?
OH, YES. THE ELBOW PATCH ONLY CAME UN-STITCHED. I'LL HAVE IT DONE IN NO TIME.

IF YOU'RE STILL HERE WHEN I RETURN, CAN I BUY YOU DINNER?
HUH? WELL...
BELIEVE ME, IT'S ONLY TO REPAY A KINDNESS YOU DID FOR YOUR FRIEND DANITA.
THINK ABOUT IT.
MORA?
YES, SEÑOR?

IF YOU HAVEN'T APOLOGIZED TO THE YOUNG LADY BY THE TIME I HAVE RETURNED, YOU'RE FIRED.

ALL FINISHED. GOOD AS NEW.
THANK YOU.

HATE TO SKIP DINNER, BUT...
NOW, HOW DO I GET OUT OF HERE?
8

CHISMOSO/GOSSIP

?!

HI! HOW'D DINNER GO? A REAL GENTLE-MAN, HUH?
GENTLEMAN MY ASS.

WHAT DO YOU MEAN? YOU DIDN'T GO?
HOW COULD I? THAT FAT FUCK AND HIS NEPHEW ALL OF A SUDDEN HAD THIS SECRET RENDEZVOUS WITH SOME SECRET DATES WHILE I JUST STOOD THERE LIKE A STUPID IDIOT WHILE THEY PRETENDED I NEVER EXISTED!
RING!

HELLO? YES! OH... HI...
I DON'T UNDERSTAND IT. THA'S REALLY NOT LIKE 'IM. HE MUSTA HAD A REASON...
HUH!

PERLA?
THAT WAS HIM. HE TOTALLY APOLOGIZED FOR THE DINNER THING...
TOLDJA! SEE, YOU THOUGHT...
...AN' HE ASKED ME TO MEET HIM AT A BAR.
GRAB THEM CAKES...

OH... WELL, I GUESS HE JUS' WANTSTA MAKE IT UP TO YOU, HUH?
YOU SURE YOU WANNA?
I ALREADY TOLD HIM I WOULD.
SEE YOU GUYS.
1242½
10

SHIT! WHAT THE HELL IS WRONG WITH ME? I AIN'T ONE OF HIS LOVED CRAZED BITCHES FALLING FOR THAT PHONEY BALONEY CHARM.

I ALSO DON'T SEE ME TURNING THIS CAR AROUND AND GOING HOME, EITHER.
FAT, STUPID IDIOT.
LITTLE LUIGI'S

SHIT, I FORGOT. I DON'T EVEN KNOW WHAT HE LOOKS LIKE. JMMM...
BROTHER JUKEBOX...

... SISTER WINE...

...MOTHER FREEDOM...

...FATHER TIME...

HEY, WHY DONTCHA COME OVER AN' HAVE A DRINK WITH US, SMILEY?
...SINCE SHE LEFT ME...
EEP! SORRY, WRONG DIABLO.

...BY MYSELF...
SHOOT...

...YOU'RE THE ONLY FAMILY...
11

GENTLEMAN OR NO GENTLEMAN, I'M OUTTA HERE.
...I'VE GOT LEFT!
WOMEN
WATCH IT!
B-BAM!

YOU ARE SO LUCKY I DON'T GOT MY BLADE...

IT'S ALL YOUR FAULT! THINGS WERE FINE TILL YOU SHOWED UP AT THE SQUARE, YOU BITCH! YOU...

...MOTHER FREEDOM...

YOU BITCH! YOU BI... YOU... OHHH...

I'VE BEEN WAITING TO DO THIS FOR A COUPLE OF WEEKS NOW...
GURK!
GINA??

NOTICE THIS FOREARM YOU ONCE SLICED? AS YOU CAN SEE, IT HAS HEALED PRETTY WELL...
GINA, SHE'S... GINA STOP!
12

GO AHEAD, PERLA. KICK HER ASS. SHE CAN'T DO ANYTHING NOW.
NO, NO! SHE'S LIKE, SICK OR SOMETHING. YOU GOTTA...
WOW. THE SLEEPER HOLD REALLY DOES WORK.
YOU GOTTA SNAP HER OUT OF IT BEFORE SOMEBODY COMES.
C'MON, GINA. HOW'S IT GO?

S-SNAP HER OUT OF IT...?
YEAH, YEAH. THAT'S IT. HURRY, BEFORE...
OH, SHIT! LET'S GO, GINA! OUT THE BACK EXIT!

I BLEW IT AGAIN, DIDN'T I, PERLA?
ARE YOU KIDDING, GINA? I DON'T KNOW HOW TO SAY IT, BUT, YOU SAVED MY MOTHER FUCKING LIFE!

I DID, PERLA? REALLY?
SHOOT YEAH! THAT GIRL WAS GONNA TURN ME INTO CARNE ASADA! IF IT HADN'T BEEN FOR YOU...

DO YOU NEED A RIDE HOME?
...NO, I BROUGHT A CAR.

I'M STILL GONNA KICK YOUR ASS. HA HA HA...
HA HA HA HA...

LITTLE LUIGI'S
13

ARE YOU SURE YOU DON'T WANT A DOCTOR TO LOOK AT YOU?
MIND YOUR OWN BUSINESS, JERK!

LOOKING FOR SOMEONE, MISS?
UH, YEAH. I NOTICED A LOTTA WRESTLERS HANG HERE. DOES RENA TITAÑON EVER COME IN?
QUEEN RENA? HERE? WHY?

I'M A FRIEND OF HERS AND I SAW HER HERE JUST A FEW MINUTES AGO. OR, I THOUGHT I SAW HER...
YOU SAW HER? QUEEN RENA?
IF YOU KNOW HER, THEN YOU KNOW RENA TITAÑON HASN'T BEEN IN THE STATES SOME SEVEN YEARS.

MAYBE WHAT YOU SAW WAS THIS AUTOGRAPHED PHOTO OF HER. GOT IT FROM HER BACK IN NINETEEN-SEVENTY.
THEE QUEEN RENA? HERE?
AWRIGHT! AWRIGHT! SO, I'M CRAZY!

BUT, DON'T YOU THINK IT WAS KINDA STRANGE THAT SHE WOULD KNOW...?
I DON'T CARE! JUST TAKE THIS NEW BOTTLE OF WINE BACK THERE AND SHUT YOUR TRAP!
14

BUT, MOM. YOU CAN'T EVEN TELL ME WHERE YOU LIVE...?
TONY, LISTEN TO ME. I TOOK A BIG CHANCE CROSSING THE BORDER TO SEE YOU. I MAY BE ENDANGERING YOUR LIFE AS WELL AS MY OWN BY BEING HERE.

AW, WHO WOULD WANT TO HURT YOU?
I MADE A LOT OF FRIENDS IN MY LIFE AS WELL AS ENEMIES. VERY POWERFUL POLITICAL ENEMIES. THE KIND THAT NEVER FORGET. THE KIND THAT WOULD STOP AT NOTHING TO HURT ME AND THOSE RELATED TO ME...

BUT, I'M OVER EIGHTEEN NOW. I COULD COME LIVE WITH YOU AND THEN NOBODY WOULD BE ABLE TO THREATEN YOU, BECAUSE I'D TEAR 'EM APART...
HEY!
15

YOU CAN'T HIDE HER FROM ME! RENA'S MY FRIEND! WE'VE BEEN TO HELL AND BACK TOGETHER! I'VE KNOWN HER LONGER THAN ANY OF YOU!
MARGARET? MARGARET??

HEY, TIO DIABLO. ISN'T THAT THE GIRL FROM THE ARENA TONIGHT?
SHHH! LET'S LEAVE 'EM ALONE AWHILE.

...AN' WHEN RENA GAVE UP HER NEWBORN SON FOR ADOPTION, SHE MADE AN AGREEMENT THAT SHE COULDN'T EVER GO NEAR HIM FOR FEAR THAT HER ENEMIES WOULD GET HER THROUGH HIM...
WOW.
I'LL BET SHE REGRETS MAKIN' THAT AGREEMENT NOW.
SCHULZ

OH, I KNOW SHE DOES. SO, ALL THESE YEARS SHE HAD TO SNEEK AROUND EVERYBODY'S BACK JUST TO SEE HIM.
HE DOESN'T HATE HER FOR ABANDONING HIM?
WHAT ABOUT DIABLO BLANCO? WHA'D YOU THINK OF HIM?
SCHULZ

I DUNNO. I NEVER SAW HIM THE WHOLE CRAZY NIGHT. I LEFT RIGHT AFTER I SAW RENA AND...
WAIT A MINUTE. THE GUY WITH THE BIG HANDS...

THAT WAS HIM? HE'S RENA'S BROTHER! BUT, I DIDN'T GET A GOOD LOOK AT HIM, 'CAUSE I DIDN'T THINK... HELP ME OUT, DANITA!
YOU MEAN, WHAT HE LOOKS LIKE? JUS' LIKE AN OL' MESKIN MAN...

AW, SHIT! NOW I KNOW I'LL NEVER BE ABLE TO SLEEP TONIGHT...
OVER AN' OL' MESKIN MAN?
SCHULZ
XXXAIME 95

BOB RICHARDSON

by Jaime "The Derek Flint of Comics" Hernandez '95

ESPPOSED/SUPPOSED

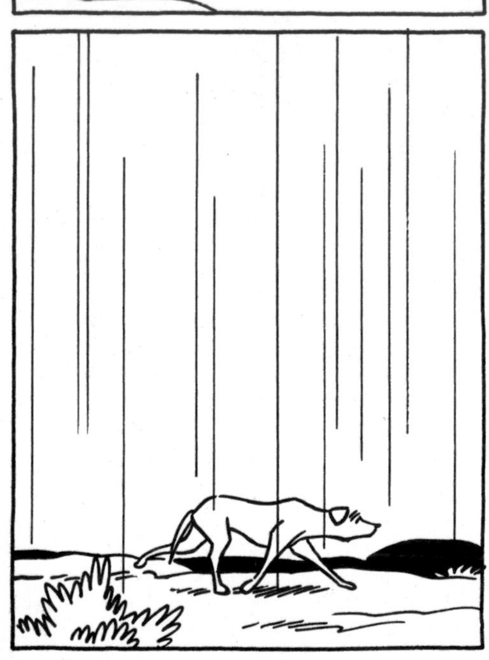

HEY, LOOK!

JUST A LONE DOG, TRAVELIN' DOWN THE ROAD...
OH, THE BONES OH, THE BONES OH, THE...
WE BETTER HURRY UP AND GET BACK BEFORE IT REALLY STARTS TO COME DOWN.

SO LONG, YOU LONE DOG YOU!
CAMP VICKI
TRESPASSERS WILL BE BULLDOGGED
2

Y'SEE, GINA. THE THING IS... I'VE ONLY EVER BEEN WITH ONE OTHER GIRL... I MEAN, LIKE REALLY BEEN WITH...
SO...?

SO, I DON'T KNOW IF I SHOULD... OR, IF I COULD BE WITH YOU, Y'KNOW...?
PERLA, YOU'RE BEING SILLY...

YOU CAN'T TELL ME WHAT I SAW IN YOUR EYES AFTER I KISSED YOU IN THAT PARKING LOT WAS ANYTHING BUT THE TENDER FLAME OF PASSION.
OK, BUT...

YOU'RE TRYING TO PUNISH YOURSELF AGAIN BECAUSE YOU SIMPLY DON'T FEEL YOU DESERVE ANY KIND OF PLEASURE.
OK, OK, OK. I DIDN'T WANT IT TO COME TO THIS, BUT, OK. HERE GOES...

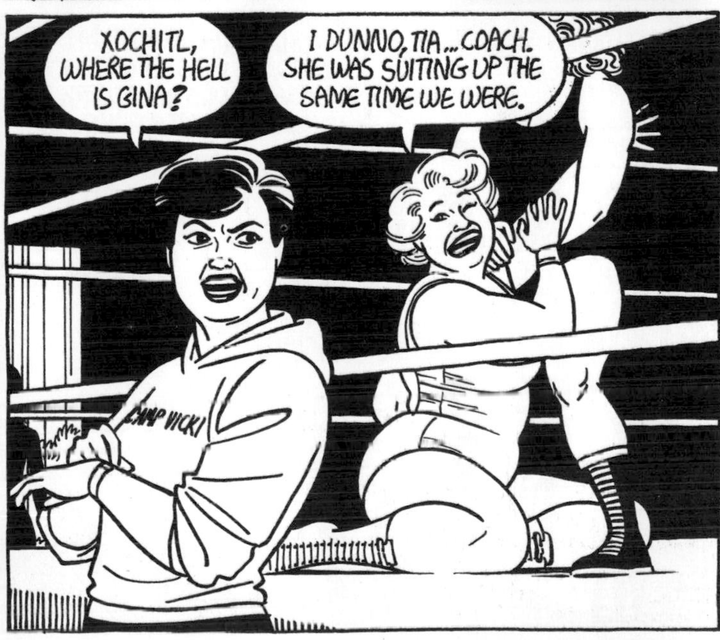
XOCHITL, WHERE THE HELL IS GINA?
I DUNNO, TIA... COACH. SHE WAS SUITING UP THE SAME TIME WE WERE.
CAMP VICKI

CAMP VICKI

SORRY I'M LATE, COACH. JUST BROKE A BOOT LACE.

CAMP VICKI
3

MY GOD, WHO WAS IN CONTROL BACK THERE? THE WISE OL' VETERAN ME, OR THE YOUNG NOVICE SHE?

OH NO!

C'MAN! SHIT!

YOU GOING SOMEWHERE, DANITA? I GET OFF IN A HALF HOUR. MAYBE WE COULD...
OH, I GOTTA GO FIND MY BOSS TO SEE IF I STILL GOT A JOB. I MISSED A LOTTA DAYS WORK, SO I... MAYBE LATER, HUH?

SO, THIS BIRTHDAY PARTY YOU'RE GOING TO; IS IT YOUR OWN?
HUH? OH... NO. JUST SOME NEIGHBORS DOWN-STAIRS WHERE I LIVE.

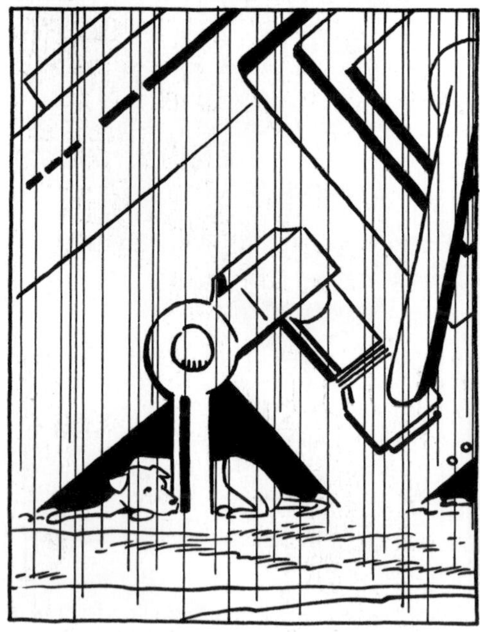

OK, NO BIGGIE. JUST GO IN THERE, TELL ENERO GARCIA YOU'RE NOT INTERESTED, THEN SPLIT. ZIP. SIMPLE.

THEY'RE ALL HERE, AS USUAL. RAIN OR SHINE, SARA'S ROCKS. UGLY OL' HAG...
SARA'S
4

HI, GUYS.
MAGGIE! I WAS JUST COMING TO SEE YOU! COME ON IN AND HAVE A DRINK! I HAVE GREAT NEWS...
ARE YOU CRAZY, ENERO? YOU KNOW SHE CAN'T COME IN HERE!

GET HER OUTTA HERE, ENERO!
HURRY, BEFORE SARA RETURNS!
WHAT'S GOING ON?
HEH HEH! C'MON, I'LL TELL YOU OUTSIDE.

MY GOD, AND THEN WHAT?
...AND THEN, LIKE A CRAZY LADY, SARA BROKE THE BROOM RIGHT ACROSS POOR RUBY'S BACK...

NO WONDER... I SAW RUBY LATER THAT NIGHT AN' SHE DIDN'T LOOK TOO HOT. THOSE HAGS...!
AND YOU THINK THEY'RE AFTER ME, TOO?
THAT'S WHAT THOSE GUYS THINK, NOT ME. I THINK THEY'RE JUST PARANOID.

WELL, I DON'T WANNA HANG OUT HERE, ANYWAY. I JUST CAME TO SEE YOU ABOUT...
...MY GREAT NEWS! GUESS WHAT? MY WIFE IS DIVORCING MY ASS!

THAT'S GREAT NEWS?
WELL, I KNOW SHE WAS THE REAL REASON WE COULDN'T BE TOGETH-ER, AND I DON'T BLAME YOU ONE BIT, BUT...

LOOK, I DON'T HAVE MUCH, BUT I REALLY THINK WE CAN DO THIS...
OK, OK, OK. I DIDN'T WANT IT TO COME TO THIS, BUT, OK. HERE GOES...

SO, WHERE DID YOUR OTHER BEER DRINKING PAL GO?
WELL... OH, HERE HE COMES.
OH, THERE HE GOES.

¡ENERO PENDEJO BUEY! YOU KNOW YOU COULDA GOT THAT LITTLE GIRLFRIEND OF YOURS SERIOUSLY HURT?
I WISH I FUCKIN' HAD! AND IF YOU EVER CALL HER MY GIRLFRIEND AGAIN...
FUCK!

WELL, I DIDN'T TELL HIM TO LEAVE HIS WIFE.
WHEW! MY SHOULDERS ARE STARTING TO FEEL LIGHTER ALREADY. WHOOSH!
MAYBE 'CAUSE I FORGOT MY RAIN-COAT BACK AT THE SQUARE. I DON'T DARE GO BACK FOR IT NOW.
GUY, DID HE HAVE TO GET SO MAD?

PERLA, YOU'RE ALIVE! WHERE YOU AT, YOU CACA HEAD? PEOPLE BEEN ASKIN' 'BOUT YOU.
I'VE BEEN... BABIES, I DON'T THINK I'M GONNA MAKE IT TO THAT BIRTHDAY PARTY TODAY...

GAW, PERLA, I DON'T WANNA GO BY MYSELF. I DON'T KNOW THESE PEOPLE...
YOU KNOW 'EM MORE'N I DO. IT'LL BE FINE. JOTOS AREN'T INTERESTED IN GIRLS, REMEMBER?

SO, UH... I DUNNO WHEN I'LL BE HOME, EXACTLY. IT MIGHT BE LATER TONIGHT, OR IT MIGHT NOT BE TILL TOMORROW. I JUST GOTTA... I DUNNO, I'LL CALL YOU LATER, OK, ESTHER BABIES? OK...?

THAT ROAD LEADS TO LITTLE LUIGI'S BAR. I'LL BET RUBY'S THERE. THAT IS, IF SHE ISN'T DEAD BY NOW...
RICHARD BASEHART SUFFERED A DELAYED DEATH AFTER ANTHONY QUINN SMACKED HIS HEAD AGAINST SOME MACHINERY IN THAT ONE MOVIE...
EDUARDO EL INDIO GOT THE SAME AFTER JUAN NUNEZ'S STICK BONKED HIM.
OR WAS IT MARIA'S FRYING PAN THAT DID HIM IN?

NEXT STOP: LITTLE LUIGI'S. I AIN'T GONNA HAVE THIS WHORE'S DEATH HAUNTING ME FOR THE REST OF MY LIFE, NO SIR.
JUST GO IN, SHAKE HANDS AN' SPLIT... AN' DON'T LOOK BACK!
6

SHE'S GOTTA BE HERE. HER KIND DON'T TAKE VACATIONS.
IS IT EVEN OPEN?

BEEP!

OH. TIA VICKI. WHAT A SURPRISE. YOU WANNA TALK TO ME AND YOU LOOK PISSED OFF. OH, HOW NICE...
CAMP VIC

HAPPY BIRTHDAY TO YOU...
ESTHER, ARE YOU SURE YOU CAN'T STAY FOR SOME CAKE?
NO, SANTIAGO. I REALLY GOTTA GO. EXPECTING A CALL FROM MY SISTER...

SEÑOR DIABLO BLANCO? SOMEONE TO SEE YOU.
HELLO, MISTER DIABLO.
DANITA! IT'S GREAT TO SEE YOU FEELING WELL AGAIN. I HOPE WELL ENOUGH TO COME BACK TO WORK FOR ME.

I KNOW I MISSED A LOTTA DAYS, BUT I... YEAH! REALLY?
WAS THERE EVER ANY DOUBT? YOU'RE MY GOOD LUCK CHARM, REMEMBER?
AND HOW'S MY MAN ELIAS TODAY?
UT! STILL A LITTLE SHY, I SEE.
7

SHRIMP, I'M NOT IN THE MOOD TO GET MAD. I JUST WANNA KNOW WHAT IT IS YOU SAID TO MY STAR WRESTLER THAT HAS TURNED HER INTO A SIX FOOT TALL BASKET CASE.
GINA? I JUST TOLD HER I WASN'T INTERESTED...

WHAT DO I LOOK LIKE, AN IDIOT? THAT GIRL IS TIED UP IN MORE KNOTS THAN SHE COULD EVER GET IN THE RING! SO, TELL ME EXACTLY WHAT YOU SAID TO HER AND I WANT NO BULLSHIT, GOT IT?
OK, OK, OK. I DIDN'T WANT IT TO COME TO THIS, BUT, OK. HERE GOES...

I-I'M GETTING MARRIED REAL SOON AN' THEY... SHE COULDN'T HANDLE IT...

TWEET!

HELLO, ESTHER? HI, IT'S ALEJANDRA. I REALLY THOUGHT YOU'D BE OUT TODAY.
NO, I'M JUST HERE WATCHING TV.
ROLL OUT THE BARREL...

WELL, I'M GLAD I CAUGHT YOU. I WANT TO WISH YOU A HAPPY BIRTHDAY FROM YOUR FATHER AND ME AND THE GIRLS...
THANK YOU.

YOUR FATHER WAS GOING TO CALL YOU HIMSELF BUT HE HAD TO WORK, SO... WELL...
HAVE PEOPLE BEEN CALLING TO WISH YOU A HAPPY BIRTHDAY?
ALL DAY.

WELL, I HAVE TO GO, BUT MAYBE WE CAN HAVE A PARTY THIS WEEKEND, OR SOMETHING? OK?
OK, ALEJANDRA. BYE.
8

MARRIED?! PERLA NEVER TOLD ME NOTHING.
WELL, SHE DIDN'T HESITATE TO TELL ME, OK, XO? OK?
GUY, YOU ACT LIKE YOU WANTED TO MARRY HER, GINA.

YEAH, MOM. IT WAS A TOTAL SURPRISE, TO ME, TOO. ISN'T IT GREAT?
BUT, ARE YOU SURE, XOCHITL?! I HAVEN'T HEARD ANY SUCH NEWS FROM PERLA'S PAPA.

ELIAS HAS BEEN LIKE THIS SINCE WE MOVED HERE. DON'T TALK MUCH, DON'T SMILE, DON'T EVEN CRY...
YOU DON'T THINK IT'S BECAUSE OF A NEW ENVI-RONMENT? IT TAKES SOME LONGER TO ADJUST.

MAYBE. BUT, NAH. HIS WHOLE LIFE HAS BEEN RUNNIN' FROM HOSTILITY AN' VIOLENCE. FIRST HIS CRAZY PAPA, THEN THAT STALKER... AN' THEN HE'S CONSTANTLY SURROUNDED BY HALF NAKED LADIES. SOME MOM, HUH?
DON'T BLAME YOURSELF, DANITA. YOU'RE DOING THE BEST ANYONE IN YOUR POSITION CAN DO.

MAGGIE SAID WHAT HE NEEDS IS A POSITIVE FATHER FIGGER TYPE HE CAN LOOK UP TO. ONE THAT'S ALWAYS AROUND...
MAG...? OH, PERLA! YES, YES! PERLA...
THUMP THUMP... THUMP THUMP... THUMP THUMP...

NOW, PERLA IS A GIRL WHO REALLY HAS HER HEAD ON STRAIGHT. I COULD TELL RIGHT AWAY WHEN I FIRST MET HER. YOU'RE VERY LUCKY TO HAVE HER AS A FRIEND.
YOU THINK SO...?
THUMP THUMP... THUMP THUMP... THUMP THU

A TRUE GEM. NEVER AFRAID TO SPEAK HER MIND. ANY MAN WOULD BE PROUD TO BE HER HUSBAND.
THUM THU THU--
SCREEEECH
CRAS
TINKLE TINKLE
9

DON'T WORRY, TIA. GINA WILL BE OVER ME BEFORE YOU CAN SAY "THE SUPER, SENSATIONAL, INTELLIGENT DESTROYER." THEN THAT GIRL IS GONNA COME THROUGH FOR YOU WITH FLYING COLORS. OR IS IT FLYING KNEE DROPS?
NOW YOU'RE TALKIN' MY LANGUAGE!
CAMP VICKI

WITH ALL THAT ASIDE, I CAN NOW TELL YOU HOW EXTREMELY HAPPY AND EXCITED I AM ABOUT YOUR ENGAGEMENT, SHRIMP.
¡SALÚD!
THANK YOU, TIA.

HEY! WHERE YOU GOING? NO FAIR!

HELP!
10

"LORD ZEUS, I WAS A SINNER. I'VE NEVER TRIED TO DENY IT...
"BUT, I DIDN'T SIN EVERY-DAY...
"WHY THEN DO YOU PUNISH ME EVERY-DAY?"

ALL I WANTED TO DO WAS WIPE MY FUCKIN' SLATE CLEAN!

HELLO? CAN I USE YOUR PHONE TO CALL A TOW TRUCK, PLEASE?
HELLO?

HELLOOO...

EXCUSE ME. NOBODY WAS OUT FRONT, SO I...
RENA?! HEY, YOU'RE STILL HERE! I THOUGHT YOU WERE GONE!
MARGARET?

I HOPE I DIDN'T INTERUPT ANYTHING. I JUST NEED TO USE A TELEPHONE, 'CAUSE...
GO HOME, MARGARET.
11

HUH?
GO HOME, MARGARET!
YOU WOULD HAVE TO LEAVE THE FRONT DOOR UNLOCKED...
DON'T LOOK AT ME! JOJO WAS STANDING BY THE DOOR!
YOU WERE CLOSER THAN I WAS!

AWRIGHT! FUCK IT!
ALL FEMALES AGAINST THE WALL, NOW!
¡AI!
IT'S ALL RIGHT, MARGARET. IT'S ME THEY WANT...

TIA VICKI! DID YOU HEAR THE GREAT NEWS ABOUT PERLA? GINA JUST TOLD ME...
YES, I DID. AND YOU'RE NOT TO BLAB IT TO ANYONE TILL SHE'S READY TO, UNDERSTAND?

FIRST, MY YOUNGER DAUGHTER BACKS OUT OF HER ENGAGEMENT AND SHE DOESN'T TELL ME. NOW MY OLDER DAUGHTER GETS ENGAGED AND I STILL HEAR IT SECOND HAND!
WELL, WHAT DO YOU EXPECT, NACHO, WHEN YOU CAN'T EVEN CALL YOUR YOUNGER DAUGHTER ON HER BIRTHDAY!

ENGAGED?! NO WONDER SHE'S AFRAID TO COME HOME! WHAT A CACA HEAD!

ENGAGED?!
12

SO, WHO'S SHE MARRYING, ANYWAY?
Y'KNOW, SHE DIDN'T SAY...

ENGAGED, HUH? I SHOULDA SEEN IT COMIN' A MILE AWAY...
THEN YOU KNOW WHO IT IS SHE'S MARRYING?

LITTLE LUIGI'S

FROM WHAT BOYD TELLS ME, YOU'RE A VERY IMPORTANT PERSON, GRANDMAMA.
YEAH, SHE'S QUEEN RENA! SHE WAS ONCE A CHAMPEEN RASSLER!
YEAH, THAT'S ME, JUST A RETIRED CHAMPEEN RASSLER.

DON'T LET HER FOOL YOU, MOON! LUIGI WAS TELLING ME HOW SHE USED TO BE LIKE, THIS IMPORTANT REVOLUTIONARY AND HOW SOME GOVERNMENTS TODAY WOULD PAY A PRETTY PENNY TO HAVE HER BROUGHT BACK TO THEM!
WHO'S GONNA PAY?
HAVEN'T FIGURED IT OUT YET.

WE'RE GONNA NEED MORE GUYS IF WE'RE GONNA DO THIS RIGHT.
CLON, GO ROUND UP YOUR BROTHERS, AND GET ANOTHER ROSCOE.
ANOTHER GUN? BUT, IT'S JUST THESE TWO GIRLS...
GET ANOTHER ROSCOE, CLON!

YOU KNOW, BOYD. YOU'RE GOING TO BREAK LUIGI'S HEART. AFTER HE TOOK YOU IN, GAVE YOU A JOB, TRUSTED YOU...
DON'T GIVE ME THAT! THAT MIDGET PAYS SHIT AND TREATS HIS EMPLOYEES SHITTIER! THIS IS MY WAY OF GETTING EVEN WITH THAT LITTLE MUSSOLINI!
13

HE'S RIGHT. YOU'RE A WAR CRIMINAL, LADY, AND WE'RE JUST DOING OUR PATRIOTIC DUTY BY PLACING YOU UNDER ARREST AND RETURNING YOU TO JAIL AND COLLECTING THE REWARD.
YOU SUCKERS REALLY DON'T KNOW WHAT YOU'RE INVOLVED IN. I FEEL SORRY FOR YOU...
SHUT UP! GIVE ME THE GUN! I'LL WATCH HER!

YEOW!
FUCK!
DON'T SHOOT!

MARGARET, I WANT YOU TO TAKE THIS AND LOCK YOURSELF IN THE BATHROOM AND DON'T COME OUT TILL I TELL YOU...
UTA...

SPACEMAN WITH A MISSION... YOU MUST MAKE A VERY BIG DECISION...

WITH THIS SOLAR BOMB YOU COULD DESTROY US...
OR SAVE THE WORLD...
OR SAVE THE WORLD...
KNOK! KNOK

OH, MY GOD!

I THINK YOU GOT THE WRONG HOUSE. THE PARTY'S DOWNSTAIRS.
HOLY SHIT! I'M SORRY! YOU GOTTA BE HER SISTER! GOD, YOU LOOK...

GASP!
SHHH...
14

NO, MOM. PERLA JUST LEFT EARLY THIS MORNING. DIDN'T SAY WHEN SHE'D BE BACK. SHE HASN'T TOLD ME ANYTHING ABOUT HER ENGAGEMENT. I HAD TO HEAR IT FROM XOCHITL.
WELL, IF SHE'S ANYTHING LIKE YOU SHE'LL BACK OUT AND NOT TELL HER FAMILY ABOUT IT, EH?
TSK!

I'LL BET YOU DIDN'T KNOW THAT ALVARO COMES TO ME ALL THE TIME ASKING WHY YOU BROKE OFF THE ENGAGEMENT.
HE COMES TO YOU? ALVARO HERNANDEZ NEVER CAME TO ANYONE IN HIS LIFE. THAT BOY DOESN'T MOVE FOR NOBODY.

DOESN'T THAT PROVE HE STILL CARES?
LOOK, MOM. I GOT COMPANY HERE. SOME FRIEND OF PERLA'S WHO CAME A LONG WAY TO SEE HER.
HOLD ON.
YOU TOLD ME YOURSELF HE NEVER ABUSED YOU.
IT'S NEVER TOO LATE TO CHANGE YOUR MIND BACK AGAIN.

UH...HOPEY? I REALLY DON'T KNOW WHEN PER...MAGGIE'S COMING HOME. COULD SHE CALL YOU...?
I DON'T KNOW WHERE I'LL BE STAYING. WE JUST GOT IN...

WELL, I GOT THIS LONG DISTANCE CALL, AN'...
I'LL JUST COME BACK.

WAIT. WHAT WAS THAT? SAY IT AGAIN...

MARGARET, I WANT YOU TO TAKE THIS AND LOCK YOURSELF IN THE BATHROOM AND DON'T COME OUT TILL I TELL YOU.
UTA...
15

SLAM!
MOON! WHAT DO WE DO NOW? SHE GOT OUR GUN!
CHARGE HER! THERE'S STILL THREE YOUNG GUYS TO ONE GRANDMAMA!

GRANDMAMA THIS!

POW! ZAP! BAM!

BOP! BIP! SOK!

BOK! TISH! POP!
BLOOP!

YOU'RE GETTIN' ME BACK FOR RAY, AIN'T YA, MAGGIE? I GUESS IT'S ONLY FAIR. ONCE I TOOK THE ONE YOU LOVED, NOW YOU GONNA GO AN' MARRY THE ONE I LOVE.

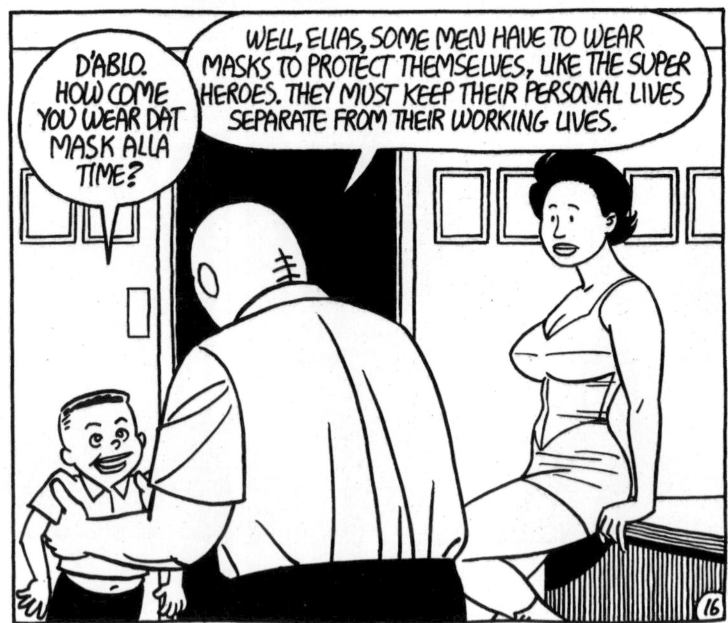
D'ABLO. HOW COME YOU WEAR DAT MASK ALLA TIME?
WELL, ELIAS, SOME MEN HAVE TO WEAR MASKS TO PROTECT THEMSELVES, LIKE THE SUPER HEROES. THEY MUST KEEP THEIR PERSONAL LIVES SEPARATE FROM THEIR WORKING LIVES.
16

IT'S ALSO TO PROTECT LOVED ONES. SOMETIMES THERE ARE THINGS IN A MAN'S PAST...
YOU AN' RENA TITAÑON MUST HAVE A LOTTA PEOPLE ALL OVER THE WORLD PRETTY MAD AT YOU, MISTER BLANCO.

MAGGIE TOL' ME HOW YOUR FAMOUS SISTER SECRETLY CAME TO THE U.S. TO SEE HER SON. I WOULDA NEVER GUESSED YOU WAS PART OF HER POLITICAL EXPLOITS. ARE YOU AS FAMOUS AS HER, TOO?
HEH. NOT HALF AS FAMOUS AS MY BIG SISTER.
SO, MAGGIE THE GEM COMES THROUGH AGAIN. SHE SAVED ME A LOT OF EXPLAINING, DANITA.
MAY I DRIVE YOU HOME?

SHE STILL AIN'T HERE.
NO, HUH?
OK.

ZOK! PAM! BING!

WOULD YOU LIKE TO MEET MY FAMOUS SISTER, DANITA? IT'S ON THE WAY TO YOUR PLACE.
NYEAWRIGHT.

YOU'RE SURE PUTTIN' A LOTTA TRUST IN ME. I'M ONLY JUST YOUR VALET.
OH, SORRY... GOOD LUCK CHARM.
DANITA, HAVE I UPSET YOU IN ANY WAY? HOW CAN I PROVE TO YOU HOW IMPORTANT YOU AND ELIAS ARE TO ME?

PERHAPS IF I SHOWED YOU MY FACE. WOULD THAT MAKE YOU FEEL MORE AT EASE?
I SEEN YOUR FACE BEFORE. IN THE LOCKER ROOM.
YOU HAVE?? YOU...
SO YOU HAVE...
I WANNA SEE IT, D'ABLO!
17

UT! WHAT'S THIS? SEEMS TO HAVE BEEN A MUDSLIDE. I'M AFRAID WE'LL HAVE TO FORGET MY SISTER...
HEY, THAT'S MAGGIE'S CAR! IT LOOKS LIKE IT SLID DOWN THE SIDE O' THAT HILL THERE!
BUT, I DON'T SEE HER...

DO YA THINK SHE COULD BE IN LITTLE LUIGI'S WITH YOUR SISTER?
Little Luigi's
TAKE ARNOLD RD.
HMM...

DANITA, COULD YOU DRIVE ELIAS AND YOURSELF HOME AND I'LL HOOK UP WITH YOU LATER? I PROMISE, I WILL CALL YOU.
OK.

WHERE'S D'ABLO GOIN', MOMMA?
SHUT UP AN' PUT ON YOUR SEAT BELT.

ZAM! BOK! BING!

WHAP! BOOM!
KLUNK!
BW

18

YOU GUYS CAN'T EVEN HANDLE ONE OLD BITCH...
TIE HER UP THIS TIME!
WHAT ABOUT YOU? WHAT ABOUT YOU?
HEY, MOON! WHA' HOPPEN, MAN?

IT'S ABOUT TIME YOU FUCKERS GOT HERE. DID YOU BRING A FUCKIN' GUN?
GOT IT RIGHT HERE.
WE EVEN BROUGHT BUTO! NO ONE'LL MESS WITH HIM!

WELL, GRANDMAMA. THE WAY YOU FIGHT, NO WONDER SOMEBODY WANTS YOU DEAD. YOU'RE SURE TO BRING A SHIT LOAD OF REWARD MONEY OUR WAY. YOU WANTED AT FORT KNOX BY ANY CHANCE?
OH, SHIT! MOON...

IT'S THE CHICK! SHE'S GOT YOUR GUN, 'MEMBER?
SHE AIN'T GOT THE GUN. IT'S PROBABLY STILL IN THE BATHROOM. GO GET IT, CLON!
YOU GET IT! IT'S YOUR GUN!
GO GET IT!

RALPH, LET ME HOLD YOUR GUN WHILE YOU TIE 'EM BOTH.
WHY DON'T I HOLD THE GUN AN' YOU TIE 'EM UP, MOON?
RALPH, TIE 'EM UP!

YEOW!
FUCK! FUCK!

TAKE THIS AND LOCK YOURSELF IN THE BATH-ROOM AND DON'T COME OUT TILL I TELL YOU.
CAN I WAIT IN THE LADIES' ROOM THIS TIME?
19

TSK! SHE STILL AIN'T HOME YET.
WELL, COULD YOU GIVE HER THIS FLYER? OUR BAND'S PLAYING IN TOWN TONIGHT AN' I'D REALLY LIKE HER TO COME, OK?
damochers rool
HI, ALE-JANDRA. HI, MARIBEL. HI, SOFIA.
HI, ESTHER! ARE YOU READY FOR ONE GLORIOUS EVENING OF SHOPPING, SHOPPING, SHOPPING? I FIGURED, WHY WAIT FOR THE WEEKEND, EH, GIRLS?
DOGPILE ON THE MASKED BONEHEAD!
HAPPY BIRTH-DAY, ESTHER. IT'S BEAUTIFUL.
THANK YOU, ALEJANDRA.
WHAT DO YOU THINK OF THESE FOR PERLA'S WEDDING GIFT?
FINE.
20

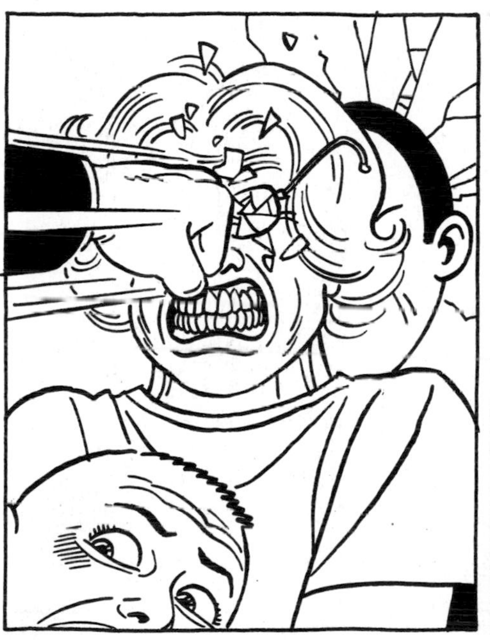

GET THE FUCKING GUN OUTTA THE MEN'S BATHROOM!
YEH...

GET THE FUCKING GUN ALREADY!
I CAN'T FIND IT!

KA-BLOO
21

WHEN IS D'ABLO COMIN' TO GET HIS CAR, MOMMA? HUH, MOMMA?
SHUT UP AN' EAT YOUR DINNER 'FORE IT GETS COLD AN' YOU DON'T WANT IT NO MORE.

PO'
♫
BIFF!
SOCKO

FLOP! BOP! PTUII!

THIS IS FUCKED! I'M GONE!
DON'T LEAVE US, MOON!

WHERE DO YOU THINK YOU'RE GOING, DICK BRAIN?
HEEEEH!

YOU KNOW, ESTHER. I'M IN NO WAY TRYING TO TAKE YOUR MOTHER'S PLACE, BUT IF THERE'S ANYTHING TROUBLING YOU AND YOU'D LIKE TO TALK ABOUT IT, MAYBE I COULD HELP AS A FRIEND...?
OK.
El Chiquito
SHAQ ATTACK!
22

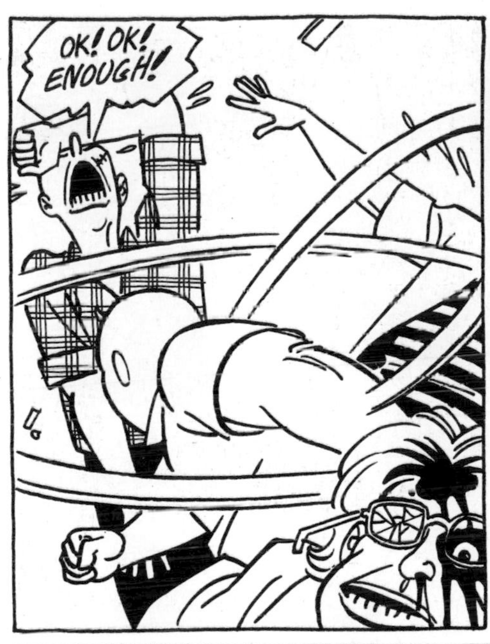
OK! OK! ENOUGH!

AW, SHIT! STOP! TIME OUT! BUTO'S DYING! WHADJA DO?
HE'S FINE. YOU GUYS HAD ENOUGH?
YES!
NO!
PIPE DOWN!

SO, PERLA TELLS ME IT'S OK THAT I BROKE OFF MY MARRIAGE AN' THEN SHE GOES OFF AN' GETS ENGAGED HERSELF. I MEAN, WHAT THE FUCK, MAN?
I DUNNO, I JUST FEEL LIKE I'M ALL BY MYSELF. I DON'T KNOW WHAT TO DO...
Colfax
TLC

COULD WE GET SOME FISH IN A TANK LIKE D'ABLO? HUH, MOMMA?
I THOUGHT I TOLD YOU TO SHUT UP AN' GO TO MOTHER FUCKIN' SLEEP AWREADY!
23

C'MERE, DOG!
LEAVE IT ALONE, IDIOT!
KLUB KRA

YOU KNEW THIS MAGGIE CHICK BACK IN L.A, HOPEY?
NO, BENNY. IN HOPPERS, CLOSE TO LOS.
AHEM!

ARE YOU GUYS SERIOUS? YOU AN' TWYLA REALLY WANNA MOVE TO L.A? WHAT'S THERE FOR YOU?
MONSTERS! MOVIES! MONSTER MOVIES! THE ACKERMANSION! THE... HOPEY, WHERE ELSE COULD YOU SEE LAWRENCE TIERNEY RIDING A BIKE DOWN HOLLYWOOD BOULEVARD?
DAMACHERS
KILL

HOPEY, YOU JUST HAVE TO COME WITH US! WE CAN'T BREAK UP THE BAND!

VENUTH!
KLUB KRAZY
THE DAMACHERS
EL DIABLO BLANCO
LUCHA LIBRE
Venus

I DIDN'T DO NOTHIN'. SNIFF
I KNOW, BABY. MOMMA'S JUS' CRUEL AN' EVIL, LIKE ALL THE REST O' THEM...
24

KNOK!
KNOK!

YOU CAN COME OUT NOW. IT'S ALL RIGHT.

BOYD WAS LIKE A SON TO ME...
I STILL DON'T KNOW HOW ALL THIS COULD HAVE HAPPENED.
IT DIDN'T HAPPEN, OK, LUIGI?
MARGARET, MY HERO! HOW ARE YOU DOING? YOU OK?

WHAT TIME IS IT?
IT'S LATE. SORRY ALL THIS HAD TO TAKE SO LONG, BUT WE HAD TO DECIDE WHAT TO DO WITH THOSE BUMS.
WHAT DID YOU DO WITH THE GUNS?

DROPPED 'EM OUT THE WINDOW. WHAT DID YOU DECIDE?
WE LET 'EM GO.
ALL EXCEPT BIG MOUTH HERE. IT'S GONNA TAKE A LOT MORE TO PERSUADE HIM TO DISAPPEAR FOR GOOD.
WHAT'S THAT SUPPOSED TO MEAN?

YOU LET 'EM GO?? YOU DIDN'T CALL THE COPS?
NO COPS. REMEMBER, MARGARET. THIS DIDN'T HAPPEN. NONE OF US WERE HERE TODAY. RIGHT, MOONIE?
FUCK YOU! WHAT ARE YOU GONNA DO TO ME?
25

DON'T WORRY, MARGARET. I DON'T THINK THOSE GUYS WILL BE COMING BACK HERE AGAIN IF THEY KNOW WHAT'S GOOD FOR THEM.
I ALSO DON'T THINK THEY'RE THE TYPE TO BRAG ABOUT HAVING BEEN BEAT UP BY TWO OLD FOLKS.
WHAT ABOUT ME??

WELL, THESE ARE GOODBYES ONCE AGAIN, MARGARET. SEE YOU IN THE FUNNY PAPERS.
OK, BUT... OK.
SEE YOU AGAIN SOMETIME, QUEENIE.
WHAT ARE YOU GONNA DO WITH ME??

I DON'T KNOW HOW I'M GONNA GET HOME. MY CAR GOT SWEPT AWAY IN A MUDSLIDE.
NO, NO, IT DIDN'T. COME THIS WAY.

PING! MY LITTLE TINY CAR JUST ENDED UP ON THE LITTLE TINY ROAD BELOW. BING! POW!
WOULD IT BE FORWARD OF ME IF I ASKED YOU FOR A RIDE BACK TO MY CAR?
TEXAS
POOTY

PERLA, I'M SORRY YOU HAD TO BE A PART OF ALL THIS, BUT YOU'RE SAFE NOW. NO ONE IS GOING TO HURT YOU ANY MORE...
I KNOW, BUT, THOSE GUYS... THAT GUY... WHAT IF HE... THEY WANTED TO KILL HER... THEY...

YOU'VE KNOWN RENA TITAÑON FOR SOME TIME SO YOU SHOULD KNOW THAT THIS WAS A WALK IN THE PARK FOR HER...
YOU WON'T SEE THOSE GUYS AGAIN, PERLA. I PERSONALLY PROMISE YOU THAT.
I SUPPOSE I SHOULD GO UP AND GET YOUR CAR KEYS FROM DANITA.
26

DON'T BOTHER TO WAKE HER. I HAVE A SPARE KEY HIDDEN IN THE WHEEL WELL.
OH, OK...
WELL, GOOD NIGHT, THEN?

WELCOME HOME, STRANGER.
HI, BABIES. WHAT'S HAPPENED IN THE WORLD SINCE I WAS AWAY?

ONLY EVERYBODY'S BEEN CALLING ASKING ABOUT YOUR ENGAGEMENT THAT YOU DIDN'T EVEN BOTHER TO TELL YOUR VERY OWN SISTER ABOUT. I HAD TO HEAR IT FROM XOCHITL.
OH... THAT.

YEAH, AN' AS YOUR VERY OWN SISTER, I ONLY GOT ONE THING TO SAY: THAT BIG WRESTLER GUY, PERLA? I GUESS HE GOTS A LOTTA MONEY, HUH?
BIG WRESTLER GUY...
EL DIABLO BLANCO. DANITA FIGURED IT OUT...

HEH! YEAH, WELL... I KNOW IT SEEMS FUNNY.
NOT FUNNY. JUST A LITTLE UNEXPECTED.
IT'S COOL.
27

OH, I ALMOST FORGOT. SOME GIRL NAMED HOPEY KEEPS COMING BY AN'...
PERLA?

CAMP VICKI
TRESPASSERS WILL BE BULLDOGGED

I DIDN'T BLAB, XOCHITL DID! AND PERSONALLY, I'M GLAD SHE DID. YOU SHOULDN'T KEEP SOMETHING LIKE AN ENGAGEMENT A SECRET FROM YOUR FAMILY. ESPECIALLY FROM YOUR POOR LONELY MOTHER, Y'KNOW?
BUT, TIA...!

I'M NOT GETTING MARRIED. I ONLY TOLD GINA THAT TO GET HER OFF MY FUCKING BACK.
BOY, AND NOW YOUR ENTIRE FAMILY IS EXPECTING A WEDDING. IF YOUR MOM'S FAMILY IS ANYTHING LIKE THE CHASCARRILLOS, THEY SURE DO LOVE A WEDDING.

28

DIABLO
PROMOCIONES
DE LUCHA
LIBRE

EEEEEEEEEE

YAAAAAH

POP!

SHIT
SHIT
SHIT
SHIT
SHIT
SHIT

BUZZZZZZ
29

...DOS A TRES CAIDAS SIN LIMITE DE TIEMPO...
...EL CAPITAN DE SU BANDO... ¡EL DIABLO BLANCO!
KNOCK KNOCK
SHE AIN'T HOME YET!
SHE AIN'T HOME YET! SHE AIN'T HOME YET!
HEY.
A-ALVARO?
30

POIK!
MAG... MARGARET! WHAT A SURPRISE! I NEVER EXPECTED TO SEE YOU...

OH, I WAS JUST DRIVING AROUND...
...THINK-ING ABOUT THINGS.
I WAS DOING A LITTLE THINKING MYSELF.
WON'T YOU HAVE A SEAT?

YOU'LL NEVER GUESS WHO I WAS THINKING ABOUT.
WHO WERE YOU THINKING ABOUT?

YOU DON'T WANT TO GUESS?
WHO WERE YOU THINKING ABOUT?

SIGH...
ACTUALLY, I WAS THINKING ABOUT MY POOR SISTER...
THE ONE THAT LIVES WITH ME...
OH? IS SHE HAVING PROBLEMS?

WELL, SURE!
TSK! IT'S SO STUPID, REALLY...
ANYWAY...
SEE, MY FAMILY'S PRETTY OLD FASHIONED. YOU KNOW, MEN WORK AND WOMEN COOK AND HAVE BABIES...

WELL, I DIDN'T EXACTLY TURN OUT LIKE THE OTHER WOMEN IN MY FAMILY, BUT MY SISTER ESTHER DID...
I MEAN, SHE DID UNTIL RECENTLY...
WHAT DID SHE DO?

WELL, I THINK SHE DID IT BECAUSE SHE'S TRYING TO PROVE THAT SHE'S INDEPEN-DENT AND HEADSTRONG LIKE HER BIG SISTER...
LIKE, IF I'M INDEPENDENT AND HEAD-STRONG, I GUESS I SHOULD BE FLATTERED...
WHAT DID SHE DO?
31

SHE BACKED OUT OF A BIG, BIG WEDDING ENGAGEMENT AND LEFT EVERYBODY WITH THEIR JAWS ON THE GROUND, THAT'S WHAT!
I SEE.
OK, SO SHE'S FIGHTING TRADITION. FINE. BUT, YOU KNOW WHAT I THINK?
I THINK SHE REALLY WANTS TO BE NORMAL AND BE MARRIED AND HAVE BABIES.
I'M NOT SAYING THAT ALL THIS BREAK TRADITION STUFF IS BULLSHIT, BUT I BELIEVE ONCE YOU'VE DONE IT LONG ENOUGH YOU WANNA SLOW DOWN AND BE NORMAL. IT'S KINDA LIKE YOU'VE EARNED IT...
SOME CALL IT MATURING, OTHERS CALL IT GETTING OLD AND BORING.
YEAH, SO I WOULDN'T BE SURPRISED IF ESTHER'S ALREADY CHANGED HER MIND AND WANTS THE ENGAGEMENT ON AGAIN. BOY, THIS MARRIAGE STUFF...
YOU DON'T APPROVE OF MARRIAGE?
IT'S FINE! IT'S JUST SO FUNNY! YOU KNOW, ESTHER CALLING OFF HERS, THEN ME... HEH HEH...
YOU? ARE YOU GETTING MARRIED?
NO! IT'S... (SIGH) THE OTHER DAY I HAD TO GIVE SOMEBODY THE BRUSH OFF AND I TOLD...HIM...LIED TO HIM THAT I WAS GETTING MARRIED SO HE'D BACK OFF...
WELL, SOMEBODY ELSE HEARD THE BOGUS NEWS AND IN LESS THAN TWENTY-FOUR HOURS MY WHOLE ENTIRE FAMILY THINKS I'M GETTING HITCHED!
OH, NO. HEH HEH...
SO, NOW THEY ALL THINK WE'RE AN ITEM...
YOU DON'T SAY...
I DON'T KNOW HOW THEY'D FIGURE THAT. I GUESS DANITA MUSTA THOUGHT...
WA... WAIT. THAT YOU AND I...??
32

WELL, YEAH. ISN'T THAT THE WEIRDEST THING YOU'VE EVER HEARD...?
WHODA... THUNK...?

I WAS AS MUCH IN THE DARK ABOUT THIS AS YOU WERE, BELIEVE ME.
AND WHEN EVERY-BODY FINDS OUT IT WAS A LIE, IT'S ME THEY'LL HATE FOR THE REST OF ETERNITY...

SEE? IT STARTED ALREADY.

MAY I SEE YOUR FACE?
I DON'T THINK THAT'S A GOOD IDEA, MARGARET.

THAT'S OK. I DON'T CARE. I SAW IT ALREADY, ANYWAY.
EVEN IF I DON'T REMEMBER WHAT I SAW...
DANITA SAW IT, TOO...

SEÑOR DIABLO. I DIDN'T THINK YOU'D BE IN TODAY, SIR.
MAPY, HOW CAN ONE PROTECT A PERSON FROM KIDNAPPERS AND GUNS BUT CANNOT PROTECT THAT SAME PERSON FROM SIMPLE HUMILIATION?

THAT'S A FUNNY ONE. I MEAN, SIMPLE HUMILIATION...?
IT'S NOT FUNNY FROM OVER HERE, I CAN TELL YOU THAT MUCH.
33

HI.
PERLA!
YOU WILL SEE HIM... ON THE MORROW... AT THE FESTIVAL... IN THE ARENA...

HE CAME! ALVARO ACTUALLY CAME TO ME AND GUESS WHAT...
WE'RE GETTING MARRIED AFTER ALL! BUT THAT'S NOT THE BEST PART...
WE'RE NOT GOING BACK TO DAIRYTOWN! WE'RE STAYING IN TEXAS!
39

ISN'T THAT SO COOL? NOW WE CAN HAVE A DOUBLE WEDDING.
WHICH REMINDS ME; DIABLO BLANCO CALLED...
OH...?
OH! HE DID, DID HE? WHAT DID HE WANT?
ACTUALLY, HE CALLED FOR DANITA...
D-DANITA?
YEAH, I FIGURE IT WAS ABOUT WORK. BUT I TOLD HIM HE WAS A LITTLE LATE...
LOOK, IT'S SO WEIRD...

THIS MORNING SHE PACKED UP HER STUFF AND HER KID AND JUST MOVED OUT. SHE DIDN'T SAY WHY, JUST BYE...

GOD, PERLA. SO MUCH HAS HAPPENED IN THE LAST TWENTY-FOUR HOURS. I KNOW THERE WAS ONE MORE THING I HAD TO TELL YOU...
OH, WELL. COME MEET YOUR FUTURE BROTHER-IN LAW.

WHERE'S D'ABLO, MOMMA?
FORGET ALL ABOUT HIM, ELIAS. HE AIN'T COMIN' WITH US.
K 19
TRACK

WE'RE GOIN' BACK TO LIVE WITH GRAMMA. DON'T YA MISS GRAMMA?
UH HUH.

MOMMA, DAT MAN OVER DERE KEEPS LOOKIN' AT US.
IGNORE 'IM AN' HE'LL GO AWAY...
TRACK 19
35

GASP
ELIAS...

IT'S HIM, MOMMA! HE CAME! HE CAME!
WHO...?
D'ABLO!

ELIAS, YA CAN'T... THIS AIN'T... IT...
YOU DIDN'T EVEN SAY GOOD BYE, DANITA.

Y-YOU AIN'T THE SAME MAN I SAW IN THE LOCKER ROOM THAT DAY. I-I NEVER SEEN YOU BEFORE IN MY WHOLE LIFE...
WHAT DO YOU SEE?

Bosier
LUPE

THE WOOLEY EYE

36

EYE

HEY!
RRRUMP

HEY, YOU LONESOME DOG, YOU. DID YOU KNOW YOU'RE A LIFE SAVER? HUH? WHAT'S YOUR NAME?

HUH?
OK, SEE YOU LATER, BYE.

IZZY? ARE YOU ALL RIGHT? SHALL I GET THE DOCTOR?
NO, DAFFY. I'M-I'M OK.
I JUST HAD A SUDDEN FLASH. I PICTURED MYSELF AS MAGGIE AND I WAS ABOUT TO HIT A BEACH.

HI.
HI. WE'LL HAVE TWO MORE OF WHAT MY FRIEND IS HAVING HERE.
THE WOOLEY EYE

YOU'RE BRAVE.
I'M NOT THAT BRAVE.
HOW ARE YOU DOING? HOW'S YOUR HEAD?
37

IT HURTS LIKE A MOTHER FUCKER...
WE SHOULD GO BACK TO THE SQUARE AND BREAK A COUPLA BROOMS OVER THOSE BIDDIES' HEADS.

HOW DO YOU KNOW ABOUT THAT? WHO THE FUCK ARE YOU, ANYWAY? EVER SINCE YOU CAME AROUND I'VE HAD NOTHING BUT TROUBLE. LIFE USED TO BE SO SIMPLE...
YA, DON'T SAY...
YIG! WHAT ARE WE DRINKING?

ESTHER'S GETTING MARRIED. ESTHER'S NOT GETTING MARRIED. PERLA'S GETTING MARRIED. ESTHER'S GETTING MARRIED. PERLA'S NOT GETTING MARRIED.

THOSE TWO THINK THEY'RE SO CUTE. MAKING FOOLS OF EVERYBODY...
I TOLD YOU SHRIMP... PERLA WAS NEVER ENGAGED IN THE FIRST PLACE, NACHO. IT WAS ALL A BIG MISUNDERSTANDING.

NICE TRY, VICKI. BUT THIS TIME SHE ANSWERS TO HER MOTHER, NOT HER AUNT.
HER MOTHER?? YOU MEAN THAT LADY THAT MOVED HER FAMILY OUT OF HUERTA BUT LEFT HER OLDEST DAUGHTER BEHIND TO BE RAISED BY HER CRAZY WRESTLER AUNT?

NACHO, I WAS HER ONLY PARENT AT A TIME WHEN SHE NEEDED PARENTS THE MOST!
ALL I KNEW WAS HOW TO BEAT PEOPLE UP, SO YOU KNOW WHAT GOOD THAT DID US.
COME ON, VICKI. THOSE WERE HARD TIMES FOR EVERYBODY.

OF COURSE THEY WERE! HER MOTHER HAD JUST GONE THROUGH A DIVORCE BECAUSE HER FATHER WAS SECRETLY LIVING WITH...
STOP IT, RIGHT NOW. I WON'T HAVE YOU TALK THAT WAY IN FRONT OF MY WIFE. LEAVE MY HOME.
38

YOU GHOUL, NACHO! DON'T YOU KNOW TO THIS DAY SHRIMP STILL BLAMES HERSELF FOR BREAKING YOU AND QUINA UP?
OUT!

DON'T LOOK AT ME LIKE THAT, ALEJANDRA. I DID IT ALL FOR YOU, REMEMBER? YOU LIKED IT THEN, OR HAVE YOU FORGOTTEN?

...WE ARE WHAT WE ARE, Y'KNOW WHAT I MEAN?
I KNOW, RUBY. IT'S SO FUNNY...
THE WOOLEY EYE

IT'S LIKE, SUDDENLY YOU WAKE UP AND FIND YOURSELF TRYING TO GET MARRIED...
I MEAN, MARRIED?? WHERE'D THAT COME FROM, HUH?
I SEE WHAT YOU'RE SAYIN'...

IT'S LIKE, YOU DON'T WANNA BE MARRIED, YOU WANNA BE LOVED.
WELL, YEAH. BUT... Y'KNOW...

I THINK I'M GONNA GO BUY ME A COUPLA BROOMS. SO LONG, PERLA.
SO LONG, RUBY. SEND 'EM TA HELL.
PUNK

WELL, IF IT AIN'T OL' BOB RICHARDSON, THE LIFE SAVER. WHADDAYA SAY, BOB?

I'M GOING TO DO EVERYTHING I POSSIBLY CAN TO MAKE PERLA AND ESTHER HAPPY...
...EVEN IF IT MEANS YOU LEAVING ME.
37

OH, ESTHER MIJA. I'M SO HAPPY FOR YOU AND I WOULD LOVE TO BE THERE BUT THE DOCTOR SAID I CAN'T MOVE FROM THIS BED FOR TWO WEEKS.
THAT'S OK, MOM. YOU GET WELL.
AND MY PERLITA...?
...LLE... LLE... LLEVA... LLEVATELO...
UH, SHE'S FINE. SHE'S PARTLY WHY I CALLED...
SHE'S NOT GETTING MARRIED.
I KNEW IT. SHE WAS NEVER GETTING MARRIED THE WHOLE TIME. HO HUM...
HOW DO YOU KNOW?
I KNOW. SHE DOES IT ALL THE TIME. SHE'S ALWAYS RESENTED ME FOR LEAVING HER WITH VICKI. HO HUM.
HOW DO YOU KNOW?
I KNOW.
MOM, I'M SURE THE DOCTOR WOULD LET YOU TRAVEL.
NO, RUBEN. THEY DON'T WANT ME THERE.
I KNOW YOU DON'T BELIEVE IT BUT IT'S THE TRUTH. HO HUM.
YOU GUYS ARE NO HELP, MANUEL AND ANGEL!
PTCH! I AIN'T GOIN' TO TEXAS.
YOU GO.
...T.J., COOL BREEZE, POPPO, HEAD... ...WE'RE THE AWSOME FOURSOME UNTIL WE'RE DEAD!
40

I'M SORRY I FORGOT YOUR BIRTH-DAY, BABIES.
MY GOD, PERLA! EVERY-BODY'S MAD AT YOU! AREN'T YOU AT ALL FREAKING OUT?
PTCH! WHAT FOR? IT AIN'T THE FIRST TIME.
PERLA, I WON'T MARRY ALVARO. THAT'LL SHOW 'EM ALL...
NO NO NO! DON'T BE A SHIT, ESTHER! MARRY HIM! TELL HIM YOU WANNA DO IT RIGHT AWAY! TOMORROW, IN FACT! I'M SERIOUS! DO IT IN CHURCH! DO IT IN COURT! DO IT IN VEGAS! DO IT ANYWHERE! JUST DO IT, BABIES!
O-OK, PERLA. OK...
OUCH.

HOPEY, TWYLA AND I ARE LEAVING RIGHT AWAY. SO, MAKE UP YOUR MIND. ARE YOU COMING, OR NOT?
I HAVEN'T SEEN MAGGIE YET AN'... JUST GIVE ME ONE HOUR! ONE HOUR!

OK, ONE HOUR! BUT IF YOU AREN'T BACK BY THEN, WE'RE GONE!
ONE HOUR!

TOCO TAXI
81-9-5171

HI! YOU LOOKING FOR THE CHASCAR-RILLOS?

I BELIEVE ESTHER'S ON HER WAY TO THE COURT-HOUSE TO GET MARRIED.
IS HER SISTER GOING, TOO? HOW DO I GET TO THE COURTHOUSE?

HOW YOU HOLDING UP, GINA?
I'M OK, COACH. I'VE BEEN BUSY CRAMMING FOR FINAL EXAMS. I'M GRADUATING SOON, Y'KNOW...
BEEP
BEE

HAVE FUN AT YOUR NIECE'S WEDDING. GIVE THEM ALL MY BEST.
C'MON, TIA! WE'RE LATE!
I'LL BE OUT IN A MINUTE, XO. I JUST HAVE TO GET MY COAT.
42

UH, COACH? YOU DIDN'T TELL XO ABOUT ME AND PERLA AND...
YOUR SEXUAL PREFERENCES ARE YOUR OWN BUSI-NESS, GINA.

DID YOU JUST HAVE ANOTHER FLASH?
YES, BUT THIS ONE IS NOT TOO CLEAR.
I'M NOT MAGGIE, BUT...
DO DOGS REALLY SEE IN BLACK AND WHITE?

RENA, DID YOU HEAR THE NEWS ABOUT YOUR BROTHER BACK IN THE STATES?
YES, AND IF THAT BOY HAD ANY SMARTS MARGARET WOULD'VE BEEN THE ONE.

43

HEY, SHRIMPO.
OH. HI, TIA.

YOU...?
LOOK, TIA. I... I'M SORRY, BUT I GOTTA GO.

I TRIED, SHRIMP. I REALLY TRIED TO BE A GOOD PARENT.

WHAT'S GONNA HAPPEN TO PERLA? EVERYBODY'S MAD AT HER AN' EVERYTHING.
SHE'S GOING TO BE FINE. I'M GOING TO TELL YOUR MOTHER ALL ABOUT THE MISTAKE.

Y-YOU'RE GONNA TALK TO HER? HAVE YOU EVER...? I MEAN, ALEJANDRA. YOU THINK YOU SHOULD...?
I THINK IT'S IMPORTANT FOR PERLA'S SAKE, DON'T YOU? I CAN'T WORRY ABOUT MYSELF RIGHT NOW...

WANNA HOLD HER
WANNA HOLD HER TIGHT...
GET TEENAGE KICKS RIGHT
THROUGH THE NIGHT...
OH YEAH...
TLAQUEPAQUE

WAIT! STOP HERE! DRIVER, STOP HERE!
WAIT TILL I PULL OVER!

EYE
44

FUCKIT! NOW WHERE'D SHE GO?
THAT'LL BE SEVEN-FORTY!

YOU DON'T WANNA BE MARRIED, YOU WANNA BE LOVED, FOOL...

WELL, WELL! THE WORLD'S GETTING SMALLER EVERYDAY! WELCOME TO "SARA'S TWO"!
ENERO, LOOK WHO'S HERE!

SHE WAS LIKE, THIS TOTALLY BEAUTIFUL STICKIN' DREAM. IT HAD TO BE THE MAGPIE...
YOU FUCKING WHORE! YO NO GOOD STINKI ROTTE WHO
DOG'S DOGS
POSTY

I LOST MY WIFE! I LOST MY KIDS! I LOST MY FUCKING HOUSE!
ALL BECAUSE OF SOME GOD DAMN NO GOOD FUCKING WHORE WHORE WHORE!
LIGHTEN UP, ENERO MAN.
SUPER SA

OH, HE'S JUST...

SLAP!
45

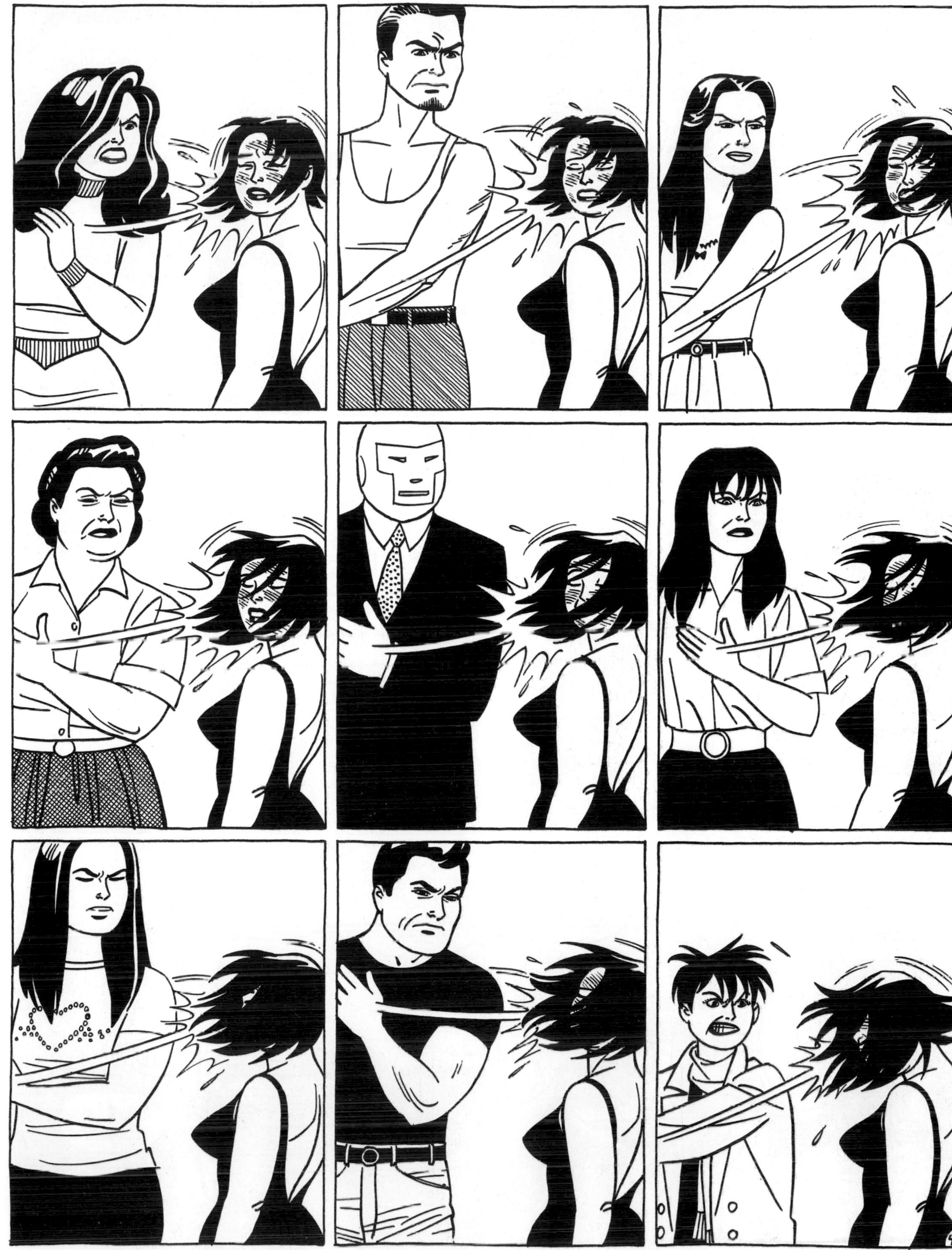
47

C'MON, MAG! RISE AN' SHINE! WE GOTTA GET GOING!
HUH? WHA...?

GET YOUR CLOTHES ON! IT'S TOUR TIME! YOU SAID YOU WANTED TO COME AN' WE'RE LEAVING RIGHT NOW!
HO-HO-HOPEY??

IT'S SO WEIRD. I HAD THIS DREAM...
TELL US ABOUT IT ON THE ROAD. HURRY, BEFORE YOUR AUNT VICKI WAKES UP.

YOU GOT YOUR TOOL BOX?
YEAH, BUT...
HI, ZERO.
HI, MONICA.
HI, TERRY.
HEY.
YOU'RE NOT ABSOLUTELY LIVID THAT MAGGIE'S COMING WITH US, TERRY DEAR?
SOMEBODY HAS TO KEEP THIS JALOPY IN WORKING ORDER.

...AN' THEN IN MY DREAM YOU GUYS LEFT ME BEHIND AN' THEN YOU GUYS BROKE UP ON THE EAST COAST AN' HOPEY GOT PREGNANT AN' I LIVED WITH THIS GUY I USED TO LIKE IN SCHOOL AN' THEN SPEEDY KILLED HIMSELF AN'...
Z
GOD, MAG! THAT MUST'VE BEEN ONE LONG ASS DREAM!

IT SEEMED LIKE FOREVER AN' IT ALL FELT SO REAL. EVERY DETAIL, SO CLEAR... SO SCARY...
...AN' YET, YOU'RE ALL HERE. AN' SPEEDY'S ALIVE...
...
OH, YEAH. AN' ALSO IN THE DREAM MONICA BECAME A MAN...
HA HA HA HA HA HA HA
AND YOU SAY THIS WAS A DREAM?
HA HA HA HA HA HA
WHAT'S SO FUNNY?
HA HA HA HA
48

APE
SEX

STILL THINKING ABOUT YOUR DREAM?
I ALREADY FORGOT MOST OF IT.

TELL ME SOMETHING, MAG: WHY DO YOU THINK I WOULD LEAVE YOU BEHIND TO GO ON TOUR AN' THEN STAY AWAY FROM YOU FOR SO LONG?
I DUNNO. IT WAS JUST A DREAM, HOPEY.

IZZY SAYS EVERY-BODY IN OUR DREAMS ARE REALLY OURSELVES IN DISGUISE.
GUY, HOPEY! I'D NEVER DO THAT TO YOU, EVER!

WHAT ABOUT SPEEDY?
RAND RACE?
SPEEDY? THERE IS NO SPEEDY.
RACE WHO?

I'M SUCH A HORRID BITCH. IT WOULD TOTALLY SERVE ME RIGHT IF YOU LEFT ME BEHIND.
49

SO, WHAT'S THE WORD?
TERRY'S FINISHING THE TOUR PLAYING WITH THE FORTY THIEVES AN' ZERO'S SELLING HIS DRUMS TO BUY BUS TICKETS HOME FOR HIM AND THAT STUPID LOOKING MONICA.
U HAU

THEN IT'S JUST YOU AND ME?
...AND THE ACTION BUS. BUT, I DON'T KNOW HOW LONG IT'LL LAST US. YOU SAID YOURSELF IT RUNS LIKE SERGEANT SCHULTZ ON A BAD DAY.

DON'T WORRY ABOUT THAT! AS LONG AS I HAVE MY TOOL BOX, THIS MONSTER WILL CONTINUE TO TAKE US WHEREVER WE WANT AS LONG AS WE WANT!
SOUNDS TO ME LIKE YOU DON'T WANNA GO HOME.

WE DON'T HAVE TO GO BACK TO CALIFORNIA! THE ACTION BUS IS OUR HOME! HELL, WE'RE SO FREE, WE'RE AS FREE AS...FREE AT LAST!
FIRST STAR TO THE LEFTIST. STRAIGHT ON TILL MORNING...
I'M LEAVIN' ON A JET PLANE...
SO LONG, IT'S BEEN GOOD TA KNOW YA...
SEE YA!
50

SLAP

MOTHER FUCKER!
...

...

51

POLIC
PLEAS
DO NO
LITTE
MY ANKLE IS KILLING ME. IT HASN'T HURT SINCE ABOUT THE TIME YOU FIRST LEFT ME TO GO ON TOUR.
THAT LONG?
THAT LONG.
the end
XAIME 81-96